Surveillance Technologies and Early Warning Systems:
Data Mining Applications for Risk Detection

Ali Serhan Koyuncugil
Capital Markets Board of Turkey, Turkey

Nermin Ozgulbas
Baskent University, Turkey

INFORMATION SCIENCE REFERENCE

Hershey · New York

Director of Editorial Content:	Kristin Klinger
Director of Book Publications:	Julia Mosemann
Acquisitions Editor:	Lindsay Johnston
Development Editor:	Joel Gamon
Publishing Assistant:	Keith Glazewski
Typesetter:	Keith Glazewski
Production Editor:	Jamie Snavely
Cover Design:	Lisa Tosheff

Published in the United States of America by
Information Science Reference (an imprint of IGI Global)
701 E. Chocolate Avenue
Hershey PA 17033
Tel: 717-533-8845
Fax: 717-533-8661
E-mail: cust@igi-global.com
Web site: http://www.igi-global.com

Library of Congress Cataloging-in-Publication Data

Surveillance technologies and early warning systems : data mining applications for risk detection / Ali Serhan Koyuncugil and Nermin Ozgulbas, editors.
     p. cm.
  Includes bibliographical references and index.
  Summary: "This book presents an alternative to conventional surveillance and risk assessment offering a multidisciplinary excursion comprised of data mining, early warning systems, information technologies and risk management and explores the intersection of these components in problematic domains"--Provided by publisher.
   ISBN 978-1-61692-865-0 (hardcover) -- ISBN 978-1-61692-867-4 (ebook) 1. Electronic surveillance. I. Koyuncugil, Ali Serhan, 1973- II. Ozgulbas, Nermin, 1968-
   TK7882.E2S87 2011
   658'.056312--dc22
                                    2010016312

British Cataloguing in Publication Data
A Cataloguing in Publication record for this book is available from the British Library.

All work contributed to this book is new, previously-unpublished material. The views expressed in this book are those of the authors, but not necessarily of the publisher.

Table of Contents

Section 1
Theoretical and Conceptual Approach to Early Warning Systems

Chapter 1

Inci Batmaz, Middle East Technical University, Turkey
Gülser Köksal, Middle East Technical University, Turkey

Chapter 2

Armand Faganel, University of Primorska, Slovenia
Danijel Bratina, University of Primorska, Slovenia

Chapter 3

Vassiliy Simchera, Research Institute of Statistics (Rosstat), Russia
Ali Serhan Koyuncugil, Capital Markets Board of Turkey, Turkey

Chapter 4

Tze Leung Lai, Stanford University, USA
Bo Shen, Stanford University, USA

Section 2
Early Warning Systems for Finance

Section 3
Early Warning Systems for Detection and Prevention of Fraud, Crime, Money Laundering and Terrorist Financing

Section 4
Early Warning Systems for Customer Services and Marketing

Detailed Table of Contents

Section 1
Theoretical and Conceptual Approach to Early Warning Systems

This section introduces basic principals of data mining, early warning systems, risk evaluation and detection in multi dimensional structure.

Inci Batmaz, Middle East Technical University, Turkey
Gülser Köksal, Middle East Technical University, Turkey

This chapter presents a formal definition of knowledge discovery in databases (KDD) process and DM, their functions and methods, used or likely to be used in early warning systems. It also presents a brief survey of overview and application papers and software in the early warning system literature.

Armand Faganel, University of Primorska, Slovenia
Danijel Bratina, University of Primorska, Slovenia

This chapter introduces the comparison of laws on data privacy protection. In this chapter, the comparison of EU comprehensive laws model and US sectoral laws model that arise from different cultural and historical background have been presented.

Chapter 3

Vassiliy Simchera, Research Institute of Statistics (Rosstat), Russia
Ali Serhan Koyuncugil, Capital Markets Board of Turkey, Turkey

This chapter deals with the divergence in statistical estimations from statistical learning point of view. In this chapter some of the approaches presented which open possibilities for the reduction of the huge gaps in modern statistical estimations of the same phenomena and its linkage with statistical learning. In addition, a solution has been given for create a single number of standards of economical information and economical indicators based on total conventional decisions via data warehouse and data mining logic for clean, comparable and standardized definitions instead of directed ones for acceptable estimations and reliable conclusions.

Chapter 4

Tze Leung Lai, Stanford University, USA
Bo Shen, Stanford University, USA

This chapter gives a review of recent developments in sequential surveillance and modeling of default probabilities of corporate and retail loans, and relates them to the development of early warning or quick detection systems for managing the risk associated with the so-called "black swans" or their close relatives, the black-necked swans.

Section 2
Early Warning Systems for Finance

This section introduces early warning systems for detection and prevention of financial crisis, stock market crashes and bankruptcies.

Chapter 5

Nermin Ozgulbas, Baskent University, Turkey
Ali Serhan Koyuncugil, Capital Markets Board of Turkey, Turkey

This chapter introduces a financial early warning system that all enterprises in need which detects signs to warn against risks and prevent from financial crisis. For this purpose, data of SMEs listed in Istanbul Stock Exchange (ISE) is processed with Chi-Square Automatic Interaction Detector (CHAID) Decision Tree Algorithm. By using this EWS, the risk profiles and risk signals have been determined for risk detection and road maps have been developed for risk prevention from financial crisis.

This chapter focuses on building a financial early warning system (EWS) to predict stock market crashes by using stock market volatility and rising stock prices. The relation of stock market volatility with stock market crashes is analyzed empirically. Also, Istanbul Stock Exchange (ISE) national 100 index data used to achieve better results from the view point of modeling purpose. Adaptive neuro fuzzy inference system (ANFIS) model was proposed to forecast stock market crashes efficiently. Also, ANFIS was explained in detail as a training tool for the EWS.

This chapter introduces a comparison of bankruptcy prediction performances of new and advanced machine learning and statistical techniques. The aim of this chapter is to compare two different machine learning techniques, one statistical approach, two types of classifier ensembles, and three stacked generalization classifiers over three related datasets.

This chapter introduces a surveillance system for bankruptcy risk of Romanian SMEs. In this context, starting from the necessity to design an early warning system, authors elaborated a new model for analysis of bankruptcy risk for the Romanian SMEs that combine two main categories of indicators: financial ratios and non-financial indicators. Analysis based on data mining techniques (CHAID) in order to identify the firms' categories accordingly to the bankruptcy risk levels. Through the proposed analysis model authors tried to offer a real surveillance system for the Romanian SMEs which can allow an early signal regarding the bankruptcy risk.

Section 3
Early Warning Systems for Detection and Prevention of Fraud, Crime, Money Laundering and Terrorist Financing

This section introduces early warning systems for detection and prevention of security, criminal and terrorist issues.

Chapter 9

Ali Serhan Koyuncugil, Capital Markets Board of Turkey, Turkey
Nermin Ozgulbas, Baskent University, Turkey

This chapter introduces a fraud detection system in social aids for social risk mitigation which has a poverty map construction facility. In this chapter, an objective targeting mechanism model and a fraud detection system model have been developed via data mining for social aids as an identifier of poverty levels which includes early warning signals for inappropriate applications. Then, these models have been used for development of a poverty map. Developed new targeting mechanism which has been based on rating approach will be an alternative to Means Test and Proxy Means Test. In addition, social aid fraud detection system has automatic update property with Intelligent System approach and the poverty map computation facility which can be used for absence of detailed data. Furthermore, Millennium Development Goals, Targeting Mechanisms, Poverty and Poverty Maps concepts have been reviewed from an analytical and objective point of view.

Chapter 10

Chia-Hui Wang, Ming Chuan University, Taiwan
Ray-I Chang, National Taiwan University, Taiwan
Jan-Ming Ho, Academia Sinica, Taiwan

This chapter introduces the generations of video surveillance systems and their applications in potential risk and crime detection. Moreover, as the surveillance video and data for safety and security are very important for all kinds of risk and crime detection, the system is required not only to data protection of the message transmission over Internet, but also to further provide reliable transmission to preserve the visual quality-of-service (QoS).

Chapter 11

Mieke Jans, Hasselt University, Belgium
Nadine Lybaert, Hasselt University, Belgium
Koen Vanhoof, Hasselt University, Belgium

This chapter discusses the application of data mining in the field of economic crime, or corporate fraud. The classification external versus internal fraud is explained and the major types of fraud within these classifications are given. Aside from explaining these classifications, some numbers and statistics are provided. After this thorough introduction into fraud, an academic literature review concerning data mining in combination with fraud is given, along with the current solutions for corporate fraud in business practice. At the end, a current state of data mining applications within the field of economic crime, both in the academic world and in business practice, is given.

Chapter 12

This chapter explores the operational data related to transactions in a financial organization to find out the suitable techniques to assess the origin and purpose of these transactions and to detect if they are relevant to money laundering. Authors' purpose is to provide an AML/CTF compliance report that provides AUSTRAC with information about reporting entities' compliance with the Anti-Money Laundering and Counter-Terrorism Financing Act 2006. Authors' aim is to look into the Money Laundering activities and try to identify the most critical classifiers that can be used in building a decision tree. The tree has been tested using a sample of the data and passing it through the relevant paths/scenarios on the tree. It is proposed that a decision tree using the classifiers identified in this chapter can be incorporated into financial applications to enable organizations to identify the High Risk transactions and monitor or report them accordingly.

Section 4
Early Warning Systems for Customer Services and Marketing

This section introduces early warning systems for customer satisfaction and promotions.

Chapter 13

This chapter introduces The Learning Management System data and the subsequent Customer Interaction System data can help to provide "early warning system data" for risk detection in enterprises. This chapter provides data from an international research project investigating on customer satisfaction in services to persons of public utility, like (education) training services and health care services, by means of explorative multivariate data analysis tools as Ordered Multiple Correspondence Analysis, Boosting regression, Partial Least Squares regression and its generalizations.

Chapter 14

This chapter introduces two models analysis – quantity (SCAN*PRO) and market share (MCI) and their power for explanatory and forecasting research using POS data for price promotions. Having dealt with more than 30 brand categories within a wider research, authors conclude that the models developed are usable for a fast decision making process within a company.

Foreword

One of the most successful application areas of data mining is in surveillance - that is, in monitoring ongoing situations to detect sudden changes or unexpected events. Such methods have extremely widespread application, from detecting epidemic disease outbreaks as quickly as possible, through fraud detection in banking, to detecting sudden changes in the condition of intensive care patients, as well as to detecting the imminent departure of manufacturing processes from acceptable operating limits, warning of potential terrorist atrocities, and the automatic analysis of video footage to detect suspicious behaviour. The aim in all such problems is to process data dynamically, as quickly as possible, to act as an early warning system so that an alert to the imminent change can be given and appropriate action can be taken.

Characteristic of such problems is that the data are *streaming data*: they keep on coming, are often multivariate, and require on-line processing. This is very different from the 'classical' statistical problem of batch mode data, which can be analysed and re-analysed in one's laboratory at leisure. This means that adaptive, sequential, *learning* algorithms are needed, and that often one will get only one chance to look at the data. The analysis has to be done immediately, and then the data are gone, and the system has to look for the next potential event.

Furthermore, surveillance problems are often characterised by *large data sets* - which makes them a very modern problem. At the extreme, the word petabyte (10^{15}) is not unusual: the Large Hadron Collider produces about 15 petabytes of data per year, which needs to be monitored for unusual data configurations, and AT&T, which uses surveillance methods to detect theft of telecomms resources, transfers some 16 petabytes per day.

A third characteristic is that the aim is to provide an *early warning*, so that a timely intervention can be made. A surveillance system to detect credit card fraud which raised an alert some three months after the transaction had occurred would be useless - even if it successfully detected all frauds and never raised a flag on legitimate transactions.

These three features of the data - its dynamic and ongoing nature, the sizes of the data sets, and the aim of providing an early warning - pose particular theoretical and practical challenges. This makes it a rich, as well as an increasingly important area, for research.

There are various approaches to surveillance. In some situations, the type of anomaly being sought is known. In such cases one can use *supervised* methods, in which one builds a system which is effective at distinguishing between data structures with the known characteristics of the anomaly and other data structures. So, for example, certain kinds of behaviour are known to be indicative of possible credit card fraud, and a system can be trained to look for such behaviour.

In contrast, in other situations, the system may hope to detect configurations which depart from the norm in various, but not completely specified ways. Outlier detection is an example, where all we know is that the observation is extreme, without being able to say in what way (on what variables) it is extreme. In such cases, *unsupervised* methods are necessary, which simply compare data points, or data configurations with the norm, to detect unusual patterns. An example would be signs of imminent disease outbreaks arising from unexpected local clusters of cases.

A wide variety of statistical tools are applied in surveillance problems, including change point analysis, forecasting methods, scan statistics, and filtering. But in some sense, the area is a relatively new one: modern data capture technology has opened up a wealth of possibilities for analysing systems as they operate, to detect unusual or dangerous events. The area is one of increasing importance, over an increasing number of domains. As a consequence, a wide range of readers will find this book of interest. The book has captured this breadth by presenting studies from a number of different areas, illustrating the range of applications and the diversity of methods which are used. It is a welcome addition to the literature.

David J. Hand
Imperial College, London

David J. Hand *is Professor of Statistics at Imperial College, London. He studied mathematics at the University of Oxford and statistics and pattern recognition at the University of Southampton. His most recent books are Statistics: a Very Short Introduction, and ROC Curves for Continuous Data. He launched the journal Statistics and Computing, and served a term of office as editor of Journal of the Royal Statistical Society, Series C. He is currently President of the Royal Statistical Society. He has received various awards and prizes for his research, including the Guy medal of the Royal Statistical Society, a Research Merit Award from the Royal Society, and the IEEE-ICDM Outstanding Contributions Award. He was elected a Fellow of the British Academy in 2003.*

Preface

Actual global situation is forced to predict the condition of achievement and should be ready to decrease the probable risk in all areas. It is possible to do that with conventional human based approach but it takes long time and the compensation of damage becomes impossible. Improvement of information technologies reflects supervision as surveillance systems and early warning systems (EWS). Operational logic of early warning systems is based on finding unexpected and extraordinary behaviors in subject area. On the other hand, data mining is the way of uncover previously unknown, useful and valuable knowledge, patterns, relations from big amount of data via sophisticated evolutionary algorithms of classical techniques such as statistics, pattern recognition, artificial intelligence, machine learning. The definitions of EWS and data mining given lead an interesting similarity. Therefore, in this book, early warning systems has been taken into consideration in both theoretical and practical mean for mainly detecting risk in financial, economical, social, security, marketing issues.

This book is a multidisciplinary study. The main components of the book are data mining, early warning systems, Information Technologies and risk management. Furthermore, this book is included the intersection and combination of these components in problematique domains. The book is mainly structured on data mining. Data mining is the most efficient and evoluationary area in Business Intelligence domain. Usage of data mining has been diffusing all areas which have big amount of data. In the book, main application area of data mining methods is early warning systems. Early warning system is a mechanism which provides proactivation via identification of critical limit values, crucial indicators, utility functions, and important factors. It is possible to mention a lot of types of early warning systems but this book is focused on early warning sytems concerning risk detection. Therefore, risk management and risk analysis or shortly risk is the last key component for this book. Risk formally defines as the expected value of the loss function. There are mainly two ways to construct a risk measure. One of them is defining a loss or utility function and the other is finding indicators which will imply risk. In this book, both of the two ways is taken into consideration while early warning system design and risk functions or indicators obtained via data mining. Furthermore, all systems are designed in IT based or aided nature. In another words, the main objective of this book is drawing a frame for risk detection via data mining and then put it in a early warning systems via Information Technologies.

The key concepts covered in this book have a very large application area in real world. Because, increasing competition has been becoming a result of globalisation and its tendecy showed that it will increase very rapidly day by day. Last global financial crisis and its extensions showed that all firms should be aware of their potancial risks and should be more proactive to produce their own solutions by themselves. On the other hand, one of the most important further reflections of financial crisis is social risk for governments. In addition, prevention of crime, proactivation for terrorist attacks can be the actual application domains in security risk perspective. Furthermore, natural disasters such as earthquakes, storms etc. and disaster recovery systems can be count in the subject area, whether included in this book or not.

It can be seen that risk detection oriented early warning systems have a very large implementation domain from the picture given above. Furthermore, last generation Business Intelligence approach data mining accelarated the accuracy of those systems. Therefore, this book will be triggered new research domains such as finance, sociology, criminology, security, earth sciences etc. Altough, there is no existing title concerning early warning systems based on data mining for risk detection. However, there are some studies (papers, proceedings etc.) on risk detection based on data mining but there is no book completely dedicated on risk detection from data mining point of view. In addition, there is no book specialized on early warning systems based on data mining. Therefore, this book is the first book in a manner of complete coverage with data mining, risk detection and early warning components.

The target audience of this book includes numerous individuals, students, academics, researchers, engineers, professionals from government and non-government institutions working in the field of data mining, knowledge discovery, risk management, IT based supervision, fraud detection, matters involving early warning in various disciplines such as information and communication sciences; insurance, banking and finance; health; social sciences; criminology; security; earth sciences; engineering etc. Therefore, this book can be identified as a practical guide of theoritical matters for solving real life problems with feasible potential systems, models and examples. From that view of point it can be used in public libraries, research organizations and academic institutes' libraries. In addition, individuals such as scientists, practitioners, managers and experts from government and non-government institutions involving risk detection will be interested in this book.

This book is divided into four sections. First section entitled 'Theoretical and Conceptual Approach to Early Warning Systems' introduces basic principals of data mining, early warning systems, risk evaluation and detection in multi dimentional structure.

Chapter 1 presents a formal definition of knowledge discovery in databases (KDD) process and DM, their functions and methods, used or likely to be used in early warning systems. It also presents a brief survey of overview and application papers and software in the early warning system literature.

Chapter 2 introduces the comparison of laws on data privacy protection. In this chapter, the comparison of EU comprehensive laws model and US sectoral laws model that arise from different cultural and historical background have been presented. The main objectives are to compare the current state of consumer's privacy protection in EU and USA, discuss legal frameworks, propose some best practice implications, and summarize perceived future trends.

Chapter 3 deals with the divergence in statistical estimations from statistical learning point of view. In this chapter some of the approaches presented which open possibilities for the reduction of the huge gaps in modern statistical estimations of the same phenomena and its linkage with statistical learning. In addition, a solution has been given for create a single number of standards of economical information and economical indicators based on total conventional decisions via datawarehouse and data mining logic for clean, comparable and standardized definitions instead of directed ones for acceptable estimations and reliable conclusions.

Chapter 4 gives a review of recent developments in sequential surveillance and modeling of default probabilities of corporate and retail loans, and relates them to the development of early warning or quick detection systems for managing the risk associated with the so-called "black swans" or their close relatives, the black-necked swans.

The second section entitled 'Early Warning Systems for Finance' introduces early warning systems for detection and prevention of financial crisis, stock market crashes and bankruptcies.

Chapter 5 introduces a financial early warning system that all enterprises in need which detects signs to warn against risks and prevent from financial crisis. Before the global financial crisis that began 2008, small and medium-sized enterprises (SMEs) have already fighted with important financial issues. The global financial crisis and the ensuring flight away from risk have affected SMEs more than larger enterprises When these effects considered, besides the issues of poor business performance, insufficient information and insufficiencies of managers in finance education, it is clear that early warning systems (EWS) are vital for SMEs for risk detection and prevention from financial crisis. The aim of this study is to develop a financial EWS for risk detection via data mining. For this purpose, data of SMEs listed in Istanbul Stock Exchange (ISE) is processed with Chi-Square Automatic Interaction Detector (CHAID) Decision Tree Algorithm. By using this EWS, the risk profiles and risk signals have been determined for risk detection and road maps have been developed for risk prevention from financial crisis.

Chapter 6 focuses on building a financial early warning system (EWS) to predict stock market crashes by using stock market volatility and rising stock prices. The relation of stock market volatility with stock market crashes is analyzed empirically. Also, Istanbul Stock Exchange (ISE) national 100 index data used to achieve better results from the view point of modeling purpose. A risk indicator of stock market crash is computed to predict crashes and to give an early warning signal. Various data mining classifiers are compared to obtain the best practical solution for the financial early warning system. Adaptive neuro fuzzy inference system (ANFIS) model was proposed to forecast stock market crashes efficiently. Also, ANFIS was explained in detail as a training tool for the EWS.

Chapter 7 introduces a comparison of bankruptcy prediction performances of new and advanced machine learning and statistical techniques. It is very important for financial institutions which are capable of accurately predicting business failure. In literature, numbers of bankruptcy prediction models have been developed based on statistical and machine learning techniques. In particular, many machine learning techniques, such as neural networks, decision trees, etc. have shown better prediction performances than statistical ones. However, advanced machine learning techniques, such as classifier ensembles and stacked generalization have not been fully examined and compared in terms of their bankruptcy prediction performances. The aim of this chapter is to compare two different machine learning techniques, one statistical approach, two types of classifier ensembles, and three stacked generalization classifiers over three related datasets.

Chapter 8 introduces a surveaillance system for bankruptcy risk of Romanian SMEs. The small and medium enterprises (SMEs) represent the backbone of the economy, playing a major economic and social role in the process of developing a dynamic economy. But the recent evolutions in the financial markets, the international financial crisis, and the increased competition on markets, the lack of financial resources and the insufficient adaptation of many firms to the requests of the European market are new threats which can determine the bankruptcies of the Romanian SMEs. In this context, starting from the necessity to design an early warning system, authors elaborated a new model for analysis of bankruptcy risk for the Romanian SMEs that combine two main categories of indicators: financial ratios and non-financial indicators. Analysis based on data mining techniques (CHAID) in order to identify the firms' categories accordingly to the bankruptcy risk levels. Through the proposed analysis model authors tried to offer a real surveillance system for the Romanian SMEs which can allow an early signal regarding the bankruptcy risk.

The third section entitled 'Early Warning Systems for Detection and Prevention of Fraud, Crime, Money Laundering and Terrorist Financing' introduces early warning systems for proactivation, detection and prevention of security, criminal and terrorrist issues.

Chapter 9 introduces a fraud detection system in social aids for social risk mitigation which has a poverty map construction facility. One of the most important concerns of social policies is social risk mitigation and fight against poverty and social aids as its extensions. In general, measurements of social events have been mostly based on subjective statements. More specifically, targeting mechanisms have been using for determination of potential social aid owners. Most popular targeting mechanisms are subjective ones as well. In this chapter, an objective targeting mechanism model and a fraud detection system model have been developed via data mining for social aids as an identifier of poverty levels which includes early warning signals for inappropriate applications. Then, these models have been used for development of a poverty map. Developed new targeting mechanism which has been based on rating approach will be an alternative to Means Test and Proxy Means Test. In addition, social aid fraud detection system has automatic update property with Intelligent System approach and the poverty map computation facility which can be used for absence of detailed data. Furthermore, Millenium Development Goals, Targeting Mechanisms, Poverty and Poverty Maps concepts have been reviewed from an analytical and objective point of view.

Chapter 10 introduces the generations of video surveillance systems and their applications in potential risk and crime detection. Moreover, as the surveillance video and data for safety and security are very important for all kinds of risk and crime detection, the system is required not only to data protection of the message transmission over Internet, but also to further provide reliable transmission to preserve the visual quality-of-service (QoS).

Chapter 11 discusses the application of data mining in the field of economic crime, or corporate fraud. The classification external versus internal fraud is explained and the major types of fraud within these classifications are given. Aside from explaining these classifications, some numbers and statistics are provided. After this thorough introduction into fraud, an academic literature review concerning data mining in combination with fraud is given, along with the current solutions for corporate fraud in business practice. At the end, a current state of data mining applications within the field of economic crime, both in the academic world and in business practice, is given.

Chapter 12 explores the operational data related to transactions in a financial organisation to find out the suitable techniques to assess the origin and purpose of these transactions and to detect if they are relevant to money laundering. Authors' purpose is to provide an AML/CTF compliance report that provides AUSTRAC with information about reporting entities' compliance with the *Anti-Money Laundering and Counter-Terrorism Financing Act 2006*. Authors' aim is to look into the Money Laundering activities and try to identify the most critical classifiers that can be used in building a decision tree. The tree has been tested using a sample of the data and passing it through the relevant paths/scenarios on the tree. It is proposed that a decision tree using the classifiers identified in this chapter can be incorporated into financial applications to enable organizations to identify the High Risk transactions and monitor or report them accordingly.

The fourth section entitled 'Early Warning Systems for Customer Services and Marketing' introduces early warning systems for customer satisfaction and promotions.

Chapter 13 introduces The Learning Management System data and the subsequent Customer Interaction System data can help to provide "early warning system data" for risk detection in enterprises. This chapter provides data from an international research project investigating on customer satisfaction in services to persons of public utility, like (education) training services and health care services, by means of explorative multivariate data analysis tools as Ordered Multiple Correspondence Analysis, Boosting regression, Partial Least Squares regression and its generalizations.

Chapter 14 introduces two models analysis – quantity (SCAN*PRO) and market share (MCI) and their power for explanatory and forecasting research using POS data for price promotions. Having dealt with more than 30 brand categories within a wider research, authors conclude that the models developed are usable for a fast decision making process within a company.

It can be seen that risk detection oriented early warning systems have a very large implementation domain from the picture given above. Furthermore, last generation Business Intelligence approach data mining accelarated the accuracy of those systems. Therefore, this book will be triggered new research domains such as data mining, statistical data analysis, statistical learning, business intelligence, information tecnologies, finance, banking, economics, governance, sociology, criminology, security, marketing etc. and their intersections. It is intended that this book will be a primary reference in all areas which need supervision and early warning approach for risk reduction via latest Business Intelligence method as Data Mining.

Ali Serhan Koyuncugil
Nermin Ozgulbas
Editors

Acknowledgment

The editors would like to acknowledge the assistance from all involved in the entire creation of chapters, review process, and revisions of the book, without whose support the project could not have been satisfactorily completed. We wish to thank all the authors who reflected their knowledge with excellent contributions, all the editorial board members who gave their support with their expertise but reviewers who were most helpful and provided invaluable, enlighted and creative comments are: Colleen McCue and Neven Vrcek. Although, we are grateful to David Hand for his visionary foreword which enriched our book with his deep knowledge, experience and expertise.

Also, special thanks to the dedicated publishing team at IGI Global. Especially to Kristin M. Klinger, Katy Peters and Erika Carter who helped to develop book proposal, Beth Ardner who helped to develop the book and Joel Gamon who helped to prepare the book for publishing.

Finally, Ali Serhan Koyuncugil would like to thank his mother Ziynet Koyuncugil, his father Suleyman Koyuncugil, his brothers Huseyin Tolga Koyuncugil and Ferhan Yilmaz Koyuncugil, Nermin Ozgulbas would like to thank her son Doga Yamac Ozgulbas, her husband Orhan Ozgulbas, her mother Meziyet Yenikose and her father Nedret Yenikose, for their patience, love and not only throughout this period but life long support. Because, we created this Project in time which is stolen from our families.

Ali Serhan Koyuncugil
Nermin Ozgulbas
Ankara, Turkey
March 2010

Section 1
Theoretical and Conceptual Approach to Early Warning Systems

Chapter 1
Overview of Knowledge Discovery in Databases Process and Data Mining for Surveillance Technologies and EWS

Inci Batmaz
Middle East Technical University, Turkey

Gülser Köksal
Middle East Technical University, Turkey

ABSTRACT

Development of more effective early warning systems (EWSs) for various applications have been possible during the past decade due to advancements in information, detection, data mining (DM) and surveillance technologies. These application areas include economy, banking, finance, health care, bioinformatics, production and service delivery, hazard and crime prevention and minimization of other social risks involving the environment, administrations, politics and human rights. This chapter aims to define knowledge discovery in databases (KDD) process in five steps: Data preparation, data preprocessing, DM, evaluation and interpretation, and implementation. DM is further explained in descriptive and predictive mining categories with their functions and methods used or likely to be used in EWSs. In addition to well-known structured data types, mining of advanced data types such as spatial, temporal, sequence, images, multimedia and hypertexts is also introduced. Moreover, it presents a brief survey of overview and application papers and software in the EWS literature.

INTRODUCTION

Early warning systems (EWSs) are designed to warn of a potential or an impending problem such as earthquakes, tsunamis, wildfires, hurricanes, pandemics, famine, human rights violations, conflicts, financial crisis, fraud and market shifts. They typically utilize a network of sensing or surveillance devices for the problem or risk detec-

DOI: 10.4018/978-1-61692-865-0.ch001

tion. Organisation for Economic Co-operation and Development [OECD] (2003) provides an analysis of many of the systemic risks that surround us.

Knowledge discovery in databases (KDD) is a general process of discovering hidden patterns in data for better decision making. A major part of KDD involves data mining (DM). DM has become a widely accepted approach for risk management. Tsumoto and Washio (2007) provide a perspective about application of DM to risk management, in general. Similarly, Baesens et al. (2009) outline a series of upcoming trends and challenges for DM, covering applications in credit risk, fraud detection and so on.

Typical applications of DM are observed in management of risks in economy, banking and financial operations, such as economic crisis prediction and fraud detection based on historical data about the economy or banking/financial operations and customers.

Environmental, public health and disaster monitoring systems use surveillance technologies such as remote sensing (satellite imaging) and the data collected are analyzed by DM approaches for early warnings. Several EWSs for health and infectious disease control exist (such the Global Outbreak Alert and Response Network (GOARN) of World Health Organization (WHO)) that make more and more use of DM methods.

Similarly, EWS applications and attempts are observed in the literature and in practice for network security, intelligence, protection against natural or man-made hazards, risks from poor product quality or competitors' threats, and so on. Gurr and Davies (1998) present original essays that examine complex political and humanitarian crisis early warning factors and develop recommendations for effective early warning and response; Carragata (1999) examines early warning signs and designing EWSs for business survival and growth; Goldstein et al. (2000) study banking and currency crises in emerging markets to identify most reliable early warning signals; Gilad (2003) discusses early warning development

for competitiveness in the market; Meier (2006) discusses an EWS for preventing environmental conflicts; Gasparini et al. (2007) analyze major earthquake EWSs; Brown (2008) focuses on remote sensing measurements and how they are used to in famine EWSs, specifically in the US Agency for International development (USAID)'s Famine EWS Network; Glantz (2009) reviews EWSs for water- and weather-related hazards; OECD (2009) presents a review and analysis of early warning and response mechanisms and instruments for preventing violence, war, and state collapse, violent conflict. There is a need to develop many others and improve the existing ones for detecting important economic and social risks including hungers, epidemics, crimes, child abuses and unemployment.

KDD and DM, in particular, can boost these developments if utilized to their full extends. The main propose of this chapter is to define the KDD process and DM with their functions and methods for EWS developers and users.

In the following, first, a brief overview of DM applications in EWSs is provided based on a review of the literature. Then, the KDD process is defined in five major steps: Data preparation, data preprocessing, DM, evaluation and interpretation, and implementation. DM is further explained in descriptive and predictive mining categories with their functions and methods. Mining of advanced data types such as images, multimedia and hypertexts, on the other hand, is presented in a separate section. Afterwards, a review of DM software used in EWSs is provided. At the end of the chapter, future research directions and concluding remarks are given.

SOME DATA MINING APPLICATIONS FOR EWS DEVELOPMENT IN THE LITERATURE

Several attempts exist in the literature for EWS development in various industries/areas by using DM approaches. These are searched mainly through the Web of Science database, and the following studies are selected to provide an idea for the range and content of the applications.

1. Economy, banking and finance

Hormozi and Giles (2004) – overviews DM operations as covered by the literature and discusses important uses of DM in risk management, fraud detection, and other banking and retail industry applications.

Toktas and Demirhan (2004) – presents DM techniques frequently used in financial risk analysis, and an early warning model that predicts failures one year prior to failure for selected banks.

Kim et al. (2004) – discusses usefulness of a frequently used DM method, artificial neural networks (ANNs) for EWS of economic crisis.

Koyuncugil and Ozgulbas (2007) – studies detecting financial early warning signs in Istanbul Stock Exchange by DM.

Chan et al. (2007) – proposes a DM framework to measure the resilience of an economy to support the EWS adopted by the International Monetary Fund to predict future financial crises.

He et al. (2007) – presents an application DM in industrial economic early warning.

Dian-Min et al. (2007) – presents a generic DM based financial fraud detection framework as a result of an extensive literature review.

Koyuncugil and Ozgulbas (2009) – presents an EWS for SMEs as a financial risk detector.

Peng et al. (2009) – uses six financial-risk-related datasets to illustrate that combination of DM techniques with chance discovery can be effective in financial risk detection.

Phua et al. (2009) – describes a technique, CASS, for generating numeric suspicion scores on streaming credit applications over both time and space. This technique is shown to rapidly detect early symptoms of identity crime.

Yang et al. (2007) – applies text mining for extracting non-structural information in corporate financial reports.

2. Health care and bioinformatics

Bull et al. (1997) – presents a methodology and the architecture of an EWS which discovers health risks, forecasts the temporal and spatial spread of epidemics, and estimates the consequences of an epidemic.

Pietravalle et al. (2002) – presents an approach based on DM to predict Septoria tritici on winter wheat using meteorological data.

Kapetanovic et al. (2004) – describes some of the commonly used and evolving bioinformatics methods and DM tools and presents examples of their application to early cancer detection, risk identification, risk assessment and risk reduction.

Tsumoto et al. (2007) – proposes the use of DM in risk management for large-scale organizations with applications in three medical domains: risk aversion of nurse incidents, infection control and hospital management.

Tsumoto et al. (2008) – proposes an application of DM to medical risk management, where DM techniques are applied to detection, analysis and evaluation of risks potentially existing in clinical environments.

Chen et al. (2008) – proposes a signal detection system based on DM for detection of the safety signal regarding the reporting of hepatotoxicity associated with the use of telithromycin.

Sintchenko et al. (2008) – proposes a framework for bioinformatics assisted biosurveillance and early warning to address the inefficiencies in traditional surveillance. It shows that particular microbial profiling and text mining approaches can enable detection of integrated infectious disease outbreak and responsive environments.

Bartels et al. (2009) – discusses data processing to document clues that predict risk of recurrence of a bladder lesion.

Li (2006) – presents a survey of EWS for environmental and public health applications.

3. Natural hazards

Jager and Kalber (2005) – introduces the GOCA (GNSS/GPS/LPS based online control and alarm system) as an EWS for natural hazards such as landslides, mining and tunneling activities, volcano monitoring and monitoring of geotechnical structures and buildings. The GOCA deformation – analysis software utilizes several DM approaches.

Cervone et al. (2006) – introduces an earthquake monitoring and forecasting system, CQuake, based on satellite derived data processed by DM approaches.

Kuenzer et al. (2007) – presents two complementing algorithms for automatic delineation of coal fire risk areas from multispectral satellite data, and automatic extraction of local fire related thermal anomalies from thermal data.

4. Network safety and management

Meng and Dunham (2006) – Traffic anomaly has been rated as an important risk indication in computer networks. This study presents a heuristic risk assessment model in a spatiotemporal environment which incorporates an anomaly detection model with user feedbacks to historical events.

Gao and Zhang (2007) – presents an intranet intrusion detection EWS model based on DM.

5. Production, service and supply chain management

Grabert et al. (2004) – presents an EWS in automotive production, which utilizes ANNs for monitoring warranty claims, and association and sequence analysis for an early detection of quality changes both in production site and car field usage.

Pettersson (2004) – discusses the use of statistical process control methods to detect increasing churn (the process of customer replacing one provider for another) rates and to monitor customer movements.

Drewes (2005) – studies timely detection of warranty defects by text mining.

Lo et al. (2006) – E-business technology has broadly been used in supply chain management to improve the relationships between business to business and between business to customers. This study proposes a framework of an e-SCM multiple-agent system for early warning of possibly lost customers.

6. Others

Patil (2005) – discusses goeinformatic hotspot systems for detection, prioritization and early warning.

Cocx et al. (2008) – presents an EWS for the prediction of criminal careers.

Cheng et al. (2008) – presents an outlier detection model of DM for improving tender evaluation of civil projects, according to which a pre-warning can be made for some risks.

Ito et al. (2009) – presents a DM approach to unusual data detection and risk management for hydroelectric power plants.

Alker (2009) – has directed a project about Conflict Early Warning Systems (CEWS), as a part of which KDD and DM are introduced to this area for increased effectiveness.

O'Brien (2004) – reports on an automated EWS called FORECITE (Forecasting of Crises and Instability Using Text-Based Events) which was developed by the US Center for Army Analysis (CAA) for monitoring and forecasting indicators associated with country instability.

KNOWLEDGE DISCOVERY IN DATABASES PROCESS AND DATA MINING

Fayyad et al. (1996) define KDD as "the nontrivial process of identifying valid, novel, potentially useful and ultimately understandable patterns in data." It consists of the following main steps: 1. Data preparation, 2. Data preprocessing, 3. DM, 4. Evaluation and interpretation, 5. Implementation. According to them, the KDD is the process of discovering patterns in large amount of data while DM is an important step in that process, which consists of applying data analysis and discovery algorithms. During the KDD process one can start at any stage depending on the quality of data mined and aim of the mining process. To illustrate, we may only want to describe data collected from available databases. In this case, we can skip the DM. In addition, there can be some visits to other stages as well. However, in any case, implementation, that is, the use of DM findings in decision making, is the final stage.

Historically DM has evolved from various disciplines. As a result it includes techniques from the areas such as databases (e.g. relational databases, data warehousing, On-Line Analytical Processing (OLAP)), information retrieval (IR) (i.e. similarity measures, clustering), statistics (e.g. Bayes' theorem, regression, maximum likelihood estimation, resampling) and artificial intelligence (AI) (e.g. ANNs, machine learning, genetic algorithms, decision trees (DTs)).

DM tasks can be divided into two main categories: descriptive and predictive. These tasks can be accomplished by using various methods based on DM functions (Han & Kamber, 2006). These functions are used to specify the types of patterns to be mined including description, clustering, association, classification, prediction, trend analysis, similarity analysis and pattern detection. The choice of DM functions and methods utilized while executing these tasks, basically, depend on the type of data mined.

Modern surveillance technologies used in EWSs provide data in various forms including digital records of economic transactions (such as credit card purchases used in fraud detection), product or process characteristics (used in process monitoring and control), Internet traffic (used in crime detection), video footages (used in security

systems), satellite images (used in environmental risk detection) and radar images (used in security and defense systems). Earliest data storages were flat files, relational and transactional databases. Afterwards, data warehouses and data marts have been created to facilitate DM operations. All of these data repositories store data systematically which leads to structured type of data. With the advances in information and electronics technologies and their wide uses with the availability of Internet, however, more complicated data types are needed to be mined. These include images, multimedia and hypertext data. These advanced data types may require both the use of methods developed for the structured data as well as the development of more elaborate DM algorithms particularly suitable both for semi-structured and unstructured (advanced) data.

In the following, we first introduce the steps of KDD process along with the methods mostly used for structured type of data. Here, we attempt to classify DM techniques with respect to the 'kinds of knowledge mined' (DM functionalities) such as association, classification, clustering and so on (Dunham, 2003). Note that this classification is neither mutually exclusive nor exhaustive in terms of the techniques covered. In other words, some techniques may be used in different stages since they serve multiple purposes. Besides, new techniques have still been emerging in some areas such as web mining and text mining (Taniar, 2007). Secondly, DM techniques employed particularly for advanced data types such as spatial, temporal, sequence, text and hypermedia data are presented. Finally, a comprehensive list of references is provided which covers most relevant studies since the year of 2000.

Data Preparation

Before any DM application, necessary data for the analysis is determined first. These data may, then, be collected from already available data repositories such as files, databases, data warehouses or data marts (Pyle, 1999). If the data set built this way becomes very large, a reduced representative form of it can be obtained by a sampling procedure. In certain situations, however, all data may not be readily available for mining. In such cases, data *farming* process can help defining characteristics which are the most suitable for DM (Kusiak, 2006). Then, one may either gather necessary data through observation or simulation of the system.

Once the data are selected, the next step is to put them into a standard representation, like a table format, where instances and variables take place in rows and columns, respectively (Giudici, 2003). After the data preprocessing described in the following section is applied, data can be described by providing summary information through frequency distributions, cross tabulations, graphics and the others, as presented in the 'descriptive data mining' section below.

Data Preprocessing

Real-world data delt with in DM applications is generally dirty, incomplete and inconsistent. Redundancies may also occur due to integrating data from various sources. The main purpose of data preprocessing step is to handle these kinds of problematic data to improve the data quality. In addition, transforming and reducing data can help to improve the accuracy and the efficiency of DM task(s) to be performed. Basic data preprocessing methods can be organized into the following categories (Pyle, 1999; Giudici, 2003; Witten, 2005):

1. *Data cleaning*: This step basically involves techniques for filling in missing values (e.g. using most probable data value, attribute mean, a global mean etc.), smoothing out noise (e.g. binning, clustering, regression etc.), handling outliers (e.g. robust regression), detecting and removing redundant data (e.g. correlation analysis). In DM applications, missing values are typically deleted, or

replaced with a representative value such as the mean or zero or with a distinctive value. Outliers in data sets are generally removed. Besides, incomplete data are either filtered out by using OLAP techniques or low filters, or deleted completely. Inconsistencies in data, on the other hand, are also treated by filters or by removing them from further analysis. Moreover, misspelled data and noise or unwanted values are eliminated from data sets too.

2. *Data transformation*: In this step, data is transformed into appropriate forms for mining. For example, ANNs and various clustering methods perform better if the data is scaled to a specified range, i.e. normalized. There are several forms of normalization like min-max, z-score and decimal scaling. Smoothing, aggregation and generalization are other kinds of transformation operations that contribute to the success of DM. Here, smoothing techniques such as binning, clustering, and regression removes noise from data. Therefore, smoothing can also be considered as a form of data cleaning. On the other hand, aggregation involves summing up data to obtain a summary of it. Generalization, on the contrary replaces low-level data with high-level ones by using concept hierarchies. To illustrate, the categorical attribute 'department' can be generalized to another one like 'faculty', and then, 'university' by generalization. It is also common to apply mathematical transformations such as logarithm on data. Other DM applications may transform categorical data to numerical, center data (i.e. subtracting data from the mean) or adjust abnormal data in such as a way that it lays within two standard deviation of the mean.

3. *Data reduction*: In this step, the size of data is reduced, where necessary, for improving the efficiency of the methods. Both generalization and aggregation methods mentioned

above can be considered as forms of data reduction. For example, the aggregation can be used for constructing the data cube to store the multidimensional summary of data for the purpose of data reduction. Another well-known data reduction technique is the dimension reduction, also called feature selection, which is used to eliminate unnecessary attributes before the application of any mining tasks. Since it is a widely used form of data reduction, there is a long list of techniques employed for this purpose literature. These include various searching methods (i.e. best-first search, beam search etc.), regression techniques (i.e. forward, backward or stepwise), analysis of variance (ANOVA), DT induction, correlation analysis (CA), ANNs, support vector machines (SVMs), rule induction by rough set theory (RST), partial least squares (PLS), subjective evaluation (SE), genetic algorithm (GA) (Larose, 2006), principal component analysis (PCA) instance-based or Naïve Bayes learning, wrapper and filter methods for classification task or some other specialized techniques (Koksal et al., 2008). Yet another data reduction method is the data compression in which transformations are applied on data to obtain a reduced representation of it. The most popular methods are principal components analysis (PCA) (Apley, 2003), Taguchi method (TM), wavelet transforms and SE. Data compression techniques can also be applied on the responses in case of having multiple responses. The use of a desirability function in multiresponse optimization is one such example. In addition, numerosity reduction techniques, on the other hand, are applied to reduce the data volume, and can be categorized into two different groups: parametric and nonparametric. In parametric methods, statistical models such as multiple linear regression (MLR) and log-linear mod-

els are developed to estimate data, and then, the estimated parameters are stored instead of the whole data set. In nonparametric methods, reduced representations of data like histograms, clusters and samples are stored instead.

4. *Discretization*: This technique can be used to reduce the number of levels of an attribute by utilizing the concept hierarchies. In this approach, data is reduced by collecting and replacing low-level concepts with high-level concepts. It produces good results when used particularly before the application of DT-based methods. This technique is specifically useful for mining large data sets having advanced data types as presented further in this chapter. In general, discretization techniques differ from each other depending on whether they are applied on continuous or categorical type of data.. For example, binning, histogram, cluster analysis, entropy-based discretization, segmentation by natural partitioning, 1R learning schema and dynamic programming are methods used for discretizing numerical data. For categorical data, on the other hand, concept hierarchies can be generated based on the number of distinct values of the attributes used for defining the hierarchy. In DM applications, discretization is extensively applied using various methods including SE, DT, discriminant analysis (DA), composite classifier based on domain expertise or object decomposition.

Descriptive Data Mining

This step involves identification of patterns and relationships that may exist in data by exploring its characteristics. Basic descriptive (exploratory) techniques used are summarization, clustering, association rule generation and sequence discovery (Dasu & Johnson, 2003; Giudici, 2003; Tan et al., 2006; Larose, 2005).

1. *Summarization* is the presentation of general properties of the data set studied. It is similar to data generalization whose basic approaches are OLAP and attribute-oriented induction (e.g. attribute removal and generalization). Besides, there are various statistical methods for summarizing data (Giudici, 2003). These techniques are basically selected depending on the number of variables involved in the analysis. Descriptive statistics (e.g. mean, median, variance, standard deviation, mode), frequency distribution, measures describing the distribution shape (e.g. coefficient of skewness, kurtosis) and measures of concentration as well as graphical displays (e.g. histogram, box plot, quantile plot) can effectively be used to describe the univariate data. For bivariate data, however, additional tools such as correlation coefficient and scatter plot are necessary to identify the relationship between two variables. For describing multivariate data, besides dependency and association measures, multidimensional graphs like a scatter plot matrix, parallel plots are needed (Martinez & Martinez, 2002). In addition, dimension reduction techniques (e.g. PCA) and transformations (e.g. wavelet, projection pursuit) can also be useful for handling multivariate data.

2. *Clustering* is the process of grouping data into classes of similar objects. The similarity among objects is usually measured by a distance measure like Euclidean and Manhattan distance. Cluster analysis can be used alone for data description (exploration) or for preprocessing before the implementation of other DM tasks such as association, classification and prediction. Major clustering methods can be classified into the following categories (Mirkin, 2005; Han & Kamber, 2006):

    a. *Partitioning methods* mainly use two algorithms: k-means and k-medoids. The k-means algorithm tries to parti-tion n objects into k clusters each of which is represented by the mean value of the objects in the cluster. The variants of k-means, called k-modes and k-prototypes, can handle categorical and mixed type of data, respectively. The k-medoids method, on the other hand, takes the most centrally located object as the representative of the cluster. So that it is more robust than k-means algorithm. For example, PAM (Partitioning Around Medoids) is a well-known k-medoids algorithm. Another common partitional technique is the Fuzzy c-Means (FCM) that uses fuzzy logic. Above two algorithms, namely, k-means and k-medoids, work very efficiently for clusters spherical in shape and for small to medium size data sets. For handling large data sets as well as clusters irregular in shape, however, sampling-based methods such as, CLARA (Clustering LARge Applications), CLARANS (Clustering Large Applications based upon RANdomized Search) and BIRCH (Balanced Iterative Reducing and Clustering using Hierarchies) are more effective. These are referred to in the 'mining advance data types' section.

    b. *Hierarchical methods* group the data into a tree of clusters by either using bottom-up (agglomerative) or top-down (divisive) approach. The agglomerative methods treat each object in the data set as a group, and then, merge them successively into the top level or a termination condition is met. In contrast, the divisive methods work in the reverse order. AGNES (AGlomerative NESting) and DIANA (Divisive ANAlysis) are two examples for these types of clustering methods.

c. *Other methods* do also exist in addition to the major clustering methods listed above. These include density-based methods that distinguish clusters as dense regions in data space surrounded by low-dens regions (e.g. DBSCAN, DENCLUE); grid-based methods that perform clustering on the data space partitioned into a finite number of cells (e.g. STING, WaveCluster); model-based methods that try to optimize the fit between the data and a mathematical model. Most of these methods have been evaluated, especially, in mining advanced data types as will be mentioned further in this chapter. Model-based methods generally follow two approaches: Statistical (e.g. COBWEB) and ANN (e.g. self organizing maps (SOMs)). Yet, there are integrated methods that attempts to merge different clustering approaches (e.g. CLIQUE adopts both grid- and density-based techniques; CURE and DBSCAN has both hierarchical and partitioning components). Further methods executed in DM applications for clustering include PCA, GA, maximal tree method (MTM), association rules, ANOVA and rule induction.

3. *Association* function tries to identify groups of items that are happening together. In other words, it attempts to show the relationships between data items. Usually, these relationships do not indicate any causality or correlation. Association algorithms assume that database consists of a set of tuples (transactions or records) which contains a set of items. Most algorithms accomplish the association task in two main steps: finding the frequent (large) item sets, and then generating 'interesting rules' of the form $X \rightarrow Y$ from them. The 'statistical interestingness' of rules are usually determined by the measures sup-

port, confidence and lift (Hand et al., 2001). While 'support' measures the frequency of occurrence, 'confidence' measures the strength of the rule generated. The lift, on the other hand, relates the confidence of a rule to the support for its consequence, that is Y. Lift values greater than, less than and equal to one show a positive, negative and no relationship at all, respectively. The most commonly used association algorithm is the Apriori (Giudici, 2003). Some modifications on the Apriori algorithm are also proposed to make it more efficient (Han & Kamber, 2006). Two such examples are partitioning the data set and then mining each separately or sampling the data set first and then mining on a subset. Association rules can be classified into several categories based on different criteria (Dunham, 2003). Advanced rules such as generalized, quantitative, and minimum item support (MIS) association rules can generate more complex rules. Generalized and multi-level association rules allow rule generation at different levels by using a concept hierarchy technique. Quantitative association rules can handle both categorical and quantitative data. MIS Apriori algorithm allows a different support threshold for each item. Correlation rules, on the other hand, attempt to identify items that are statistically correlated.

Predictive Modeling

1. *Classification* is the well-known DM function accomplished in two basic steps: constructing a model that describes important classes in a given labeled data set (training sample) by using the methods like DTs, ANNs, and so on, and then, categorizing a new data set (testing sample), whose classes are not known, depending on the model built. Examples of classification applications are pattern recognition, medical diagnosis, faults

in industry applications like that. Major classification algorithms can be listed as follows (Dunham, 2003):

a. *S-based* algorithms use statistical techniques such as MLR and Bayesian Classifier (BC). Generalized linear models (GLM) are special type of regression models that are particularly useful for modeling categorical response variable such as logistic and Poisson regression (Larose, 2006). MLR, as GLM does, enable to model the relationship between the dependent variable (response) and predictors. The difference between them is that MLR assumes continuous dependent variable while GLM works with categorical dependent variable. The BC is based on the well-known Bayes' theorem. A simple form of it is called Naïve Bayesian Classifier (NBC), which assumes that the effect of an attribute value on a given class is independent of the values of the other attributes (Larose, 2006). While NBC simplifies the computations by assuming class conditional independence, Bayesian Belief Networks (BBN), uses graphical models, allow representing dependencies among attribute subsets.

b. *Decision Tree-based (DT-based)* algorithms, first, construct a tree to model the training data. Then, the tree is applied to the testing data for classification. These algorithms automatically generate rules by using if-then type structures. The most familiar DT induction algorithm is ID3. It is based on the information gain, called entropy, to measure the amount of uncertainty or randomness in the data set. Another DT algorithm, C4.5 which improves ID3 by dealing with missing data, continuous type data, pruning and rule generation.

The algorithm C5.0 is a commercial version of C4.5. Clementine, the DM component of SPSS, uses C5.0 algorithm for classification modeling. C5.0 algorithm is similar to C4.5 in DT induction but differs in generating rules. CHAID (CHi-Squared Automatic Interaction Detection) is one of the earliest DT algorithms. It only works on categorical values, and uses chi-square test to determine splitting and pruning. The algorithm CART (Classification and Regression Tree) creates a binary DT. It uses entropy as ID3 algorithm does. Others include statistical batch-based and instance-based (ID5R) DT learning. These algorithms perform considerably well for small to medium databases. There are other algorithms, however, suitable for large databases such as SLIQ and SPRINT (Scalable PaRallelizable Induction of DTs). A disadvantage of DT-based algorithms is overfitting that may occur due to modeling noise in training data. To overcome this problem, and thus, improve the classification accuracy 'tree pruning' is employed. This technique enables to identify the branches of tree that represent noise in data and remove them. These methods have also been employed especially for advanced DM such as spatial and temporal mining.

c. *Artificial Neural Network-based (ANN-based)* systems are very successful particularly for modeling nonlinear relationships (Fu, 1994). They consist of a set of connected input-output units each of which has a weight. These weights are updated during the learning phase. Learning an ANN involves numerical optimization of usually nonlinear functions. The choice of optimization method depends on the nature of problem. Levenberg-Marquart (LM), quasi-Newton and conjugate-gradient (CG) algorithms are local optimization methods while simulated annealing (SA) and GA are the global ones. Perceptron is the simplest form of an ANN, and used for classifying data into two classes. A multi-layer perceptron (MLP) combines percep-trons into a network structure. The most popular learning algorithm used in ANNs is the backpropagation (BP), which performs learning on a MLP feed-forward ANN by gradient descent (GD) optimization technique. Another widely used form of ANNs is the radial basis function (RBF). In fact, RBFs are three-layer feedforward NNs that generate output as a linear combina-tion of the basis functions computed by the hidden units. They employed supervised learning and can be used both for classification and predic-tion functions. A competitive ANN (CompetNN), on the other hand, learns to group input patterns into clusters, and adopt winner-take-all approach. SOM and learning vector quantization (LVQ) are examples for unsupervised competitive ANNs while ARTMAP and Fuzzy ARTMAP are examples for supervised competitive ANNs. Probabilistic NN (PNN) and Bayesian NN (BNN) are two other types of ANNs. Although BP is a widely used ANNs' learning algorithm, it requires a long computing time. PNN developed to solve this problem; it involves one pass, hence, result in quick learning. BNN, on the other hand, uses a paral-lel distributed approach for upgrading belief values in causal network struc-ture according to the Bayes' theorem. It uses both forward and backward propagation. Generally, ANNs do not generate if-then type rules. This aspect is one of their disadvantages over the DT. To overcome this problem, some algorithms have been developed, for example, rectangular basis function network (RecBFN).

d. *Other* classification algorithms include k-nearest-neighbors (KNN), GA, rough set theory (RST), fuzzy set theory (FST), SVM, entropy network (EN) and association rules-based methods. KNN is a distance-based algorithm that uses similarity or distance mea-sures to perform classification. It is an instance-based (also called lazy learners) type classifier, which is also used for prediction. GA (Zhai et al., 2002) learns by genetic evaluation. RST and FST are good at finding out relationships that may exist within noisy data. Note that RST can only be applied to discrete type variables. SVM algorithms are mixture of linear modeling and instance-based learning. They determine a few critical bound-ary instances, called support vectors, from each class and construct a linear discriminant function that separates the classes as widely as possible. Yet, there are others like PRISM, attribute decomposition approach (ADA), modi-fied breath-first search of an interest graph (MIG), genetic programming (GP) and breadth-oblivious-wrapper (BOW) which is a hill-climbing search procedure (Koksal et al., 2008).

e. *Combining techniques:* The classifier accuracy can be improved by combin-ing results with the use of a weighted linear combination of different clas-sification techniques. This approach is called combination of multiple classi-fiers (CMC) (Witten, 2005; Fu, 1994;

Sharkey, 1996). Boosting and bagging (bootstrap aggregation-BANN) are two examples for this type. While the models take equal weights in bagging (i.e. the final output is the average of individual models' output), successful models take more weights in boosting. As a result CMC decreases the expected error by reducing the overall variance. Another approach may be a combination of alternative techniques in such a way to obtain a completely new classification method, called stacked generalization (stacking). It applies the concept of metalearner to determine how best to combine the outputs of alternative classification techniques. Boosting and stacked generalization (NN and DT) methods are also used for the purpose of classification.

f. *Mixed techniques* have also been attempted for improving the performance of classification function (Koksal et al., 2008). For example, FST is used in combination with RBF NN; RST and linear programming (LP) are mixed up. DT and ANN are used in a hybrid manner; Taguchi method (TM) is applied to select parameters of an ANN; a Fuzzy Decision Support System (FDSS) is developed based on GA learning; FST is used in combination with RST; SVM and DT algorithms are integrated for the purpose of classification. One special method obtained as a result of mixing methods is the neuro-fuzzy system (NFS), which is based on a fuzzy system trained by an ANN learning algorithm. It combines the inexact reasoning ability of fuzzy set theory and the self-adaptation and -organization ability of ANN to obtain a more powerful computational structure. The NFS is also called as

fuzzy neural network (FNN). Modern NFSs are usually represented as special multilayer feedforward ANNs such as adaptive neural fuzzy inference systems (ANFIS). It is a three-layer feedforward ANN in which the first layer represents input variables, the middle (hidden) layer represents fuzzy rules and the third layer represents output variables. Fuzzy sets are encoded as (fuzzy) connection weights. Note here that a NFS can be interpreted as a system of fuzzy rules as well.

2. *Prediction* and classification functions try to predict future values of continuous and categorical type of data, respectively. Below, the DM methods used for prediction function are summarized.

a. *S-based* techniques include some well-known statistical methods for prediction task such as MLR (Larose, 2006) and GLM as stated above. Nonlinear regression (NLR) is an alternative to MLR when the assumed model is not linear in its parameters. Time series analysis (TSA), on the other hand, helps to model data obtained through time by considering time dependencies. Robust regression (RR) methods provide flexibility when white noise assumption regarding error term in MLR is not satisfied. Response surface methodology (RSM) is a process that leads to optimization of the dependent variable. It starts with MLR modeling in current operating conditions by using statistically designed experiments, and, then continues with the steepest ascent (descent) to reach the optimum response. Mathematical analysis of neighborhood of the optimum point is the final. Above methods tries to develop well-defined mathematical relations between the variables besides determining the most significant factors. The aim of ANOVA, however, is only to determine the important factors and their interactions affecting the response variation most. Nonparametric approaches provide us methods that are free of parametric assumptions. Classical regression methods seek point estimates of the model parameters. By contrast, in Bayesian regression (BR), the uncertainty is categorized in the parameter vector through a probability distribution. Then the posterior distribution of the parameters vector is expressed by the use of Bayes' theorem. Computational disadvantage of BR is coped with the availability of fast computers.

b. *DT-based:* CART is a DT algorithm used also for prediction.

c. *ANN-based:* MLP with BP (GD) learning is widely preferred ANN method in DM studies for the purpose of prediction. Other extensively used MLP based methods include MLP with LM and MLP with CG. Besides, MLP with BP (SA) learning is used when global optimization is needed. Recurrent NN Feedforward BP, RBF and BNN are other ANN-based methods utilized for the purpose of predictive modeling. Modular ANN (MANN) contains several expert networks and a gating network which determines the expert to be called for each training sample. Here, expert networks are ANNs that can perform as good as human experts can do. Each expert and gating networks are feedforward networks like a perceptron or a RBF network, and all networks have the same number of inputs and outputs. In this structure, the overall output error is propagated backward to expert and gating networks, and are adjusted accordingly. Computational NN (ComputNN) can learn by examples and can map very complex nonlinear functions without stating any functional relationship. A Polynomial Network (PN) builds nonlinear models efficiently by using a similar approach that ANNs generally use. Each input parameter is placed into a polynomial, and different combinations of polynomials attempt to minimize the error between the derived and expected output. Since PN does not use BP, it runs more quickly than any ANN. General Regression NN (GRNN) tries to approximate mathematical functions. PN and GRNN have similar architectures that depend on radial basis networks. However, PN perform classification whereas GRNN perform regression for prediction. Fuzzy ARTMAP NN is an NFS also used for prediction.

d. *Others:* Case-based reasoning (CBR), fuzzy adaptive network (FAN), ANFIS, TM, info-fuzzy network (IFN), GP and abductive network (AN) are other methods used for prediction (Koksal et al., 2008). Here, CBR solves new problems by adapting previously successful solutions to similar problems. An AN consists of a set of interconnected nodes whose computations can differ from one another and can be very complex. Abductive modeling searches for the node types and the architecture of their interconnections which minimize the predictive error. FAN, in other words, neural fuzzy approach, combines the ability of fuzzy sets for modeling vaguely defined systems, and the learning ability of an ANN. Finite element method (FEM) is used for finding approximate solutions of partial differential equations and integral equations. Fuzzy regression (FR) is relatively new method used for prediction. Bagging (bootstrap aggregated (BANN)) is a combining technique as described above, used also for prediction. In some studies, above listed techniques are used in combination for the same purpose. As an example, both FST and ANN are used in combination; TM is used for selecting ANN parameters.

Evaluation and Interpretation

The KDD process outlined above tries to uncover previously unknown structures that may reside in data. It basically includes data organization and descriptive and/or predictive modeling stages. Depending on needs of data sets and also depending on research objectives, one can start at any stage and continue with the others as long as there are research questions left to be answered. Thus, KDD is an iterative process in nature. Besides, there is not an only one way of mining data sets. One may try several methods for describing or modeling data. Therefore, assessing the utility and reliability, and then, interpretation of the information discovered in the (descriptive and/or predictive) modeling should be a complementary stage in a KDD process (Giudici, 2003). Evaluation of the DM methods to reach a final decision, that is selecting the best model, requires comparison of results obtained from various DM methods. Several criteria are used for this purpose including measures for assessing their performance and accuracy as well as assessing time and resource requirements. To obtain reliable results, knowledge extracted should be evaluated and interpreted correctly (Dunham, 2003). The output provided by today's DM software however is so complex that a human expert interpretation is a must. In any case, visual techniques can provide better understanding of the results obtained. These include two- or three-dimensional graphs such as bar charts, pie charts, line graphs, box plots, scatter plots etc.

The DM process stages 1-4 described above provides tools for better understanding the relations (i.e. learning) in data. The next step involves implementation of the results obtained from the KDD process into the decision making process (Giudici, 2003). Kusiak (2006) proposes a framework for more structured and transparent decision making based on the knowledge provided by different DM algorithms. This framework uses decision making constructs called as decision tables, decision maps, atlases and library. The matrix consist of rules versus attributes (generated by DM algorithms) is put into more structured form which is then used to be the building block of a decision table. The decision table here is defined as "a collection of knowledge needed to make decisions in a particular area." Several decision tables are combined to form a decision maps, and then, in an atlas.

Implementation

The KDD process described above provides tools for better understanding of the relations in data. The final KDD step involves implementation of the results obtained into the domain area (Giudici, 2003). Note here that implementation is the stage that distinguishes DM from any kind of data analysis. However, typical output of a DM analysis cannot be readily understood by its users. Kusiak (2006) proposes a framework for more structured and transparent decision making based on decision making constructs called decision tables, decision maps, atlases, and library. Moreover, in EWSs, time is a key factor necessitating correct interpretation and dissemination of the DM results in shorter times. Hence, special implementation approaches need to be developed for EWSs.

MINING ADVANCED DATA TYPES

Algorithms listed in the previous sections are suitable for mining structured data, which are stored in flat files, relational databases, transactional databases, data warehouses or data marts. In fact, real life applications involve data which requires more complex data formats such as objects, hypertexts, images, multimedia and so on, to be used. These data are usually stored in repositories such as object-oriented databases, object-relational databases and application-oriented databases (e.g. spatial databases, temporal databases) (Wu & Li, 2003).

Mining these type of advanced data needs new DM functionalities to be introduced in addition to the ones (e.g. association, clustering, classification and prediction) defined for structured data types. These include sequence discovery, trend analysis, and similarity analysis. These functionalities are implemented either by modifying the existing algorithms or developing totally new algorithms. In this section, we present DM functions and their corresponding methods that are particularly suitable for advanced data types.

Mining Spatial Data

Spatial data contain information regarding objects that occupy in space (Dunham, 2003). As a result, spatial data contains location information (e.g. address, latitude/longitude, coordinates in the Cartesian system) of objects in addition to their nonspatial features. Database in which spatial data such as maps, images, satellite data, are stored is called as spatial database. Spatial DM aims at finding out useful spatial patterns hidden in spatial data(bases). Spatial DM have been applied in various areas including geographic information systems (GIS), geology, environment, agriculture, climate science, medicine, robotics (Dunham, 2003). Geoinformatic surveillance for spatial and temporal hotspot detection based on raster maps is an evolving research area in developing

EWSs for various social and environmental risks (Patil, 2005).

Spatial data is more complicated compared to nonspatial data. Besides, spatial databases contains gross amount of both spatial and nonspatial data. These special characteristics cause difficulties in accessing and managing spatial data that are stored in spatial databases. In order to overcome these difficulties, spatial DM utilizes database technologies such as querying, reporting and OLAP operations as well as DM techniques (Han & Kamber, 2006). Among the spatial queries there are basic ones such as region query, range query, nearest neighbor query, distance scan query as well as spatial selection, aggregation and join (e.g. map overlay). In addition to these information processing techniques, OLAP operations such as drill down or roll up, can be used for analytical processing of data. Thus, descriptive DM on spatial data can effectively be applied by constructing spatial data cubes and by using spatial OLAP techniques.

There are also other approaches that are used to improve the efficiencies of spatial DM algorithms. These include generalization and specialization of spatial or nonspatial data depending on concept (i.e. spatial) hierarchies (Dunham, 2003). These approaches help to establish relationships at any level of the hierarchy. *Progressive refinement* is one such approach that leads more accurate results from approximate ones by filtering out data. *Nearest neighbor* distance, on the other hand, enables to determine objects which are close each other. STING is a kind of hierarchical clustering technique that partition the area studied into rectangular grids. Then, statistical information (e.g. descriptive statistics) is stored into each grid. All these techniques can also be applied as preprocessing of spatial data before accomplishing any DM task by using DM functions.

Due to peculiarities of spatial data, development of efficient spatial DM algorithms necessitates the invention of special data representations and data structures. A common approach is to represent a spatial object by the minimum bounding rectangle (MBR), which is the minimum rectangle embodying the object (Dunham, 2003). Instead of only one rectangle, several smaller nonoverlapping MBRs with the same or different sizes, which enclose the whole object, can also be used for representing spatial data.

There are several data structures used to store spatial data. The well-know ones are R-tree, quad tree and k-D tree (Dunham, 2003). R-tree is used to store data objects represented by MBRs. In this approach MBRs can overlap which may lead to a nested representation of spatial objects. The root node of the R-tree stores the top object that contains all the others. The layers, on the other hand, store ones that are contained at the same level of decomposition of the top object. Quad tree is another data structure that decomposes the space in which a spatial object occupies into quadrants hierarchically. The number of quadrants is determined according to the precision level needed. However, the quadrants should be nonoverlapping and regular in shape. Yet, another form of data structure is the k-D tree. It is a form of binary search tree that can store not only spatial but also any multidimensional data. It stores the top object representing the whole place/space to the root node as R-tree does. Then, the top object is continually partitioned along different dimensions until each division contains only one object.

Spatial Data Functionalities

In the following, we present algorithms used for implementing different DM functions applied on spatial data.

a.   *Spatial Association*: generate rules where some objects implies the other(s) (Dunham, 2003). In order to qualify an association rule be a *spatial association rule*, it must contain some spatial attributes (predicates) in either antecedent or consequent part. Special predicates include distance information (e.g. near,

close to, far away), topological relations (e.g. intersect, overlap), spatial orientations (e.g. right of, east of) (Han & Kamber, 2006). As an example, dormitories locating in the campus are expensive. Basic methods for implementing spatial association analysis utilize traditional approaches like Apriori. Because spatial databases contain huge number of objects, association rules considerable in number can be generated for spatial relationships among these objects. In order to make these algorithms work efficiently, the progressive refinement approach (Han & Kamber, 2006) or generalizations (Dunham, 2003) mentioned above are used.

b.   *Spatial Clustering*: is expected to have the following basic features: must be able to handle very large multidimensional data and clusters having irregular shapes as well as must not be influenced by the existence of outliers. In addition to the clustering algorithms which are also suitable for spatial data presented for structured data types (Han & Kamber, 2006), there are ones particularly developed for spatial data (Ladner et al., 2002). These new ones include CLARANS extensions, SD(CLARANS), DBCLASD, BANG and WaveCluster (Dunham, 2003). Both extensions of CLARANS use the approaches of reducing the size of the data. SD(CLARANS) first uses the clustering algorithm CLARANS to cluster objects depending on their spatial attributes, and then, tries to describe the objects in the cluster using nonspatial attributes. BANG is a density-based algorithm which uses a k-D tree like structure to identify clusters. WaveCluster treats the data as signals. Then a transformation such as wavelet can be used to determine clusters. Shekhar and Vatsavai (2003) provide application of clustering algorithms such as k-medoid for geospatial data.

c. *Spatial Classification*: tries to classify objects depending on their spatial or nonspatial attributes or both (Dunham, 2003). In order to improve the efficiencies of the algorithms sampling, generalization or progressive refinement techniques are utilized. Spatial DT approach describes the classes based on the most relevant spatial and nonspatial attributes of the nearby objects. Then, a DT is constructed by using these attributes. Particularly, an ID3 extension algorithm constructs a neighborhood graph to classify objects.

d. *Spatial Trend Analysis*: attempts to detect "regular changes in one or more nonspatial attribute values for spatial objects as you move away from another spatial object" (Dunham, 2003). It studies the trend in nonspatial or spatial data changing with space (Han & Kamber, 2006). Regression and correlation analysis are usually used to apply spatial trend analysis.

Mining Temporal Data

The *sequence data* involves attributes related to ordered activities (Han & Kamber, 2006). *Temporal (time-varying) data* is a kind of sequence data consisting of values of attributes that change with time (Dunham, 2003). The main difference between spatial data and time-varying data is that spatial attributes are static while time is dynamic. Besides, time can be represented in one dimension while space is represented in at least two dimensions. Temporal databases can be categorized according to the representation type of time: snapshot, transactional time, valid time or bitemporal (uses both valid time and transactional time representation) databases. Some examples related to temporal data are images and sensor data collected by satellites, monitoring of products produced in a dynamic production process, heartbeats recorded continuously for a patient after surgery or treatment.

Several techniques have been used to model temporal data (Dunham, 2003). The most common ones include finite state recognizer (FSR), Markov models (MMs), hidden Markov models (HMMs), recurrent neural networks (RNNs). Here, both FSR and MM are directed graphs. HMM is similar to MMs in that HMM satisfies the Markov property but HMM may not correspond to observable states. RNNs, on the other hand, are used both for recognition and prediction of temporal data. However, it is rather difficult to train and use compared to the feedforward NNs.

As with spatial DM, temporal DM utilizes elaborate DM techniques such as trend analysis, similarity analysis, pattern detection, periodicity analysis, prediction in addition to well-known database features like querying. Temporal queries include intersection, inclusion, containment (Dunham, 2003).

In the following section, we present different approaches and algorithms developed specifically for implementing DM functions which can be applied on temporal data.

Temporal Data Functionalities

As stated above, temporal data is a sequence data but the reverse may not be true, so that algorithms developed for sequence data may also used for time series data as well. Here, we need to distinguish the terms *series* and *sequence*. A sequence is defined as "an ordered list of sets of items or values" whereas a series is "an ordered list of values"; subsequence, on the other hand, is the "one that can be obtained by removing some items and any resulting empty item sets from the original sequence" (Han & Kamber, 2006).

In DM studies, temporal data usually recall time series data, which is defined as "a set of attribute values over a period of time" (Dunham, 2003). It can be of type discrete or continuous. DM functions peculiar to time series and sequence data can be listed as follows (Laxman & Sastry, 2006):

a. *Trend Analysis* is a part of time series analysis which tries to partition a time series into four basic components: trends, cycles, seasonal and random (Box et al., 2008; Wei, 2006). Trend, here, is "the general direction in which a time series is moving over a long interval of time" (Han & Kamber, 2006). It can be modeled by using a linear or non-linear mathematical model. Usually simple methods help us to detect (estimate) trends. One of them is the free-hand method which is a subjective approach. More objective methods include smoothing techniques and least squares method. Detecting components other than trend requires more elaborate technique to be used. For example, autocorrelation function can be utilized for detecting seasonal patterns that may emerge at a particular time of year. Transformations can contribute pattern detection by reducing the number of dimensions or stabilizing the variance.

b. *Prediction* involves forecasting future values of attributes. Typical methods used for implementing the prediction DM function are autoregression, autoregressive moving average (ARMA) and autoregressive integrated moving average (ARIMA). ARIMA models are used if the data is not stationary (Box et al., 2008; Wei, 2006).

c. *Similarity Analysis* matchs patterns to determine if they differ only slightly (Han & Kamber, 2006). It uses a similarity measure such as Euclidian distance. There are different kinds of similarity searches. Whole sequence matching matches the two sequences completely. Subsequence matching, on the other hand, searches for all data sequences similar to the given. One special type of subsequent matching looks for the longest similar subsequences between two sequences. Examples for similarity analysis include medical diagnosis, cardiogram analysis, image processing, and stock market analysis. To improve the efficiencies of the algorithms for subsequence matching or similarity search in large databases, data independent transformations such as discrete Fourier transformation (DFT) or discrete wavelet transformation (DWT) can be first applied data. Then, a multidimensional indexing (e.g. R-tree) can be constructed by using, for example, the first few Fourier coefficients. There are also advanced methods to deal with gaps and differences in offsets and amplitudes.

d. *Pattern Detection* identifies "a given pattern that occurs in the sequence" (Dunham, 2003). In fact, it tries to classify the pattern(s) (if exist) in the sequence using the given set of patterns. Therefore, pattern detection can be considered as a classification function. The simplest pattern detection algorithms have been developed for word processing and spell checking. These involve string matching algorithms such as Knuth-Morris-Pratt (KMP) and Boyer-Moore (BM). The KMP uses FSM for pattern recognition. BM is an improvement on the KMP. On the contrary of string matching problems, many real life applications require fuzzy pattern matching. *Sequential pattern mining* is defined as "the mining of frequently occurring patterns related to time or other sequences" (Wang & Yang, 2005). This kind of mining can be used, for example, for customer retention or weather prediction. Methods for implementing sequential pattern mining usually use approaches similar to that of Apriori. These include ArpioriAll, sequential discovery using equivalence classes (SPADE) and generalized sequential patterns (Han & Kamber, 2006).

e. *Periodicity Analysis* deals with recurrent patters in time series (Wang & Yang, 2005). Hence, it is a special kind of sequential pattern mining applied on temporal data. Examples include seasonal precipitation amounts, daily energy consumptions, and yearly wages. There are three types of basic periodic patterns: full, partial and cycling periodic pattern.

f. *Temporal Association Rules* are generated after the data is clustered depending on time to examine the change in association rules over time. There are different types of rules are generated by using sliding windows. Episode rules are generalized association rules applied to sequences of events. Sequence association rules use sequences in rules. Sequence association rule generation is interested in finding sequence association rules with minimum support and confidence. As an example, buying behavior of customers can be predicted over time by using sequence association rules.

Mining Text Data

Textual DM is relatively immature area of DM compared to the ones introduced above (i.e. mining in databases, mining spatial and temporal data). However, there has been a growing need on the development of new DM techniques in analyzing and mining text data because of increasing amount of documents collected and stored in the electronic mediums. The main aim of text mining is to "extract useful information from data sources through the identification and exploration of interesting patterns" (Feldman & Sanger, 2007). Here, "data sources" refer to the document collections such as news articles, research papers, manuscripts, electronic mail messages, electronic books and web pages. The text data are semi-structured type data in that it may contain some structured information (e.g. title, date, authors) as well as unstructured information (e.g. body of the text).

Earliest technique developed to process unstructured data is the IR (e.g. text indexing methods) (Han & Kamber, 2006). Given the user specified input (i.e. keywords), IR techniques concerns with placing related documents

(Thuraisingham, 2003). The success of retrieval operation is usually evaluated by the measures: precision and recall. Here, precision and recall are defined as the percentage of retrieved document, actually, relevant to the query, and the percentage of documents relevant to the query, actually, retrieved, respectively.

There are two basic methods of IR: keyword-based and similarity-based (Han & Kamber, 2006). Keyword-based IR attempts to find relevant documents containing a keyword or an expression provided. Similarity-based IR, on the other hand, cares for locating similar documents. Similarity of documents or similarity between a given document and keywords are measured by their relative frequencies stored in a "term frequency matrix." Another one used for determining the degree of similarity is the cosine measure. In addition, to improve the efficiency of these techniques, indexing techniques such as latent semantic indexing, inverted index, signature files are also employed.

In spite of its unique features listed, IR is not a sufficient tool for accomplishing the text mining tasks. Obviously, more advanced treatments are needed to analyze and identify interesting patterns in textual data. These include data preprocessing and DM functionalities such as association, classification and clustering. In the following, first, we introduce text mining preprocessing. Next, the DM functions as applied to documents are presented.

The main purpose of text mining preprocessing is to convert the semi-structured format of text data into structured one. It significantly differs from the conventional data preprocessing of KDD. Note here that text mining algorithms works on the feature-based representations of documents. There are four basic features used to represent documents: characters, words, terms and concepts (Feldman & Sanger, 2007). The task of text preprocessing is to elaborate the existing features leading to a structured document. There are two approaches for text preprocessing. Natural language processing (NLP) is the domain-dependent approach while text categorization (or classification) (TC) and information extraction (IE) are domain-dependent ones. These later two techniques are also referred to as "tagging". Implementation of these techniques (i.e. TC or IE) creates the "tagged-formatted" structure of the text preprocessed, thus, creating a structured document as a result.

Below, text DM functionalities are briefly described.

a. *Text Classification* is defined as "given a set of categories (subjects or topics) and a collection of text documents, the process of finding the correct topic for each document" (Feldman & Sanger, 2007). Applications include spam filtering, text indexing, and web page categorization. There are two main approaches to text classification. In knowledge engineering approach, experts in the domain develops rules for classifying a document into a subject or topic. For example, the CONSTRUE system is constructed by this approach. Machine learning approach, however, automatically builds the classifier by supervised learning. The following algorithms can be used for classifying textual data: NB, Bayesian LR, DT (e.g. ID3, C4.5, CART), decision rule classifiers, regression, the Rocchio method, NN, k-nearest neighbor, SVM, bagging and boosting (Feldman & Sanger, 2007).

b. *Clustering* is grouping the given unlabeled document with/out any prior information (Feldman & Sanger, 2007). Clustering applications include document retrieval, image segmentation and pattern classification. Before clustering textual data, documents are represented by vectors. Next, dimension reduction is applied. Then, cluster descriptions are generated to help further automatic processing. Afterwards, one of the clustering methods such as k-means, hierarchical agglomerative clustering, minimal spanning tree, nearest neighbor, is applied.

Mining Multimedia Data

A multimedia data consists of a large number of objects such as audio, video, hypertext and image data. These types of data are becoming more available due to extensive use of electronic instruments such as audio-video equipments, cell phones, CD ROMS, in recent years. Internet database, for example, contains such data. In addition to the classical multidimensional analysis of multimedia data, similarity search, association, clustering, classification and prediction DM functions are also applied to mine the multimedia data (Han & Kamber, 2006).

Before conducting rigorous DM applications on multimedia data, usually data preprocessing techniques like data cleaning, data focusing and feature selection, are employed. Following preprocessing, multidimensional data analysis may be managed by constructing a multidimensional data cube. A data cube of multimedia data contains additional dimensions such as the size of image or video, height and width of an image, and color. Concept hierarchies may also be relevant in such as analysis.

Similarity search can be applied either by using data description or data content. Data descriptions may include size, creation date and time, keywords, and so on. Content, on the other hand, may be consisting of information such as color, texture, and shape. Similarity search for content may depend on examples or features of multimedia objects. Applications of content similarity searches include medical diagnosis, weather prediction.

In addition to OLAP and similarity analysis, association rules can be generated for the multimedia data. These may be related to associations between image and nonimage content, image content and spatial relations. Because multimedia data contains several objects having many features, as a result of association mining association rules in considerable number can be generated. In such a case, using resolution refinement approach may help to improve the process. Besides association rule generation, classification and prediction functions are also applied multimedia data particularly in astronomy and geology (Kamath, 2003). One of the methods utilized for this purpose is the DT. Djeraba and Fernandez (2003) also applied k-medoids algorithm for clustering image data.

Mining Word Wide Web

World-wide web (www) is a distributed information service environment containing data about banks, education, firms, industries, government and so on (Han & Kamber, 2006). Web mining is "the process of applying DM techniques to the pattern discovery in Web data" (Chang et al., 2001). Since the invention of the internet, search in www has been very popular to retrieve information. Many algorithms have been developed for this purpose (Marko & Larose, 2007). The earliest ones are based on keywords which have essentially insufficiencies. These problems have been mostly overcome with the help of the developments in text mining techniques. One such algorithm developed is the hyperlink induced topic search (HITS) which utilizes the hub(s) to identify most relevant pages for the search (Han & Kamber, 2006). A hub, here, is a web page containing links to the most significant sites related to a common topic. An example for keyword and HITS based search engines are Yahoo and Google, respectively. Besides the searching activities, classification of web documents is also a relevant web mining function. Methods similar to the text data classification can also be utilized for this purpose.

Web mining is generally conducted by three ways: web content mining, web structure mining and web usage mining (Chang et al., 2001; Han & Kamber, 2006; Dunham, 2003). Since web content and structure mining are related to each other, usually, there are two categories: web content and usage mining. Web content mining is the process of analyzing www data including text and multimedia data (Thuraisingham, 2003).

Therefore all techniques listed above for mining text and multimedia data can be used for the web content analysis. Web usage mining, on the other hand, is the process of analyzing access patterns of users' to the web pages. For this purpose weblog records are analyzed to determine associations between the web pages and the users. Such analysis, for example, can be helpful in locating potential customers of e-commerce. Furthermore, business intelligence can be developed through web mining to handle threats and anti-terrorist attacks (Thuraisingham, 2003).

DM SOFTWARE USED IN EWS

DM software used in EWSs vary from simple spreadsheet applications (such as Excel™) and database management systems (such as ORACLE™) to statistical software (such as SAS™ and SPSS™), DM software (such as SAS/EM™ and SPSS Clementine™), general purpose software (such as MATLAB™), high-level languages (such as C/C++) and special purpose software. The special purpose software solutions are designed for use in a particular EWS. For example, SAP AG™ provides an EWS that can be used for all applications in logistics. Similarly, InforSense Text Analytics™ is a text mining software that can be used in EWSs for manufacturers to identify common faults as well as in security and intelligence applications. Wallace and Cermack (2004) illustrates the use of an EWS running on SAS/Text Miner™ and SAS/QC™ to monitor incoming free form text warranty and call center data in a systematic manner, for an automotive supplier. There are also special purpose software programs used for risk detection by governments and large international organizations. ADVISE (Analysis, Dissemination, Visualization, Insight, and Semantic Enhancement) is such a program within the United States Department of Homeland Security Threat and Vulnerability Testing and Assessment (TVTA). It is reported to be a massive

DM system that processes a wide variety of data in the form of any electronic information used to assess the probability of a suspect being a terrorist (Burleson, 2009). Similarly, several software solutions based on general purpose software and high-level languages are being developed and used in ongoing research projects on risk management of geohazards using DM (International Centre for Geohazards [ICG], 2009). Among other examples, a software system currently used in Indian National Tsunami EWS has a data warehousing and DM and dissemination module for storing and analyzing and quick retrival of data at the time of a tsunami event (Kumar et al., 2009).

FUTURE RESEARCH DIRECTIONS

Several research directions can be described for the development of EWSs using KDD and DM. Considering successful results of the current DM applications in EWSs, it should be expected that DM is adapted also to less explored areas such as risk detection in food supply networks, harvest failure and unemployment. Mining of advanced data types such as raster maps, time varying images and hypertexts is also challenging. Further contributions are needed in processing and analyzing these data both for DM and EWS development. On the other hand, surveillance technologies keep improving for faster collection of more accurate, reliable and multifaceted data. As the data types vary with these improvements, data preparation and preprocessing approaches of the KDD process and DM approaches need to improve accordingly. Furthermore, evaluation, interpretation and implementation of DM results require more attention by the researchers, since typical output of a DM analysis cannot be readily understood by its users. Moreover, in EWSs, time is a key factor necessitating correct interpretation and dissemination of the DM results in shorter times. Hence, automating the interpretation and dissemination or implementation of the results can be considered as an important research area.

CONCLUSION

Application of DM, in particular, and KDD, in general, has proven to increase effectiveness of EWSs. In this chapter, KDD process and DM as an important part of it are defined thoroughly with their functions and methods as well as their extensions for advanced data types. This background together with the overview of application examples and software used in the literature can be used as a reference by the researchers and practitioners interested in detection and management of various types of risks.

REFERENCES

Alker, H. R. (2009). *Conflict Early Warning Systems*. Received August 1, 2009 from http://www.usc.edu/dept/LAS/ir/cews/

Apley, W. (2003). Principal componets and factor analysis. In Ye, N. (Ed.), *The handbook of data mining*. Upper Saddle River, NJ: Lawrence Erlbaum Associates Publisher.

Baesens, B., Mues, C., Martens, D., & Vanthienen, J. (2009). 50 years of data mining in OR: Upcoming trends and chalanges. *Journal of the Orepational Research Society, 60*, 16–23. doi:10.1057/jors.2008.171

Bartels, P. H., Montironi, R., Scarpelli, M., Bartels, H. G., & Alberts, D. S. (2009)... *Analytical and Quantitative Cytology and Histology, 31*(3), 125–136.

Box, G. E. P., Jenkins, G. M., & Reinsel, G. C. (2008). *Time series analysis, forecasting and control*. New York: Wiley.

Brown, M. E. (2008). *Famine early warning systems and remote sensing data*. Berlin: Springer.

Bull, M., Kundt, G., & Gierl, L. (1997). Discovering of health risks and case-based forecasting of epidemics in a health surveillance systems. In Komorowski, J., & Zytkow, J. (Eds.), *Principles of Data Mining and Knowledge Discovery, 1263* (pp. 68–77). Berlin: Springer-Verlag.

Burleson, R. (2009). *Information to insight in a counterterrorism context*. Retrieved August 1, 2009, from http://www.ipam.ucla.edu/publications/gss2005/gss2005_5484.pdf

Caragata, P. J. (1999). *Business early warning systems:Corporate Governance for the New Millennium*. Wellington, New Zealand: Butterworths.

Cervone, G., Kafatos, M., Napoletani, D., & Singh, R. P. (2006). An early warning systems for coastal earthquakes. *Advances in Space Research, 37*, 636–642. doi:10.1016/j.asr.2005.03.071

Chan, N. H., Wong, H. Y., & Wong, H. Y. (2007). Data mining of resilience indicators. *IIE Transactions, 39*(6), 617–627. doi:10.1080/07408170600899565

Chang, G., Healey, M. J., McHugh, J. A. M., & Wang, J. T. L. (2001). *Mining the world wide web: An information search approach*. Boston: Kluwer Academic Publisher.

Chen, Y., Guo, J. J., Healy, D. P., Lin, W. D., & Patel, N. C. (2008). Risk of hepatotoxity associated with the use of telithromycin: A signal detection using data mining algorithms. *The Annals of Pharmacotherapy, 42*(12), 1791–1796. doi:10.1345/aph.1L315

Cheng, T. X., Qi, X., & Jiang, W. T. (2008). The DM based DSS for risk pre-warning in tender evaluation of civil projects. In Xia, G. P. & Deng, X. Q. (Eds.), *Proceedings of the 38th International Conference on Compuers and Industrial Engineering,* (Vol. 1-3, pp. 487-492). Beijing: Publishing House Electronics Industry.

Cocx, T., Kosters, W. A., & Laros, J. F. J. (2008). An early warning system for the prediction of criminal careers. In Gelbukh, A., & Morales, E. F. (Eds.), *Mexican international conference on artifical intelligence 2008: Lecture notes in artifical intelligence* (pp. 77–89). Berlin: Springer-Verlag.

Dasu, T., & Johnson, T. (2003). *Exploratory data mining and data cleaning*. New York: Wiley-Interscience. doi:10.1002/0471448354

Dian-Min, Y., Xiao-Dan, W., Yue, L., & Chao-Hsien, C. (2007). Data mining-based financial fraud detection: Current status and key issues. In Qi, E. (Ed.), *Proceedings of the 14th International Conference on Industrial Engineering and Engineering Management, Vols A and B – Building core competencies through IE&EM* (pp. 891-896). Beijing: Chine Machine Press.

Djeraba, C., & Fernandez, G. (2003). Mining image data. In Ye, N. (Ed.), *The handbook of data mining* (pp. 637–656). Mahwah, NJ: Lawrence Erlbaum Associates Publisher.

Drewes, B. (2005). Some industrial applications of text mining. In Sirmakessis, S. (Ed.), *Knowledge mining: Proceesings of the NEMIS 2004 final conference* (pp. 233–238). Berlin: Springer.

Dunham, M. H. (2003). *Data mining introductory and advanced topics*. Upper Saddle River, NJ: Prentice Hall/Pearson Education.

Fayyad, U. P., Piatetsky-Shapiro & Smith, P. (1996). From data mining to knowledge discovery in databases. *AI Magazine*, 37–57.

Feldman, R. (2003). Mining text data. In Ye, N. (Ed.), *The handbook of data mining* (pp. 481–518). Mahwah, NJ: Lawrence Erlbaum Associates Publisher.

Feldman, R., & Sanger, J. (2007). *The text mining handbook*. Cambridge, MA: Cambridge University Press.

Fu, L. M. (1994). *Neural networks in computer intelligence*. New York: McGraw-Hill.

Gao, W., & Zhang, G. (2007). An IDS early-warning model based on data mining technology. In *ISCRAM CHINA 2007: Proceedings of the Second International Workshop on Information Systems for Crisis Response and Management* (pp. 99-104). Harbin, China: Harbin Engineering University.

Gasparini, P., Manfredi, G., & Zschau, J. (2007). *Earthquake early warning systems*. Berlin: Springer. doi:10.1007/978-3-540-72241-0

Gilad, B. (2003). *Early warning: using competitive intelligence to anticipate market shifts, control risk, and create powerful strategies*. New York: AMACOM.

Giudici, P. (2003). *Applied data mining: statistical methods for business and industry*. New York: John Wiley.

Glantz, M. H. (2009). *Heads up!: early warning systems for climate-, water- and weather-related hazards*. Tokyo: United Nations University Press.

Goldstein, M., Reinhart, C., & Kaminsky, G. (2000). *Assessing financial vulnerability: an early warning system for emerging markets*. Washington, DC: Institute for International Economics.

Grabert, M., Prechtel, M., Hrycej, T., & Gunther, W. (2004). An early warning systems for vehicle related quality data. In Perner, P. (Ed.), *Advances in Data Mining – Applications in Image mining, Medicine and Biotechnology, Management and Environment Control, and Telecommunications, 3275* (pp. 88–95). Berlin: Springer-Verlag.

Gurr, J. L., & Davies, T. R. (1998). *Preventive measures: building risk assessment and crisis early warning systems*. Lanham, MD: Rowman and Littlefield Publishers, Inc.

Han, J., & Kamber, M. (2006). *Data mining: concepts and techniques*. San Francisco: Morgan Kaufmann Publishers.

Hand, H., Mannila, H., & Smyth, P. (2001). *Principles of data mining*. Cambridge, MA: MIT Press.

He, Y., Huang, Z., & Liu, J. S. (2007). An application of self-organizing data mining method in early-warning of industrial economy. In Xu, J., Jiang, Y. & Yan, H. (Eds.), *Proceedings of 2007 International Conference on Management Science and Engineering Management* (pp. 163-167). Liverpool, UK: World Acad Union-World Acad Press.

Hormozi, A. M. & Giles, S. (2004). Data mining: A compatetive wepon for banking and retail industries. *International Systems Management*, 62-71.

International Centre for Geohazards (ICG). (2009). *Project 12: monitoring, remote sensing and early warning systems*. Retrieved August 1, 2009 from http://www.geohazards.no/projects/project12_monitor.htm

Ito, N., Onoda, T., & Yamasaki, H. (2009). Interactive abnormal condition sign discovery for hydroelectric power plants. In Chawla, S., Washio, T., Minato, S. I., Tsumoto, S., Onoda, T., Yamada, S., & Inokuchi, A. (Eds.), *New Frontiers in Applied Data Mining, 5433* (pp. 181–192). Berlin: Springer-Verlag. doi:10.1007/978-3-642-00399-8_16

Jager, R., & Kalber, S. (2005). GNSS/GPS/LPS based online control and alarm system (GOCO) – Mathematical models and technical realization of a system for natural and geotechnical deformation monitoring and hazard prevention. In Cygas, D. & Froehner, K. D. (Eds.), *6th International Conference Environmental Engineering, Vols 1 and 2* (pp. 882-890).

Kamath, C. (2003). Mining science and engineering data. In Ye, N. (Ed.), *The handbook of data mining* (pp. 550–572). Mahwah, NJ: Lawrence Erlbaum Associates Publisher.

Kapetanovic, I. M., Rosenfeld, S., & Izmirlian, G. (2004). Overview of connonly used Bioinformatics methods and their applications. *Annals of the New York Academy of Sciences, 1020*, 10–21. doi:10.1196/annals.1310.003

Kim, T. Y., Oh, K. J., Shon, I., & Hwang, C. (2004). Usefulness of artificial neural networks for early warning system of economic crisis. *Expert Systems with Applications, 26*, 583–590. doi:10.1016/j.eswa.2003.12.009

Koksal, G., Batmaz, I., & Testik, M. C. (2008). *Data mining processes and a review of their applications for product and process quality improvement in manufacturing industry. Technical report No: 08-03, Supported by TÜBİTAK, Industrial Engineering Department.* Ankara: METU.

Koyuncugil, A. S., & Ozgulbas, N. (2007). Detecting financial early warning signs in Istanbul stock exchange by data mining. [IJBR]. *International Journal of Business Research, 5*(3).

Koyuncugil, A. S., & Ozgulbas, N. (2009). Early warning system for SMEs as a financial risk detector. In Rahman, H. (Ed.), *Data mining applications for empowering knowledge societies* (pp. 221–240). Hershey, PA: Information Science Reference.

Kuenzer, C., Zhang, J., Voigt, J. L., Mehl, H., & Wagner, W. (2007). Detecting unknown coal fires: synercy of coal fire risk area delination and improved thermal anomaly extraction. *International Journal of Remote Sensing, 28*(20), 4561–4585. doi:10.1080/01431160701250432

Kumar, T. S., Kumar, C. P., Kumar, B. A., Mulukutla, S., & Vittal, T. S. (2009). *Geospatial technology solution for Indian national tsunami early warning system.* August 1, 2009 from http://www.gisdevelopment.net/application/natural_hazards/floods/mwf09_srinivasa.htm

Kusiak, A. (2006). Data mining: Manufacturing and service applications. *International Journal of Production Research, 44*(18/19), 4175–4191. doi:10.1080/00207540600632216

Ladner, R. Show, & Abdelguerfi, K. (2002). *Mining spatio-temporal information systems.* Boston: Kluwer Academic Publisher.

Larose, D. T. (2005). *Discovering knowledge in data.* Mahwah, NJ: Wiley and Sons.

Larose, D. T. (2006). *Data mining methods and models.* Mahwah, NJ: Wiley and Sons.

Laxman, S., & Sastry, P. S. (2006). A survey of temporal data mining. *Sadhana, 3*, 173–198. doi:10.1007/BF02719780

Li, C. S. (2006). Survey of early warning systems for environmental and public health applications. In Wong, S., & Li, C. S. (Eds.), *Life science data mining.* Singapore: World Scientific Publishing. doi:10.1142/9789812772664_0001

Lo, W. S., Hong, T. P., Jeng, R., & Liu, J. P. (2009). Intelligent agents in supply chain management as an early warning mechanism. In *2006 IEEE International Conference on Systems, Man, and Cybernetics, Vols 1-6, Proceedings* (pp. 2161-2166). New York: IEEE Pub.

Marko, Z., & Larose, D. T. (2007). *Data mining the web.* Mahwah, NJ: Wiley and Sons. doi:10.1002/0470108096

Martinez, W. L., & Martinez, A. R. (2002). *Computational statistics handbook with MATLAB.* Boca Raton, FL: Chapman and Hall.

Meier, P. (2006). *Towards an early warning system for preventing environmental conflicts. Natural Resources Related Conflict Management in Southeast Asia.* Khon-Khaen, Thailand: Institute for Dispute Resolution.

Meng, Y., & Dunham, M. H. (2006). Online mining of risk level of traffic anomalies with user's feedbacks. In *2006 IEEE International Conference on Granular Computing,* (pp. 176-181). New York: IEEE Pub.

Mirkin, B. (2005). *Clustering for data mining: a data recovery approach.* New York: Chapman and Hall.

O'Brien, S. P. (2003). *Near-term forecasts of crisis and instability using text-based events.* Bethesda, MD: Center for Army Analysis, Report Number: A363824.

Organisation for Economic Co-operation and Development (OECD). (2009). *Conflict and fragility preventing violence, war and state collapse: the future of conflict early warning and response.* Paris: OECD Publishing.

Organization for Economic Cooperation and Development (OECD). (2003). *Emerging systemic risks in the 21st century: an agenda for action.* Paris: OECD Publishing.

Patil, G. P. (2005). Geoinformatic hotspot systems (GHS) for detection, prioritization, and early warning. In *Proceedings of the 2005 national conference on digital government research* (pp. 116-117). Digital Government Society of North America.

Peng, Y., Kou, G., & Shi, Y. (2009). Knowledge-rich data mining in financial risk detection. Allen, G. Seidel, E., Dongarra, J., Nabrzyski, J., VanAlbada, G. D. & Sloot, P. M. A. (Eds.), *Computational Science, ICCS 2009, Part II, LNCS 5545* (pp. 534–542). Berlin: Springer-Verlag.

Pettersson, M. (2004). SPC with applications to churn management. *Quality and Reliability Engineering International, 20,* 397–406. doi:10.1002/qre.654

Phua, C., Gayler, R., Lee, V., & Smith-Miles, K. (2009). On the communal analysis suspicion scoring for identity crime in streaming credit applications. *European Journal of Operational Research, 195,* 595–612. doi:10.1016/j.ejor.2008.02.015

Pietravalle, S., Van der Bosch, F., Shaw, M. W., & Parker, S. R. (2002). Towards an earl warning system for winter wheat disease severity. In *BCPC Conference – Pests & Diseases 2002,* (Vol. 1-2, pp. 897-902).

Pyle, D. (1999). *Data preparation for data mining.* San Francisco, CA: Morgan Kaufmann Publishers.

Sharkey, A. J. K. (1996). On combining artificial neural nets. *Connection Science, 8*(3), 299–314. doi:10.1080/095400996116785

Shekhar, S., & Vatsavai, R. R. (2003). Mining geospatial data. In Ye, N. (Ed.), *The handbook of data mining* (pp. 520–548). Mahwah, NJ: Lawrence Erlbaum Associates Publishers.

Sintchenko, V., Gallego, B., Chung, G., & Coiera, E. (2009). Towards bioinformatics assisted infectious disease control. BMC *Bioinformatics, 10*(2). Retrieved August 1, 2009, from http://www.biomedcentral.com/1471-2105/10/S2/S10

Tan, P. N., Steinbach, M., & Kumar, V. (2006). *Introduction to data mining.* New York: Pearson Education.

Taniar, D. (Ed.). (2007). *Research and trends in data mining technologies and applications.* Hershey, PA: IGI Global.

Thuraisingham, B. (2003). *Web data mining with applications in business intelligence and counter-terrorism.* Boca Raton, FL: CRC Press. doi:10.1201/9780203499511

Toktas, P., & Demirhan, M. B. (2004). *Risk analizinde veri madenciliği uygulamaları.* Paper presented at the meeting of the YA/EM'200-Yöneylem Araştırması/ Endüstri Mühendisliği-XXIV Ulusal Kongresi, Gaziantep-Adana.

Tsumoto, S. Maksuoka, K. & Yokoyama, S. (2008) Application of data mining to medical risk management – art. No. 697308. In Dasarathy, B. V. (Ed.), *Data Mining, Intrusion Detection, Information Assurance, and Data Networks Security, 6973* (pp. 97308-97308). Bellingham, WA: Spei-Int. Soc. Optical Engineering.

Tsumoto, S., Tusumoto, Y., Matsuoka, K., & Yokoyama, S. (2007). Risk mining in medicine: Application of data mining to medical risk management. In Zhong, N., Liu, J. M., Yao, Y. Y., Wu, J. L., Lu, S. F., & Li, K. C. (Eds.), *Web Intelligent Meets Brain Informatics, 4845* (pp. 471–493). Berlin: Springer-Verlag. doi:10.1007/978-3-540-77028-2_28

Tsumoto, S., & Washio, T. (2007). Risk mining – Overview. In Washio, T., Satoh, K., Takeda, H., & Inokuchi, A. (Eds.), *New frontiers in artificial intelligence* (pp. 303–304). Berlin: Springer-Verlag. doi:10.1007/978-3-540-69902-6_26

Wallace, J., & Cermack, T. (2004). Text mining warranty and call center data: Early warning for product quality awareness. *SUGI 29 Proceedings, Analytics, 003-29*. Cary, NC: SAS Institute Inc. Retrieved August 1, 2009, from http://www2.sas.com/proceedings/sugi29/003-29.pdf

Wang, W., & Yang, J. (2005). *Mining sequential patterns from large data sets*. New York: Springer.

Wei, W. W. S. (2006). *Time series analysis: univariate and multivariate methods*. Boston: Addison-Wesley.

Witten, I. H. (2005). *Data mining: practical machine learning tools and techniques*. Boston: Morgan Kaufman.

Wu, T., & Li, X. (2003). Data storage and management. In Ye, N. (Ed.), *The handbook of data mining* (pp. 393–408). Mahwah, NJ: Lawrence Erlbaum Assoc. Publishers.

Yang, J. M., Liang, P. H., & Chen, A. H. (2007). Applying text mining for extracting non-structural information in corporate financial report- A study of financial early-warning system. *Proceedings of Bussiness and Information, 4*. Retreived August 1, 2009, from http://ibacnet.org/bai2007/proceedings/Papers/2007bai7427.doc

Zhai, L., Khoo, L., & Fok, S. (2002). Feature extraction using rough set theory and genetic algorithms—an application for the simplification of product quality evaluation. *Computers & Industrial Engineering, 43*(4), 661–676. doi:10.1016/S0360-8352(02)00131-6

ADDITIONAL READING

Abonyi, J., & Feil, B. (2007). *Cluster analysis for data mining and system identification*. Boston, MA: Birkhäuser.

Akerkar, R. (2008). *Building an intelligent web: theory and practice*. Boston, MA: Bartlett Publishers.

Asian Development Bank. (2005). *Early warning systems for financial crises: applications to East Asia*. New York: Palgrave Macmillan.

Berry, M. J. A., & Linoff, G. S. (2004). *Data mining techniques: for marketing, sales, and customer relationship management*. Indianapolis, IN: Wiley Publisher.

Berry, M. W. (Ed.). (2004). *Survey of text mining*. New York: Springer.

Bettini, C., Jajodia, S., & Wang, S. (2000). *Time granularities in databases, data mining, and temporal reasoning*. New York: Springer.

Bramer, M. (2007). *Principles of data mining*. London: Springer.

Chakrabarti, S. (2003). *Mining the web: discovering knowledge from hypertext data*. San Francisco, CA: Morgan Kaufmann Publishers.

Chakrabarti, S. (2009). *Data mining: know it all*. Burlington, MA: Elsevier/Morgan Kaufmann Publishers.

Chattamvelli, R. (2009). *Data mining methods*. Oxford, UK: Alpha Science International.

Cios, K. J. (2000). *Medical data mining and knowledge discovery.* New York: Physica-Verlag.

Feldman, R., & Sanger, J. (2007). *The text mining handbook: advanced approaches in analyzing unstructured data.* Cambridge, NY: Cambridge University Press.

Harvey, J. M., & Han, J. (Eds.). (2009). *Geographic data mining and knowledge discovery.* Boca Raton, FL: Chapman & Hall/CRC.

Hsu, W., Lee, M. L., & Wang, J. (2008). *Temporal and spatio-temporal data mining.* Hershey, PA: IGI Publishers.

Jafar, A. (2009). *Introduction to early warning through data mining.* Retrieved November 9, 2009 from http://www.isi.edu/~adibi/InternationalRelation.htm

Kamath, C. (2009). *Scientific data mining: a practical perspective.* Philadelphia, PA: Society for Industrial and Applied Mathematics.

Kantardzic, M. M., & Zurada, J. (Eds.). (2005). *Next generation of data-mining application.* Hoboken, NJ: Wiley-Interscience.

Kao, K., & Poteet, S. R. (Eds.). (2007). *Natural language processing and text mining.* London: Springer. doi:10.1007/978-1-84628-754-1

Kononenko, I., & Kukar, M. (2007). *Machine learning and data mining: introduction to principles and algorithms.* Chichester, UK: Horwood Publishing.

Kovalerchuk, B., & Vityaev, E. (2002). *Data mining in finance: Advances in relational and hybrid methods.* Boston, MA: Kluwer Academic Publishers.

Last, M., Kandel, A., & Bunke, H. (2004). *Data mining in time series databases.* Singapore: World Scientific Publishers.

Last, M., Szczepaniak, P. S., Volkovich, Z., & Kandel, A. (Eds.). (2006). *Advances in web intelligence and data mining.* Berlin: Springer. doi:10.1007/3-540-33880-2

Lawrence, K. D., Kudyba, S. & Klimberg, (Eds.) (2008). *Data mining methods and applications.* Boca Raton, FL: Auerbach Publications.

Little, B. (2009). *Data mining: method, theory, and practice.* Southampton, UK: WIT Press.

Liu, B. (2007). *Web data mining: exploring hyperlinks, contents, and usage data.* Berlin: Springer-Verlag.

Maimon, O., & Rokach, L. (2005). *Data mining and knowledge discovery handbook.* New York: Springer Science+Business Media, Inc.

Marakas, G. M. (2003). *Modern data warehousing, mining, and visualization: core concepts.* Upper Saddle River, NJ: Prentice Hall.

McCue, C. (2007). *Data mining and predictive analysis: intelligence gathering and crime analysis.* Burlington, MA: Butterworth-Heinemann.

Nigro, H. O., Gonzalez-Cisaro, S., & Xodo, D. (Eds.). (2008). *Data mining with ontologies: implementations, findings and frameworks.* Hershey, PA: Information Science Reference.

Nisbet, R., Elder, J., & Gary, M. (2009). *Handbook of statistical analysis and data mining applications.* Burlington, MA: Elsevier Academic Pres.

Olson, D., & Shi, Y. (2007). *Introduction to business data mining.* Boston: McGraw-Hill/Irwin.

Olson, D. L., & Delen, D. (2008). *Advanced data mining techniques.* Berlin: Springer-Verlag.

Perner, P. (2006). *Advances in data mining: applications in e-commerce, medicine, and knowledge management.* Berlin: Springer-Verlag.

Petersen, J. K. (2000). *Understanding surveillance technologies: spy devices, their origins and applications.* Boca Raton, FL: CRC Press. doi:10.1201/9781420038811

Refaat, M. (2007). *Data preparation for data mining using SAS*. San Francisco, CA: Morgan Kaufmann Publishers.

Roddick, J. F., & Hornsby, K. (Eds.). (2001). *Temporal, spatial and spatio-temporal data mining*. New York: Springer. doi:10.1007/3-540-45244-3

Roddick, J. F., Hornsby, K., & Spiliopoulou, M. (2001). An updated bibliograpy of temporal spatial, and spatio-temporal data mining research. In Roddick, J. F., & Hornsby, K. (Eds.), *Temporal, spatial and spatio-temporal data mining* (pp. 147–163). New York: Springer. doi:10.1007/3-540-45244-3_12

Rokach, L., & Maimon, O. (2008). *Data mining with decision trees: theroy and applications*. Hackensack, NJ: World Scientific.

Rosenfeld, A., Doermann, D., & DeMenthon, D. (Eds.). (2003). *Video mining*. Boston, MA: Kluwer Academic.

Scime, A. (Ed.). (2005). *Web mining: applications and techniques*. Hershey, PA: Idea Group.

Sirmakessis, S. (Ed.). (2004). *Text mining and its applications: results of the NEMIS Launch Conference*. New York: Springer-Verlag.

Sirmakessis, S. (2005). *Knowledge mining*. London: Springer. doi:10.1007/3-540-32394-5

Soukup, T., & Davidson, I. (2002). *Visual data mining: techniques and tools for data visualization and mining*. New York: Wiley Publishers.

Stein, A., Shi, W., & Bijker, W. (Eds.). (2008). *Quality aspects in spatial data mining*. Boca Raton, FL: Chapman & Hall/CRC. doi:10.1201/9781420069273

Sullivan, D. (2001). *Document warehousing and text mining*. New York: John Wiley.

Sumathi, S., & Sivanandam, S. N. (2006). *Introduction to data mining and its applications*. Berlin: Springer.

Taniar, D. (Ed.). (2008). *Data mining and knowledge discovery technologies*. Hershey, PA: IGI Global.

Wei, C. P., Piramuthu, S., & Shaw, M. J. (2003). Knowledge discovery and data mining. *In* Holsapple, C.W. (Ed.), *Handbook on knowledge management 2* (pp. 157-189). Berlin: Springer-Verlag, 157-189.

Wu, X., & Kumar, V. (Eds.). (2009). *The top ten algorithms in data mining*. Boca Raton, FL: Chapman & Hall/CRC.

Ye, N. (Ed.). (2003). *The handbook of data mining*. Mahwah, NJ: Lawrence Erlbaum Associates Publishers.

Zhang, Z., & Zhang, R. (2009). *Multimedia data mining: a systematic introduction to concepts and theory*. Boca Raton, FL: CRC Press.

Zhu, X., & Davidson, I. (Eds.). (2007). *Knowledge discovery and data mining: challenges and realities*. Hershey, PA: Information Science Reference.

KEY TERMS AND DEFINITIONS

Early Warning System (EWS): A system or mechanism designed to warn of a potential or an impending problem or risk.

Knowledge Discovery in Databases (KDD): The process of discovering useful and interesting information in huge data.

Data Mining (DM): A step in KDD where knowledge discovery methods are applied.

Clustering: The process of creating similar object groups.

Association: Association identifies items that are happening together.

Spatial Mining: Exploring patterns in spatial data like images, graphs, maps, and satellite data.

Temporal Mining: Mining data involving time-varying component.

Text Mining: The process of extracting useful information from document collections.

Multimedia Mining: Exploring objects such as audio, video, image and hypertext data.

Web Mining: Involving in applying data mining methods to web data.

Similarity Analysis: Searching for patterns that are slightly different from each others.

Trend Analysis: Identification the general direction of a time series over a long time period.

Pattern Detection: Classifying patterns in a sequence given a set of patterns.

Chapter 2
Data Mining and Privacy Protection

Armand Faganel
University of Primorska, Slovenia

Danijel Bratina
University of Primorska, Slovenia

ABSTRACT

Modern data mining tools search databases for hidden patterns, finding predictive information that is otherwise not evident. There exist four models for privacy protection, which depending on their application, can be complementary or contradictory. This chapter deals with the comparison of EU comprehensive laws model and US sectoral laws model that arise from different cultural and historical background. The main objectives are to compare the current state of consumer's privacy protection in EU and USA, discuss legal frameworks, propose some best practice implications, and summarize perceived future trends. We must not forget that consumers have the right to communicate and interact, and also to keep the control over their personal data, even after they disclosed it to others.

INTRODUCTION

The speed of information and communication technologies development creates improvements in consumer's life. Personal data of consumers spreading around are available and offer data basis for proliferation of data transactions. Besides the benefits, risks for consumers' privacy are becoming more and more real. Solove (2008) provided a comprehensive overview of privacy, as one of the most important concepts of our time, yet also one of

the most elusive. As rapidly changing technology makes information increasingly available, scholars, activists, and policymakers have struggled to define privacy, with many conceding that the task is virtually impossible. There are several difficulties involved in discussions of privacy and ultimately provides a provocative resolution. He argues that no single definition can be workable, but rather that there are multiple forms of privacy, related to one another by family resemblances. His theory bridges cultural differences and addresses historical changes in views on privacy.

DOI: 10.4018/978-1-61692-865-0.ch002

The Charter of Fundamental Rights of the European Union (EC, 2000b) recognizes in Article 8 the right to the protection of personal data. This fundamental right is set forth in a European Union legal framework on the protection of personal data consisting in particular of the Data Protection Directive 95/46/EC (EC, 1995) and the ePrivacy Directive 2002/58/EC (EC, 2002) as well as the Data Protection Regulation 45/2001 (EC, 2001) relating to processing by Community institution and bodies. This legislation presents several substantive provisions imposing obligations on data controllers and recognizing rights of data subjects. It also prescribes sanctions and appropriate remedies in cases of breach and establishes enforcement mechanisms to make them effective.

It is quite possible that this system could prove insufficient when personal data is disseminated globally through information and communication technologies networks and the processing of data crosses several jurisdictions, often outside the European Union. In such situations the current rules may be considered to apply and to provide a clear legal response. However, considerable practical obstacles may exist as a result of difficulties with the technology used involving data processing by different actors in different locations.

Data mining is been used to track consumer activities and use that information for future marketing purposes. When entering a web site, it is often needed a personal identification, revealing some data about yourself. Not every consumer is aware of the possible use of his/her information. The history of transactions and individual preferences is collected, stored, analyzed to evaluate buying behaviors. It is done for improving the marketing of new products and promotions directly to the customer's personal e-mail address. Collecting personal data to evaluate consumer needs and improve consumer service makes great business sense, but in the internet the threat of a security breach is very high. The transfer of personal data across the internet without adequate protection

causes concern for many officials and citizens (Tran & Atkinson, 2002).

Modern data mining tools search databases for hidden patterns, finding predictive information that is otherwise not evident. They predict future trends and behaviours, allowing organizations to make decisions based on prospective analyses. In response to the obvious privacy concerns with this practice, computer scientists in recent years have work on "privacy preserving" methods of data mining – methods that would preserve individual privacy while still providing researchers with the information they want.

Despite the fact that democratic societies value and institutionalize privacy, governments have also to provide for the disclosure of information necessary to the rational and responsible conduct of public affairs and to support fair dealing in business affairs. Officials must engage in surveillance of properly identified anti-social activity to control illegal or violent acts (Westin, 2003). Personal level data based systems (e.g. security, anti-terror systems) need to recover personal data and early warning systems have to be managed in a way that does not enter in conflict with general human rights. Managing this tension among privacy, disclosure, and surveillance in a way that preserves civility and democracy, and copes successfully with changing social values, technologies, and economic conditions, is the central challenge of contemporary privacy definition and protection (Westin, 1967).

Bygrave (2002) explained why data protection laws deserve extensive study. First reason is data protection laws practical significance (both actual and potential); they can affect the heart of organizational activity. The second reason is their normative importance because such laws emphasize that account be taken of values, needs and interests, different from increased organizational effectiveness or maximization of financial profit, when processing personal data. Partially, the normative and practical importance of the laws is mirrored in the burgeoning focus on rights to privacy and private life, with which data protection laws are closely linked.

This qualitative study is based in interpretativism, influenced by Guba & Lincoln's (2005) constructivist epistemology. Approach is qualitative grounded on subjective assumptions made from document analysis, literature review, scrutinizing regulative frameworks, and critical reflection. The main objectives are to compare the current state of consumer's privacy protection in EU and USA, discuss legal frameworks, propose some best practice implications, and summarize perceived future trends.

BACKGROUND

We can map four models for privacy protection, which depending on their application, can be complementary or contradictory. In most countries, several models are used simultaneously. In the countries that protect privacy most effectively, all of the models are used together to ensure privacy protection (Privacy International, 2007): *Comprehensive Laws*: Several countries adopted a general law that governs the collection, use and dissemination of personal information by both the public and private sectors. An oversight body was appointed to ensure compliance. This is the preferred model for most countries adopting data protection laws and was adopted by the European Union to ensure compliance with its data protection regime. A variation of these laws, which is described as a co-regulatory model, was adopted in Canada and Australia. Under this approach, industry develops rules for the protection of privacy that are enforced by the industry and overseen by the privacy agency; *Sectoral Laws*: Other countries (i.e. United States), avoided to enact general data protection rules in favour of specific sectoral laws governing. Enforcement is achieved through a range of mechanisms. Problem with this approach is that it requires that new legislation be introduced with each new technology

so protections frequently lag behind. There is also the problem of a lack of an oversight agency. In many countries, sectoral laws are used to complement comprehensive legislation by providing more detailed protections for certain categories of information, such as telecommunications, police files or consumer credit records; *Self-Regulation*: Data protection can also be achieved, at least in theory, through various forms of self-regulation, in which companies and industry bodies establish codes of practice and engage in self-policing. However, in many countries, especially the United States, these efforts have been disappointing, with little evidence that the aims of the codes are regularly fulfilled. Adequacy and enforcement are the major problem with these approaches. Industry codes in many countries have tended to provide only weak protections and lack enforcement. *Technologies of Privacy*: Due to recent development of commercially available technology-based systems, privacy protection has also moved into the hands of individual users. Users of the internet and of some physical applications can employ a range of programs and systems that provide varying degrees of privacy and security of communications. These include encryption, anonymous remailers, proxy servers and digital cash. Users should be aware that not all tools effectively protect privacy. Some are poorly designed while others may be designed to facilitate law enforcement access.

According to Li & Sarkar (2006), we can usually determine three parties when describing the privacy problem in data mining: the data owner (the organization that owns the data) who has complete access to the data and wants to discover knowledge from the data without compromising the confidentiality of the data; individuals who provide their personal information to the data owner and want their privacy protected; and the data miner (insider or outsider) who, with access only to the data released by the data owner, performs data mining for the data owner. In this study, they focus on situations where the data owner hires the data miner as a third party due to the need for data-mining expertise or resources, and has to consider the data miner as a potential data snooper. The data owner can also be a not-for-profit organization (e.g., government agency) that is obligated to release the data, more likely in summarized or perturbed forms, to the public or some professional organizations. In that case, anyone who has the access to the released data can be regarded as a potential data snooper (Adam & Wortmann, 1989).

Data privacy as a consumer's right is regulated and enforced in European Union. The EU Parliament adopted 155 amendments in 2008, to the Amending Directive 2002/22/EC on universal service and users' rights relating to electronic communications networks, Directive 2002/58/EC concerning the processing of personal data and the protection of privacy in the electronic communications sectors and Regulation (EC) No 2006/2004 on consumer protection cooperation (EC, 2008). The main goal was to adapt the regulatory framework for electronic communications by strengthening certain consumer and user rights and by ensuring that electronic communications are trustworthy, secure and reliable and provide a high level of protection for individuals' privacy and personal data. One of the objectives was to enhance the protection of individuals' privacy and personal data in the electronic communications sector, in particular through strengthened security-related provisions and improved enforcement mechanisms. Customers should also be kept well informed of possible types of actions that the providers of electronic communications services may take to address security threats or in response to a security or integrity incident, since such actions could have a direct or indirect impact on the customer's data, privacy or other aspects of the service provided. Directive 97/66/EC (EC, 1997) of the European Parliament and of the Council of 15 December 1997 concerning the processing of personal data and the protection of privacy in the telecommunications sector ensures the subscrib-

ers' right to privacy with regard to the inclusion of their personal information in a public directory.

In the United States of America and some other countries they followed another approach. The idea of self-regulation involves the voluntary adhesion on the part of companies to develop standards at the industry level. But consumers could feel that without legal guarantees, the efforts of self-regulation are not enough as they lack enforcement mechanism that is expected in commercial transactions. Should governments therefore pass laws to back up self-regulators initiatives by the private sector or should they regulate the protection of on-line consumer specifically? There should be ensured balance between consumer protection and safeguarding constitutional rights of freedom of speech and expression. Another important question to consider is how to create an environment where the rights of citizens are protected while avoiding unnecessary restrictions on trans-border flow of personal data that could inhibit the potential growth of e-commerce.

When approaching all these problems governments have several possibilities. A light handed regulatory approach, as history showed that too much regulation was not good for the industry. Strong government leadership is recommended, particularly in encouraging use of e-commerce technologies in dealing with government. Not to forget consumer education by increasing public awareness by educating them of their rights, risks and responsibilities. Strategies for content regulation may involve the use of technological measures such as blocking or filtering software.

Johnson & Post (1996) offer a solution to the problem of Internet governance. Given the internet's unique situation, with respect to geography and identity, Johnson and Post believe that it becomes necessary for the internet to govern itself. Instead of obeying the laws of a particular country, internet citizens will obey the laws of electronic entities like service providers. Instead of identifying as a physical person, Internet citizens will be known by their usernames or email addresses. Since the internet defies geographical boundaries, national laws will no longer apply. Instead, an entirely new set of laws will be created to address concerns like intellectual property and individual rights. Johnson and Post propose a law for cyberspace which regulates all internet based transactions regardless of where their real life participants reside, where their server is located or what their domain name is. As former US FCC Commissioner Abernathy (2001) remembered: "…government is a service industry, and we should act like it. You are our customers – you deserve responsiveness, timeliness, and well-reasoned results…".

PRIVACY PROTECTION HISTORY AND DEVELOPMENT

Consumer's Concerns

Modern consumer protection has to adapt to different legislations, regulations and practices. The aim is to protect consumer from fraud, protect economic interests in the country and to educate consumers about their rights. Economic legislation has been historically established centuries before computers and internet era, when most goods had physical origin. Important legal and regulatory challenges appeared as the technology developed, especially regarding information and data transfer. Other concerns to which consumer is exposed involve privacy and security and different jurisdiction rules and practices, connected with internet activities. Data mining can occur on numerous occasions, whenever consumer uses a credit card, exposes his/her bank account details, or makes a call from mobile phone. Disclosure of consumer habits, shopping patterns and health problems, using data matching from available sources, can righteously cause feelings of unprotectedness and vulnerability. Even if country adopts data privacy legislation about data transfer on internet, effec-

tive enforcement due to jurisdiction difficulties still remains questionable.

Advanced development of internet technologies, expanded capabilities of collecting, warehousing and treating data, interconnected data basis and cross-border data transfer enabled increased threat to privacy; at the same time all these caused greater concern and influenced citizen consciousness regarding privacy and elementary human rights. As Webb deducted, our control over personal data changed, because information technology allows data of greater amounts and increasing sensitivity to be collected and analysed by both public and private sectors (Webb, 2003).

As Sookman (2000) warns, the systematic collection of information made possible by information technologies gives rise to the real danger of the gradual erosion of individual liberties through the automation, integration and interconnection of many small, separate record keeping systems, each of which alone may seem innocuous, and wholly justifiable. The improvements in information handling capability also give rise to the tendency to use more data and to disguise less. New technologies create new types of records and analysis never before possible. Different techniques are used to collect personal data. Whenever a telephone call is made, goods are purchased using a credit card, health services are procured, or the Internet is surfed, data is captured and recorded. A great deal of information is unknowingly volunteered by individuals such as by filling out a questionnaire or registration form. And finally, we as consumers are sometimes willing to disclose a great deal of personal information about themselves in return for free products or give-aways.

Due to concern regarding the influence of information technologies for privacy and the ability of international information flow, first privacy laws appeared simultaneously with the development of information technologies in early seventies in some European countries. Most of this regulation was oriented mainly to the information privacy. It regulated collecting and managing of data and their further propagating and merging (Crompton, 2002).

From the beginning there were a lot of differences between these legal approaches, but thanks to the increasing amount of cross-boarder data exchange, it was necessary to accept international rules, which could represent efficient and uniform framework for data and privacy protection.

First international agreement in this direction was made by the member countries the OECD - Organisation for Economic Co-operation and Development reached a consensus on issues related to the protection of privacy to promote the free flow of information across their borders and to prevent legal issues related to the protection of privacy from creating obstacles to the development of their economic and social relations. In 1980, OECD council adopted the privacy guidelines that were intended to form the basis of legislation in the organization's member states and for support in countries that did not prepare such regulation yet. At the core of the guidelines is a set of eight principles to be applied to both the public and private sectors: the collection limitation principle, the data quality principle, the purpose specification principle, the use limitation principle, the security safeguards principle, the openness principle, the individual participation principle and the accountability principle (OECD, 2007).

According to the guidelines there should be limits to the collection of personal data and any such data should be obtained by lawful and fair means and, where appropriate, with the knowledge or consent of the data subject. Between other rules, personal data should be relevant to the purposes for which they are to be used, and, to the extent necessary for those purposes, should be accurate, complete and kept up-to-date; they should not be disclosed, made available or otherwise used for purposes other than those specified in accordance with except: with the consent of the data subject; or by the authority of law. An individual should have the right: to obtain from a data controller, or otherwise, confirmation of whether or not the data controller has data relating to him; to have communicated to him, data relating to him within a reasonable time; at a charge, if any, that is not excessive; in a reasonable manner; and in a form that is readily intelligible to him.

One year later, the member states of the Council of Europe (1981) accepted similar guidelines in the Convention for the Protection of Individuals with regard to Automatic Processing of Personal Data. The purpose of this convention: "…is to secure in the territory of each Party for every individual, whatever his nationality or residence, respect for his rights and fundamental freedoms, and in particular his right to privacy, with regard to automatic processing of personal data relating to him (data protection)." In the convention is written that every member state should take the necessary measures in its domestic law to give effect to the basic principles for data protection.

United Nations General Assembly adopted in 1990 the Guidelines concerning computerized personal data files. The procedures for implementing regulations concerning computerized personal data files were left to the initiative of each State subject to these guidelines. Stated principles concerning the minimum guarantees that should be provided in national legislations are following (United Nations, 1990): principle of lawfulness and fairness (information about persons should not be collected or processed in unfair or unlawful ways); principle of accuracy (the obligation to conduct regular checks on the accuracy and relevance of the data recorded and to ensure that they are kept as complete as possible); principle of the purpose – specification (the purpose which a file is to serve and its utilization in terms of that purpose should be specified, legitimate and, when it is established, receive a certain amount of publicity or be brought to the attention of the person concerned); principle of interested-person access (the right to know whether information concerning a person is being processed and to obtain it in an intelligible form); principle of non-discrimination (data likely to give rise to unlawful or arbitrary discrimination should not be compiled); power to make exceptions (only if they are necessary to protect national security, public order, public health or morality, as well as, inter alia, the rights and freedoms of others, especially persons being persecuted - humanitarian cause); principle of security (to protect the files against both natural dangers, such as accidental loss or destruction and human dangers, such as unauthorized access, fraudulent misuse of data or contamination by computer viruses); supervision and sanctions (the law of every country shall designate the authority which, in accordance with its domestic legal system, is to be responsible for supervising observance of the principles set forth above); transborder data flows (information should be able to circulate as freely as inside each of the territories concerned); Field of application (principles should be made applicable, in the first instance, to all public and private computerized files as well as, by means of optional extension and subject to appropriate adjustments, to manual files).

Basic principles that are to be found in almost every guidelines, directives and frameworks imply that personal information must be (Dodig-Crnkovic, 2006): obtained fairly and lawfully; used only for the original specified purpose; adequate, relevant and not excessive to purpose; accurate and up to date; and destroyed after its purpose is completed.

Similar conclusions have been made at the the 27th International Conference of Data Protection and Privacy Commissioners, held in Montreux from 14 - 16 September 2005 at the invitation of the Swiss Federal Data Protection Commissioner. They adopted a final declaration aimed at strengthening the universal nature of data protection principles. It has been stressed that more than at any time in the past, data protection has become the focus of debate and constitutes a major challenge which has emerged as a result of the globalization of our societies and the development of information technologies. Information may be covered by different data protection laws, and in some cases there may be no protective mechanism whatsoever. It is often impossible, or at least very difficult, for data subjects to enforce their rights because their data are scattered to the four corners of the world. They proposed following principles for data protection (FDPIC, 2005): lawful and fair data collection and processing; accuracy; purpose-specification and limitation; proportionality; transparency; individual participation and in particular the guarantee of the right access of the person concerned; non-discrimination; responsibility; independent supervision and legal sanction; and adequate level of protection in case of transborder flows of personal data.

Regulation on Privacy Protection in the European Union

In 1995, the European Union joined with similar directive 95/46/EC (EC, 1995) of the European parliament and of the Council. Member states took the obligation that they shall neither restrict nor prohibit free flow of personal data between member states for reasons connected with the protection of the fundamental rights and freedoms of natural persons, and in particular their right to privacy with respect to the processing of personal data and on the free movement of such data (EC, 1995). Each member state had to apply the national provisions it adopts pursuant to this directive to the processing of the personal data. Personal data, appearing on internet comply under this directive too. In Article 17 directive commands member states to provide that the controller must implement appropriate technical and organizational measures to protect personal data against accidental or unlawful destruction or accidental loss, alteration, unauthorized disclosure or access, in particular where the processing involves the transmission of data over a network, and against all other unlawful forms of processing to ensure a level of security appropriate to the risks represented by the processing and the nature of the data to be protected.

Directive 95/46/EC (EC, 1995) in Article 6 implies that all personal data should be processed fair and lawful; collected for specified, explicit and legitimate purposes and not further processed in a way incompatible with those purposes. Further processing of data for historical, statistical or scientific purposes shall not be considered as incompatible provided that member states provide appropriate safeguards; adequate, relevant and not excessive in relation to the purposes for which they are collected and/or further processed; accurate and, where necessary, kept up to date; every reasonable step must be taken to ensure that data which are inaccurate or incomplete, having regard to the purposes for which they were collected or for which they are further processed, are erased or rectified; kept in a form which permits identification of data subjects for no longer than is necessary for the purposes for which the data were collected or for which they are further processed. Member states shall lay down appropriate safeguards for personal data stored for longer periods for historical, statistical or scientific use. Conforming to directive, personal data can be processed only when there is unequivocal agreement with the owner of data, data subject. Information collector has to acknowledge data subject, which data are being gathering and for what purpose. They must be informed also about the possibilities to access data and the right to correct them. Transfer across European Union borders is possible only if third country assures corresponding level of security.

In December 1997 European Parliament accepted Directive 97/66/EC (EC, 1997), which particularised and complemented Directive 95/46/EC to the special rules regarding the protection of privacy and personal data in the sector of telecommunications. This directive provides for the harmonisation of the provisions of the member states required to ensure an equivalent level of protection of fundamental rights and freedoms, and in particular the right to privacy, with respect to the processing of personal data in the telecommunications sector and to ensure the free move-

ment of such data and of telecommunications equipment and services in the European Union. In Article 5 there is a rule about confidentiality of the communications, saying that member states shall ensure via national regulations the confidentiality of communications by means of a public telecommunications network and publicly available telecommunications services. In particular, they shall prohibit listening, tapping, storage or other kinds of interception or surveillance of communications, by others than users, without the consent of the users concerned, except when legally authorised. Article 11 is dealing with directories of subscribers; personal data contained in printed or electronic directories of subscribers available to the public or obtainable through directory enquiry services should be limited to what is necessary to identify a particular subscriber, unless the subscriber has given his unambiguous consent to the publication of additional personal data. The subscriber shall be entitled, free of charge, to be omitted from a printed or electronic directory at his or her request, to indicate that his or her personal data may not be used for the purpose of direct marketing, to have his or her address omitted in part and not to have a reference revealing his or her sex, where this is applicable linguistically.

Directive 97/66/EC had to be adapted to developments in the markets and technologies for electronic communication services in order to provide an appropriate level of protection of personal data and privacy for users of publicly available electronic communications services, regardless of the technologies used. So the Directive 97/66/EC was repealed and replaced by Directive 2002/58/EC (EC, 2002), concerning the processing of personal data and the protection of privacy in the electronic communications sector (Directive on privacy and electronic communications). Internet offers its users new possibilities and new risks regarding their personal data and privacy. Purpose of this directive is to minimize the processing of personal data and whenever it is a possibility to use anonymous and pseudonymous data. Basic principles of Directive 2002/58/EC are following: confidentiality of the communications (member states shall ensure the confidentiality of communications and the related traffic data by means of a public communications network and services. They shall prohibit listening, tapping, storage or other kind of interception or surveillance of communications and the related traffic data by persons other than users, without the consent of the users concerned, except when legally authorised); traffic data (are giving good picture of individual's habits, contacts, interests, activities and therefore represent sensitive data. Directive imposes to erase or make anonymous traffic data relating to users processed and stored by the provider of a public communications network or service, when it is no longer needed for the purpose of transmission of a communication); location data (may only be processed when they are made anonymous, or with the consent of the user); unsolicited communications (electronic contact details in the context of the sale of a product or service may be used for the purpose of sending an electronic mail provided that customers clearly and distinctly are given the opportunity to object, free of charge and in an easy manner in case the customer has not initially refused such use). The use of so-called spyware, web bugs, hidden identifiers and other similar devices can enter the user's terminal in order to gain access to information, to store hidden information or to trace the activities of the user and may seriously intrude upon the privacy of these users. It is allowed only for legitimate purposes, with the knowledge of the users concerned. Member states can legally intercept electronic communications if this is necessary for the protection of public security, defence, state security and the enforcement of criminal law.

After the September 11, 2001, the attitude toward privacy changed throughout the world. Dilemma between individual's privacy and state security is more and more expressed. Directive 2002/58EC allows member states to adopt legislative measures providing for the retention of data through different communication devices as mobile phones, internet etc. for a limited period of time, while the Directive 95/46/EC demands that data should be erased immediately or altered into anonymous right after the cause of their collection has terminated. Terrorism counter fight generated laud calls from member states to increase the control over citizens and for the prolongation of the location and traffic data retention.

Directive 2006/24/EC on the retention of data generated or processed in connection with the provision of publicly available electronic communications services or of public communications networks were accepted in March 2006. Data must now be stored for a period of 6 to 24 months, while member states may adjust maximum retention periods at will. The fact that no guideline on cost reimbursement was approved raises the danger of fragmentation in the single market for the important telecoms sector. The directive is no longer limited to the fight against terrorism and organized crime, but now includes all serious crimes, as defined by each individual member state. The EU Parliament included in the types of data to be retained the telephone calls location data, SMS and internet use. This includes unsuccessful call attempts if the company already stores such data. Directive is not a law by itself, member states have to implement minimal guidelines in their respective regulation.

Gutwirth et al. (2009) said that the recognition of data protection as a fundamental right in the legal order of European Union has been welcomed for many reasons. Due to considerations regarding the legitimacy of the EU data protection framework because from the start the Data Protection Directive (EC, 1995) was based on a double logic: the achievement of an internal market (free movement and personal data) and the protection of fundamental rights and freedoms of consumers. In legal terms the economic perspective and internal market arguments prevailed.

Data and Privacy Security in USA

Forth amendment of the US constitution indirectly mentions privacy, saying that "the right of the people to be secure in their persons, houses, papers, and effects, against unreasonable searches and seizures, shall not be violated, and no Warrants shall issue, but upon probable cause, supported by Oath or affirmation, and particularly describing the place to be searched, and the persons or things to be sized" (US, 1791).

The Freedom of Information Act – FOIA (US, 1966) generally provides that any person has a right, enforceable in court, to obtain access to federal agency records, except to the extent that such records are protected from public disclosure. Enacted in 1966, the FOIA established and ensured an informed citizenry, vital to the functioning of a democratic society, needed to check against corruption and to hold the governors accountable to the governed.

Privacy Act of 1974, 5 U.S.C. § 552a, establishes a code of fair information practices that governs the collection, maintenance, use, and dissemination of personally identifiable information about individuals that is maintained in systems of records by federal agencies. A system of records is a group of records under the control of an agency from which information is retrieved by the name of the individual or by some identifier assigned to the individual. The Privacy Act requires that agencies give the public notice of their systems of records by publication in the Federal Register. The Privacy Act prohibits the disclosure of information from a system of records absent the written consent of the subject individual, unless the disclosure is pursuant to one of twelve statutory exceptions. The Act also provides individuals with a means by which to seek access to and amendment of their records, and sets forth various agency record-keeping requirements (US, 1974).

Strong resistance is to be found in the US against the adoption of general legislation for the private sector. The US Privacy Act of 1974

applies only to Federal Government, and not to the private sector; its implementation has been limited in the absence of appointed authority to oversee and enforce compliance (Raab, 2005). Broadly stated, the purpose of the Privacy Act is to balance the government's need to maintain information about individuals with the rights of individuals to be protected against unwarranted invasions of their privacy stemming from federal agencies' collection, maintenance, use, and disclosure of personal information about them. The Act focuses on four basic policy objectives (US, 1974): to restrict disclosure of personally identifiable records maintained by agencies; to grant individuals increased rights of access to agency records maintained on themselves; to grant individuals the right to seek amendment of agency records maintained on themselves upon a showing that the records are not accurate, relevant, timely, or complete; to establish a code of "fair information practices" which requires agencies to comply with statutory norms for collection, maintenance, and dissemination of records.

Federal Agencies have to deliver demanded information, acknowledge public about different kinds of collections run through federal register, how the information is been used, they have to assure the relevance of collected information. Information can not be used for other purposes as primarily stated. Federal systems of records about individuals can be opened to others in cases when: the purpose of investigation is similar as primary purpose of information gathering; for statistical research; for legislative appointed purposes; if the court decided; if it is urgent from medical standpoint (US, 1974).

The Electronic Communications Privacy Act of 1986 - ECPA was enacted by the United States Congress to extend government restrictions on various forms of wire and electronic communications. New provisions were added prohibiting access to stored electronic communications. ECPA prohibits unlawful access and certain disclosures of communication contents. Additionally, the law prevents government entities from requiring disclosure of electronic communications from a provider without proper procedure. The ECPA also included so-called pen/trap provisions that permit the tracing of telephone communications (US, 1986). Law requires court decision about the control of electronic communications, or consent of at least one participant in the communication process. Later, the ECPA was amended, and weakened to some extent, by some provisions of the PATRIOT Act.

In 1987, the US Congress enacted Computer Security Act of 1987 (US, 1987), reaffirming that the National Institute for Standards and Technology – NIST, a division of the Department of Commerce,

was responsible for the security of unclassified, non-military government computer systems; to perform research and to conduct studies, as needed, to determine the nature and extent of the vulnerabilities of computer systems, and to devise techniques for the cost effective security and privacy of sensitive information in federal computer systems and to improve it in the public interest, and hereby creates a means for establishing minimum acceptable security practices for such systems, without limiting the scope of security measures planned or in use.

Before September 11 2001, US had very severe regulative, which controlled the spreading of information between different agencies. It was considered that such spreading of information breaks human rights and state agencies had to comply with this acts. After September 11, US accepted a package of anti terrorist acts. USA PATRIOT Act of 2001 (US, 2001) and Homeland Security Act of 2002 (US, 2002) increase the power of electronic surveillance and interception of data. Both acts endanger online privacy of innocent individuals, as they allow tracking and storing of IP addresses and insight of investigators in financial and other transactions of every citizen. Such surveillance diminishes individual's privacy on account of state security. USA PATRIOT Act

(US, 2001), meaning Uniting and Strengthening America by Providing Appropriate Tools Required to Intercept and Obstruct Terrorism, among other purposes increases the ability of law enforcement agencies to search telephone, e-mail communications, medical, financial, and other records. The Homeland Security Act – HAS of 2002, created the US Department of Homeland Security. The HSA includes many of the organizations under which the powers of the USA PATRIOT Act are exercised. It also created the new cabinet-level position of the Secretary of Homeland Security.

The Privacy Act has limited effectiveness, which can be best described as critical, because it allows data brokers to accumulate huge databases that the government is legally prohibited from creating. When the government needs information, it can be requested from the data broker. When this happens, the personal information would be subject to the Privacy Act, but law enforcement and intelligence agencies have special exemptions under the Act that limit access, accuracy, and correction rights. Yet another limitation is that the Privacy Act only applies to federal, not state or local government agencies, and the fact that the Act has a number of major exemptions, including one that exempts agencies when they disclose information for any routine use that is compatible with the purpose for which the agency gathered the data (Solove & Hoofnagle, 2005).

The US sectoral approach to data protection has produced a patchwork of federal and state laws and self-regulatory programmes. Although participation in the safe harbor is optional, its rules are binding for those US companies that decide to join, and compliance with the rules is backed up by the law enforcement powers of the Federal Trade Commission and (for airlines) of the US Department of Transportation (EC, 2000a).

As mentioned already, Privacy Act and acts regarding the protection of personal data is in power only for state agencies; private companies do not have to adequate to the regulative. Purpose of Safe Harbor principles was mainly to content request of European Union to apply appropriate standard of data protection regarding data transfer from European Union states, demanded in Directive 95/46/EC. Principles had to be accepted because of fluid flow of information from company to company on both sides of Atlantic. On July 27, 2000, the European Commission issued its decision in accordance with Article 25.6 of the Directive that the Safe Harbor Privacy Principles provide adequate protection (EC, 2000a).

These principles should offer a high level of protection, demanded by European directive, on voluntary basis. They have to provide: notice - individuals must be informed about the purposes for which information about them has been collected; choice - individuals must have the opportunity to opt out of the collection and forward transfer of their data to third parties; onward transfer - an organization may only disclose personal information to third parties consistent with the principles of notice and choice; security - reasonable efforts must be made to prevent loss of collected information; data integrity - data must be relevant and reliable for the purpose it was collected for; access - individuals must be able to access information held about them, and correct or delete it if it is inaccurate; enforcement - there must be effective mechanisms of enforcing these rules.

Differences between the USA and EU

We could say that the most visible difference between the USA and EU is the absence of comprehensive data privacy legislation regulating the USA private sector and of a data protection authority, which should oversee the regulation of privacy protection. Of course these differences do not imply that the in the USA they are not interested in obtaining high level of privacy regime. The comprehensive, bureaucratic nature of data privacy regulation in EU partly originates from traumas of totalitarian oppression lived in first hand experience (Bygrave, 2004). Abuses like these have increased the EU's desire to enact

strong data protection laws which protect the safety and identity of its citizens. With the invention of the Internet, there was a similar call for stricter privacy laws in the USA to protect individuals' information. However, this American trend came to an abrupt halt with the attacks of September 11, 2001. As a result, a conflict of ideals was created between the EU and USA where Europeans wish to protect information to avoid the follies of the past, while the American government is continually seeking information to learn of possible terrorist activities or plans of future attacks. This struggle between privacy and security has affected the transfer of important data from the EU to the USA. A strict EU Data Protection Directive has made it difficult for the USA to gather information in the post 9/11 era without violating EU law (Shea, 2008).

Heisenberg (2005) argues that EU became the global leader in setting data privacy standards. She traced the origins of the stringent EU privacy laws, the responses of the USA and other governments, and the reactions and concerns of a range of interest groups. Analyzing the negotiation of the original 1995 EU Data Protection Directive, the 2000 Safe Harbor Agreement, and the 2004 Passenger Name Record Agreement, Heisenberg showed that the degree to which business vs. consumer interests were factored into governments' positions was the source not only of USA-EU conflicts, but also of their resolution.

Zwick & Dholakia (2001) proposed a study of different approaches to privacy in the EU and USA electronic markets, discussing property rights versus civil rights. In the regulation model, consumer is seen as a citizen to be protected and marketer as a potential violator of righths that should be regulated. In the self-regulation model, consumer is homo economicus – maximizer of benefits and marketer an exchange partner that also seeks to maximize his benefits. Important difference between the USA and EU in the field of privacy protection is the expected level of privacy. While in the USA exist several laws that protect privacy, they re not as concrete as those in EU. Patriot Act and Homeland Security Act caused great loss of citizens' privacy. The EU is still strongly supporting their charter to protect privacy. Of course in EU all the governments have to agree on the law, when trying to accept a new act and it makes it easier to pass and implement legislation. Sedita and Subramanian (2006) emphasize that USA and EU are not the only countries that consider and enact such legislation.

Newman & Bach (2004) defined two distinct self-regulatory trajectories – *legalistic self-regulation* in the USA and *coordinated self-regulation* in the EU. They expressed the expectations that the instruments of institutionalized legalism will shape the dynamics of self-regulation in USA. The government is unlikely to actively induce and steer collective action within the business community. Government attempts to leverage its buying power to create markets for public goods may even enhance competition among self-regulators alternatives. In EU, the European Commission will make use of its control over R&D funds to sponsor self-regulatory initiatives and the executive branch is also likely to play a role in the creation of intermediary institutions should business alone fail. The EU executive branch will thus play a catalytic role in the process of self-regulation, in USA it is more a hands-off executive. The judiciary, by contrast, should not play as significant role in EU.

Flavian & Guinaliu (2006) pointed out that public sector measures regarding internet privacy, security and trust followed two lines of action: measures of legal nature and communication policies.

In relation to the legal measures, they assessed that the measures exercised in the USA and Europe have had no significant effect, because of the lack of resources and the heterogeneous nature of legislation between different countries. Two causes of this ineffectiveness are: a) the lack of equilibrium between the regulations' intentions and the resources assigned to them, and b) the

heterogeneous nature of legislation between different countries. In the USA, there is a great deal of inconsistency, because while activities such as spamming are harshly prosecuted in some states, in others exists greater tolerance. In EU, privacy protection is more homogeneous, since it emanates from directives issued for this purpose (e.g. Directive 2002/58/EC of the European Parliament). Concerning the communication policies, there have been various awareness-raising campaigns among internet users (e.g. 1st Worldwide Internet Security Campaign, www.worldwidesecure.org). Up to now, government communication strategies do not appear to have a significant effect. For this reason, more direct measures need to be taken, such as giving users the training they need through free courses in collaboration with the private sector. Indeed, some researchers have shown that more computer-savvy individuals make internet purchases with greater frequency.

Solutions and Recommendations

In order to resolve the conflict between data mining and privacy protection, researchers in the data-mining community have proposed various methods. Agrawal and Srikant (2000) have considered building a decision tree classifier from data where the confidential values have been perturbed. Evfimievski et al. (2002) presented a framework for mining association rules from transaction data that have been randomized to preserve individuals' privacy. Estivill-Castro and Brankovic (1999) introduced methods aimed at finding a balance between the individuals' right to privacy and the data-miners' need to find general patterns in huge volumes of detailed records. In particular, they focused on the data-mining task of classification with decision trees, basing their security-control mechanism on noise-addition techniques used in statistical databases because (1) the multidimensional matrix model of statistical databases and the multidimensional cubes of On-Line Analytical Processing (OLAP) are essentially the same, and

(2) noise-addition techniques are very robust. The main drawback of noise addition techniques in the context of statistical databases is low statistical quality of released statistics.

Several studies on privacy preserving mining can be found, i.e. Atallah et al. (1999), and Verykios et al. (2004), who discussed that huge repositories of data contain sensitive information that must be protected against unauthorized access. The protection of the confidentiality of this information has been a long-term goal for the database security research community and for the government statistical agencies. Recent advances in data mining and machine learning algorithms have increased the disclosure risks that one may encounter when releasing data to outside parties. A key problem, and still not sufficiently investigated, is the need to balance the confidentiality of the disclosed data with the legitimate needs of the data users. Every disclosure limitation method affects, in some way, and modifies true data values and relationships.

This stream of research tends to approach the privacy issue from a data miner's standpoint, focusing on techniques for mining those data sets where confidential values are deleted or perturbed due to privacy concerns. We believe, however, it is more important to approach the issue from the standpoint of an organization that owns data, because the primary concern of a data miner is to discover useful knowledge from the data, while an organization has to set privacy protection as its first priority.

Li & Sarkar (2006) recognized that in order to respond to growing concerns about privacy of personal information, companies that use their customers' records in data-mining activities are forced to take actions to protect the privacy of the individuals involved. A common practice for many companies today is to remove identity-related attributes from the customer records before releasing them to data miners or analysts. Li & Sarkar investigated the effect of this practice and demonstrated that many records in a data set could be uniquely identified even after identity-related attributes are removed. They proposed a perturba-

tion method for categorical data that can be used by organizations to prevent or limit disclosure of confidential data for identifiable records when the data are provided to analysts for classification, a common data-mining task. The proposed method attempted to preserve the statistical properties of the data based on privacy protection parameters specified by the company.

Wang, et al. (2004) investigated data mining as a technique for masking data; therefore, termed data mining based privacy protection. This approach incorporates partially the requirement of a targeted data mining task into the process of masking data so that essential structure is preserved in the masked data. Wang & Liu (2008) researched further and stated that privacy preservation in data mining demands protecting both input and output privacy. The former refers to sanitizing the raw data itself before performing mining. The latter refers to preventing the mining output (model/pattern) from malicious pattern-based inference attacks. The preservation of input privacy does not necessarily lead to that of output privacy. This work studies the problem of protecting output privacy in the context of frequent pattern mining over data streams.

Witzner et al. (2006) argued that the perspective of controlling or preventing access to information has become inadequate and obsolete, overtaken by the ease of aggregating and searching across multiple databases, to reveal private information from public sources. To replace this outlived framework, they proposed that issues of privacy protection as viewed in terms of data access should be re-conceptualized in terms of data use. They presented a technology infrastructure, which required supplementing legal and technical mechanisms for transparency and accountability of data use.

FUTURE RESEARCH DIRECTIONS

Despite the high level of privacy protection in European Union, remains the openness of global information exchange as a very difficult nut to crack. We could recognize privacy as an international issue, and the urgent need for an international harmonization. Directive 95/46/EC, 97/66/EC and 2002/58/EC of the European Union represent a sound basis for the establishment of privacy protection in other countries outside European Union too. Kennedy, et al. (2009) reported the state of the data protection laws in Asia, and stated that many countries today still have no or extremely limited data protection laws. This could be due to the cultural attitudes towards the concept of autonomy and the right of certain governments to monitor and scrutinise its people in certain countries. But if they want to remain economically viable, the businesses and government of these countries must be able to provide protections which are at least similar to those afforded by the data protection laws of their business counterparts. Greenleaf (1996) predicted that directive 95/46/EC could "be a valuable model for countries currently without data protection laws".

Canada passed data protection legislation in 2000 to prevent potential blockage of data transfer from companies inside European Union. Australia is currently weighing numerous options regarding privacy legislation. Several changes have been proposed that would significantly shift the balance between freedom of speech and privacy in Australia because they would extend to the media and private individuals as well as governments and businesses - especially important because Australia has no express right of free speech (Hughes, et al., 2008).

Waters (2008) said useful progress has been made on directories of contacts, agreements between regulators and templates for referral of complaints. Similarities with OECD (2007) Working Party on Security and Privacy work on cross border enforcement have been recognized, so they are trying to harmonize processes. Greenleaf (2008) is critical to the APEC framework defining that "privacy principles set the lowest standards

of any international privacy agreement; and it has no meaningful enforcement requirements", while Waters (2008) sees the positive influence in gradual development of higher privacy standards in Asia, especially looking to the overall framework, including implementation and enforcement aspects.

Lundheim & Sindre (1994) pointed to the fact, that privacy on organizational levels is a cultural construct and important cultural diversity should be considered, when approaching privacy needs and interests, while on personal level we can talk about physiological need when discussing privacy.

Clifton, et al. (2002) wrote about privacy preserving data mining, or how to get valid data mining results without learning the underlying data values. They provided a framework and metrics for discussing the meaning of privacy preserving data mining, as a foundation for further research in this field. Fule & Roddick (2004) argue that the process of generating rules through a mining operations becomes an ethical issue when the results are used in decision making processes that effect people, or when mining consumer data unwittingly compromises the privacy of those consumers.

Gutwirth et al. (2009) evaluated current European Union data protection law against the background of the introduction of increasingly powerful, miniaturized, ubiquitous and autonomic forms of computing. Their book assesses data protection and privacy law by analyzing the actual problems (trans-border data flows, proportionality of the processing, and sensitive data) and identifying lacunae and bottlenecks, while at the same time looking at prospects for the future (web 2.0., RFID, profiling) and suggesting paths to rethink and reinvent fundamental principles and concepts.

CONCLUSION

Consumers are entitled to communicate and interact, and also to keep the control over their personal data, even after they disclosed it to others. Despite severe legislation has been adopted in most countries regarding the data transfer, there is a shortage of regulation about data storage.

Technology is making gigantic progress in electronic communication sector and transborder data transfer is taking advantage of quickly developing possibilities. An improvement of legislative consistency, modernizing specific provisions to align them with technology and market developments has been made in recent decades, but there still remain different approaches to this issue, because of historical and cultural reasons.

European Union does not believe that competition on the market could solve the needs of citizens and protect users' rights. That's why specific provisions were included in European regulatory scheme to safeguard universal services, user's rights and the protection of personal data. US sectoral laws model has to adapt to new technologies, when they appear and this is the main reason, why they always lay back. Self-regulation has proved to be of little use, as there are always certain companies, that don't care about ethics and individual's rights. We argue that self-regulatory attempts do not comply adequately with the privacy protection standards and that legislative intervention, like in EU, should be necessary to enhance further online exchange of personal information.

Privacy regulation fragmentation is a problem that cannot be solved individually by a country. When a framework or minimum harmonization clauses are proposed, each country implements those minimal criteria at its own discretion. An intragovernmental dialogue is needed for further development of these issues, with the help of international organizations. Not to forget, consumer consent is the answer to many questions. Consumers should be informed about the use of data collected about them and whether or not it will be disclosed to third parties. Pressures toward increased privacy protection are being exercised also by companies, which noticed that the lack

of consumer trust in preservation of their privacy represents a barrier to their business effectiveness.

REFERENCES

Abernathy, K. Q. (2001). *Speech to WCA*, June 25. Retrieved July 13, 2009, from http://www.fcc.gov/Speeches/Abernathy/2001/spkqa101.html

Adam, N. R., & Wormann, J. C. (1989). Security-control methods for statistical databases: A comparative study. *ACM Computing Surveys, 21*(4), 515–556. doi:10.1145/76894.76895

Agrawal, R., & Srikant, R. (2000). Privacy-preserving data mining. *2000 ACM SIGMOD International Conference Management of Data, 29*(2), (pp.439-450). New York: ACM Press.

Atallah, M., Elmagarmid, A., Ibrahim, M., Bertino, E., & Verykios, V. (1999). Disclosure limitation of sensitive rules. In *Proceedings of the 1999 Workshop on Knowledge and Data Engineering Exchange,* (pp. 45-52). Los Alamitos, CA: IEEE Computer Society.

Bygrave, L. A. (2002). *Data protection law - approaching its rationale, logic and limits (Information law series Vol: 10)*. The Hague, The Netherlands: Kluwer Law International.

Bygrave, L. A. (2004). Privacy protection in a global context – A comparative overview. *Scandinavian Studies in Law, 47*, 319–348.

Clifton, C. Kantarcioglu. M. & Vaidya, J. (2002). Privacy for data mining. In *National Science Foundation Workshop on Next Generation Data Mining*, Baltimore, MD.

Council of Europe. (1981). *Convention for the protection of individuals with rRegard to automatic processing of personal data*. Strassburg, January 28. ETS no. 108. Retrieved July 13, 2009, from http://conventions.coe.int/treaty/EN/Treaties/Html/108.htm

Crompton, M. (2002). *Under the gaze, privacy identity and new technologies.* International Association of Lawyers, 75th Anniversary Congress, Sydney. Retrieved July 13, 2009, from http://www. privacy.gov.au/news/speeches/sp104notes.doc

Dodig-Crnkovic, G. (2006). *Privacy and protection of personal integrity in the working place.* Department of Computer Science and Electronics, Mälardalen University, Västerås, Sweden, February 2006. Retrieved July 13, 2009, from http:// danskprivacynet.files.wordpress.com/2008/08/ privacy_personalintegrity_workplace.pdf

EC – European Commission. (1995). *Directive 95/46/EC of the European Parliament and of the Council of 24 October 1995 on the protection of individuals with regard to the processing of personal data and on the free movement of such data,* No L 281/31. Retrieved July 13, 2009, from http://ec.europa.eu/justice_home/fsj/privacy/ docs/95-46-ce/dir1995-46_part1_en.pdf

EC – European Commission. (1997). *Directive 97/66/EC of the European Parliament and of the Council the Council, December 1997 concerning the processing of personal data and the protection of privacy in the telecommunications sector.* Retrieved July 13, 2009, from http://www.legaltext. ee/text/en/T50023.htm

EC – European Commission. (2000a). Data protection: Commission adopts the "safe harbor" decision – Adequate protection for personal data transfer to US. *Single Market News, 23* (October 2000). Retrieved July 13, 2009, from http:// ec.europa.eu/internal_market/smn/smn23/ s23mn27.htm

EC – European Commission. (2000b). *The Charter of Fundamental Rights of the European Union.* Retrieved July 13, 2009, from http://www. eucharter.org/

EC – European Commission. (2001). *Regulation (EC) No 45/2001 of the European Parliament and of the Council of 18 December 2000 on the protection of individuals with regard to the processing of personal data by the institutions and bodies of the Community and on the free movement of such data.* Retrieved July 13, 2009, from http://europa. eu/legislation_summaries/information_society/ l24222_en.htm

EC – European Commission. (2002). *Directive 2002/58/EC of the European Parliament and of the council of July 2002, concerning the processing of personal data and the protection of privacy in the electronic communications sector (Directive on privacy and electronic communications).* Retrieved July 13, 2009, from http://mineco.fgov. be/internet_observatory/pdf/legislation/directive_2002_58_en.pdf

EC – European Commission. (2008). *Opinion 2/2008 on the review of the Directive 2002/58/ EC on privacy and electronic communications (ePrivacy Directive).* Retrieved July 13, 2009, from http://ec.europa.eu/justice_home/fsj/privacy/docs/wpdocs/2008/wp150_en.pdf

Estivill-Castro, V., & Brankovic, L. (1999). Data swapping: Balancing privacy against precision in mining for logic rules. In Mohania, M., & Min Tjoa, A. (Eds.), *DaWaK'99 Proceedings – Data Warehousing and Knowledge Discovery* (pp. 389–398). Berlin: Springer.

FDPIC - Federal Data Protection and Information Commissioner. (2005). Montreux declaration: The protection of personal data and privacy in a globalised world: a universal right respecting diversities. In *27th International Conference of Data Protection and Privacy Commissioners,* Montreux (14 - 16 September 2005). Retrieved July 13, 2009, from http://www.privacy.org.nz/ assets/Files/22718821.pdf

Flavian, C., & Guinaliu, M. (2006). Consumer trust, perceived security and privacy policy. *Industrial Management & Data Systems, 106*(5), 601–620. doi:10.1108/02635570610666403

Fule, P., & Roddick, J. F. (2004). Detecting privacy and ethical sensitivity in data mining results. In V. Estivil-Castro (Ed.), *Twenty-Seventh Australasian Computer Science Conference (ACSC2004).* Dunedin, Australia: Australian Computer Society, Inc.

Greenleaf, G. W. (1996). Privacy and Australia's New Federal Government. *Australasian Privacy Law & Policy Reporter, 3*(1), 1-3 and 4-7.

Greenleaf, G. W. (2009). Five years of the APEC privacy framework: Failure or promise? *Computer Law & Security Report, 25*(1), 28–43. doi:10.1016/j.clsr.2008.12.002

Guba, E. G., & Lincoln, Y. S. (2005). Paradigmatic controversies, Contradictions, and emerging confluences. In Booth, C., & Harrington, J. (Eds.), *Developing Business Knowledge* (pp. 295–319). London: SAGE.

Gutwirth, S., Poullet, Y., De Hert, P., de Terwangne, C., & Nouwt, S. (2009). *Reinventing data protection?* Berlin: Springer. doi:10.1007/978-1-4020-9498-9

Heisenberg, D. (2005). *Negotiating privacy: The European Union, The United States, and personal data protection (Politics/Global Challenges in the Information Age).* Boulder, CO: Lynne Rienner Publishers.

Hughes, G., Dawson, S., & Brookes, T. (2008). Considering new privacy lLaws in Australia. *IEEE Security and Privacy, 6*(3), 57–59. doi:10.1109/MSP.2008.60

Johnson, D. R., & Post, D. G. (1996). Law and borders - The rise of law in cyberspace. *Stanford Law Review, 48*(5), 13–67. doi:10.2307/1229390

Kennedy, G., Doyle, S., & Lui, B. (2008). Data protection in the Asia-Pacific region. *Computer Law & Security Report, 25*(1), 59–68. doi:10.1016/j.clsr.2008.11.006

Linn, A. (2005). Amazon has a big memory. *Philadelphia Inquirer,* E12.

Lundheim, R., & Sindre, G. (1993). Privacy and computing: A cultural perspective. In Sizer, R. et al. (Eds.), *Security and Control of Information Technology in Society, IFIP WG 9.6 Working Conference,* St. Petersburg, Russia. New York: Elsevier Science Publishers.

Newman, A. L., & Bach, D. (2004). Self-regulatory trajectories in the shadow of public power: Resolving digital dilemmas in Europe and the U.S. *Governance: An International Journal of Policy, Administration, and Institutions, 17*(3), 387–413.

OECD – Organisation for Economic Co-operation and Development. (2007). *Recommendation on Cross-Border Co-operation in the Enforcement of Laws Protecting Privacy.* Paris: OECD – Committee for Information, Computer and Communications Policy.

Privacy International. (2007). *Overview of privacy.* Retrieved July 9, 2009, from http://www.privacyinternational.org/article. shtml?cmd[347]=x-347-559062

Raab, C. D. (2005). The future of privacy protection. In Mansell, R., & Collins, B. S. (Eds.), *Trust and crime in information societies* (pp. 282–318). Cheltenham, UK: Edward Elgar Publishing Ltd.

Sedita, S., & Subramanian, R. (2006). Trends and issues in global information security – a comparison of US and EU cybercrime laws. In *Proceedings of the Conference on Trends in Global Business- Doing Business in the European Union: Yesterday, Today and Tomorrow* (pp. 214-228). Hamden, NJ: Quinnipiac University.

Shea, C. (2008). A need for a swift change: The struggle between the European Union's desire for privacy in international financial transactions and the United States' need for security from terrorists as evidenced by the Swift scandal. *Journal of High Technology Law*, *8*, 143.

Solove, D. J. (2008). *Understanding Privacy*. Cambridge, MA: Harvard University Press.

Solove, D. J., & Hoofnagle, C. J. (2005). *A model regime of privacy protection* (Version 2.0). GWU Law School Public Law Research Paper No. 132. GWU Legal Studies Research Paper No. 132. Retrieved July 9, 2009, from at SSRN: http://ssrn.com/abstract=699701

Sookman, B. B. (2000). *Sookman: Computer, Internet and Electronic Commerce Law*. Toronto, Canada: Carswell Legal Publications.

Tran, E., & Atkinson, M.-A. (2002). Security of personal data across national borders. *Information Management & Computer Security*, *10*(5), 237–241. doi:10.1108/09685220210446588

United Nations. (1990). *Guidelines concerning Computerized personal data files*. Geneva: UN, Office of the high commissioner for human rights. Retrieved July 13, 2009, from http://www.unhchr.ch/html/menu3/b/71.htm

US – United States. (1791). *The United States Constitution*. Washington, DC: US Department of Justice. Retrieved July 13, 2009, from http://www.usconstitution.net/const.html

US – United States. (1966). *The Freedom of Information Act*. Washington, DC: US Department of Justice. Retrieved July 13, 2009, from http://www.usdoj.gov/oip/foia_guide07.htm

US – United States. (1974). *The Privacy Act*. Washington, DC: US Department of Justice. Retrieved July 13, 2009, from http://www.usdoj.gov/opcl/1974privacyact-overview.htm

US – United States. (1986). *The Electronic Communications Privacy Act of 1986*. Washington, DC: US Department of Justice. Retrieved July 13, 2009, from http://www.usiia.org/legis/ecpa.html

US – United States. (1986). *The Computer Security Act of 1987*. Washington, DC: US Department of Justice. Retrieved July 13, 2009, from http://epic.org/crypto/csa/csa.html

US – United States. (2001). *Uniting and Strengthening America by Providing Appropriate Tools Required to Intercept and Obstruct Terrorism Act of 2001* (USA PATRIOT Act). Washington, DC: US Department of Justice. Retrieved July 13, 2009, from http://www.gpo.gov/fdsys/pkg/PLAW-107publ56/content-detail.html

US – United States. (2002). *Homeland Security Act of 2002*. Washington, DC: US Department of Homeland Security. Retrieved July 13, 2009, from http://www.dhs.gov/xlibrary/assets/hr_5005_enr.pdf

Verykios, V. S., Elmagarmid, A. K., Bertino, E., Saygın, Y., & Dasseni, E. (2004). Association rule hiding. *IEEE Transactions on Knowledge and Data Engineering*, *16*(4), 434–447. doi:10.1109/TKDE.2004.1269668

Wang, K., Yu, P. S., & Chakraborty, S. (2004). Bottom-up generalization: A data mining solution to privacy protection. In *Fourth IEEE International Conference on Data Mining (ICDM'04)* (pp. 249-256). Brighton, UK: IEEE.

Wang, T., & Liu, L. (2008). Butterfly: Protecting output privacy in stream mining. *2008 IEEE 24th International Conference on Data Engineering* (pp. 1170-1179). Cancun, Mexico: ICDE.

Waters, N. (2008). *The APEC Asia-Pacific privacy initative – a new route to effective data protection or as Trojan horse for self-regulation*? Paper 59. University of New South Wales, Faculty of Law Research Series. Retrieved July 13, 2009, from http://law.bepress.com/cgi/viewcontent.cgi?article=1134&context=unswwps

Webb, P. (2003). A comparative analysis of data protection laws in Australia and Germany. *Journal of Information, Law and Technology, 2*. Retrieved July 13, 2009, from http://www2.warwick.ac.uk/fac/soc/law/elj/jilt/2003_2/webb/

Westin, A. F. (1967). *Privacy and freedom*. New York: Athenenum.

Westin, A. F. (2003). Social and political dimensions of privacy. *The Journal of Social Issues, 59*(2), 431–453. doi:10.1111/1540-4560.00072

Witzner, D. J., Abelson, H., Berners-Lee, T., Hanson, C., Hendler, J., Kagal, L., et al. (2006). *Transparent accountable data mining: New strategies for privacy protection*. MIT CSAIL Technical Report-2006-007. Retrieved July 13, 2009, from http://dig.csail.mit.edu/2006/01/tami-privacy-strategies-aaai.pdf

Zwick, D., & Dholakia, N. (2001). Contrasting European and American approaches to privacy in electronic markets: Property right versus civil right. *Electronic Markets, 11*(2), 116–120. doi:10.1080/101967801300197034

ADDITIONAL READING

Aquisti, A., Gritzalis, S., Lambrinoudakis, C., & De Capitani di Vimercati, S. (2008). *Digital privacy: theory, technologies, and practices*. Boca Raton: Auerbach Publications.

Bygrave, L. A. (2002). *Data protection law - Approaching its rationale, logic and limits* (information law series Volume 10). The Hague: Kluwer Law International.

Carey, P. (2004). *Data protection: A practical guide to UK and EU law*. Oxford: Oxford University Press.

Falch, M., Henten, A., & Skouby, K. E. (2001). Consumer related legal aspects of electronic commerce: the case of Denmark. In Bloch Rasmussen, L. Beardon C. and Munari S. (Eds.), *Computers and networks in the age of globalization* (pp. 43-52). Dordrecht: Kluwer Academic Publishers.

Greenleaf, G. W. (2009). Five years of the APEC privacy framework: Failure or promise? *Computer Law & Security Report, 25*(1), 28–43. doi:10.1016/j.clsr.2008.12.002

Gutwirth, S., Poullet, Y., De Hert, P., de Terwangne, C., & Nouwt, S. (2009). *Reinventing Data Protection?* Berlin: Springer. doi:10.1007/978-1-4020-9498-9

Kuhn, M. (2007). *Federal dataveillance: Implications for constitutional privacy protections (Law and Society)*. El Paso: LFB Scholarly Publishing LLC.

Kuner, C. (2007). *European data protection law: Corporate regulation and compliance*. Oxford: Oxford University Press.

Reed, C., & Angel, J. (Eds.). (2007). *Computer Law: the Law and Regulation of Information Technology*. Oxford: Oxford University Press.

Schwartz, P. M., & Solove, D. J. (2008). *Information privacy: Statutes and regulations, 2008-2009 Supplement*. New York: Aspen Publishers, Inc.

Singleton, S., & Ustaran, E. (2007). *e-privacy and online data protection*. Haywards Heath: Tottel Publishing.

Solove, D. J. (2008). *Understanding privacy*. Cambridge: Harvard University Press.

Sookman, B. B. (2000). *Sookman: Computer, internet and electronic commerce law*. Toronto: Carswell Legal Publications.

KEY TERMS AND DEFINITIONS

Data Mining: The process of automatically searching large volumes of data for patterns.

Data Protection: Class of laws that commonly go by the name of data protection law, used in European jurisdictions.

Privacy: An individual or group's right to control the flow of sensitive information about themselves.

Privacy protection: Class of laws that that commonly go by the name of data protection laws in USA, Canada and Australia.

Comprehensive Law: General law that governs the collection, use and transfer of personal information by both the public and private sectors.

Sectoral Law: Specific law for each sector.

Self-Regulation: Established codes of practice and engage in self-policing of companies and industry.

Consumer: Individual who purchases, uses, maintains, and disposes of products and services.

Chapter 3
On the Nature and Scales of Statistical Estimations Divergence and its Linkage with Statistical Learning

Vassiliy Simchera
Research Institute of Statistics (Rosstat), Russia

Ali Serhan Koyuncugil
Capital Markets Board of Turkey, Turkey

ABSTRACT

Besides the well-known commonplace, and sometimes also simply fantastic reasons for the existing breaks in the estimations of one and the same phenomena, substitution of concepts, manipulations, intentional distortions, all possible manipulations and frank lie there are their own technological reasons in the statistics for the similar breaks, which are being generated by some sort of circumstances of insurmountable force, which one should differ from well-known posy reasons, and therefore to consider in a special order. Predetermined objectively by conditioned divergence of the theoretical and empirical distributions, gaps between a nature and phenomenon, shape and its content, word and deed, these reasons (different from subjective reasons), limited by the extreme possibilities of human existence, can be overcome through the expansion of humans knowledge's, which assumes reconsideration of the very basis of the modern science. Below we present some of the approaches towards such a reconsideration, which opens possibilities for the reduction of the huge gaps in modern statistical estimations of the same phenomena and its linkage with statistical learning.

INTRODUCTION

General condition of success for any research is the convergence of theoretical assumptions to the facts being observed, and vise versa the facts being observed to the theoretical assumptions. No matter whether we talk about inductive or deductive researches, determined or undetermined facts and theirs cause – effect connections, natural scientific or socio-economic researches, reliable or less reliable data – the condition always remains

DOI: 10.4018/978-1-61692-865-0.ch003

the same. Convergence of theory and practice, forecasts and facts, their adequacy or inadequacy are set by identifications of existing in nature and familiar to science of theoretical and empirical distributions. Convergence at the level of the necessary and sufficient conditions in contrast to abstract ideals is being checked by known criteria of statistical agreement (or in case of its absence) by trial-and-error method and likelihood criteria and common sense. This is the way as many centuries ago the imaginations and theories is tested by facts and practices, and in turn facts and practices is tested by theory and imaginations. And there is nothing else that human mind could invent either in the past nor today.

Where a theory relies on the facts and facts relies on theory it is possible to carry out a statistical experiment, which can and indeed gives a significant results with clear sense and paramount scientific and practical importance, and where does not – such an experiment is impossible, and there is no point to initiate this experiment as its results will be false. Unfortunately we should state here that a first case (rather in natural science than in public science) by various reasons, and mainly for a general reason of the limit of knowledge and resources of their realization, is restricted and ultimate, and each successful experiment is interpreted as unique success, while a second case, because of the ignorance of the law of the limited knowledge, is not restricted and infinite. As a result we have domination in a science of simple and mainly false surveys results which are worthless and insignificant, and as a general consequence – depreciation of the efficiency of the science and knowledge's, and total ignorance of them.

The correction of a general situation perhaps requires not only changes in the existing unsatisfactory market treatment, and correction of the negligible treatment towards fundamental researches and labor-intensive experimental results, but raising the systematic level of the knowledge production itself and its application according to

the exact form of the identified processes and events in a way their endogen necessity in the world around us. This is the cause of scientific experiment stagnation and further the science as a whole. We should not criticize the external circumstances but think on how to clear a science itself from futile imitation accumulated during centuries, reconsideration of the statistical experiment basis – this is what one should start from and what indeed can help to correct the unsatisfactory situation in the modern science.

This means that phenomena and events in the world around us their content, dynamic and structure should not adapt to a format of scientific experiment that is its usual paradigms, algorithms and interpretations but in contrast – the format of scientific experiment itself its set of ideological potential must constantly alter and adapt to a world around us, to catch and produce a future tendencies its fast going and dominantly differently directed and therefore contradictive changes and give it a shape of essential construction which helps not only for better understanding but also transform our world in efficient and reasonable ways.

Conceiving the situation this way one should start from fundamental basis of the modern scientific experiment, its theoretical hypothesis the basis of which is multivariate statistical distributions and their approximating functions and laws. Depending on how full and certain these functions and laws reflect the structure and dynamic of modern world, the tendencies of its alteration, so this is a degree which define how these functions and laws are applicable today in order to influence the modern events in a constructive way, providing each time the possibilities for effective decision making.

The constructive answer to this question demands reconsideration of the whole variety of the existing types of univariate and multivariate distributions their inventory, adaptation and identification applicable to a modern problems solving for production, labor and life. The first step towards obtaining such an answer is typology of present (or in any case most commonly used) distribution functions and laws of observed phenomena and their systematization with regard to problems solving of multivariate distributions as most important and significant ones. There are a lot of distribution functions, but they are separated and can not be united. Part of these functions (linear, normal, power-series, exponential and others distribution functions) acceptable on the level of required and sufficient conditions are approximating observed empirical facts, and have clear substantial interpretation of parameters and sense of the results being received on their basis and these functions are widespread. The other part (the most part) of these functions (logistic, maximum likelihood, and in particular nonlinear and nonparametric distribution functions) are less proved theoretically, and inadequately or even does not reflect the existing empirical distributions and require as a rule robust work while their identification and appliance of them to the problem solving of multivariate analysis.

There is also one, some kind of off-balance part of multivariate distribution functions, aimed towards chaotic, partly robust and partly non parametric and further fuzzy distributions, which as a rule lack of any theoretical basis and badly or no way approximating the respective empirical data observed and demand a development of substantially different approaches to their construction. Here we can attribute the synthesis combinatorial problem of distribution function, constructing the unknown hybrid functions on the basis of the existing known ones. In view of exceptional complexity these two tasks are just mentioned here.

The overcoming of the existing gaps between theoretical and empirical multivariate distribution functions assumes the typology's ground and representation of these distributions and functions by their resolving powers which are defined by attributes and criteria of necessary and sufficient equivalence. Nowadays one of the most popular ways of using multivariate distributions is data mining. Therefore, data mining has the same gaps mentioned.

BACKGROUND

It is possible to review data mining under two separate headings as Statistics and Information Technologies. At the beginning of data mining concept discovered in 1990's IT perspective mostly underlined but in 2000's analytical or statistical point of view of data mining has been becoming most integral part of data mining. Hastie et al. (2001) emphasized the statistical view of data mining with statistical learning concept. Rao (2001) linked statistics and data mining with more strong ties and mentioned data mining as a future of statistics. On the other hand, Moss and Atre (2003) mentioned the difference between Classical Statistics and data mining.

Data mining mostly interested in big data sets. Therefore, finance is one of the most suitable implementation areas of data mining because of the huge data produces with transactions. Kovalerchuk and Vityaev (2002) inspected the implemantation domains of finance in data mining with examples and emphasized that stock prices, currency rates and bankruptcy predictions, claim management, customer profiling and money laundry some of the implemantation domains of data mining. In addition, data mining successfully applied to financial performance and distress prediction. Koyuncugil and Ozgulbas (2006a) emphasized the problems of Turkish SMEs and suggested financial profiling as a first step of solutions. Then, the authors determined the financial profiles of 135 SMEs listed in İstanbul Stock Exchange (ISE) according to 2004 ISE data. Koyuncugil and Ozgulbas (2006b) defined a financial performance measure for Turkish SMEs with 2004 ISE data. Koyuncugil and Ozgulbas (2006c) defined the factors which effected financial failers of ISE listed SMEs with 2000-2005 data via CHAID (Chi-Square Automatic Interaction Detector) decision tree algorithm which is one of the most update data mining methods. Ozgulbas and Koyuncugil (2006) and Ozgulbas et al. (2006) determined weak and strenght sides of SMEs in financial mean, financial performance level with 2000-2005 data via data mining.

One of the most efficient facilities of data mining is Early Warning Systems because of its definition. Data mining aims to discover hidden relations, covered patterns and then use them for prediction of future behaviours. This definition of data mining makes it the most efficient tool for Early Warning Systems. Therefore, many recent studies in early warning domain has been using data mining. Koyuncugil (2006) developed an early warning system for manipulation and insider trading detection in Stock Exchange Markets and proved that the system works successfully with real data.

Simchera (2003a) is given examples of systematic errors, which are made at improper identification of direct and reversed numbers modules, recursive and discursive rates, direct and reversed exchange rates as well as effective interest rates, annuities and bills with recourse, and also numerous examples on collecting and publishing various estimates 9such as GDP, life standards etc.) on the basis of the same methods and estimates with the application of different methods. The module increase direct number for example consumer price index with value of 1.25 is 0.25, whilst module of reversed number for example index of consumer inflation would be 0.2 (1/1.25), in everyday practice it is considered to be equal to 0.25 module, which is not right and in turn illustrates as demonstrative as possible the most spread example of typical routine "misspell" in statistics that is in other words – to judge anything with the same value and present the same thing with different numbers. And from this quite small "misspell" grows fraud in statistics. Keen and Smith (2007) are given with exceptional arguments the examples of fraud in the estimates of British tax calculations; in the working paper of Ruhashyankiko and Yehoue (2006) and in working paper by Mauro (2002) authors argue the corruption in the private sector of economy and its effect on economic growth reduction. The persuasive estimate of debt dynamics and imbalances are given in the working paper by Meredith (2007) and measurement of financial market liquidity is considered in the working paper of Sarr and Lybek (2002).

Booth et al. (1999) based on excellent models the authors illustrate the insolvent insurers estimations for portfolio investments, funds and exchange rates, derivatives, pension funds. In the work of Vaitilingam (2007) there are examples of such estimate, in particular examples ob divergence of estimates for actuarial indices, based on sample observations (covering 30 companies - Dow Johns Indices up to 500 companies – Standards and Poor's Index) and mass observations (covering thousands of companies (400 million companies all over the world).

In general the methodology of distortion and publishing of unreliable estimates and explanations of cause and sources of fraud in statistics are given in significant work by OECD (2003, 2008).

MAIN THRUST

Simchera (2003a) and Simchera (2008) are reviewed nine types of distributions within two categories (category of linear and category of nonlinear distributions). The adequate choice of which is the first condition for an efficient minimization of fundamental estimation discrepancies in the modern statistics and arising on these basis deep delusions and undisguised lies. At the same time we can mark out within linear six and within nonlinear three types of distributions. Here are six respective linear distributions:

$$y_x = a_0 + a_1 x_1 \text{ – functional distribution;} \quad (1)$$

$$\Phi(x)\frac{1}{\sigma\sqrt{2\pi}}e\frac{-(x-a)^2}{2\sigma^2} - \text{normal distribution;}$$

(2)

f(x)= a_0+x - power-series distribution; (3)

$$\varphi(x,b) = \frac{1}{b}e^{x/b}(x \geq 0) - \text{exponential distribution;}$$

(4)

f(x)=(1/b)e$^{-(x-a)/b}$[+e$^{-(x-a)/b}$]$^{-2}$ – logistic distribution;

(5)

f(x)=x/b^{c-1}e$^{(-xb)}$[1/bΓ(c)] – multivariate distribution.

(6)

Without such identification all statistical estimations (and further expectations, forecasts etc.) are shifted and have only illustrative meanings. Nowadays, estimation word coincides another concept different from statistics. This new concept is data mining. There are a lot of definitions of data mining. Because data mining is an evolutionary area. One of the most common definition: 'Data mining is the process of extracting previously unknown, valid and actionable information from large databases and then using the information to make crucial business decisions (Cabena et al., 1997).' Data mining is not a single step analysis. Data mining is a sequential multi analysis and multi task process. But, mainly the core of the whole data mining process is called data mining. On the other hand, the process takes place as 'Knowledge Discovery' as well. Data mining step of the knowledge discovery process mostly means modified multivariate statistical analysis methods. These methods automized, scaled to analyze huge data sets via modification. Therefore, it is possible to define data mining as an evolution of statistical methods via Information Technologies and automated processes.

Data mining mainly has two different point of view:

1. Statistical,
2. Information Technologies.

Data mining from statistical point of view calls 'Statistical Learning'. Statistical learning let us know what data tells instead of subjective sayings. Data mining, automatic extraction of predictional strategic knowledge is mostly based on multivariate statistical methods. Discovery process aims to extract valuable knowledge from hidden, covered, unknown patterns or relations. Patterns usually imply two concepts as similarities and dissimilarities. Profiles, specifications, identifications and unique properties can be determined by dissimilarities or divergence. In addition, divergences can be play a key role for determination of early warning signals for anomalies, errors and fraud. Therefore, divergence is not one of the concerns of only statistics but data mining too.

Yet there is also more powerful reason for divergence of the existing statistical estimations which are discrepancies in the conceptual scaling reflecting different ideologies of perceptions of the same phenomena. Especially in relief such discrepancies project at the joint of various world view sciences and epochs sometimes containing in the same definitions and classifications and even in symbols and measures completely different indicative view and value sense. The phenomenon in question comes out visually and instructively at their most on the example of widening the gaps between statistical information and socio-economic disinformation which are in temporary crisis circumstances go beyond all sensible apogees, turning even old time lie into the definite value. What has really happened here, what causes, except sheer self-interest which give rise (this process continues) to such terrible condition of socio-economic information?

From technological point of view we have to deal today what on the one hand the capacity and flows of economical information for the period of globalization (1991-2008) would increase tenfold. On the other hand – for a mentioned period the credibility and quality of published data and consequently a quality of decisions made of their bases decreased drastically. As a result some countries and world as a whole instead of expected transition from manual control to automatic one have got into manipulative management.

In total of published data the volume of primary data has significantly reduced a lot of valuable and demanded information are consumed by commercial classified information and corruption, we have lost many sources and spheres of primary data, the level of data comparability had fallen, virtually the possibilities for testing them for convergence, precision and credibility are taken out of public access. Information is dominantly collecting for information itself that is why it works with reduced efficiency. The Internet is a convincing example which shows that it servicing itself and its providers for 97, 5% and only for the rest 2, 5% it is commercial network and information service. The understanding of that the people and the worlds nations need not information typologies but information itself is substituted and lost.

How to turn the contemporary situation for the better, to overcome the accumulated information gaps, misbalances, obstructions and through this to provide freed space and resources for collection, processing and distribution of credible information on the basis of which one only can provide crucial improvement of total socio-economic situation in the countries to organize the real transition from today's reforms to the reforms of forthcoming efficient transformation. Simchera (2003b) is given general answer to this question in his work. Below with use of additional information we give following concise answer to this question.

There are a lot of economical estimations but they are uncoordinated and mainly doubtful and incomparable. The gaps between existing indicators (due to conceptual differences of their understanding and coverage, material divergence in prices, exchange rates etc.) reach sometimes multiple values and strike off any possibility to its

wise application. All socio-economic parameters gathered and published today are pretty often characterizing mainly not real situation in the world but represent only calculation effect, and in many cases even less – that is statistical calculations errors. On the basis of such deliberately incorrect and even false data one should not make that conclusions and assumptions which are made in modern statistical science.

The science loses even more in its potential due to data manipulating practices which became rather standard than exception, substitution of one parameters for the others, aberration of not only size and meaning but the sense of the phenomena in question, that is what confirm the today's crisis estimations. There is no other brunch of the science where measurements would be more contradictive, estimations divergent and results just useless for a practice, than it is in the economic science. This is why it is logical not accidental that much of published data should be taken out of 'circulation' as useless. Consequently one should not understand all of the above as total result which shows that with this level of divergence, incorrectness there is less point to calculate and publish statistical data than not to. This fully concerns to calculations and publications of market statistical data which not only distort but also misrepresent all normal perceptions about real situation in modern economy, and virtually turn all published estimations into economical phantoms and threaten of credibility loss to all conclusions and values of modern science.

Subjective evaluations, interpretations and conclusions generally can be very far away from what data tells us objectively. In addition, the data can be directed, dirty, missing, unstandardized and uncomparable. Therefore, there are some necessary steps for acceptable decision making process:

1. Data must be realiable.
2. Analysis must be suitable for the aim (s) and the data.

3. The evaluation of the results of the analysis must be correctly
4. Conclusions must be in an objective manner

In case of missing at least one of the necessary steps given above, then, the gap between estimations and the realizations will be statistically or scientifically unacceptable.

THE GAP BETWEEN ESTIMATIONS AND REALIZATIONS WITH NUMERICAL EXAMPLES

Here are examples illustrating gaps in economical estimations, which directly point to the sources of bad informational situation in the world and from our point of view due to this fundamental reason – situation of modern economical science.

According to official statistics GNP growth in the USA in constant prices of 2000 (with regard to statistical calculation errors) in 2007 in comparison with 2000 accounted for 1,18 times (increase 2,3% per year); (in 1991-1999 – 1,18) for the period 1981-2007 – it would be 1,93 points (2,4% per year); national wealth's estimation of growth are 1,16; 1,18 and 1,72 points respectively. These are actual estimations of growth. And here are the figures – phantoms which substitute the quite humble figures against their background of real rates of the USA economical growth. The growth of the wide spreading Dow Jones Index (share rates of 30 largest companies in the world) for the same period accounted for 1,22; 3,8 and 7,1 times (the points fixed for this index at the end of 1990 were 2892, and at the end of 1999 – 10 991; 2007 – 13 368; June 2009 – 8 501), the Standard and Poor's Index (500 companies) – 1,3; 2,1 and 19,0 times (the points fixed for this index at the end of 2003 – 1 109; 2007 – 1 479; June 2009 – 923) respectively, and the growth for Nasdaq (5 000 technology companies) – only from the middle of 1996 has exceeded 153 times (the points fixed

for this index at the end of 2003 – 2 010; 2007 – 2 654; June 2009 – 1 796).

In other G-7 countries the gaps between real rates and phantom – rates are approximately the same. In England in particular with the GNP growth for the period 1991-1998 in 1,25 times increase (for the period 1981-1998 - 1,49 times increase) the stock exchange FTSE index showed growth of 2,7 and 9,1 times. The exception was France where while GDP growth for the period 1991-1998 was 1,13 times its stock exchange CAC – 40 index showed growth of "just" 2,7 times. Even if we take estimations of GDP's of G-7 countries in current prices, the gaps between them and stock exchange increases would stay fantastic and destroy representations of any dignity.

In addition, here are some others kind of phantoms. The real indicators of the USA's GDP with most favorable calculations – today would be $14,0 (in 2003 – $11,0; 1990 – $5,8) bill. doll. Indicators of national wealth are $28,3, $24,8 and $14,8 bill. doll. respectively; considering real financial assets $39,5, $33,2 and $22,4 bill. Doll (U.S. Census Bureau, 2009). The capitalization value of USA's companies (price multiplied by quantity of issued shares) on financial markets estimated, before crisis 2008, for $200-$215 trill., annual turnover of shares – $100-$120 trill. The crisis only for a last half of 2008 and first half of 2009 has devaluated these assets to 40-50% and yet it is going to devaluate them to 30-35% in forthcoming months, equalizing them with estimations of real assets, which turns all fund market in the USA into a phantom. The phantoms are also modern indicators for banks assets. The real assets for 1000 largest banks are estimated for $20 (in 2003 - $12,7) trill. The derivatives (fictitious capital) of all world's banks exceed $400 (in 2003 - $100) trill., while their equity capitals account for only $30-$25 and $19,5-$18,5 (in the USA -$14-$10) trill. respectively. On the assumptions of estimations of U.S. Federal Deposit Insurance Corporation (2007) consolidated real assets of commercial banks (at the end of 2007

– 7 282 banks in the USA), investment institutions or investment banks (total number 1 251 at the end of 2007) and credit unions (8 101 at the end of 2007) excluding mutual benefit societies which would not exceed $14 till. (to be precise $13.792,5 bill.) in the pre-crisis year, including assets of commercial banks - $11 176,5 bill., and credit unions - $753,4 bill. (National Credit Union Administration, 2007). And these quite credible estimates in comparison with analogues estimates on assets of some separately taken American banks are also appearing to be phantoms. The allied assets of JP Morgan accounted for $97,5 trill. (62,5% over the world's GDP), while its real equity capital accounted for $2,5 trill. (2,6% of the assets). Respectively estimations of Goldman & Sachs are $50 trill. (83,3% of world's GDP) and $1,5 trill (3% of assets). Even the assets of largest bank holding HSBC (Hong Kong-Shanghais Bank, Corp.) are phantoms, the fictitious assets of which (in 2000 accounted for $6,5, and in 2008 - $108 trill.) exceeds the equity capital for almost 10-50 times more (Bank of Russia, 1999). According to market rates virtually all modern transnational companies including American pride – Ford and biggest world's bank – HSBC which real capitalization in good times would exceed trillion of US dollars – are bankrupts, whilst according to leading rating agencies they still have higher ratings than actually solvent companies in China, Brazil, India or Russia.

Against the background of real GDP's volume accounted for about $60 trill. in 2008, it is absurd how estimates of fictitious capital look like, the guaranteed part of which in the same year would overrun $6*10^{14}$ that is $600 trill., while unguaranteed part $3*10^{15}$ that is $3 quadrillion, including the USA with $175 and $900 trill. At last the phantoms are the inadmissibly different by module, scope and contents indicators of GDP, inflation, national wealth in various countries. Finally, it is just ridiculous how in the form of phantoms – marginal's are presented today the audition estimations for capitalization of world's leading companies which have fallen drastically at once to 7-10% from the initial value following the world's crisis.

The mixing of own capitals with attracted ones, real values with fictitious values, the parameters mentioned above and many other parameters of financial assets cause quite serious concerns and according to specialists' opinion require not only cardinal revision but also international legislative control. The above examples illustrate not only destructive but also demoralizing role of market representations about fundamentals of modern economical life and processes of economic developments of different countries and nations. They cause apprehension in a whole world and persuasively point at necessity of fundamental revision of all modern practices of economical estimations, and a new approach to the principals of economic measurements. Especially loud voices for this decision are coming out from the USA which is a motherland of financial pyramids and financial bubbles the burst of which can destroy not only the US but the rest of contemporary financial and economical system. When Alan Greenspan was speaking at the White House on 5th of April, that were unheard appeals to study statistics of world's financial markets, scrutinize and reveal the consequences of the growth of financial bubbles in the world's economy.

The way out from this situation one can see in revision of core structure of a whole variety of market expectations their conventional agreements and standardization of their methods for comparative calculations. For provision of practical realization of this way out the authorities should preliminary to take concrete solutions on the following basis:

- on the basis of the international standards of calculation and account one should organize the inventory and fundamental revaluation of all international and national assets and on this base one should take all fictitious assets out of balance turnover which dilute real representations in economy and excludes in principle the possibilities to coordinate it on a fair basis;

- instead of floating exchange rates one should introduce fixed ones which reflect real interaction of prices by all line of produced and consumed products, services and capitals;

- one should find corporative indices and fund market ratings as useless and cancel them due to they distort situation with global market estimations;

- on the principally new basis should be constructed and introduced into international turnover the single world's indices, which would representatively reflect the dynamics of world's fund and foreign exchange rates markets;

- on the basis of transparency and free accessibility, public watch and personal responsibility, with compensation of damage and lost profits one should reconsider the principles of IMF and World Bank work, and in case of failure to implement the liabilities – one should develop conditions to seize their activity as the international institutions – regulators of the international financial relationships;

- under the auspices of UN one should establish an International commission on causes qualifications and regulation of world's financial crisis consequences with the functions to determine a size of material loss and moral damage caused by the monetary authorities of the US and other countries – satellites due to failure to take the necessary measures for prevention of their negative consequences and rights to discover in accordance with international law all persons guilty for breaking the rules of financial business leading to a global default, mass bankruptcies which exceed all calculated losses of almost every country and nation in all world wars.

The presented examples – are documentary approved facts of the informational distortion. However in today's practice the economy has to deal not with distorted information but with outspoken call to world's economical society what is in legal parlance called fraud, in the form of forgery, which is done by betrayal of trust – the deeds which are qualified as crime and penalties are severe. This could be a decision.

CONCLUSION AND FUTURE STUDIES

To overcome the differences in modern economic conditions and eliminate the existing unjustified in many cases multiple and even by a factor of ten divergences in economical estimations which distort economical representation and excluding possibilities of their efficient practical use in the development of the international standards one should organize and implement special work on the correction of fundamental divergences in the economic estimations, restitution of incomparable parameters, standardization of methods of their calculations and publications on comparable basis and degrees of credibility claimed beforehand. In other words one should create a single number of standards of economical information and economical indicators based on total conventional decisions. All information in the world, all economical or rather all other indicators must be built and published on this basis. There is no country which must not and cannot be exception unless it claims to be included into the existing borders of the single world socio-economic space. The conditions and consequences of its activity and life first of all should be transparent and explicit in estimations. A "non-transparent" country cannot and has no moral rights to claim transparency from other countries and first of all from its own citizens.

In this connection a total international standardization for all multiplicity of mutually demanded socio-economical parameters shall not mean the automatic unification of every possible other multiplicities, which are characterizing an objectively existing national flavour and specificity of development for every single country. On the contrary the modern standardization should initially take into account the necessity for an existence, maintenance and multiplication of various numbers of national indicators considering them as fundamental origins and solid ground for their own development and existence. That is why what has been done today in the sphere of international standardization of national indicators is only the first level not the top of the enormous work which must be done in every single country and in a whole world in behave of increase of their convergence and guaranteed provision for that level of the mutual subject understanding in the world which is only possible on the basis of the international standardization of the national indicators.

Thus it is rather proposed than excluded that all preceding work of the International Statistical Institute (ISI), UN's League of Nations and other international organizations which has been made during XIX-XX centuries in the field of international standardization with regard to the stated position should be reconsidered and all used in the modern world international standards should be re-standardized. Perhaps against the background of the statistical standards flaws revealed by a crisis the international organizations should initiate and perform this very work. And data mining can be the main tool for this work. The big picture given above shows the need of clean, comparable and standardized definitions instead of directed ones for acceptable estimations and reliable conclusions. Clean, comparable data and standardized definitions lead us the datawarehouse logic or data mining infrastructure or basis.

Indicators, proportions, ratios, rates and the other kind of statistics can be the first signals in case of evaluating them in a proper way. We should note that all the raw data, processed data must be clear, transparent and has equal definition for reliable comparison. Therefore, existing data stock can be collect with the same definition and standarts. Actually, UN has standard definitions for indicators, methodologies and data preparation. Eurostat (European Union Statistical Office) has standards as well for European Union member and candidate countries. Furthermore, Eurostat statistical standards are mostly a subset of UN standards and widely there are no contradiction between UN and Eurostat standarts. Therefore, it is easy to merge UN and Eurostat data with some little justifications. UN country data infrastructure can become the base for unified statistical indicators datawarehouse. Coordinator can be the ISI as mentioned above for much more updated scientifically standards. Furthermore, practice of counteraction against legalization of statistical divergence can be use for occupational objectivity. Therefore, practice of disclosure, critical assessment and correction of statistical divergence being revealed. The effective tools of counteraction are law on legal responsibility and legal protection for statisticians (currently not in use).

REFERENCES

Bank of Russia. (1999). *Russia bulletin on banking statistics, 11*, 19.

Booth, P., Chadburn, R., Haberman, S., James, D., Khorasanee, Z., Plumb, R. H., & Rickayzen, B. (1999). *Modern actuarial theory and practice*. Boca Raton, FL: Chapman and Hall/CRC.

Cabena, P., Hadjinian, P., Stadler, R., Verhees, J., & Zanasi, A. (1997). *Discovering Data Mining: From Concept To Implementation*. Upper Saddle River, NJ: Prentice Hall PTR.

Hastie, T., Tibshirani, R., & Friedman, J. H. (2001). *The elements of statistical learning*. Berlin: Springer.

Keen, M., & Smith, S. (2007). VAT fraud and evasion: What do we know, and what can be done? IMF Working Paper, WP/07/31.

Kovalerchuk, B., & Vityaev, E. (2002). *Data mining in finance*. Hingham, MA: Kluwer Academic Publiher.

Koyuncugil, A. S. (2006). *Fuzzy data mining and its application to capital markets*. Unpublished doctoral dissertation, University of Ankara, Turkey.

Koyuncugil, A, S., & Ozgulbas, N. (2006a). Is there a specific measure for financial performance of SMEs. *The Business Review, Cambridge, 5*(2), 314–319.

Koyuncugil, A, S., & Ozgulbas, N. (2006b). Financial profiling of SMEs: An application by data mining. *European Applied Business Research (EABR) Conference*.

Koyuncugil, A. S., & Ozgulbas, N. (2006c). Determination of factors affected financial distress of SMEs listed in ISE by data mining. In *3rd Congress of SMEs and Productivity*, KOSGEB and Istanbul Kultur University (pp.159-170).

Mauro, P. (2002). *The persistence of corruption and slow economic growth*, IMF Working Paper, WP/02/213.

Meredith, G. (2007). *Debt dynamics and global imbalances: some conventional views reconsidered*, IMF Working Paper, WP/07/4.

Moss, L. T., & Atre, S. (2003). *Business intelligence roadmap: the complete project lifecycle for decision-support applications* (p. 576). Reading, MA: Addison-Wesley Publishing.

National Credit Union Administration. (2007). *National Credit Union Administration Year-end Statistics, 2007; Statistics on Banking, 2007*. Retrieved from http://www.census.gov/compendia/statab/tables/09s1136.xls

OECD. (2003). The measure of non-observed economic activity. In *The Guide*. Paris: OECD.

OECD. (2008). The measure of non-observed economic activity. In *The Guide*. Paris: OECD.

Ozgulbas., et al. (2006).Identifying the effect of firm size on financial performance of SMEs. *Economics & International Business Research Conference*, Miami, FL.

Ozgulbas, N., & Koyuncugil, A. S., (2006). Profiling and determining the strengths and weaknesses of SMEs listed in ISE by the data mining decision trees algorithm CHAID. *10th National Finance Symposium*, Izmir, Turkey.

Rao, C. R. (2001). Statistics: reflections on the past and visions for the future. *Communications in Statistics Theory and Methods, 30*(11), 2235–2257. doi:10.1081/STA-100107683

Ruhashyankiko, J., & Etienne, B. Y. (2006). *Corruption and technology-induced private sector developpment*. IMF Working Paper, WP/06/198.

Sarr., A., & Lybek, T. (2002). *Measuring liquidity in financial markets*. IMF Working Paper, WP/02/232.

Simchera, V. M. (2003a). *Introduction to financial and actuarial calculations*. Moscow: Financy i Statistika Publishing House.

Simchera, V. (2003a). *M* (pp. 91–116). Federalizm Magazine.

U.S. Federal Deposit Insurance Corporation. (2007). *Statistics on Banking*, Tables 696, 1136. U.S. Federal Deposit Insurance Corporation. Retrieved from http://www.fdic.gov/index.html.

U.S.Census Bureau. (2009). Statistical Abstract of the United States: 2008, Table 651, *Statistical abstract of the United States: 2008*. www.census.gov.

Vaitilingam, R. (2007). *Guide to using the financial pages*. London: FT Pitman Publishing.

KEY TERMS AND DEFINITIONS

Estimation: Actuarial estimations defined as estimations on risks and their probable outcomes within uncertainty circumstances; estimations of current (nominal without regard to risk and modern imputed) costs of assets being borrowed with use of stochastic methods with their documentary proved representations in standard forms (usually legislatively approved actuarial reports).

Divergence: In other words, statistical divergence estimations for fraud, evasion, manipulation, phantoms, etc. Estimations of deliberately unobserved and artificially concealed phenomena which register gaps between real and imaginary values. For instance, between purchasing power parity of currencies and their exchange rates and also between real or fictitious capitals (derivatives). Normally they are set with use of two or more alternative statistical methods numbers of their calculations.

Statistical Learning: Data mining mainly has two differet point of views as Statistical and Information Technologies. Data mining from statistical point of view calls Statistical Learning. Statistical Learning let users know what data tells instead of subjective sayings.

Data Mining: Collection of evolved statistical analysis, machine learning and pattern recognition methods via intelligent algorithms which are using for automated uncovering and extraction process of hidden predictional information, patterns, relations, similarities or dissimilarities in (huge) data.

Datawarehouse: Special structured database which provides fast access to clean (ready to analyze) data in all types such as numeric, image, voice etc. together in unified nature. Mainly, knows as data provider for data mining and the other business intelligence applications.

Chapter 4
Black–Necked Swans and Active Risk Management

Tze Leung Lai
Stanford University, USA

Bo Shen
Stanford University, USA

ABSTRACT

This chapter gives a review of recent developments in sequential surveillance and modeling of default probabilities of corporate and retail loans, and relates them to the development of early warning or quick detection systems for managing the risk associated with the so-called "black swans" or their close relatives, the black-necked swans.

INTRODUCTION

Taleb (2007) proposed the Black Swan Theory to explain high-impact, hard-to-predict and rare events, which are far beyond the realm of normal expectations, i.e., black swans. He did not consider, however, what to do with the black swan's cousin, the black-necked swan. The black-necked swan, unlike the Australia-bound black swan, is born covered in white, but its neck gradually darkens from 3 months onward. Hence there is the "black-necked swan problem" concerning whether a given swan born white will stay white. And yet, an even harder problem is when and where it might possibly turn black (See Figure 1).

DOI: 10.4018/978-1-61692-865-0.ch004

Risk management should take into consideration the possible appearances of these "black swans" and "black-necked swans". Once in a while a driver gets a traffic ticket; he/she starts to watch out for a few weeks and then forgets about everything until another traffic violation. Good risk management practice entails active vigilance and continuous monitoring of the financial situation and relevant macroeconomic variables. Early warning systems, surveillance technologies, and accurate, up-to-date and easily accessible databases are important tools to support this kind of active risk management.

This chapter describes statistical models and methods for on-line surveillance and early warning/quick detection of risk associated with "black-necked swans" and even "black-swans".

Figure 1. Black-necked swan

Traditional risk management considers risks associated with adverse events that occur with substantially higher, albeit small, probability. We first give a brief review of a number of important ideas in traditional risk management that is mostly passive and precautionary in nature. We then refine some of these ideas for active risk management, which also involves sequential detection of structural changes and surveillance of financial risks. In this connection, recent advances in on-line surveillance and sequential detection are also reviewed. We conclude with some remarks and further discussion of the advantages of active over passive risk management in today's complex financial markets.

MEASURES OF FINANCIAL RISKS AND THE BASEL ACCORD

In this section, we first summarize different categories of financial risks and commonly used risk measures; a classic reference on these topics is Jorion (2004). Then we review the regulatory background underlying statistical methods for risk management, focusing primarily on the Basel Accord. The Basel Accord was developed in 1988 by the Basel Committee on Banking and Supervision (2005, 2006) and was later widely endorsed by banks in G10 countries. It provides a unified statistical approach to measuring the risks in banks and specifying the amount of capital needed to hedge against these risks. The first Basel Accord introduced 8% as the minimum solvency ratio,

defined to be the ratio of capital to risk-weighted assets. We focus primarily on the internal ratings models, introduced by the second Basel Accord (Basel II), which use rigorous statistical models to calibrate the solvency ratio for each bank.

Categories of Financial Risks

The main types of financial risks are: market risk, credit risk, liquidity risk, operational risk, and legal risk. Market risk is the risk that the value of an investment, largely equity, interest rate, currency or commodity, will decrease due to changes in prices and the market. Credit risk is the risk due to uncertainty in a counter party's (also called an obligor's) ability to meet its obligations. Liquidity risk is the risk that an asset cannot be sold due to lack of liquidity in the market, usually associated with widening bid-ask spread. Operational risk is the risk of loss arising from execution of a company's business functions caused by people, procedures or systems. This includes human error and fraud. Legal risk is the risk of potential loss arising from the uncertainty of legal proceedings, such as bankruptcy laws.

Commonly Used Risk Measures

There is no single risk measure that is appropriate for every risk management application. We review several measures and briefly summarize their pros and cons.

Value at Risk. Value at risk (VaR) is a downside risk measure that focuses on losses. It measures the maximum loss of a financial institution's position due to market movements over a given holding period with a prescribed confidence level. Specifically, $VaR_\alpha = \inf\{y: P(L > y) \le 1 - \alpha\}$, where L denotes the loss. Although it is widely used in risk management, VaR is not a coherent measure in that it does not satisfy subadditivity, e.g., diversification may not reduce VaR.

Expected Shortfall. A coherent measure is a function ρ that satisfies the following conditions for any two loss variables Z_1 and Z_2, it satisfies:

- Monotonicity: If $Z_1 \geq Z_2$, then $\rho(Z_2) \geq \rho(Z_1)$.
- Sub-additivity: $\rho(Z_1 + Z_2) \leq \rho(Z_1) + \rho(Z_2)$.
- Positive Homogeneity: $\rho(\alpha Z) = \alpha\rho(Z)$ for $\alpha \geq 0$.
- Translation Invariance: $\rho(Z + a) = \rho(Z) + a$ for any real number a.

The expected shortfall is a coherent risk measure that was introduced to address the lack of subadditivity of VaR. When the distribution function of L is continuous, the expected shortfall is defined as the conditional expectation of L given that it exceeds the $100(1 - \alpha)\%$ VaR.

CrashMetrics. This is a stress-testing tool introduced by Wilmott (2006) for evaluating the performance of a portfolio of N risk assets over a range of large price movements, and is motivated by the pattern of high correlations between the asset returns in extreme markets. Letting x denote the return on a standard index, e.g., S&P 500, covering the stock during a crash, the *crash coefficient* κ_i of the ith stock is defined by $\Delta S_i / S_i$, i.e., the coefficient relating the return $\Delta S_i / S_i$ on the ith asset to x. Suppose there are M contracts available with which to hedge a portfolio. Let Δ_i^k denote the delta of the kth hedging contract, which is the derivative of the value of the contract with respect to the price of the ith asset, $k=1, \ldots, M$, $i=1,\ldots, N$. Let Γ_{ij}^k denote the gamma, which is the second partial derivative of the value of the kth hedging contract with respect to the prices of the ith and jth assets. Denote the bid-offer spread by $C_k > 0$, meaning that if one buys (sells) the contract and immediately sells (buys) it back, one loses the amount C_k. Suppose we add a number λ_k of each of the available hedging contracts to our original position. Our portfolio then has a first-order exposure of

$$x(D + \sum_{k=1}^{M} \lambda_k \sum_{i=1}^{N} \Delta_i^k \kappa_i S_i),$$

where D is the delta of the original portfolio, and a second-order exposure of

$$\frac{1}{2} x^2 (G + \sum_{k=1}^{M} \lambda_k \sum_{i=1}^{N} \sum_{j=1}^{N} \Gamma_{ij}^k \kappa_i S_i \kappa_j S_j),$$

where G is the gamma of the original portfolio (see Wilmott (2006, 722)).

Not only does the portfolio change by these amounts for a crash of size x but it also loses a guaranteed amount

$$\sum_{k=1}^{M} | \lambda_k | C_k$$

since we cannot close out new positions without losing out on the bid-offer spread. The total change in the portfolio with the static hedge in place is

$$x(D + \sum_{k=1}^{M} \lambda_k \sum_{i=1}^{N} \Delta_i^k \kappa_i S_i) + \frac{1}{2} x^2 (G + \sum_{k=1}^{M} \lambda_k \sum_{i=1}^{N} \sum_{j=1}^{N} \Gamma_{ij}^k \kappa_i S_i \kappa_j S_j) - \sum_{k=1}^{M} | \lambda_k | C_k$$

which represents the exposure to the crash and is called the Crash Metric(see Wilmott (2006, 723)).

Basel Accord and Internal Ratings Model

Unlike Basel I, which sets the capital requirement of a debt to be 8% of the total exposure, Basel II decomposes the expected credit loss $E(L_c)$ for a loan to be $E(L_c) = EAD \times LGD \times PD$, where PD is the probability of default, LGD is the expected loss given default as a fraction between 0 and 1, and EAD is the exposure at default. Basel II allows each bank to use either a standard model or its own internal ratings model. The standard model is based on Schonbucher's model that assumes the ith obligor to have standardized asset level

$$V_i = \sqrt{\rho}Z + \sqrt{1-\rho}\varepsilon_i,$$

where Z is a common hidden factor shared by all obligors. Default for the ith obligor occurs if $V_i < k$ and therefore the default probability is the same for all obligors in the same risk class. Letting I_i denote the indicator variable of the event $\{V_i < k\}$, Schonbucher (2000) has shown that for a large number M of obligors in the same risk class,

$$\lim_{M \to \infty} P\{\frac{\sum_{i=1}^{M} I_i}{M} \le x\} = \Phi[-\frac{1}{\sqrt{\rho}}\Phi^{-1}(PD) + \sqrt{\frac{1-\rho}{\rho}}\Phi^{-1}(x)]$$

where Φ denotes the standard normal distribution function. This formula is used to set the capital requirements for retail loans if the bank adopts Basel II's standard model.

SEQUENTIAL DETECTION AND SURVEILLANCE

The risk measures in the previous section are used to quantify the risks in a financial system at a prescribed time, e.g. one week later in a 1-week VaR. Active risk management uses sequential surveillance to continuously monitor certain risk measures and related market variables so that there is minimal delay in detecting abrupt changes in the financial system. There is an extensive literature in statistics and engineering on the subject of quick detection, with low false alarm rates, of an abrupt change in the underlying stochastic system that generates the observed data.

Beginning with Shewhart's (1925,1931) seminal work on quality control charts, sequential change-point detection has evolved from industrial quality control to automated fault detection. In recent years, the theory has been further extended from single to multiple change-points, as in the case of surveillance applications. In this section, we will review recent developments in three major directions of the field, namely, detection of a single change-point with known baseline, or with unknown baseline, and detection of multiple change-points. For active risk management, the third direction is most relevant although it is the least developed.

Sequential Detection with Known Baseline

We first define the sequential change-point detection problem within a statistical framework. Observing a stochastic sequence X_1 , X_2,... and denoting a change-point by v, we want to test the null hypothesis that under P_0, the conditional density function of X_n given $X_1,..., X_{n-1}$ is $f0(\cdot|X_1, \cdots, X_{n-1})$ for every $n \ge 1$ against the alternative hypothesis that under $P(v)$, the conditional density function is $f_0(\cdot | X_1, \cdots, X_{n-1})$ for $n < v$ and $f_1(\cdot| X_1, \cdots, X_{n-1})$ for $n \ge v$. When f_0 is known, we call it known baseline and otherwise unknown baseline. Lai (1995,1998) has given a comprehensive review of the case where X_1, X_2... are independent. Bansal & Papantoni-Kazakos (1986) specialized in the case where X_t $t < v$ and X_t $t \ge v$ are independent of each other but are stationary ergodic. The stopping rule is said to be minimax if among all rules T with a lower bound on the Average Run Length (ARL), $E_0 T \ge \gamma$, it asymptotically minimizes the maximum expected time delay (see Lorden (1971)).

$$\bar{E}_1 T = \text{ess sup}v \ge 1 E \left[(T - v + 1)^+ | X_1,..., X_{v-1}\right];$$

The CUSUM scheme introduced by Page (1954) can be generalized to

$$N = \inf\{n : \max_{n-m_a \le k \le n} \sum_{t=k}^{n} \log \frac{f_1(X_i | X_1,..., X_{i-1})}{f_0(X_i | X_1,..., X_{i-1})} \ge c\}$$

which is a special case of the more general "window-limit GLR scheme" introduced by Lai (1995), that assumes the f_1 to be indexed by an unknown parameter θ:

$$N = \inf\{n > \tilde{M} : \max_{n-M \le k \le n-\tilde{M}} \sup_{\theta \in \Theta} \sum_{t=k}^{n} \log \frac{f_\theta(X_t \mid X_1,\ldots,X_{t-1})}{f_{\theta_0}(X_t \mid X_1,\ldots,X_{t-1})} \ge c\}$$

This rule has attractive statistical and computational properties; see Lai (1995) and Lai & Shan (1999) for discussion.

Sequential Detection when Pre- and Post- Change Parameters are Unknown

In recent years, there has been much interest in applying Bayesian models to change-point detection when the baselines are not completely defined. Bayesian detection of change-points was started by Shiryaev (1963, 1978) who introduced a geometric prior distribution on the unknown change point v, assuming the observations X_t to be independent with known density function f_0 for $t < v$, and f_1 for $t \ge v$, a loss of c for each observation taken at or after v and a loss of 1 for a false alarm before v. He used optimal stopping theory to show that the Bayes rule triggers an alarm as soon as the posterior probability that a change has occurred exceeds some fixed level. Since

$$P\{v \le n \mid X_1,\ldots,X_n\} = R_{p,n} / (R_{p,n} + p^{-1}),$$

where p is the parameter of the geometric distribution $P\{v = n\} = p(1 - p)^{n-1}$ and

$$R_{p,n} = \sum_{k=1}^{n} \prod_{i=k}^{n} \{f_1(X_i) / (1 - p)f_0(X_i)\},$$

the Bayes rule declares at time

$$N(\gamma) = \inf\{n \ge 1 : R_{p,n} \ge \gamma\}$$

that a change has occurred. Pollak (1987) has extended Shiryaev's approach to the case where f_1 is indexed by an unknown parameter θ, putting a prior distribution on this unknown parameter and assuming that f_θ belongs to an exponential

family. Lai & Xing (2009b) have recently shown how the Bayesian detection rule can be further extended to the case where the baseline parameters are unknown again assuming the observations are independent with density function from an exponential family indexed by θ.

Multiple Change-Points and Sequential Surveillance

The extension from single to multiple change-point detection schemes has made the framework more suited to applications in engineering and finance, as most of the underlying stochastic processes where data are generated in these two fields undergo more than one change throughout their lifetime. Assume an m-dependent exponential family

$$f_\theta(y_t \mid y_{t-1},\ldots,y_{t-m}) \propto \exp\{\theta^T(y_t,\ldots,y_{t-m}) + A(\theta)\}$$

Suppose that the parameter vector θ may undergo occasional changes such that for $t > 1$, the indicator variables

$$I_t := I_{\{\theta_t = \theta_{t-1}\}}$$

are independent Bernoulli random variables with $P(I_t = 1) = p$, as in Chernoff & Zacks (1964) and Yao (1984). When there is a parameter change at time t (i.e., $I_t = 1$), the changed parameter θ_t is assumed to be sampled from the prior density function

$$\pi(\theta; a_0, \mu_0) = c(a_0, \mu_0) \exp\{a_0 \mu_0^T \theta - a_0 \psi(\theta)\}$$

where $c(a_0, \mu_0)$ is the normalizing constant. The simplicity of this conjugate family plays an important role in the recursive formulas for the filters $\theta_t \mid Y_t$, letting Y_t denote $(y_1,\ldots,y_t)$ and $Y_{i,j}$ denotes $(y_i,\ldots,y_j)$ for $i \le j$.

As shown by Lai & Xing (2009a) in the case when the y_i are independent, or earlier by Lai, et al. (2005) in autoregressive models, an important variable is the most recent change time K_t up to t, i.e., $K_t = \max\{s \le t: I_s = 1\}$. Denoting conditional densities by $f(|)$, note that

$$f(\theta_t \mid Y_t) = \sum_{i=1}^{t} p_{it} f(\theta_t \mid Y_{i,t}, K_t = i),$$

where $p_{it} = P(K_t = i | Y_t)$. It follows that

$$f(\theta_t \mid Y_{i,t}, K_t = i) = \pi(\theta_t; a_0 + t - i + 1, \overline{Y}_{i,t}),$$

where $\overline{Y}_{i,j} = \left(a_0\mu_0 + \sum_{k=i}^{j} y_k\right) / (a_0 + j - i + 1)$

for $j \ge i$. Combining these two equations yields

$$f(\theta_t \mid Y_t) = \sum_{i=1}^{t} p_{it} \pi(\theta_t; a_0 + t - i + 1, \overline{Y}_{i,t}).$$

We next provide a recursive formula for p_{it} by noting that $\sum_{i=1}^{t} p_{it} = 1$ and

$$p_{i,t} \propto p_{it}^* := \begin{cases} p(y_t \mid I_t = 1) & \text{if} \quad i = t \\ (1-p)p_{i,t-1}f(y_t \mid Y_{i,t}, K_t = i) & \text{if} \quad i \le t - 1 \end{cases}$$

Combining $f(y_t \mid Y_{i,t-1}, K_t = i)$ with the above yields

$$p_{it}^* := \begin{cases} p\pi_{0,0} / \pi_{t,t} & \text{if} \quad i = t \\ (1-p)p_{i,t-1}\pi_{i,t-1} / \pi_{i,t} & \text{if} \quad i \le t - 1 \end{cases}$$

where $\pi_{0,0} = c(a_0, \mu_0)$ and $\pi_{i,j} = c(a_0 + j - i + 1, \overline{Y}_{i,j})$. As a modification of Shiryaev's rule that stops at the smallest n for which

$$P(v \le n | Y_n) \ge \delta_{p,c},$$

Lai & Xing (2009c) proposed a stopping rule which declares at time n that a change-point has occurred in the time interval between $n - k(p)$ and n if

$$\sum_{i=n-k(p)}^{n} p_{in} \ge \eta_p,$$

and described how the threshold should be chosen. For small p, the BCMIX (bounded complexity mixture) approximation introduced by Lai & Xing (2009a) can be applied to the recursive formulas for $\theta t | Yt$. The subject of sequential surveillance, although still in its infancy, has been recognized as a potentially fundamental tool for financial risk management (see Frisen (2008)).

PROBABILITY ESTIMATES FOR EARLY WARNING OF IMPENDING ADVERSITY

The preceding sequential detection and surveillance schemes, presented in the simplified model of a multi-parameter exponential family, can be extended to more complex stochastic models and then applied to detect which components of a financial system and which factors in the external market have undergone adverse structural changes. This is an important ingredient of active risk management proposed by Lai & Xing (2010). Another important ingredient of active risk management is early warning of impending financial distress or crisis so that the financial institution can avert severe damage or disaster. The importance of these early warning systems (EWS) is widely recognized after the recent financial crisis. We first give a brief review of the literature on EWS and then describe a new statistical approach to this problem.

An Overview of Early Warning Systems

Whereas quick detection and sequential surveillance are related to detecting change- points after their occurrence, the problem of early warning is to use relevant data and Bayesian modeling to evaluate the probability of adverse events, issuing early warnings when the probability exceeds some threshold. In the field of industrial quality control that motivated much of the work of sequential change-point detection, *control charts with warning lines* were introduced by Dudding & Jennett (1942), who proposed to draw warning lines within the control limits of the Shewhart control chart, declaring the occurrence of a change-point if k out of a sequence of n consecutive points fall outside the warning lines; see also Weiler (1954) and Ishikawa (1982). Although financial EWS are much more complex than these control charts with warning lines, the underlying principles are similar. Whereas the objective of Shewhart's (1925,1931) control chart is to signal that the system is no longer in a state of statistical control, the warning lines within the control limits serve to give warning that the system appears to be progressing towards the out-of-control state. The warning suggests that corrective action should be taken to reverse such progression.

The currency crises in the 1990s, starting with the European currency crises in 1992, followed by the Mexican peso crisis in 1994, and culminating with the Asian currency crises in 1997-98 and the Russian currency crisis in 1998, led to various attempts to construct EWS for predicting the probability of the next crisis. Economic theories providing explanations for such crises had been proposed by Krugman (1979), Flood & Garber (1984), Velasco (1987), Blackburn & Sola (1993), Gerlach & Smets (1995), Ozkan & Sutherland (1995), and Eichengreen et al. (1995). Based on these theories, EWS for financial crises were initially designed to monitor macroeconomic fundamental variables and to predict a potential financial crisis within a relatively long time horizon (e.g., a year), and subsequently to address fast deterioration in economic conditions. Examples of the former are Eichengreen et al. (1996) using probit models, and Edwards (1998) using GARCH models of volatility. Examples of the latter include Oh et al. (2006), Lin et al. (2008), and Koyuncugil & Ozgulbas (2008,2009). These papers use data

mining and machine learning algorithms such as neural networks, genetic algorithms, fuzzy logic, classification and regression trees, hierarchical cluster analysis, and segmentation algorithms. Recent advances in statistical learning algorithms such as Friedman's (2001) gradient boosting, Tibshirani's (1997) Lasso and its enhancements provide powerful tools to develop the next generation of EWS, as described by Lai & Xing (2010). Here we briefly introduce an empirical Bayes methodology introduced in the last decade which offers a new approach to constructing EWS, details of which are given in Lai & Xing (2010).

Modeling Default Probabilities for Retail and Corporate Loans

An example of empirical Bayes models for early warning of adverse events in financial risk management is PD (probability of default) modeling required by Basel II for a bank's internal models for measuring its credit risk. Lai & Wong (2009) have recently proposed a Markovian time series model that incorporates covariates intrinsic to the phenomenon of payment delinquency for retail loans. For retail loans, default means delinquency, i.e., overdue payment for longer than 90 days. For corporate loans, default means bankruptcy of the obligor. The default probabilities of corporate bonds, which are liquid instruments traded at a large daily volume, are estimated by three credit rating agencies, namely, Moody, Standard & Poor, and Fitch, and are used to produce assessments of the financial health of a company. A class of default probability models called *reduced-form* models relies heavily on the covariates of a firm to model the default intensity function. A powerful approach to this modeling problem is empirical Bayes via generalized linear mixed models, extending the work of Lai & Wong (2009); details can be found in Lai & Xing (2010). An important set of covariates, introduced by Altman (1968) and Altman & Hotchkiss (2006), includes the following accounting ratios that are often called *Altman's Z scores*:

- $X1$ = Working capital/Total assets

Total assets is the sum of all tangible assets of the firm while the working capital is the difference between current assets and current liabilities; hence $X1$ measures the net liquid assets of the firm relative to the total capitalization.

- $X2$ = Retained earnings/Total assets

Retained earnings refer to the gross balance of the firm throughout its life; firms with high $X2$ levels finance their assets mostly with plowed-back profits without issuing too many debts.

- $X3$ = Earnings before interest and taxes/Total assets

This is a measure of the net productivity of the firm's assets before taxes.

- $X4$ = Market value of equity/Book value of total liabilities

This measure tells the relative health of a firm, noting that $X4 < 1$ means default.

- $X5$ = Sales/Total assets

This is the capital turnover ratio and quantifies the sales generating ability of the firm's assets.

CONCLUSION

The modeling and operational issues of risk management have attracted widespread attention and discussion after the recent financial turmoil, but for how long would this public awareness last? Supposedly, black-necked swans may be born at any time, and the practice of active risk management

should adapt accordingly. Disaster has manifested itself in different forms in the past, and provided valuable lessons and insights to avert, or at least adequately respond to them in the future. This is the objective of active risk management, which needs the support of surveillance technologies and early warning systems and which is the theme of Lai & Xing's (2010) forthcoming book.

REFERENCES

Altman, E. (1968). Financial ratios, discriminant analysis and the prediction of corporate bankruptcy. *The Journal of Finance, 23*, 189–209.

Altman, E., & Hotchkiss, E. (2006). *Corporate financial distress and bankruptcy* (3rd ed.). New York: John Wiley & Sons.

Bansal, R., & Papantoni-Kazakos, P. (1986). An algorithm for detecting a change in a stochastic process. *IEEE Transactions on Information Theory, 32*(2), 227–235. doi:10.1109/TIT.1986.1057160

Basel Committee on Banking Supervision. (2005). *An explanatory note on the Basel II IRB risk weight functions*. Retrieved from http://www.bis.org/bcbs/irbriskweight.pdf.

Basel Committee on Banking Supervision. (2006). *Basel II: International convergence of capital measurement and capital standards: A revised framework*. Retrieved from http://www.bis.org/publ/bcbs128.htm.

Blackburn, K., & Sola, M. (1993). Speculative currency attacks and the balance of payments crises. *Journal of Economic Surveys, 7*, 119–144. doi:10.1111/j.1467-6419.1993.tb00162.x

Chernoff, H., & Zacks, S. (1964). Estimating the current mean of a normal distribution which is subject to changes in time. *Annals of Mathematical Statistics, 35*, 999–1018. doi:10.1214/aoms/1177700517

Dudding, B. P., & Jennett, W. J. (1942). *Quality control charts, British Standard 600R*. London: British Standards Institution.

Edwards, S. (1998). Interest rate volatility, contagion and convergence: An empirical investigation of the cases of Argentina, Chile and Mexico. *Journal of Applied Econometrics, 1*, 55–86.

Eichengreen, B., Rose, A., & Wyplosz, C. (1995). Exchange market mayhem: The antecedents and aftermath of speculative attacks. *Economic Policy, 21*, 249–312. doi:10.2307/1344591

Eichengreen, B., Rose, A., & Wyplosz, C. (1996). Contagious currency crisis. *Scandinavian Economic Review, 98*, 463–484. doi:10.2307/3440879

Flood, R., & Garber, P. (1984). Collapsing exchange rate regimes: Some linear examples. *Journal of International Economics, 17*, 1–13. doi:10.1016/0022-1996(84)90002-3

Friedman, J. (2001). Greedy function approximation: The gradient boosting machine. *Annals of Statistics, 29*, 1189–1232. doi:10.1214/aos/1013203451

Frisen, M. (2008). *Financial surveillance*. New York: Wiley.

Gerlach, S., & Smets, F. (1995). Contagious speculative attacks. *European Journal of Political Economy, 11*, 5–63. doi:10.1016/0176-2680(94)00055-O

Ishikawa, K. (1982). *Guide to quality control*. Tokyo: Asian Productivity Organization.

Jorion, P. (2004). *Value at risk* (3rd ed.). New York: McGraw-Hill.

Koyuncugil, A. S., & Ozgulbas, N. (2008). A data mining model for detecting financial and operational risk indicators of SMEs. *World Academy of Science. Engineering and Technology, 46*, 88–91.

Koyuncugil, A. S., & Ozgulbas, N. (2009). An intelligent financial early warning system model based on data mining for SMEs. In *IEEE Proceedings of the 2009 International Conference on Future Computer and Computation,* (pp. 662-666.)

Krugman, P. (1979). A model of balance-of-payments crises. *Journal of Money, Credit and Banking, 11*, 311–325. doi:10.2307/1991793

Lai, T. L. (1995). Sequential change point detection in quality control and dynamical systems. *Journal of the Royal Statistical Society. Series B. Methodological, 57*, 613–658.

Lai, T. L. (1998). Information bounds and quick detection of parameter changes in stochastic systems. *IEEE Transactions on Information Theory, 44*, 2917–2929. doi:10.1109/18.737522

Lai, T. L., Liu, H., & Xing, H. (2005). Autoregressive models with piecewise constant volatility and regression parameters. *Statistica Sinica, 15*, 279–301.

Lai, T. L., & Shan, J. Z. (1999). Efficient recursive algorithms for detection of abrupt changes in signals and systems. *IEEE Transactions on Automatic Control, 44*, 952–966. doi:10.1109/9.763211

Lai, T. L., & Wong, S. P. (2009). Statistical models for the Basel II internal ratings-based approach to measuring credit risk of retail products. *Statistics and Its Interface, 1*, 229–241.

Lai, T. L., & Xing, H. (2009a). *A simple Bayesian approach to multiple change-points. To appear in*. Statistica Sinica.

Lai, T. L., & Xing, H. (2009b). *Sequential change-point detection when the pre- and post-change parameters are unknown. To appear in*. Sequential Analysis.

Lai, T. L. & Xing, H. (2009c). A Bayesian approach to sequential surveillance in exponential families. To appear in *Communications in Statistics, Theory and Methods* (Special issue in honor of S. Zacks).

Lai, T. L., & Xing, H. (2010). *Risk management and surveillance: Financial models and statistical methods.* Boca Raton, FL: Chapman & Hall/CRC.

Lin, C. S., Khan, H. A., Chang, R. Y., & Wang, Y. C. (2008). A new approach to modeling early warning systems for currency crises: Can a machine-learning fuzzy expert system predict the currency crises effectively? *Journal of International Money and Finance, 27,* 1098–1121. doi:10.1016/j.jimonfin.2008.05.006

Lorden, G. (1971). Procedures for reacting to a change in distribution. *Annals of Mathematical Statistics, 42,* 1897–1908. doi:10.1214/aoms/1177693055

Oh, K. J., Kim, T. Y., & Kim, C. (2006). An early warning system for detection of financial crisis using financial market volatility. *Expert Systems: International Journal of Knowledge Engineering and Neural Networks, 23,* 83–98. doi:10.1111/j.1468-0394.2006.00326.x

Ozkan, F. G., & Sutherland, A. (1995). Policy measures to avoid a currency crisis. *The Economic Journal, 105,* 510–519. doi:10.2307/2235508

Page, E. S. (1954). Continuous inspection schemes. *Biometrika, 41,* 100–114.

Pollak, M. (1985). Optimal detection of a change in distribution. *Annals of Statistics, 18,* 1464–1469.

Schonbucher, P. J. (2000). *Factor models for portfolio credit risk.* Manuscript, Department of Statistics, Bonn University.

Shewhart, W. A. (1925). The application of statistics as an aid in maintaining quality of manufactured product. *Journal of the American Statistical Association, 20,* 546–548. doi:10.2307/2277170

Shewhart, W. A. (1931). *Economic control of quality of manufactured product.* New York: D. Van Nostrand Company.

Shiryaev, A. N. (1963). On optimum methods in quickest detection problems. *Theory of Probability and Its Applications, 8,* 22–46. doi:10.1137/1108002

Shiryaev, A. N. (1978). *Optimal stopping rules.* Berlin: Springer.

Taleb, N. N. (2007). *The black swan: The impact of the highly improbable.* New York: Random House.

Tibshirani, R. (1997). The Lasso method for variable selection in the Cox model. *Statistics in Medicine, 16,* 385–395. doi:10.1002/(SICI)1097-0258(19970228)16:4<385::AID-SIM380>3.0.CO;2-3

Velasco, A. (1987). Financial crises and balance of payments crises: A simple model of the southern cone experience. *Journal of Development Economics, 27,* 263–283. doi:10.1016/0304-3878(87)90018-6

Weiler, K. (1954). A new type of control chart, limits for means, ranges and sequential runs. *Journal of the American Statistical Association, 40,* 298–514. doi:10.2307/2280936

Wilmott, P. (2006). *Paul Wilmott on quantitative finance.* London: John Wiley & Sons.

Yao, Y. (1984). Estimation of a noisy discrete-time step functions: Bayes and empirical Bayes approach. *Annals of Statistics, 12,* 1434–1447. doi:10.1214/aos/1176346802

KEY TERMS AND DEFINITIONS

Black-Necked Swan: Impending rare events

Change Point: A deviation in stochastic process

Multiple Change-Point: possibly more than one change-point.

Altman Z-scores: Selected accounting ratios reflecting corporate health

Default: Corporate debt exceeding capital

Basel Accord: International banking agreement on capital reserve for loan underwriting

Sequential Detection: Detection of faults or other change-points on-line, i.e., during the system's operation

Section 2
Early Warning Systems
for Finance

Chapter 5
Financial Early Warning System for Risk Detection and Prevention from Financial Crisis

Nermin Ozgulbas
Baskent University, Turkey

Ali Serhan Koyuncugil
Capital Markets Board of Turkey, Turkey

ABSTRACT

Risk management has become a vital topic for all enterprises especially in financial crisis periods. All enterprises need systems to warn against risks, detect signs and prevent from financial distress. Before the global financial crisis that began 2008, small and medium-sized enterprises (SMEs) have already fought with important financial issues. The global financial crisis and the ensuring flight away from risk have affected SMEs more than larger enterprises When we consider these effects, besides the issues of poor business performance, insufficient information and insufficiencies of managers in finance education, it is clear that early warning systems (EWS) are vital for SMEs for detection risk and prevention from financial crisis. The aim of this study is to develop and present a financial EWS for risk detection via data mining. For this purpose, data of SMEs listed in Istanbul Stock Exchange (ISE) and Chi-Square Automatic Interaction Detector (CHAID) Decision Tree Algorithm were used. By using EWS, we determined the risk profiles and risk signals for risk detection and road maps for risk prevention from financial crisis.

INTRODUCTION

The financial crisis and keep away from risk have affected nearly all countries and firms. The last financial crisis that began in the latter half of 2008 has been called by leading economists the worst financial crisis since the Great Depression of the 1930s. This global financial crisis caused to the

failure of key businesses, declines in consumer wealth estimated in the trillions of U.S. dollars, a significant decline in economic activity, decrease liquidity, and increase risk. World Bank reported that rates of average economic growth in the developing world declined from 6.4 to 4.5 percent in 2009, according as global financial crises (WB, 2009a). Also, firms have affected in different degrees, depending on their size, location and risk features. In such a context, small and

DOI: 10.4018/978-1-61692-865-0.ch005

medium-sized enterprises (SMEs) that have heavy dependence on bank credit, and limited recourse to finance affected more then bigger firms.

SMEs are defined as independent firms which employ less than a given number of employees. In general, one of three defining measurements is used for statistical definitions of a SME; number of employees, turnover, and the size of the balance sheet. These measurements vary across national statistical systems. For example, the most frequent upper limit is 250 employees, as in European Union, while the United States considers SMEs to include firms with fewer than 500 employees. Financial assets are also used to define SMEs. In Europe, firms with annual turn-over less than €50 million or with annual balance sheet less than €43 million are defined as SMEs. SMEs play a significant role in all economies and are the key generators of employment and income, and drivers of innovation and growth. Access to financing is the most significant challenges for the creation, survival and growth of SMEs, especially innovative ones. The problem is strongly exacerbated by the financial and economic crisis as SMEs have suffered a double shock: a drastic drop in demand for goods and services and a tightening in credit terms, which are severely affecting their cash flows (OECD, 2009a). As a result, all these factors throw SMEs in financial distress.

Risk management has become a vital topic for all institutions, especially for SMEs, banks, credit rating firms, and insurance companies. The financial crisis has pushed all firms to active risk management and control financial risks. Strategically, asset/liability management systems are important tools for controlling a firm's financial risks. But, it is not enough for to understand and manage the financial risks that can cause insolvency and distress. Managers need also to manage operational risks that can arise from execution of a company's business functions, and strategic risks that can undermine the viability of their business models and strategies or reduce their

growth prospects and damage their market value (Berliet, 2009).

All enterprises need Early Warning System (EWS) to warn against risks and prevent from financial distress. But, when we consider the issues of poor business performance, insufficient information and insufficiencies of managers in finance education, it is clear that EWS is vital for SMEs. Benefits of an EWS can summarize as early warning before financial distress, road maps for good credit rating, better business decision making, and greater likelihood of achieving business plan and objectives.

The aim of this chapter is to present an EWS based on data mining. For this purpose, an EWS model was developed for SMEs for risk detection and an implementation was presented for demonstration of EWS. Data of SMEs listed in Istanbul Stock Exchange (ISE) and Chi-Square Automatic Interaction Detector (CHAID) Decision Tree Algorithm were used for implementation. Remaining of this chapter is organized as follows: Section 2 presents definition and financial issues of SMEs. Section 3 contains impacts of financial crisis on SMEs. In Section 4, EWSs are presented as a solution for SMEs. Implementation of data mining for early warning system and methodology is presented in Section 5. Section 6 provides the results of the study. Concluding remarks, future implementations based on EWS and strategies were suggested in the Conclusion Section.

SMES AND FINANCIAL ISSUES

SMEs are defined as enterprises in the non-financial business economy (NACE, Nomenclature statistique des activités économiques dans la Communauté européenne (Statistical classification of economic activities in the European Community)) that employ less than 250 persons. The complements of SMEs - enterprises that employ 250 or more persons -are large scale enterprises (LSEs).

Within the SME sector, the following size-classes are distinguished:

- Micro enterprises, employing less than 10 persons
- Small enterprises, employing at least 10 but less than 50 persons
- Medium-sized enterprises that employ between 50 and 250 persons.

This definition is used for statistical reasons. In the European definition of SMEs two additional criteria are added: annual turnover should be less than 50 million €, and balance sheet total should be less than 43 million € (Commission Recommendation, 2003/361/EC).

When overall world economy is considered, it is noted that SMEs constitute 95% of total enterprises in the world (OECD, 2009b). According to the Annual Report on EU Small and Medium Sized Enterprises, 99.8% of the enterprises are defined as SMEs and employ approximately 88 million people in the European Union (EU-27: Austria, Belgium, Bulgaria, Cyprus, Czech Republic, Denmark, Estonia, Finland, France, Germany, Greece, Hungary, Ireland, Italy, Latvia, Lithuania, Luxemburg, Malta, the Netherlands, Poland, Portugal, Romania, Slovakia, Slovenia, Spain, Sweden and the United Kingdom) in 2007. There were over 20 million enterprises in the European Union in 2007. Only about 43,000 of these were large scale enterprises (LSEs), i.e. 0.2% of all enterprises. Within the SME sector, the vast majority (92%) are micro enterprises, having less than 10 occupied persons. So, the typical European firm is a micro firm. There are about 1.4 million small enterprises, representing 7% of the total stock. About 1% of all enterprises (220,000) are medium-sized enterprises (Audretsch, et al., 2009). The numbers and percentage of SMEs in some countries can be seen in Table 1

Table 1. Numbers of enterprises in some countries

COUNTRIES	YEAR	ENTERPRISES					
		MICRO	SMALL	MEDIUM	SMEs	LSEs	TOTAL
Numbers							
Iceland	2004	21,700	900	100	22,700	100	22,800
Switzerland	2004	260,000	30,000	5,000	294,000	1,000	295,000
Norway	2004	214,000	17,000	2,000	233,000	1,000	234,000
Liechtenstein	2001	5,500	4,500	3,500	13,500	2,500	16,000
USA	2005	14,049,000	468,000	191,000	14,709,000	36,000	14,745,000
Japan	2001	n/a	n/a	n/a	4,690,000	13,000	4,703,000
EU-27	2007	18,788,000	1,402,000	220,000	20,409,000	43,000	20,452,000
Percentage (%)							
Iceland	2004	95	4	0	100	0	100
Switzerland	2004	88	10	2	100	0	100
Norway	2004	92	7	1	100	0	100
Liechtenstein	2001	34	28	22	84	16	100
USA	2005	95	3	1	100	0	100
Japan	2001	n/a	n/a	n/a	100	0	100
EU-27	2007	92	7	1	100	0	100

Source: EIM on the basis of EUROSTAT

Beside the vast majority of enterprises are SMEs, SMEs grow faster then LSEs. As can be seen in Table 2, during the period under consideration (2002-2007), the number of SMEs grew by 11% or over 2 million, and the number of large enterprises by 4%, which is equivalent to 2,000.

SMEs are the backbone of all economies. The direct contribution of SMEs to economic wealth can be measured by their contribution to turnover (or gross premiums written) or to value added. In EU countries turnover is about equal in all SMEs size classes. As Table 3 shows, turnover or gross premiums written is about 4.5 thousand billion Euro, and in percentages roughly 20% in each classes. The distribution of micro, small and medium-sized enterprises to value added is: 21%-19%-18%. The contribution of micro, small and medium-sized enterprises to employment is 30%-21%-17%. These statistics show that total percentage of turnover or gross premiums written is 58%, value added at factor cost is 58%, and number of employees is 67% in SMEs. So, it is clear that the contributions of SMEs to economic wealth are higher than LSEs in Europe. But when we compare the labour productivity, it's seen that SMEs have a lower labour productivity than large enterprises. Thus, SMEs contribute a considerably lower share to value added (58%) than to employment (67%).

In OECD counties, it is accounting that SMEs constitute 97% of total enterprises, between 40 and 60% of GDP, and up to 70% of employment (OECD, 2005). Also, in Turkey, SMEs play a major role in Turkish economy and constitute 99.89% of total enterprises, account for 77% of

total employment, and 38% of total value added (TSI, 2002).

Before the global financial crisis, SMEs have already fought with important issues. Access to financing is the most significant issue of SMEs. When we review the scientific studies and the reports about SMEs, it is seen that the majority of the studies findings match up with these issues. We present some of these studies to underline these issues and emphasize the financial perspective of SMEs.

The study of Beck, et al. (2008) was conducted for characterizing bank financing to SMEs around the world. They used data from a survey of 91 banks in 45 countries. They found that banks perceived the SME segment to be highly profitable, but perceived macroeconomic instability in developing countries and competition in developed countries as the main obstacles. Summary of results and suggestions of the study are:

- To serve SMEs banks have set up dedicated departments and decentralized the sale of products to the branches.
- Loan approval, risk management, and loan recovery functions remain centralized.
- Compared with large firms, banks are less exposed to small enterprises, charge them higher interest rates and fees, and experience more non-performing loans from lending to them.
- There are some differences in SMEs financing across government, private, and foreign-owned banks — with the latter be-

Table 2. Number of enterprises by size, EU-27, 2002-2007

enterprIses	number of enterprIses		change	
	2002	2007	Number	%
SMEs	18,348,000	20,409,000	2,062,000	11
LSEs	41,000	43,000	2,000	4
TOTAL	18,389,000	20,452,000	2,063,000	

Source: EIM on the basis of EUROSTAT

Table 3. Turnover of enterprises, EU-27, 2007

	UNIT	ENTERPRISES					
		MICRO	**SMALL**	**MEDIUM**	**SMEs**	**LSEs**	**TOTAL**
Levels							
Turnover or gross premiums written	mln €	4,402,000	4,504,000	4,564,000	13,471,000	9,917,000	23,388,000
Value added at factor cost	mln €	1,251,000	1,132,000	1,070,000	3,453,000	2,537,000	5,990,000
Number of employees	units	38,890,000	27,062,000	21,957,000	87,909,000	42,895,000	130,805,000
Percentages							
Turnover or gross premiums written	%	19	19	20	58	42	100
Value added at factor cost	%	21	19	18	58	42	100
Number of employees	%	30	21	17	67	33	100

Source: EIM on the basis of EUROSTAT

ing more likely to engage in arms-length lending — the most significant differences are found between banks in developed and developing countries.

- Banks in developing countries tend to be less exposed to SMEs, provide a lower share of investment loans, and charge higher fees and interest rates.
- The lending environment is more important than firm size or bank ownership type in shaping bank financing to SMEs.

The latest survey of The Observatory of European SMEs that established for monitoring of the economic performance of SMEs in Europe was carried out end of 2006 and early 2007 in EU 27 counties, and as well as in Norway, Iceland and Turkey. Besides, general characteristics of firms, perceptions on business competition, human resources problems, data on internationalization and innovation constraints, issues of SMEs were reported by this survey (The Observatory of European SMEs, 2007). The main findings are:

- Exports: Fewer than one in ten EU SMEs (8%) reported turnover from exports, which was significantly lower than the respective share of large enterprises (28%). The main export obstacle for SMEs was the lack of knowledge of foreign markets (13% of exporting SMEs mentioned this as their prime obstacle), followed by import tariffs in destination countries and the lack of capital (both 9%).
- Relocation/Subsidiaries Abroad: Only 5% of EU SMEs have reported that they have subsidiaries or joint ventures abroad. These foreign business partnerships seem to have a positive direct impact on employment in the home countries of EU SMEs: 49% of the involved SMEs confirmed that their partnership does not affect employment in their home country, while 18% reported that it increases and 3% that it decreases their respective employment in the home country. The main reason for SMEs to invest abroad is the geographic proximity as supplier to other enterprises.

- Strategies against Increasing Competition: While two thirds of SMEs in the EU believe that competition in their markets has increased over the past two years, the primary strategy of SMEs to face increasing competition is the improvement of product quality. SMEs would only consider in last resort strategies to increase working hours, looking for new markets abroad or cutting production costs.
- Innovation: New products in enterprise portfolio: About 3 in 10 SMEs indicated that they have new products or that they do have income from new products. The share of SMEs which reported innovations is higher in the old EU Member States than in the new Member States.
- Barriers to Innovation: SMEs regard four factors as constituting equally important barriers to innovation: problems in access to finance, scarcity of skilled labour, a lack of market demand and the high cost of human resources.
- Energy Efficiency: Comprehensive systems for energy efficiency are much less in place in SMEs (4%) than in large enterprises (19%); the same applies for simple measures to save energy, which are used by 30% of SMEs but 46% of large enterprises.
- Dependency from Regional Markets: The survey confirms that SMEs (89%) are much more dependant on the regional labour market than large enterprises (77%).
- Availability of an Appropriate Workforce: More than half of SME managers said that they have recruitment problems. A primary problem is the availability of an appropriate workforce; excessive wage demands are a relatively distant second issue. Finding and hiring the appropriate workforce is a challenge for many SMEs in the EU. Especially in the new Member States, a significant number of jobs remain unfilled.

- Administrative Regulations: Beyond the limitations of the demand side, the most important individual business constraint reported by SMEs is the compliance with administrative regulations; 36% of EU SMEs reported that this issue constrained their business activities over the past two years. This judgment is linked to the appraisal that 44% of SMEs consider themselves as operating in an over-regulated environment. Furthermore, SMEs perceive an overall deterioration in terms of administrative regulations.

Economic stagnation, high inflation, instability, frequent change in economic measures, globalization, access to finance, low competitive power have effected financial risk and financial performance of SMEs According to European Commission (2003), main financial issues of SMEs are:

- Many SMEs have consistently considered access to finance to be a problem. This relates to access to equity as well as access to debt financing.
- In spite of the growing importance of alternative sources of debt financing, the majority of European SMEs still depend on banks and this is not expected to change in the near future.
- In most countries, the importance of short-term financing is usually higher for SMEs than for large enterprises, a feature that correlates to the need of SMEs for (relatively) more working capital.
- The majority of SMEs maintain a relationship with just one bank, usually covering a relatively small credit amount (< 100,000 euro).
- Concerning the costs of financing, SMEs have a competitive disadvantage compared to LSEs. Usually interest rates as well as bank charges are higher to SMEs.

- The reasons for not obtaining bank financing differ between size classes: lack of collateral mostly affects micro and small enterprises, while poor business performance and insufficient information are the main reason for medium-sized firms,
- Poor business performance,
- Insufficient information,
- Insufficiencies of managers in finance education.

Financing has always been a key area of work for the OECD Working Party on SMEs (WPSMEE). In June 2004, the theme Financing Innovative SMEs in a Global Economy was discussed by Ministers at the 2nd OECD SME Ministerial Meeting in Istanbul. In March 2006, the Brasilia Conference on Better Financing for Entrepreneurship and SME Growth assessed the SME "financing (debt and equity) gap". The OECD Brasilia Action Statement for SME and Entrepreneurship Financing, which was issued at the end of the Conference, stressed that the financing gaps are not insurmountable and can be mitigated by a series of actions. The WPSMEE has been pursuing research in this area and carried out work in 2007-2008 on Financing Innovative and High Growth SMEs. In late October 2008 on the occasion of its 34th Session WPSMEE delegates engaged in a preliminary exchange of views on the impact of the global crisis on SME and entrepreneurship financing, and discussed the strategies so far adopted by governments in dealing with the problem and what should be done next (OECD, 2009c).

Paranque (1995) aimed to show that the terms of the debate on the capitalization of small manufacturing firms ought to be clarified. Author called these firms as undercapitalized, because in relative terms their capital spending is often similar, or even greater, than that of their larger competitors. Earnings of these firms are depleted by the higher depreciation charges for maintaining their fixed assets. Also, undercapitalization is due to the fact that firms in this category have poor access to capital markets.

Danset, et al. (1998) examined the financial structures and performance of SMEs versus LSEs by using BACH data bank which is the most advanced publicly available database for comparisons in this field. Study covered the period 1990-1996 and concerned 9 countries, namely Austria, Belgium, France, Germany, Italy, Portugal, Spain, Japan and United States. The results showed that there was no link between financial structure and profitability that used as performance indicator.

Maher, et al (2000) examined some of the strengths, weaknesses, and economic implications associated with various corporate governance systems in OECD countries. Then discussed the various mechanisms employed in different systems (e.g. the market for corporate control, executive remuneration schemes, concentrated ownership, and cross-shareholdings amongst firms) and assess the evidence on whether or not they are conducive to firm performance and economic growth. For example, they showed how the corporate governance framework can impinge upon the development of equity markets, R&D and innovative activity, and the development of an active SME sector, and thus impinge upon economic growth. Several policy implications are identified.

Sogorb (2001) aimed to test the relevance of the different financing theories for explaining capital structure choice in the Small and Medium Enterprises (SMEs) sector. They carried out an empirical analysis over a panel data of 3962 non – financial Spanish SMEs. Results showed that the financing decision in these companies could be explained by the main capital structure theories: Fiscal Theory, Trade – Off Theory and Pecking Order Theory. Among all these theories, some caveats are worth to be stressed and the hierarchically theory seems to fit completely in the explanation of SMEs debt policy.

Requejo (2002) aimed to examine the importance of the different theoretical proposals that explain a firm's capital structure. The contrast was carried out from a structural equation model on the database of the Business Strategies Survey for Spanish firms in 1998. The results revealed a greater importance in financial constraints as determinants of capital structure, in the sense that SMEs together with firms not belonging to any business group, recently created firms and those with a smaller market share have less possibility of deferring required investments and leverage. The preference for internal financing and the average debt ratio of the sector were also capital structure determinants.

Arias, et al. (2003) provided an empirical examination of the pecking order theory on capital structure in the field of Small and Medium Enterprises (SMEs). Results showed that firms that have many growth opportunities and small cash flows had more debt in their capital structure. These results didn't change when different SME definitions or sample sizes were used.

Bukvik and Bartlett (2003) aimed to identify financial problems that prevented the expansion and development of SMEs in Slovenia, Bosnia and Macedonia. In their studies, they applied a survey on 200 SMEs which was active in 2000-2001. As a result of the study; the major financial problems of SMEs in these countries were defined as high cost of capital, insufficient financial cooperation, the bureaucratic processes of banks, SMEs' lack of information on financial subjects and delay in the collection of the payment.

Abouzeedan and Busler (2004) reviewed the firm performance models and pointed out their individual strengths and weaknesses that would help both academic researchers and professional users to understand and appreciate how and when to use these various models. They divided theoretical models for Small and Medium-size Enterprise (SME) performance into two categories. First part was firm dynamics theories and performance prediction models, like Stochastic Theories, Learning Model Theories and Hazard Modeling Theories. In the second part they examined the performance prediction models of SMEs, which

include Z-Scores, ZETA-Scores, Neural Networks (NN) and the SIV models, among others.

Ogujiuba, et al. (2004) discussed the critical causes of the risk-averse behavior of banks in funding small and medium enterprises (SMEs) in Nigeria, monetary policy and financial stability implications of SMEs "Credit Crunch" were evaluated. This paper showed that capital matters for the response of bank lending to economic shocks and highlights the need for a sound, stable and efficient financial sector to assist SMEs.

Bhaird, et al. (2005) presented an empirical examination of firm characteristic determinants of the capital structure of a sample of 299 Irish small and medium sized firms. The results suggested that age, size, level of intangible activity, ownership structure and the provision of collateral are important determinants of the capital structure in SMEs. Seemingly Unrelated Regression approach (SUR) was used to examine industry effects and to test the stability of parameter estimates across sectors. Results suggested that the influence of age, size, ownership structure and provision of collateral were constant across SMEs.

Sormani (2005) researched the financial problems of small businesses in the UK. The study emphasized the cash flow and unpaid invoices of SMEs. According to this study, there were two main suggestions for SMEs in UK. First one was managing cash flow for the financial health of SMEs, and the other one was taking into account the time between issuing an invoice and receiving payment in order to run efficiently.

Daskalakis and Psillaki (2005) aimed to obtain the main determinants of capital structure of Small and Medium Enterprises (SMEs) for Greece and France, and compare and analyze any emerging differences between the two countries. They applied panel data methodology on the Greek and French firms, derived from the ICAP and the DIANE databases respectively. The results showed that the SMEs in both countries seem to behave in a very similar way. Specifically, for both countries, the asset structure and the profitability seem to have a negative relationship with the firm leverage, whereas the firm size and growth were positively related to their debt ratio. The main conclusion was that there were great similarities in the determinants of the SMEs' capital structure for Greece and France.

Larsen and Bjerkeland (2005) analysed the differences of unexpected loan losses between SMEs and LSEs in Norway. Study covered all companies in the period of 1998-2001. Results showed that unexpected loan losses have been lower for loans to SMEs than for those to LSEs.

Bitszenis and Nito (2005) determined the financial problems of SMEs while evaluating the obstacles and problems encountered by entrepreneurs in Albania. It was determined that the most important financial problems were lack of financial resources and taxation faced by SMEs in Albania.

Mohnen and Nasev (2005) examined firm growth in the German SME-sector using a sample of companies obtained by a survey of two well known German SME networks – Arbeitsgemeinschaft selbstandiger Unternehmer (ASU) and Bundesverband Junger Unternehmer (BJU). Results showed that growth was negatively related to firm size and age. This study confirmed that firms under limited liability displayed higher growth rates than firms under full liability. Also the results showed that the human capital of employees and the entrepreneur had a significant impact on growth.

Sarno (2005) presented how small and medium enterprises located in the less developed regions of Southern Italy face higher liquidity constraints compared to the firms in the Central-Northern Italian regions. The results showed the existence of a bottleneck of financial resources devoted to current finance production that limits the accumulation of working capital even when faced with favorable market opportunities.

Sanchez and Marin (2005) analyzed the management characteristics of Spanish SMEs according to their strategic orientation and the consequences in terms of firm performance and business efficiency. The study was conducted on 1,351 Spanish SMEs. The results confirmed the expected relationship between management characteristics and performance of SMEs in Spain.

Sogorb-Mira (2005) aimed to test how firm characteristics affect Small and Medium Enterprise (SME) capital structure. They carried out an empirical analysis of panel data of 6482 non-financial Spanish SMEs during the five years period 1994–1998. Results suggested that non-debt tax shields and profitability were both negatively related to SME leverage, while size, growth options and asset structure influence positively SME capital structure.

Tagoe, et al. (2005) examined the impact of financial sector liberalization policies on financial management of SMEs in Ghana by using six case studies. It was found that the main financial challenge facing SMEs was access to affordable credit over a reasonable period.

Tsuruta, et al. (2005) aimed to find the factors that affected the distress of SMEs in Japan. Data was obtained from Credit Risk Information Database for SMEs during 1996-2002. The study covered 2787 bankrupt firms. According to analysis the higher trade credit ratio and lower trade credit growth rate have negative effects to survive of the distressed firms.

Bhaird, et al. (2006) presented an empirical description of the capital structures of a sample of 299 Irish small and medium sized enterprises. The sources of finance used by respondents were delineated by internal and external sources and viewed through a life cycle model. Multivariate regression results indicated that there were relationships between age, size, sector and intangible assets and the means of collateral used to secure debt financing. Also they reported SME owners' attitudes towards and perception of sources of finance. It was found that the respondents' desire for independence and control, and the perceived lack of information asymmetries in debt markets were explained the financing choices of SMEs.

Canovas and Solano (2006) analyzed the effect of banking relationship on interest rates and probability that guarantees must be provided in a sample of SMEs. Data obtained from Sistema de Analisis de Balances Espanoles (SABE) Database during 1999–2000 and study covered 184 SMEs. ANOVA test was used for analysis. The results indicated that SMEs that work with fewer banks obtain debt at a lower cost. The study seemed to suggest that concentrated banking relationships reduce the uncertainty of leading to risky firms.

Klapper, et al. (2006) tested competing theories of capital structure choices using firm-level data on firm borrowings. The study covered privately owned, young and small and medium sized enterprises concentrated in the service sector. Statistical tests found a positive firm size effect on financial intermediation. Larger firms had higher leverage ratios (both short term and long term), including higher use of trade credit. There was also a negative influence of profitability on leverage ratios. Also, firms operating in a competitive environment had higher leverage ratios. It was found that SMEs were very active in creating jobs. Results suggested a new type of firm that was more market and profit-oriented.

Nguyen, et al. (2006) aimed to identify the determinants influencing the capital structure of SMEs in Vietnam. Results showed that SMEs employ mostly short-term liabilities to finance their operations. The capital structure of SMEs was positively related to growth, business risk, firm size, networking, and relationships with banks; but negatively related to tangibility.

Koyuncugil and Ozgulbas (2006a) emphasized the financial problems of SMEs in Turkey, examined their suggestions on solutions in addition to the stock markets of SMEs, and expressed that the first step to solve problems was to identify the financial profiles of SMEs. Researchers identified the financial profiles of SMEs with the method of data mining by using the data of 135 SMEs in Istanbul Stock Exchange (ISE). As a result of the study, the most important factor that affects the

financial performance of SMEs was determined as the capital structure of finance. At the end of the study, the basic suggestion towards the SMEs is concentrated on debt financing to increase the financial performance.

In another study that was realized by Koyuncugil and Ozgulbas (2006b) on operations of SMEs in ISE; a criterion of the financial performance for SMEs were identified due to factors that affects the financial risk and performance of SMEs. As a result of the study, return on equity was determined as a criterion for the measurement of the financial performance of SMEs.

Once again in another study, that was hold by Koyuncugil and Ozgulbas (2006c) on operations of SMEs between the years of 2000-2005 in ISE; the identification of the financial factors that affected the financial failures of SMEs was aimed. CHAID (Chi-Square Automatic Interaction Detector) Decision Tree Algorithm was used in the study. The result of the study was identified as the financial failure of SMEs was affected by the productivity of equity, profit margin, the administration of payments and the finance of tangible assets. In various studies that were realized by Ozgulbas and Koyuncugil (2006) and Ozgulbas, Koyuncugil & Yilmaz (2006) with the same set of data, showed that the success of the firms were not only based on the financial strength of SMEs, but also based on the scale of the SMEs such as the higher success of middle scale firms than the small scale firms.

Inegbenebor (2006) focused on the role of entrepreneurs and capacity to access and utilize the fund of SMEs in Nigeria. The sample of study was consisted of 1255 firms selected to represent 13 identified industrial subsectors. The results of the study were showed that the capacity of SMEs to access and utilize the fund were weak in Nigeria.

Kang (2006) analyzed the role of the SMEs in Korean economy. According to the study, SMEs have been hit hard by the economic slowdown and also faced some deep structural problems. The main financial problem of SMEs in Korea was heavy dept financing. Many SMEs are over-burdened with debt. Also SMEs are saddled with excess capacity, and they suffer from growing overseas competition. All these factors are affected the profitability of SMEs in Korea.

Lopez (2007) attempted to create an objective model that allowed evaluating SMEs loan performance by using the literature on business finance. Lopez suggested his model for understanding the factors of default risk of small business loans and helping to access the credit.

Teruel and Solano (2007) presented empirical evidence about the effects of working capital management on the profitability of a sample of small and medium-sized Spanish firms. Authors collected a panel data of 8,872 SMEs covering the period 1996-2002. The results demonstrated that managers can create value by reducing their firm's number of days accounts receivable and inventories. Equally, shortening the cash conversion cycle also improves the firm's profitability.

Daskalakis, et al. (2008) investigated the capital structure determinants of small and medium sized enterprises (SMEs) using a sample of Greek and French firms. They assessed the extent to which the debt to assets ratio of firms depends upon their asset structure, size, profitability and growth rate. The results showed that the SMEs in both countries exhibit similarities in their capital structure choices. Asset structure and profitability had a negative relationship with leverage, whereas firm size was positively related to their debt to assets ratio. Growth was statistically significant only for France and positively related to debt.

Koyuncugil and Ozgulbas (2008a) detected strengths and weaknesses of SMEs listed in ISE by using A CHAID Decision Tree application that is one of a data mining method. The results showed that productivity of equity and assets, financing of assets, management of account receivables and liquidity were the weaknesses of SMEs.

Studies that summarized above showed that SMEs are in financial problems, due to the economical condition of country, underdevelopment of money and capital markets that can provide financial sources to SMEs, and insufficiency of financial administration and administrator.

THE IMPACT OF FINANCIAL CRISIS ON SMES

Even in 'normal' economic conditions SMEs are more vulnerable, and the impact of financial crisis is perceived severely in SMEs than LSEs. The reasons of the oversensitivity of SMEs are (OECD, 2009c):

- it is more difficult for them to downsize as they are already small;
- they are individually less diversified in their economic activities;
- they have a weaker financial structure (i.e. lower capitalisation);
- they have a lower or no credit rating;
- they are heavily dependent on credit and
- they have fewer financing options.

Access to financing is the most significant challenges for survival and growth of SMEs. With the impact of the financial and economic crisis, financing problems have strongly exacerbated and SMEs faced sharply tighter credit and higher interest rates which are severely affected cash flows. The global financial crisis broke out in September 2008, had serious impacts on the economies like economic slow-down and recession. In many countries, GDP growth declined dramatically. Also, the financial crisis caused export growth to drop sharply, and the rising unemployment rate tightened the liquidity of funds throughout the all enterprises, especially impacting export-oriented SMEs.

European Association of Craft, Small and Medium-sized Enterprises (UEAPME) managed a survey on 10 European countries (Austria (AT), Germany (DE), Spain (ES), Finland (FI), France (FR), Ireland (IE), Lithuania (LT), Netherlands

(NL), Poland (PL) and United Kingdom (UK)) in June 2009 to find the difficulties, and effects of financial and economic crisis on SMEs (UEAPME, 2009). According to this survey:

- The overall situation on access to finance for SMEs was significantly worse than a year before.
- About 4% of all SMEs are reporting that they have not access to finance at all.
- Some countries are reporting significant problems on access to working capital.
- Risk premium is significantly above its rate in normal times.
- Banks ask SMEs for more collateral and more information to assess the risks of clients.
- Finally, as regards the impact of the financial crisis on the real economy.
- 48% of all SMEs reduced their investments due to the crises.
- 33% of all SMEs have negative impacts on employment.

The OECD Working Party on SMEs and Entrepreneurship (WPSMEE) has started a research on the impact of the global crisis on SMEs and entrepreneurs' access to finance. WPSMEE was conducted a survey among member and non-member countries in January and February 2009. Twenty-nine countries, the European Commission and the European Investment Fund responded to the questionnaire. The main results of this survey are (OECD, 2009c):

- Extended payment delays on receivables, especially in times of reduced sales, are leading rapidly to a depletion of working capital in many countries.
- Increased insolvency rates appear to confirm SMEs' increased inability to obtain short-term financing.
- The stagnation in lending is true even of banks in countries where governments

have deliberately strengthened banks' balance sheets to allow them to grant additional credit to SMEs and/or where credit guarantee schemes exist.
- Confronted with worsening access to credit, SMEs are exploring alternative sources of finance such as the mobilization of reserves, self-financing and factoring.
- Global venture capital fundraising slowed down between 2007 and 2008.

World Bank conducted "Financial Crisis Survey" to measure the effects of the financial crisis on firms. Survey covered six countries from Eastern Europe and Central Asia; Bulgaria, Hungary, Latvia, Lithuania, Romania and Turkey. The 42 indicators shown below were developed to measure the effects of the crisis on key elements of the private economy: sales, employment, finances, and expectations about the future. Interviews for the Financial Crisis Survey took place in June and July 2009. All of 1,686 firms interviewed were previously surveyed by Enterprise Surveys in 2008/2009 as part of its ongoing research effort. This pre-crisis data was used as a baseline for estimating the impact of the crisis. This study didn't contained the SMEs but the results were very important for showing the impact of financial crisis, for this reason some main results of survey is presented in Table 4 (WB, 2009b).

Another study was conducted in China for detecting the impacts of the current financial crisis on SMEs. According to the report of ADB Institute about China's SMEs, the current financial crisis has had two big impacts on SMEs in China. The crisis has resulted in a sharply decreasing external need for export-oriented SMEs and more severe financial difficulties for all SMEs overall (ADBI, 2010). Similar studies done in different countries like Romania (Roxana, 2009), Indonesia (Wahyu & Swadaya, 2009), South Korea (The Hankyoreh, 2009) and Japan (Shirakawa, 2009) detected same affects of financial crisis on SMEs.

Table 4. Results of World Bank's financial crisis survey

RESULTS	COUNTRIES					
	Bulgaria	Hungary	Latvia	Lithuania	Romania	Turkey
% of firms closed	0.69	0.00	4.54	1.01	3.28	5.79
% of firms with increased sales, compared to the same month in 2008	14.09	6.14	4.86	5.35	9.15	14.75
% of firms with decreased sales, compared to the same month in 2008	66.33	63.05	88.47	86.84	73.27	71.68
Net change in sales in June 2009, compared to the same month in 2008	-20.53	-15.44	-41.07	-40.73	-25.20	-23.79
Weighted difference in share of sales that were domestic	-0.93	-3.78	-4.37	7.46	-0.70	-5.78
Weighted difference in share of sales that were indirect exports	133.20	-22.01	-14.69	-94.14	0.00	-32.88
Weighted difference in share of sales that were direct exports	-38.85	-5.61	-5.56	-47.18	36.86	-13.13
% of firms using less capacity	76.79	55.28	71.60	74.12	36.25	61.84
Difference in capacity utilization	-24.80	-5.88	-23.34	-23.07	-2.69	-15.09
% of firms decreased number of permanent workers	48.62	51.93	66.10	62.47	49.82	60.17
% of firms decreased number of temporary workers	7.72	13.46	17.73	21.83	15.35	9.15
% of firms filed for re organization	15.31	1.27	27.78	3.28	25.17	25.09
% of firms filed for insolvency or bankruptcy	0.49	2.48	0.16	2.10	3.13	1.88
% of firms applied for direct state aid	6.58	2.50	6.41	11.75	0.97	26.69
% of firms main effect is an increase in debt level	3.90	2.69	7.59	11.05	7.88	6.39
% of firms main effect is reduced access to credit	4.63	0.86	2.29	3.23	5.49	6.42
% of firms main effect is a drop in demand for its products or services	78.12	70.32	75.43	70.77	78.47	71.30
Proportion of working capital financed from internal funds	78.15	52.78	72.00	54.91	64.16	N/A
Share of debt denominated in foreign currency	21.40	35.30	39.50	20.73	31.18	21.75
Share of short term liabilities	49.30	69.44	49.17	80.09	56.91	66.44
% of firms overdue for more than 3 months in the last year	28.98	34.67	40.59	40.66	29.62	36.65
% of firms that restructured liabilities in the last year	12.02	19.16	25.90	26.66	4.90	16.83

SMEs need special attention, because they are essential for economic growth in all countries. The financial crisis adversely impacts most of the SMEs, because SMEs are more vulnerable than LSEs, and involve higher risk and weaker financial structures. SMEs need simple, flexible, and efficient solution created for non-expert financier for detecting risk signals and preventing from distress.

A SOLUTION FOR SMES: EARLY WARNING SYSTEM

Today, SMEs need to think about global dimensions of their business earlier than ever. Especially in developing countries, in addition to the administrative insufficiencies of SMEs, the permanent threat towards SMEs from globalization, competition, economical conditions and financial crisis have caused distress and affect their performance.

The failure of a business is an event which can produce substantial losses to all parties like creditors, investors, auditors, financial institutions, stockholders, employees, and customers, and it undoubtedly reflects the economics of the countries concerned. When a business with financial problems is not able to pay its financial obligations, the business may be driven into the situation of becoming a non-performing loan business and, finally, if the problems cannot be solved, the business may become bankrupt and forced to close down. Those business failures inevitably influence all businesses as a whole. Direct and indirect bankruptcy costs are incurred which include the expenses of either liquidating or an attempting to reorganize businesses, accounting fees, legal fees and other professional service costs and the disaster broadens to other businesses and the economics of the countries involved (Warner, 1977; Westerfield, et al., 2008, Terdpaopong, 2008).

The awareness of factors that contribute to making a business successful is important; it is also applicable for all the related parties to have an understanding of financial performance and bankruptcy. It is also important for a financial manager of successful firms to know their firm's possible actions that should be taken when their customers, or suppliers, go into bankruptcy. Similarly, firms should be aware of their own status,

of when and where they should take necessary actions in response to their financial problems, as soon as possible rather than when the problems are beyond their control and reach a crisis.

Therefore, to bring out the financial distress factors into open as early warning signals have a vital importance for SMEs as all enterprises. There is no specific method for total prevention for a financial crisis of enterprises. The important point is to set the factors that cause the condition with calmness, to take corrective precautions for a long term, to make a flexible emergency plan towards the potential future crisis.

An early warning system (EWS) is a monitoring and reporting system that alerts for the probability of problems, risks and opportunities before they affect the financial statements of firms. EWSs are used for detecting financial performance, financial risk and potential bankruptcies. EWSs give a chance to management to take advantage of opportunities to avoid or mitigate potential problems. Nearly, all of the financial EWSs are based on financial statements. Balance sheets and income tables are the data sources that reflect the financial truth for early warning systems. In essence, the early warning system is a financial analysis technique, and it identifies the achievement analysis of enterprise due to its industry with the help of financial ratios.

The efforts towards the separation of distressed enterprises started with the z-score that are based on the usage of ratios by Beaver (1996) for single and multiple discriminant analysis of Altman in 1968. The examples of other important studies that used multi variable statistical models, are given by Deakin (1972), Altman, et al. (1977), Taffler and Tisshaw (1977) with the usage of multiple discriminant model; are also given by Zmijewski (1984), Zavgren (1985), Jones (1987), Pantalone and Platt (1987), with the usage of logit ve probit models; are at the same time given by Meyer and Pifer (1970) with the usage of multiple regression model.

Financial early warning systems are grouped under three main categories in literature:

- The models towards the prediction of profits of enterprise,
- The ratio based models towards the prediction of bankrupt/distress of enterprise,
- Economic trend based models towards the prediction of bankrupt/ distress of enterprise.

In literature, there were some EWS studies done before. But the system must design according to the needs of SMEs managers. Therefore, system must be easy to understand and easy to use, must design according to financial and operational risk factors (as banks and BASEL II requirements), and must be intelligence for using update data. Some of these studies conducted in SMEs, banks, insurers, i.e. are presented below.

Brockett and Cooper (1990) developed an EWS by using Neural Network Method. The model was developed with 24 variables firstly, and then the numbers of variables were decreased to 8. These variables were equities, capitalization ratio, return on assets, turnover of assets, account receivables / equities, chainging of loses, debt/current assets.

Lee and Urritia (1996) compared the models of logit, hazard, Neural Networks and discriminant for developing an early warning system. They found different indicators or signs for each model. Also they determined that forecast power of all models were same.

Barniv and Hathorn (1997) developed an early warning model based on logistic regression by evaluating the studies of Trieschmann and Pinches (1973), Ambrose and Seward (1998), and Barniv and McDonald (1992) in insurance firms.

Laitinen and Chong (1999) presented a model for predicting crises in small businesses using early-warning signals. Study summarised the results of two separate studies carried out in Finland (with 72 per cent response) and the UK (26 per cent) on the decision process of corporate analysts (Finland) and bank managers (UK) in predicting the failure of small and medium-sized enterprises (SMEs). Both studies consisted of seven main headings and over 40 sub-headings of possible factors leading to failure. Weighted averages were used for both studies to show the importance of these factors. There were significant similarities in the results of the two studies. Management incompetence was regarded as the most important factor, followed by deficiencies in the accounting system and attitude towards customers. However, low accounting staff morale was considered a very important factor in Finland but not in the UK.

Yang, et al. (2001) used Artificial Neural Networks (ANN) for detecting financial risk of banks as an early warning, and tested the method.

Salas and Saurina (2002) compared the determinants of problem loans of Spanish commercial and savings banks in the period 1985-1997, taking into account both macroeconomic and individual bank level variables. The GDP growth rate, firms, and family indebtedness, rapid past credit or branch expansion, inefficiency, portfolio composition, size, net interest margin, capital ratio, and market power are variables that explain credit risk. The findings raised important bank supervisory policy issues: the use of bank level variables as early warning indicators, the advantages of bank mergers from different regions, and the role of banking competition and ownership in determining credit risk.

Edison (2003) developed an operational early warning system (EWS) that can detect financial crises. The system monitored several indicators that tend to exhibit an unusual behavior in the periods preceding a crisis. When an indicator exceeded (or falls below) a threshold, then it was said to issue a "signal" that a currency crisis may occur within a given period. The model was tested in 1997/1998 crises, but several weaknesses to the approach were identified. The paper also evaluated how this system can be applied to an individual country. The results suggested that an early warning system should be thought of as a useful diagnostic tool.

El-Shazly (2003) investigated the predictive power of an empirical model for an early warning system of currency crises. EWS employed qualitative response models within a signals framework that monitors the behavior of key economic variables and issues a warning when their values exceed certain critical levels. Author conducted a case study in Egypt. Results showed that this model, and in particular the extreme value model, captured to a good extent the turbulence in the foreign exchange market and the onset of crises.

Jacobs (2003) presented an EWS for six countries in Asia. Financial crises were distinguished in three types; currency crises, banking crises, and debt crises. The significance of the indicator groups was tested in a multivariate logit model on a panel of six Asian countries for the period 1970-2001. Author founded that some currency crises dating schemes outperform others by using EWS.

Berg, et al. (2004), developed early warning system models of currency crisis for Mexican and Asian crises. Since the beginning of 1999, IMF staff has been systematically tracking, on an ongoing basis, various models developed in-house and by private institutions, as part of its broader forward-looking vulnerability assessment. This study examined in detail at the performance of these models in practice. The forecasts of the in-house model were statistically and economically significant predictors of actual crises. On the whole, the short-horizon private sector models examined performed poorly out of sample, despite stellar in-sample performance.

Brockett, et al. (2006) examined the effect of statistical model and neural network methods to detect financially troubled life insurers. They considered two neural network methods; back-propagation (BP), and learning vector quantization (LVQ), two statistical methods; multiple discriminant analysis, and logistic regression analysis. The results showed that BP and LQV outperform the traditional statistical approaches.

Abumustafa (2006) detected early warning signs for predicting currency crises in Egypt, Jordan and Turkey. The study proposed real exchange rate, exports, imports, trade balance/gross domestic product (GDP), foreign liabilities/foreign assets, domestic real interest rate, world oil prices, and government consumption/GDP as indicators to predict currency risk. The results showed that all crises were predictable, and EWSs should use for detecting crises.

Kyong, et al. (2006) presented the construction process of a daily financial condition indicator (DFCI), which can be used as an early warning signal using neural networks and nonlinear programming. The procedure of DFCI construction was completed by integrating three sub-DFCIs, based on each financial variable, into the final DFCI. The study, then examined the predictability of alarm zone for the financial crisis forecasting in Korea.

Katz (2006) proposed to use EWS and early warning signs. Study listed often common warning signs and the best ways to solve the problems. These are: payroll taxes, sales tax, and other fiduciary obligations; communications with executive management and company leaders; accounts receivable; customers and product profitability; accounts payable; inventory, management; for capital-intensive or manufacturing operations; and checks as an indicator of problems.

Koyuncugil and Ozgulbas (2007a) aim to develop d a financial early warning model for the SMEs listed in Istanbul Stock Exchange (ISE) in Turkey by using data mining. Authors conducted another study (2007b) and detected early warning signs for financial risk. A data mining method, Chi-Square Automatic Interaction Detector (CHAID) decision tree algorithm, was used in the study for financial profiling and detecting signs. The study covered 697 SMEs listed in ISE between 2000 and 2005. As a result of the study, the covered SMEs listed in ISE were categorized into 19 financial profiles and it was determined that 430 of them had poor financial performance, in other words

61.69%. According to the profiles of SMEs in financial distress, Return on Equity (ROE) will be a financial early warning signal for SMEs listed in ISE.

Koyuncugil and Ozgulbas (2008b) emphasized the affect and importance of operational risk in financial distressed of SMEs, beside the financial risk. Authors developed an early warning model that qualitative (operational) and quantitative (financial) data of SMEs taken into consideration. During the formation of system; an easy to understand, easy to interpret and easy to apply utilitarian model that is far from the requirement of theoretical background was targeted by the discovery of the implicit relationships between the data and the identification of effect level of every factor. This model was designed by data mining.

Koyuncugil and Ozgulbas (2009a) developed a financial early warning model that detected operational risk factors for hedging financial risk. For this purpose study used CHAID (Chi-Square Automatic Interaction Detector) decision trees. The study covered 6.185 firms in Organized Industrial Region of Ankara in 2008. It was found that firms should emphasize the educational background of managers, status of managers, annual turnover, operating length of firms, makers of financial strategies, expenditure of energy, knowledge about BASEL-II, quality standards, and usage of credit as operational risk factors for hedging operational risk and raising financial performance.

Koyuncugil and Ozgulbas (2009b) to develop an intelligent financial early warning system model based on operational and financial risk factors by using data mining for SMEs in Turkey. This model was aimed to not remain in theoretical structure, be practicable for SME, and available for the utilization of SMEs managers. According to model, financial data of Turkish SMEs was obtained by means of financial analyses of balance sheets and income statements through Turkish Central Bank. Operational data couldn't be access by balance sheets and income statements was collected by a

field study from SMEs. Next step of model was analyzed the financial and operational data by data mining and detecting early earming signs.

Karim (2008) successful predicted a majority of banking crises in emerging markets and advanced countries in 1970-2003. Karim also, suggested that logit was the most appropriate approach for global EWS and signal extraction for country specific EWS.

Davis and Karim (2008) searched to assess whether early warning systems based on the logit and binomial tree approaches on the UK and US economies could have helped to warn about the crisis. The study suggested that a broadening of approaches of macro prudential analysis was appropriate for early warning.

DATA MINING MODEL AND AN IMPLEMENTATION FOR EARLY WARNING SYSTEM

The identification of the risk factors by clarifying the relationship between the variables defines the discovery of knowledge. Automatic and estimation oriented information discovery process coincides the definition of data mining. Data mining is the process of sorting through large amounts of data and picking out relevant information. Fawley, et al. (1992) has been described data mining as "the nontrivial extraction of implicit, previously unknown, and potentially useful information from data". Also, Hand, et al. (2001) decribed data mining as "the science of extracting useful information from large data sets or databases". Data mining, the extraction of hidden predictive information from large databases, is a powerful new technology with great potential to help companies focus on the most important information in their data warehouses. Data mining tools predict future trends and behaviors, allowing businesses to make proactive, knowledge-driven decisions. The automated, prospective analyses offered by data mining move beyond the analyses of past events provided by retrospective tools typical of decision support systems. Data mining tools can answer business questions that traditionally were too time consuming to resolve. They scour databases for hidden patterns, finding predictive information that experts may miss because it lies outside their expectations (Thearling, 2009).

During the developing EWS; an easy to understand, easy to interpret and easy to apply utilitarian model that is far from the requirement of theoretical background is targeted by the discovery of the implicit relationships between the data and the identification of effect level of every factor. Because of this reason, the ideal method to financial early warning system is the data mining method that is started to be used frequently nowadays for financial studies.

Data mining is used by business intelligence organizations, and financial analysts to get information from the large data sets. Data mining in relation to enterprise resource planning is the statistical and logical analysis of large sets of transaction data, looking for patterns that can aid decision making (Monk and Wagner, 2006). Today, data mining technology integrated measurement of different kinds of is moving into focus to measure and hedging risk. Data mining techniques have been successfully applied like fraud detection and bankruptcy prediction by Tam and Kiang (1992), Lee et al. (1996), Kumar et al(1997), strategic decision-making by Nazem and Shin (1999) and financial performance by Eklund et al. (2003), Hoppszallern (2003), Derby (2003), Chang et al. (2003), Kloptchenko et a., (2004), Magnusson et al. (2005). Also, some earlier studies of Koyuncugil and Ozgulbas (2006a, 2006b, 2006c, 2007a, 2007b, 2008a, 2008b, 2009a, 2009b) Ozgulbas and Koyuncugil (2006, 2009) conducted on financial performance, financial risk and operational risk of Small and Medium Enterprises (SMEs) and hospitals by data mining.

Fayyad *et al.* (1996), proposed main steps of DM:

- Retrieving the data from a large database.
- Selecting the relevant subset to work with.
- Deciding on the appropriate sampling system, cleaning the data and dealing with missing fields and records.
- Applying the appropriate transformations, dimensionality reduction, and projections.
- Fitting models to the preprocessed data.

Data mining techniques can yield the benefits of automation on existing software and hardware platforms, and can be implemented on new systems as existing platforms are upgraded and new products developed. When data mining tools are implemented on high performance parallel processing systems, they can analyze massive databases in minutes. The most commonly used techniques in data mining are (Thearling, 2009; Koyuncugil, 2006):

- **Artificial neural networks**: Non-linear predictive models that learn through training and resemble biological neural networks in structure.
- **Decision trees**: Tree-shaped structures that represent sets of decisions. These decisions generate rules for the classification of a dataset. Specific decision tree methods include Classification and Regression Trees (CART) and Chi Square Automatic Interaction Detection (CHAID).
- **Genetic algorithms**: Optimization techniques that use process such as genetic combination, mutation, and natural selection in a design based on the concepts of evolution.
- **Nearest neighbor method**: A technique that classifies each record in a dataset based on a combination of the classes of the k record(s) most similar to it in a historical dataset. Sometimes called the k-nearest neighbor technique.

- **Rule induction**: The extraction of useful if-then rules from data based on statistical significance.

Decision trees are tree-shaped structures that represent sets of decisions. The decision tree approach can generate rules for the classification of a data set. Specific decision tree methods include Classification and Regression Trees (CART) and Chi Square Automatic Interaction Detection (CHAID). CART and CHAID are decision tree techniques used for classification of a data set. They provide a set of rules that can be applied to a new (unclassified) data set to predict which records will have a given outcome. CART typically requires less data preparation than CHAID (Lee & Siau, 2001).

Developing an EWS for SMEs focused segmentation methods. The main approach in analysis is discovering different risk levels and identifying the factors affected financial performance. By means of Chi-Square metrics CHAID is able to separately segment the groups classified in terms of level of relations. Therefore, leaves of the tree have not binary branches but as much branches as the number of different variables in the data. So, it was deemed convenient to use CHAID algorithm method in the study.

CHAID modeling is an exploratory data analysis method used to study the relationships between a dependent measure and a large series of possible predictor variables those themselves may interact. The dependent measure may be a qualitative (nominal or ordinal) one or a quantitative indicator. For qualitative variables, a series of chi-square analyses are conducted between the dependent and predictor variables. For quantitative variables, analysis of variance methods are used where intervals (splits) are determined optimally for the independent variables so as to maximize the ability to explain a dependent measure in terms of variance components (Thearling, 2009).

Model of EWS

The model of EWS based on data mining and data flow diagram of the EWS is shown in Figure 1.

The steps of the EWS are:

- Preparation of data collection
- Implementation of DM method
- Determination of risk profiles
- Identification for current situation of SMEs from risk profiles and early warning signs
- Description of roadmap for SMEs

The details of the EWS are given below:

I. Preparation of Data Collection

Financial data that are gained from balance sheets: Items of balance sheets will be entered as financial data and will be used to calculate financial indicators of system:

Figure 1. Data flow diagram of the EWS

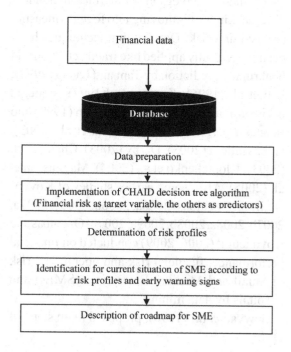

- Calculation of financial indicators like in Table 5
- Reduction of repeating variables in different indicators to solve the problem of Collinearity / Multicollinearity
- Imputation of missing data
- Solution of outlier and extreme value problem

II. Implementation of DM Method

In the scope of the methods of data mining,

- Logistic regression,
- Discriminant analysis,
- Cluster analysis,
- Hierarchical cluster analysis,
- Self Organizing Maps (SOM),
- Classification and Regression Trees (C&RT),
- CHi-Square Automatic Interaction Detector (CHAID)

can be the principal methods, in addition to this several classification/segmentation methods can

Table 5. Financial indicators

Financial Variables
Current Ratio
Quick Ratio (Liquidity Ratio)
Absolute Liquidity
Inventories to Current Assets
Current Liabilities to Total Assets
Debt Ratio
Current Liabilities to Total Liabilities
Long Term Liabilities to Total Liabilities
Equity to Assets Ratio
Current Assets Turnover Rate
Fixed Assets Turnover Rate
Days in Accounts Receivables
Inventories Turnover Rate
Assets Turnover Rate
Equity Turnover Rate
Profit Margin
Return on Equity
Return on Assets

be mentioned. However, during the preparation of an early warning system for SMEs, one of the basic objectives is to help SME administrators and decision makers, who does not have financial expertise, knowledge of data mining and analytic perspective, to reach easy to understand, easy to interpret, and easy to apply results about the risk condition of their enterprises. Therefore, decision tree algorithms that are one of the segmentation methods can be used because of their easy to understand and easy to apply visualization. Although, several decision tree algorithms have widespread usage today, CHAID is separated from other decision tree algorithms because of the number of the branches that are produced by CHAID. Other decision tree algorithms are branched in binary, but CHAID manifests all the different structures in data with its multi-branched characteristic. Hence; the method of CHi-Square Automatic Interaction Detector (CHAID) is used in the scope of this study.

Assume that $X_1, X_2, ..., X_{N-1}, X_N$ denote discrete or continous independent (predictor) variables and Y denotes dependent variable as target variable where $X_1 \in [a_1, b_1]$, $X_2 \in [a_2, b_2]$, ..., $X_N \in [a_N, b_N]$ and $Y \in \{Poor, Good\}$. While 'Poor' shows poor financial performance in red bar and 'Good' shows good financial performance in green bar.

Figure 2 given below shows CHAID decision tree.

In Figure 2 we can see that only 3 variables of N have a statistically significant relationship with the target Y.

- X_1 has most statistically significant relation with target Y.
- X_2 has statistically significant relation with X_1 where $X_1 \leq b_{11}$
- X_3 has statistically significant relation with X_1 where $b_{11} < X_1 \leq b_{12}$.

Figure 2. CHAID decision tree

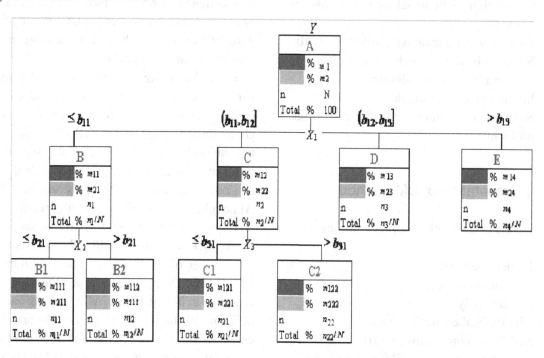

III. Determination of Risk Profiles

CHAID algorithm organizes Chi-square independency test among the target variable and predictor variables, starts from branching the variable which has the strongest relationship and arranges statistically significant variables on the branches of the tree due to the strength of the relationship. An example of a CHAID decision tree is seen in Figure 2. As it is observed from Figure 2, CHAID has multi-branches, while other decision trees are branched in binary. Thus, all of the important relationships in data can be investigated until the subtle details. In essence, the study identifies all the different risk profiles. Here the term risk means the risk that is caused because of the financial failures of enterprises.

Figure 2 shows that there are six risk profiles;

- Profile B1 shows that
  - There are n_{11} samples where $X_1 \leq b_{11}$ and $X_2 \leq b_{21}$

  - $\% m_{111}$ has poor financial performance,
  - $\% m_{211}$ has good financial performance
- Profile B2 shows that
  - There are n_{12} samples where $X_1 \leq b_{11}$ and $X_2 > b_{21}$
  - $\% m_{112}$ has poor financial performance,
  - $\% m_{212}$ has good financial performance
- Profile C1 shows that
  - There are n_{21} samples where $b_{11} < X_1 \leq b_{12}$ and $X_3 \leq b_{31}$
  - $\% m_{121}$ has poor financial performance,
  - $\% m_{221}$ has good financial performance
- Profile C2 shows that
  - There are n_{21} samples where $b_{11} < X_1 \leq b_{12}$ and $X_3 > b_{31}$
  - $\% m_{122}$ has poor financial performance,
  - $\% m_{222}$ has good financial performance
- Profile D shows that
  - There are n_3 samples where $b_{12} < X_1 \leq b_{13}$
  - $\% m_{13}$ has poor financial performance,
  - $\% m_{23}$ has good financial performance

- Profile E shows that
  - There are n_4 samples where $X_1 > b_{13}$
  - % m_{14} has poor financial performance,
  - % m_{24} has good financial performance

If all of the profiles are investigated separately,

Profile B1 shows that if any firm's variables X_1 and X_2 have values where $X_1 \leq b_{11}$ and $X_2 \leq b_{21}$, poor financial performance rate or in another words risk rate of the firm will be $R_{B1} = m_{111}$.

Profile B2 shows that if any firm's variables X_1 and X_2 have values where $X_1 \leq b_{11}$ and and $X_2 > b_{21}$, poor financial performance rate or in another words risk rate of the firm will be $R_{B2} = m_{112}$.

Profile C1 shows that if any firm's variables X_1 and X_3 have values where $b_{11} < X_1 \leq b_{12}$ and $X_3 \leq b_{31}$ poor financial performance rate or in another words risk rate of the firm will be $R_{C1} = m_{121}$.

Profile C2 shows that if any firm's variables X_1 and X_3 have values where $b_{11} < X_1 \leq b_{12}$ and $X_3 > b_{31}$ poor financial performance rate or in another words risk rate of the firm will be $R_{C2} = m_{122}$.

Profile D shows that if any firm's variable X_1 have values where $b_{12} < X_1 \leq b_{13}$ poor financial performance rate or in another words risk rate of the firm will be $R_D = m_{13}$.

Profile E shows that if any firm's variable X_1 have values where $X_1 > b_{13}$ poor financial performance rate or in another words risk rate of the firm will be $R_E = m_{14}$.

IV. Identification for Current Situation of SME According to Risk Profiles and Early Warning Signs

The part of study until this point is based on the identification of risk profiles from all of the data. In the scope of the data that is about the past of SMEs, the part of the study until this point defines the relationships between financial risk and variables, and also the risk profiles.

At this step, risk profiles that all of the firms belong to are identified in the study. This identification is realized with taking the group of variables in the risk profiles into consideration.

All of the firm will look at the values of their own enterprises, in the light of the statistically significant variables in the decision tree. According to Figure 2 these variables are X_1, X_2 and X_3. The firm compares the values of X_1, X_2 and X_3 between decision tree and firms. Then, they can identify their risk profile. For example if any firm has $X_1 > b_{13}$. Therefore, the risk profile of the firm must be Profile E.

According to the risk profiles of SMEs, it is possible to detect the early warning signs that show highest financial risk.

V. Description of Roadmap for SMEs

According to Figure 2 we can easily determine the risk grades of the firms. Assume that, the risk rates of the firms in the order of E > D > C2 > C1 > B2 > B1. Therefore, the best risk profile will be B1. Then, every firm tries to be in Profile B1. There are two variables X_1 and X_2 related with profile B1. If any firm want to be in Profile B1, the firm must make arrangements to make values $X_1 \leq b_{11}$ and $X_2 \leq b_{21}$.

Enterprise will identify the suitable road map after defining its risk profile. The enterprise can identify the path to reach upper level risk profile and the indicators that require privileged improvement in the light of the priorities of the variables in the roadmap. Furthermore, enterprise can pass to upper level risk profiles step by step at the same time can reach to a targeted risk profile in the upper levels for improving indicators due to this target. For example, any firm in Profile E has the biggest risk rate. The firm must be rehabilitating first the variable X_1 to decrease it between (b_{12}, b_{13}). Therefore, the firm will be in profile D and so on.

Implementation

I. Preparation of Data Collection

Implementation covered SMEs quoted in ISE in 2007. Data on balance sheets and income statements of such firms are available online at the web site of ISE (URL: http://www.imkb.gov.tr/). Total number of firms listed in ISE was 296 in 2007. Since scope of our study only covered micro, medium, and small-scaled enterprises, which are often referred to as SMEs, those 131 firms were classified to identify the firms, which can be categorized as a SME. We based on SME definition of the EU in an attempt to participate to Turkey's efforts to align with the EU acquits and to ensure comparability of the analysis provided herein. The thresholds used to classify SME on basis of the EU's SME definitions are €50 million.

Financial data of SMEs in Table 6 was collected from balance sheets of SMEs

II. Implementation of DM Method

CHAID algorithms are developed on basis of two groups of variables, namely target variable and predictor variables that will explain the target variable. In the study financial performance is explained by means of all variables of a SME, including financial variables. Therefore, the financial performance indicator is considered as the target variable and all financial variables (see Table 6) are considered as the predictor variables.

III. Determination of Risk Profiles

As can be seen from Figure 3, which explain SMEs profiling and financial performance statuses based

Table 6. Financial variables and their definitions

Ratios	Definition
Return on Equity	Net Income / Total Assets
Return on Assets	Net Income/ Total Equity
Profit Margin	Net Income/ Total Margin
Equity Turnover Rate	Net Revenues / Equity
Total Assets Turnover Rate	Net Revenues / Total Assets
Inventories Turnover Rate	Net Revenues / Average Inventories
Fixed Assets Turnover Rate	Net Revenues / Fixed Assets
Tangible Assets to Long Term Liabilities	Tangible Assets / Long Term Liabilities
Days in Accounts Receivables	Net Accounts Receivable/ (Net Revenues /365)
Current Assets Turnover Rate	Net Revenues/ Current Assets
Fixed Assets to Long Term Liabilities	Fixed Assets / Long Term Liabilities
Tangible Assets to Equities	Tangible Assets /Equities
Long Term Liabilities to Constant Capital	Long Term Liabilities / Constant Capital
Long Term Liabilities to Total Liabilities	Long Term Liabilities / Total Liabilities
Current (Short Term) Liabilities to Total Liabilities	Current Liabilities / Total Liabilities
Total Debt to Equities	Total Debt / Equities
Equities to Total Assets	Total Equity/Total Assets
Debt Ratio	Total Dept/Total Assets
Current Account Receivables to Total Assets	Current Account Receivables/ Total Assets
Inventories to Current Assets	Total Inventories / Current Assets
Absolute Liquidity	(Cash,Banks,Marketable Sec.,Acc. Rec.)/ Current Liab.
Quick Ratio (Liquidity Ratio)	(Cash, Marketable Sec.,Acc. Rec.)/ Current Liab.
Current Ratio	Current Assets/ Current Liabilities

on CHAID method, although it was possible to superficially categorize the covered SMEs into two groups as SMEs with good financial performance and with bad financial performance with CHAID method it was possible to categorize the covered SMEs in 5 different profiles in terms of level of financial performance. These profiles show us what financial indicators should focus on for good financial performance as well as those profiles those SMEs should take example to improve their financial performances.

IV. Identification for Current Situation of SME from Risk Profiles and Early Warning Signs

As you can see in Figure 3 and Table 7, it was determined that 60 SMEs out of 131 covered SMEs had good financial performance while 71 of them had poor financial performance. Results showed that 54.19% of the covered SMEs financially distress.

As required under CHAID method SMES profiling is based on return on assets (ROA) ratio, which has the strongest relation with the financial performance (p<0.000). As you can see in Figure 3 and Table 7-8, SMEs with ROA lower than and equal to 0.0002 and profit margin lower than and equal to 0.001 are grouped in the 1st profile. All of 49 SMEs had poor financial performance and

were in financial distress while SMEs in other profiles had varying financial performances.

SMEs with ROA lower than and equal to 0.002, but profit margin higher than 0,001 are grouped in the 2nd profile. In this profile 66.67% of SMEs were in financial distress. In the 3rd profile, ROA was higher than 0.002, but absolute liquidity was lower than and equal to 0.01. All of 19 SMEs had low financial performance in the 3rd profile. SMEs with ROA higher than 0.002, but absolute liquidity were between 0.01 and 0.03 are grouped in the 4th profile. 25% of the SMEs were in financial distress in 4th profile. In the last profile, ROA was higher than 0.002, and absolute liquidity was higher than 0.01. All of the 56 SMEs had good financial performance in this profile.

According to the distressed SMEs or in another words risk profile of SMEs, ROA, profit margin and absolute liquidity were early warning signs for the SMEs.

If;
ROA was lower than and equal to 0.002
If;
ROA was lower than and equal to 0.002, and Profit margin was lower than 0.001,
If;
ROA was higher than 0.002, and
Absolute liquidity was lower than 0.01,
financial distress were indispensable for SMEs.

Table 7. Financial performance of SMEs

Profiles	FINANCIAL PERFORMANCE					
	Good		Poor		Total	
	n	%	n	%	n	%
1	0	0	49	100	49	100
2	1	33.33	2	66.67	3	100
3	0	0	19	100	19	100
4	3	75	1	25	4	100
5	56	100	0	0	56	100
Total	60	45.81	71	54.19	131	100

Figure 3. CHAID decision tree and financial profiles of SMEs

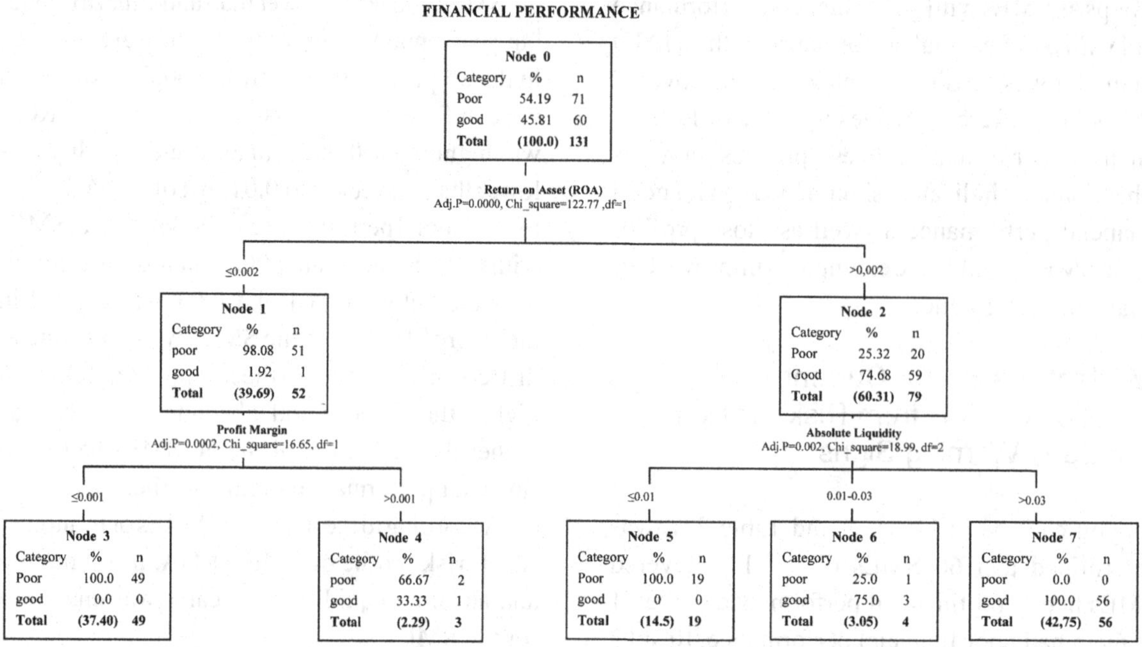

FINANCIAL PERFORMANCE

Node 0		
Category	%	n
Poor	54.19	71
good	45.81	60
Total	**(100.0)**	**131**

Return on Asset (ROA)
Adj.P=0.0000, Chi_square=122.77 ,df=1

≤0.002

Node 1		
Category	%	n
poor	98.08	51
good	1.92	1
Total	**(39.69)**	**52**

Profit Margin
Adj.P=0.0002, Chi_square=16.65, df=1

≤0.001

Node 3		
Category	%	n
Poor	100.0	49
good	0.0	0
Total	**(37.40)**	**49**

>0.001

Node 4		
Category	%	n
poor	66.67	2
good	33.33	1
Total	**(2.29)**	**3**

>0,002

Node 2		
Category	%	n
Poor	25.32	20
Good	74.68	59
Total	**(60.31)**	**79**

Absolute Liquidity
Adj.P=0.002, Chi_square=18.99, df=2

≤0.01

Node 5		
Category	%	n
Poor	100.0	19
good	0	0
Total	**(14.5)**	**19**

0.01-0.03

Node 6		
Category	%	n
poor	25.0	1
good	75.0	3
Total	**(3.05)**	**4**

>0.03

Node 7		
Category	%	n
poor	0.0	0
good	100.0	56
Total	**(42,75)**	**56**

Table 8. Profiles of SMEs

PROFILES	ROA	PROFIT MARGIN	ABSOLUTE LIQUDITY
1	≤ 0.002	≤0.001	
2	≤0.002	>0.001	
3	>0.002		≤0.01
4	>0.002		0.01-0.03
5	>0.002		>0.01

Table 9. Road maps

ROAD MAPS	PROFILES	ROA	ABSOLUTE LIQUDITY
1	5	>0.002	>0.01
2	4	>0.002	0.01-0.03

V. Description of Roadmap for SME

According to Figure 3, risk profiles of SMEs were determined. Therefore, the best risk Profile that contained SMEs without risk was 5. Then, every firm tries to be in Profile 5. There were two variables ROA and absolute liquidity related with Profile 5, as seen in Table 9. If any SME want to be in Profile 5, the SME must make arrangements to make values ROA >0.002 and absolute liquidity >0.01.

Second best Profile was 4. There were two variables ROA and absolute liquidity related with Profile 4. If any SME wants to be in Profile 4, the SME must make arrangements to make values ROA >0.002 and absolute liquidity between 0.01 and 0.03.

CONCLUSION

Early warning system is a technique of analysis that is used to predict the achievement condition of enterprises and to decrease the risk of financial crisis. By the application of this technique of analysis, the condition and possible risks of an enterprise can be identified with quantity. An EWS for risk detection of SMEs was introduced in this chapter. Firstly, definition and financial issues of SMEs, impacts of financial crisis on SMEs and EWSs were discussed in the background of chapter. Then, EWS model based on data mining and an implementation on SMEs were presented. Model of EWS was developed by using Chi-Square Automatic Interaction Detector (CHAID) Decision Tree Algorithm. Implementation of EWS applied with real data of SMEs and data of SMEs listed in Istanbul Stock Exchange (ISE) in 2007 was used for this purpose.

Risk management has become a vital topic for all institutions, especially for SMEs, banks, credit rating firms, and insurance companies. The financial crisis has pushed all firms to active risk management and control financial risks. All enterprises need EWS to warn against risks and prevent from financial distress. But, when we consider the issues of poor business performance, insufficient information and insufficiencies of managers in finance education, it is clear that EWS is vital for SMEs. Benefits of an EWS can summarize as early warning before financial distress, road maps for good credit rating, better business deci-

sion making, and greater likelihood of achieving business plan and objectives.

Developing practical solutions will not only help to SMEs but also to the economies of countries. Having information about their financial risk, monitoring this financial risk and knowing the required roadmap for the improvement of financial risk are very important for SMEs to take the required precautions. Data mining, that is the reflection of information technologies in the area of strategical decision support, develops a system for finding solutions to the financial administration as one of the most suitable application area for SMEs as the vital point of economy.

In this study, we developed a financial EWS based on financial risk. But, it is not enough for to understand and manage the financial risks that can cause insolvency and distress. Managers need also to manage operational risks that can arise from execution of a company's business functions, and strategically risks that can undermine the viability of their business models and strategies or reduce their growth prospects and damage their market value. For this reason we suggest to develop EWS that contain all kind of risk factors.

Some of the contributions EWSs that are expected can be summarized as:

- Determine financial performance and position of firms
- Determine financial strategies by minimum level of finance education and information
- Financial and operational risk detection
- Roadmaps for risk reduction
- Prevent for financial distress
- Decrease the possibility of bankruptcy
- Decrease risk rate
- Efficient usage of financial resources
- By efficiency
- Increase the competition capacity
- New potential for export
- Decrease the unemployment rate
- More taxes for government
- Adaptation to BASEL II Capital Accord

EWSs should develop and implement in every business, to provide information relating to the actions of individual officers, supervisors, and specific units or divisions. In deciding what information to include in their early warning system, business should balance the need for sufficient information for the system to be comprehensive with the need for a system that is not too cumbersome to be utilized effectively. The system should provide supervisors and managers with both statistical information and descriptive information about the function of business.

Other application areas of EWSs are marketing, fraud detection, manipulation, and health. Also, EWS based on data mining should give signs about natural risks (rainfall, landslides, volcanic eruption, earthquakes, floods, drought, tornados); lifecycle risks (illness, injury, disability, hungers, food poisoning, pan epidemics, old ages and death); social risks (crimes, domestic violences, drug addiction, terrorism, gangs, civil strife, war, social upheaval, child abuses); economic risks (unemployment, harvest failure, resettlement, financial or currency crisis, market trading shocks); administrative and political risks (ethnic discrimination, ethnic conflict, riots, chemical and biological mass destruction, administrative induced accidents and disasters, political induced malfunction on social programs, coup); and environmental risks (pollution, deforestation, nuclear disasters, soil salinities, acid rains, global warming).

REFERENCES

Abouzeedan, A., & Busler, M. (2004). Typology analysis of performance models of small and medium size enterprises (SMEs). *Journal of International Entrepreneurship, 2*(1-2), 155–177. doi:10.1023/B:JIEN.0000026911.03396.2d

Abumustafa, N. I. (2006). Development of an early warning model for currency crises in emerging economies: An empirical study among Middle Eastern countries. *International Journal of Management, 23*(3), 403.

ADBI Institute. (2010), *Enterprise risk management during the global financial crisis: Sharing global experience.* Presented at 2nd Annual Thought Leadership Conference, Bejing.

Altman, E. (1968). Financial ratios, discriminant analysis and the prediction of corporate bankruptcy. *The Journal of Finance,* (September): 589–609. doi:10.2307/2978933

Altman, E. I., Haldeman, G., & Narayanan, P. (1977). Zeta Analysis: A new model to identify bancrupcy risk of corporations. *Journal of Banking & Finance,* (June): 29–54. doi:10.1016/0378-4266(77)90017-6

Arias, C. A., Martinez, A. C., & Gracia, J. (2003). *Capital structure and sensitivity in SME definition: A panel data investigation.* Retrieved December, 2009, from http://ssrn.com/abstract=549082.

Audretsch, D., van der Horst, R., Kwaak, T., & Thurik, R. (2009). *First section of the annual report on EU small and medium-sized enterprises.* Retrieved December, 2009, from http://ec.europa.eu/enterprise/policies/sme/files/craft/sme_perf_review/doc_08/spr08_anual_reporten.pdf

Barniv, R., & Hathorn, J. (1997). The merger or insolvency alternative in the insurance industry. *The Journal of Risk and Insurance, 64*(1), 89–113. doi:10.2307/253913

Beaver, W. (1966). Financial ratios as predictors of failure. *Journal of Accounting Research, 4,* 71–111. doi:10.2307/2490171

Beck, T., Kunt, A., & Peria, M. S. (2008). *Bank financing for SMEs around the world, Policy Research Working Paper*, 4785. Retrieved October, 2009, from https://www.researchgate.net/publication/23970207_Bank_Financing_for_SMEs_around_the_World_Drivers_Obstacles_Business_Models_and_Lending_Practices

Berg, A., Borensztein, E., & Pattillo, C. (2004). *Assessing early warning systems: How have they worked in practice? IMF Working Paper*, March 2004. Retrieved October, 2009, from http://www.ksri.org/bbs/files/research02/wp0452.pdf.

Berliet, J. (2008). *Lessons from the financial crisis for directors and CEOs of insurance companies, risk management: The current financial crisis, lessons learned and future implications*. Institute of ActuARies

Bhaird, C., & Lucey, B. (2006). *Capital structure and the financing of SMEs: Empirical evidence from an Irish survey*. Working Paper, Retrieved October, 2009, from http://www.cebr.dk/upload/ciaranmacanbhaird.pdf

Bhairdi, C., & Lucey, B. (2005). Determinants of the capital structure of SMEs: A seemingly unrelated regression approach. *Small Business Economics*. doi:.doi:10.1007/s11187-008-9162-6

Bitzenis, A., & Nito, E. (2005). Obstacles to entrepreneurship in a transition business environment: The case of Albania. *Journal of Small Business and Enterprise Development, 12*(4), 564–578. doi:10.1108/14626000510628234

Brockett, P. L., Golden, L. L., Jang, J., & Yang, C. (2006). A comparison of neural network, statistical methods and variable. *The Journal of Risk and Insurance, 73*(3), 397–419. doi:10.1111/j.1539-6975.2006.00181.x

Bukvic, V., & Bartlett, W. (2003). Financial barriers to SME growth in Slovenia. *Economic and Business Review, 5*(3), 161–181.

Canovas, G. H., & Solano, P. M. (2006). Banking relationships: Effect on debt terms for Spanish firms. *Journal of Small Business Management, 44*(3), 315–334. doi:10.1111/j.1540-627X.2006.00174.x

Chang, S., Chang, H., Lin, C., & Kao, S. (2003). The effect of organizational attributes on the adoption of data mining techniques in the financial service industry: An empirical study in Taiwan. *International Journal of Management, 20*(1), 497–503.

Commission Recommendation of 6 May 2003 Concerning the Definition of Micro, Small and Medium-sized Enterprises (2003/361/EC), L 124/36 2003. *Official Journal of the European Union*. Retrieved December, 2009, from http://eur-lex.europa.eu/LexUriServ/LexUriServ.do?uri=OJ:L:2003:124:0036:0041:en:PDF

Danset, R. (1998). *Comparison between the financial structures of SME versus large enterprises*. Final Report for the DG II European Community.

Daskalakis, N., & Psillaki, M. (2005). *The determinants of capital structure of the SMEs: Evidence from the Greek and the French firms*. Paper presented at the XXIInd Symposium on Banking and Monetary Economics, Strasbourg.

Daskalakis, N., & Psillaki, M. (2008). Do countries or firm factors explain capital structure? Evidence from SMEs in France and Greece. *Applied Financial Economics, 18*(2), 87–97. doi:10.1080/09603100601018864

Davis, E. P., & Karim, D. (2008). Could early warning systems have helped to predict the subprime crisis? *National Institute Economic Review, 206*(1), 35–47. doi:10.1177/0027950108099841

Deakin, E. B. (1972). A discriminat analysis of predictors of business failure. *Journal of Accounting Research, 10*(1), 167–179. doi:10.2307/2490225

Derby, B. L. (2003). Data mining for improper payments. *The Journal of Government Financial Management, 52*(1), 10–13.

Edison, H. J. (2003). Do indicators of financial crises work? An evaluation of an early earning system. *International Journal of Finance & Economics, 8*(1), 11–53. doi:10.1002/ijfe.197

Eklund, T., Back, B., Vanharanta, H., & Visa, A. (2003). Using the self- organizing map as a visualization tool in financial benchmarking. *Information Visualization, 2*(3), 171–181. doi:10.1057/palgrave.ivs.9500048

El-Shazly, A. (2006). Early warning of currency crises: An econometric analysis for Egypt. *The Middle East Business and Economic Review, 18*(1), 34–48.

EU. Europen Commission. (2003). *2003 Observatory of European SMEs: SMEs in Europe.* Technical Paper No.7.

European Association of Craft. Small and Medium-Sized Enterprises (UEAPME). (2009). *European SME Finance Survey.* Retrieved October, 2009, from http://www.ueapme.com/IMG/pdf/090728_SME-finance_survey.pdf

Fayyad, G., Piatetsky-Shapiro, P., & Symth, P. (1996). From data mining to knowledge discovery in databases. *AI Magazine, 17*(3), 37–54.

Frawley, W., Piatetsky-Shapiro, G., & Matheus, C. (1992). Knowledge discovery in databases: An overview. *AI Magazine,* (Fall): 213–228.

Hand, D., Mannila, H., & Smyth, P. (2001). *Principles of data mining.* Cambridge, MA: MIT Press.

Hodorogel, R. G. (2009). The economic crisis and its effects on SMEs. *Theoretical and Applied Economics, 5*(34), 79–89.

Inegbenebor, A. U. (2006). Financing small and medium industries in Nigeria-case study of the small and medium industries equity investment scheme: Emprical research finding. *Journal of Financial Management and Analysis, 19*(1), 71–80.

Jacobs, L. J., & Kuper, G. H. (2004). *Indicators of financial crises do work! An early-warning system for six Asian countries.* CCSO Working Paper 13. Department of Economics, University of Groningen, the Netherlands.

Jones, F. (1987). Current techniques in bankruptcy prediction. *Journal of Accounting Literature, 6,* 131–164.

Karim, D. (2006). *Comparing early warning systems for banking crises.* Unpublished doctoral dissertation, Brunel University, UK.

Katz, M. (2006). *Multivariable Analysis: A Practical Guide for Clinicians.* New York: Churchill-Livingstone. doi:10.1017/CBO9780511616761

Klapper, L., Allende, V. S., & Zaidi, R. (2006). *A firm level analysis of small and medium size enterprise financing in Poland.* World Bank Policy Research Working Paper No: 3983.

Kloptchenko, A., Eklund, T., Karlsson, J., Back, B., Vanhatanta, H., & Visa, A. (2004). Combining data and text mining techniques for analysing financial reports. *Intelligent Systems in Accounting Finance and Management, 12*(1), 29–41. doi:10.1002/isaf.239

Koyuncugil, A. S. (2006). *Fuzzy Data Mining and its application to capital markets.* Unpublished doctoral dissertation, Ankara University, Ankara.

Koyuncugil, A. S., & Ozgulbas, N. (2006a). *Financial profiling of SMEs: An application by Data Mining. The European Applied Business Research (EABR).* Conference, Clute Institute for Academic Research.

Koyuncugil, A. S., & Ozgulbas, N. (2006b). Is there a specific measure for financial performance of SMEs? *The Business Review, Cambridge, 5*(2), 314–319.

Koyuncugil, A. S., & Ozgulbas, N. (2006c). *Determination of factors affected financial distress of SMEs listed in ISE by Data Mining. In 3ʳᵈ Congress of SMEs and Productivity.* Istanbul: KOSGEB and Istanbul Kultur University.

Koyuncugil, A. S., & Ozgulbas, N. (2007a). *Developing financial early warning system via data mining.* Paper presented in 4ᵗʰ Congress of SMEs and Productivity, Istanbul.

Koyuncugil, A. S., & Ozgulbas, N. (2007b). Detecting financial early warning signs in Istanbul Stock Exchange by data mining. *International Journal of Business Research,* VII(3), Koyuncugil, A. S., & Ozgulbas, N. (2008a). Strengths and weaknesses of SMEs listed in ISE: A CHAID Decision Tree application. *Journal of Dokuz Eylul University. Faculty of Economics and Administrative Sciences, 23*(1), 1–22.

Koyuncugil, A. S., & Ozgulbas, N. (2008b). Early warning system for SMEs as a financial risk detector. H. Rahman (Ed), *Data mining applications for empowering knowledge societies* (pp. 221-240). Hershey, PA: Idea Group Inc. Global.

Koyuncugil, A. S., & Ozgulbas, N. (2009a). *Measuring and hedging operational risk by data mining.* Paper presented in the World Summit on Economic-Financial Crisis and International Business, Washington, DC.

Koyuncugil, A. S., & Ozgulbas, N. (2009b). An intelligent financial early warning System model based on data mining for SMEs. *International Conference on Future Computer and Communication, Kuala Lumpur, Malaysia.*

Kumar, N., Krovi, R., & Rajagopalan, B. (1997). Financial decision support with hybrid genetic and neural based modeling tools. *European Journal of Operational Research, 103,* 339–349. doi:10.1016/S0377-2217(97)00124-0

Kyong, J. O., Tae, Y. K., Chiho, K., & Suk, J. L. (2006). Using neural networks to tune the fluctuation of daily financial condition indicator for financial crisis forecasting. In *Advances in Artificial Intelligence.* DOI: 10.1007/11941439_65 Volume 4304/2006

Laitinen, K., & Chong, H. G. (1998). Early warning system for crisis in SMEs: Preliminary evidence from Finland and the UK. *Journal of Small Business and Enterprise Development, 6*(1), 89–102. doi:10.1108/EUM0000000006665

Larsen, K., & Bjerkeland, K. M. (2005). Are unexpected loan losses for small enterprises than for large enterprises? *Norges Bank Economic Bulletin, 76*(3), 126–133.

Lee, K. C., Han, I., & Kwon, Y. (1996). Hybrid neural network models for bankruptcy predictions. *Decision Support Systems, 18,* 63–73. doi:10.1016/0167-9236(96)00018-8

Lee, S. J., & Siau, K. (2001). A review of data mining techniques. *Industrial Management & Data Systems, 101*(1), 41–46. doi:10.1108/02635570110365989

Lopez, A. S. (2007). *Improving access to credit of SME's in Puerto Rico: Exploring variables to Forceast small business loan events.* Retrieved October, 2009, from http://selene.uab.es/dep-economia-empresa/Jornadas/Papers/4-12-2007/Alizabeth_Sanchez.pdf

Maher, M., & Andersson, T. (2000). *Corporate governance: Effects on firm performance and economic growth, convergence and diversity of corporate governance regimes and capital markets.* London: Oxford University Press.

Meyer, P. A., & Pifer, H. W. (1970). Prediction of bank failures. *The Journal of Finance*, 25(4), 853–886. doi:10.2307/2325421

Mohnen, A., & Nasev, J. (2005). *Growth of small and medium-sized firms in Germany*. Retrieved October, 2009, from http://ssrn.com/abstract=852785

Monk, E., & Wagner, B. (2006). *Concepts in Enterprise Resource Planning* (2nd ed.). Boston: Thomson Course Technology.

Nazem, S., & Shin, B. (1999). Data mining: New arsenal for strategic decision making. *Journal of Database Management*, 10(1), 39–42.

Nguyen, D. K., & Ramachandran, N. (2006). Capital structure in small and medium sized enterprises: The case of Vietnem. *ASEAN Economic Bulletin*, 23(2), 192–208. doi:10.1355/AE23-2D

Nomenclature statistique des activités économiques dans la Communauté européenne (NACE). (n.d.). Retrived October, 2009, from http://epp.eurostat.ec.europa.eu/statistics_explained/index.php/SMEs

OECD. (2005). *SME and Entrepreneurship Outlook*. Centre for Entrepreneurship, SMEs and Local Development OECD.

OECD. (2009a). *Policy responses to the economic crisis: Investing in innovation for long-term growth*. Retrieved December 2009, from http://www.oecd.org/dataoecd/59/45/42983414.pdf.

OECD. (2009b). *The observatory of European SMEs, 2007 observatory survey*. Retrieved from http://ec.europa.eu/enterprise/policies/sme/facts-figures-analysis/sme-observatory/index_en.htm#h2-2007-observatory-survey

OECD. (2009 c). *The impact of the global crisis on SME and entrepreneurship financing and policy Responses*. Retrieved December 2009, from http://www.oecd.org/dataoecd/40/34/43183090.pdf

Ogiujiba, K. K., Ohuche, F. K., & Adenuga, A. O. (2004). *Credit availability to small and medium scale enterprises in Nigeria: Importance of new capital base for banks*. Retrieved October, 2009, from http://129.3.20.41/eps/mac/papers/0411/0411002.pdf

Ozgulbas, N., & Koyuncugil, A. S. (2006). Profiling and determining the strengths and weaknesses of SMEs listed in ISE by the Data Mining Decision Trees Algorithm CHAID. In *10th National Finance Symposium, Izmir*.

Ozgulbas, N., Koyuncugil, A. S., & Yilmaz, F. (2006). Identifying the effect of firm size on financial performance of SMEs. *The Business Review, Cambridge*, 5(2), 162–167.

Pantalone, C., & Platt, M. (1987). Predicting failures of savings and loan associations. *AREUEA Journal*, 15, 46–64.

Paranque, B. (1995). *Equity and rate of return: Are small manufacturing firms handicapped by their own success?* Paper presented at the meeting International Council for Small Business 40th World Conference, Sydney.

Requejo, M. (2002). *SME vs. large enterprise leverage: Determinants and structural relations*. Retrieved October, 2009, from http://ssrn.com/abstract=302400 or DOI: 10.2139/ssrn.302400

Ross, S., Westerfield, R., & Jaffe, J. (2008). *Corporate finance* (8th ed.). New York: McGraw Hill Ryerson Limited.

Salas, V., & Saurina, J. (2002). Credit risk in two institutional regimes: Spanish commercial and savings banks. *Journal of Financial Services Research*, 22(3), 203–224. doi:10.1023/A:1019781109676

Sanchez, A., & Marin, G. S. (2005). Strategic orientation, management characteristics, and performance: A study of Spanish SMEs. *Journal of Small Business Management*, 43(3), 287–309.

Sarno, D. (2005). Liquidity constraint on the production of firms in Southern Italy. *Small Business Economics, 25*(2), 133–146. doi:10.1007/s11187-003-6452-x

Shirakawa, M. (2009). Coping with financial crisis - Japan's experiences and current global financial crisis. *BIS Review,* 23.

Sogorb-Mira, F. (2001). *On capital structure in the small and medium enterprises: The Spanish case.* working paper series, Instituto de Estudios Europeos – Universidad San Pablo CEU, Madrid. Retrieved October, 2009, from http://ssrn.com/abstract=277090 or DOI: 10.2139/ssrn.277090.

Sogorb-Mira, F. (2005). How SME uniqueness affects capital structure: Evidence from A 1994–1998 Spanish data panel. *Small Business Economics, 25*(5), 447–457. doi:10.1007/s11187-004-6486-8

Sormani, A. (2005). Debt causes problems for SMEs. *European Venture Capital & Capital Equity Journal, 1,* 1.

SPSS. (2001). *AnswerTree 3.0 User's Guide.* Chicago: SPSS Inc.

Taffler, R. J., & Tisshaw, H. (1977). Going, going, gone-four factors which factors which predict. *Accountancy,* (March), 50-54.

Tagoe, N., Nyarko, E., & Amarh, E. A. (2005). Financial challenges facing urban SMEs under financial sector liberalization in Ghana. *Journal of Small Business Management, 43*(3), 331–343.

Tam, K. Y., & Kiang, M. Y. (1992). Managerial applications of neural networks: The case of bank failure predictions. *Decision Sciences, 38,* 926–948.

Teruel, P. J. G., & Solano, P. M. (2007). Effects of working capital management on SME profitability. *International Journal of Managerial Finance, 3*(2), 164–177. doi:10.1108/17439130710738718

The Hankyoreh. (2009). *The financial crisis and South Korea one year after.* Retrieved October, 2009, from http://english.hani.co.kr/arti/english_edition/e_business/376783.html

Thearling, K. (2004). *Data mining and analytic technologies.* Retrieved October, 2009, from hhtp://www.thearling.com/.

Tsuruta. D., & Xu, P. (2005). *Capital structure and survival of financial distressed SMEs in Japan.* Retrieved April, 2009, From (2005). http://www.rieti.go.jp/users/uesugi-iichiro/cf-workshop/pdf/tsuruta-xu.pdf

Turkish Statistic Institute (TSI). (2002). *General industrial enterprise census, April 2006.* Retrieved April, 2009, from hhtp://www.die.gov.tr/TURKISH/SONIST/GSIS/ gsisII141003.pdf

Wahyu, I., & Swadaya, B. (2009). *Impact the financial crisis for SMEs in Indonesia.* Paper presented at the Regional Conference on the Impact of Financial Crisis on Vulnerable Sectors: Civil Society Voices and ASEAN, Jakarta.

Warner, J. (1977). Bankruptcy costs: some evidence. *The Journal of Finance, 32,* 337–347. doi:10.2307/2326766

World Bank. (WB). (2009a). *The financial crisis: Implications for developing countries.* Retrieved December, 2009, from http://econ.worldbank.org/WBSITE/EXTERNAL/EXTDEC/0,contentMDK:21974412~isCURL:Y~pagePK:64165401~piPK:64165026~theSitePK:469372,00.html

World Bank. (WB). (2009b). *Survey: Eastern European businesses report long-term impact of financial crisis.* Retrieved December, 2009, from http://www.enterprisesurveys.org/FinancialCrisis/

Yang, B., Ling, X. L., Hai, J., & Jing, X. (2001). An early warning system for loan risk assessment using artificial neural Networks. *Knowledge-Based Systems, 14*(5-6), 303–306. doi:10.1016/S0950-7051(01)00110-1

Zavgren, C. (1985). Assessing the vulnerability to failure of American industrial firms: A logistics analysis. *Journal of Accounting Research, 22*, 59–82.

Zmijewski, M. E. (1984). Methodological issues related to the estimation of financial distress prediction models. *Journal of Accounting Research,* (Supplement), 59–82. doi:10.2307/2490859

KEY TERMS AND DEFINITIONS

Data Mining: Collection of evolved statistical analysis, machine learning and pattern recognition methods via intelligent algorithms which are using for automated uncovering and extraction process of hidden predictional information, patterns, relations, similarities or dissimilarities in (huge) data.

CHAID (CHi-Square Automatic Interaction Detector): One of the most popular and updated decision tree algorithm in data mining methods which is using for segmentation and it uses Chi-square metric as its

Early Warning System (EWS): A system which is using for predicting the success level, probable anomalies and is reducing crisis risk of cases, affairs transactions, systems, phenomenons, firms and people. Furthermore, their current situations and probable risks can be identified quantitatively.

Financial Risk: Risk shows that a firm is unable to meet its financial obligations. Financial risk is primarily a function of the relative amount of debt that the firm uses to finance its assets.

Financial Performance: Measure and evaluate of how well a company is using financial resources to be profitable.

Financial Distress: A stage before bankruptcy where a company's creditors are not being paid or are paid with significant difficulty.

Financial Crisis: Crisis in the financial sector and the financial markets.

Risk Management: Identification and evaluation of risk, and then selection and adaptaion of the most appropriate method for hedging risk.

Business Performance: Efficiency of financial, human, material and all resources of a business.

Small and Medium Enterprises (SMEs): Firms with annual turn-over less than €50 million or with annual balance sheet less than €43 million are defined as SMEs in Europe.

Chapter 6
Designing an Early Warning System for Stock Market Crashes by Using ANFIS

Murat Acar
ISE Settlement and Custody Bank Inc., Turkey

Dilek Karahoca
Bahcesehir University, Turkey

Adem Karahoca
Bahcesehir University, Turkey

ABSTRACT

This chapter focuses on building a financial early warning system (EWS) to predict stock market crashes by using stock market volatility and rising stock prices. The relation of stock market volatility with stock market crashes is analyzed empirically. Also, Istanbul Stock Exchange (ISE) national 100 index data used to achieve better results from the view point of modeling purpose. A risk indicator of stock market crash is computed to predict crashes and to give an early warning signal. Various data mining classifiers are compared to obtain the best practical solution for the financial early warning system. Adaptive neuro fuzzy inference system (ANFIS) model was proposed to forecast stock market crashes efficiently. Also, ANFIS was explained in detail as a training tool for the EWS. The empirical results show that the fuzzy inference system has advantages to gain successful results for financial crashes.

INTRODUCTION

Failures in financial systems may cause financial crises and then the latter may develop into economic fundamental crises that might not be always inevitable results. Economic crises are characterized by sharp falls in both asset prices and currency values. Failures could lead to a stock market crash that is often defined as a sharp dip in share prices of equities listed on the stock exchanges. Rising stock prices and excessive economic optimism may also cause a stock market crash. Although there is no a numerically specific definition of a stock market crash, it can be defined as double-digit percentage losses in a stock market index over a period of several days.

DOI: 10.4018/978-1-61692-865-0.ch006

Stock market crashes can provoke recessions, lead to failures in the financial system or consume years of savings and pensions instantaneously. Testing for the existence of log-periodic behavior and attempting to forecast crashes are thus important for financial regulators, risk and portfolio managers, policy makers and financial institutions (Cajueiro, et al., 2009). Generally, in any given field, crashes are extremely difficult to forecast accurately. Forecasting of crashes is one of the most popular research topics in finance. Many theoretical and empirical studies have been done to forecast crashes and many models have been developed to predict the occurrence of such crashes.

With increasing globalization and financial integration, crises in a country could make other countries highly vulnerable to shocks. The United States (US) subprime mortgage crisis also hit the Turkish economy in 2008. The Istanbul Stock Exchange (ISE) decreased from 54708 to 26864 in 2008 because of the rapid decrease in foreign markets and insufficient fresh money entrance. The ISE is the only securities exchange in Turkey. The ISE is a dynamic and growing emerging market with an increasing number of publicly traded companies, state-of-the-art technology and strong foreign participation. The ISE provides a transparent and fair trading environment not only for domestic participants, but also for foreign issuers and investors (http://www.ise.org/). Iseri indicates that the ISE has very high chaotic phenomena. So prediction on chaotic phenomena is very complex (Iseri, et al., 2008). Investors are intensely interested in market directions and possibilities of stock market crashes. Therefore behavior patterns of risky market days should be defined. Relationships among variables derived from the historical financial data should be discovered and a financial early warning system (EWS) should be constructed to forecast stock market crashes. Financial early warning systems have evolved considerably during the last decade thanks to data mining.

Data mining is the automatization of the process of finding interesting patterns in datasets. Methodologies in data mining come from machine learning and statistics. Machine learning is connected to computer science and artificial intelligence and is concerned with finding relations and regularities in data that can be translated into general truths. The aim of machine learning is the reproduction of the data-generating process, allowing analysts to generalize from the observed data to new, unobserved cases (Giudici, 2003).

Early warning systems in finance are vital tools for monitoring and detecting events in financial markets to predict upcoming financial crises. The world financial crisis in 2008 has put an emphasis on the importance of prediction of crises in both academic and industrial senses. It's now more necessary to develop an efficient and predictive model to give early warning signals and to anticipate crises. From a policy perspective, EWS models that help to reliably anticipate financial crises constitute an important tool for policy makers if they are employed carefully and sensibly. Many financial crises over the past few decades had devastating social, economic and political consequences. Developing reliable EWS models therefore can be of substantial value by allowing policy makers to obtain clearer signals about when and how to take pre-emptive action in order to mitigate or even prevent financial turmoil. It should be stressed that EWS models cannot replace the sound judgment of the policy maker to guide policy, but they can play an important complementary role as a neutral and objective measure of vulnerability (Bussiere & Fratzscher, 2006).

Forecasting simply means understanding which variables lead or help to predict other variables, when many variables interact in volatile markets. This means looking at the past to see what variables are significant leading indicators of the behavior of other variables. It also means a better understanding of the timing of lead–lag relations among many variables, understanding the statistical significance of these lead–lag relationships, and learning which variables are the more important ones to watch as signals for further developments in other returns (McNelis, 2005).

In this study, the main motivation is developing reliable EWS by using ANFIS. High stock market volatility and excessive stock prices make stock markets more risky. ISE national 100 index data was used to measure the dynamic change of volatility of ISE. A model was developed to predict the occurrence of such crises by using stock market volatility and rising stock prices or rising ISE national 100 index. Five variables as input variables and one variable as an output variable were included in the model. The output variable is a risk indicator of crisis which represents the probability of a stock market crash. If the probability is strong, it should be interpreted as a warning signal that a stock market crash is more likely to happen. Adaptive neuro fuzzy inference system (ANFIS) is used in the model to give early warning signals and these signals help forecasting any stock market crashes before it happens. Also, simple logistic, logistic regression, and artificial neural networks of multi layer Perceptron was used for benchmarking purpose.

The rest of the chapter is organized as follows: Section 2 surveys the related works with developing EWS. In section 3, variables and data mining methods are explained. Respectively, Section 4 reports the results of data mining classifiers and detailed explanation of the ANFIS model. Finally, conclusions are drawn in Section 5.

BACKGROUND

There are various types of financial crises: currency crises, banking crises, sovereign debt crises, private sector debt crises, equity market crises. Most of the early warning systems was developed so far have tried to predict currency crises, banking crises or both. Previous early warning systems of financial crises have been used methods that

fall into two broad categories. One approach uses logit or probit models, whereas the other extracts signals from a range of indicators (Bussiere & Fratzscher, 2006).

The advantage of logit or probit model is to represent all the information contained in the variables by giving the probability of the crisis. The disadvantage is that it cannot gauge the precise forecasting ability of each variable though it can give the significance level of each variable. In other words, the ability of the correct signal and false alarm for each variable cannot be seen exactly from the model. On the other hand, the signal approach can show the contribution of each variable for the crisis prediction. Besides, it can also offer a summary indicator by calculating the conditional probability given the number of indicators used for signaling (Lin, et al., 2006).

Frankel and Rose (1996) use a panel of annual data for over one hundred developing countries from 1971 through 1992 to characterize currency crashes. They define a currency crash as a large change of the nominal exchange rate that is also a substantial increase in the rate of change of the nominal depreciation. They examine the composition of the debt as well as its level, and a variety of other macroeconomic, external and foreign factors. Factors are significantly related to crash incidence, especially output growth, the rate of change of domestic credit, and foreign interest rates. A low ratio of foreign direct investment to debt is consistently associated with a high likelihood of a crash.

Kaminsky, et al. (1998) examines the empirical evidence on currency crisis and proposes a specific early warning system. This system involves monitoring the evolution of several indicators that tend to exhibit an unusual behavior in periods preceding a crisis. When an indicator exceeds a certain threshold value, this is interpreted as a warning "signal" that a currency crisis may take place within the next 24 months. The threshold values are calculated so as to strike a balance between the risk of having many false signals and the risk of missing the crisis altogether. Also, since the group of indicators that are issuing signals would be identified, this helps provide information about the source(s) of problems that underlie a crisis.

Peltonen's study (2006) analyzes the predictability of emerging market currency crises by comparing the often used probit model to a multilayer perceptron artificial neural network (ANN) model. The main result of the study is that both the probit and the ANN model are able to correctly signal crises reasonably well in-sample, and that the ANN model slightly outperforms the probit model. In contrast to the findings in the earlier literature on currency crises, the ability of the models to predict currency crises out-of-sample is found to be weak. Only in the case of the Russian crisis (1998) both models are able to signal its occurrence well in advance. In addition, certain economic factors are found to be related to the emerging market currency crises. These factors are the contagion effect, the prevailing de facto exchange rate regime, the current account and government budget deficits, as well as real gross domestic product (GDP) growth.

Until now, however, a few studies have been done on stock market crises. Kim and et al. (2004) studied for modeling EWSs by training classifiers for the distinctive features of economic crises. An economic crisis always makes it possible to consider EWS as a pattern classifier between critical and normal economic situations. To find a better classifier for training EWSs, logistic discrimination (LD) model, decision tree (DT), support vector machine (SVM), neuro-fuzzy model (NF), and artificial neural networks (ANN) are considered among various classifiers. Each of these classifiers has its own strength and weakness, which might work either positively or negatively during training EWS. Kim defines five classifiers to compare in terms of their performances, which is done by building EWS based on each classifier for Korean economy, which had experienced a severe economic crisis in 1997. As a concluding remark of his studies, ANN is suggested as a better clas-

sifier and is argued that its major drawback, over fitting might work positively for training EWS.

Levy (2008) also analyzes stock market crashes. He states that stock market crashes are traumatic events that affect the lives of millions of people around the globe and have tremendous economic implications. Crashes are not only dramatic, but often completely unexpected. Levy suggests that spontaneous market crashes can be explained by a 'social phase transition' mechanism similar to statistical mechanics phase transitions. The analysis suggests that dramatic crashes are a robust and inevitable property of financial markets. It also implies that market crashes should be preceded by an increase in price volatility, as empirically observed. Thus market crashes are a fundamental and unavoidable part of our world. However, he thinks early warning systems can be developed that may help minimize the damages. In the preceding section, data modeling and executed data mining methods are given in detail.

MATERIAL AND METHODS

Information Extraction

In this study, ISE national 100 index data is used to measure the dynamic change of volatility. Data set covers during the December 2007-December 2008. All variables are derived from ISE national 100 index (x_t) which are used to estimate early warning signals. Input variables are computed by using equations (1-5). Kim and et al.'s (2004) detailed analysis to select input variables to measure the volatility and their analysis. It is expected that the stock market must have shown a sudden increase of volatility as it headed into the crisis. Indeed, five input variables are considered to measure such a sudden volatility increase.

1. Istanbul Stock Exchange national 100 index (x_t),
2. Daily rise and fall rate (p_t),

3. Ten-day moving average of rise and fall rate ($\overline{p}_t$),
4. Ten-day moving variance of rise and fall rate (s_t^2)
5. Ratio of moving variance (r_t).

The frequency and amplitude of p_t reflects a sudden volatility increase of the stock market due to the coming crisis. The other variables $\overline{p}_t$, s_t^2 and r_t add an additional dimension to the volatility analysis. Clearly, s_t^2 measures the amount of variation of p_t, and r_t is found to be very useful to obtain specific dates of sudden volatility increase. In fact, one can easily observe that s_t^2 starts to increase from September and there was an obvious signal or flag at September 16 by r_t (i.e. r_t exceeds 4 on that date) which is an early warning signal. The variable $\overline{p}_t$ is included since it is a variable to smooth out fluctuations over the recent 10 days and then it would help creating a stable indicator. Note that a rather short period of 10 days for moving average is taken into account in order to obtain the visibly clear non-stationary of p_t. These input variables are calculated by formulas presented as follows:

$$[x_t] \tag{1}$$

$$[p_t=(x_t-x_{t-1})/x_{t-1}] \tag{2}$$

$$[\overline{p}_t = \sum_{i=t-9}^{t} p\,i/10] \tag{3}$$

$$[s_t^2=(1/10) \sum_{i=t-9}^{t} (pi - \overline{pt})^2] \tag{4}$$

$$[r_t=s_t^2/s_{t-1}^2] \tag{5}$$

The output variable or the stock market crash risk indicator contains normalized results of the multiplication of Istanbul Stock Exchange national 100 index (x_t) and the ten-day moving variance of rise and fall rate (s_t^2) values:

$$[\textit{the result}= x_t * s_t^2] \tag{6}$$

After normalization of the result values, the following rule set can be obtained:
If the result<0.2 then output=0.2,
Else If the result<0.4 then output=0.4,
Else If the result<0.6 then output=0.6,
Else If the result<0.8 then output=0.8,
Else output=1.

So the output variable was clustered into five intervals which are 0.2, 0.4, 0.6, 0.8 and 1. The output value 1 means the most risky value in the stock market and if the output value is 1, a stock market crash likely will happens in the following days. Actually, 5 to 8 output class is accepted well form for classification purpose. Therefore, dataset clustered 5 classes to obtain well form fuzzy classes. But, when the dataset coverage is good enough, it is better to use k-means, fuzzy c-means or another clustering technique to partitioning classes dynamically.

All input and output data is divided into three parts as training data set(498 Records), testing data set(498 Records) and checking data set(498 Records). Training data is used for model building, testing data is used for model validation and checking data is used for model evaluation.

In the following section, definitions of data mining methods are given which are used in this study. Following data mining methods are Adaptive neuro fuzzy inference system (ANFIS), Simple logistic (SL), Logistic regression (LR), and Multilayer perceptron (MLP). Matlab and Weka were used as data mining tools. Weka has not ANFIS thus, ANFIS was performed in Matlab and others were performed in Weka (Witten & Frank, 2005).

The MATLAB is a high-performance language for technical computing. It integrates computation, visualization, and programming in an easy-to-use environment where problems and solutions

Figure 1. Istanbul Stock Exchange national 100 index of 2008 (xt)

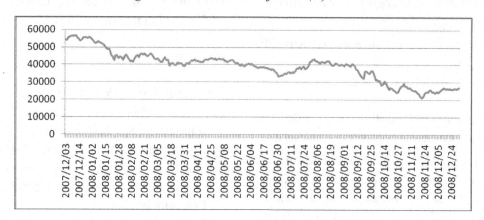

are expressed in familiar mathematical notation. Typical uses include math and computation, algorithm development, data acquisition, modeling, simulation, and prototyping, data analysis, exploration, and visualization, scientific and engineering graphics, application development, including graphical user interface building (The MathWorks, 2008a).

In this study, Fuzzy Logic Toolbox was used for rule generation. Fuzzy Logic Toolbox software is a collection of functions built on the MATLAB technical computing environment. It provides tools for you to create and edit fuzzy inference systems (FISs) and rules within the framework of MATLAB (The MathWorks, 2008b; Sivanandam, 2007).

The Weka workbench is a collection of state-of-the-art machine learning algorithms and data preprocessing tools. It is designed so that you can quickly try out existing methods on new datasets in flexible ways. It provides extensive support for the whole process of experimental data mining, including preparing the input data, evaluating learning schemas statistically, and visualizing the input data and the result of learning. As well as a wide variety of learning algorithms, it includes a wide range of preprocessing tools. This diverse and comprehensive toolkit is accessed through a common interface so that its users can compare different methods and identify those that are most

appropriate for the problem at hand. Weka was developed at the University of Waikato in New Zealand, and the name stands for Waikato Environment for Knowledge Analysis (WEKA). The system is written in Java and distributed under the terms of the GNU General Public License. It runs on almost any platform and has been tested under Linux, Windows, and Macintosh operating systems—and even on a personal digital assistant. It provides a uniform interface to many different learning algorithms, along with methods for pre- and post-processing and for evaluating the result of learning schemas on any given dataset (Witten & Frank, 2005).

Next section argues the ANFIS structure and architecture for how we can generate fuzzy rules for obtaining best prediction results.

Adaptive Neuro Fuzzy Inference System (ANFIS)

A Fuzzy Logic System (FLS) can be seen as a non-linear mapping from the input space to the output space. The mapping mechanism is based on the conversion of inputs from numerical domain to fuzzy domain with the use of fuzzy sets and fuzzifiers, and then applying fuzzy rules and fuzzy inference engine to perform the necessary operations in the fuzzy domain. The result is transformed back to the arithmetical domain using defuzzifiers.

The ANFIS approach uses Gaussian functions for fuzzy sets and linear functions for the rule outputs. The parameters of the network are the mean and standard deviation of the membership functions (antecedent parameters) and the coefficients of the output linear functions (consequent parameters). Fuzzy inference systems (FISs) are also known as fuzzy rule-based systems, fuzzy model, fuzzy expert system, and fuzzy associative memory. This is a major unit of a fuzzy logic system. The decision-making is an important part in the entire system. The FIS formulates suitable rules and based upon the rules the decision is made. This is mainly based on the concepts of the fuzzy set theory, fuzzy IF–THEN rules, and fuzzy reasoning. FIS uses "IF. . . THEN. . . " statements, and the connectors present in the rule statement are "OR" or "AND" to make the necessary decision rules. The basic FIS can take either fuzzy inputs or crisp inputs, but the outputs it produces are almost always fuzzy sets. When the FIS is used as a controller, it is necessary to have a crisp output. Therefore in this case defuzzification method is adopted to best extract a crisp value that best represents a fuzzy set. The most important two types of fuzzy inference method are Mamdani and Takagi–Sugeno method. Takagi–Sugeno method is used in this study. The Sugeno fuzzy model was proposed by Takagi, Sugeno, and Kang in an effort to formalize a system approach to generating fuzzy rules from an input–output data set. Sugeno fuzzy model is also known as Sugeno–Takagi model (Jang, 1992;1993).

A typical fuzzy rule in a Sugeno fuzzy model has the format

IF x is A and y is B THEN $z = f(x, y)$, $\qquad$ (7)

where A, B are fuzzy sets in the antecedent; $Z = f(x, y)$ is a crisp function in the consequent. Usually $f(x, y)$ is a polynomial in the input variables x and y, but it can be any other functions that can appropriately describe the output of the system within the fuzzy region specified by the antecedent of the rule. When $f(x, y)$ is a first-order polynomial, we have the *first-order* Sugeno fuzzy model. When f is a constant, we then have the *zero-order* Sugeno fuzzy model, which can be viewed either as a special case of the Mamdani FIS where each rule's consequent is specified by a fuzzy singleton, or a special case of Tsukamoto's fuzzy model where each rule's consequent is specified by a membership function of a step function centered at the constant. Moreover, a zero-order Sugeno fuzzy model is functionally equivalent to a radial basis function (RBF) network under certain minor constraints. The first two parts of the fuzzy inference process, fuzzifying the inputs and applying the fuzzy operator, are exactly the same. The main difference between Mamdani and Sugeno is that the Sugeno output membership functions are either linear or constant. A typical rule in a Sugeno fuzzy model has the following form (Jang, 1993; 1996):

IF Input 1 = x AND Input 2 = y, THEN Output is $z = ax + by + c$. $\qquad$ (8)

For a zero-order Sugeno model, the output level z is a constant ($a = b = 0$). The output level z_i of each rule is weighted by the firing strength w_i of the rule (Jang, 1996).

Rule 1: If X is A_1 and Y is B_1, then $f_1 = p_1 x + q_1 y + r_1$

Rule 2: If X is A_2 and Y is B_2, then $f_2 = p_2 x + q_2 y + r_1$ (9)

The fuzzy reasoning mechanism is summarized in Figure 2. Weighted averages are used in order to avoid extreme computational complexity in defuzzification processes.

The ANFIS learning algorithm is used to obtain these parameters. This learning algorithm is a hybrid algorithm consisting of the gradient descent and the least-squares estimate. Using this hybrid algorithm, the rule parameters are recursively

Figure 2. First-order Sugeno fuzzy model

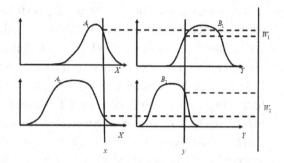

$$f_1 = p_1x + q_1y + r_1$$
$$f_2 = p_2x + q_2y + r_2$$

$$\Rightarrow \quad t = \frac{w_1 + f_1 + w_2 f_2}{w_1 + w_2}$$

$$= \overline{w_1} f_1 + \overline{w_2} f_2$$

updated until an acceptable error is reached. Iterations have two steps, one forward and one backward. In the forward pass, the antecedent parameters are fixed, and the consequent parameters are obtained using the linear least-squares estimate. In the backward pass, the consequent parameters are fixed, and the output error is back-propagated through this network, and the antecedent parameters are accordingly updated using the gradient descent method.

In the designing of ANFIS model, the number of membership functions, the number of fuzzy rules, and the number of training epochs are important factors to be considered. If they were not selected appropriately, the system will over-fit the data or will not be able to fit the data. Adjusting mechanism works using a hybrid algorithm combining the least squares method and the gradient descent method with a mean square error method. The aim of the training process is to minimize the training error between the ANFIS output and

the actual objective. This allows a fuzzy system to train its features from the data it observes, and implements these features in the system rules. ANFIS has the following layers as represented in Figure 3.

ANFIS Algorithm

Layer 0: It consists of plain input variable set.

Layer 1: Each node in this layer generates a membership grade of a linguistic label. For instance, the node function of the i-th node may be a generalized bell membership function:

$$\mu_{A_i}(x) = \frac{1}{1 + \left[\left(\dfrac{x - c_i}{a_i}\right)^2\right]^{b_i}}$$

(10)

Figure 3. ANFIS architecture

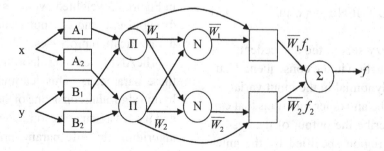

where x is the input to node i; A_i is the linguistic label (small, large, etc.) associated with this node; and $\{a_i, b_i, c_i\}$ is the parameter set that changes the shapes of the membership function. Parameters in this layer are referred to as the premise parameters.

Layer 2: The function is a T-norm operator that performs the firing strength of the rule, e.g., fuzzy conjunctives AND and OR. The simplest implementation just calculates the product of all incoming signals.

$$w_i = \mu A_i(x)\mu B_i(y), i = 1, 2. \tag{11}$$

Layer 3: Every node in this layer is fixed and determines a normalized firing strength. It calculates the ratio of the jth rule's firing strength to the sum of all rules firing strength.

$$\overline{w_i} = \frac{w_i}{w_1 + w_2}, i = 1, 2. \tag{12}$$

Layer 4: The nodes in this layer are adaptive and are connected with the input nodes (of layer 0) and the preceding node of layer 3. The result is the weighted output of the rule j.

$$\overline{w_i} f_i = \overline{w_i}(p_i x + q_i y + r_i) \tag{13}$$

where $\overline{w_i}$ is the output of layer 3, and $\{p_i, q_i, r_i\}$ is the parameter set. Parameters in this layer are referred to as the consequent parameters.

Layer 5: This layer consists of one single node which computes the overall output as the summation of all incoming signals.

$$\text{Overall Output} = \sum_i \overline{w_i} f_i = \frac{\sum_i w_i f_i}{\sum_i w_i} \tag{14}$$

The basic learning rule of ANFIS is the back-propagation gradient descent which calculates error signals (the derivative of the squared error

with respect to each node's output) recursively from the output layer backward to the input nodes. This learning rule is exactly the same as the back-propagation learning rule used in the common feed-forward neural networks (Jang, 1992, 1993, 1996).

Simple Logistic (SL) Curve

The Simple logistic (SL) curve model is widely used for fitting curves and constructing models to predict some unknown variables. The most important characteristic of simple logistic model is that it is symmetric about the point of inflection. This feature represents that the process which will happen after the point of inflection is the mirror image of the process that happened before the point. The model for the simple logistic curve is controlled by three coefficients, a, b, and L is expressed as

$$y_t = L / 1 + ae^{-bt} \tag{14}$$

where y_t is the value of interest, L is the maximum value of y_t, a describes the location of the curve, and b controls the shape of the curve. To estimate the parameters for a and b, the equation of the simple logistic model is transformed into a linear function using natural logarithms. The linear model is expressed as

$$y_t = \ln(y_t/L - y_t) = -\ln(a) + bt \tag{15}$$

where the parameter a and b are then estimated using a simple linear regression (Trappey, 2008).

Logistic Regression (LR)

Linear regression can be used to approximate the relationship between a continuous response variable and a set of predictor variables. However, the response variable is often categorical rather than continuous. For such cases, linear regression is not appropriate, but the analyst can turn to an analogous method, logistic regression (LR), which is similar to linear regression in many ways. Logistic regression refers to methods for describing the relationship between a categorical response variable and a set of predictor variables. Logistic regression assumes that the relationship between the predictor and the response is non-linear. In linear regression, the response variable is considered to be a random variable $Y = \beta_0 + \beta_1 x + \varepsilon$ with conditional mean $\pi(x) = E(Y|x) = \beta_0 + \beta_1 x$. The conditional mean for logistic regression takes on a different form from that of linear regression (Larose, 2005).

Multilayer Perceptron (MLP)

Neural network models can be used for nonlinear classification. They connected many simple Perceptron like models in a hierarchical structure. This can represent nonlinear decision boundaries. There are two aspects to how to learn a multilayer perceptron: learning the structure of the network and learning the connection weights. It turns out that there is a relatively simple algorithm for determining the weights given a fixed network structure. This algorithm is called back propagation. However, although there are many algorithms that attempt to identify network structure, this aspect of the problem is commonly solved through experimentation—perhaps combined with a healthy dose of expert knowledge. Sometimes the network can be separated into distinct modules that represent identifiable subtasks (e.g., recognizing different components of an object in an image recognition problem), which opens up a way of incorporating domain knowledge into the learning process. Often a single hidden layer is all that is necessary, and an appropriate number of units for that layer are determined by maximizing the estimated accuracy (Witten & Frank, 2005).

BENCHMARKING DATA MINING METHODS

When tried to compare two or more different artificial learning methods on the same problem to see which one is the better, it has been needed to benchmark success and failure parameters. It seems simple, to estimate the error using cross-validation (or any other suitable estimation procedure), perhaps repeated several times, and choose the scheme whose estimate is smaller. This is quite sufficient in many practical applications: if one method has a lower estimated error than another on a particular dataset, the best we can use the former method's model. However, it may be that the difference is simply caused by estimation error, and in some circumstances it is important to determine whether one schema is really better than another on a particular problem. This is a standard challenge for machine learning researchers. If a new learning algorithm is proposed, its proponents must show that it improves on the state of the art for the problem at hand and demonstrate that the observed improvement is not just a chance effect in the estimation process. This is a job for a statistical test that gives confidence bounds, the kind we met previously when trying to predict true performance from a given test-set error rate. If there were unlimited data, we could use a large amount for training and evaluate performance on a large independent test set, obtaining confidence bounds just as before. However, if the difference turns out to be significant we must ensure that this is not just because of the particular dataset we happened to base the experiment on. What we want to determine is whether one scheme is better or worse than another on average, across all possible training and test datasets that can be drawn from the domain. Because the amount of training data naturally affects performance, all datasets should be the same size: indeed, the experiment might be repeated with different sizes to obtain a learning curve.

Table 1. A confusion matrix for positive and negative tuples

Actual class		Predicted Class	
		C_1	C_2
	C_1	true positives	false negatives
	C_2	false positives	true negatives

Using training data to derive a classifier or predictor and then to estimate the accuracy of the resulting learned model can result in misleading overoptimistic estimates due to overspecialization of the learning algorithm to the data. Instead, accuracy is better measured on a test set consisting of class-labeled tuples that were not used to train the model. The accuracy of a classifier on a given test set is the percentage of test set tuples that are correctly classified by the classifier. In the pattern recognition literature, this is also referred to as the overall recognition rate of the classifier, that is, it reflects how well the classifier recognizes tuples of the various classes.

The confusion matrix (CM) is a useful tool for analyzing how well your classifier can recognize tuples of different classes. A confusion matrix for two classes is shown in Table 1. Given m classes, a confusion matrix is a table of at least size m by m. An entry, $CM_{i,j}$ in the first m rows and m columns indicates the number of tuples of class i that were labeled by the classifier as class j. For a classifier to have good accuracy, ideally most of the tuples would be represented along the diagonal of the confusion matrix, from entry $CM_{1,1}$ to entry $CM_{m,m}$, with the rest of the entries being close to zero. The table may have additional rows or columns to provide totals or recognition rates per class (Fawcat, 2003).

Given two classes, we can talk in terms of positive tuples versus negative tuples. True positives (TP) refer to the positive tuples that were correctly labeled by the classifier, while true negatives (TN) are the negative tuples that were correctly labeled by the classifier. False positives

(FP) are the negative tuples that were incorrectly labeled. Similarly, false negatives (FN) are the positive tuples that were incorrectly labeled. These terms are useful when analyzing a classifier's ability. Sensitivity is also referred to as the true positive (recognition) rate (that is, the proportion of positive tuples that are correctly identified), while specificity is the true negative rate (TNR) (that is, the proportion of negative tuples that are correctly identified). The counts in a confusion matrix can also be expressed in terms of percentages. The true positive rate (TPR) or sensitivity is defined as the fraction of positive examples predicted correctly by the model (Han & Kamber, 2006):

$$sensitivity\ (TPR) = TP/(TP + FN) \tag{16}$$

Similarly, the true negative rate (TNR) or specificity is defined as the fraction of negative examples predicted correctly by the model.

$$specificity\ (TNR) = TN/(TN + FP) \tag{17}$$

Accuracy is a function of sensitivity and specificity:

$$accuracy = sensitivity*pos/(pos+neg)\ + speficity*neg(pos+neg) \tag{18}$$

Precision determines the fraction of records that actually turns out to be positive in the group which the classifier has declared as a positive class. The higher the precision is, the lower the number of false positive errors committed by the classifier.

$$precision = TP/(TP + FP) \tag{19}$$

Recall is defined:

$$recall = TP/(TP + FN) \tag{20}$$

F-score, which is defined as the harmonic mean of recall and precision:

F_score=recall x precision /(recall+precision)/2

$$(21)$$

Correctness is the percentage of correctly classified instances. RMSE denotes the root mean square error (RMSE) for the given dataset and method of classification. Correctness and RMSE values show important variety. Lower RMSE systems tend to make less incorrect classifications than the others and it indicates reliability in further testing of data.

In classification problems, it is commonly assumed that all tuples are uniquely classifiable, that is, that each training tuple can belong to only one class. Yet, owing to the wide diversity of data in large databases, it is not always reasonable to assume that all tuples are uniquely classifiable. Rather, it is more probable to assume that each tuple may belong to more than one class. How then can the accuracy of classifiers on large databases be measured? The accuracy measure is not appropriate, because it does not take into account the possibility of tuples belonging to more than one class.

Rather than returning a class label, it is useful to return a probability class distribution. Accuracy measures may then use a second guess heuristic, whereby a class prediction is judged as correct if it agrees with the first or second most probable class. Although this does take into consideration, to some degree, the nonunique classification of tuples, it is not a complete solution.

ROC curves are a useful visual tool for comparing two classification models. The name ROC stands for Receiver Operating Characteristic (ROC). ROC curves come from signal detection theory that was developed during World War II for the analysis of radar images. An ROC curve shows the trade-off between the true positive rate or sensitivity (proportion of positive tuples that are correctly identified) and the false-positive rate (proportion of negative tuples that are incorrectly identified as positive) for a given model. That is, given a two-class problem, it allows us to visualize

the trade-off between the rate at which the model can accurately recognize 'yes' cases versus the rate at which it mistakenly identifies 'no' cases as 'yes' for different "portions" of the test set. Any increase in the true positive rate occurs at the cost of an increase in the false-positive rate. The area under the ROC curve is a measure of the accuracy of the model (Hanley & McNeil, 1982).

In order to plot an ROC curve for a given classification model, M, the model must be able to return a probability or ranking for the predicted class of each test tuple. That is, we need to rank the test tuples in decreasing order, where the one the classifier thinks is most likely to belong to the positive or 'yes' class appears at the top of the list. Naive Bayesian and backpropagation classifiers are appropriate, whereas others, such as decision tree classifiers, can easily be modified so as to return a class probability distribution for each prediction. The vertical axis of an ROC curve represents the true positive rate. The horizontal axis represents the false-positive rate. An ROC curve for M is plotted as follows. Starting at the bottom left-hand corner (where the true positive rate and false-positive rate are both 0), we check the actual class label of the tuple at the top of the list. If we have a true positive (that is, a positive tuple that was correctly classified), then on the ROC curve, we move up and plot a point. If, instead, the tuple really belongs to the 'no' class, we have a false positive. On the ROC curve, we move right and plot a point. This process is repeated for each of the test tuples, each time moving up on the curve for a true positive or toward the right for a false positive. The closer the ROC curve of a model is to the diagonal line, the less accurate the model. If the model is really good, initially we are more likely to encounter true positives as we move down the ranked list. Thus, the curve would move steeply up from zero. Later, as we start to encounter fewer and fewer true positives, and more and more false positives, the curve cases off and becomes more horizontal. To assess the accuracy of a model, we can measure the area under the curve (AUC). Several software packages are able to perform such calculation. The closer AUC is to 0.5, the less accurate the corresponding model is. A model with perfect accuracy will have an area of 1.0 (Hanley & McNeil, 1982).

RESULTS

In this section various data mining classifiers were compared to obtain the best practical solution for the financial early warning system. We should again underline that it is possible to foresee whether the market is close to a stock market crash by monitoring the market's volatility. Market volatility is expected to peak just before the market crash. The input variables are taken into account mainly because they can effectively measure the volatility change of stock market. This effect may be pronounced in advance, as illustrated by numerical simulation, and in confirmation with the empirical findings. The value of the stock market crash risk indicator closely shows the possibility of an upcoming crisis. The possibility of a crisis is as high as the value.

Rule based models and curve fitting models have high level of precision, however they demonstrate poor robustness when the dataset is changed. In order to provide adaptability of the classification technique, neural network based alteration of fuzzy inference system parameters is necessary. The results prove that, ANFIS method combines both precision of fuzzy based classification system and adaptability (back propagation) feature of neural networks in classification of data.

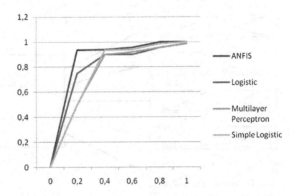

Figure 4. The ROC curves of selected methods

Receiver operating characteristics (ROC) curve analysis conveys information about performance from all possible combinations and of misclassification costs and class distributions. The Receiver Operating Characteristic (ROC) curve, which is obtained by altering threshold level, is typically used to visualize the performance and robustness of the method. The ROC curve indicates how the prediction rate changes as the thresholds are varied to generate more or fewer false alarms. The ROC curve is a plot of prediction accuracy against the false positive probability that tradeoffs prediction accuracy against the analyst workload. The ROC curves for selected methods are illustrated on Figure 4.

The ANFIS approach uses Gaussian functions for fuzzy sets and linear functions for the rule outputs. The initial parameters of the network are the mean and standard deviation of the membership functions (antecedent parameters) and the coefficients of the output linear functions (consequent parameters). The ANFIS learning algo-

Table 2. Behnchmarking the data mining methods

Method	Sensitivity	Precision	Recall	F-Measure	ROC Area
ANFIS	0,97	0,95	0,97	0,96	0,988
Logistic regression	0,90	0,92	0,90	0,91	0,988
MultilayerPerceptron	0,85	0,87	0,85	0,86	0,996
SimpleLogistic	0,87	0,90	0,87	0,89	0,994

Figure 5. FIS model

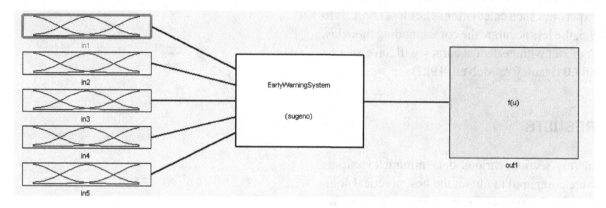

rithm is then used to obtain these parameters. This learning algorithm is a hybrid algorithm consisting of the gradient descent and the least-squares estimate. Using this hybrid algorithm, the rule parameters are recursively updated until an acceptable error is reached. Iterations have two steps, one forward and one backward. In the forward pass, the antecedent parameters are fixed, and the consequent parameters are obtained using the linear least-squares estimate. In the backward pass, the consequent parameters are fixed, and the output error is back-propagated through this network, and the antecedent parameters are accordingly updated using the gradient descent method.

In the designing of ANFIS model in Figure 5, the number of membership functions, the number of fuzzy rules, and the number of training epochs are important factors to be considered. If they are not selected appropriately, the system will overfit the data or will not be able to fit the data. Adjusting mechanism works using a hybrid algorithm combining the least squares method and the gradient descent method with a mean square error method. ANFIS creates membership functions for each variable input.

The aim of the training process is to minimize the training error between the ANFIS output and the actual objective. This allows a fuzzy system to train its features from the data it observes, and implements these features in the system rules.

The results indicate that ANFIS has a pretty good means to model of the EWS. The 78 of 83 test samples were correctly classified. Average training error is 0.0498, average testing error is 0.0653 and average checking error is 0.0587. The results of experiment show that the accuracy rate of the neuro fuzzy model is approximately 95%.

We prefer Sugeno-type for computational efficiency. The output of each rule is a linear combination of input variables and a constant term. The final output is the weighted average of each rule's output. The basic learning rule of the proposed network is based on the gradient descent and the chain rule. Takagi and Sugeno's fuzzy is a fuzzy system with crisp functions in consequent, which perceived proper for multifaceted applications. Due to crisp consequent functions, ANFIS method requires a rather uncomplicated form of scaling implicitly. The ANFIS has the advantage of good applicability as it can be interpreted as local linearization modeling and that form of state estimation is straightforwardly applicable to different systems.

Figure 6 shows the fuzzy inference rules which are obtained by the model for predicting stock market crashes. As mentioned before, 5 inputs are fed into ANFIS model and one variable output is

Figure 6. FIS rules

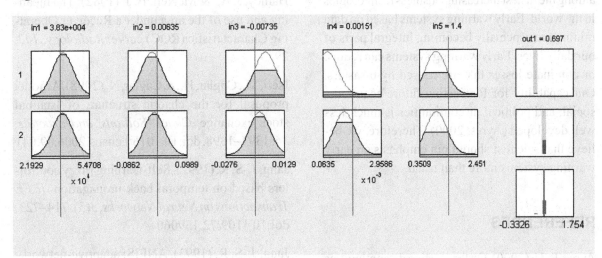

obtained at the end. The last node (rightmost one) calculates the summation of all outputs.

FUTURE RESEARCH DIRECTIONS

As we considered in the data preparation phase, dataset clustering process should have to be done dynamically like to create fuzzy clusters according to the output variable. By this way, ANFIS method may minimize the root mean squared error of the forecasts. Also, previous works of (Kim et al.,2006) and this study shows that neuro fuzzy approach good enough to predict financial crises by using different economical characteristics. In order to forecast economical situations before the crisis, we have to develop new economical indicators for tracking the stability of economic systems. In Turkey, ISE has not represents all economic developments in advance. Therefore, other economical metrics and indicators should have to be taken into account to develop more powerful EWS forecasting system. Because stock market crashes triggers the economical crashes but vice versa is true too.

CONCLUSION

In this chapter, we presented a new methodology of early warning system for stock market crashes and this new methodology is able to provide excellent early warning information. We have constructed early warning systems by using various data mining classifiers. The empirical results show that the proposed ANFIS model is the most successful. ISE national 100 index data is non-linear and ANFIS can model non-linear system successfully. Consequently, the model learns patterns from the dataset and these patterns can help us decide upcoming stock market crashes and so the model is capable of indicating crash risks effectively. One disadvantage of the ANFIS method is that the complexity of the algorithm is high when there are more than a number of inputs fed into the system. However, when the system reaches an optimal configuration of membership functions, it can be used efficiently against large datasets. Based on the accuracy of the results of the study, it can be stated that the ANFIS model can be used as an alternative to current financial early warning systems to predict stock market crashes. ANFIS was used as a part of a new and progressive technology, data mining and data mining is among the fastest increasing business technologies in the world. Early warning systems based on data mining are especially becoming integral parts of our daily lives. Early warning systems can reduce or eliminate losses that are caused by disasters. Our capability for forecasting future economic, social, and political discontinuities is much less well developed (Ayres, 2000). Therefore, we believe that scientist should put emphasis on early warning systems more than usual.

REFERENCES

Ayres, R. U. (2000). On forecasting discontinuities . *Technological Forecasting and Social Change*, *65*, 81–97. doi:10.1016/S0040-1625(99)00101-8

Bussiere, M., & Fratzscher, M. (1996). Towards a new early warning system of financial crises. *Journal of International Money and Finance*, *25*, 953–973. doi:10.1016/j.jimonfin.2006.07.007

Cajueiro, D. O., Tabak, B. M., & Werneck, F. K. (2009). Can we predict crashes? The case of the Brazilian stock market. *Physica A*, *388*, 1603–1609. doi:10.1016/j.physa.2008.12.010

Fawcett, T. (2003). *ROC graphs: notes and practical considerations for data mining researchers*. Technical Report HPL-2003–4. Palo Alto, CA: HP Laboratories.

Frankel, J. A., & Rose, A. K. (1996). Currency crashes in emerging markets: An empirical treatment. *Journal of International Economics*, *41*(3-4), 351–366. doi:10.1016/S0022-1996(96)01441-9

Giudici, P. (2003). *Applied data mining*. New York: John Wiley & Sons.

Han, J., & Kamber, M. (2006). *Data mining: Concepts and techniques*. San Francisco, CA: Morgan Kaufmann Publishers.

Hanley, J. A., & McNeil, B. J. (1982). The meaning and use of the area under a Receiver Operating Characteristic (ROC) curve. *Radiology*, *143*, 29–36.

Iseri, M., Caglar, H., & Caglar, N. (2008). A model proposal for the chaotic structure of Istanbul stock exchange. *Chaos, Solitons, and Fractals*, *36*, 1392–1398. doi:10.1016/j.chaos.2006.09.041

Jang, J.-S. R. (1992). Self-learning fuzzy controllers based on temporal back propagation. *IEEE Transactions on Neural Networks*, *3*(5), 714–723. doi:10.1109/72.159060

Jang, J.-S. R. (1993). ANFIS: adaptive-network-based fuzzy inference system. *IEEE Transactions on Systems, Man, and Cybernetics*, *23*(3), 665–685. doi:10.1109/21.256541

Jang, J.-S. R. (1996). Input selection for ANFIS learning. In *Proceedings of the IEEE International Conference on Fuzzy Systems*, (pp.1493-1499).

Kaminsky, G., Lizondo, S., & Reinhart, C. (1998). Leading indicators of currency crisis. *International Monetary Fund Staff Papers*, *45*(1).

Kim, T. Y., Oh, K. J., Sohn, I., & Hwang, C. (2004). Usefulness of artificial neural networks for early warning system of economic crisis . *Expert Systems with Applications*, *26*, 583–590. doi:10.1016/j.eswa.2003.12.009

Larose, D. T. (2005). *Data mining methods and models*. New York: John Wiley & Sons. doi:10.1002/0471756482

Levy, M. (2008). Stock market crashes as social phase transitions. *Journal of Economic Dynamics & Control*, *32*, 137–155. doi:10.1016/j.jedc.2007.01.023

Lin, C., Khan, H. A., Wang, Y., & Chang, R. (2006). A new approach to modeling early warning systems for currency crises: Can a machine-learning fuzzy expert system predict the currency crises effectively? *CIRJE-F, 411*.

McNelis, P. D. (2005). *Neural networks in finance: Gaining predictive edge in the market*. New York: Elsevier Academic Press.

Peltonen, T. A. (2006) Are emerging market currency crises predictable? A test. *European Central Bank, Working Paper Series*, No. 571.

Sivanandam, S. N., Sumathi, S., & Deepa, S. N. (2007). *Introduction to fuzzy logic using matlab*. Berlin: Springer. doi:10.1007/978-3-540-35781-0

The Istanbul Stock Exchange. (2009). Retrieved 2009, from http://www.ise.org

The MathWorks. (2008a). *MATLAB: Getting Started Guide*.

(2008b). *The MathWorks*. Fuzzy Logic Toolbox User's Guide.

Trappey, C. V., & Wu, H. (2008). An evaluation of the time-varying extended logistic, simple logistic, and Gompertz models for forecasting short product lifecycles. *Advanced Engineering Informatics, 22*, 421–430. doi:10.1016/j.aei.2008.05.007

Witten, I. H., & Frank, E. (2005). *Data mining: Practical machine learning tools and techniques* (2nd ed.). San Francisco, CA: Morgan Kaufmann Publishers.

ADDITIONAL READING

Alvarez-Plata, P., & Schrooten, M. (2004). Misleading indicators? The Argentinean currency crisis. *Journal of Policy Modeling, 26*(5), 587–603. doi:10.1016/j.jpolmod.2004.01.008

Bayoumi, T., & Eichengreen, B. (1994). *One money or many? Analyzing the prospects for monetary unification in various parts of the world, Princeton Studies in International Finance, No. 76*. International Finance Section, Department of Economics, Princeton University.

Bayoumi, T., & Eichengreen, B. (1997). Optimum currency areas and exchange rate variability: Theory and evidence compared . In Cohen, B. (Ed.), *Research Frontiers in International Economics*. Princeton: Princeton University Press.

Berg, A., & Pattillo, C. (1999a). *Are currency crises predictable? A Test*. IMF.

Berg, A., & Pattillo, C. (1999b). Predicting currency crises: The indicators approach and an alternative.

Berg, A., & Pattillo, C. (1999c). *What caused the Asian crises: An early warning system approach, Brown, M. & Harris C (1994). Neurofuzzy adaptive modeling and control*. England: Prentice Hall International.

Brown, M. (1996). *An introduction to fuzzy and neurofuzzy systems*. England: Prentice Hall International.

Chang, R., & Velasco, A. (2001). A model of currency crises in emerging markets. *The Quarterly Journal of Economics*, 489–517. doi:10.1162/00335530151144087

Chung, J.K., Shin, T.C., Hsiao, N.C., Tsai, Y.B., Lee, W.H.K. & Teng T.L. (1999). Development of an integrated earthquake early warning system in Taiwan case for the hualien area earthquakes. Terrestrial *Atmospheric and Oceanic Sciences*, 719-736.

Demirguc-Kunt, A., & Detragiache, E. (2000). Does deposit Insurance increase banking system stability? An empirical investigation, *Econometric Society World Congress 2000* Contributed Papers 1751, Econometric Society.

Dermirguc-Kunt, A., & Detragiache, E. (1997). *The determinants of banking crises in developing and developed countries, IMF Working Paper 106*. Washington, D.C.: International Monetary Fund.

Edison, H. J., & Warnock, F. E. (2003). A simple measure of the intensity of capital controls. *Journal of Empirical Finance, 10*(1-2), 81–103. doi:10.1016/S0927-5398(02)00055-5

Eichengreen, B. & Arteta, C. (2000). *Banking crises in emerging markets: Risks and red herrings.*

Eichengreen, B., & Rose, A. K. (1998). Contagious currency crises: channels of conveyance. In: Ito, T., Krueger, A. (Eds.), Changes in Exchange Rates in Rapidly Developing Countries, University of Chicago Press, 29–55.

Eichengreen, B., & Wyplosz, C. (1993). The unstable EMS. *Brookings Papers on Economic Activity, 1*, 51–144. doi:10.2307/2534603

Eichengreen, B., & Wyplosz, C. (1998). The stability pact: More than a minor nuisance? *Economic Policy, 26*, 65–114. doi:10.1111/1468-0327.00029

Eichengreen, B. J., Rose, A., & Wyplosz, C. (1996). Contagious currency crises: First tests. *The Scandinavian Journal of Economics, 98*, 463–494. doi:10.2307/3440879

Frankel, J. A., & Rose, A. K. (1996). Currency crashes in emerging markets: An empirical treatment. *Journal of International Economics, 41*(3-4), 351–366. doi:10.1016/S0022-1996(96)01441-9

Gaines, B. R., & Compton, P. (1995). Induction of ripple-down rules applied to modeling large databases. *Journal of Intelligent Information Systems, 5*(3), 211–228. doi:10.1007/BF00962234

Glick, R., & Moreno, R. (1999). *Money and credit, competitiveness, and currency crises in Asia and Latin America, Papers 99-01.* Economisch Institut voor het Midden en Kleinbedrijf.

Glick, R., & Rose, A. (1998). Contagion and trade: why are currency crisis regional. *Journal of International Money and Finance, 18*(4), 603–617. doi:10.1016/S0261-5606(99)00023-6

Gochoco-Bautista, M. S. (2000). Periods of currency pressure: Stylized facts and leading indicators. *Journal of Macroeconomics, 22*(1), 125–158. doi:10.1016/S0164-0704(00)00126-9

Jang, J., Sun, C., & Mizutani, E. (1997). *Neurofuzzy and soft computing, A computational approach to learning and machine intelligent.* USA: Prentice Hall International.

Kamin, S. B., Schindler, J. W., & Samuel, S. L. (2001). *The contribution of domestic and external factors to emerging market devaluation crises: An early warning system approach, International Finance Discussion, Paper No. 711.* Washington, D.C.: Board of Governors of the Federal Reserve System.

Kaminsky, G., Lizondo, S., & Reinhart, C.M. (1998). Leading indicators of currency crisis. International Monetary Fund Staff Papers, 45(1).

Kaminsky, G., & Reinhart, C. (2000). On crises, contagion, and confusion. *Journal of International Economics, 51*(1), 145–168. doi:10.1016/S0022-1996(99)00040-9

Kaminsky, G. L., & Reinhart, C. M. (1996). *The twin crises: The causes of banking and balance-of-payments problems.* Washington, DC: Board of Governors Federal Reserve System.

Kaminsky, G. L., & Reinhart, C. M. (1999). The twin crises: the causes of banking and balance-of-payments problems . *The American Economic Review, 89*(3), 473–500. doi:10.1257/aer.89.3.473

Kaminsky, G. L., & Schmukler, S. L. (1999). What triggers market jitters? A Chronicle of the Asian crisis. *Journal of International Money and Finance, 18*(4), 537–560. doi:10.1016/S0261-5606(99)00015-7

Krugman, P. (1979). A model of balance-of-payments crises . *Journal of Money, Credit and Banking, 11*, 311–325. doi:10.2307/1991793

Lanoie, P., & Lemarbre, S. (1996). Three approaches to predict the timing and quantity of LDC debt rescheduling. *Applied Economics*, *28*(2), 241–246. doi:10.1080/000368496328876

Lin, C. S. (2008). A new approach to modeling early warning systems for currency crises: Can a machine-learning fuzzy expert system predict the currency crises effectively? *Journal of International Money and Finance*, *27*(7), 1098–1121. doi:10.1016/j.jimonfin.2008.05.006

Marchesi, S. (2003). Adoption of an IMF programme and debt rescheduling. *Journal of Development Economics*, *70*(2), 403–423. doi:10.1016/S0304-3878(02)00103-7

Milesi-Ferretti, G. M., & Razin, A. (1998). Sharp reduction in current account deficits: an empirical analysis. *European Economic Review*, *42*.

Nauck, D., Klawonn, F., & Kruse, R. (1997). *Foundations of neuro-fFuzzy systems*. England: John Wiley & Sons.

Obstfeld, M., & Rogoff, K. (1986). Rational and self-fulfilling balance-of-payments crises. *The American Economic Review*, *76*(1), 72–81.

Olson, D. L., & Delen, D. (2008). *Advanced data mining techniques*. Springer.

Simoudis, E. (1996). Reality check for data mining. *IEEE Expert*, *11*(5), 26–33. doi:10.1109/64.539014

Son, S., Oha, K. J., Kim, T. Y., & Kim, D. H. (2009). An early warning system for global institutional investors at emerging stock markets based on machine learning forecasting. *Expert Systems with Applications*, *36*(3), 4951–4957. doi:10.1016/j.eswa.2008.06.044

KEY TERMS AND DEFINITIONS

Adaptive Neuro Fuzzy Inference System (ANFIS): ANFIS is a non-linear mapping system that utilized advantages of neuro fuzzy and radial basis functions neural network for generating fuzzy rules for forecasting the results.

Data Mining (DM): DM is an approach to handle very large data sets for segmentation, classification, clustering, etc., purpose for detecting useful patterns and extracting information.

Stock Market Crashes (SMC): SMC is an unstable declining trend of the stock markets.

Economical Crisis (EC): EC is a declining trend and risky situation that internal and external economic markets triggered each other like domino effect.

Early Warning System (EWS): EWS may be useful to tracking any economical or environmental systems' behaviors to detect anomalies or any different trends for making proactive decisions.

Chapter 7

Bankruptcy Prediction by Supervised Machine Learning Techniques:
A Comparative Study

Chih-Fong Tsai
National Central University, Taiwan

Yu-Hsin Lu
National Chung Cheng University, Taiwan

Yu-Feng Hsu
National Sun Yat-Sen University, Taiwan

ABSTRACT

It is very important for financial institutions which are capable of accurately predicting business failure. In literature, numbers of bankruptcy prediction models have been developed based on statistical and machine learning techniques. In particular, many machine learning techniques, such as neural networks, decision trees, etc. have shown better prediction performances than statistical ones. However, advanced machine learning techniques, such as classifier ensembles and stacked generalization have not been fully examined and compared in terms of their bankruptcy prediction performances. The aim of this chapter is to compare two different machine learning techniques, one statistical approach, two types of classifier ensembles, and three stacked generalization classifiers over three related datasets. The experimental results show that classifier ensembles by weighted voting perform the best in term of predication accuracy. On the other hand, for Type II errors on average stacked generalization and single classifiers perform better than classifier ensembles.

INTRODUCTION

Bankruptcy prediction has been a major research topic in accounting and finance for at least a century since corporate bankruptcy can affect the economy of every country seriously. Therefore, timely and correctly predicting bankruptcy is a great importance to various stakeholders (e.g. management, investors, employees, shareholders

DOI: 10.4018/978-1-61692-865-0.ch007

and other interested parties) as it provides them some early warnings (Shin, et al, 2005; Lensberg, et al, 2006; Van Gestel et al., 2006; Hua et al. 2007).

Financial failure always occurs when the firm has chronic and serious losses, owns negative net worth that the market value of assets is less than total liabilities, and/or in a situation which is firm's inability to pay debts as they come due. The common assumption underlying bankruptcy prediction is that a firm's financial statements appropriately reflect all these characteristics. Therefore, almost all prior researches (such as Deakin, 1972; Ohlson, 1980; Richardson, et al., 1998; Van Gestel et al. 2006; Hua et al., 2007; Alfaro et al., 2008) have predicted financial distress through several classification techniques by using financial ratios (e.g. leverage, size of firm, and current liquidity) and data originating from these statements.

However, traditional statistics such as univariate approaches (Beaver, 1966), multivariate approaches, linear multiple discriminant approaches (MDA) (Altman, 1968; Altman, et al., 1977), and multiple regression (Meyer & Pifer, 1970) typically rely on the linearity assumption, as well as normality assumptions which is difficult to apply to the real world problem. To develop a more accurate and generally applicable prediction model, machine learning and artificial intelligence techniques including neural networks, decision trees, genetic algorithm (GA), support vector machine (SVM), etc., have been successfully applied in corporate financial bankruptcy forecasting recently (Wu et al., 2007; Hua et al., 2007; Huang et al., 2008; Alfaro et al., 2008). Especially, the neural network models trained by the back-propagation learning algorithm and decision trees are the popular techniques used for financial and accounting literatures.

The consideration of prior studies has been to identify the single best model for predicting financial distress. However, many researches have realized that there exists limitation on using a single classification technique. This observation has motivated the relatively recent studies utiliz-

ing classifiers combinations (i.e. Multi-classifier system or ensembles) for better accuracy (Zhou & Zhang, 2002; Kim, et al., 2002; West, et al., 2005; Tsai & Wu, 2008; Nanni & Lumini, 2009). Besides classifier ensembles, stacked generalization is another advanced learning approach which estimates the errors of using one single technique and then corrects those errors to maximize the accuracy (Wolpert, 1992; Tsai, 2003).

Although the two approaches may provide more accurate prediction results in various domains, there are very few researches comparing with different models based on these machine learning techniques to examine their prediction performances. Therefore, this paper develops a classifier ensemble and stacked generalization model, respectively and employs a multilayer perception neural network, decision trees, and logistic regression as the baseline classifiers to assess the accuracy and Type I/II errors of these models.

The remainder of this paper is organized as follows. Section 2 reviews the predictors of bankruptcy and describes the concept of pattern classification and different classification techniques. Section 3 describes the development of different models and the evaluation methods of them. In Section 4, the experiments are based on comparing the prediction performance of models in terms of average prediction accuracy and the type I and type II errors over three well-known and public downloadable datasets. Finally, the conclusion is made in Section 5.

LITERATURE REVIEW

Bankruptcy Prediction

Factors of Bankruptcy

According to the definition of Beaver (1966), financial failure is defined as the inability of a firm to pay its financial obligations as they mature. In other words, a firm is said to have failed when any of the following events have occurred: bankruptcy, bond default, an overdrawn bank account, or nonpayment of a preferred stock dividend. Among of these, the latter three events will also result in bankruptcy. Therefore, bankruptcy always occurs in the situation that the firm suffers from continuous losses, owns the negative, or is not able to pay debts as they come due.

Bankruptcy of a business firm is a great event which can produce substantial losses to creditors and stockholders. Therefore, a model which predicts potential business failures as early as possible would serve to reduce such losses by providing sufficient warning to these interested parties (Deakin, 1972; Ohlson, 1980; Shin et al., 2005; Van Gestel et al., 2006; Hua et al. 2007). In many prior related studies, the common assumption underlying bankruptcy prediction is that a firm's financial statements appropriately reflect all bankruptcy situations. Therefore, the financial ratios in statements are always better predictors of bankruptcy prediction (Altman, 1968; Deakin, 1972; Ohlson, 1980; Richardson et al., 1998; Van Gestel et al. 2006; Hua et al., 2007; Alfaro et al., 2008).

Beaver (1966) examines the predictive ability of six groups of financial ratios including cash-flow ratios, net-income ratios, debt to total assets ratios, liquid-assets to total assets ratios, liquid-assets to current debt ratios, and turnover ratios in predicting financial failure. Ohlson (1980) indicates that the company size, financial structure, firm performance, and current liquidity are four basic factors as being statistically significant in affecting the probability of failure. Deakin (1972) employs a discriminant analysis to predict business failure using four categories contain fourteen ratios.

Modeling Bankruptcy Prediction

To predict corporate bankruptcy, several classification techniques are suggested to employ. In the early work, univariate approaches used ratio analysis; multivariate approaches combined multiple ratios and characteristics to predict financial distress (Deakin, 1972; Ohlson, 1980; Pastena & Ruland, 1986). Otherwise, multiple discriminant analysis and multiple regressions attempt to identify the most efficient hyperplane to linearly separate between successful and non-successful firms (Beaver, 1966; Altman, 1968; Meyer & Pifer, 1970; Altman et al., 1977). Balcaen & Ooghe (2006) review 35 years of studies on business failure, and discriminate four general types of classical statistical methods including univariate analysis, risk index methods, multivariate discriminant analysis, and conditional probability models applied in corporate failure prediction.

However, traditional statistics typically rely on the linear separability, and normality assumptions. Recent researches focus on machine learning techniques which are sophisticated nonlinear model, such as artificial neural networks and decision trees, to increase predication accuracy of the models (Park & Han, 2002; Shin & Lee, 2002; Shin, Lee, & Kim, 2005; Hua et al., 2007; Huang et al., 2008; Alfaro et al., 2008).

Particularly, Pendharkar (2008) compares the result of artificial neural networks to other competitive intelligent techniques such as inductive machine learning and genetic algorithms. Salcedo-Sanz et al. (2005) propose genetic programming for the prediction of possible bankruptcy of the insurance companies.

Compare to some researches focus on identifying the single best model, more and more studies utilize classifiers ensembles to reduce the generalization error of a single model and increase the accuracy for financial decision problems (West et al., 2005; Tsai & Wu, 2007; Nanni & Lumini, 2009). Specifically, Breiman (1996) and Breiman (1999) confirm that the ensembles of predictors have demonstrated the potential to reduce the generalization error of a single model from 5% to 70%.

On the other hand, stacked generalization is another advanced machine learning approach which estimates the errors of using one single technique and then corrects those errors to maximize the accuracy (Wolpert, 1992; Tsai, 2003). However, these two advanced machine learning techniques have not been applied in the domain of financial distress prediction simultaneously to compare their prediction performances with single baseline predication models. Therefore, this paper develops a classifier ensemble and stacked generalization model, respectively and employs a multilayer perception neural network, decision trees, and logistic regression as the baseline classifiers to assess the prediction accuracy and Type I/II errors of these models.

Machine Learning

Pattern Classification

Pattern classification is the scientific discipline whose goal is to classify unknown patterns based on current knowledge or statistical information extracted from patterns into a number of categories or classes (Theodoridis & Koutroumbas, 2006). In general, pattern classification contains supervised learning or classification and unsupervised learning or clustering techniques.

Supervised learning techniques calculate the value of some variables, and classifies according to results. In other words, supervised learning means that if a set of training data are available, the classifier is designed by exploiting this a priori known information (Theodoridis & Koutroumbas, 2006). The popular algorithms of supervised learning techniques include decision trees, artificial neural networks, and so on (Tou & Gonzalez, 1974; Han & Kamber, 2001). The followings describe the well-known and widely used classification techniques in bankruptcy prediction.

Multilayer-Perceptron (MLP) Neural Networks

Neural Networks (NNs) are a class of input-output models capable of learning through a process of trial and error, and collectively constitute a particular class of nonlinear parametric models where learning corresponds to statistical estimation of model parameters (Li & Tan, 2006). Neural networks can be regarded as a black box system, which is not required to understand its internal architecture for the final output decision. It is an information processing paradigm that is inspired by the way of the biological nervous system, such as the brain to process information.

Neural Networks can be distinguished into single-layer perception and multilayer perceptron (MLP). The multilayer perceptron consists of multiple layers of simple, two taste, sigmoid processing nodes or neurons that interact by using weighted connections. The MLP network may contain several intermediary layers between input and output layers. Such intermediary layers are called hidden layers and composed of number of nodes embedded in these layers, which are called hidden nodes. Based on prior research results (Zhan, et al., 1998; Hung, et al. 2006), multilayer perception is a relatively accurate neural network model.

Decision Trees

A decision tree is constructed by many nodes and branches on different stages and various conditions. It is a very popular and powerful tool for many prediction and classification problems since it can produce a number of decision rules. Several algorithms of decision trees have been developed, such as C4.5 and C5.0. Among them, classification and regression trees (CART) developed by Breiman et al. (1984) is a non-parametric statistical method to construct a decision tree to solve classification and regression problems (Deconinck et al., 2005; Lee et al., 2006). CART is a single procedure that can be used to analyze either categorical or continuous data using the same technology. When the dependent variable is categorical, CART produces a classification tree, when it is continuous it will read to a regression tree.

According to Breiman et al. (1984), CART can be summarized into three stages. In the first step, a maximal tree is growing by using a recursive partitioning technique to select variables and split points using a splitting criterion. In the next step the overgrown tree, which shows overfitting, is pruned. Cross-validation or a testing sample will be used to provide estimates of future classification errors for each subtree. The last stage is to select the optimal tree, which corresponds to a tree yielding the lowest cross-validated or testing set error rate.

Logistic Regression

Logistic regression is a widely used statistical modeling technique in which the probability of a dichotomous outcome is related to a set of potential independent variables (Cox & Snell, 1989; Hosmer & Lemeshow, 1989) and it is used to forecast the value of two class labels or sequence variables (Ozdamar, 2004). Although it is one of traditional statistical techniques, the logistic regression model does not necessarily require the assumptions of discriminant analysis. However, Harrell & Lee (1985) found that logistic regression is as efficient and accurate as discriminant analysis even though the assumptions of discriminant analysis are satisfied. Logistic regression models have been widely discussed in social research, medical research, design, control, financial decision-making, market segmentation, and customer behaviors (Kay et al., 2000; Wei & Chiu, 2002; Kane & Velury, 2004; Stanley & De-Zoort, 2007) and has also been explored by Daily & Dalton (1994), Richardson, et al. (1998), and Laitinen & Laitinen (2000) in building corporate financial distress prediction models.

Classifier Ensembles

Many researchers have realized that there exist limitations on using single classification techniques. Therefore, relatively recent researches utilize multiple classifiers known as classifier ensembles for better accuracy, and the superiority of these approaches with multiple classifiers and features over single classification techniques have been proved (Zhou & Zhang, 2002; Kim et al., 2002; West et al., 2005; Tsai & Wu, 2008; Nanni & Lumini, 2009).

In particular, Hayashi & Setiono (2002) indicate increased accuracy diagnosing hepatobiliary disorders from ensembles of 30 MLP neural networks. Hu & Tsoukalas (2003) and Sohn & Lee (2003) tested both bagging and boosting ensembles, and provide a reduction in generalization error for the bagging neural network ensemble of 6.3% relative to the single neural network model. The main idea of using ensembles is that the combination of classifiers (e.g. neural network, naïve Bayes, Genetic algorithm, Fuzzy logic, etc.) can lead to an improvement in the performance of a pattern recognition system in terms of better generalization and/or in terms of increased efficiency and clearer design (Canuto et al., 2007).

There are two families of combining multiple classifiers: serial combination and parallel combination. The serial combining method is based on combining classifiers sequentially. That is, the input of the i-th classifier is based on the output of the i-1-th classifier (Kimura & Shridhar, 1991). However, the parallel combining method is based on combining classifiers in parallel. If an input is given, multiple classifiers classify it concurrently, and then the classification results from them are integrated by a combination method, such as majority voting, weighted voting, bagging, and boosting, etc. (Kim et al., 2002).

Figure 1. Architecture of stacked generalization

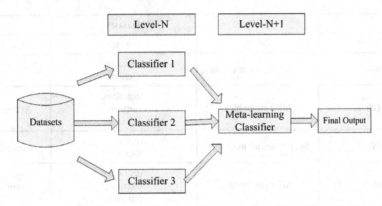

Stacked Generalization

Stacked generalization proposed by Wolpert (1992) is another advanced machine learning approach (Hu & Tsoukalas, 2003). The aim of stacked generalization is to estimate the error of using one single technique and then corrects those errors to maximize the accuracy (Wolpert, 1992; Tsai, 2003). Stacked generalization is based on combining a number of trained classifiers, and finding out a system to improve the generalization performance from the beginning to end by using some partitions of a given dataset. In other words, stacked generalization is composed of multi-level training stages (in general, two levels of training). That is, level-N classifiers are trained and can produce some classification results (by giving a testing set), and then, these results will become new training data for constructing the level-N+1 classifiers. Finally, the final classification result can be obtained from the level-N+1 classifiers. Figure 1 shows a modular classifier system which is based on stacked generalization and combines the outputs of several level-N classifiers using a level-N+1 classifier to produce the final output.

Related Work

Table 1 compares some related work published from 2005 to 2009 in terms of the classifier constructed, the dataset used, evaluation mea-

sure considered, etc. Detailed reviews of related studies can be referred to Kumar & Ravi (2007) and Tsai (2008).

Regarding Table 1, classifier ensembles based on MLP have been considered to improve the predication performance of single classifiers. However, other classifier ensembles have not been examined. In addition, there is no related study constructing stacked generalization for comparisons. On the other hand, the Australian, German, and Japanese datasets are widely used as the benchmarks.

EXPERIMENTAL SETUP

The Datasets

In this work, we use three bankruptcy prediction related datasets to conduct the experiments, which are Australian, German, and Japanese datasets. In literatures, these datasets are widely used for experiments and simulations (Hoffmann et al., 2007; Hsieh, 2005; Huang et al., 2007; Martens et al., 2007; Nanni & Lumini, 2008; Ong et al., 2005; Tsai & Wu, 2008b; West, 2000; West et al., 2005). Table 2 shows the detailed information of these datasets. In particular, 5-fold cross validation is considered for each dataset during training and testing the developed models. For detailed infor-

Table 1. Comparisons of related work

Work	Classifier	Dataset	Evaluation
Chuang & Lin (2009)	MLP	German	Accuracy; Type I/II errors
Luo et al. (2009)	Support vector machines	Australian; German	Accuracy
Nanni & Lumini (2009)	MLP ensembles	Australian; German; Japanese	Accuracy; Type I/II errors
Lin et al. (2008)	Support vector machines	Australian; German	Accuracy; statistical analysis
Tsai & Wu (2008)	MLP ensembles	Australian; German; Japanese	Accuracy; Type I/II errors
Hua et al. (2007)	Support vector machines; logistic regression	Shang-hai Stock Exchanges	Accuracy; statistical analysis
Huang et al. (2007)	Support vector machines	Australian; German	Accuracy; statistical analysis
Lee et al. (2006)	MLP; decision trees; logistic regression	Taiwan	Accuracy
Tsakonas et al. (2006)	MLP	Greek	Accuracy; Type I/II errors
Lee et al. (2005)	Cluster; MLP	Korea	Accuracy; Type I/II errors
West et al. (2005)	MLP ensembles	Australian; German	Accuracy; statistical analysis

mation of the variables over these three datasets, please refer to their websites.

For the Japanese dataset, the data samples contain positive and negative instances of people who were and were not granted credit. Similarly, the German and Australian datasets are used to classify people into good or ad credit risk groups. It should be noted here that there is no exact answer to what factors (variables) can well represent (non)bankruptcy in literature and this is out the scope of this paper. In addition, this paper does not consider feature selection to filter out unrepresentative variables during the data pre-process-

ing step in order to obtain better prediction performances (Tsai, 2009).

Single Classifiers

In the bankruptcy prediction domain, multi-layer perceptron (MLP) neural networks, decision trees (CART) and logistic regression are widely used. Detailed reviews of these techniques can be referred to Kumar & Ravi (2007) and Tsai (2008).

Therefore, for the single classification techniques considered in this paper are the MLP neural network, decision trees (CART) and logistic

Table 2. Information of the three datasets

Dataset	No. of variables	No. of Samples	Non-bankruptcy	Bankruptcy
Japanese	15	653	296	357
German	20	999	699	300
Australian	14	690	307	383

Table 3. The optimal parameters of neural network

Datasets	Training epochs	No. of hidden layer neurons	Average accuracy
Australian	100	8	0.855
German	100	16	0.734
Japanese	50	12	0.811

regression. In particular, the construction of the neural network model is more complex since some important parameters, such as the training epoch and the number of hidden layer nodes must carefully set up. Consequently, we set up four different learning epochs (50, 100, 200, and 300) and five different numbers of the hidden layer nodes (8, 12, 16, 24, and 32) in order to obtain the 'best' MLP classifier for comparisons. Table 3 shows the optimal parameters of the MLP model over the three datasets. These models will be used as one of the baseline prediction models. In addition, we will use these models to construct more advanced prediction models, which are MLP ensembles and stacked MLP classifiers.

Classifier Ensembles

As classifier ensembles are based on combining multiple classifiers, there are two different methods for the combination, which can result in homogeneous and heterogeneous classifier ensembles.

To construct heterogeneous classifier ensembles, the three different single classifiers are combined. That is, the 'best' MLP, CART, and LR models are combined based on their 5-fold cross validation results respectively.

On the other hand, for homogeneous classifier ensembles, first of all, we consider one 'best' classifier which provides the highest rate of accuracy over the three single classifiers. The 'best' classifier can be decided after the prediction result of single classifiers is obtained, say X classifier (i.e. one of MLP, CART, and LR).

In particular, using 5-fold cross validation results in 5 different X classifiers (and results), represented by X_1, X_2, X_3, X_4, and X_5. Then, we can select and combine three models of X which provide the top three highest rates of accuracy.

In addition, the majority voting and weighted voting combination methods are considered in homogeneous and heterogeneous classifier ensembles respectively for further comparisons.

As a result, there are four different models developed in this type of models. They are majority voting based homogeneous and heterogeneous classifier ensembles and weighted voting based homogeneous and heterogeneous classifier ensembles.

Stacked Generalization

To design stacked classifiers, two-level of classifiers need to be constructed. For the level-N classifiers, they are based on the single MLP, CART, and LR classifiers. Then, for the creation of the level-N+1 classifier, we also apply MLP, CART, and LR individually. That is, we would like to examine which combination can perform the best to identify the best stacked classifiers for comparisons.

Evaluation Methods

To evaluate the prediction performance of these prediction models, we consider average prediction accuracy rates and Type I/II error rates. They can be measured by a confusion matrix shown in Table 4.

Prediction accuracy can be obtained by

$$\text{Prediction accuracy} = \frac{a + d}{a + b + c + d}$$

The Type I error is the error of not rejecting a null hypothesis when the alternative hypothesis is the true state of nature. On the other hand, the Type II error is defined as the error of rejecting a null hypothesis when it is the true state of nature.

For the bankruptcy prediction domain, the Type I error is the rate of prediction errors of a classifier, which incorrectly classifies the non-bankruptcy group into the bankruptcy group. Opposed to the Type I error, the Type II error presents the rate of prediction errors of a classifier to incorrectly classify the bankruptcy group into the non-bankruptcy group. Therefore, the Type II error is more critical which contain higher risks for financial institutions.

EXPERIMENTAL RESULTS

Prediction Accuracy

For the prediction accuracy of the constructed models, Table 5 to 7 show the rate of average prediction accuracy of single baseline classifiers, classifier ensembles, and stacked classifiers over the three datasets respectively.

Regarding Table 5, the performance of logistic regression is better than the MLP and CART classifiers over two and three datasets respectively. On average, the LR classifier performs the best. On the other hand, MLP and CART does not have a significant difference.

As we can see that the combination method of classifier ensembles by weighted voting performs the best. In particular, the homogeneous classifier ensemble performs the best over the German and Australian datasets, and the heterogeneous classifier ensemble for the Japanese dataset.

The result of Table 7 is similar to the one of single baseline classifiers that the level N+1

Table 4. Confusion Matrix

↓actual \ predicted→	Bankruptcy	Non-bankruptcy
Bankruptcy	(a)	II (b)
Non-bankruptcy	I (c)	(d)

Table 5. Prediction accuracy of single baseline classifiers

	MLP	CART	LR
German	72.9%	73.3%	75.9%
Australian	85.65%	85.07%	86.23%
Japanese	83.97%	82.9%	83.97%
Avg.	80.84% (2)	80.42% (3)	82.03% (1)

Table 6. Prediction accuracy of classifier ensembles (CE)

	Homo. CE	Homo. CE (weighted voting)	Hetero. CE	Hetero. CE (weighted voting)
German	87.11%	87.34%	82.47%	85.44%
Australian	90.17%	90.75%	89.17%	89.59%
Japanese	87.66%	87.97%	87.87%	93.02%
Avg.	88.31% (3)	88.69% (2)	86.5% (4)	89.35% (1)

Table 7. Prediction accuracy of stacked generalization (SG)

	SG-MLP	SG-CART	SG-LR
German	64.5%	63%	65.1%
Australian	87.68%	86.23%	88.41%
Japanese	84.73%	83.97%	84.73%
Avg.	78.97% (2)	77.73% (3)	79.41% (1)

Figure 2. Comparisons of three best classification methods

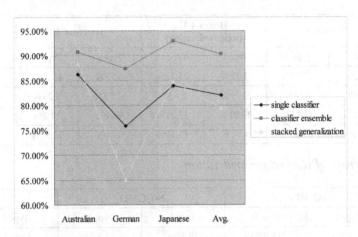

classifier based on LR (i.e. SG-LR) performs the best and slightly better than MLP (i.e. SG-MLP). On the other hand, SG-CART performs the worst over the three datasets.

Figure 2 compares the best classifiers of these three kinds of classification methods over the three datasets. Classifier ensembles perform the best over the three datasets. It is interesting to note that, these three classification methods perform badly based on the German dataset, which implies that this dataset is much more difficult to predict. On the other hand, although the single classifier does not perform better than stacked generalization over the Australian and Japanese datasets, it slightly outperforms stacked generalization on average.

Type I/II Errors

Besides comparing prediction accuracy rates of these models, we also examine the Type I/ II errors of them. Table 8 to 10 show the Type I/II errors of single classifiers, classifier ensembles, and stacked generalization over the three datasets respectively.

Regarding Table 8, LR can provide the lowest Type II error rate and MLP for the Type I error. Although CART performs the worst on average, it performs the best in terms of the Type I and II errors over the Japanese and Australian datasets respectively.

The result shows that classifier ensembles by weighted voting can provide the lowest Type I/II error rates, in which homogeneous and heterogeneous classifier ensembles do not have a big difference.

On average, the level N+1 classifier of stacked generalization based on LR outperforms the other classifiers in terms of the Type II error. For the Type I error, MLP as the level N+1 classifier performs the best.

Table 8. Type I/II errors of single baseline classifiers

	MLP		CART		LR	
	Type I	Type II	Type I	Type II	Type I	Type II
German	52.7%	15.96%	57.16%	22.53%	52.46%	11.64%
Australian	14.43%	14.42%	18.58%	11.98%	12.42%	14.93%
Japanese	21.13%	27.84%	19.04%	30.74%	25.68%	21.4%
Avg.	29.42%	19.41%	31.59%	21.75%	30.19%	15.99%

Table 9. Type I/II errors of classifier ensembles (CE)

	Homo. CE		Homo. CE (weighted voting)		Hetero. CE		Hetero. CE (weighted voting)	
	Type I	Type II	Type I	Type II	Type I	Type II	Type I	Type II
German	6.32%	27.48%	7.02%	25.12%	6.73%	41.22%	6.85%	31.92%
Australian	11.61%	8.16%	9.99%	8.43%	12.58%	9.29%	12.51%	8.44%
Japanese	12.88%	12.01%	12.21%	12.01%	9.61%	14.2%	9.61%	4.86%
Avg.	10.27%	15.88%	9.74%	15.19%	9.64%	21.57%	9.66%	15.07%

Table 10. Type I/II errors of stacked generalization

	SG-MLP		SG-CART		SG-LR	
	Type I	Type II	Type I	Type II	Type I	Type II
German	12.42%	14.93%	17.35%	12.11%	13.68%	12.22%
Australian	21.26%	19.2%	24.17%	24.74%	21.26%	18.18%
Japanese	25.68%	21.4%	19.65%	28.93%	25.68%	21.4%
Avg.	36.45%	18.51%	37.06%	21.93%	36.87%	17.27%

Figure 3 and 4 compare the Type I and II errors of the best classifiers of these three classification methods respectively. Similar to predication accuracy, classifier ensembles can provide the lowest rate of Type I and II errors on average. However, these three classification methods do not have a big difference in the Type II error, i.e. less than 5%. Again, by using the German dataset, the single classifier and classifier ensemble perform badly in term of the Type I and II errors respectively, which indicate that this dataset is difficult to predict.

CONCLUSION

To effectively predict business failure or bankruptcy is always one major research problem in accounting and finance fields. As related work has constructed numbers of different machine

Figure 3. Type I errors of three best classification methods

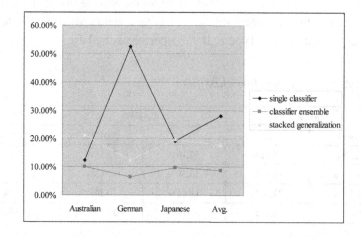

Figure 4. Type II errors of three best classification methods

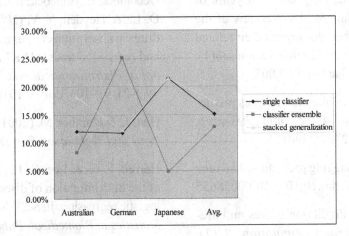

learning based prediction models, there is no a comparative study to examine the prediction performance of the models by advanced machine learning techniques, such as classifier ensembles and stacked generalization.

This comparative study allows us to understand that classifier ensembles by weighted voting perform the best in term of predication accuracy. In particular, homogeneous and heterogeneous classifier ensembles do not have a significant difference over the three datasets. On the other hand, as Type II errors are the most critical for financial institutions, it is interesting that on average stacked generalization and single classifiers perform better than classifier ensembles. These experimental results indicate that in practical related financial institutions should construct classifier ensembles and stacked classifiers for prediction accuracy and Type II errors respectively in order to make more effective decisions.

There are several issues to be considered in the future. First, hybrid machine learning techniques can be applied to construct the prediction models. That is, they are based on combining two or more machine learning techniques. In particular, the clustering and classification techniques are serially combined. Second, feature selection or dimensionality reduction can be performed during the data pre-processing step in order to filter out unrepresentative features, which are likely to degrade the prediction performance. Finally, some real case(s) can be involved to examine the performance of these models in terms of prediction accuracy and Type I/II errors.

ACKNOWLEDGMENT

This research is partially supported by National Science Council of Taiwan (NSC 96-2416-H-194-010-MY3).

REFERENCES

Alfaro, E., Garcia, N., Gamez, M., & Elizondo, D. (2008). Bankruptcy forecasting: An empirical comparison of AdaBoost and neural network. *Decision Support Systems*, *45*(1), 110–122. doi:10.1016/j.dss.2007.12.002

Altman, E. I. (1968). Financial rations, discriminant analysis and the prediction of corporate bankruptcy. *The Journal of Finance*, *23*(4), 589–609. doi:10.2307/2978933

Altman, E. I., Haldeman, R. G., & Narayanan, P. (1977). ZETATM analysis. A new model to identify bankruptcy risk of corporations. *Journal of Banking & Finance*, *1*(1), 29–54. doi:10.1016/0378-4266(77)90017-6

Balcaen, S., & Ooghe, H. (2006). 35 years of studies on business failure: An overview of the classic statistical methodologies and their related problems. *The British Accounting Review, 38*(1), 63–93. doi:10.1016/j.bar.2005.09.001

Beaver, W. H. (1966). Financial ratios as predictors of failure. *Journal of Accounting Research, 4*(3), 71–111. doi:10.2307/2490171

Breiman, L. (1996). Bagging predictors. *Machine Learning, 24*, 123–140. doi:10.1007/BF00058655

Breiman, L. (1999). Prediction games and arcing algorithms. *Neural Computation, 11*(7), 1493–1517. doi:10.1162/089976699300016106

Breiman, L., Friedman, J., Olshen, R., & Stone, C. (1984). *Classification and regression trees.* Wadsworth.

Canuto, A. M. P., Abreu, M. C. C., De Melo Oliverira, L., Xavier Jr, J. C., & Santos, A. D. M. (2007). Investigating the influence of the choice of the ensemble members in accuracy and diversity of selection-based and fusion-based methods for ensembles. *Pattern Recognition Letters, 28*(4), 472–486. doi:10.1016/j.patrec.2006.09.001

Chuang, C. L., & Lin, R. H. (2009). Constructing a reassigning credit scoring model. *Expert Systems with Applications, 36*(3), 1685–1694. doi:10.1016/j.eswa.2007.11.067

Cox, D. R., & Snell, E. J. (1989). *Analysis of binary data.* London: Chapman & Hall.

Daily, C. M., & Dalton, D. R. (1994). Bankruptcy and corporate governance: The impact of board composition and structure. *Academy of Management Journal, 37*(6), 1603–1617. doi:10.2307/256801

Deakin, E. (1972). A discriminant analysis of predictors of business failure. *Journal of Accounting Research, 10*(1), 167–179. doi:10.2307/2490225

Deconinck, E., Hancock, T., Commans, D., Massart, D. L., & Heyden, Y. V. (2005). Classification of drugs in absorption classes using the classification and regression trees (CART) methodology. *Journal of Pharmaceutical and Biomedical Analysis, 39*(1-2), 91–103. doi:10.1016/j.jpba.2005.03.008

Han, J., & Kamber, M. (2001). *Data mining: Concepts and Techniques.* San Diego.

Harrell, F. E., & Lee, K. L. (1985). A comparison of the discrimination of discriminant analysis and logistic regression. In Se, P. K. (Ed.), *Biostatistics: Statistics in Biomedical, Public Health, and Environmental Sciences.* Amsterdam: North-Holland.

Hayashi, Y., & Setiono, R. (2002). Combining neurla network predictions for midical diagnosis. *Computers in Biology and Medicine, 32*(4), 237–246. doi:10.1016/S0010-4825(02)00006-9

Hoffmann, F., Baesens, B., Mues, C., Gestel, T. V., & Vanthienen, J. (2007). Inferring descriptive and approximate fuzzy rules for credit scoring using evolutionary algorithms. *European Journal of Operational Research, 177*, 540–555. doi:10.1016/j.ejor.2005.09.044

Hosmer, D. W., & Lemeshow, S. (1989). *Applied logistic regression.* New York: Wiley Publications.

Hsieh, N. C. (2005). Hybrid mining approach in the design of credit scoring models. *Expert Systems with Applications, 28*, 655–665. doi:10.1016/j.eswa.2004.12.022

Hu, M. Y., & Tsoukalas, C. (2003). Explaining consumer choice through neural networks: the stacked generalization apporach. *European Journal of Operational Research, 146*(3), 650–660. doi:10.1016/S0377-2217(02)00368-5

Hua, Z., Wang, Y., Xu, X., Zhang, B., & Liang, L. (2007). Predicting corporate financial distress based on integration of support vector machine and logistic regression. *Expert Systems with Applications, 33*(2), 434–440. doi:10.1016/j.eswa.2006.05.006

Huang, C. L., Chen, M. C., & Wang, C. J. (2007). Credit scoring with a data mining approach based on support vector machines. *Expert Systems with Applications*, *33*(4), 847–856. doi:10.1016/j.eswa.2006.07.007

Huang, S. M., Tsai, C. F., Yen, D. C., & Cheng, Y. L. (2008). A hybrid financial analysis model for business failure prediction. *Expert Systems with Applications*, *35*(3), 1034–1040. doi:10.1016/j.eswa.2007.08.040

Hung, S. Y., Yen, D. C., & Wang, H. Y. (2006). Applying data mining to telecom churn management. *Expert Systems with Applications*, *31*(3), 515–524. doi:10.1016/j.eswa.2005.09.080

Kane, G. D., & Velury, U. (2004). The role of institutional ownership in the market for auditing services: an empirical investigation. *Journal of Business Research*, *57*(9), 976–983. doi:10.1016/S0148-2963(02)00499-X

Kay, O. W., Warde, A., & Martens, L. (2000). Social differentiation and the market for eating out in the UK. *International Journal of Hospitality Management*, *19*(2), 173–190. doi:10.1016/S0278-4319(00)00015-3

Kim, E., Kim, W., & Lee, Y. (2002). Combination of multiple classifiers for the customer's purchase behavior prediction. *Decision Support Systems*, *34*(2), 167–175. doi:10.1016/S0167-9236(02)00079-9

Kimura, F., & Shridhar, M. (1991). Handwritten numeral recognitioni based on multiple algorithms. *Pattern Recognition*, *24*(10), 969–983. doi:10.1016/0031-3203(91)90094-L

Kumar, P. R., & Ravi, V. (2007). Bankruptcy prediction in banks and firms via statistical and intelligent techniques – a review. *European Journal of Operational Research*, *180*(1), 1–28. doi:10.1016/j.ejor.2006.08.043

Laitinen, E. K., & Laitinen, T. (2000). Bankruptcy prediction: application of the Taylor's expansion in logistic regression. *International Review of Financial Analysis*, *9*(4), 327–349. doi:10.1016/S1057-5219(00)00039-9

Lee, K., Booth, D., & Alam, P. (2005). A comparison of supervised and unsupervised neural networks in predicting bankruptcy of Korean firms. *Expert Systems with Applications*, *29*(1), 1–16. doi:10.1016/j.eswa.2005.01.004

Lee, T. S., Chiu, C. C., Chou, Y. C., & Lu, C. J. (2006). Mining the customer credit using classification and regression tree and multivariate adaptive regression splines. *Computational Statistics & Data Analysis*, *50*(4), 1113–1130. doi:10.1016/j.csda.2004.11.006

Lensberg, T., Eilifsen, A., & McKee, T. E. (2006). Bankruptcy theory development and classification via genetic programming. *European Journal of Operational Research*, *169*(2), 677–697. doi:10.1016/j.ejor.2004.06.013

Li, C. T., & Tan, Y. H. (2006). Adaptive control of system with hysteresis using neural networks. *Journal of Systems Engineering and Electronics*, *17*(1), 163–167. doi:10.1016/S1004-4132(06)60028-5

Lin, S. W., Ying, K. C., Chen, S. C., & Lee, Z. J. (2008). Particle swarm optimization for parameter determination and feature selection of support vector machines. *Expert Systems with Applications*, *35*(11), 1817–1824. doi:10.1016/j.eswa.2007.08.088

Luo, S. T., Cheng, B. W., & Hsieh, C. H. (2008). Prediction model building with clustering-launched classification and support vector machines in credit scoring. *Expert Systems with Applications*, *36*(4), 7562–7566. doi:10.1016/j.eswa.2008.09.028

Martens, D., Baesens, B., Gestel, T. V., & Van-thienen, J. (2007). Comprehensible credit scoring models using rule extraction from support vector machines. *European Journal of Operational Research*, *183*(3), 1466–1476. doi:10.1016/j.ejor.2006.04.051

Meyer, P. A., & Pifer, H. W. (1970). Prediction of bank failure. *The Journal of Finance*, *25*(4), 853–868. doi:10.2307/2325421

Nanni, L., & Lumini, A. (2009). An experimental comparison of ensemble of classifiers for bankruptcy prediction and credit scoring. *Expert Systems with Applications*, *36*(2), 3028–3033. doi:10.1016/j.eswa.2008.01.018

Ohlson, J. A. (1980). Financial ratios and the probabilistic prediction of bankruptcy. *Journal of Accounting Research*, *18*(1), 109–131. doi:10.2307/2490395

Ong, C.,S., Huang, J.J., & Tzeng, G., H. (2005). Building credit scoring models using genetic programming. *Expert Systems with Applications*, *29*, 41–47. doi:10.1016/j.eswa.2005.01.003

Ozdamar, K. (2004). *Paket programlar ile istatistiksel veri analizi 1*. Eskisehir, Turkey: Kaan Kitabevi.

Park, C. S., & Han, I. (2002). A case-based reasoning with the feature weights derived by analytic hierarchy process for bankruptcy prediction. *Expert Systems with Applications*, *23*(3), 255–264. doi:10.1016/S0957-4174(02)00045-3

Pastena, V., & Ruland, W. (1986). The merger/Bankruptcy alternative. *Accounting Review*, *61*(2), 288–302.

Pendharkar, P. C. (2008). A threshold varying bisection method for cost sensitive learning in neural networks. *Expert Systems with Applications*, *34*(2), 1456–1464. doi:10.1016/j.eswa.2007.01.011

Richardson, F. M., Kane, G. D., & Lobingier, P. (1998). The impact of recession on the prediction of corporate failure. *Journal of Business Finance & Accounting*, *25*(1-2), 167–186. doi:10.1111/1468-5957.00182

Salcedo-Sanz, S., Fernandez-Villacanas, J. L., Segovia-Vargas, M. J., & Bousono-Calzon, C. (2005). Genetic programming for the prediction of insolvency in non-life insurance companies. *Computers & Operations Research*, *32*(4), 749–765. doi:10.1016/j.cor.2003.08.015

Shin, K. S., Lee, T. S., & Kim, H. J. (2005). An application of support vector machines in bankruptcy prediction model. *Expert Systems with Applications*, *28*(1), 127–135. doi:10.1016/j.eswa.2004.08.009

Shin, K. S., & Lee, Y. J. (2002). A genetic algorithm application in bankruptcy prediction modeling. *Expert Systems with Applications*, *23*(3), 321–328. doi:10.1016/S0957-4174(02)00051-9

Sohn, S. Y., & Lee, S. H. (2003). Data fusion, ensemble and clustering to improve the classification accuracy for the severity of road traffic accidents in Korea. *Safety Science*, *41*(1), 1–14. doi:10.1016/S0925-7535(01)00032-7

Stanley, J. D., & DeZoort, F. T. (2007). Audit firm tenure and financial restatements: An analysis of industry specialization and fee effects. *Journal of Accounting and Public Policy*, *26*(2), 131–159. doi:10.1016/j.jaccpubpol.2007.02.003

Theodoridis, S., & Koutroumbas, K. (2006). *Pattern recognition*. Amsterdam: Academic Press.

Tou, J. T., & Gonzalez, R. C. (1974). *Pattern Recognition Principles*. Reading, MA: Addison-Wesley.

Tsai, C. F. (2003). Stacked generalization: a novel solution to bridge the semantic gap for content-based image retrieval. *Online Information Review*, *27*(6), 442–445. doi:10.1108/14684520310510091

Tsai, C. F. (2008). A review of bankruptcy prediction models: the machine learning perspective. In Peters, H., & Vogel, M. (Eds.), *Machine Learning Research Progress*. New York: Nova Science Publishers.

Tsai, C. F. (2009). Feature selection in bankruptcy prediction. *Knowledge-Based Systems, 22*(2), 120–127. doi:10.1016/j.knosys.2008.08.002

Tsai, C. F., & Wu, J. W. (2008). Using neural network ensembles for bankruptcy prediction and credit scoring. *Expert Systems with Applications, 34*(4), 2639–2649. doi:10.1016/j.eswa.2007.05.019

Tsakonas, A., Dounias, G., Doumpos, M., & Zopounidis, C. (2006). Bankruptcy prediction with neural logic networks by means of grammar-guided genetic programming. *Expert Systems with Applications, 30*(3), 449–461. doi:10.1016/j.eswa.2005.10.009

Van Gestel, V., Baesens, B., Suykens, J. A. K., Van den Poel, D., Baestaens, D. E., & Willekens, M. (2006). Bayesian kernel based classification for financial distress detection. *European Journal of Operational Research, 172*(3), 979–1003. doi:10.1016/j.ejor.2004.11.009

Wei, C. P., & Chiu, I. T. (2002). Turning telecommunications call details to churn perdiction: A data mining approach. *Expert Systems with Applications, 23*(2), 103–112. doi:10.1016/S0957-4174(02)00030-1

West, D. (2000). Neural network credit scoring models. *Computers & Operations Research, 27*(11/12), 1131–1152. doi:10.1016/S0305-0548(99)00149-5

West, D., Dellana, S., & Qian, J. (2005). Neural network ensemble strategies for financial decision applications. *Computers & Operations Research, 32*(10), 2543–2559. doi:10.1016/j.cor.2004.03.017

Wolpert, D. H. (1992). Stacked generalization. *Neural Networks, 5*(2), 241–259. doi:10.1016/S0893-6080(05)80023-1

Wu, C. H., Tzeng, G. H., Goo, Y. J., & Fang, W. C. (2007). A real-valued genetic algorithm to optimize the parameters of support vector machine for predicting bankruptcy. *Expert Systems with Applications, 32*(2), 397–408. doi:10.1016/j.eswa.2005.12.008

Zhan, G., Patuwo, B. E., & Hu, M. Y. (1998). Forecasting with artificial neural network: The state of the art. *International Journal of Forecasting, 14*(1), 35–62. doi:10.1016/S0169-2070(97)00044-7

Zhou, D., & Zhang, J. (2002). Face recognition by combining several algorithms. *Pattern Recognition, 3*(3), 497–500.

KEY TERMS AND DEFINITIONS

Bankruptcy Prediction: Predicting whether a new customer will be bankrupt to issue a loan.

Machine Learning: Developing algorithms to allow computers to change behavior based on data.

Classifier Ensembles: Combining multiple classifiers in a parallel manner, in which each of these classifiers take the same unknown instance to make their own outputs for further combination and then the final output can be produced.

Stacked Generalization: A multi-level learning architecture to improve the classification performance.

Chapter 8
Data Mining Used for Analyzing the Bankruptcy Risk of the Romanian SMEs

Laura Giurca Vasilescu
University of Craiova, Romania

Marian Siminica
University of Craiova, Romania

Cerasela Pirvu
University of Craiova, Romania

Costel Ionascu
University of Craiova, Romania

Anca Mehedintu
University of Craiova, Romania

ABSTRACT

The small and medium enterprises (SMEs) represent the backbone of the economy, playing a major economic and social role in the process of developing a dynamic economy. But the recent evolutions in the financial markets, the international financial crisis, the increased competition on markets, the lack of financial resources and the insufficient adaptation of many firms to the requests of the European market are new threats which can determine the bankruptcies of the Romanian SMEs. In this context, starting from the necessity to design an early warning system, we will elaborate a new model for analysis of bankruptcy risk for the Romanian SMEs that combine two main categories of indicators: financial ratios and non-financial indicators. The authors' analysis is based on data mining techniques (CHAID) in order to identify the firms' categories accordingly to the bankruptcy risk levels. Through the proposed analysis model they try to offer a real surveillance system for the Romanian SMEs which can allow an early signal regarding the bankruptcy risk.

DOI: 10.4018/978-1-61692-865-0.ch008

INTRODUCTION

The importance of small and medium enterprise (SMEs) as the basis for establishing and developing a modern, dynamic and knowledge-based economy is widely recognized. Generally, small and medium companies are more dynamic and flexible than the corporations, being able to respond quickly in a competitive market and to adapt to the structural changes in the global economy. But the integration process, the globalization and the new financial crisis imposes a higher adaptation effort for the SMEs, in general and for the Romanian SMEs, in particular.

After 1990, Romania has made considerable progress in setting up an extensive policy framework to support the SME sector. There were developed a range of institutions, policy instruments, programs and resources in order to assist the small and medium enterprise development in Romania accordingly with the EU regulations. In 2002, Romania, together with other candidate countries, signed the Maribor Declaration and engaged to harmonize its policies for supporting the competitiveness of local companies to the provisions of the Lisbon Strategy. As an expression of Romania's international engagement, the National Development Plan 2007-2013 highlights the importance of restructuring and developing existing SMEs and the creation of new enterprises and defines the priority measures as improving the business environment, supporting access to financial resources and providing support services to and entrepreneurs. In the same time, the Ministry for SMEs, Trade and Business Environment (MSMETBE) is also responsible for ensuring Romania's compliance with its obligations under the European Charter for Small Enterprises.

Along with the positive evolutions in the Romanian economy (economic growth of 8.3% in 2004 and 7.9% in 2006), the SMEs sector from Romania registered an ascendant trend in the last years. In 2007, the SMEs predominated in the Romanian economy having a substantial contribution to the GDP (70%), to the budget incomes (about 60%) and playing a main role in job creation (60.7% of active population) accordingly with the Annual Report of MSMETBE, 2008.

But not all Romanian SMEs are prepared for acting their role of economy engine. The lack of their competitiveness is caused mostly by the lack of adaptation to the European standards or their incapacity to attract financing sources for investment in new technologies, new products and implementing the quality and the environment protection systems (Giurca et al., 2008). Despite the Government's measures to generate a favorable background for the development of the SMEs and to improve their access to financing sources, there are still many deficiencies on the financial market. Therefore, the largest part of the planned investments is done on the basis of their own funds followed by the banking credit and other non-reimbursing sources as budget allocation or grants offered by EU.

The financial crisis represents another new threat for SMEs financing and growth. The clear signs about the global credit crunch make the access to external finance becoming much more difficult and very expensive.

Most of the Romanian small and medium sized enterprises are affected by the financial crisis mainly because of lower demand; the limited financial resources and the high dependence on a single credit institution; the difficult lending conditions; the dependence on the large firms because of the sub-contracting system; the high volatility of the exchange rate, etc. Also, the Romania SMEs have to face a financial deadlock partly because of the state through its debts towards the private sector and on the other hand, by other companies that become indebted, being created a vicious circle. Other effects of the financial crisis upon SMEs are the increasing unemployment, reduction of exports, lower investments, the reduction of the incomes to the state budget, and finally, yet importantly, the psychological effect of the market difficulties.

In the circumstances imposed by the financial crisis, the Romanian SMEs have to face the new challenges and should adapt their strategy to the new conditions. Therefore, an early warning system that could reveal the economic-financial situation and prevent the financial difficulties, could offer these firms a major advantage in the market competition.

On the other hand, the development of the informatics technologies and the using of the informatics applications for evaluation the risk and assisting the decisions generated a considerable volume of data to be analyzed. This fact was possible because the development of the data basis and also because of the evolutions of the storage media, which have the capacity to keep huge amounts of data (Soava et al., 2008).

As technique of exploitation and analysis of important amounts of data in order to find out patterns or rules with a signification, data mining can facilitate the discovering, in data apparently without any relation, of relations through can be anticipated the possible problems or can be solved the studied problems.

Data mining is the process of analyzing data from different perspectives and summarizing it into useful information through the following stages: extract, transform and load transaction data onto the data warehouse system; store and manage the data in a multidimensional database system; provide data access to business analysts and information technology professionals; analyze the data by application software, present the data in a useful format, such as a graph or table. Therefore, in our study we will use the data mining as operation to extract the interesting information and previous unknown and which can represent an only phases in the complex process of discovering the knowledge in the data basis.

The main objective of the chapter is to elaborate a new model for analysis of bankruptcy risk for the Romanian SMEs which combine the two main categories of indicators: financial ratios and non-financial indicators. The analysis is based on

data mining techniques in order to identify the firms' categories accordingly to the bankruptcy risk levels.

BACKGROUND

The experience of the EU member states demonstrates that a well developed SMEs sector is able to ensure and support the stability and the macro-economic growth. In fact, the economic and social importance of the SMEs sector - considered as backbones of the economy - is recognized in the economic literature (Newberry, 2006; Biggs, 2002; Peneder, 2000). Thus, there are brought numerous arguments in favor of SMEs contribution to the development of economy: creation of new jobs (Birch, 1987), contribution to the GDP, key factor of the industrial development (Acs & Audretsch, 1987); add dynamism and flexibility to the business environment; contribute to the improvements of the economic performances; the SMEs are considered a considerable source of innovative activities (Thurik, 1996; Nooteboom, 1994; Jones & Tilley, 2003) and contribute to the stimulation of entrepreneurship (Acs et al., 1996); the increase of competitiveness (Song & Parry, 1997) and exports (Lefebre & Lefebre, 2000).

Moreover, the SMEs are easier to be managed and administrated, have an increased flexibility and a better adaptability to the market, permit a better communication among the employees, exploit a specific know how, benefit by a local solidarity. But despite these advantages, there are also disadvantages generated by the insufficient capital necessary for their development; high level of centralization; the fact that they can not take advantages from the scale economies; the lack of a strategically implication; the vulnerability to the continuous modifications from the economic environment (Szathmary-Miclea, 2003).

Accordingly with the Romanian legislation, the small and medium enterprises are structured in the followings three categories: micro-enterprises (less than 9 employees and a net turnover/total assets less than 2 million Euro); small firms (between 10 and 49 employees and a net turnover/total assets less than 10 million Euro); medium firms (between 50 and 249 employees and a net turnover less than 50 million Euro/total assets less than 43 million Euro).

In structure, the micro-enterprises dominate the SME sector (88.4%) while the small firms represent 9.6% and the medium firms represent 2%, in 2007. In relative terms, the most substantial share is the one of the SMEs belonging to the services sector (75.5%) followed by industry (12.2%) and constructions sector (9.4%) (MSMETBE, 2008).

Accessing the financing resources represent one of the main challenging factors for the Romanian SMEs. Besides, the international financial crisis generated new dimensions of the financing problems and new challenges for the SMEs. The necessity to stimulate the access of SMEs to the financing sources represents a concern for many specialists who underlined the deficiencies registered in this field (Berger & Udell, 2005; Beck, 2007, Carbo-Valverde et al., 2008).

In Romania, the main causes which limits the access of SMEs to the financing funds are the followings: the lack of guarantees, the limited experience in business field, the lack of information, the high interest rates, the terms and conditions inappropriate for the SMEs, the lack of managerial skills at the firms level (Pirvu et al, 2008). Also, from the credit institutions view, the main deficiencies are related to the lack of flexible credit programs, the limited experience of banks in SMEs financing and the lack of financing capital. Moreover, the financial crisis imposed new restrictions to the banks which modified the conditions for offering loans to the firms. In these conditions, there should be improved the legislative framework in order to introduce a system of credits based on guarantees and on the development of the National Credit Guarantee Fund for SMEs (FNGCIMM). All these measures could determine the decrease of risk and the credit could be ensured by the debtor guarantees or by the guarantee fund. The reduction of risk will have as effect the decrease of credit cost, thus the SMEs could overtake the restrictions imposed by the banks.

In the new context, should be found new alternative solutions for financing (venture capitals, micro-credits, financial mezzanine, business angels) that contribute to the reduction of risks (Sanders & Wegener, 2006; Giurca, 2008; Zavatta, 2008). On other hand, the difficulties in accessing the financial resources determine the SMEs to administrate properly their assets and to adopt solution for increasing the efficiency of their activity.

The increased competition on the internal and external market, the uncontrolled expansion of the firms based on banking credits, insufficient adaptation of many firms to the requests of the European market and the recent international financial crisis are the main causes that can determine the bankruptcies of the SMEs (Ionascu & Radu, 2008). In fact, the definition of the concept of bankruptcy represent one of most difficult tasks of the researches in this field taking into consideration the complex aspects of this phenomenon. Some specialists (Ooghe & Van Wymeersch, 2006) take into consideration two aspects of the firms which face financial difficulties: the economic (firm that can not fulfill its economic objectives: maximizing the market value – in conditions of social and economic restraints) and the juridical one (from this point of view, resulting a classification of the firms in difficulties: bankruptcy firms and firms for which the bankruptcy can not be avoided). Therefore, the bankruptcy can be defined, from the economic view, the situation when a firm can not adapt to the economic environment or from the juridical view, when the firm is in situation of payments incapacity, determined by the juridical procedure.

Others specialists (Casta & Zerbib, 1979) use three approaches of the bankruptcy concept, respectively: juridical (the insolvency), economical (the absence of profitability and efficiency) and financial (the payment incapacity of debts). Also, the financial bankruptcy can be defined taking into consideration three possible situations: when the equities are negative; when the firm can not face the debts; when the firm's activity is carried or is liquidated under the surveillance of a law court (Pastena & Ruland, 1986).

There were established criteria for defining the bankruptcy firms taking into consideration the banking approach, respectively, the existence of difficulties in payment of the installments, or the renegotiation of the payment term for the debts (Ward & Foster, 1997).

Taking onto consideration the different approaches, the bankruptcy, from the juridical view, can be defined as the state of a firm, at a moment, caused by the impossibility to pay the debts and against which there was initiated a procedure of reorganization or juridical liquidation. This definition is not always useful in practice for the financial annalists, because it involves the will of the creditors or of the firm to initiate in court the bankruptcy procedures. In that sense, more useful is the definition from the financial perspective, accordingly with the bankruptcy can be defined as a degradation of the financial situation of the firm, reflected in the reduction or the lack of profitability, solvency, liquidity and payment capacity, as well as on the deterioration of the level of other relevant financial ratios. As well, the bankruptcy risk can be defined as the probability that the firm will end its activity in the future under the unfavorable action of several internal or external factors.

The models for forecasting the bankruptcy risk were developed in mostly market economies and can be structures as follows: the first stage in US, in the 60' (such as Beaver, 1966; Altman, 1968) and brought back after the famous bankruptcy cases registered in the last years; the second stage developed in the Continental European countries (Conan & Holder, 1979; Bilderbeek, 1979, Grammatikos & Gloubos, 1984, Bardos, 1998) in parallel with the evolutions from English-Saxon school

(Edmister, 1972; Diamond, 1976; Deakin, 1977, Springate, 1978, Ohlson, 1982, Zavgren, 1983) and Japan (Koh & Killough, 1980, Koh, 1992, Shirata, 1999) and the third stage from the Eastern European countries (including Romania) which regard the using of some modern techniques of analysis and prognosis (Manecuta & Nicolae, 1996, Bailesteanu, 1998, Ivonciu, 1998, Anghel, 2000; Siminica, 2005).

The models proposed till present have the disadvantage that they can be applied just in the economies (or the activity sector) where it was made the statistical study and their use can not be generalized. Moreover, the period characterized by economic instability determine the correlations of the scoring function elaborated, which limit temporally the using of these models or impose their updating at regular period of times.

The methods which use the scoring function are methods of statistical forecasting for the firms' bankruptcy which have as objective the evaluation in a synthetically way of the financial situation of the firms. These methods are based on the following principle: the potential bankruptcy situation manifested through some particularities which differentiate it from a normal situation, thus the analyzed firm will be included in the group of firms considered healthy or in difficulty. In order to use efficiently the scoring function, the following conditions should be followed: using of scoring in dynamic; using of many scores; using of adapted scoring; comparison of the firms' scoring with the average scoring of the sector (Szathmary-Miclea, 2003).

A special attention should be paid to the indicators used in order to evaluate the financial situation of a firm. Therefore for the study of bankruptcy risk there will be selected those financial ratios which separate more clearly the bankruptcy firms from the low bankruptcy risk ones. Thus, we selected 15 ratios, grouped in 4 categories, such as: profitability ratios; risk ratios; liquidity and solvability ratios, rotation ratios.

Besides the financial ratios, the analysis of the non financial indicators is imposed by the fact that the financial indicators has as informational source the classical records which indicate periodically, *posteriori,* the final financial results without any explanation regarding the way these were obtained. Confronted with the increased competition and other challenges, the managers look for new information sources regarding the key factors which determine the firms' performance. In these conditions, the performance analysis should be extended to the qualitative aspects of the firms and the non-financial indicators could offer important information regarding the real situation of the firms (Buse et al., 2006).

One of the problems the Romanian firm, especially the SMEs, have to face is the fact that many times the managers do not recognize the signs of possible risk and failure in their business. Therefore, the recognition of some early warning signals of financial distress could help the managers to adopt some measures and solutions in order to avoid them.

Early warning system (EWS) is a technique of analysis used to predict the achievement condition of enterprise and to decrease the risk of financial crisis (Koyuncugil & Ozgulbas, 2009). Therefore the EWS should assist the SMEs to be prepared for the future changes and to anticipate them, representing an useful financial management's instrument. But the recent financial crisis revealed the weaknesses of the system and raised doubts about the efficiency of the models based mostly on financial ratios (the models towards the prediction of profits of enterprise; the ratio based models towards the prediction of bankrupt/distress of enterprise, economic trend based models towards the prediction of bankrupt/distress of enterprise (Koyuncugil & Ozgulbas, 2007).

In this context, it is necessary to combine the financial ratios and non-financial indicators in order to provide an appropriate early warning system closer to the firm's environment which can reveal different risk levels and consequently, identify the main determining factors.

But as more data about firms is gathered, this make impossible the study and interpretation of all data to find useful information. In this context, data mining is becoming an increasingly important tool to transform this data into information.

Generally, data mining is the efficient discovery of valuable, non-obvious information from a large collection of data (Ponniah, 2001) or it is the process of extracting hidden patterns from large amounts of data. The goal of any data mining operation is to understand the business, discern new patterns and possibilities and also turn these into actions.

Data mining is the process of analyzing data from different perspectives and summarizing it into useful information - information that can be used in order to increase revenue, reduce the costs, or both. Data mining enables the firms to determine relationships among internal factors (such as price, product positioning, staff skills) and external factors (such as economic indicators, competition, customer) (Rygielski et al., 2002, Kusiak & Smith, 2007, Trumbach et al, 2006). Besides, it enables them to determine the impact on sales, customer satisfaction and corporate profits. Therefore, data mining tools can predict behaviors and future risks, like financial distress (Sun & Li, 2008), bankruptcy (Ravi Kumar & Ravi, 2006), allowing businesses to make proactive, knowledge-driven decisions (Ponniah, 2001).

The main scope of data mining consists of:

- Automated prediction of trends and behaviors. Data mining allow the process of finding predictive information in large databases. Questions that traditionally required extensive analysis can now be answered directly from the data;
- Automated discovery of previously unknown patterns. Data mining tools sweep through databases and identify previously hidden patterns.

The application of the data mining techniques can be done from the perspective of an upward or downward approach. In the downward approach, the effort is oriented towards the confirmation or non-confirmation of some ideas (hypothesis) formulated before through others means. The upward approach intends to extract new knowledge and information from the available data and the search can be controlled or uncontrolled.

The most important techniques of data mining are the followings:

1. Neural Networks:
    ○   can supply solutions, especially of predictive nature, for problems with a high complexity and volatility;
    ○   the typical cases of successful use of neural networks include: setting up the prices on the real estate market, evolution of exchange rates on the financial markets, analysis of the credits etc.;
    ○   a neural networks can solve a certain type of problem after a learning process. The learning processes permit the network to identify automatically a set of correlations used afterwards for predictions.

2. Decision Trees:
    ○   it is a technique applicable for both classification and prediction;
    ○   the result presents a hierarchy of logical rules established through the exploration of a basis of examples;
    ○   the rules are obtained as effect of subdivision more and more detailed of the examples, in function of the content of the attributes;
    ○   Specific decision tree methods include Classification and Regression Trees (CART) and Chi Square Automatic Interaction Detection (CHAID). CART and CHAID are decision tree techniques used for clas-

sification of a dataset. They provide a set of rules that can be applied to a new (unclassified) dataset to predict which records will have a given outcome. CART segments a dataset by creating 2-way splits while CHAID segments using chi square tests to create multi-way splits;

3. Case-based reasoning:
    ○   it search for answers for the new problems in the experiences from the past;
    ○   facing a new situation, there will be searched the similar known cases and the conclusions will be applied in the new situation;
    ○   the method can be applied both for classification and predictions;

4. Genetic algorithms:
    ○   apply the main mechanisms of natural selection in order to encourage the conservation and reproduction, from a numerous population, of the most performing, the best adapted individuals;
    ○   the population is formed from a set of possible solutions of a problem; the most adapted individual, is therefore, the best solution;
    ○   the genetic algorithm allows the finding of the optimal solution (through predictions or classifications).

5. Clustering:
    ○   permits the identifying of a the existent groups in the ensemble of the analyzed data;
    ○   the groups result automatically from the processing, without a starting point (a certain criteria or a feature);
    ○   it is a techniques which have the capacity to reveal hidden characteristics from a set of registering;
    ○   the automatic detection of cluster is recommendable as starting technique

for a data mining project. The results are going to be explored with other techniques in order to get more completed information.

6. Association analysis:
   ○ try to find the rules that describe the frequent appearance together of heterogeneous objects;
   ○ the results get a certain and simple form which encourage their understanding and application;
   ○ the techniques can be applied for non direct searching for information (it can be applied to commercial transaction).

From all these techniques, the CHAID algorithm (Chi-square Automatic Interaction Detection) is an effective approach for getting a quick but meaningful segmentation where segments are defined in terms of demographic or other variables that are predictive of a single categorical dependent variable (Magidson & Vermunt, 2004).

The original CHAID algorithm was introduced by Kass (1980) for nominal dependent variables. CHAID is a recursively partitions method used in exploratory analyses that relate a potentially large number of categorical predictor variables to a single categorical nominal dependent variable. It was extended to ordinal dependent variables by Magidson (1993) who illustrated how this extension could be used to take advantage of fixed scores such as profitability, for each category of the dependent variable when such scores are known, as well as how to estimate meaningful scores when category scores are unknown.

Specifically, the algorithm proceeds as follows (Hoare, 2004):

• *Preparing predictors.* The first step is to create categorical predictors out of any continuous predictors by dividing the respective continuous distributions into a number of categories with an approximately equal number of observations. For cat-

egorical predictors, the categories (classes) are "naturally" defined.

• *Merging categories.* The next step is to cycle through the predictors to determine for each predictor the pair of (predictor) categories that is least significantly different with respect to the dependent variable; for classification problems (where the dependent variable is categorical as well), it will compute a *Chi*-square test (Pearson *Chi*-square); for regression problems (where the dependent variable is continuous), F tests.

• *Selecting the split variable.* The next step is to choose the split the predictor variable with the smallest adjusted p-value, i.e., the predictor variable that will yield the most significant split; if the smallest adjusted p-value for any predictor is greater than some alpha-to-split value, then no further splits will be performed, and the respective node is a terminal node. Continue this process until no further splits can be performed.

CHAID "builds" non-binary trees (i.e., trees where more than two branches can attach to a single root or node), based on a relatively simple algorithm that is particularly well suited for the analysis of larger datasets which is the case of SMEs. Also, because the CHAID algorithm will often effectively yield many multi-way frequency tables it has been particularly popular in marketing research, in the context of market segmentation studies.

USING DATA MINING FOR ANALYZING THE BANKRUPTCY RISK OF THE ROMANIAN SMES

Issues and Controversies

The present economic and financial crisis and the increased competition on the internal and international markets cause new challenges for the

Romanian firms which have to adapt to the new circumstances. The lack of possibilities to adapt to the market evolutions can lead to financial failures and even bankruptcies for the firms. In fact, the bankruptcy risk is determined by both internal (such as internal errors, inappropriate investment management, low productivity, losses in the operational activity, indebtedness) and external factors (economic environment factors). Both of these factors have a convergent effect in the degradation process (Hlaciuc et al., 2008).

The analysis of the causes that can determine the bankruptcy of firms has revealed their diversity and has underlined the idea that bankruptcy is not a sudden phenomenon caused by conjuncture, but is determined also by the progressive degradation of the financial situation of the firms. Moreover, the small and medium firm are more exposed to the bankruptcy risk because their insufficient equities and the lack of financial resources.

The need for development of the SMEs imposes an easier access to the financing sources, especially banking credits. But at present, the SMEs have a limited access to the credits. The loans are guaranteed with real guarantees which have values higher than the credit amount. As well, the banks accept as guarantees for the credits only real estates, which in the condition of the crisis, registered decreases of the markets values.

The Ministry for SMEs, Trade and Business Environment from Romania estimates that 40% of the SMEs (about 240,000 firms) could get bankruptcy in 2009. The most affected are the start-ups but also the firms which are not capitalized, do not have a business plan and depend by contracts on the large firms. On activity sectors, 45% from the firms on services, tourism and food industry declared bankruptcy after 2 years since the European integration and 75% of the real estate firms are expected to close their activity. Besides the fact that many firms will declare insolvable, the main danger is that the number of new born firms will decrease dramatically.

Therefore, a new analysis model that could allow the evaluation of the SMEs economic-financial situation and the prediction of possible financial difficulties, become an important basis for taking preventive measures in order to avoid the bankruptcies.

Data Analysis

For elaboration of the model, the first step was the collection of necessary data regarding the Romanian SMEs from Dolj county (12,496 firms) using the data basis from the Ministry of Public Finance, in the year 2007.

Another important stage was the selection and calculation of the financial ratios. Very often, there are used the solvency and liquidity ratios because the evolution of these indicators in time reflect the dynamic of the health financial situation of the firms. As well, the profitability registered by a firm for the investment is a determinant factor of the firm's financial situation and solvency.

The liquidity of a firm depends on the efficiency of using its assets. Thus when the inventories and claims increase faster than the sales and short term debts, the liquidity will be affected negatively. As well, the investment made by the firm can affect its liquidity: higher the weight of the fixed assets, lower the liquidity and vice versa. But the structure of the firm's assets depends, more on the specific of the firm's activity and less on the decisions and preferences of the managers.

The firms which pay more attention to the assets management have more chances to survive because they get higher assets profitability then other firms in difficulty, which will be forced to sell part of the assets or to restructure in order to finance their activity.

Therefore for the study of bankruptcy risk there will be selected those financial ratios which separate more clearly the bankruptcy firms from the low bankruptcy risk ones. Thus, for the study there were be selected the most discriminant financial ratios, grouped in 5 classes, in function of the risks involved, as follows:

- 1st class: very high risk;
- 2nd class: high risk;
- 3rd class: medium risk;
- 4th class: low risk;
- 5th class: very low risk.

From the ensemble of financial ratios, we selected 15 ratios, grouped in 4 categories, such as:

- *Profitability ratios:*
  - Return on Investment (Operating profit/Total assets);
  - Return on Equity (Net profit/Total Equity);
  - Operating Profit Margin (Operating Profit/Operating Expenses);
  - Return on Turnover (Operating Profit/Turnover);
- *Risk ratios:*
  - Financial Stability Ratio (Invested Capital or Long term Capital/Total Capital);
  - Debt Ratio (Total Debt/Total Capital);
  - Capital Assets Financing (Invested Capital/Fixed Assets);
- *Liquidity and solvability ratios:*
  - Current Liquidity (Current Assets/Current Liabilities);
  - Quick Ratio (Current Assets – Inventories/Current Liabilities);
  - General Solvability (Total assets/Total Liabilities);
  - Patrimonial Solvability (Total Equity/Total Capital);
- *Rotation Ratios:*
  - Account Receivable Turnover Rate (Accounts Receivable x 365/Turnover);
  - Debt Turnover Rate (Debts x 365/Turnover);
  - Current Assets Turnover Rate (Current Assets x 365/Turnover);
  - Total Assets Turnover Rate (Total Incomes/Total Assets).

In order to include the firms in one of the 5 classes, first of all, there should be done the classification in function of the 15 financial ratios. The intervals taken into consideration are presented in the Figure 1.

Thus, each firm was included in a risk zone in function of the value of each indicator. There are numerous cases of firms that, in function of the value of each financial ratio analyzed, were included in different risk classes. In order to establish the risk classes for each firm, taking into consideration all financial ratios, there was determined the modal value (the most often found value) of this. For the firms that registered more modal values, there was calculated the weighted arithmetic mean of the individual risk classes, the resulted value representing the risk classes where the firm was included.

Besides the financial ratios, in our analysis there were introduced the non-financial indicators. The using of the non-financial indicators has as purpose the achievement of the progresses made through the application of specific measures which ensure the success of the firm. The ensemble of these measures is named *non financial process,* which supposes the following stages:

a. The existence of disturbing factors able to bring about a real shock in its operational environment;
b. The discovering of old system's insufficiencies;
c. Defining the key factors which determine the success of the firm;
d. Defining the performance measures which are objective and quantifiable;
e. Putting in practice of these measures;
f. Evaluation of a new system.

Figure 1. Classification intervals for the 15 financial ratios

Nr. crt.	Ratio	Activity sector	1	2	3	4	5
1	Return on Investment	All	< 0	0 - 6	6 - 12	12 - 18	> 18
2	Return on Equity	All	< 0	0 – 7	7 - 14	14 - 21	> 21
3	Operating Profit Margin	Trade	< 0	0 - 3	3 - 6	6 - 9	> 9
		Others	< 0	0 - 5	5 - 10	10 - 15	> 15
4	Return on Turnover	Trade	< 0	0 - 2	2 - 4	4 - 7	> 7
		Others	< 0	0 - 4	4 - 8	8 -12	> 12
5	Financial Stability Ratio	All	< 0	0 - 25	25 - 50	50 - 75	> 75
6	Debt Ratio	All	100 -	70 - 100	40 - 70	20 – 40	0 – 20
7	Capital Assets Financing	All	< 0	0 - 50	50 - 90	90 - 130	> 130
8	Current Liquidity	All	< 100	100 - 120	120 - 140	140 - 160	> 160
9	Quick Ratio	All	< 20	20 - 50	50 - 80	80 - 100	> 100
10	General Solvability	All	< 100	100 - 150	150 - 200	200 - 250	> 250
11	Patrimonial Solvability	All	< 0	0 - 25	25 - 40	40 - 70	> 70
12	Account Receivable Turnover Rate	All	> 180	100 - 180	40 - 100	10 - 40	< 10
13	Debt Turnover Rate	All	> 180	100 - 180	40 - 100	10 - 40	< 10
14	Current Assets Turnover Rate	Trade	> 180	120 - 180	60 - 120	30 - 60	< 30
		Others	> 300	180 - 300	120 - 180	60 - 120	< 60
15	Total Assets Turnover Rate	All	< 0.7	0.7 – 1.4	1.4 – 2.1	2.1 - 3	>3

For each firm, the process start through the appearance of a shock in its operational environment, shock that lead to the conclusion that the used methods did not produce the expected effects. In that way, the managers become aware of the increased competition and the possible loss of clients. In the same time, the shock was perceived as a driver and it leads towards the new modalities of administration, measuring and control of the production process.

In order to attenuate the insufficiencies of the control process – apparent or not – the firm should determine the factors that can offer a competition advantage, named key factors of success. This involves an important investment in time for defining these factors by the managers, as well the characteristics which permit the firm to survive in a competition environment and even to growth.

The 10 non-financial indicators that will be considered in the analysis are the followings:

1. *Management quality.* The evaluation criteria for this indicator are the followings:

   ○ the character, integrity and behavior of the managers;
   ○ the training experience in the activity field and in management positions;
   ○ the existence in the management team of at least one person qualified in the financial-accounting activity;
   ○ the membership of the managers in professional associations;

2. *Relations and market reputation.* The evaluation criteria for this indicator are the followings:

   ○ the development perspective on short and long term of the activity sector;
   ○ the major problems the sectors is confronted with (technological changes, government norm, environment changes, etc);
   ○ the advantages/opportunities offered by the economic sector;
   ○ the facilities/difficulties to get into the market (capital, loyalty to the trade, technology, government policies);

- the existence of the substitution products;
3. *Offered products.* The followings criteria were taken into consideration:
    - if there are necessity products, they resist on the market a longer period of time, or they are luxury products;
    - how long the client delivery the products on the market, respectively, offer services and if they are well received by the buyers;
    - if the products, respectively the services, can be sold separately or they depend on other products and services;
    - in what stage of the life cycle is the product: at the beginning, maturity or decline stage;
    - value weight of the products/services in the total incomes of the client;
4. *Clients portfolio.* The following appreciation criteria are considered:
    - the important internal and external clients, the weight of the sales in the total sales of the firm, dependency on the main clients and their geographical repartition;
    - the clients are concentrated in a viable sector, in a sector with problems or with particularities;
    - the cashing period of the clients;
    - how are regulated the contractual relations;
    - if there are delayed payments, the value, weight, frequency and on what periods of time;
5. *Suppliers portfolio.* The evaluation criteria are the followings:
    - if the client depends on one supplier;
    - how is made the payment (payment order, ticket order, exchange liability);

- if the supplying is made unconditioned and the suppliers offers guarantees;
- if there are replacement products for acquisitions;
- if there are delayed payments to the suppliers, value, weight, frequency and for what periods of time;
6. *Clients' satisfaction* which were evaluated in function of the following criteria:
    - very high satisfaction;
    - high satisfaction;
    - medium satisfaction;
    - low satisfaction;
    - no satisfaction;
7. *Promptness in delivery.* The evaluation criteria are the followings:
    - if the delivery were done immediately;
    - if the deliveries were done in less than 3 days;
    - if the deliveries were done between 3 and 10 days;
    - if the deliveries were done between 10 and 15 days;
    - if the deliveries were done in more than 15 days;
8. *Quality of products/services offered*, evaluated in function of the following criteria:
    - if the offered products/services are of very high quality;
    - if the offered products/services are of high quality;
    - if the offered products/services are of medium quality;
    - if the offered products/services are of low quality;
    - if the offered products/services does not correspond as quality;
9. *History of business in the present sector* is evaluated in function of the following criteria:
    - if the business period is more than 5 years;

- ○ if the business period is between 3 and 5 years;
- ○ if the business period is between 1 and 3 years;
- ○ if the if the business period is between 6 months and 1 year;
- ○ if the business period is less than 6 months;

10. *Shareholders quality* which is evaluated in function of the following criteria:
- ○ if the main shareholders are multinational corporations or national companies well known;
- ○ if the main shareholders have a good prestige;
- ○ if the main shareholders are convergent;
- ○ if the shareholders are very dispersed;
- ○ if the shareholders are divergent.

In the next stage, we used the data mining techniques for analysis the financial ratios and non-financial indicators for the firms.

In order to apply the data mining process it is necessary to follow a succession of steps:

- define business objectives which ensure the understanding of the application framework and of the previous relevant information and the identification of the purpose of the KDD (Knowledge Discovery in Databases) process from the users' view;
- data preparation (data selection, preprocessing of data and data transformation) which refer to the followings:
  - ○ creation of a group of target data which suppose the selection of a group of data or focusing on a subset of data samples on which will be achieved the result;
  - ○ preparing the data for processing;
  - ○ reduction and projection of the data which consist on finding the useful characteristics for representing the

data accordingly with the established task;

- perform data mining (the knowledge discovery engine applies the selected algorithm to the prepared data). This refers to the searching of the interesting patterns in a form of specific representation or in a set of such representations: rules or classification trees, regression, clustering, association rules and others. Accordingly with the purpose of the process of discovering of the knowledge from data, there will be used one of the specific methods for exploring the data. An important role can be played by the user which can correct the performances from the previous steps;
- evaluate results, present discoveries (in the form of visual navigation, charts, graphs, texts) incorporate usage of discoveries (the results of the discovery are assembled so that they can be exploited to improve the business). At this stage, there is necessary the interpretation of extracted patterns and it is possible to come back to any of the previous stages for future iterations. After this, should be consolidated the extracted knowledge and incorporated in another system for future actions or simple documentation and reporting of them towards the interested parts. In this stage, should be tried to solve the potential conflicts with the previous accepted knowledge.

In essence, our study concerns the determination of some classification rules for the elements of a group in classes known *a priori*. These rules, after validation, will be used for framing new elements in new classes and following the same studied characteristics. Therefore, we will use CHAID because it is one of the methods suitable to the objectives of our study and it has the advantage of simplicity in comparison with other possible methods to be used.

For instance, it is not the case to use the clustering method for analysis because this can be used in the situation the classes are not known *a priori*. CHAID can be seen as the opposite of clustering, in the sense that the CHAID analysis starts with the overall database, and then splits it according to the most important variable until it achieves homogeneous sub-groups that cannot be split any further. A major advantage of this technique is that the results can be presented as an easy-to-read classification tree; each split in the tree being accredited to a single variable (e.g. credit worthiness, income, age, etc).

The Neural Networks can be used but they present two major disadvantages, as follows:

- being an analytic technique based on a process of so-called learning from existing data, this operation can last longer and it has the disadvantage that is very dependent on the existing data;
- the way to get the result is not always very clear.
- The Genetic algorithms can be also used but they involve a longer period of time till finding the proper solution.
- Therefore, the CHAID technique fulfilled all the requirements necessary for its application in our study, as follows:
- the dependent variable is categorical with more than two states which are known *a priori*;
- the predictors are categorical and continuous;
- there is a high number of registering but it responds most appropriate to the solicitations of our study;
- it permits the creation of a link between the predictor variables and the dependent one through a classification algorithm, that is easy to be represented as a tree with more that two ramifications at every node.

In our study, the CHAID method was used in order to obtain some classification rules for grouping the firms in function of several parameters in the 5 risk classes (1 – very high risk, 2 – high risk, 3 – medium risk, 4 – low risk, 5 – very low risk) regarding the risk bankruptcy. It was used a data basis with 12,496 firms which included the 15 financial ratios, determined on the information from the SMEs' balance sheets of the year 2007 and 10 non-financial indicators, determined in a previous research from a market research on the analyzed firms.

The processing of data was done in two variants in order to determine the classification rules:

- a first variant for the 15 financial ratios;
- a second variant for the 15 financial ratios and the 10 non-financial indicators.

The using of two variants has the purpose to determine the possibilities of improvement the classification based on the non-financial indicators.

For the classification tree was chosen the maxim level of 10 nodes and for the validation of the results was used the cross validation method with 10 sample folds.

Results and Discussions

In the first variant (for the 15 financial ratios), the using of CHAID method led to the selection of 11 from the 15 financial ratios, grouped in a decision tree with 161 nodes, 4 depth. The parameters of the classification tree (including just the financial ratios) are presented in Figure 2.

Taking into consideration the whole tree there can be identified the levels for early warning signals in function of the first variable considered as being the most significant. As result of CHAID method, the first selected financial ratio was the Patrimonial Solvability Ratio.

Therefore, for value of Patrimonial Solvability Ratio less than - 9%, the risk is very high, more

Figure 2. The parameters of the classification tree (financial ratios)

Results	Independent Variables Included	1. Patrimonial Solvability	
		2. Total Debt Turnover Rate	
		3. Current Liquidity	
		4. Return on Equity	
		5. Operating Profit Margin	
		6. Capital Assets Financing	
		7. Financial Stability Ratio	
		8. Current Assets Turnover Rate	
		9. Account Receivable Turnover Rate	
		10. Return on Turnover	
		11. Quick Ratio	
	Number of Nodes		161
	Number of Terminal Nodes		107
	Depth		4

than 95% of these firms being included in the 1st risk class (3597 from 3769 firms) and this is the last early warning level because the firms from this class are very close to bankruptcy.

For values of the Patrimonial Solvability Ratio between -9% and 1% inclusive, there are 1202 firms, from which, 761 firms (63.3%) are included in the 1st risk class and 304 firms (25.3%) are included in the 2nd risk class. Because it can not be identified clearly the risk class for these firms, in analysis was introduced a second financial ratio: Operating Profit Margin. For negative values of this ratio, from the 619 firms, 548 firms (88.5%) were included in the 1st risk class. For value between 0 and 3% of the Operating Profit Margin, it can not be clearly identified the risk class. From this reason, the CHAID method introduced in analysis a third ratio, respectively the Return on Equity. Thus, for values of this rate less than 4%, 70 from the 93 firms (75.3%) are included in the 1st risk class. When the Return on Equity is above 4%, most of the firms (116 from the 144 firms) are included in the 2nd risk class.

If the Operating Profit Margin ranges between 3% and 24%, it can not be established precisely the risk class, the supplementary financial ratio included in analysis being the Return on Equity. Thus, if this ratio is less than 34%, 93 from the 110 firms (84.5%) are included in the 1st risk class. If the Return on Equity is more than 34%,

83 from the 142 firms (58.5%) are included in the 2nd risk class.

For the values of the Patrimonial Solvability Ratio between 1% and 8% inclusive, the most firms are included in the 2nd risk class, (793 from 1271 firms). For an accurate framing, there was introduced the second financial ratio, respectively, the Operating Profit Margin. If the level of this ratio is less than -4%, 77.3% of the firms (92 from 119 firms) were included in the 1st risk class.

For values between -4% and 0, the firms were distributed mostly in the 1st and 2nd risk classes which imposed the introduction of a supplementary ratio for their differentiation, respectively the Return on Equity ratio. Accordingly with this ratio, the firms that registered values less than -17% were included mostly in the 1st risk class and those that registered values more than -17%, were included in the 2nd risk class. For values of the Operating Profit Margin between 0% and 12% inclusive, the majority of the firms (623 from 776 firms, that is 80.3%) were included in the 2nd risk class. For values of the Operating Profit Margin more than 12%, it can not be identified precisely the risk class, being introduced a third ratio: Capital Assets Financing. Therefore, of the level of this ratio is less than 88%, most of the firms were included in the 2nd risk class while, for values above 88%, the majority of the firms are included in the 5th risk class.

For the firms with values of the Patrimonial Solvability Ratio between 8% and 18% inclusive, the including in the risk class was done in function of the Operating Profit Margin. If the level of this ratio is less than 4%, the majority of firms (91 from 126 firms) were included in the 1st risk class. If the Operating Profit Margin had values between - 4% and 24%, the majority of firms (660 from 1018 firms) were included in the 2nd risk class. If the Operating Profit Margin was more than 24%, the firms are distributed in several risk classes and their separation was made in function of a third ratio: Total Debt Turnover Rate.

For the firms with values of the Patrimonial Solvability Ratio between 18% and 31% inclusive, the inclusion in the risk class was made in function of the level of the Operating Profit Margin. When the level of this ratio was less than 0, 130 firms from the 180 firms were included in the 1st risk class. If the level of the Operating Profit Margin was between 0 and 3%, 62.6% of the firms (109 from 174 firms) were included in the 2nd risk class. For values between 3% and 6%, the majority of firms were included in the 3rd risk class. If the Operating Profit Margin registered values between 6% and 12%, it was necessary the introduction of another financial ratio for separation the firms on risk classes, respectively the Total Debt Turnover Rate. If the Operating Profit Margin registered values between 12% and 24%, the inclusion of firms in the risk class was done in function of the level of Capital Assets Financing. The firms with a Operating Profit Margin more than 24%, were included mostly in the 5th risk class (148 from the 240 firms).

The firms with values of the Patrimonial Solvability Ratio between 31% and 50% inclusive were included in the risk classes in function of the level of the Return on Turnover, as follows:

- if the Return on Turnover is less than 0, 100 from the 146 firms were included in the 1st risk class;

Figure 3. Risk (financial ratios)

Method	Estimate	Std. Error
Resubstitution	0.192	0.004
Cross-Validation	0.206	0.004

Growing Method: CHAID
Dependent Variable: Risk class 07

- if the Return on Turnover is between 0 and 6%, 146 from the 249 firms were included in the 3rd risk class;
- if the Return on Turnover is between 6% and 11%, it can not be established precisely the risk class, being necessary another ratio: Total Debt Turnover Rate;
- if the Return on Turnover is more than 11%, 455 firms from the 637 firms (71.4%) are included in the 5th risk class.

The firms with values of the Patrimonial Solvability Ratio above 50% were included mostly in the 5th risk class (2076 from 2518 firms, respectively 82.4%) and this is the first level of early warning signals.

Therefore, in function of the value of the financial ratios, for every firm it can be identified warning signals regarding a possible financial distress.

The estimations regarding the risk of an erroneous classification are presented in the Figure 3.

The correct classification of the firms was achieved in proportion of 88.1%. The highest classification errors was determined for the risk class 4 – low risk (where the correct classification was just 14.3%) and for the risk class 3 – medium risk (where the correct classification was 29.1%) (Figure 4).

The using of CHAID method after there was added the non-financial indicators led to the selection of 11 financial ratios and of all non-financial indicators (Figure 5).

As a result of applying the CHAID method, the most relevant financial ratio for including the

Figure 4. Classification (financial ratios)

Observed	Predicted					
	1	2	3	4	5	Percent Correct
1	4813	104	9	0	134	95.1%
2	201	1762	121	0	154	78.7%
3	162	393	392	31	370	29.1%
4	22	21	58	51	205	14.3%
5	99	144	134	38	3078	88.1%
Overall Percentage	42.4%	19.4%	5.7%	1.0%	31.5%	80.8%

Growing Method: CHAID
Dependent Variable: Risk class

firms in the risk classes was maintained the Patrimonial Solvability Ratio. At the second level, besides the two financial ratios used before (Operating Profit Margin and Return on Turnover) there were included two non-financial indicators: management quality and promptness in delivery which separate the firms in the hypothesis of a Patrimonial Solvability Ratio less than -35%, respectively, between -9% and 1%. At the third level, another 7 non-financial indicators are used: history of business in the present sector, suppliers portfolio, quality of products/services offered, offered products, relations and market reputation,

clients' portfolio, clients' satisfaction. The 10th non-financial indicator included in analysis (shareholders quality) appears on the 4th node of the tree.

It should be underlined the fact that the number of the financial ratios is still 11, just one financial ratio Return on Equity was replaced by the General Solvability. There were included all non-financial indicators.

It can be noticed a low improvement of the classification accuracy. The error classification risk decreased with 0.009 for resubstitution respectively with 0.007 for cross-validation (Figure 6).

Figure 5. The parameters of the classification tree (financial ratios and non-financial indicators)

Results	Independent Variables Included		
		1. Patrimonial Solvability	Financial
		2. Management quality	Non-financial
		3. Capital Assets Financing	Financial
		4. Total Debt Turnover Rate	Financial
		5. Offered product	Non-financial
		6. Current Liquidity	Financial
		7. Operating Profit Margin	Financial
		8. Promptness in delivery	Non-financial
		9. General solvability	Financial
		10. Return on Turnover	Financial
		11. Suppliers portfolio	Non-financial
		12. History of business in the present sector	Non-financial
		13. Financial Stability Ratio	Financial
		14. Current Assets Turnover Rate	Financial
		15. Account Receivable Turnover Rate	Financial
		16. Quality of products/services offered	Non-financial
		17. Clients portfolio	Non-financial
		18. Relations and market reputation	Non-financial
		19. Shareholders quality	Non-financial
		20. Quick Ratio	Financial
		21. Clients' satisfaction	Non-financial
Number of Nodes			179
Number of Terminal Nodes			116
Depth			5

Figure 6. Risk (financial ratios and non-financial indicators)

Method	Estimate	Std. Error
Resubstitution	0.183	0.003
Cross-Validation	0.199	0.004

Growing Method: CHAID
Dependent Variable: Risk Class

The precision of classification increased with 0.9% per total (Figure 7). On categories, the precision of classification decreased a little for the risk class 1 (with -0.2%) and for the risk class 2 (with -1.1%) and increased for the other categories:

- with 4.1% for 3 risk category;
- with 8.4% for 4 risk category;
- with 1.9% for 5 risk category.

It can be concluded that the adding of 10 non-financial indicators lead to an increase of the classification accuracy. Finally, 1218 firms (9.75% from total number of firms) changed their risk class.

Solutions and Recommendations

Our analysis is based on data mining techniques (CHAID) in order to identify the firms' categories accordingly to the bankruptcy risk levels. Using of data mining for risk analysis of the small and medium enterprises is recommended because the high number of these firms; their diversity which involve a high volume of data that can not be analyzed with classical methods.

The combination of the financial and non-financial indicators through CHAID increased the precision of identification the risk levels that could represent a signal for financial managers regarding the financial distress. The next steps should be the monitorization of the risk, taking into consideration the possible new challenges and the managers should adopt the appropriate decisions on the short, medium and long term in order to prevent the failure.

The early warning model for detecting the bankruptcy risk is useful for the firms but also for other stakeholders, as follows:

- financial banking institutions for the credit analysis and establishing the guarantees;
- non-financial banking institutions – such as National Credit Guarantee Fund for SMEs - as support to offer the credit guarantees to the SMEs;
- the state institutions involved in administration of the structural funs for analysis the financial capacity of the SMEs to implement projects;
- local public administration for elaboration the local budget;
- central public administration for estimation of the revenues collected from the taxes to the state budget;

Figure 7. Classification (financial ratios and non-financial indicators)

Observed	Predicted					
	1	2	3	4	5	Percent Correct
1	4802	184	14	1	59	94.9%
2	203	1,736	185	1	113	77.6%
3	142	352	448	38	368	33.2%
4	20	15	55	81	186	22.7%
5	80	123	89	57	3144	90.0%
Overall Percentage	42.0%	19.3%	6.3%	1.4%	31.0%	81.7%

Growing Method: CHAID
Dependent Variable: Risk class

- other stakeholders (suppliers, clients) for analysis and determination of the risk generated by the business with the respective firms. Moreover, based on these information, the potential investors can take decision regarding the capital investment in the firms;

Also, it should be taken into consideration that in the business environment, complex data mining projects may require the coordinate efforts of various experts, stakeholders or departments throughout an entire organization in order to identify the risk factors and to adopt a strategy for decrease the risks.

FUTURE RESEARCH DIRECTIONS

Data mining has become an indispensable technology for businesses and researchers in many fields and it is becoming increasingly popular as a business information management tool which it is expected to reveal knowledge structures that can guide decisions in conditions of limited certainty.

Data mining extracts useful information from the large data sets now available to industry and science and this collection surveys the most recent advances in the field and draw directions for future research.

It should be taken into consideration that the results obtained after applying the algorithms of data mining can offer answers for two main categories of problems: prediction and description (Delmater, 2001). Even the limits between the prediction and description can be descriptive; the distinction between them is useful in order to understand the global objective of the discovering.

The prediction classifies the registers treated in function of a behavior or a future estimated value (Han, 2001): a collection of examples, based on previous data, where the values of forecasting variable are already known; there is built a model to explain the observed behavior. Applying

this model on the registers to be processes can be obtained a prediction of the behavior or their values in the future.

The objective of prediction can be achieved through the following elementary methods for data exploitation (Krzysztof, 2007):

- for prediction: classification, which suppose finding a function which include an article of data in one or more predefined classes and regression that is used in order to forecast of a value for a continue variable based on the others variables' values, assuming a linear or non-linear model of dependence;
- for description: clustering - identify a finite group of categories or clusters for describing the data; summarizing suppose a compact description of a subgroup of data; the association rules suppose finding a model to describe the significant dependents between the variables; detection of changes and deviation get to the discover of the most significant changes of data in the period between two consecutive measurements.

The ultimate goal of data mining is prediction - and predictive data mining is the most common type of data mining and one that has the most direct business applications. The term Predictive Data Mining is usually applied to identify data mining projects with the goal to identify a statistical or neural network model or set of models that can be used to predict some response of interest.

In our study, we tried to underline the predictive character of data mining. In these circumstances, once identified the classification rules on the basis of the decision tree, they can be used for classification in one of the 5 risk categories of firms which were not included in our study. If this fact is achieved repeatedly in different moments, it can be monitorized the way of modification of the risk class for the analyzed firms.

The method can be reapplied in the next years in order to identify those indicators which maintain their significance for classification and their position in the tree (identification of those parts which are stable in time). Also, in the analysis of the classification tree, it is necessary that on the interval of values for some of the selected variables, a part of the tree to be pruned because either the specific interval of values can be found in very rare cases, or the result is the inclusion of the firms in very close risk classes using other variables which are not stable in time.

In the perspective of analysis for the year 2008, it is possible to increase the importance of the non-financial indicators taking into consideration the economic instability generated by the financial crisis. Therefore, a future research direction is to establish how the crisis affected the SMEs, the financial and non-financial indicators.

In order to increase the classification accuracy, there could be included in analysis some modern financial ratios (such as Economic Value Added, Market Value Added). Also, others non-financial indicators (such as: quality of services ante and post sale, cost of services ante and post sale, technological advantages, relation with the bank, etc.) could be included in analysis in order to give a better estimation to the effects of the financial crisis on the Romanian SMEs.

CONCLUSION

The recent trends revealed that the SMEs are sensible to the evolutions of the economic cycle. Small and medium sized enterprises are not a lonely island but a vivid ensemble which function in direct connection with what is happening at national, European and international economy level. Thus, the SMEs are the first developing entities when the economy is on the right path but also the first ones to pay the price of economic recession.

The SMEs are affected by the financial crisis because two main motives: their limited resources and the high dependence on a credit institution which, in general, ensure the financial support for their activity. Moreover, the limited access to the banking credits will reduce the capacity of SMEs to attract financial resources in order to co-finance the projects from structural funds. Unfortunately, many times the Romanian managers prefer the bankruptcies to a recovering plan for their business.

The circumstances imposed by the financial crisis determine the Romanian SMEs to permanently adapt their strategy in order to face the new challenges. Therefore, an analysis model that could reveal the economic-financial situation and prevent the financial difficulties, offer these firms a major advantage in the market competition.

Many models for forecasting the bankruptcy risk were developed in mostly market economies till present but they have the disadvantage their use can not being generalized to another economies, besides the one where it was made the statistical study. Moreover, the period characterized by economic instability determine the correlations of the scoring function elaborated, which limit temporally the using of these models or impose their updating at regular period of times.

Therefore, we elaborated a new model for analysis the bankruptcy risk for Romanian SMEs based on financial (15 financial ratios) and non-financial indicators (10 indicators), the firms being classified in 5 risk classes. The including of the non-financial indicators was determined by the fact that the financial ratios has as informational source the classical records (financial statements) which indicate periodically the final financial results without any explanation regarding the way these were obtained.

We used CHAID method for processing the data in two variants in order to determine the classification rules: a first variant for the 15 financial ratios and a second variant for the 15 financial ratios and the 10 non-financial indicators. Also, the using of two variants could determine the possibilities of improvement the classification. In fact, the inclusion in the analysis of the 10 non-financial indicators leads to an increase of the classification accuracy.

In conclusion, the using of the data mining for detecting the bankruptcy risk of the Romania SMEs contribute to the development of the scientific knowledge in this field but has also a practical utility because the following advantages:

- permits an approach in a forecasting and retrospective view of the bankruptcy risk; for the financial diagnostic of the firm or from the perspective of the surveillance of the risks by the stakeholders;
- the model is based on both financial and non-financial indicators in order to forecast the firms' difficulties;
- the model will permit the classification of the firms with similar characteristics in one of the five identified risk zones: very high, high, medium, low and very low;
- it allows a multidisciplinary approach of the bankruptcy risk, through using data mining (CHAID) in analysis of the firms' difficulties;
- the elaboration of the model request the study of the risky firms' characteristics, which represent an important information source for analysis the financial behaviors of the firms;
- ensure a better efficiency in financing through banking credits or structural funds because the model will permit a faster analysis of the various financial and non-financial indicators by the banks or other stakeholders.

Also, the using of CHAID method presents the followings advantages:

- one of the major advantages of the CHAID is the explicit character of the result. A classification tree CHAID can be understood also by the researchers and business people, and the last ones can intervene and modify the tree accordingly with their practical experience;
- the capacity to restrict the creation of the classification tree using low quality data;
- the possibility to quickly identify and understanding of the predictor variables;
- the easiness to implement the method, taking into consideration that the rules expressed by the CHAID tree can be integrated directly into logical expressions, which permits an immediate application ;
- the facility to build a classification tree starting from categorical or continuous variable in any combination;
- the method ensure protection for soverfitting and administrate the missing data;
- CHAID does not need a too high calculation power or special knowledge for its application.

Therefore, through the proposed analysis model based on CHAID method we try to offer a real surveillance system for the Romanian SMEs which can allow an early warning regarding the bankruptcy risk, useful for the firms but also an important signal for the stakeholders. The model could represent an important step for further researches taking into consideration the possible consequences caused by the financial crisis on the SMEs and the possibility to adopt preventing measures in the conditions of risk.

REFERENCES

Acs, Z., & Audretsch, D. (1987). Innovation, market structure and firm size. *The Review of Economics and Statistics*, *69*(4), 567–575. doi:10.2307/1935950

Acs, Z., Carlsson, B., & Thurik, A. R. (1996). *Small business in the modern economy*. Oxford, UK: Basil Blackwell Publishers.

Altman, E. (1968). Financial ratios, discriminant analysis and the prediction of corporate bankruptcy. *The Journal of Finance, 23*(3), 589–609. doi:10.2307/2978933

Anghel, I. (2000). Predictia falimentului intreprinderilor romanesti – Scorul Anghel. *Tribuna Economica, 40*, 33–35.

Bailesteanu, G. (1998). *Diagnostic, risc si eficienta in afaceri*. Timisoara, Romania: Editura Mirton.

Bardos, M. (1998). Detecting the risk of company failure at the Banque de la France. *Journal of Banking & Finance, 22*, 1405–1419. doi:10.1016/S0378-4266(98)00062-4

Beaver, W. H. (1966). Financial ratios as predictors failure. *Empirical Research in Accounting: Selected Studies. Supplement to Journal of Accounting Research, 4*, 71–111. doi:10.2307/2490171

Beck, T. (2007). *Financing Constraints of SMEs in developing countries: Evidence, determinants and solutions*. Working Paper. World Bank.

Berger, A., Udell, G. (2005). A more complete conceptual framework for financing of small and medium enterprises. *World Bank Policy Research Working*, Paper 3795.

Biggs, T. (2002). *Is small beautiful and worthy of subsidy? Literature Review*. IFC.

Bilderbeek, J. (1979). De continuïteitsfactor als beoordelingsinstrument van ondernemingen. *Accountancy en Bedrijfskunde Kwartaalschrift, 4*(3), 58–61.

Birch, D. L. (1987). *Job creation in America: How our smallest companies put the most people to work*. New York: Free Press.

Buse, L., Pirvu, C., Siminica, M., & Circiumaru, D. (2006). A model for assessing the performances of the company using financial and non-financial measures. *Brno International Conference on Applied Business Research 2006* (pp. 130-138). Brno, Czech Republic: Mendel University and Forestry.

Carbó-Valverde, S., Fernández, R. F., & Udell, G. F. (2008). *Bank lending, financing constraints and SME investment*. Federal Reserve Bank of Chicago, Working papers.

Casta, J. F., & Zerbib, J. P. (1979). Prévoir les défaillances des entreprises. *Revue Française de Comptabilité, 97*, 506–527.

Conan, J., & Holder, M. (1979). *Variables explicatives de performances et contrôle de gestion dans les PMI*. Thèse d'Etat en Sciences de Gestion Université, Universite Paris Dauphine.

Deakin, E. (1977). *Business Failure Prediction: an empirical analysis, Financial Crisis Institutions and Marlets in a Fragile Environment*. Chichester, UK: John Wiley&Sons.

Delmater, R., & Hancock, M. (2001). *Data mining explained: A manager's guide to customer-centric business intelligence*. Digital Press.

Diamond, H. (1976). *Pattern recognition and detection of corporate failure*. PhD Dissertation, New York University.

Edmister, R. (1972). An empirical test of financial ratio for Small business failure prediction. *Journal of Financial and Quantitative Analysis, 2*, 1477–1493. doi:10.2307/2329929

Giurca Vasilescu, L. (2008). A SWOT Analysis of the SMEs Development in Romania. *Journal of Applied Economic Sciences, 4*(6), 396–404.

Giurca Vasilescu, L., Pirvu, C., & Tapordei, D. (2008). Challenges for the Romanian SMES regarding the cmpetitiveness. *microCAD. International Scientific Conference* (pp. 91-98). Miskolc, Hungary: University of Miskolc.

Grammatikos, T., & Gloubos, G. (1984). Predicting bankruptcy of industrial firms in Greece. *Spoudai, The University of Piraeus Journal of Economics, Business. Statistics and Operations Research, 3-4*, 421–443.

Han, J., & Kamber, M. (2006). *Data mining: Concepts and techniques* (2nd ed.). New York: Elsevier Publisher.

Hlaciuc, E., Socoliuc, M., & Mates, D. (2008). Bankruptcy risk analysis through financial management. *Buletin stiintific, Publicatie stiintifica de informare a academiei fortelor terestre, 2* (26).

Hoare, R. (2004). *Using CHAID for classification problems*. Paper presented at New Zealand Statistical Association 2004 Conference, Wellington.

Ionascu, C. M., & Radu, C. (2008). Comparative analysis at the level of countries from European Union regarding the development potential of companies population. *Annals of University of Craiova. Economic Sciences Series, 36*(1), 203–210.

Ivonciu, P. (1998). Analiza riscului de faliment prin metoda scorurilor. *Revista finante banci, asigurari, 4*, 17-19.

Jones, O., & Tilley, F. (2003). *Competitive advantage in SME's: Organising for innovation and change*. New York: John Wiley & Sons.

Kass, G. V. (1980). An exploratory technique for investigating large quantities of categorical data. *Applied Statistics, 29*(2), 119–127. doi:10.2307/2986296

Koh, H. (1992). The sensitivity of optimal cutoff points the misclassification costs of type I and type II errors in the going concern prediction. *Journal of Business Finance & Accounting, 19*(2), 187–197. doi:10.1111/j.1468-5957.1992.tb00618.x

Koh, H., & Killough, L. (1980). The use of multiple discriminant analysis in the assessment of the going concern status of an audit client. *Journal of Business Finance & Accounting, 17*(2), 179–192. doi:10.1111/j.1468-5957.1990.tb00556.x

Koyuncugil, A. S., & Ozgulbas, N. (2007). Detecting financial early warning signs in Istanbul Stock Exchange by data mining. *International Journal of Business Research, 7*(3).

Koyuncugil, A. S., & Ozgulbas, N. (2009). Early warning system approach to SMEs Based on data Mining as a financial risk detector. In H. Rahman (Ed), *Data mining applications for empowering Knowledge societies* (pp.221-240). Hershey, PA: Idea Group Inc., USA

Krzysztof, J. C., Pedrycz, W., Swiniarski, R. W., & Kurgan, L. A. (2007). *Data mining: A knowledge discovery approach*. Springer.

Kusiak, A., & Smith, M. (2007). Data mining in design of products and production systems. *Annual Reviews in Control, 31*, 147–156. doi:10.1016/j.arcontrol.2007.03.003

Lefebvre, E., & Lefebvre, L. A. (2000). *SMEs, exports, and job creation: A firm level analysis. CIRANO and Polytechnique de Montreal*. Retrieved from http://www.strategis.ic.gc.ca/SS1/ra/op26_e.pdf

Magidson, J. (1993). The use of the new ordinal algorithm in CHAID to target profitable segments. *The Journal of Database Marketing, 1*, 29–48.

Magidson, J., & Vermunt, J. K. (2004). An extension of the CHAID tree-based segmentation algorithm to multiple dependent variables, ed. Classification – the ubiquitous challenges, studies in classification, data analysis and knowledge organization. In *Proccedings of the 28th Annual Conference of the Gesellchaft für Classification e.V.* (pp.176-183). University of Dortmund.

Manecuta, C., & Nicolae, M. (1996). Construirea si utilizarea functiei scor pentru diagnosticarea eficientei agentilor economici. *Revista Finante. Credit si Contabilitate, 5,* 47–54.

Ministry for SMEs, Trade and Business Environment (MSMETBE).(2008). *Annual report.*

Newberry, D. (2006). *The role of small and medium sized enterprises in the futures of emerging economies.* World Resource Institute.

Nooteboom, B. (1994). Innovation and diffusion in small firms: Theory and evidence. *Small Business Economics, 6*(5), 327–347. doi:10.1007/BF01065137

Ohlson, J. A. (1980). Financial ratios and the probabilistic prediction of bankruptcy. *Journal of Accounting Research, 18*(1), 109–131. doi:10.2307/2490395

Ooghe, H., & Van Wymeersch, C. (2006). *Traité d'analyse financière.* Intersentia/Anthemis.

Pastena, V., & Ruland, W. (1986). The merger/bankruptcy alternative. *Accounting Review,* (April): 288–301.

Peneder, M. (2001). *Entrepreneurial competition and industrial organization.* Cheltenham, UK: Edward Elgar.

Pirvu, C., Giurca Vasilescu, L., & Mehedintu, A. (2008). *Banking financing for Romanian SMEs – challenges and opportunities. Munich Personal RePEc Archive.* MPRA.

Ponniah, P. (2001). *Data warehousing fundamentals: Comprehensive guide for IT professionals.* New York: John Wiley & Sons, Inc., (Electronic).

Ravi Kumar, P., & Ravi, V. (2007). Bankruptcy prediction in banks and firms via statistical and intelligent techniques – A review. *European Journal of Operational Research, 180,* 1–28. doi:10.1016/j.ejor.2006.08.043

Rygielski, C., Wang, J. C., & Yen, D. C. (2002). Data mining techniques for customer relationship management. *Technology in Society, 24*(4), 483–502. doi:10.1016/S0160-791X(02)00038-6

Sanders, T., & Wegener, C. (2006). *Meso finance filling the financial service gap for small business in developing countries.* Retrieved from http://www.bidnetwork.org/download.php?id=40005

Shirata, C. Y. (1999). *Financial ratios as predictors of bankruptcy in Japan: an empirical research.* Tsubuka College of Technology.

Siminica, M. (2005). Model de analiză a riscului de faliment la nivelul firmelor industriale româneşti. *Revista de Politica Ştiinţei şi Scientometrie,* CNCSIS, 1-6.

Soava, G., Mehedintu, A., Buligiu, I., & Buse, R. (2008). *Sisteme informatice economice. Teorie şi aplicaţii.* Craiova, Romania: Editura Universitaria.

Song, M., & Parry, M. (1997). A cross-national comparative study of new product development processes: Japan and the USA. *Journal of Marketing, 61*(2), 1–18. doi:10.2307/1251827

Springate, G. (1978). *Predicted the possibility of failure in a Canadian firm. Unpublished MBA research project.* Simon Fraser University.

Sun, J., & Li, H. (2008). Data mining method for listed companies' financial distress prediction. *Knowledge-Based Systems, 21,* 1–5. doi:10.1016/j.knosys.2006.11.003

Szathmary-Miclea, C. (2003). *Evaluarea si gestionarea riscului in intreprinderile mici si mijlocii* (de Vest, U., Ed.). Timisoara, Romania.

Thurik, A. R. (1996). Introduction: economic performance and small business. *Small Business Economics, 8*(5), 327–328. doi:10.1007/BF00389551

Trumbach, C. C., Payne, D., & Kongthon, A. (2006). Technology mining for small firms: Knowledge prospecting for competitive advantage. *Technological Forecasting and Social Change, 73*, 937–949. doi:10.1016/j.techfore.2006.05.018

Ward, T. J., & Foster, B. P. (1997, July). A Note on Selecting a Response Measure for Financial Distress. *Journal of Business Finance & Accounting, 24*(6), 869–879. doi:10.1111/1468-5957.00138

Zavatta, R. (2008). *Financing technology entrepreneurs & SMEs in developing countries.* Retrieved June 2008, from http://www.infodev.org/en/Publication.542.html

Zavgren, C. (1983). The prediction of corporate failure: The state of the art. *Journal of Accounting Literature, 2*, 1–33.

ADDITIONAL READING

ADaM (Data Mining and Image Processing Toolkits). Retrieved from http://www.datamining.itsc.uah.edu/adam/

Altman, E. I. (1993). *Corporate financial distress and bankruptcy: A complete guide to predicting and avoiding distress.* New York, USA: Wiley and Sons Publishing House.

Ayadi, R. (2006). *The New Basel Capital Accord and SME financing: SMEs and the new rating culture.* Centre for European Policy Studies.

Barrow, C., Brown, R., & Clarke, L. (2001). *The business enterprise handbook: A complete guide to achieving profitable growth for all entrepreneurs and SMEs.* Kogan Page Ltd.

Berry, M., & Linoff, G. (2000). *Mastering data mining.* John Wiley & Sons.

Bigus, J. P. (1996). *Data mining with neural networks: solving business problems from application development to decision support.* Hightstown, NJ, USA: McGraw-Hill, Inc.

Buse, L., Siminica, M., & Circiumaru, D. (2007). The use of the statistical methods in the evaluation of the financial risk. *Analele Universității din Craiova, seria Științe Economice, 35*(1), 1-15.

Chen, S. Y., & Liu, X. (2005). Data mining from 1994 to 2004: an application-orientated review. *International Journal of Business Intelligence and Data Mining, 1*(1), 4–21. doi:10.1504/IJBIDM.2005.007315

Ching, W. K., & Kwok-Po, M. (2003). *Advances in datamining.* Singapore: World Scientific Publishing Co. Re. Ltd.

Cull, R., Davis, L. E., Lamoreaux, N. R., & Rosenthal, J. L. (2005), Historical financing of small-and medium-size enterprises. *NBER Working Paper*, 11695.

Enea, I., Radu, C., Ionascu, C., & Murarita, I. (2007). *Statistica. Teorie si Aplicatii.* Craiova, Romania: Editura Universitaria.

Foster, P. F., & Stine, R. A. (2001). *Variable selection in data mining: Building a predictive model for bankruptcy.* Warton Financial Institution Center, University of Pennsilvania.

Friedman, J. (2003). *The elements of statistical learning: Data mining, inference and prediction.* Springer Series in Statistics, Springer.

Gattiker, U. E. (2008). Early warning system for home users and small- and medium-sized enterprises: eight lessons learned. *International Journal of System of Systems Engineering, 1*(1-2), 149–170. doi:10.1504/IJSSE.2008.018136

Giudici, P. (2003). *Applied data mining. Statistical methods for business and industry.* UK: John Wiley & Sons Ltd.

Giurca Vasilescu, L. (2007). *Gestiunea financiară a întreprinderii*. Craiova, Romania: Editura Universitaria.

Giurca Vasilescu, L. (2008). Risk and performances of the Romanian companies - Possible effects on financial stability. *5th International Symposium on Business Administration*, (pp. 319-329). Canakkale: Onsekiz Mart University

Grice, J. S., & Dugan, M. T. (2001). The limitations of bankruptcy prediction models: some cautions for the researcher. *Review of Quantitative Finance and Accounting, 17*(2), 151–166. doi:10.1023/A:1017973604789

Han, J., & Kamber, M. (2006). *Data mining: Concepts and techniques* (2nd ed.). Elsevier Publisher.

Hastie, T., Tibshirani, R., & Friedman, J. (2001). *The elements of statistical learning: Data mining, inference, and prediction*. Springer Verlag.

Ionascu, C.M. (2007). Statistical analysis of the correlation between GDP, productivity and brute investments at the level of Oltenia region. *Revista tinerilor Economiști, 1*(9), 133-137.

Kantardzic, M. (2003). *Data mining: Concepts, models, methods, and algorithms*. John Wiley & Sons.

Kovalerchuk, B., & Vityaev, E. (2000). *Data mining in finance*. Hingham, MA, USA: Kluwer Academic Publisher.

Koyuncugil, A. S., & Ozgulbas, N. (2008). A data mining model for dtecting financial and operational risk indicators of SMEs. *Proceedings of World Academy Of Science. Engineering and Technology, 36*, 88–91.

Koyuncugil, A. S., & Ozgulbas, N. (2009). Risk modeling by CHAID Decision Tree Algorithm. *Journal of ICCES, 199*(1), 1–8.

Krzysztof, J. C., Pedrycz, W., Swiniarski, R. W., & Kurgan, L. A. (2007). *Data mining: A knowledge discovery approach*. Springer.

Larose, D. T. (2006). *Data mining methods and models*. John Wiley & Sons.

Linoff, G. S. (2007). *Data analysis using SQL and Excel*. John Wiley & Sons.

Meghana, A., Demirguc-Kunt, A., & Maksimovic, V. (2006). How important are financing constraints? The role of finance in the business environment. *World Bank Policy Research Working*, Paper 3820.

Mehedintu, A. (2007). *Sisteme informatice economice. Teorie și aplicații*. Craiova, Romania: Editura Universitaria.

Militaru, V. (2003). Studiu comparat asupra tehnicilor de data mining utilizate în rezolvarea problemelor de regresie si clasificare. *Revista Informatica Economica, 3*(27), 105–111.

Mitrut, C., & Constantin, D. L. (2006). Current issues concerning regional policy and SMEs in Romania. *South-Eastern Europe Journal of Economics, 2*, 209–221.

Myatt, G. J. (2006). *Making sense of data: A practical guide to exploratory data analysis and data mining*. John Wiley.

O'Regan, P. (2006). *Financial information analysis* (2nd ed.). John Wiley & Sons.

Olson, D. L. (2005). *Introduction to business data Mining*. Mcgraw-Hill College.

Perez, M. (2006). Artificial neural networks and bankruptcy forecasting: a state of the art. *Journal Neural Computing & Applications, 15*(2), 154–163. doi:10.1007/s00521-005-0022-x

Pirvu, C. (2008). *Managementul si calculatia costurilor. Modele de optimizare si prognozare*. Craiova, Romania: Editura Universitaria.

Pochet, C. (2002). Institutional complementarities within corporate governance systems: a comparative study of bankruptcy rules. *Journal of Management and Governance, 6,* 343–381. doi:10.1023/A:1021219200695

Ratner, B. (2003). *Statistical modeling and analysis for database marketing: Effective techniques for mining big data.* Chapman & Hall. doi:10.1201/9780203496909

Rodger, J. A. (2003). *Utilization of data mining techniques to detect and predict accounting fraud: a comparison of neural networks and discriminant analysis, Managing data mining technologies in organizations: techniques and applications.* Hershey, PA: Idea Group Publishing.

Rud, O. P. (2000). *Data mining cookbook: Modeling data for marketing, risk and customer relationship management (Datawarehousing).* John Wiley & Sons.

Shin, K. S., & Lee, Y. J. (2002). A genetic algorithm application in bankruptcy prediction modeling. *Expert Systems with Applications,* Springer-Verlag, Berlin, 23(3), 321-328.

Siminica, M. (2008). *Diagnosticul financiar al firmei.* Craiova, Romania: Ed. Universitaria.

Siminica, M., & Cîrciumaru, D. (2005). Alternative methods for assessing the bankruptcy risk. *The International Conference "The Impact of European Integration on the National Economy"* (pp. 474-480). Cluj-Napoca: Universitatea Babeş Bolyai, Facultatea de Ştiinţe Economice

Siminica, M., Marcu, N., & Bandoi, A. (2009). The development of a bankruptcy prognosis model regarding Romanian companies between theory and practice. *Metalurgia International, 14*(7), 114–117.

Soares, C., Peng, Y., Meng, J., Washio, T., & Zhou, Z. H. (2008). *Applications of data mining in e-business and finance.* IOS Press.

Tan, P. N., Steinbach, M., & Kumar, V. (2005). *Introduction to data mining.* Pearson Addison Wesley. Weka 3: Data mining software in Java, Retrieved from http://www.cs.waikato.ac.nz/ml/weka/

Williams, G. (2009). Data mining desktop survival guide. Retrieved from http://www.togaware.com/datamining/survivor/index.html

Witten, I., & Eibe, F. (2005). *Data mining: Practical machine learning tools and techniques* (2nd ed.). Morgan Kaufmann.

KEY TERMS AND DEFINITIONS

Data Mining: Data mining is the process of extracting hidden patterns from a large collection of data in order to understand the business, discern new possibilities and turn these into actions.

CHAID: A type of decision tree technique which can be used for prediction: classification and for detection of interaction between variables.

Early Warning Systems: A technique of analysis used to predict the possible challenges a firm can face and to decrease the risk of financial distress.

Bankruptcy Risk: The risk that a company will be unable to meet its debt obligations and the probability that the firm will end its activity in the future under the unfavorable action of internal or external factors.

Small and Medium Enterprises: Companies with the number of employees and turnover below certain limits (less than 249 employees and a net turnover less than 50 million Euro or total assets less than 43 million Euro).

Financial Ratios: Ratios of two numerical values selected from an enterprise's financial statements.

Non-Financial Indicators: Indicators which regard the qualitative aspects of the firm's activity (management quality, shareholders quality, clients' portfolio, quality of products/services offered, etc.) and characterize better the performances of the firm because they deal with causes rather than effects.

Section 3
Early Warning Systems for Detection and Prevention of Fraud, Crime, Money Laundering and Terrorist Financing

Chapter 9
Social Aid Fraud Detection System and Poverty Map Model Suggestion Based on Data Mining for Social Risk Mitigation

Ali Serhan Koyuncugil
Capital Markets Board of Turkey, Turkey

Nermin Ozgulbas
Baskent University, Turkey

ABSTRACT

After last global financial crisis, one of the most important concerns of the governments became unemployment. Higher unemployment rates haves been forcing governments to develop some policies. Some of these policies has been included financial policies while some of them included social policies. One of the most important concerns of social policies is social risk mitigation and fight against poverty and social aids as its extensions. In general, measurement of social events have been mostly based on subjective statements. More specifically, targeting mechanisms have been using for determination of potential social aid owners. Most popular targeting mechanisms are subjective ones as well. In this chapter, an objective targeting mechanism model and a fraud detection system model have been developed via data mining for social aids as an identifier of poverty levels which includes early warning signals for inappropriate applications. Then, these models have been used for development of a poverty map. Developed new targeting mechanism which has been based on rating approach will be an alternative to Means Test and Proxy Means Test. In addition, social aid fraud detection system will be updated automatic with Intelligent System property and the poverty map computation approach can be used for absence of detailed data. Furthermore, Millenium Development Goals, Targeting Mechanisms, Poverty and Poverty Maps concepts have been reviewed from an analytical and objective point of view.

DOI: 10.4018/978-1-61692-865-0.ch009

INTRODUCTION

One of the most important elements of social life is solidarity under risky situations. Social Security System presents solidarity in instituional mean in country level. Social security may be accept as system, organization, necessity, solidarity and as service tool of the government when individuals face to danger. In some countries, social security has a wider mean than the others. According to ILO, actual norms of social security covers support for economical and social protection, health protection, family life with kids arising from income loss because of disease, motherhood, working force loss, unemployment, disability and old age by public programs. Elements of social security can be count as social solidarity, neediness, public programs, obligations and participation. Therefore, social security can be define as a solidarity organization based on obligation of participation which against dangers faced by the individuals of society via public programs.

First bases of social security institutions has been established in 1880. First compulsory insurance about social security dangers has been established in German on 1883 by government. Then the other insurance types established conseqeuntly such as

- insurance on disease has been started in 1883,
- insurance on occupational accidents has been started in 1884,
- insurance on disability and older age has been started in 1889.

In other countries, establishment and improvement of the insurance almost in the same years:

- In Austria,
  - Insurance on occupational accidents has been started in 1887,

  - Insurance on disease has been established in 1888. Social Security and related legislations have been started
- In Hungary in 1891,
- In Norway and France in 1894,
- In Finland in 1895,
- In Italy in 1898,
- In Spain in 1900,
- In Japan and in England in 1903,
- In Latin America, USA and Canada in 1930.

Second World War has been a milestone about Social Security. Following years after war have been became the beginning point of Social Security Gold Age. In 1952, coverage and the norms of the social security have been defined with aggreement number 102 entitled 'Minimum Norms of Social Security' by ILO. Today, all developed countries have been applying nine insurance activities included by aggrement number 102. Those nine insurance acitivities are

- Occupational accidents
- Occupational diseases
- Disease
- Motherhood
- Unemployment
- Family payments
- Old age
- Death
- Disability.

In developing countries unemployment and family payments haven't been appllying widely but the others. These advancements have been the first steps of the providing establihment and organizing of social security system. Re sharing of income has been foreseen with solidarity and cooperation principles.

One of the main components of social security system is social services. Social services are all systematic and regular activities and programs which have properties such as protective, proactive, rehabilitative, able to change, able to improve with the aim of improving people's life standards via providing help

- To the ones for their needings because of social deficincy arising out of control
- To the ones for making themselves more adequately and prevention of dependency to another ones
- For strengthening the family relations
- To individuals, families, groups and societies for realiziation of their social functions accurately.

Another main component of social services is social aid. Social aid is determined as according to the Local measures lack of afford of living costs belongs to his/her and based deprivation detection and control and aim to make those ones self – sufficient with temporary or continously, systematic and regularly complimentary aids.

According to the table given above, all social aids beneficiary determination criterias based on poverty measurements. Of course there are a lot of approaches to poverty and prosperity as well but most up to date and accepted standards can be taken as Millenium Development Goals. Therefore, Millenium Development Goals have been take into consideraition as a poverty coverage.

In most of the studies dealt with poverty determination have been using subjective 'expert opinions' or basic statistical methods. Of course, let the social aids to deserving ones very important but not enough. In social aids, timing is one one the important elements. So, fast decision making process one of the vital elements too. In addition, multidimensional nature will take into consideration for accurate decision making as well. In social aid, all the citizens must be evaluated. Therefore, countrywide personal data in mutidimensional nature will be evaluated in poverty determination. It means, the number of the records should be equal the population size in poverty determination. In addition, dynamic

nature of the population must be considered for accurate decisions. So, computation approach must be fast, enable to process huge data sets and sensitive to changes. These necessities let us to data mining. Data mining is the most efficient computation approach to analysis huge data sets.

In this chapter, objective targeting mechanism computation, poverty maps construction and fraud detection in social aids have been given. From Millenium Development Goals point of view determination of poverty and poverty maps as an extension have been determined via data mining.

BACKGROUND

Sustainable Development and its extension Development Indicators are one of the good starting point for evaluating Social Risk Mitigation. It is possible to talk about many different Development Indicators but 'Millenium Development Goals' are generally accepted one.

Basically, the main idea of Millennium Development Goal (MDG)s constructed as a conclusion of international conferences and summits held in 1990's. Then, they were evaluated and first set of indicators defined as International Development Goals. Member states of United Nations (UN) accepted the Millenium Declaration and introduced the Millennium Development Goals which are given Table 1 as part of implementing Millenium Declaration in September 2000. The goals have been commonly accepted as a framework for measuring development progress (UN, 2010; Worldbank, 2010a).

Millennium Development Goals given in Table 1 shows that the first goal for development indicated as eridicate the extreme poverty and the hunger. According to the definition of Worldbank, 'Poverty is hunger. Poverty is lack of shelter. Poverty is being sick and not being able to see a doctor. Poverty is not having access to school and not knowing how to read. Poverty is not having a job, is fear for the future, living one day at a

Table 1. Millenium development goals

Goal 1.	Eradicate extreme poverty and hunger
Goal 2.	Achieve universal primary education
Goal 3.	Promote gender equality and empower women
Goal 4.	Reduce child mortality
Goal 5.	Improve maternal health
Goal 6.	Combat HIV/AIDS, malaria, and other diseases
Goal 7.	Ensure environmental sustainability
Goal 8.	Develop a global partnership for development

time. Poverty is losing a child to illness brought about by unclean water. Poverty is powerlessness, lack of representation and freedom.' (Worldbank, 2010b). More detailed definition and explanations about the poverty concept are given below.

The most meaningful definition of poverty was defined by Rowentree and Berengula in 1901. According to this definition the poverty is the lack of income for fulfilling the minimum physical needings (Field 1983). In 1960's a poverty measure was defined as the bunch of food and non-food goods for fullfilling minimum needings (Lipton and Ravallion, 1993). Actually, the definition of the poverty has been developed but the consumption is still one of the most widely used poverty indicator (Nunan, et al., 2002). In 1970's, needing concept merge with satisfaction then poverty concept turn into more qualitative nature and more qualitative indicators. These indicators are malnutrition, sheltering, wearing and reach facility to health services. Therefore, United Nations Development Program (UNDP) developed Human Development Index as an alternative for income/consumption measurements. In Human Development Index, more qualitative dimensions of human poverty takes into consideration as life expectancy, literacy in adults, reaching facilities to health services and clean water, and low weight childs under five age in serious level (Nunan, et al., 2002).

'Basic needs' concept was determined for operational use of UN's poverty concept. Basic needs concept widely used in ILO's global conferences in 1976 and then World Bank was began to use the concept. Basic needs concept can be determined as realization of honorable live right becomes with human being in universal level. Basic needs was determined as

- Minimum needs for a family's private consumption,
- Safe drinking water, sewerage, electricity, health, education etc.,
- Pariticipation to the decisions effecting themselves,
- Satisfaction of basic needs in basic human rights framework,
- Consideration of need strategy based on employment as both goal and tool (Worlbank, 2003).

Human Development Report 2001 emphasized the necessity of wider definition for poverty which covers vulnerability and risk concepts (Nunan, et al., 2002). In later studies, vulnerability determined as the probability of fall down under poverty limit (World Bank, 2003). According to the World Bank the poverty is determined as the situation of couldn't reach the minimum life standard. Nunan, et al. (2002) has been determined the poverty was the situation of couldn't reach economical, social and the other standards for human properity. Falkingham and Namazie (2002) evaluated the poverty from economists' and political analyts' point of view.

Zastrow and Bowker (1984) determined the factors as the reason of poverty:

- High unemployment
- Negative physical health
- Physical disability
- Emotional problems
- High health expenditures
- Alcholism
- Drug addiction
- Large family

- Fired from work because of otomation
- Deprived of working skills
- Low education level
- Families which have little childs and have women responsibles
- Increasing life expenses while income stability
- Guilty against race
- Labeled as condemned or mentally sick
- Divorced, be abandoned and dead of husband/wife
- Gambling
- Sex crimes
- Victim of crime
- Negative ethical values about work
- Unavailability of job because of seeking conditions
- Low waged job
- Mental retardation
- Retirement because of age

OECD (2001) determined the basic dimensions of the poverty with five articles given below:

- Economical facilities
- Humanatarian facilities
- Political facilities
- Socio-cultural facilities
- Protective facilities

It is hard to determine and measure the poverty concept because of its dynamic and relativistic nature. Therefore, its different dimensions have been investigated seperately. In another words, the main logic has been based on identifying the deprivations included by the poverty concept. This approach resulted as different definitions such as;

- Berengula and Pescetto (2003) determined 'absolute poverty' concept,
- Falkingham and Namazie (2002) determined relative poverty concept,
- Berenguela and Pescetto (2003) emphasized subjective poverty concept

- OECD (2001), DPT – CPO (2001) and McMichael (2000) considered rural poverty concept
- UNDP developed and Morrisson (2002) and Nunan, et al. (2002) evaluated humanitarian poverty concept
- Especially World Bank considered gender poverty and feminization of poverty concepts
- International Council of Nurses (2004) evaluated youth and elder poverty concepts.

Measurement of the poverty has been discussing as much as its definition. Poverty limits are the most useful tools for measurement of the poverty. Poverty limit is the the line which is seperated poor and non-poor persons according to the countries poverty definition. Poverty limits identified with the income or consumption which covers minimum nourishment needs and the other necessary expenses. As an example we may assume the ones who live under poverty limits as the ones who earn under avearage annual income. On the other hand, someone takes poor ones as who take daily colaries under average calories (International Council of Nurses, 2004). A lot of institutions such as UNDP have been been trying to measure the poverty and have been using poverty indicators as a strategy for reducing national poverty. MJainly, poverty indicattors based on countries' poverty definitions, factors effects poverty and perception about poverty. Actually, poverty is a multi dimensional concept. Therefore, it is possible to measure the poverty with multi dimensional indicators. According to the UNDP (1997b), classification of the poverty indicators are given below:

- Income indicators: There are two main income measures of poverty. These are poverty interventions and Gross National Product.
- Social indicators: The biggest advantage of social indicators is their ability on di-

rect measurement of necessary goods and services for human prosperity (e.g. income measured in indirect way).

- Indicators on poverty of facilities: Protection from disease, adequate nourishing, reproductive health, personal safety etc. can count as facilities for saving persons from poverty. There are different indicators for measurement for these items. Human Development 1996 Report was combined these different indicators in one index (UNDP, 1997a).

One of the most important concerns of poverty measurement is determining the the ones who will have social aid. The main idea of social aid and social service programs is providing support who couldn't find another way provide necessary needings. Some countries are using income test which covers a big portion of population like aged, disabled, unemployment etc. In alot of countries, for the ones who covers whether in social security programs use social aid programs based on income test. Social aid covers some groups such as aged and orphans provided by Public or non-Public Institutions (Ortiz, 2001). In addition, there is a specific definition for determination of the ones in need for social aid as targeting mechanism. Targeting mechanism is a mechanism which provides objective selection criterias for beneficiary families of social aids. Targeting mechanisms can be differ according to country's social, economical and geographical properties. On the other hand, the main logic almost the same in all targeting mechanisms as scorin formulas based on social, economical and the other necessary indicators. Hence, objective and transparent conditions can be provided in target population selection.

The aim of the targeting models is discovering the poor households in a accurate and efficient way. There are 4 basic targeting methods (Ortiz, 2001; Legovini, 1999):

- **Categorical targeting:** It is the most easy targeting methods. In categorical targeting, programs utilize all people in selected geographical area or group. Therefore, it is possible to support non-poor ones too.
- **Means Test:** Means test targeted programs utilize the households whose income under a determined limit. Means test better than categorical targeting but it is more expensive than categorical targeting. Means test can use both direct transfer programs and wage programs (Legovini, 1999; Coady, et al., 2003).

Means test model is using in a lot of social aid programs. Utilizations defined as a function of person's or a family's income and assets in official means test applications. Some means test models don't cover some income sources and assets. Especially, houses and agricultural areas don't covered. If offcial means test doesn't suitable for implementation then informal approaches or proxy means test can be used for beneficiary selection. These tests cover some alternative indicators and tools such as household size and structure, geographical area, age, disabilities etc (Ortiz, 2001).

- **Proxy Means Test (Alternative tools test – Rating formula):** It is subset of Means Test. Targeting is made by gathering information, computing indicators and collecting tools which are concerning income/poverty of beneficiaries. It is based on recurrences. It may be give reasonable results for Local decision makers or Local NGO. Number of the countries using Proxy Means Test has been increasing but still the other tests are using widely. This test is a system which includes a rating formula based on observations of the properties such as residence of the household, quality of the house, durable goods ownership, demographical structure of household, education level and employment status of the adults. Indicators and the weights which are using for computing the rates is genarating from the statistical analysis (mainly regression and principal component analysis) results of the detailed household surveys. In addition, Type 1 and Type 2 errors should be weighted in rating. In general, gathered information is partially confirmed with house visits or documents. Means test is more efficient than Proxy means test (Coady, et al., 2003, Legovini, 1999).

- **Personal Choice:** It usually uses for preventnig for ethical issues. Because some obligations put such as working for food, low waged job etc. This program is not suitable for preventing poverty but hunger. On the other hand, this mechanism is low costed in managerial mean. In addition, it is very suitable in crisis because of its automated targeting nature (Legovini, 1999; Coady, et al., 2003).

In social aid programs, it is possible to take more than one methods as a targeting method according to needings. Merging methods can help to maximize the efficiency and minimize the managerial costs. From this view of point for a better targeting mechanism must take into account both qualitative and quantitative properties. Furthermore, multi dimensional nature of the poverty must be summarized with

- clear,
- easy to understand,
- comparable,
- transparent

indicators as a successful separator between poor and non-poor ones. According to this framework, efficient poverty implied indicators in another words well defined targeting mechanism must be discovered from huge data sets such as

census of population. Discovering knowledge from huge data sets coincides the definition of data mining. Data mining is one of the most efficient approach of discovering knowledge from huge data sets.

Data mining describes a collection of techniques that aim to find useful but undiscovered patterns in collected data. The goal of data mining is to create models for decision-making that predict future behavior based on analyses of past activity. Data mining supports knowledge discovery, defined by Piatetsky-Shapiro and Frawley (1991) as '... the nontrivial extraction of implicit, previously unknown, and potentially useful information from data...' (Berson, et al., 2000). Bolshavoka, et al. (2005) indicated that "the fast growth of data collections in sciences and business applications as well as the need to analyze and extract useful knowledge from this data leads to a new generation of tools and techniques grouped under the term data mining". Data mining is the process of sifting through the mass organizational (internal and external) data to identify patterns critical for decision support. Data mining techniques have been successfully applied like fraud detection and bankruptcy prediction by Tam and Kiang (1992), Lee, et al. (1996), Kumar, et al. (1997), strategic decision-making by Nazem and Shin (1999) and financial performance by Eklund, et al. (2003), Hoppszallern (2003), Derby (2003), Chang, et al. (2003), Kloptchenko, et al, (2004), Magnusson, et al. (2005). Koyuncugil and Ozgulbas conducted studies on financial performance and financial risk of Small and Medium Enterprises (SMEs) and hospitals by data mining. They determined;

- a specific measure for financial performance (Koyuncugil & Ozgulbas 2006a),
- the financial profile of SMEs (Koyuncugil & Ozgulbas, 2006b)
- the financial profile of hospitals (Ozgulbas & Koyuncugil, 2007).

It is clear that data mining will be the main method for poverty level determination with new developed hybrid targeting mechanism. In addition, some indicators or signals will be defined for social risk mitigation. In another words, we need a set of indicators which implies potential risk for make us proactive. When we use this indicators in a system logic, we are talking about Early Warning Systems. EWS use for predicting the success level, probable anomalies and for reducing crisis risk of cases, affairs transactions, systems, phenomenons, firms and people. In addition their current situations and probable risks can be identified quantitatively (Koyuncugil, 2009).

A lot of governments don't recognized the symptoms of social risk and explotions until face them. And when signal start occurring, responsibles don't know how to manage. By identifying some early warning signs of social risk, decision makers can prevent or at least manage risks. Some studies about early warning systems used by data mining and other analytical methods are presented below. There are a lot of application areas of early warning systems but most of the important early warning studies dealt with financial issues. Early warning systems that are used to examine financial failure and risk are investigated for banking sector by Gaytan and Johnson (2002). Collard (2002) underlined the importance of early warning system and presented early warning signs that concerned business failure and risk. Mena (2003) mentioned credit card fraud detection via data mining. Gunter and Moore (2003) studied to develop an early warning model for detecting the financial condition of bank. Jacops and Kuper (2004) presented an early warning system for six countries in Asia which has been calculated the probability of a financial crisis. Apoteker and Barthelemy (2005) focused on financial crises in emerging markets and they dealt with country risk signaling by newly developed non-parametric methodology. Liu, et al. (2006) identified an early warning system on financial crises happened worldwide by fuzzy C-means method. A novel

anomaly detection scheme that uses a data mining to handle computer network security problems is proposed by Shyu, et al. (2006). One of the most important study towards the purpose of this study is the design of an early warning system based on data mining about the examination of in capital market was realized by Koyuncugil (2006). Koyuncugil determined the success of designed early warning system by testing the system with actual data. Some of the studies dealt with SMEs and stock exchanges such as

- Factors affected financial distress and risk (Ozgulbas & Koyuncugil, 2006; Koyuncugil & Ozgulbas, 2006c),
- Financial early warning signals for stock market crisis (Koyuncugil & Ozgulbas, 2007)

can be taken into account as fundamental studies for early warning approached risk detection studies based on data mining.

Kamin, et al. (2007) used early warning systems in emerging markets of 26 countries to identify the roles of domestic and external factors in emerging market crises. Tan and Quektuan (2007), hase been used Genetic Complementary Learning (GCL) for early warning system for stock market and bank failures. Beside these empirical studies given above, Koyuncugil and Ozgulbas (2008) developed a financial early warning system model based on data mining for SMEs as a risk detector as an advancement.

Poverty level is one of the most important identifiers of social aid and early warning signals are very important for proactivation as well. In addition, regional details have big impotance for policy making. Therefore, poverty levels and early warning signals will be a base of development policies for both country and Local level. Especially in Local studies, one of the most important problems is defining the priorities among the geographical zones. Poverty maps provide visual information about poverty. According to Worldbank (2010c),

Poverty mapping, the spatial representation and analysis of indicators of human well being and poverty within a region, is useful in a variety of ways such as

- Highlighting geographic variations
- Simultaneously displaying different dimensions of poverty and/or its determinants
- Understanding poverty determinats
- Selecting and designing interventions
  - Selecting interventions
  - Designing interventions
    - Geographic targeting of resources
    - Designing interventions with regional variants
    - Informing decentralization
    - Fostering participation at the local level.

SOCIAL AID FRAUD DETECTION SYSTEM FOR SOCIAL RISK MITIGATION

After global financial crisis, wide spread unemployment has been becoming one of the most important issues of all countries whether developed or not. High level unemployment has been triggered mass poverty and inceeased poverty levels. One of the most important problems or danger of the increasing poverty level is social risk. Social risk could be show itself in different scales from protest meetings to social explosions and the worst case for social risk can be identified as looting or fighting between poor and non-poor ones. Of course, worst cases can be considered very far away right now but it must be take into consideration because of increasing poverty level. At this point, social aids play very important role for social risk mitigation. Fair social aids distribution will be one of the emergency switch of income distribution gap between poor and non-poor ones. Therefore, in evaluation process

of social aid applications, there will be objective norms to discriminate the ones whether really in need of social aid or not. In statistical mean it is possible to identify this situation Type I and Type II errors according to the Hypothesis Tests Theory:

- Acceptance of application which belongs to non-poor one
- Rejection of application which belongs to poor one

Case I shows acceptance of fraudient application. In this case, fraud applications prevent to reach the ones in need of the social aid. Therefore, minimization of the fraudient applications can be one of the measures of the accuracy of the social aid system. Case II shows rejection of right application. In this case, fairness of the social aid system will be damaged. Therefore, minimization of the rejection of applications which belong to poor ones can be another measure of the accuracy of the social aid system. Therefore, an efficient social aid system must be minimized wrong decisions. It means it must be discriminate poor and non-poor ones in evaluation process for a fair decision process. Altough, timing is another basic elements in decision making process. Discriminate the fraudient aplication from deserved ones in limited time is forced to use early warning mechanism. Therefore, to bring out the fraudient applications into open as early warning signals have a vital importance for social risk mitigation. Nearly, all of the former social aid detection systems have been based on subjective 'expert opinions. Observations of the experts and declarations of the social aid applicants are the data sources that reflect the decision making. However, these decisions ignore the multidimensional nature of the poverty in objective manner. Therefore, fair, accountable, transparent and comparable system can only provide accurate results.

Determination of the indicators of fraud by clarifying the relationships between the variables defines the discovery of knowledge from the poverty variables. Automatic and estimation oriented information discovery process coincides the definition of data mining. During the formation of system;

- fair,
- accountable,
- transparent,
- comparable,
- easy to use,
- easy to understand,
- easy to interpret

model that is far from the complexity is targeted by the discovery of the implicit relationships between the data and the identification of effect level of every factor. Because of this reason, the ideal method to develop early warning system is the data mining method that is started to be used frequently nowadays for strategic decision making process. Therefore, the objective of this study was determined as using data mining to a fraud detection system which has early warning properties.

According to the framework given above social aid fraud detection system will be

- Identified the fraudient behaviours
- Determined the profiles of the ones who deserve social aid
- Determined the profiles of the profiles who don't deserve the social aid
- Determined the early warning signals and indicators in fraudient applications
- Constructed poverty maps.

Mainly, system is based on determination of objective norms and indicators which imply poverty. In another words, it will be very similar to targeting mechanism. Therefore, it is possible to talk about data mining based targeting mechanism. Means Test and Proxy Means Test are most popular targeting mechanisms. In this study, an alternative rate based targeting mechanism will

be developed which will have properties of both Means Test and Proxy Means Test. System will be assigned scores according to both quantitaive and qualitative properties. Hence, the method which will be used for poverty determination can be use for all types of data. The system will be included three main difference and advantages than similar ones:

The new hybrid targeting mechanism: The system will be determined the poverty levels with an hybrid targeting mechanism which will assign poverty scores. Targeting mechanism calls hybrid because of its nature which includes Means Test and Proxy Means Test properties at the same time.

Data mining as a computing method: System will be evaluated both quantitative and qualitative data at the same time. Therefore, poverty determination method must be suiatble for both quantitative and qualitative data. In addition, the method will be scalable for huge data sets. As a result we should deal with method(s) which can be enable to analysis quantitative and qualitative huge data sets. Analysing huge data sets must be one of the necessities but not the only one. Hybrid targeting mechanism must be involved prediction nature and computations should be automated for the efficiency of the system. As a result, the method must be enables to analysis huge data sets and has automated prediction property. Nowadays, the most popular approach of analysing huge data sets calls data mining. Hence, data mining methods will take into consideration in system development.

Intelligent early warning mechanism: Statistically significant poverty indicators and profiles determined by the System can be used as early warning signals for identified values. Cut points, threshold values from one profile to another profile can be identify as early warning signals. At the same time, early warning signals show risk signals for social risk detection.

Objective, transparent, comparable indicators: In general, poverty determinations based on 'expert' opinions. Therefore, it is hard to talk about comparable standards, objective evaluation and transparency. One expert accept application which was rejected by another expert.

METHODS

The main method will be CHAID Decision Tree algorithm for determination of important variables in poverty identification and determination of early warning signals in fraudient behaivours. Then, K-nearest Neighbour method will be implemented for povery map construction. Details about these methods are given below.

CHAID Decision Tree

In this study CHAID decision trees – one of the data mining algorithms -, which is one of the best ways to identify profiles of the poverty and determine fraudient characteristics thereof, were used. One of the data mining algorithm decision trees are used in profiling as a predictive model that, as its name implies, can be viewed as a tree. Specifically each branch of the tree is a classification question and the leaves of the tree are partitions of the dataset with their classification (Berson et. al., 2000).

With the series of rules obtained from decision trees would be possible to create profiles of firms and then classify firms in terms of levels of financial management by using such profiles. For each profile the most important financial and key indicators, which require improvement for reaching to an upper profile level, will be determined. By this way it will be possible to identify the structure of the poverty levels for strategies to be followed, and early warning indicators and signals could be improved.

There are different decision tree algorithms such as C4.5, C 5, C&RT and CHAID. C&RT and CHAID are the most popular decision tree algorithms. In addition, CHAID differentiate from the others with branching style. CHAID has

multi branchs (more than two), while the others have binary branchs. Therefore, CHAID gives all sub-details or minor differences in investigating data set. CHi-square Automatic Interaction Detector (CHAID) uses Chi-square metric as its name implies (Koyuncugil, 2006).

K-Nearest Neighbour

In classification process, a new object with input vector y will be examined with k closest training points to y and the object will be assigned to the class which has the majority of points among this k (Hand, et al., 2001).

K-nearest neighbour is a very straightforward method and it uses for classification of new object. K-nearest neighbour is a memory based method and doesn't need a model for fitting. Assume that x_0 query point was given and x_r, r=1,...,k denotes training data points. In this method, closest distance between x_0 and x_r takes into account. Then, x_0 will be assigned to class which has majority of points among these k points. As an exmaple, x_0 query point is a member of O Class according to 7-nearest neighbour according to Figure 1 (Hand, et al., 2001; Hastie, et al., 2001, Koyuncugil, 2006).

Properties assumed that real valued and Euclid Distance:

$$d_i = \|x_{(i)} - x_0\|$$

will be used as a facility.

Typically, all properties will be transformed into N(0,1) distribution. Hence, it will be possible to compare measurements of different units (Hastie, et al., 2001, Koyuncugil, 2006).

Data and Variables

According to data sources of Millenium Development Goals, poverty indicators given below is take into account for possible data and variables are given below:

Figure 1. 7 – nearest neigbour of x_0 query point

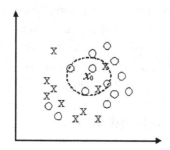

- Demographic data
- Consumption/income indicators
- Gender statistics and indicators
- Health indicators
- Data on children
- Other social indicators

SOCIAL AID FRAUD DETECTION SYSTEM AND POVERTY MAP

Flow diagram and explanations of the steps of the data mining based fraud detection system is given in Figure 2.

Steps of the System

Step 1. Survey Sampling

There are two main approaches in data gathering for Poverty Level Determination determination as

1. Data gathering from complete coverage researchs (Census of Population),
2. Data gathering from sampling researchs.

In Census of Population all people covered in the country. On the other hand, there are limitations for gathering detailed data. Therefore, mainly Census of Population will be a base for Poverty Level Determination and main indicators/variables will be provided. In sampling researchs,

details which couldn't collected in Census of Population will be collected. Therefore, in Poverty Level Determination construction a mixed data will take into consideration as complete coverage (population) and sample.

Administrative records can provide official information. But these records couldn't enough for poverty determination. Detailed personal information should be provided with sampling surveys for better discrimination between poor and non-poor ones. Census records will be the sampling framework. Of course it is possible to define another data source except Population Census database but in many developing and less developed countries population registry systems are not updated. Therefore, for developed countries or for the countries which have updated population registry systems other data sources can used as sampling framework. Therefore, representantive sample for population will be selected from census database (or from any other complete coverage data sources which are provided personal information) for sampling survey. Survey questionaire will be included questions on poverty determination which is determined according to Millenium Development Goals and other internationaly accepted and comparable indicators. Data provided from sampling survey will be used for training data in data mining model development.

Step 2. Poverty Model Development

CHAID Decision Tree which is one of the most updated data mining methods will be used as a main method for poverty model development. Early Warning System approach of Koyuncugil and Ozgulbas (2008) will be used for poverty model development. According to this approach CHAID decesion tree algorithm will be used as a main method. Assume that $X_1, X_2, ..., X_{N-1}, X_N$ denote discrete or continous independent (predictor) variables and Y denotes dependent variable as target variable in CHAID algorithm where $X_1 \in [a_1, b_1], X_2 \in [a_2, b_2], ..., X_N \in [a_N, b_N]$ and $Y \in$

Figure 2. System flow diagram

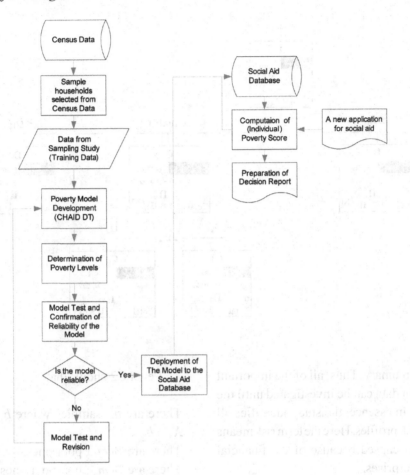

{Poor, Not Poor}. While 'Poor' shows poor ones in red bar and 'Not Poor' shows not poor ones in green bar in CHAID decision tree in Figure 3.

CHAID Decision Tree in Figure 3 was taken into consideration for computing the individual poverty scores. CHAID decision tree determined the variables which effect the poverty level. Then, statistically significant variables in CHAID Decision Tree will take into consideration in determination of poverty level process for individuals. Their location in decision tree will be determined, then their scores will be computed with weights in CHAID Decision Tree.

Only 2 variables of N have a statistically significant relationship with the target Y in Figure 3:

X_1 has most statistically significant relation with target Y.

X_2 has statistically significant relation with X_1 where $b_{11} < X_1 \leq b_{12}$

Step 3. Determination of Poverty Levels

CHAID algorithm organizes Chi-square independency test among the target variable and predictor variables, starts from branching the variable, which has the strongest relationship and arranges statistically significant variables on the branches of the tree due to the strength of the relationship. An example of a CHAID decision tree is seen in Figure 3. As it is observed from Figure 3, CHAID has multi-branches, while other decision trees

Figure 3. CHAID decision tree

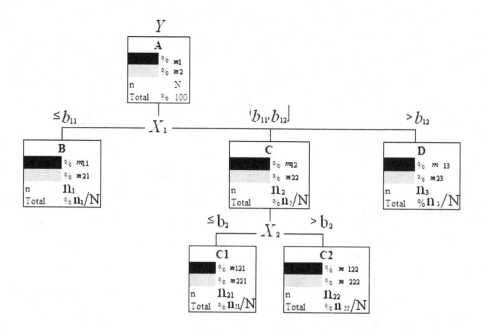

are branched in binary. Thus, all of the important relationships in data can be investigated until the subtle details. In essence, the study identifies all the different risk profiles. Here the term risk means the risk that is caused because of the financial failures of enterprises.

Figure 3 shows that there are four different risk levels that two of them (B and D) influenced only one variable (X_1) and the rest (C1 and C2) influenced two variables $(X_1$ and $X_2)$. Details about 4 different poverty levels are given below:

Level B shows that:

There are n_1 samples where $X_1 \leq b_{11}$
There are % m_{11} poor ones,
There are % m_{21} non-poor ones

Level C1 shows that:

There are n_{21} samples where $b_{11} < X_1 \leq b_{12}$ and $X_2 \leq b_2$
There are % m_{121} poor ones,
There are % m_{221} non-poor ones

Level C2 shows that:

There are n_{22} samples where $b_{11} < X_1 \leq b_{12}$ and $X_2 > b_2$
There are % m_{122} poor ones,
There are % m_{222} non-poor ones

Level D shows that:

There are n_3 samples where $X_1 > b_{12}$
There are % m_{13} poor ones,
There are % m_{23} non-poor ones

Levels given above show that different poverty levels has been influenced different variables or different values of same variables. It means that different poverty levels have different structures and need different policies. If all of the profiles are investigated separately,

Level B shows that if any household's variables X_1 have values where $X_1 \leq b_{11}$, poverty rate or in another words risk rate of the poverty of the households in this level will be $R_B = m_{11}$. It means anyone (or household) has a $X_1 \leq b_{11}$ property is a poor one with % m_{11} percent.

Level C1 shows that if any household's variables X_1 and X_2 have values where $b_{11} < X_1 \leq b_{12}$ and $X_2 \leq b_2$ poverty rate or in another words risk rate of the poverty of the households in this level will be $R_{C1} = m_{121}$. It means anyone (or household) has $b_{11} < X_1 \leq b_{12}$ and $X_2 \leq b_2$ properties is a poor one with % m_{121} percent.

Level C2 shows that if any household's variables X_1 and X_2 have values where $b_{11} < X_1 \leq b_{12}$ and $X_2 > b_2$ poverty rate or in another words risk rate of the poverty of the household in this level will be $R_{C2} = m_{122}$. It means anyone (or household) has $b_{11} < X_1 \leq b_{12}$ and $X_2 > b_2$ properties is a poor one with % m_{121} percent.

Level D shows that if any household's variable X_1 have values where $X_1 > b_{12}$, then poor financial performance rate or in another words risk rate of poverty of the households in this level will be $R_D = m_{13}$. It means anyone (or household) has $X_1 > b_{12}$ property is a poor one with % m_{13} percent.

Poverty interventions can be determined according to the levels given above.

Step 4. Model Test and Confirmation of Reliability of the Model

Statistically significant variables (e.g. X_1 and X_2) and poverty levels (e.g. B, C1, C2 and D) which were obtained via CHAID method will be examined with survey via field study. Model results will be compared with household properties whether the model discriminate the poor and non-poor ones accurately.

Step 5. Revision of the Model

In case of the model couldn't discriminate the poor and non-poor ones correctly then the model will be constructed again.

Step 6. Deployment of the Model to the Social Aid Database

Poverty levels which were determined by survey sampling will be matched with social aid database according to the key variables.

Step 7. Computation of (Individual) Poverty Score

In social risk mitigation, the ones who need in social aid should be selected carefully. Type and Type II errors must be considered for a fair final decisioin. Therefore, statistically signifant variables according to the CHAID decision tree will be considered for computation of individual poverty scores. CHAID decision tree will be given different poverty levels with statistically significant variables.

In social aid applications, applicants will be fill out a form which includes statiscially significant variables determined by CHAID. Then, applicant's poverty level will be defined according to poverty levels determined by CHAID.

As an example, applicant's properties will be queried according to the obtained statistically significant variables (e.g. X_1 and X_2) and household's poverty level will be determined according to the values of statistically significant variables such as B, C1, C2 or D. Then, poverty rate of poverty level will be assigned as household's poverty rate.

Step 8. Reporting and Database Registry

Then, final decision will be reported while applicants data registered to the social aid database.

Development of Poverty Maps

Sample data (obtained from survey sampling in Step 1) can be gathered in Urban/Rural, Geographical Zones, Provinces, District or for more details in more little locations. In sampling reseach more detailed data can provide more reliable and accurate results. On the other hand, research cost forced to decreased the sample size. Therefore, there will be a trade off between cost and sample size. Hence, adequate statistical significancy and the budget will draw the framework. Therefore, we should make some analysis for decision making on sub-locations. Because, sample reseach covers only limited locations according to the research design. As an example, a sample research on province level couldn't provide information about district level. So, we should make analysis for determination of poverty level on districts. A general algorithm given below from country to district level can provide information about poverty level for all sub-locations.

In this study, social aid database will be used as primary data source for poverty map construction. In social aid database, all records have poverty level in personal details. In addition, all records have location information. Therefore, it is possible to identify a poverty level according to the records in database. On the other hand, database couldn't in include records for all locations country wide or for all detailed locations. Assume that X1, X2, ..., XN-1, XN determined as important variables for PL=1, 2, ..., M different poverty levels and sample research was designed for country prediction with S sample of size with d = A sensitivity. Therefore, it is possible to predict country level poverty with country wide distributed S samples. In addition, assume that there are i= 1, 2, ..., I provinces and j= 1, 2, ..., J districts in country where Zij denotes poverty level of the jth district of ith province. Zij will be computed via K-nearest neighbour analysis as

Zij = K-nearest neighbour i = 1 to I, j = 1 to J.

Then, Zij values will be registered to the social aid database. Hence, poverty maps can be provided list based with a little database query or in a visual nature with a GIS support.

Determination of Early Warning Indicators and Signals for Social Risk Mitigation

Statistically significant poverty variables, poverty levels, cut-points or interventions from one level to the another level, poverty rates or poverty risk rates has been determined according to the CHAID decision tree given Figure 3.

Statisticall significant variables can be identified as early warning indicators as well. In addition, values of the variables can be identified as risk signasl as well. Because, poverty related variables identified the household's poverty level and it means variation in this values can be changed the poverty level. Therefore, cut points of statistically significant variables from one level to another level are drawing limit values between better or worst poverty level. Therefore, these cut points are obtaining early warning signals in transition from one poverty level to another poverty level. Then, risk signals for households (individuals) can be easily determined according to the poverty levels and values of statistically significant variables. On the other hand, CHAID decision tree will not be adequate for determination of geographical early warning signals. Poverty levels Zij in poverty map will be helped to seperate the geographical zeon form the others. Then, summarization will be realized in district level.

CONCLUSION

One of the popular sayings about globalisation is 'Globalisation turns the world into a little village'. It is possible to think that one of the biggest triggers of globalisation is improvement in Communication and Information Technologies. Of course, reflections of globalisation not only into tecnologies but almost every part of life and daily life as well. Especially in last two decades, a lot of changes has been realized in every part of life and managerial approach of goverments as well until global financial crisis. Market economy rules sharpened, social policies and sharpened market economy effects on people ignored. As a result, every part of life restructured according to the profit-loss balance. This approach strethgened the financial markets, tools and derivatives while real sector tools got weakened. Finally, the financial bubble inflated and exploided. Then, global financial crisis occured in 2006 and is still influncing the financial markets, country economics, real economy, supply-demand balance, profit-loss balance and finally huge unemployment. Governments has been thinking on to rehabilate the damages of financial crisis while trying to solve the effects of huge unemployment. Because, higher unemployment rate is one of the most important triggers of social risk. Of course, there are a lot faces of global financial crisis but this chapter dealt with social risk mitigation which has been ignored for developed countries but emerging and less-developed countries in globalization process.

In general social security and particularly social aid has been discussing since U.S. President Obama's Health Reform proposal on September 9, 2009. Because, this proposal includes health insurance whether afford it or not which is one of the main components of social aid. This proposal underlined the importance of social policies while still the effects of global financial crisis progressing. Because, the limited resources decreasing day by day and its influence on the population increasing as a contradiction. Then the importance of the income distribution getting higger while the difference between poverty and the prosperity drawing the huge gaps. As a result social policies has been becoming day by day and of course with objective decision making processes. Therefore, the motivation of this chapter designed for the prevention of further effects of the financial crisis on the society and for usage of analytical methods in social policy making with objective, compa-rable, transparent, well defined, measurable and fair indicators or norms instead of subjective ones.

In this chapter, new alternative targeting mechanism suggestion developed with system approach for poverty level detection and poverty map construction facility. It means that there are two main components of the System as

- **Social aid fraud detection system** which includes targeting mechanism for poverty level determination. Developed targeting mechanism in fraud detection system provides statistically significant variables which effect poverty level in an order of importance level. As a property of CHAID decision algorithm, all different subsets of the same variable unhidding according to their importance level. Therefore, limit values are obtaining as cut points for different poverty levels. These cut points provide early warning signals in the transition from one poverty level to the another one. It means, system can discriminate and select the suitable ones in social aid applications. Thefore, inproper applications can detect as misuse or fraud. As a result a fraud detection system developed for social applications which gives early warning signals in inproper applications.
- **Poverty map construction facility** which provides location specific poverty determination for regional poverty mitigation policy making for social risk mitigation. Therefore, it makes possible risk reduction according to geographical locations.

This chapter provides fraud detection system suggestion with early warning property and poverty map construction facility. Further studies will be included application of the system with real data or hypothetic data. It is believe in that this chapter will be triggered usage of data mining and other business intelligence methods in poverty and other social studies for objective results.

REFERENCES

Apoteker, T., & Barthelemy, S. (2005). Predicting financial crises in emerging markets using a composite non-parametric model. *Emerging Markets Review, 6*(4), 363–375. doi:10.1016/j.ememar.2005.09.002

Berenguela, R., & Pescetto, C. (2003). *Improving the measurement of poverty in the Americas health adjusted poverty lines: background materials – a literature review.* Pan American Health Organization. Working Paper (Draft).

Berson, A., Smith, S., & Thearling, K. (2000). *Building Data Mining Applications for CRM.* New York: McGraw-Hill.

Bolshakova, N., Azuaje, F., & Cunningham, P. (2005). An integrated tool for microarray data clustering and cluster validity assessment. *Bioinformatics (Oxford, England), 21*(4), 451–455. doi:10.1093/bioinformatics/bti190

Chang, S., Chang, H., Lin, C., & Kao, S. (2003). The effect of organizational attributes on the adoption of data mining techniques in the financial service industry: An empirical study in Taiwan. *International Journal of Management, 20*(4), 497–503.

Coady, D., Grosh, M., & Hoddinott, J. (2003). *The targeting of transfers in developing countries: review of experience and lessons.* World Bank.

Collard, J. M. (2002). Is your company at risk? *Strategic Finance, 84*(1), 37–39.

Derby, B. L. (2003). Data mining for improper payments. *The Journal of Government Financial Management, 52,* 10–13.

DPT - CPO. (2001). Rehabilitation of income distribution and fight against poverty, Special Interest Group Report, Ankara, Turkey.

Eklund, T., Back, B., Vanharanta, H., & Visa, A. (2003). Using the self-organizing map as a visualization tool in financial benchmarking. *Information Visualization, 2*(3), 171–181. doi:10.1057/palgrave.ivs.9500048

Falkingham, J., & Namazie, C. (2002). *Measuring health and poverty: A Review of approaches to identifying the poor.* London: DFID Publishing.

Field, F. (1983). *The minimum wage.* London: Policy Studies Institute.

Gaytan, A., & Johnson, A. J. (2002). *A review of the literature on early warning systems for banking crises.* Central Bank of Chile Working Papers no: 183.

Gunther, J., W. & Moore, R. R. (2003). Early warning models in real time. *Journal of Banking, 27*(10), 1979–2001. doi:10.1016/S0378-4266(02)00314-X

Hand, D. J., Mannila, H., & Smyth, P. (2001). *Principles of data mining.* Cambridge, MA: MIT Press.

Hastie, T., Tibshirani, R., & Friedman, J. H. (2001). *The elements of statistical learning.* New York: Springer New York Inc.

Hoppszallern, S. (2003). Healthcare benchmarking. *Hospitals & Health Networks, 77,* 37–44.

International Council Of Nurses. (2004). *Nurses: Working with the poor; Against Poverty. Information and action tool kit.* Geneva, Switzerland: International Council of Nurses.

Jacobs, L. J., & Kuper, G. H. (2004). *Indicators of financial crises do work! An early-warning system for six Asian countries.* CCSO Working Paper 13. Department of Economics, University of Groningen, the Netherlands.

Kamin, S. B., Schindler, J., & Samuel, S. (2007). The contribution of domestic and external factors to emerging market currency crises: An Early Warning System. *International Journal of Finance & Economics*, *12*(3), 317–322. doi:10.1002/ijfe.314

Kloptchenko, A., Eklund, T., Karlsson, J., Back, B., Vanhatanta, H., & Visa, A. (2004). Combining data and text mining techniques for analysing financial reports. *Intelligent Systems in Accounting Finance and Management*, *12*(1), 29–41. doi:10.1002/isaf.239

Koyuncugil, A. S. (2006). *Fuzzy Data Mining and its application to capital markets*. Unpublished doctoral dissertation, Ankara University, Ankara.

Koyuncugil, A. S. (2009). *The financial crisis and its impact on international business from statistics and data mining approached early warning systems perspective*. Paper presented at the Financial Crisis and its Impact on International Business Panel Discussion in World Summit on Economic-Financial Crisis and International Business (WSEFCIB2009), Washington, DC.

Koyuncugil, A. S., & Ozgulbas, N. (2006a). *Financial profiling of SMEs: An application by Data Mining. The European Applied Business Research (EABR)*. Conference, Clute Institute for Academic Research.

Koyuncugil, A. S., & Ozgulbas, N. (2006b). Is there a specific measure for financial performance of SMEs? *The Business Review, Cambridge*, *5*(2), 314–319.

Koyuncugil, A. S., & Ozgulbas, N. (2006c). *Determination of factors affected financial distress of SMEs listed in ISE by Data Mining. In 3rd Congress of SMEs and Productivity*. Istanbul: KOSGEB and Istanbul Kultur University.

Koyuncugil, A. S., & Ozgulbas, N. (2007). Detecting financial early warning signs in Istanbul Stock Exchange by data mining. *International Journal of Business Research*, *7*(3), Koyuncugil, A. S., & Ozgulbas, N. (2008). Early warning system for SMEs as a financial risk detector. H. Rahman (Ed), *Data mining applications for empowering knowledge societies* (pp. 221-240). Hershey, PA: Idea Group Inc.

Kumar, N., Krovi, R., & Rajagopalan, B. (1997). Financial decision support with hybrid genetic and neural based modeling tools. *European Journal of Operational Research*, *103*, 339–349. doi:10.1016/S0377-2217(97)00124-0

Lee, K. C., Han, I., & Kwon, Y. (1996). Hybrid neural network models for bankruntcy predictions. *Decision Support Systems*, *18*, 63–73. doi:10.1016/0167-9236(96)00018-8

Legovini, A. (1999). *Targeting methods for social programs. Poverty & Inequality Technical Note 1*. Washington, DC: Inter-American Development Bank.

Lipton, M., & Ravallion, M. (1995). Poverty and policy. In Behrman, J., & Srinivasan, T. N. (Eds.), *Handbook of development economics*. Amsterdam: Elsevier.

Liu, S., & Lindholm, C. K. (2006). Assessing early warning signals of currency crises: A fuzzy clustering approach. *Intelligent Systems in Accounting. Financial Management*, *14*(4), 179–184.

Magnusson, C., Arppe, A., Eklund, T., & Back, B. (2005). The language of quarterly reports as an indicator of change in the company's financial status. *Information & Management*, *42*, 561–570. doi:10.1016/S0378-7206(04)00072-2

McMichael, A. J. (2000). The urban environment and health in a world of increasing globalization: issues for developing countries. *Bulletin of the World Health Organization*, *78*(9), 1117–1126.

Mena, J. (2003). *Investigative data mining for security and criminal detection*. New York: Elsevier Science.

Morrisson, C. (2001). *Health, education and poverty reduction. Policy Brief No.19*. OECD Development Centre.

Nazem, S., & Shin, B. (1999). Data mining: New arsenal for strategic decision making. *Journal of Database Management, 10*(1), 39–42.

Nunan, F., Grant, U., Bahigwa, G., Muramira, T., Bajracharya, P., Pritchard, D., & Vargas M. J. (2002). *Poverty and the environment: Measuring the links*. Environment Policy Department Issue Paper No. 2

OECD. (2001). *Poverty reduction. The DAC guidelines*. Retrieved December, 2009, from http://www.oecd.org/poverty.

Ortiz, I. D. (2001). *Social protection in Asia and the Pacific*. Asian Development Bank.

Ozgulbas, N., & Koyuncugil, A. S. (2006). Profiling and determining the strengths and weaknesses of SMEs listed in ISE by the Data Mining Decision Trees Algorithm CHAID. In *10th National Finance Symposium, Izmir*.

Ozgulbas, N., & Koyuncugil, A. S. (2009). Financial profiling of public hospitals: An application by Data Mining. *The International Journal of Health Planning and Management, 24*(1), 69–83. doi:10.1002/hpm.883

Piatetsky-Shapiro, G., & Frawley, W. (Eds.). (1991). *Knowledge discovery in databases*. Cambridge, MA: AAAI/MIT Press.

Shyu, M. L., Chen, S. C., Sarinnapakorn, K., & Chang, L. (Eds.). Foundations and novel approaches in data mining. *Studies in Computational Intellegence*, 9.

Tam, K. Y., & Kiang, M. Y. (1992). Managerial applications of neural networks: The case of bank failure predictions. *Decision Sciences, 38*, 926–948.

Tan, Z., & Quektuan, C. (2007). Biological brain-inspired genetic complementary learning for stock market and bank failure prediction. *Computational Intelligence, 23*(2), 236–242. doi:10.1111/j.1467-8640.2007.00303.x

UN. (2010). *United nations millennium declaration*. Retrieved January 2010, from http://www.un.org/millennium

UNDP. (1997a). *Poverty measurement: Behind and beyond the poverty line*. Technical Support Document. Poverty Reduction. Module 3.

UNDP. (1997b). *Poverty indicators*. Technical Support Document. Poverty. Module 1.

World Bank. (2003). *Turkey, poverty and coping after crises*. Human Development Unit Europe and Central Asia Region Report No: 24185- TR Vol.1-2.

Worldbank. (2010a). *Official list of MDG indicators*. Retrieved January 2010, from http://siteresources.worldbank.org/DATASTATISTICS/Resources/MDGsOfficialList2008.pdf.

Worldbank. (2010b). *Overview: Understanding, measuring and overcoming poverty*. Retrieved January 2010, from http://web.worldbank.org/WBSITE/EXTERNAL/TOPICS/EXTPOVERTY/0,contentMDK:20153855~menuPK:373757~pagePK:148956~piPK:216618~theSitePK:336992,00.html)

Worldbank. (2010c). *What can poverty maps be used for?* Retrieved January 2010, from http://web.worldbank.org/WBSITE/EXTERNAL/TOPICS/EXTPOVERTY/EXTPA/0,contentMDK:20239110~menuPK:462100~pagePK:148956~piPK:216618~theSitePK:430367,00.html

Zastrow, C., & Bowker, L. (1984). *Social problems*. Chicago: Nelson-Hall.

KEY TERMS AND DEFINITIONS

Data Mining: Collection of evolved statistical analysis, machine learning and pattern recognition methods via intelligent algorithms which are using for automated uncovering and extraction process of hidden predictional information, patterns, relations, similarities or dissimilarities in (huge) data.

CHAID (CHi-Square Automatic Interaction Detector): One of the most popular and updated decision tree algorithm in data mining methods which is using for segmentation and it uses Chi-square metric as its name implies.

K-Nearest Neighbour: One of the classical, memory based classification method of new object which doesn't need a model for fitting in data mining methods collection.

Early Warning System (EWS): A system which is using for predicting the success level, probable anomalies and is reducing crisis risk of cases, affairs transactions, systems, phenomenons, firms and people. Furthermore, their current situations and probable risks can be identified quantitatively.

Early Warning Signals: Signals produced in probable risky situations by an early warning system.

Fraud Detection System: A system detects probable misuse or fraud in any application domain.

Social Risk: Probable anomaly in society in different scales from protest meetings to social explosions and the worst case for social risk can be identified as looting or fighting between poor and non-poor ones.

Social Aid: According to the local measures lack of afford of living costs belongs to his/her and based deprivation detection and control and aim to make those ones self – sufficient with temporary or continously, systematic and regularly complimentary aids.

Targeting Mechanism: Specific definition for determination of the ones in need for social aid. The aim of the targeting models is discovering the poor households (individuals) in a accurate and efficient way.

Poverty Map: Spatial representation and analysis of indicators of human well being and poverty within a region.

Chapter 10
Collaborative Video Surveillance for Distributed Visual Data Mining of Potential Risk and Crime Detection

Chia-Hui Wang
Ming Chuan University, Taiwan

Ray-I Chang
National Taiwan University, Taiwan

Jan-Ming Ho
Academia Sinica, Taiwan

ABSTRACT

Thanks to fast technology advancement of micro-electronics, wired/wireless networks and computer computations in past few years, the development of intelligent, versatile and complicated video-based surveillance systems has been very active in both research and industry to effectively enhance safety and security. In this chapter, the authors first introduce the generations of video surveillance systems and their applications in potential risk and crime detection. For effectively supporting early warning system of potential risk and crime (which is load-heavy and time-critical), both collaborative video surveillance and distributed visual data mining are necessary. Moreover, as the surveillance video and data for safety and security are very important for all kinds of risk and crime detection, the system is required not only to data protection of the message transmission over Internet, but also to further provide reliable transmission to preserve the visual quality-of-service (QoS). As cloud computing, users do not need to own the physical infrastructure, platform, or software. They consume resources as a service, where Infrastructure-as-a-Service (IaaS), Platform-as-a-Service (PaaS), Software-as-a-Service (SaaS), and pay only for resources that they use. Therefore, the design and implementation of an effective communication model is very important to this application system.

DOI: 10.4018/978-1-61692-865-0.ch010

INTRODUCTION

In the past few years, the application studies of intelligent and versatile video camera were very active in both research and industry due to the fast advancement of micro-electronics, communication networks and computer vision technologies. Now, video surveillance systems have played an important role in the early warning of potential risk (such as fire accident, flood disaster, and debris flow) and potential crime (such as a man to tail after an old woman or to spy on a bank truck) to protect lives and properties.

In this chapter, we introduce the generations of video surveillance systems and their applications in the potential risk and crime detection. For supporting these load-heavy and time-critical applications, a system with collaborative video surveillance and distributed visual data mining would be necessary. The concept of collaborative video surveillance was first presented in (Wang, et al., 2003). Start from the collaborative commerce based on Internet Web-based information system for providing users ubiquitous video surveillance services. We treat the surveillance data and service as a kind of digitized product in E-marketplaces.

By collaborating different surveillance data with different value-added services, diverse applications for the early warning of potential risk and crime can be provided. Notably, these value-added services are distributed and may require visual data mining techniques (Simoff, et al., 2008). In this chapter, the design and implementation of an effective communication model to support collaborative video surveillance are introduced. As the visual mining data for safety and security is very important for all kinds of risk and crime detection, our system will protect the surveillance information transmission on public and prevalent Internet by Diffie-Hellman key exchange algorithm and AES encryption (Wang, Li, Liao, 2007; FIPS-197). Moreover, open-loop error control of forward erasure correction (FEC) is applied for reliable transmission of live surveillance video to preserve the perceptual quality.

The main objectives of this chapter are to illustrate a framework for effective detection of potential risk and crime via visual data mining of real-time surveillance videos and then to describe the development of this early warning system (EWS) using related information technologies.

BACKGROUND

Video surveillance services have been active for decades to protect lives and properties of individuals, enterprises and governments such as homeland security, office-building security and traffic surveillance on highways. Video surveillance systems have evolved to the third generation (Fong & Hui, 2001; Liang & Yu, 2001; Marcenaro, et al., 2001). In the third-generation systems as shown in Figure 1, all applied devices and technologies are digital. The digital camera can further compress the video data to save the bandwidth for providing users ubiquitous video surveillance services through the prevalent Internet (Ho, et al., 2000). Therefore, we can aggregate different surveillance information from different cameras to provide users more value-added surveillance services (Fong & Hui, 2001; Liang & Yu, 2001; Juang & Chang, 2007) such as fire accident, flood disaster, and debris flow. More details are presented later in this book chapter.

The major advantage from the third-generation surveillance systems over previous generations is their highly increasing functionalities in video surveillance services. For example, by collaborating with distributed visual data mining functions that support by different service nodes, we can create new and diverse "digitized products (services)" for supporting different applications. For example, by applying services such as face-recognition, moving object tracking, abandoned object identification and emerging data mining technologies (OpenIVS, 2009; Xie, et al., 2006)

Figure 1. Basic architecture of the third generation surveillance systems

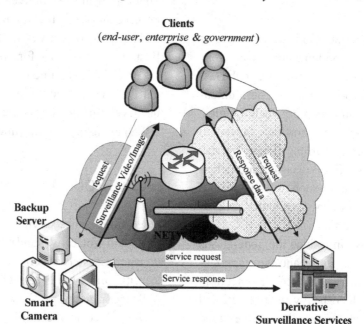

as shown in Figure 2, an early warning system (EWS) can be constructed to find out if there is a man who is tailing after an old woman or spying on a bank truck. We can also apply the same services to construct security systems, intelligent

Figure 2. Architecture example for collaborative commerce of distributed surveillance services

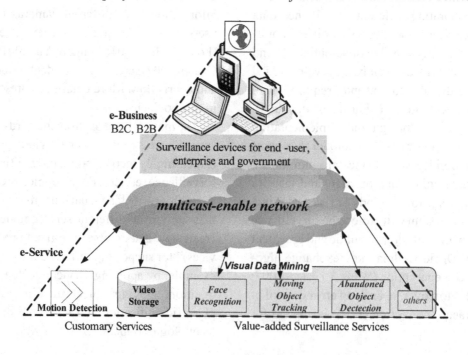

Figure 3. Proposed core service architecture for ubiquitous video surveillance over Internet

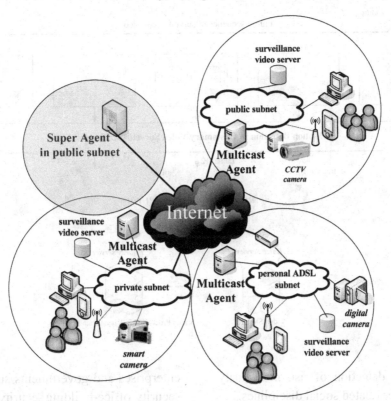

transportation systems (ITS) and biometric systems in airports, parking lots and offices.

In Figure 2, users who request the surveillance services are on top of the architecture. Diversified surveillance services are put on the bottom of the architecture including the live/stored surveillance video streaming service and the motion detection service. For supporting ubiquitous surveillance services in the middle of the architecture, we must collaborate with the ISP (Internet Service Provider) networks (i.e. B2B E-commerce) to send messages to the subscribed users (i.e. B2C E-commerce) through their PSTN phones, fax machines, cellular or VoIP phones. By collaborating the media streaming service, users can watch live/recorded surveillance videos immediately through wired/wireless Web-devices connected to Internet (Bao & Liao, 2005; RFC-3489). The proposed architecture of customary service is illustrated in Figure 3.

To reduce network workload, we apply multicast communication for the surveillance video delivery. Furthermore, an effect and efficient motion detection method is proposed to reduce redundant traffic and storage. By the proposed architecture, users may apply further the services from other video/image processing and/or mining techniques shown in Figure 4 to identify the motion objects while an alarm is set to reduce the redundant processing overhead. Our proposed schemes can help the system remit the performance penalty from network congestion from Internet. Therefore, our system architecture is more suitable for collaborating with those experts, which have the domain expertise on the delicate video/image processing/mining techniques to provide value-added services in E-marketplaces on the Internet.

Our proposed communication model for collaborative video surveillance and distributed visual data mining can provide effective architecture

Figure 4. Architecture of value-added services invoked by motion detection in surveillance video

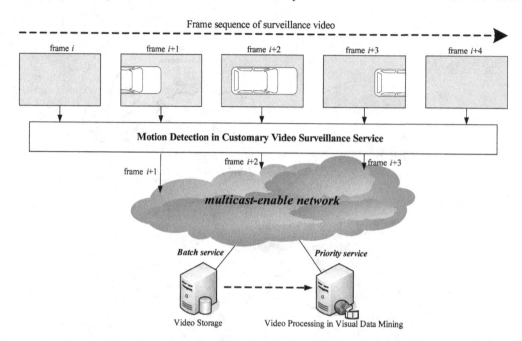

CVS-DVDM OF POTENTIAL RISK AND CRIME DETECTION

CVS-DVDM is abbreviation of "collaborative video surveillance for distributed visual data mining". CVS-DVDM is used to provide an effective early warning system of not only the potential risks (e.g. fire accident, flood disaster, and debris flow), but also the crime detections such as a main tails behind an old lady, or a man spies on a bank truck). CVS-DVDM is the main focus of this chapter and details of issues and solutions are presented in the following.

Generations of Video Surveillance and Issues

Video surveillance services are active for decades to protect lives and properties of individuals,

of EWS for the detection of risk in security, criminal and other related social disciplines.

enterprises and governments such as homeland security, office-building security, airport security, traffic surveillance on highways, and etc. Due to the technology advancements in digital media compression, computer computation and wired/ wireless communications, video surveillance is evolved to the third-generation surveillance system (Fong & Hui, 2001) with digital camera to deliver bandwidth-saving compressed-video over computer networks and distribution of intelligence among network nodes connected by heterogeneous communication.

In the first-generation surveillance system, they applied analog devices and technologies throughout all system. Analog video (CCTV, closed-circuit television) camera captured the observed scene and transmitted the video signal via analog communication cables to specific locations. The second-generation surveillance systems began to apply digital technologies in some back-end components, such as automatic event detection and alarm generation via real-time processing of digital video data.

In third-generation surveillance systems as shown in Figure 1, the digital camera can further compress the video data to save the bandwidth for applied communication networks. The major advantage from third-generation surveillance systems over previous generations is highly increasing functionality in diversified video surveillance services, such as aggregating surveillance information from different cameras to provide users value-added surveillance services (Fong & Hui, 2001), extracting different information from a surveillance video of single camera (Liang & Yu, 2001; Xie, et al., 2006) through techniques of image processing and computer vision, and providing users ubiquitous video surveillance (UVS) services (OpenIVS, 2009) through the prevalent wired/wireless Internet access.

Nowadays, the installation number of third-generation surveillance systems has been tremendously more increasing than ever via individuals, communities, organizations, companies and government. However, most of these widely-deployed video surveillance systems provide their users some intelligent surveillance services via client-server architecture over IP networks. It's well-known that delivering surveillance videos in client-server network architecture will incur service bottleneck at server side due to resource consumption of network bandwidth and computing power. Meanwhile, another scalability issue of further creating new diversified video surveillance services among existent video surveillance systems will also come from the client-server architecture.

IP multicast is a one-to-many protocol, originally designed for multimedia conferencing and very suitable for multiple accessing applications for multimedia data such as scalable video surveillance services. Different with IP unicast, IP multicast serves only single traffic no matter how many clients sending their requests. IP multicast is very useful for large-scale real-time network applications for single data source. However, in order to avoid service abuse and malicious attack

of flooding traffic, Internet Service Providers (ISP) usually disable multicast forwarding ability on routers. Thus, IP multicast data cannot pass through the Internet and Internet becomes IP multicast islands.

Thus, Multicast Backbone (MBone) arises as a virtual network for connecting IP multicast islands over Internet. On each of these islands, there is a host running an IP multicast routing demon and these islands are connected with one another via IP unicast tunnels. The idea of MBone is applied further to construct the application-layer multicast (ALM) for CVS-DVDM to perform EWS of potential risk and crime detection.

Collaborative Video Surveillance (CVS) and Applications

To effectively collaborate the isolated video surveillance systems in different generations for producing more diversified value-added applications, not only the ALM overlay network is required for CVS in large scale on Internet, but also some subsystem components are needed to provide interoperability within different generations of video surveillance. These subsystem components were proposed and called "customary video surveillance services". Besides, the ALM overlay network is composed of two types of forwarding agents to achieve ubiquitous and reliable video surveillance services. The architectures of ALM overlay network and customary video surveillance services for CVS are presented in details as follows.

ALM Overlay Network

Multicast agent (MA) and super agent (SA) are the two types of forwarding agent for CVS. Basically, they are used to internet connect multicast islands to help CVS to achieve collaboration from different video surveillance services. An operational example of MA is shown in Figure 5. There is a MA located in subnet A, which can be denoted

Figure 5. Framework of collaborative video surveillance

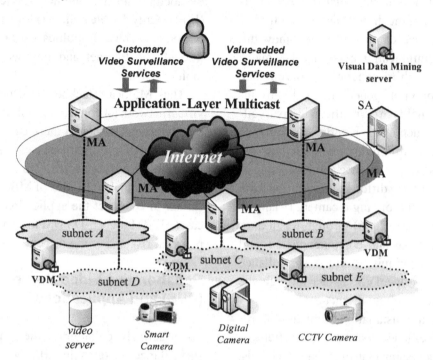

as sMA (source MA), and sMA is responsible to receive the multicast video from surveillance camera and then forwarding it to other MAs, said destination MAs (dMA), in different subnets (e.g. subnets B, C, D and E). Then, the subscriber can have the live surveillance video via MA.

However, since the NAT technology (RFC 3489) has been widely used to provide the Internet access from private networks. In proposed CVS, for example, a sMA located behind a NAT device is not possible to receive CVS service requests to deliver its outbound surveillance video. Thus, the super agent (SA) located in public network helps CVS to achieve ubiquity to forward surveillance videos from the sMAs located in private networks, no matter the dMAs are located in either public or private networks. That's to say, SA serves as a public proxy to solve this NAT traversal problem for CVS.

Besides, the reason why SA is called "super" agent is that it has to not only maintain the administrative information of MAs such as their

configuration and inbound/outbound connections with other MAs, but also provide the mapping information between video surveillance spot and sMA, which the dMA can directly connect to for its local CVS subscriber receiving surveillance videos. SA also serves as an oracle to effectively response all kinds of service requests.

Customary Video Surveillance Services

Customary video surveillance services are basic video surveillance services with consideration of scalability and reliability. They are provided by 3 kinds of different subsystems: Compressed Video Pumping Server (CVPS), Video Recording and Querying Server (VRQS), Web Browsing Viewer and Manager (WBVM). These subsystems are listed and summarized as follows (see Figure 6):
CVPS:

• Compress the captured video from surveillance camera, which is not smart camera.

Figure 6. Customary video surveillance services in UVS subnets

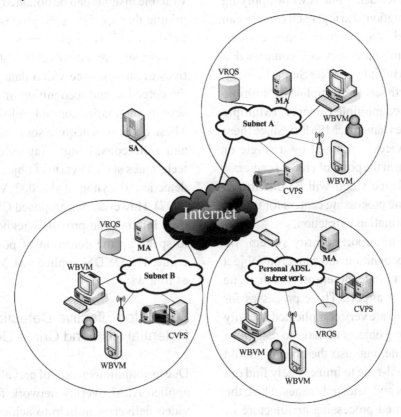

- Attach FEC packets to compressed video packets to achieve reliable video streaming service over Internet.
- Then multicast video packets with FEC packets to Internet to achieve scalable and reliable CVS service.

VRQS:

- Record surveillance videos to storage.
- Provide query interfaces for reviewing stored surveillance videos

WBVM:

- Provide users' interfaces to view surveillance videos of either live or stored data.
- Provide administration functions within above-mentioned subsystems and agents,

such as the settings of CVPS, the information of SA and the mapping information between a CVPS and its MA.

As the results from applying both ALM overlay network and customary video surveillance service to effectively collaborate video surveillance services, four kinds of video surveillance service disciplines are extended and categorized from proposed CVS framework as shown in Figure 5. The first service discipline is "a single service comprises a single camera" (Single Service Single Camera, SSSC). Most of current video surveillance service belongs to SSSC. The second service discipline is "a single service comprises multiple cameras" (Single Service Multiple Cameras, SSMC). Tracking a vehicle between succeeding smart cameras in a tunnel can be categorized into SSMC.

The third service discipline is while applying the idea of information sharing: each camera can share its captured image with multiple services. This leads to "multiple services comprised a single camera" (Multiple Services Single Camera, MSSC). The fourth service discipline is "multiple services comprised multiple cameras" (Multiple Services Multiple Cameras, MSMC). Since there are multiple services composed by a single or multiple cameras, at the point of view of cameras, captured surveillance video will be distributed over more than one processing centers for further surveillance information extraction.

For example, in airport security system, we need to do face recognition and dangerous object recognition from a single camera or more than one cameras located in airport. These processes for one or more images are very complicated not only because the varying objects we have to recognize in a complex scene, but also the objects should be processed in real-time to immediately find out the potential risks and detected crimes. Thus, the proposed distributed processing architecture of CVS model as shown in Figure 5 can effectively provide all kinds of service disciplines listed above for EWS of potential risk and crime detection.

Besides, as the applications of video surveillance service are growing than ever, value-added and diversified collaborative video surveillance (CVS) services can be produced by integrating with other full-fledged applications on Internet without the loading over the popular surveillance spots.

Detection of Potential Risk and Crime Using DVDM

Video surveillance usually consists of collecting, analyzing and summarizing video information about particular surveillance spots like highways, parking lots, building, malls, retail stores, offices, homes and etc. We can apply diversified video surveillance services to protect assets and to detect potential risk events and crimes. Furthermore, valuable insights can be obtained from video data mining that applies video processing techniques to find out visual cues or events.

Petrushin & Khan (2006) state that objectives of surveillance video data mining include the detection and recognition of object or event, activity summarization and real-time monitoring. These objectives acquire sophisticated, complex and time-consuming image/video processing techniques such as various objects' tracking and detections (Beynon, et al., 2003; Venetianer, et al., 2007). However, our proposed CVS architecture over Internet can provide backbone for DVDM to speed up the detection of potential risk and crime. The DVDM applied on CVS is introduced as follows:

DVDM for Effective Detection of Potential Risk and Crime Detection

Due to ubiquitous access of prevalent Internet, the applied ALM overlay network for surveillance video delivery can help to achieve surveillance video in scalability without constrains of the numbers of users, cameras and services. While a surveillance task, which applied above-mentioned models of SSSC, SSMC, MSSC and MSMC, can be decomposed into isolated service agents for independent DVDM jobs, CVS architecture can easily distribute surveillance video data to these service agents to complete their mining jobs in parallelism. Moreover, if a job can be split into independent processes, these independent processes are also feasible to be parallelism in our proposed CVS to speed up the time-constrained EWS for effective detection of potential risk and crime.

FUTURE RESEARCH DIRECTIONS

In this chapter, a framework of collaborative video surveillance is presented for distributed visual data mining. It can effectively detect the potential risk and crime in early warning system to protect people's assets in an active way. For applying on prevalent and public Internet with heterogeneous networks via wired and wireless access links, this framework has to consider issues of ubiquity, security, reliability and stability. The primary solutions for ubiquity, security, scalability and reliability of CVS-DVDM are presented. However, while a popular MA has to relay large video traffic to many other Mas in the proposed CVS-DVDM, the overloading issue of ALM applied is not considered in this chapter. Because load balancing issue was an active research in real-time media streaming through multicast overlay network, CVS-DVDM may apply previous load-balancing schemes to achieve both of service qualities in scalability and stability.

CONCLUSION

In this chapter, an architecture of collaborative video surveillance for distributed visual data mining of potential risk and crime detection has been presented. The proposed architecture has the ability to efficiently integrate independent surveillance systems that locate in public or private networks. Besides, security issue is considered in the proposed architecture. In the future, we are going to extend multicast agent with support of load sharing, to efficiently reduce loading to a popular sMA and its network.

REFERENCES

Bao, C. W., & Liao, W. (2005). Performance analysis of reliable MAC-layer multicast for IEEE 802.11 Wireless LANs. In *Communications, 2005, ICC 2005, IEEE International Conference,* (Vol. 2, pp.1378 – 1382).

Beynon, V. H., & Seibet, P. D. (2003). Detecting abandoned packages in a multi-camera video surveillance system. In *2003 IEEE International Conference on Advanced Video and Signal Based Surveillance (AVSS'03)*, Miami, FL. FIPS-197, National Inst. Of Standards and Technology, Federal Information Processing Standard 197. (2001, November). *Advanced Encryption Standard.* Retrieved from http://csrc.nist.gov/publications/fips/fips197/fips-197.pdf

Fong, A. C. M., & Hui, S. C. (2001). Web-based intelligent surveillance system for detection of criminal activities. *Journal of Computing & Control Engineering, 12*(6), 263–270. doi:10.1049/cce:20010603

Ho, J. M., Chang, R. I., Juang, J. Y., & Wang, C. H. (2000). Design and implementation of a web-based surveillance system using internet multicast communications. In *SoftCOM 2000.* Washington, DC: IEEE.

Juang, C. F., & Chang, C. M. (2007). Human body posture classification by a neural fuzzy network and home care system application. *IEEE Transactions on Systems, Man, and Cybernetics, 37*(November), 984–994.

Liang, L. F., & Yu, S. Y. (2001). Real-Time duplex digital video surveillance system and its implementation with FPGA. In *Proceedings off International Conference on ASIC,* (pp. 471-473).

Marcenaro, L. F., et al. (2001). Distributed architectures and logical-task decomposition in multimedia systems. In *Procedings of IEEE,* (pp.1419-1440).

OpenIVS. (2009). Retrieved 2009, http://OpenIVS.dyndns.org

Petrushin, V. A., & Khan, L. (Eds.). (2006). *Multimedia data mining and knowledge discovery.* London: Baker & Taylor Books. RFC-3489. (n.d.). *STUN - Simple Traversal of User Datagram Protocol (UDP) Through Network Address Translators (NATs).*

Simoff, S., Böhlen, M. H., & Mazeika, A. (Eds.). (2008). *Visual data mining: Theory, techniques and tools for visual analytics*. Berlin: Springer.

Venetianer, Z., & Yin, L. (2007). Stationary target detection using the object video surveillance system. In *2007 IEEE Conference on Advanced Video and Signal Based Surveillance*, (pp. 242-247).

Wang, C. H., Chang, R. I., & Ho, J. M. (2003). An effective communication model for collaborative commerce of Web-based surveillance services. In *IEEE International Conference on E-Commerce* (CEC 2003), 24-27 June, (pp. 40 -44).

Wang, C. H., Li, M. W., & Liao, W. (2007). A distributed key-changing mechanism for secure voice over IP (VOIP) service. In *IEEE 2007 International Conference on Multimedia & Expo (ICME 2007)*, July 2-5, Beijing, China.

Xie, J., Nandi, A., & Gupta, S. A. K. (2006). Improving the reliability of IEEE 802.11 broadcast scheme for multicasting in mobile ad hoc networks. *Proceedings of Communications IEE*, *153*(2), 207–212. doi:10.1049/ip-com:20045271

KEY TERMS AND DEFINITIONS

Early Warning System: Integration of information to allows us to detect and rectify potential problems at an early stage.

Collaborative Video Surveillance: Treatment of each surveillance data or function as a digitial product in collaborative commerce to provide users different video surveillance services.

Visual Data Mining: Integration of the techniques of visual and data mining to use data mining techniques for visual data or to use visual techniques in data mining.

Cloud Computing: A new supplement, consumption and delivery model for Internet-based computer services.

Chapter 11
Data Mining and Economic Crime Risk Management

Mieke Jans
Hasselt University, Belgium

Nadine Lybaert
Hasselt University, Belgium

Koen Vanhoof
Hasselt University, Belgium

ABSTRACT

Economic crime is a billion dollar business and is substantially present in our current society. Both researchers and practitioners have gone into this problem by looking for ways of fraud mitigation. Data mining is often called in this context. In this chapter, the application of data mining in the field of economic crime, or corporate fraud, is discussed. The classification external versus internal fraud is explained and the major types of fraud within these classifications will be given. Aside from explaining these classifications, some numbers and statistics are provided. After this thorough introduction into fraud, an academic literature review concerning data mining in combination with fraud is given, along with the current solutions for corporate fraud in business practice. At the end, a current state of data mining applications within the field of economic crime, both in the academic world and in business practice, is given.

INTRODUCTION

Fraud is a billion dollar business, as several research studies reveal. Among them are important surveys by the Association of Certified Fraud Examiners (ACFE, 2008) and PriceWaterhouse&Coopers (PwC, 2007). These reports demonstrate the magnitude of fraud that companies must deal

with today. Economic crime, or corporate fraud, is generally speaking to be divided in internal fraud (fraud from within the company), and external fraud (fraud from outside targeting the company). At the Background section, a complete classification overview is provided, along with some fraud theories and some numbers.

At the same breath as fraud, data mining is often called, whether it is relevant or not. However, to link fraud to data mining, a lot of questions

DOI: 10.4018/978-1-61692-865-0.ch011

raise to the surface. About which kind of fraud are we talking? Is it internal or external fraud? Are all kinds of fraud to be linked with data mining? And if so, what data mining technique are we talking about? And equally important, what kind of data is used? And what is the purpose of the data mining? Is the aim to detect fraud, or to prevent fraud, or both? To have a clear overview of the current state of data mining in relation to economic crime, we look at all these aspects, to end with an unmistakable summary of current data mining applications for fraud mitigation. We refer to Jans, et al. (2009) as the original source of the following thoughts.

BACKGROUND

What is Economic Crime?

There are many definitions of fraud, depending on the point of view considering. According to The American Heritage Dictionary, (Third Edition), fraud is defined as "a deception deliberately practiced in order to secure unfair or unlawful gain" (p.722). We can conclude that fraud is deception. Whatever industry the fraud is situated in or whatever kind of fraud you visualize, deception is always the core of fraud.

In a nutshell, Davia, et al. (2000) summarize: "Fraud always involves one or more persons who, with intent, act secretly to deprive another of something of value, for their own enrichment". Also Wells (2005) stresses deception as the linchpin to fraud.

Corporate Fraud Classification

The most prominent classification in fraud is corporate versus non-corporate fraud. Corporate fraud is fraud in an organizational setting, whereas non-corporate fraud encompasses all remaining frauds. For instance, a citizen cheating with his income taxes is certainly fraud, but is no part of corporate fraud. Economic crime is equal to corporate fraud. Accordingly, an overview of corporate fraud classifications is given.

Within corporate fraud, the most important distinction is Bologna & Lindquist (1995)'s internal versus external fraud classification. This classification is based on whether the perpetrator is internal or external to the victim company. Frauds committed by vendors, suppliers or contractors are examples of external fraud, while an employee stealing from the company or a manager cooking the books are examples of internal fraud. What is seen as internal fraud, following this definition, is in fact the same as '*occupational fraud and abuse*'; the type of fraud the ACFE investigates in their Reports to the Nation.

In their 2008 Report to the Nation on Occupational Fraud and Abuse, the ACFE defines this type of economic crime as: "The use of one's occupation for personal enrichment through the deliberate misuse or misapplication of the employing organization's resources or assets" (ACFE, 2008). This definition encompasses a wide variety of conduct by executives, employees, managers, and principals of organizations. Violations can range from asset misappropriation, fraudulent statements and corruption over pilferage and petty theft, false overtime, using company property for personal benefit to payroll and sick time abuses (Wells, 2005). Although this type of fraud encompasses many kinds of irregularities, notice that it only covers internal corporate fraud. For example, fraud against the government (non-corporate fraud) and fraud perpetrated by customers (external corporate fraud) are not included. Since one has to be internal to a company and abuse its occupation to commit internal fraud, we put internal fraud and occupational fraud and abuse as equivalents. A combination of internal and external fraud can also occur, for example when an employee collaborates with a supplier to deprive the company. This is however categorized under occupational fraud and abuse as corruption.

Corruption is one of the three categories the ACFE distinguishes within internal fraud: asset misappropriation, corruption, and financial statement fraud. However, there are numerous other ways of classifying fraud. Bologna & Lindquist (1995) mentioned in their first edition of *Fraud Auditing and Forensic Accounting*, in addition to other classifications, statement fraud versus transaction fraud. The authors define statement fraud as "the intentional misstatement of certain financial values to enhance the appearance of profitability and deceive shareholders or creditors" (Bologna & Lindquist, 1995). Transaction fraud on the other hand is intended to embezzle or steal organizational assets. According to these definitions, we can classify ACFE's financial statement fraud as statement fraud and ACFE's corruption and asset misappropriation as transaction fraud. Davia, et al. (2000) distinguish two related types of fraud: financial statement balance fraud and asset-theft fraud. The authors state that the main difference between the former and the latter is that there is no theft of assets involved in financial statement balance fraud. Well-known examples of this type of fraud are Enron and WorldCom. We see this classification (financial statement balance fraud vs. asset-theft fraud) as an equivalent of Bologna & Lindquist (1995)'s statement and transaction fraud.

Singleton, et al. (2006) give more classifications of fraud - all classifying corporate fraud. A first classification is fraud for versus against the company. The former contains frauds intended to benefit the organizational entity, while the latter encompasses frauds that intend to harm the entity. Examples of fraud for the company are price fixing, corporate tax evasion and violations of environmental laws. While these frauds are in the benefit of the company at first, in the end the personal enrichment stemming from these frauds are the real incentives. Frauds against the company are only intended to benefit the perpetrator, like embezzlement or theft of corporate assets. Pay attention to the fact that not all frauds fit conveniently into this schema, for example arson for profit, planned bankruptcy and fraudulent insurance claims. These frauds may also fall partly under external fraud (in case of the fraudulent insurance claims).

Another distinction Singleton, et al. (2006) refers to is management versus non-management fraud, also a classification based on the perpetrator's characteristics. These different classifications all present another dimension and can display some overlap. In Figure 1 the overview by Jans, et al. (2009) of how to see the different classifications and their relations to each other is depicted. Some assumptions are made and explained below.

Because the focus of this chapter is economic crime, alias corporate fraud, this overview is accordingly limited to corporate fraud classifications. The most prominent distinction is the internal versus external fraud, since all other classifications are situated within internal fraud. As already pointed out, occupational fraud and abuse is seen as an equivalent of internal fraud. Figure 1 also shows that all classifications left, apply only to corporate fraud. This explains why all are embedded in internal fraud. Only fraud against the company has a common field with external fraud. The rectangle of fraud against the company is open at the bottom, pointing that all external corporate frauds are a form of fraud against the company. The reasoning is that someone external to the company would not benefit from any type of fraud committed for the company, and consequently commits always fraud against the company.

Within internal fraud, three different classifications are incorporated. As a start, a distinction between statement fraud and transaction fraud (including ACFE's corruption and asset misappropriation) is made, respectively financial statement balance fraud and asset-theft fraud in terms of Davia, et al. (2000). A second distinction is based upon the occupation level of the fraudulent employee: management versus non-management fraud. It is assumed that managers

Figure 1. Corporate fraud classification overview (Adapted fromJans, et al. (2009))

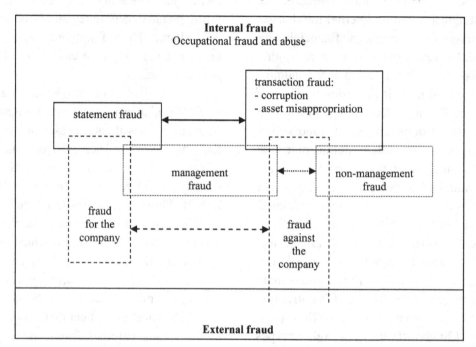

can commit both statement and transaction fraud, yet non-management is in this view restricted to transaction fraud only. The last classification in this overview is fraud for versus fraud against the company. Although fraud for the company does not necessarily need to be statement fraud, an overlap is realistic. Another assumption is made with the classification for versus against. Contrary to fraud against the company, only managers are believed to be in an advantageous position to commit fraud for the company, hence the overlap with only management fraud. This is in contrast to fraud against the company, which is believed to be committed by both managers and non-managers. A last assumption is made concerning the nature of statement fraud. All statement fraud is assumed to be committed to improve the company's appearance and never to harm the company. Accordingly, statement fraud is assumed to always be profiled as fraud for the company, never against the company (Jans, et al., 2009).

Cost of Fraud: Some Numbers

Several research studies on economic crime report shocking numbers. Concerning internal fraud, two elaborate surveys, one conducted in the United States by the ACFE (ACFE, 2008), and one worldwide by Pricewaterhouse&Coopers (PwC, 2007), yield the following information about corporate fraud:

The ACFE study conducted in 2007-2008 in the United States reported that company's estimate a loss of seven percent of annual revenues to fraud. Applied to the US$ 14,196 billion of United States estimated Gross Domestic Product in 2008, this would translate to approximately US$ 994 billion in fraud losses for the United States. The PwC worldwide study revealed that 43 percent of the companies surveyed had fallen victim to economic crime in the years 2006 and 2007. The average financial damage to these companies was US$ 2.42 million per company over two years.

These numbers all concern internal fraud. There are however also large costs from external fraud.

Four important domains afflicted by fraud are regularly discussed: telecommunications, automobile insurance, health care and credit cards. On these domains, we found the following numbers:

Globally, telecommunications fraud is estimated at about US$ 55 billion (Abidogum, 2005). For the second domain, the automobile insurance fraud problem, Brockett, et al. (1998) cited already in 1998 an estimation of the National Insurance Crime Bureau (NICB) that the annual cost in the United States is US$ 20 billion. At the website of the NICB nowadays we read: "Insurance industry studies indicate 10 percent or more of property/casualty insurance claims are fraudulent" (NICB, 2009). Concerning health care insurance claims fraud, the United States National Health Care Anti-Fraud Association (NHCAA) estimates conservatively that of the nation's annual health care outlay, at least 3 percent is lost to outright fraud. This is $68 billion. Other estimates by government and law enforcement agencies place the loss as high as 10 percent or US$ 170 billion (NHCAA, 2009). Concerning the fourth domain, credit card fraud, Bolton & Hand (2002) cite estimates of US$ 10 billion losses worldwide for Visa/Mastercard only.

Prevention Versus Detection

When discussing data mining in a context of economic crime, there is another clarification to be made, apart from what type of fraud we are dealing with. Whether data mining is used for fraud prevention or fraud detection is an important distinction. When making a statement about data mining and fraud mitigation at the end of this chapter, we take this distinction into account.

Bologna & Lindquist (1995) state that prevention should take precedence over detection. The authors mean by fraud prevention creating a work environment that values honesty. This includes hiring honest people, paying them competitively, treating them fairly, and providing a safe and secure workplace. In the *Accountant's Guide to Fraud Detection and Control*, Davia, et al. (2000) state that it is management's responsibility to allocate resources and emphasis to fraud-specific internal controls and to proactive fraud-specific examinations. These approaches are examples of prevention on one hand and detection on the other. The authors point out that it is a mistake to think in terms of one versus the other. Strong internal controls as fraud prevention are very important, but they are best reinforced by following fraud-specific examinations.

By the way Bologna & Lindquist (1995) and Davia, et al. (2000) describe the combination of fraud prevention and detection, a general description of risk management is given. This confirms why both detection and prevention are important to include in our summary about data mining and economic crime risk management.

APPLICATION OF DATA MINING FOR ECONOMIC CRIME RISK MANAGEMENT

Issues, Controversies, Problems

Employing data mining for the goal of fraud detection poses extra challenges as opposed to standard data mining tasks. Paass, et al. (2007) summarize these challenges. In fraud detection one has to deal with a highly skewed distribution of the defrauded transactions within the population as opposed to the legitimate transactions. The percentage of fraud cases is always very low and fraud is, fortunately, the exception to the rule. A second characteristic of fraud research is that labeled data is sparse. Based on the quantity of conducted research on supervised data, labeled data is apparently easier to access in cases of external fraud, or financial statement fraud. (see table below) A third characteristic is the issue of false negatives that can be included in training data as 'non-fraudulent' instead of 'fraudulent'. Paass, et al. (2007) also mention trivial rules as typical to fraud detection, hereby referring to rules to discover only known fraud schemes. The last two characteristics are concept drift and interpretability. Concept drift refers to the adaptive behavior of frauds, being able to respond to new legislation and new detection methods. Fawcett & Provost (1997) amongst others paid particularly attention to this characteristic in their study, but still is concept drift a research topic that needs to be much further explored in Adaptive Information Systems. The last characteristic of interpretability points to the limitation to data mining techniques that allow the researcher to interpret the outputted rules in order to decide whether the new pattern discovered actually describes fraud or not.

We wish to make up a balance about the use of data mining for economic crime risk management. Before we can perform this exercise, several aspects have to be taken into account. One issue is already addressed: there are several forms of fraud, such as there are internal and external kinds of fraud. This distinction is important to make, because we find a discrepancy in the use of data mining in these two domains of economic crime. The underlying reason for this deviation is the type of input data available, forming the basis for data mining.

Based on the input data, there are two categories of learning: supervised and unsupervised learning. In supervised learning, the class to be learned is present in the data set. In the fraud detection problem, this translates in a data set containing examples of both fraudulent and legitimate records. This means that all the records available are labeled as 'fraudulent' or 'non-fraudulent'. After building a model using these training data, new cases can be classified as fraudulent or legitimate. Of course, one needs to be confident about the true classes of the training data, as this is the foundation of the model. This problem of false negatives is explicitly addressed in a study of Artis, et al. (2002). Another practical issue that is related to the classification supervised versus unsupervised is the availability of labeled data, which is often

minimized unjustly. Furthermore, this method is only able to detect frauds of a type which has previously occurred. In contrast, unsupervised methods don't make use of labeled records. These methods seek for accounts, customers, suppliers, etc. that behave 'unusual'. The issue is that in cases of internal fraud, one often has no access to a supervised data set to learn from, while in cases of external fraud, such data sets are easier to build. This difference will be reflected in the current way of managing economic crime risk in the domain of external fraud and the domain of internal fraud, as will become clear later in this chapter.

Aside from dividing data in the groups supervised versus unsupervised, there is yet another dimension to make. The field of data mining encompasses many techniques, like K-means clustering, decision trees, neural networks etc. These techniques serve different tasks, like for example classification, clustering, and anomaly detection. Mainly, data mining tasks can be divided in two subgroups: predictive tasks and descriptive tasks. With predictive tasks, the objective is to predict the value of one attribute, based on the values of other attributes. This is what classification techniques pursue. Predictive tasks make a prediction for every observation. In this context, the prediction will be about the fraudulent or legal character of a case. Descriptive tasks however, do not pronounce upon every observation, but describe the data set as a whole. It aims to describe the underlying relationships in the data set. Examples of descriptive tasks are pattern recognition, anomaly detection, and correlations. (Tan, et al., 2006; Jans, et al., 2009) Because of the great difference in output, we will take into account which task is served, when making statements about the use of data mining for risk management.

In the next sections of 'Solutions and Recommendations' the applicability of data mining in terms of mitigating economic crime is reviewed. We take into account whether or not data mining is currently used, whether this is only in a theoretical phase, or also implemented in research, whether the applicability of data mining is in the academic field, or in business practice, whether fraud detection or fraud prevention is the aim, and what kind of data mining task is used. To make statements about this topic, we have to look both at business practice and at academic research, because those fields unfortunately not always operate on the same level. We start with solutions and recommendations on the problem of economic crime from a practitioner's perspective, and turn later to the solutions and recommendations from an academic perspective. We end with a conclusive overview of the current applicability of data mining for economic crime risk management.

Solutions and Recommendations Business Practice

The above mentioned studies of PwC and the ACFE investigate by means of surveys, which are the most occurring means or methods that lead to fraud detection, or are believed to do so by the CFO's. The following are the findings of both studies.

About the way fraud is detected, both studies of PwC and the ACFE stress the importance of tips. At the PwC study, no less than 43% of the fraud cases is detected by means of tips (whistleblowing, internal tip-offs and external tip-offs). The respondents of the ACFE study even reported a number of 46.2%. According to the ACFE report, an anonymous fraud hotline anticipates a lot of fraud damage. In the cases reviewed, organizations that had such hotlines, suffered a median loss of US$ 100.000, whereas organizations without hotlines had a median loss of US$ 250.000, presenting a reduction of 60% in fraud loss. Tips and hotlines are associated with a company's fraud culture. These numbers suggest that a company can detect and deter fraud by setting an appropriate tone at the top (and down). Another recent study, performed by Ernst&Young, also addresses the effectiveness of a Code of Conduct, expressing

a company's culture (E&Y, A Survey into Fraud Risk Mitigations in 13 european Countries, 2007). However, as a second best detection method, the company's control system comes forward. This is represented in several aspects, from internal audit to fraud risk management, but all together these methods contribute to fraud detection. At the PwC study, the corporate controls were responsible for the detection of 34% of the reported frauds. At the ACFE study, internal audit and internal control together revealed 39.4% of the reported cases. So also corporate control, after chance related means, can have a measurable impact on detecting fraud. The more control measures a company puts in place, the more incidents of fraud will be uncovered. The use of data mining is situated in the field of these corporate control methods.

Another study, performed by Ernst&Young, mentions more explicitly both preventing and detecting fraud. This is contrary to the previous mentioned studies, which mainly cover fraud detection. The global survey by Ernst&Young in 2006 revealed similar insights as the other studies on fraud detection. On fraud prevention, respondents identify internal controls as the key factor to prevent and detect fraud (Ernst&Young, 2006). Also the ACFE study stresses the importance of improving the internal control system. Hence it is no surprise internal control is currently the most prevalent mean companies use to mitigate internal fraud. In the following paragraphs, some information about internal control is given.

To start with, the Committee of Sponsoring Organizations of the Treadway Commission (COSO) was formed in 1985 to commission the Treadway Commission to perform its task. The task at hand was to study the causes of fraudulent reporting and make recommendations to reduce its incidence. In response to this recommendation, COSO developed an internal control framework, issued in 1992 and entitled "Internal Control - Integrated Framework". This work has been updated later on, but the definition of internal control, according to the COSO framework, stayed defined as:

a process, effected by the entity's board of directors, management, and other personnel, designed to provide reasonable assurance regarding the achievement of objectives in the following categories:

- *Effectiveness and efficiency of operations*
- *Reliability of financial reporting*
- *Compliance with applicable laws and regulations*

If we look at the definition, it is clear why internal control is important as a protection against fraud. The achievement of the first category is to encounter transaction fraud, the second to encounter statement fraud and the third category achievement is to protect the organization against fraud for the company. Following this broad definition, internal control can both prevent and detect fraud. And although this definition is stemming from the foundation of the National Commission on Fraudulent Financial Reporting, also other classes of fraud than fraudulent financial reporting can be encountered. However, the definition is clear about its reasonable - not absolute - assurance regarding the objectives. We can conclude that internal control is a means to protect an organization against internal fraud, but given the rising prevalence of fraud it is still not sufficient as a stand-alone tool. Also the numbers provided by the PwC and ACFE surveys reveal that internal control comes off worse than chance means as a detection tool. However, these studies also emphasize the extra value of well-functioning internal control systems (Jans, et al., 2009).

The internal control framework of COSO is the broadest existing framework on this topic. Some industries have taken this framework and customized it to their specific needs, for instance the banking industry. In this environment, Basel II is created, with its own internal control section. It is however based on COSO and hence is a variant of this framework. It is beyond the scope

and the goal of this chapter to address all existing internal control frameworks. We believe that by addressing the settings of COSO, the general business practice in terms of internal control are covered. Our main interest in this framework is however whether data mining takes part in it or not. Finding an answer on this question, we first take a closer look to the content of the internal control framework.

In her framework, COSO identifies the following five components as part of internal control:

- The control environment,
- The entity's risk assessment process,
- The information system,
- Control activities, and
- Monitoring of controls.

The control environment encompasses the management's overall attitude, awareness and actions regarding internal control and its importance in the entity. The entity's risk assessment process comprehends the entity's process of identifying risks and apprehending an appropriate strategy towards these risks. Further, the entity should have access to an effective information system. This is an information system that guards the accurate reporting of transactions and provides a complete audit trail. Control activities are established by management to ensure that specific objectives are achieved. This need exists because of the information asymmetry already mentioned in the context of agency theory. The last component of internal control is monitoring. Employees need to know that non-compliance with controls is likely to be detected (deterrence effect). Monitoring controls also provides feedback concerning these controls.

Looking at these five components defined by COSO, we see internal control encompasses a wide variety of actions. Aside from qualitative actions like a control environment and a risk assessment process, also actions based on quantitative data are desired. The control activities for example may require some data analyzing. The techniques applied to this end are however to be categorized as reporting tools, another category of data analyzing techniques than data mining. Reporting techniques are primarily oriented toward extracting quantitative and statistical data characteristics such as means, minima and maxima. These techniques facilitate useful data interpretations by combining some descriptive statistics, and can help to get better insights into the processes behind the data. These interpretations and insights are the sought knowledge. Although the traditional data analyzing techniques can indirectly lead us to knowledge, it is still created by human analysts. This is contrary to data mining techniques, where the knowledge is extracted out of the data by means of machine learning.

The above paragraphs all deal with how business practice mitigates internal fraud. The COSO framework is a response on internal fraud and is encapsulated in several legislations. The discussion of all related legislation is however not directly relevant to this chapter and consequently beyond the scope of this chapter. About external fraud, there exists, to our knowledge, no such framework. Consequently, we do not have any information about how companies protect themselves against external fraud. Obviously, certain business domains as credit card companies, banking companies, telecommunication or insurance companies, are occupied with this challenge and probably allocate a lot of resources to counter this threat. However, we do not have any access to information that would justify a statement on this topic. That way, we can only make conclusions for the applicability of data mining for internal fraud risk reduction in business practice. Although it is dangerous to generalize, and exceptions always exist, we can say that generally speaking, business practice does not apply (yet) any data mining in their fight against internal fraud. About the fight against external fraud, we have to distance ourselves from a conclusion.

SOLUTIONS AND RECOMMENDATIONS ACADEMIC RESEARCH

Research Studies

Not only business practice has searched for solutions to reduce economic crime risk, also the academic community has investigated this topic. In this section an overview of the academic literature concerning fraud prevention and detection is given. We take into account both fraud detection and fraud prevention (although almost all articles found address the problem of fraud detection). To gain a clear overview, Table 1 is created. Aside from the division internal versus external fraud, the type of fraud is shown in more detail. Within external fraud we make a distinction between automobile insurance, telecommunications, health care, and credit card. The table provides us with the author(s) in alphabetical order, the application domain, whether it concerns internal or external fraud, whether the objective is fraud detection or prevention, which technique is used, and what task this technique serves.

Concerning the techniques used, an intensively explored method is the use of neural networks. The studies of Hilas & Mastorocostas (2008), Krenker, et al. (2009) and Davey, et al. (1996) (telecommunications fraud), Dorronsoro, et al. (1997) (credit card fraud), and Fanning & Cogger (1998), Green & Choi (1997) and Kirkos, et al. (2007) (financial statement fraud) all use neural network technology for detecting fraud in different contexts. Lin, et al. (2003) apply a fuzzy neural net, also in the domain of fraudulent financial reporting. Both Brause, et al. (1999) and Estévez, et al. (2006) use a combination of neural nets and rules. The latter use fuzzy rules, where the former use traditional association rules. Also He, et al. (1997) apply neural networks: a multilayer perceptron network in the supervised component of their study and Kohonen's self-orga-

Table 1. Fraud detection/prevention literature overview (©2009, Jans, Lybaert & Vanhoof. Used with permission)

Author	Application Domain	Internal/ External	Detection/ Prevention	Technique	Task
Bermúdez *et al.* (2007)	Automobile Insurance Fraud	External	Detection	Skewed Logit Link and Bayesian Analyses	Predicitve
Bolton and Hand (2001)	Credit Card Fraud	External	Detection	Peer Group Analysis and Break Point Analysis	Predictive
Bonchi *et al.* (1999)	Fiscal Fraud	External	Detection	Decision Tree	Predictive
Brause *et al.* (1999)	Credit Card Fraud	External	Detection	Rules and Neural Network	Predictive
Brockett *et al.* (1998)	Automobile Insurance Fraud	External	Detection	Kohonen's Self-Organizing Map	Predictive
Brockett *et al.* (2002)	Automobile Insurance Fraud	External	Detection	Principal Component Analysis	Predictive
Burge and Shawe-Taylor (2001)	Telecommunications Fraud	External	Detection	Unsupervised Neural Network	Predictive
Cahill *et al.* (2002)	Telecommunication Fraud	External	Detection	Profiling by means of signatures	Predictive
Cortes *et al.* (2002)	Telecommunications Fraud	External	Detection	Dynamic Graphs	Predictive
Cox *et al.* (1997)	Telecommunications Fraud	External	Detection	Visual Data Mining	Descriptive
Davey *et al.* (1996)	Telecommunications Fraud	External	Detection	Neural Network	Predictive
Derrig and Ostaszewski (1995)	Automobile Insurance Fraud	External	Detection	Fuzzy Set Theory	Descriptive
Deshmukh and Talluru (1998)	Financial Statement Fraud	Internal	Detection	Rule-based Fuzzy Reasoning System	Predictive
Dorronsoro *et al.* (1997)	Credit Card Fraud	External	Detection	Neural Network	Predictive
Estévez *et al.* (2006)	Telecommunications Fraud	External	Detection and Prevention	Fuzzy Rules and Neural Network	Predictive
Ezawa and Norton (1996)	Uncollectible Telecommunications Accounts	External	Detection	Bayesian Neural Network	Predictive
Fan (2004)	Credit Card Fraud	External	Detection	Decision Tree	Predictive
Fanning and Cogger (1998)	Financial Statement Fraud	Internal	Detection	Neural Network	Predictive
Fawcett and Provost (1997)	Telecommunications Fraud	External	Detection	Rules, Monitors and Linear Threshold Unit	Predictive
Fawcett and Provost (1999)	Telecommunications Fraud	External	Detection	Activity Monitoring	Predictive
Green and Choi (1997)	Financial Statement Fraud	Internal	Detection	Neural Networks	Predictive
He *et al.* (1997)	Health Care Insurance Fraud	External	Detection	Neural Network	Predictive
He *et al.* (1997)	Health Care Insurance Fraud	External	Detection	Kohonen's Self-Organizing Map	Descriptive
Hilas and Mastorocostas (2008)	Telecommunications Fraud	External	Detection	Neural Network and Clustering	Predictive
Hilas (2009)	Telecommunication Fraud	External	Detection	Rule based expert system	Predictive

continued on following page

Table 1. continued

Author	Application Domain	Internal/ External	Detection/ Prevention	Technique	Task
Hoogs *et al.* (2007)	Financial Statement Fraud	Internal	Detection	A Genetic Algorithm Approach	Predictive
Juszczak *et al.* (2008)	Credit Card Fraud	External	Detection	Many different classification techniques	Predictive
Kim and Kwon (2006)	Insurance Fraud	External	Detection	Insurance Fraud Recognition System (Korea)	Predictive
Kirkos *et al.* (2007)	Financial Statement Fraud	Internal	Detection	Decision Tree, Neural Network and Bayesian Belief Network	Predictive
Krenker *et al.* (2009)	Telecommunications Fraud	External	Detection	Bidirectional Artificial Neural Network	Predictive
Lin *et al.* (2003)	Financial Statement Fraud	Internal	Detection	Fuzzy Neural Network	Predictive
Maes *et al.* (2002)	Credit Card Fraud	External	Detection	Neural Network and Bayesian Belief Network	Predictive
Major and Riedinger (2002)	Health Care Insurance Fraud	External	Detection	Electronic Fraud Detection (EFD)	Predictive
Murad and Pinkas (1999)	Telecommunications Fraud	External	Detection	Three Level Profiling	Predictive
Panigrahi *et al.* (2009)	Credit Card Fraud	External	Detection	Dempster-Shafer theory & Bayesian learning	Predictive
Pathak *et al.* (2003)	Insurance Fraud	External	Detection	Fuzzy logic based expert system	Predictive
Phua *et al.* (2004)	Automobile Insurance Fraud	External	Detection	Meta-classifiers	Predictive
Quah and Sriganesh (2008)	Credit Card Fraud	External	Detection	Self-Organizing Maps	Descriptive
Rosset *et al.* (1999)	Telecommunications Fraud	External	Detection	Rules	Predictive
Sánchez *et al.* (2008)	Credit Card Fraud	External	Detection and Prevention	Fuzzy Rules	Descriptive
Stolfo *et al.* (2000)	Credit Card Fraud and Intrusion	External	Detection	Meta-classifiers	Predictive
Tsung *et al.* (2007)	Telecommunications Fraud	External	Detection	Batch Library Method	Predictive
Viaene *et al.* (2002)	Automobile Insurance Fraud	External	Detection	Logistic Regression, k-Nearest Neighbor, Decision Tree, Bayesian Neural Network, SVM, Naive Bayes, and tree- augmented Naive Bayes	Predictive
Viaene *et al.* (2005)	Automobile Insurance Fraud	External	Detection	Bayesian Neural Network	Predictive
Viaene *et al.* (2007)	Automobile Insurance Fraud	External	Detection	Logistic Regression	Predictive
Whitrow *et al.* (2009)	Credit Card Fraud	External	Detection	SVM, Random Forests, Logistic Regression, Quadratic Discriminant, Naïve Bayes, Decision Tree, k-Nearest Neighbor	Predictive
Xing and Girolami (2007)	Telecommunications Fraud	External	Detection	Latent Dirichlet Allocation	Predictive
Yang and Hwang (2006)	Health Care Insurance Fraud	External	Detection	Frequent Pattern Mining	Predictive

nizing maps for the unsupervised part. Like He, et al. (1997) apply in their unsupervised part, Brockett, et al. (1998) apply Kohonen's self-organizing feature maps (a form of neural network technology) to uncover phony claims in the domain of automobile insurance. This is also what Zaslavsky & Strizhak (2006) suggest later, in 2006, in a methodological paper to detect credit card fraud. Quah & Sriganesh (2008) follow this suggestion in an empirical paper on understanding spending patterns to decipher potential fraud cases. A Bayesian learning neural network is implemented for credit card fraud detection by Maes, et al. (2002) (aside to an artificial neural network), for uncollectible telecommunications accounts (which is not always fraud) by Ezawa & Norton (1996), for financial statement fraud by Kirkos, et al. (2007) and for automobile insurance fraud detection by Viaene, et al. (2005) and Viaene, et al. (2002).

In Viaene, et al. (2005)'s field of automobile insurance fraud, Bermúdez, et al. (2007) use an asymmetric or skewed logit link to fit a fraud database from the Spanish insurance market. Afterwards they develop Bayesian analysis of this model. In a related field Major & Riedinger (2002) presented a tool for the detection of medical insurance fraud. They propose a hybrid knowledge/statistical-based system, where expert knowledge is integrated with statistical power. More recently Panigrahi, Kunda, Sural, & Majundar (2009) employed a fraud detection system consisting of four components, including rule-based and Bayesian learning. Another example of combining different techniques can be found in Fawcett & Provost (1997). A series of data mining techniques for the purpose of detecting cellular clone fraud is hereby used. Specifically, a rule-learning program to uncover indicators of fraudulent behavior from a large database of customer transactions is implemented. From the generated fraud rules, a selection has been made to apply in the form of monitors. This set of monitors profiles legitimate customer behavior and indicate anomalies. The outputs of the monitors, together with labels on an account's previous daily behavior, are used as training data for a simple Linear Threshold Unit (LTU). The LTU learns to combine evidence to generate high-confidence alarms. The method described above is an example of a supervised hybrid as supervised learning techniques are combined to improve results. In another work of Fawcett & Provost (1999), Activity Monitoring is introduced as a separate problem class within data mining with a unique framework. Fawcett & Provost (1999) demonstrate how to use this framework among other things for cellular phone fraud detection.

Another framework presented, for the detection of healthcare fraud, is a process-mining framework by Yang & Hwang (2006). The framework is based on the concept of clinical pathways where structure patterns are discovered and further analyzed.

The fuzzy expert systems are also experienced within a couple of studies. So there are Derrig & Ostaszewski (1995), Deshmukh & Talluru (1998), Pathak, et al. (2003) and Sánchez, et al. (2009). The latter extract a set of fuzzy association rules from a data set containing genuine and fraudulent credit card transactions. These rules are compared with the criteria which risk analysts apply in their fraud analysis process. The research is therefore difficult to categorize as 'detection', 'prevention' or both. We adopt the authors' own statement of contribution in both fraud detection and prevention. Derrig & Ostaszewski (1995) use fuzzy clustering and therefore apply a data mining technique performing a descriptive task, where the other techniques (but Sánchez, et al. (2009)) perform a predictive task.

Stolfo, et al. (2000) delivered some interesting work on intrusion detection. They provided a framework, MADAM ID, for Mining Audit Data for Automated Models for Intrusion Detection. Although intrusion detection is associated with fraud detection, this is a research area on its own and we do not extend our scope to this field. Next to MADAM ID, Stolfo, et al. (2000) discuss the results of the JAM project. JAM stands for Java Agents for Meta-Learning. JAM provides an integrated meta-learning system for fraud detection that combines the collective knowledge acquired by individual local agents. In this particular case, individual knowledge of banks concerning credit card fraud is combined. Also Phua, et al. (2004) apply a meta-learning approach, in order to detect fraud and not only intrusion. The authors base their concept on the science fiction novel Minority Report and compare the base classifiers with the novel's 'precogs'. The used classifiers are the naive Bayesian algorithm, C4.5 and back propagation neural networks. Results from a publicly available automobile insurance fraud detection data set demonstrate that the stacking-bagging performs better in terms of performance as well as in terms of cost savings.

Rule-learning and decision tree analysis is also applied by different researchers, e.g. Hilas C. S. (2009), Kirkos, et al. (2007), Fan (2004), Viaene, et al. (2002), Bonchi, et al. (1999), and Rosset, et al. (1999). Viaene, et al. (2002) actually apply different techniques in their work, from logistic regression, k-nearest neighbor, decision trees and Bayesian neural network to support vector machine, naive Bayes and tree-augmented naive Bayes. Also in Viaene, et al. (2007), logistic regression is applied.

Link analysis takes a different approach. It relates known fraudsters to other individuals, using record linkage and social network methods (Wasserman & Faust 1998). Cortes, et al. (2002) find the solution to fraud detection in this field. The transactional data in the area of telecommunications fraud is represented by a graph where the nodes represent the transactors and the edges represent the interactions between pairs of transactors. Since nodes and edges appear and disappear from the graph through time, the considered graph is dynamic. Cortes, et al. (2002) consider the subgraphs centered on all nodes to define communities of interest (COI). This method is inspired by the fact that fraudsters seldom work in isolation from each other.

To continue with link analysis, Kim & Kwon (2006) report on the Korean Insurance Fraud Recognition System that employs an unsupervised three-stage statistical and link analysis to identify presumably fraudulent claims. The government draws on this system to make decisions. The authors evaluate the system and offer recommendations for improvement.

Bolton & Hand (2001) are monitoring behavior over time by means of Peer Group Analysis. Peer Group Analysis detects individual objects that begin to behave in a way different from objects to which they had previously been similar. Another tool Bolton & Hand (2001) develop for behavioral fraud detection is Break Point Analysis. Unlike Peer Group Analysis, Break Point Analysis operates on the account level. A break point is an observation where anomalous behavior for a particular account is detected. Both the tools are applied on spending behavior in credit card accounts.

Also Murad & Pinkas (1999) focus on behavioral changes for the purpose of fraud detection and present three-level-profiling. As the Break Point Analysis from Bolton & Hand (2001), the three-level-profiling method operates at the account level and it points any significant deviation from an account's normal behavior as a potential fraud. In order to do this, 'normal' profiles are created (on three levels), based on data without fraudulent records. To test the method, the three-level-profiling is applied in the area of telecommunication fraud. In the same field, also Burge & Shawe-Taylor (2001) use behavior profiling for the purpose of fraud detection by using a recurrent neural network for prototyping calling behavior. Two time spans are considered at constructing the profiles, leading to a current behavior profile (CBP) and a behavior profile history (BPH) of each account. In a next step the Hellinger distance is used to compare the two probability distributions and to give a suspicion score on the calls.

In credit card fraud detection Withrow, et al. (2009) aggregate transaction data over a period of time, consequently also being able to work with profiles. Their method is particularly interesting in that it aggregates information of transactions and therefore this method is more robust to the presence of mislabeled data, a common problem in fraud databases. The authors compare several classifying techniques, but aggregation seems particularly effective when a random forest is used.

Other related work is done by Cahill, et al. (2000). They designed a fraud signature, based on data of fraudulent calls, to detect telecommunications fraud. For scoring a call for fraud its probability under the account signature is compared to its probability under a fraud signature. The fraud signature is updated sequentially, enabling event-driven fraud detection. Another technique for building signatures (profile signatures) is used by Xing & Girolami (2007). The authors employ Latent Dirichlet Allocation to build user profile signatures. As in the studies of Murad & Pinkas (1999) amongst others, a significant unexplainable deviation from the normal acitivity of a signature is assumed to be highly correlated to fraud risk. Edge & Dampaio (2009) provide a recent survey of signature based methods for detecting financial fraud.

A brief paper of Cox, et al. (1997) combines' human pattern recognition skills with automated data algorithms. In their work, information is presented visually by domain-specific interfaces. The idea is that the human visual system is dynamic and can easily adapt to ever-changing techniques used by fraudsters. On the other hand, machines have the advantage of far greater computational capacity, suited for routine repetitive tasks.

Four last studies we would like to mention, are those of Tsung, et al. (2007), Brockett, et al. 2002), Hoogs, Kiehl, Lacomb, & Senturk (2007) and Juszczak, Adams, Hand, Whitrow, & Weston (2008). Tsung, et al. (2007) applies manufacturing batch techniques to the field of fraud detection. They use the batch library method. Brockett, et

al. (2002) use a principal component analysis of RIDIT scores to classify claims for automobile bodily injury. Hoogs, et al. (2007) present a genetic algorithm approach to detect financial statement fraud. They find that exceptional anomaly scores are valuable metrics for characterizing corporate financial behavior and that analyzing these scores over time represents an effective way of detecting potentially fraudulent behavior. Juszczak, Adams, Hand, Whitrow, & Weston (2008) at last apply many different classification techniques in a supervised two-class setting and a semi-supervised one-class setting in order to compare the performances of these techniques and settings.

By looking at Table 1, we arrive at the conclusion that merely all academic research is conducted in the field of external fraud. There is clearly a gap in the academic literature concerning internal fraud. Only six articles on internal fraud are found and they all address the same kind of internal fraud: statement fraud. There is no research performed in mitigating transaction fraud, including corruption and asset misappropriation, the most prevalent kind of internal fraud according to both the ACFE and PWC surveys (ACFE, 2008; PwC, 2007). Aside from this, there are almost no studies found that focus on fraud prevention; the majority aims at fraud detection. Consequently, almost all studies use predictive data mining techniques, as opposed to descriptive data mining.

The literature review above all concerns studies conducted in real life. However, in our summary statement about data mining and economic crime risk management, we also wish to take theoretical frameworks into account. This is dealt with in the following subsection.

Academic Theory

The only theory (without practical implementation) in academic literature we found concerning the use of data mining for mitigating economic crime, is based on Table 1. The authors of this table, Jans, et al. (2009), used this as the starting point to create a conceptual framework to reduce internal fraud risk. The deduction of this framework from academic work and business practice, which is to be found in the original article in *The International Journal of Digital Accounting Research,* will be summarized in the following paragraphs.

As stated before, internal fraud is currently dealt with by internal control, where data analyzing primarily occurs by reporting tools. It is at that point, Jans, et al. (2009) combine academic research with practical insights. Data mining tools are currently not implemented in the internal control framework. The conviction that a framework, based on data mining techniques, could be of additional value to internal control in mitigating fraud, was the starting point for the IFR² framework as a complement of the existing internal control environment. The focus of this framework is on both fraud detection and fraud prevention.

The insights of academic research about data mining and fraud detection and prevention of Table 1 were used to construct the IFR² Framework. However, this framework is in the field of internal fraud, as opposed to the bulk of academic research. Because there are elements of distinction between found academic research and the aim of the IFR² Framework, existing methods of working could not just be copied. Two major differences between the IFR² Framework objective and existing work is that the framework 1) focuses on internal fraud which typically involves unsupervised data, and 2) focuses on fraud risk reduction instead of fraud detection. This is a contribution to the literature, where the use of data mining for (especially external) fraud detection is investigated. These differences had their effect on the framework, which will differ from the framework (although never explicitly registered!) used in existing literature. The IFR² framework is presented in Figure 2.

The IFR² Framework starts with selecting a business process with an advanced IT integration. An organization should select a business process which it thinks is worthwhile investigating. This selection can be motivated by different aspects: a business process that has a great cash flow, one that is quite unstructured, one that is known for misuses, or one that the business has no feeling with and wants to learn more about. Also the implementation of advanced IT, according to Lynch & Gomaa (2003), is a breeding ground for employee fraud. So selecting a business process with an advanced IT integration is a good starting point to encounter this stream of frauds (Jans, et al., 2009).

After the selection of an appropriate business process, data has to be collected, manipulated and enriched for further processing. This is comparable to the step "Data preparation" in Chien & Chen (2008)'s framework for personnel selection. The manipulation of data refers to the cleaning of data, merging connected data, transforming data into interpretable attributes and dealing with missing values. Although background knowledge may be required for executing this step, these are mainly technical transactions in that they still present operational data (Jans, et al., 2009).

During the third step, transformation of the data, the operational data will be translated into behavioral data. This translation builds - even more than the second step - upon domain knowledge and is not just a technical transformation (Jans, et al., 2009).

The core of the framework is then to apply a descriptive data mining approach for getting more insights in this behavioral data. This is where the IFR² framework remarkably differs from the followed methodologies in the existing literature. In the existing academic literature, almost all research applies a data mining technique with a predictive task. The explanation for the IFR² approach is twofold. Existing work predicts whether an observation is fraudulent or not. This can be explained by their focus on fraud detection. The IFR² Framework, however, is interested in all information, captured in the data that helps reducing the fraud risk, and is not only interested in the class 'fraudulent/legal'. In

Figure 2. The IFR² framework (©2009, Jans, Lybaert & Vanhoof. Used with permission)

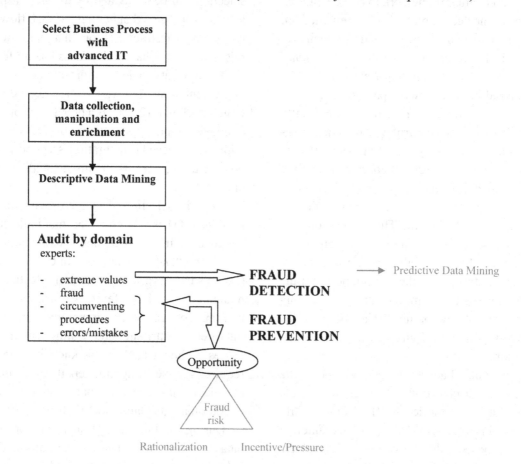

order to retrieve more information and patterns in data, a descriptive data mining approach has to be pursued (Jans, et al., 2009).

Another characteristic of internal fraud risk reduction is the presence of unsupervised data sets, liable to this stream of research. As mentioned before, there are almost no supervised data sets available in the context of internal fraud. This fact also accounts for the use of descriptive data mining instead of predictive data mining. An advantage of the use of descriptive data mining techniques is that it is easier to apply on unsupervised data. Thus for overcoming the exclusion of types of fraud where supervised data is difficult to obtain, the use of descriptive data mining techniques is recommended (Jans, et al., 2009).

The core of the IFR² Framework - to use descriptive data mining - is also motivated by the higher intrinsic value a description of the data set under investigation provides than just a prediction of fraudulent versus legal. A description of the data set as a whole can bring insights to light that were not clear before. All extra insights an analyst can gain are valuable to a better understanding of what is going on, leading to a better position to mitigate internal fraud. When one only focuses on predicting the fraud class, one is not open minded enough to notice other interesting patterns. Association rules, clustering and anomaly detection are appropriate candidates for describing the data set. These can ultimately lead to observations or outliers, seeming interesting to take a closer look at. This is what happens in the fifth step of our methodology (Jans, et al., 2009).

The fifth step is the audit of interesting observations by domain experts. The descriptive from the former step should provide the researchers a recognizable pattern of procedures of the selected business process. In addition, some other patterns of minor groups of observation in the data can arise, interesting to have a closer look at. By auditing these observations, one can acquire new insights in the business process. As a general rule, one will always select outliers or extreme values to take a closer look at. Observations defined as outlier can normally be brought back to one of the following four cases: the observation is an extreme value but very logic when looked into, the observation is fraudulent, the observation is the result of circumventing procedures or it is simply a mistake. The regular observations will not draw our attention (Jans, et al., 2009).

Observations defined as an outlier because they contain extreme values -but can be explained- are not of interest for the purpose of internal fraud risk reduction. (Think for example at the purchase of a mainframe at the same department as the purchases of CDs.) Nevertheless, they can occur. The other three categories (fraud, circumventing procedures and mistakes) on the other hand are of interest. If a fraudulent observation comes to attention as an outlier, this is part of fraud detection. A fraud case can be interesting for adjusting current practice in the business process. If enough similar fraud cases are uncovered, a supervised fraud detection method can be elaborated for this specific fraud, based on a new data set. In this particular case, one can find well elaborated and tested methods in the existing literature. At this stage of investigation, predictive data mining tasks are recommended to search specifically for this type of fraud. The other two categories which can be at the origin of an outlier, circumventing procedures and making mistakes, are important in the light of fraud prevention. By making a mistake and realizing nobody notices or by circumventing

procedures, a window of opportunity to commit fraud can develop. Opportunity, aside from rationalization and incentive or pressure, is one of the three elements of Cressey's fraud triangle. Also according to Albrecht, et al. (1984) "fraud scale" and even according to Hollinger and Park's theory, opportunity is an element of influence on fraud risk (Wells, 2005). Being able to select those cases where procedures are circumvented or mistakes are made, is an important contribution to taking away this opportunity and hence to prevent future fraud. The way in which this is dealt with, is up to the company. Internal controls can be adapted, persons can be called to account, procedures can be rewritten or other measures can be taken. This follow-up is not part of the framework anymore (Jans, et al., 2009).

The IFR² Framework just described, is to our knowledge currently the only theory without practical implementation yet. The difference with the research studies described before is that this framework addresses all internal fraud, including statement fraud, which is not covered by the research studies. Further does this framework focus both on fraud detection and prevention, as opposed to a heavy stress on detection in the research studies? On the other hand, this framework contains for the moment only theory, practical research still has to follow.

FUTURE RESEARCH DIRECTIONS

The future will make clear whether business practice picks up the suggestion of academic literature to use data mining techniques for fighting external fraud. Maybe they do already, but this is not visible as an outsider.

Further research is needed to investigate whether (internal) transaction fraud is also suitable to mitigate by means of data mining techniques or not. This research could be embedded in the theoretical IFR² Framework. When more academic research is conducted in this area, question is still

Figure 3. Current state of data mining application for economic crime risk management in academic research

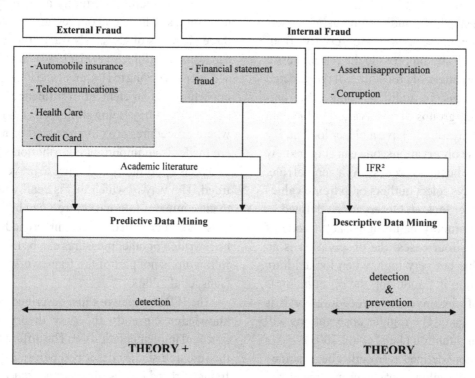

whether or not business practice will expand their COSO framework on internal control with a data mining part or not.

CONCLUSION

In this chapter an overview of issues concerning data mining and economic crime, along with solutions from both business practice and academic research, is given. Several aspects that are important but easily forgotten or abandoned in this context are treated first. Some characteristics of input data, like whether there is a supervised data set at hand or not, have a great impact on the topic. Further is the task that the data mining technique serves also very deterministic. Also, what kind of fraud is better suited to investigate by means of data mining? And last, when combining data mining with

economic crime, are we talking about business practice initiatives, or about academic research? All these issues are taken into account to make a clear statement on the current applicability of data mining for economic crime risk management. Economic crime is hereby limited to corporate fraud only, and risk management encompasses both fraud detection and fraud prevention.

A first division we made, was to look at business practice and academic research separately. We arrived at the conclusion that business practice has a formal framework to mitigate internal fraud (by means of internal control), but that this framework does not encompass the use of data mining. How business practice reacts on the threat of external fraud, we cannot make a statement about, because of lack of information.

When turning to academic literature to find an answer on whether or not academics found ways to counter economic crime by means of data mining, another division came to light. We can conclude that there has been a lot of research in conducting a data mining approach in a fraud context, but the focus is heavily on external fraud or on financial statement fraud. The latter is a type of internal fraud, characterized by the ability to possess supervised data sets on this type of fraud, just like external fraud. Probably, it is this characteristic that explains the stress of data mining tasks on predictive data mining.

If we look at the remainder of internal fraud, we only find a theoretical framework, the IFR[2] Framework, not applied yet in a real life situation. Another difference is that this framework suggests a descriptive data mining approach, as opposed to the predictive data mining in the bulk of academic literature. Further, this theoretical framework has the intention to work proactively by both fraud detection and fraud prevention, yet another distinction with academic research studies.

We depicted the current situation of data mining applications for economic crime risk management, found in academic work, in Figure 3. We named the most occurring types of external fraud, as we did with internal fraud. External fraud is mostly categorized in one of the following four types: automobile insurance fraud, telecommunications fraud, health care fraud, or credit card fraud. Based on studies of Ernst& Young (2006), PriceWaterhouse&Coopers (2007) and ACFE (2008), internal fraud is generally to divide in three types: financial statement fraud, asset misappropriation, and corruption. The former is a statement fraud, while the latter two are examples of transaction fraud, according to the division of Bologna & Lindquist (1995). We can conclude that transaction fraud, a type of internal fraud, is the only type of fraud which is currently not researched academically by means of applying a data mining technique, apart from the IFR[2] Framework as an assist on further research.

REFERENCES

Abidogum, O. (2005). *Data mining, fraud detection and mobile telecommunications: Call patterns analysis with unsupervised neural networks*. PhD Thesis, University of the Western Cape, Capetown, South Africa.

ACFE. (2008). *2008 report to the nation on occupational fraud and abuse*. Austin, TX: Association of Certified Fraud Examiners.

Albrecht, W., Howe, K., & Romney, M. (1984). *Deterring fraud: The internal auditor's perspective*. Altamonte Springs, FL: Institute of Internal Auditors Research Foundation.

Artis, M., Ayuso, M., & Guillen, M. (2002). Detection of automobile insurance fraud with discrete choice models and misclassified claims. *The Journal of Risk and Insurance, 69*, 325–340. doi:10.1111/1539-6975.00022

Bermúdez, L., Pérez, J., Ayuso, M., Gómez, E., & Vázquez, F. (2007). A Bayesian dichotomous model with asymmetric link for fraud in insurance. *Insurance, Mathematics & Economics, 42*, 779–886. doi:10.1016/j.insmatheco.2007.08.002

Bologna, G., & Lindquist, R. (1995). *Fraud auditing and forensic accounting*. New York: John Wiley & Sons.

Bolton, R., & Hand, D. (2001). *Unsupervised profiling methods for fraud detection*. Credit Scoring & Credit Control VII.

Bonchi, F., Giannotti, F., Mainetto, G., & Pedreschi, D. (1999). A classification based methodology for planning audit strategies in fraud detection. *Fifth ACM SIGKDD International Conference on Knowledge Discovery and Data Mining*. San Diego, CA: ACM Press.

Brause, R., Langsdorf, T., & Hepp, M. (1999). Retrieved July 6, 2009, from Goethe Universität - Frankfurt am Main: http://www.uni-frankfurt.de

Brockett, P., Derrig, R., Golden, L., & Levine, A., & M., A. (1998). Using Kohonen's self-organizing feature map to uncover automobile bodily injury claims fraud. *The Journal of Risk and Insurance, 69,* 245–274. doi:10.2307/253535

Brockett, P., Derrig, R., Golden, L., Levine, A., & Alpert, M. (2002). Fraud classification using principal component analysis of RIDITs. *The Journal of Risk and Insurance, 69,* 341–371. doi:10.1111/1539-6975.00027

Burge, P., & Shawe-Taylor, J. (2001). An unsupervised neural network approach to profiling the behavior of mobile phone users to use in fraud detection. *Journal of Parallel and Distributed Computing, 61,* 915–925. doi:10.1006/jpdc.2000.1720

Cahill, M., Lambert, D., Pinheiro, J., & Sun, D. (2000). *Detecting fraud in the real world.*

Chien, C.-F., & Chen, L. (2008). Data mining to impove personnel selection and enhance human capital: A case study in hig-technology industry. *Expert Systems with Applications, 34,* 280–290. doi:10.1016/j.eswa.2006.09.003

Cortes, C., Pregibon, D., & Volinsky, C. (2002). Communities of interest. *Intelligent Data Analysis, 6,* 211–219.

Cox, K., Eick, S., Wills, G., & Brachman, R. (1997). Visual data mining: Recognizing telephone calling fraud. *Data Mining and Knowledge Discovery, 1,* 225–231. doi:10.1023/A:1009740009307

Davey, N., Field, S., Frank, R., Barson, P., & McAskie, G. (1996). The detection of fraud in mobile phone networkds. *Neural Network World, 6,* 477–484.

Davia, H., Coggins, P., Wideman, J., & Kastantin, J. (2000). *Accountant's Guide to Fraud Detection and Control.* New York: John Wiley & Sons.

Derrig, R., & Ostaszewski, K. (1995). Fuzzy techniques of pattern recognition. *The Journal of Risk and Insurance, 62,* 447–482. doi:10.2307/253819

Deshmuck, A., & Talluru, L. (1998). A rule-based fuzzy reasoning system for assessing the risk of management fraud. *International Journal of Intelligent Systems in Accounting Finance & Management, 7,* 223–241. doi:10.1002/(SICI)1099-1174(199812)7:4<223::AID-ISAF158>3.0.CO;2-I

Dorronsoro, J., Ginel, F., Sanchez, C., & Santa Cruz, C. (1997). Neural fraud detection in credit card operations. *IEEE Transactions on Neural Networks, 8,* 827–834. doi:10.1109/72.595879

Edge, M. E., & Dampaio, P. R. (2009). A survey of signature based methods for financial fraud detection. *Computers & Security, 28,* 381–394. doi:10.1016/j.cose.2009.02.001

Estévez, P., Held, C., & Perez, C. (2006). Subscription fraud prevention in telecommunications using fuzzy rules and neural networks. *Expert Systems with Applications, 31,* 337–344. doi:10.1016/j.eswa.2005.09.028

E&Y. (2006). *9th Global fraud survey, fraud risk in emerging markets.* Technical Report, Ernst&Young.

E&Y. (2007). *A survey into fraud risk mitigations in 13 European Countries.* Technical Report, Ernst&Young.

Ezawa, K., & Norton, S. (1996). Constructing Bayesian networks to predict uncollectible telecommunications accounts. *IEEE Expert: Intelligent Systems and Their Applications, 11,* 45–51.

Fan, W. (2004). Systematic data selection to mine concept-drifting data streams. In *Tenth ACM SIGKDD International Conference on Knowledge and Discovery and Data Mining,* Seattle, (pp. 128-137).

Fanning, K., & Cogger, K. (1998). Neural network detection of management fraud using published financial data. *International Journal of Intelligent Systems in Accounting Finance & Management, 7*, 21–41. doi:10.1002/(SICI)1099-1174(199803)7:1<21::AID-ISAF138>3.0.CO;2-K

Fawcett, T., & Provost, F. (1997). Adaptive fraud detection. *Data Mining and Knowledge Discovery, 1*, 291–316. doi:10.1023/A:1009700419189

Fawcett, T., & Provost, F. (1999). Activity monitoring: Noticing interesting changes in behavior. *Fifth ACM SIGKDD: International Conference on Knowledge Discovery and Data Mining*, (pp. 53-62). New York: ACM Press.

Green, B., & Choi, J. (1997). Assessing the risk of management fraud through neural network technology. *Auditing, 16*, 14–28.

He, H., Wang, J., Graco, W., & Hawkins, S. (1997). Application of neural networks to detection of medical fraud. *Expert Systems with Applications, 13*, 329–336. doi:10.1016/S0957-4174(97)00045-6

Hilas, C., & Mastorocostas, P. (2008). An application of supervised and unsupervised learning approaches to telecommunications fraud detection. *Knowledge-Based Systems, 21*, 721–726. doi:10.1016/j.knosys.2008.03.026

Hilas, C. S. (2009). Designing an Expert System for Fraud Detection in Private Telecommunications Networks. *Expert Systems with Applications, 36*, 11559–11569. doi:10.1016/j.eswa.2009.03.031

Hoogs, B., Kiehl, T., Lacomb, C., & Senturk, D. (2007). A genetic algorithm approach to detecting temporal patterns indicative of financial statement fraud. *Intelligent Systems in Accounting. Financial Management, 15*, 41–56.

Jans, M., Lybaert, N., & Vanhoof, K. (2009). *International Journal of Digital Accounting Research*, 1-29.

Juszczak, P., Adams, N., Hand, D., Whitrow, C., & Weston, D. (2008). Off-the-peg and bespoke classifiers for fraud detection. *Computational Statistics & Data Analysis, 52*, 4521–4532. doi:10.1016/j.csda.2008.03.014

Kim, H., & Kwon, W. (2006). A multi-line insurance fraud recognition system: A government-led apporach in Korea. *Risk Management & Insurance Review, 9*, 131–147. doi:10.1111/j.1540-6296.2006.00090.x

Kirkos, E., Spathis, C., & Manolopoulos, Y. (2007). Data mining techniques for the detection of fraudulent financial statements. *Expert Systems with Applications, 32*, 995–1003. doi:10.1016/j.eswa.2006.02.016

Krenker, A., Volk, M., Sedlar, U., Bester, J., & Kos, A. (2009). Bidirectional Artificial Neural Networks for Mobile Phone Fraud Detection. *ETRI Journal, 31*, 92–94. doi:10.4218/etrij.09.0208.0245

Lin, J., & Hwang, M., & becker, J. (2003). A fuzzy neural network for assessing the risk of fraudulent financial reporting. *Managerial Auditing Journal, 18*, 657–665. doi:10.1108/02686900310495151

Lynch, A., & Gomaa, M. (2003). Understanding the potential impact of information technology on the susceptibility of organizations to fraudulent employee behaviour. *International Journal of Accounting Information Systems, 4*, 295–308. doi:10.1016/j.accinf.2003.04.001

Maes, S., Tuyls, K., Vanschoenwinkel, B., & Manderick, B. (2002). Credit card fraud detection using Bayesian and neural networks. In *First International NAISO Congress on Neuro Fuzzy Technologies*, Havana, Cuba.

Major, J., & Riedinger, D. (2002). EFD: A hybrid knowledge/statistical-based system for the detection of fraud. *The Journal of Risk and Insurance, 69*, 309–324. doi:10.1111/1539-6975.00025

Murad, U., & Pinkas, G. (1999). Unsupervised profiling for identifying superimposed fraud. *Lecture Notes in Computer Science, 1704*, 251–262.

National Health Care Anti-Fraud Association (NHCAA). (2009). *Anti-Fraud Resource Center - Fighting Health Care Fraud: An Integral Part of Health Care Reform.* Retrieved July 1, 2009, from National Care Anti-Fraud Association: http://www.nhcaa.org

National Insurance Crime Bureau (NICB). (2009). *Theft & Fraud Awareness - Fact Sheets - Insurance Fraud.* Retrieved July 1, 2009, from National Insurance Crime Bureau: http://www.nicb.org

Paass, G., Reinhardt, W., Rüping, S., & Wrobel, S. (2007). Data Mining for Security and Crime Detection. *NATO Advanced Research Workshop on Security Informatics & Terrorism - Patrolling the Web.* Beer-Sheva, Israel.

Panigrahi, S., Kunda, A., Sural, S., & Majundar, A. (2009). Credit Card Fraud Detection: A Fusion Approach Using Dempster-Shafer Theory and Bayesian Learning. *Information Fusion, 10*, 354–363. doi:10.1016/j.inffus.2008.04.001

Pathak, J., Vidyarthi, N., & Summers, S. (2003). A fuzzy-based algorithm for auditors to detect element of fraud in settled insurance claims. *Odette School of Business Administration Working Paper No. 03-9.*

Phua, C., Alahakoon, D., & Lee, V. (2004). Minority report in fraud detection: Classification of skewed data. *SIGKDD Explorations, 6*, 50–59. doi:10.1145/1007730.1007738

PwC. (2007). *Economic Crime: People, culture and controls. The 4th biennial global economic crime survey.* New York: PriceWaterhouse&Coopers.

Quah, J., & Sriganesh, M. (2008). Real-time credit card fraud detection using computational intelligence. *Expert Systems with Applications, 35*, 1721–1732. doi:10.1016/j.eswa.2007.08.093

Rosset, S., Murad, U., Neumann, E., Idan, Y., & Pinkas, G. (1999). Discovery of fraud rules for telecommunications: Challenges and solutions. In *Fifth ACM SIGKDD: International Conference on Knowledge Discovery and Data Mining,* (pp. 409-413). New York: ACM Press.

Sánchez, D., Vila, M., Cerda, L., & Serrano, J. (2009). Assocation rules applied to credit card fraud detection. *Expert Systems with Applications, 36*, 3630–3640. doi:10.1016/j.eswa.2008.02.001

Singleton, T., Singleton, A., Bologna, J., & Lindquist, R. (2006). *Fraud Auditing and Forensic Accounting.* New York: John Wiley & Sons.

Stolfo, S., Fan, W., Lee, W., Prodromidis, A., & Chan, P. (2000). Cost-based modeling for fraud and intrusion detection: Results from the JAM project. In *DARPA Information Survivability Conference & Exposition 2,* (pp. 1130-1144). New York: IEEE Computer Press.

Tan, P.-N., Steinbach, M., & Kumar, V. (2006). *Introduction to Data Mining.* New York: Pearson Education, Inc.

Tsung, F., Zhou, Z., & Jiang, W. (2007). Applying manufacturing batch techniques to fraud detection with incomplete customer information. *IIE Transactions, 39*, 671–680. doi:10.1080/07408170600897510

Viaene, S., Ayuso, M., Guillén, M., Gheel, D., & Dedene, G. (2007). Strategies for detecting fraudulent claims in the automobile insurance industry. *European Journal of Operational Research, 176*, 565–583. doi:10.1016/j.ejor.2005.08.005

Viaene, S., Dedene, G., & Derrig, R. (2005). Auto claim fraud detection using Bayesian learning neural networks. *Expert Systems with Applications, 29*, 653–666. doi:10.1016/j.eswa.2005.04.030

Viaene, S., Derrig, R., Baesens, B., & Dedene, G. (2002). A comparison of state-of-the-art classification techniques for expert automobile insurance claim fraud detection. *The Journal of Risk and Insurance, 69*, 373–421. doi:10.1111/1539-6975.00023

Wasserman, S., & Faust, K. (1998). *Social Network Analysis: Methods and Applications*. Cambridge, UK: Cambridge University Press.

Wells, J. (2005). *Principles of Fraud Examination*. Chichester, UK: John Wiley & Sons.

Withrow, C., Hand, D., Juszczak, P., Weston, D., & Adams, N. (2009). Transaction Aggregation as a Stragey for Credit Card Fraud Detection. *Data Mining and Knowledge Discovery, 18*, 30–55. doi:10.1007/s10618-008-0116-z

Xing, D., & Girolami, M. (2007). Employing Latent Dirichlet Allocation for Fraud Detection in Telecommunications. *Pattern Recognition Letters, 28*, 1727–1734. doi:10.1016/j.patrec.2007.04.015

Yang, W.-S., & Hwang, S.-H. (2006). A process-mining framework for the detection of healthcare fraud and abuse. *Information and Security, 18*, 48–63.

Zaslavsky, V., & Strizhak, A. (2006). Credit card fraud detection using self-organizing maps. *Expert Systems with Applications, 31*, 56–68.

KEY TERMS AND DEFINITIONS

Fraud: The act of intentional deception, hereby depriving someone else for (personal) enrichment.

Corporate Fraud: Fraud in an organizational setting.

Economic Crime: In this chapter we put economic crime equal to corporate fraud.

Internal Fraud: Corporate fraud where the perpetrator is internally related to the victim company, like for instance an employee.

External Fraud: Corporate fraud where the perpetrator is externally related to the victim company, like for instance a client or supplier.

Risk Management: All actions a company takes on managing or reducing its risks. In the context of this chapter, risk management is narrowed down to fraud prevention and fraud detection.

Chapter 12
Data Mining in the Investigation of Money Laundering and Terrorist Financing

Ibrahim George
Macquarie University, Australia

Manolya Kavakli
Macquarie University, Australia

ABSTRACT

In this chapter, the authors explore the operational data related to transactions in a financial organisation to find out the suitable techniques to assess the origin and purpose of these transactions and to detect if they are relevant to money laundering. The authors' purpose is to provide an AML/CTF compliance report that provides AUSTRAC with information about reporting entities' compliance with the Anti-Money Laundering and Counter-Terrorism Financing Act 2006. Their aim is to look into the Money Laundering activities and try to identify the most critical classifiers that can be used in building a decision tree. The tree has been tested using a sample of the data and passing it through the relevant paths/scenarios on the tree. The success rate is 92%, however, the tree needs to be enhanced so that it can be used solely to identify the suspicious transactions. The authors propose that a decision tree using the classifiers identified in this chapter can be incorporated into financial applications to enable organizations to identify the High Risk transactions and monitor or report them accordingly.

INTRODUCTION

The Australian Transaction Reports and Analysis Centre (AUSTRAC) is Australia's anti-money laundering and counter-terrorism financing (AML/CTF) regulator and specialist financial intelligence unit (FIU). An AML/CTF compliance report provides AUSTRAC with information about reporting entities' compliance with the *Anti-Money Laundering and Counter-Terrorism Financing Act 2006* (AML/CTF Act), the regulations and the AML/CTF Rules. It is required under the AML/CTF Act in Part 3 Division 5, which came into effect on 12 June 2007. A reporting entity is a person who provides a 'designated service' as defined in the AML/CTF Act. Examples of reporting entities include banks and other financial institutions, remittance service providers, foreign exchange

DOI: 10.4018/978-1-61692-865-0.ch012

dealers, debit and stored value card providers, bullion dealers and casinos and other gambling service providers.

Data mining (also called data or knowledge discovery) is the process of analysing data from different perspectives and summarizing it into useful information (Luo, 2008). It is an analytic process designed to explore data in search of consistent patterns and/or systematic relationships between variables, and then to validate the findings by applying the detected patterns to new subsets of data. The ultimate goal of data mining is prediction. The process of data mining consists of three stages: (1) the initial exploration, (2) validation/verification that involves model building or pattern identification, and (3) deployment that involves the application of the model to new data in order to generate predictions.

Data mining allows users to analyse data from many different dimensions or angles, categorize it, and summarize the relationships identified. In this paper our aim is to explore the operational data, which are related to transactions done in a financial organisation and find out the suitable techniques to assess the origin and purpose of these transactions and if they are relevant to money laundering to be able to provide an AML/CTF compliance report. Research studies in this area are mainly on the technologies used to implement Data Mining and Artificial intelligence solutions such as using agent based systems (Wu, 2004) and there are no examples of such reporting systems in the current academic literature.

BACKGROUND

Money Laundering

Money laundering involves moving illicit funds, which may be linked to drug trafficking or organized crime, through a series of transactions or accounts to disguise origin or ownership. There are many countries suffering from the consequences of money laundering. China, for example, is facing severe challenge on money laundering with an estimated 200 billion RMB laundered annually (Wang & Yang, 2007) Money laundering is the process undertaken to conceal the true origin and ownership of the profits of criminal activities. These profits can be the proceeds from crimes such as:

- Drug trafficking;
- Fraud;
- Tax evasion;
- Illegally trading in weapons;
- Enforced prostitution;
- Slavery; and
- People smuggling.

Who Launders Money?

Money launderers can be people who committed some or all of the profitable crimes, or criminals who provide specialized services in money laundering to other criminals.

Do Financial Organisations have to Deliberately Set Out to Launder Money to be a Money Launderer?

Under Australian Law, financial organizations can also be a money launderer if they engage in a transaction, and a reasonable person would know that the money or assets involved are the proceeds of criminal activities. This applies regardless of whether the proceeds of criminal activities are on the organisation's side of the transaction or not.

Why do People Want to Launder Money?

People launder money so they can keep and spend the profits of crime. Some crimes are very profitable, and people who are interested in making money out of a crime are as enterprising as participants in the legitimate economy. Money launderers will make considerable efforts to ensure that they keep and can use their profits by making the money appear legitimate.

What Happens to Laundered Money?

Money that is laundered can be used to:

- fund further criminal enterprises and keep criminals in business;
- buy or set up legitimate businesses which can make even more money (and be used to launder more funds);
- buy expensive goods such as luxury cars and houses;
- invest in retirement savings or the share market; and
- pay bribes to corrupt officials, and create an appearance of legitimate wealth.

In general, money laundering follows a three-stage process (Austrac E-learning, 2009). They are as follows:

1. **Placement:** During the *Placement* phase, profits of crime enter the general economy. Criminals put their money into things such as: accounts, assets, jewels, bullion, cars, houses, or securities.
2. **Layering:** During the *Layering* phase, the source of the money and ownership is disguised. Money is transferred, invested, sent to different accounts, sent offshore to tax or financial havens co-mingled with other assets or put in trusts.
3. **Integration:** During the *Integration* phase, the money appears to be legitimate, and evidence of its origin and ownership has been disguised. Money may have been invested in businesses, real estate, companies, overseas investments, bonds or a family trust.

What is Terrorist Financing?

Terrorists seek to influence policy and people through the use of illegal force. Terrorist financing refers to the money raised to fund global terrorist activities. Money used for terrorist financing may be raised through legal or illegal activities. It is usually transferred through banking systems in small, unobtrusive sums. It looks very similar to legitimate banking activity.

Data Mining

Data mining is the process of exploration of raw data to find meaningful relationships between different parameters of that data. From this definition we identify the following:

Data Mining is a Process

Data mining is not a one-time activity of a single business analyst, but rather a commitment of an organization to leverage its business data on an ongoing basis and to continuously and iteratively improve its business practices based on a new level of understanding of its data.

Data Mining is Complimentary to Decision Support Tools

Today's decision support tools are 'assumption-driven' in the sense that the business professionals use them to verify their hypothesis about the data. Data mining tools are 'discovery-driven' and complimentary to assumption-driven tools. Data mining tools are hypothesis generators; they analyze corporate data automatically to discover new insight into business experiences.

Data Mining Finds Buried Knowledge

Over the last few years data mining has sometimes been overhyped with respect to finding hidden treasures using these new algorithms and methodologies. Experience has shown that data mining is most effective in finding buried knowledge which provides additional insight into business practices.

Data Mining Delivers Understanding to Business Professionals

The new breed of data mining tools is geared towards business professionals, business analysts, and marketing professionals - not the statistician or artificial intelligence expert. Data mining tools do not necessarily replace statisticians, but they empower knowledge workers to more deeply understand business data without having to comprehend details of statistical analysis or intricacies of artificial intelligence.

In this research we will be focusing on the operational data, which are related to transactions done in a financial organization and find out the suitable techniques to assess whether the transactions are Money Laundry born or not.

DATA MINING PROCESS

Issues

Data mining is a technique that discovers previously unknown relationships in data (Campos et al, 2005). Data can be any numbers, or text that can be processed by a computer. Today, organizations are accumulating vast and growing amounts of data in different formats and different databases. This includes:

1. Operational or transactional data such as, sales, cost, inventory, payroll, and accounting
2. Non-operational data, such as industry sales, forecast data, and macro economic data
3. Meta data - data about the data itself, such as logical database design or data dictionary definitions

Kleissner (1998) refers to Data mining as a new decision support analysis process to find buried knowledge in corporate data and deliver understanding to business professionals. Decision tree learning is one of the most widely used methods for inductive inference since the 1960s. Since then, numerous researches have conducted research to improve the accuracy, performance, etc. (e.g., Yang et al, 2007). Most of the research done in the area is about the technological aspects of the deployment of Data Mining into applications.

The tasks of data mining (Luo, 2008) are very diverse and distinct because many patterns exist in a large database. Different methods and techniques are needed to find different kinds of patterns. Based on the patterns we are looking for, tasks in data mining can be classified into summarization, classification, clustering, association and trend analysis, as follows:

Summarization. Summarization is the abstraction or generalization of data. A set of task-relevant data is summarized and abstracted. This results in a smaller set which gives a general overview of the data, usually with aggregate information.

Classification. Classification is a type of supervised learning that consists of a training stage and a testing stage (Chen, 2006). Accordingly the dataset is divided into a training set and a testing set. The classifier is designed to "learn" from the training set classification models governing the membership of data items. Accuracy of the classifier is assessed using the testing set. Classification derives a function or model which determines the class of an object based on its attributes. A set of objects is given as the training set. In it, every object is represented by a vector of attributes along with its class. A classification function or model is constructed by analyzing the relationship between the attributes and the classes of the objects in the training set. This function or model can then classify future objects. This helps us develop a better understanding of the classes of the objects in the database.

Clustering. Clustering identifies classes-also called clusters or groups-for a set of objects whose classes are unknown. The objects are so clustered that the intraclass similarities are maximized and the intraclass similarities are minimized. This is done based on some criteria defined on the attributes of the objects. Once the clusters are decided, the objects are labeled with their corresponding clusters. The common features for objects in a cluster are summarized to form the class description.

Trend analysis. Time series data are records accumulated over time. For example, a company's sales, a customer's credit card transactions and stock prices are all time series data. Such data can be viewed as objects with an attribute time. The objects are snapshots of entities with values that change over time. Finding the patterns and regularities in the data evolutions along the dimension of time can be then used in relevant applications.

Data Mining Systems for the Detection of Money Laundering

The task of finding and charting associations between crime entities such as persons, weapons, and organizations often is referred to as entity association mining (Lin & Brown, 2003) or link analysis (Sparrow, 1991) in law enforcement. As described by Chen (2006), Law enforcement officers and crime investigators throughout the world have long used link analysis to search for and analyze relationships between criminals. Examples include the Federal Bureau of Investigation (FBI) in the investigation of the Oklahoma City Bombing case and the Unabomber case to look for criminal associations and investigative leads (Schroeder et al., 2003).

The goal of link analysis is to find out how crime entities that appear to be unrelated at the surface are actually linked to each other. Three types of link analysis approaches have been suggested, as explained by Chen (2006): *heuristic-based*, *statistical-based*, and *template-based*.

Heuristic-based approaches rely on decision rules used by domain experts to determine whether two entities in question are related. In the FinCEN system of the U.S. Department of the Treasury, Goldberg and Senator (1998) investigated the links or associations between individuals in financial transactions using a set of heuristics, such as whether the individuals have shared addresses, shared bank accounts, or related transactions to detect money laundering transactions and activities. The COPLINK Detect system (Hauck et al., 2002) employed a statistical-based approach called Concept Space (Chen & Lynch, 1992) measuring the weighted co-occurrence associations between records of entities (persons, organizations, vehicles, and locations) stored in crime databases. An association exists between a pair of entities if they appear together in the same criminal incident. The more frequently they occur together, the stronger the association is. Zhang et al. (2003) proposed to use a fuzzy resemblance function to calculate the correlation between two individuals' past financial transactions to detect associations between the individuals who might have been involved in a specific money laundering crime. If the correlation between two individuals is higher than a threshold value these two individuals are regarded as being related.

SOLUTION

As we mentioned before, money laundering life cycle goes through three stages: Placement, Layering and Integration. The decision tree developed as part of this research is mainly done in the Placement phase where the fund is being entered into the economy by being transferred into a bank account. However, Data Mining should be applied on transactions throughout their life cycle. The reason for that is some transactions may not be detected in one of the phases but then later on detected in the next one.

In addition to having specific data mining activities for each phase separately, it would be very beneficial to use the data warehousing capabilities available in organizations now to have another layer of data mining activities done at the warehouse level. In case of large organizations, the creation of Data Marts with targeted parameters of data would be useful to conduct those data mining activities. Different technologies can be used in this area to suit the Data Mining activities being done. In general, this will have two benefits:

- The higher chance the fraudulent transactions are detected.
- The more associations and relationships are discovered which enables the enhancement of current decision trees, logic and rules, etc...

The aim of this research is to look into the Money Laundering activities and try to identify the most critical classifiers that can be used in building a decision tree. A decision tree is a decision support tool that uses a tree-like graph of decisions and their possible consequences. Decision trees help identify a strategy most likely to reach a goal.

In this paper, a decision tree is generated to explore the logic behind the transactions. Decision trees can be incorporated into financial applications to enable organizations to identify the High Risk transactions and monitor or report them accordingly. Decision tree classifiers organize decision rules learned from training data in the form of a tree.

In our research we have identified a number of the classifiers that are anticipated as the ones that are mostly efficient in differentiating between different categories of customers and their transactions. The Classifiers are:

1. Client Type; it is essential to know the type of customer, whether being an individual or a business client. The reason for that is the rules applying to the Individuals are different to the ones applied to business going down the tree branches. This is due to the different financial products. Also, the expected patterns and volumes of transactions are not the same for the different types of clients.

2. Country of residence; this classifier is a major one on the tree. For clients, whether individuals or businesses, they are considered higher risk if they are overseas residents. For individual clients, this means that the residential address is an overseas one. For businesses, this will take the form of the main place of business is conducted overseas. The overseas clients are considered higher risk due to the fact that tracking any overseas transactions cannot be as simple as tracking the local transactions.

3. Country Risk Level; countries worldwide have been categorized into a number of categories that determine the level of risk of transactions being transferred with any of those categories.

4. Local or overseas transactions; as mentioned earlier, the overseas transactions are harder to track, therefore they are considered higher risk than the ones transferred within Australia. Therefore they are given Higher Risk rating.

5. Transaction pattern; for individual accounts, creating a pattern for the transactions of a certain account can be used to identify the transactions that do no follow that pattern, the irregular ones. The transactions that do not follow the pattern for the account is considered a higher risk one than the other ones that do follow the pattern for the account.

6. Transaction volume; for business accounts, the volume and monetary amounts of transactions should correspond to the type and size of the business. If the volume of transactions for an account starts to appear not corresponding to the size of the business, this is then flagged as a higher risk transaction.

Table 1. Classifiers and ratings

Classifier	Lower Risk (1)	Higher Risk (2)
Residency	Australian	Overseas
Country Risk level	Low	High
Transaction	Local	Overseas
Transaction matching account pattern? (Individual)	Yes	No
Transaction corresponds to business size? (Business)	Yes	No

Using those classifiers, transactions will be given different ratings in order to identify the ones that have higher potential of being a fraudulent transaction.

The aim of this research is to reach that stage where each transaction is assessed and given a risk rating that shows whether that transaction is a potentially fraudulent one. It is expected that different risk ratings will have different strategies to deal with throughout the life cycle of the account.

Methodology

We have developed a decision tree using a number of classifiers, and then conducted testing by passing the data through the tree logic and check the results. Based on the results of the initial testing, some of the classifiers have been removed from the tree and replaced by a number of new ones and further experimentation has been conducted. This process has been repeated a number of times until the current results have been achieved.

On the decision tree, 5 levels of risk are allocated to transactions:

1. Very High Risk: the highest risk rating, indicating the transaction is of extremely high risk of being a fraudulent one.
2. High Risk: indicates that transaction is of considerable risk.
3. Neutral: indicates a classification cannot be given to the transaction. However, this does not mean that the transaction cannot be a

fraudulent one. It only indicates that there is a less chance for it to be fraudulent.
4. Low Risk: Indicates that the transaction is relatively a low risk one.
5. Very Low Risk: Indicates that the transaction has the lowest risk of being a fraudulent one.

Transactions are rated according to the following rating for each of the classifiers in Table 1:

As indicated in Table 2, the Lower Risk is given 1 point while the Higher Risk is given 2 points. The sum of points for each transaction is then calculated to reach the overall grade, which is mapped to the risk level as per the table below:

Please note that one of the future enhancements to be done on the tree is to have a weighting assigned to each of the classifiers as this will give a better indication of the risk level of the transaction. This was not conducted as part of this research as it required further research to be conducted to specify the weighting of each of the classifiers.

The CRISP-DM methodology (CRISP-DM, 2009) is considered the industry standard for

Table 2. Risk level

Risk level	Overall Grade
Very Low Risk	4
Low Risk	5
Neutral	6
High Risk	7
Very High Risk	8

data mining exercises and used in this research. Below follows a brief outline of the phases of this methodology:

Business Understanding: In this phase, we have done some readings on the different aspects and phases of Money Laundering in order to understand how data mining can be used to assist in the detection of fraudulent transactions.

Data Understanding: The data used in this research was obtained from the Wealth Management area of the Commonwealth Bank. In this phase, we attempted to understand the different aspects and parameters of the data in order to use it in the best possible way in the research.

Data Preparation: The data was obtained from the team looking at the AML/CTF solutions for the Commonwealth Bank; therefore most of the parameters/classifiers on the data were of good quality and did not require too many changes to prepare the data for the data mining exercise.

Modeling: In this phase, the classifiers chosen to be used in the creation of the decision tree are as follows:

1. Client Type: Individual or Business
2. Country of Residence Australian or Overseas
3. Country Risk Level for Overseas Individuals and Business
4. Local or overseas transaction.
5. Transaction is within account transactions pattern for Individual clients.
6. Transaction matches the size of business for Business clients.

Evaluation In this phase, we have tested the decision trees built across some of the data to identify if applying the tree logic would deliver the results anticipated.

Deployment Deployment was not considered as part of this research and is not one of the research objectives; however, it is suggested as the future work.

Experimentation

Classifiers at three levels have been used to construct the decision tree, as follows:

1. Customer

Customer profiling is essential to identify the High Risk ones and monitoring their transactions in a closer manner than other lower risk customers. A number of classifiers can be used in doing that:

For Individuals:

a. Residential address: members with Australian addresses are in the lower risk group than customers with overseas addresses.
b. Countries can be classified into different risk levels according to their implementation in AML/CTF measures. This indicates the countries where information cannot be traced to identify the legitimacy of transactions and funds transfers as opposed to others that do not implement adequate measures. Countries with less AML/CTF measures are considered in the higher risk group and therefore all dealings with transactions from and to those countries are given higher risk ratings. Accordingly, customers dealing with any of those countries can be considered to be in the higher risk group, even if they have residential address in Australia.

For Businesses:

a. Principal place of business: business with overseas principal place of business are considered higher risk
b. Businesses that have charitable operations are higher in risk.

2. Account

A number of classifiers can be used to assess the account's risk:

a. Creating a certain pattern wherever possible for the account will enable the system to identify the transactions that do not follow the pattern and highlight it for further monitoring.
b. Accounts with multiple signatories are considered higher risk than the ones with single signatory.
c. Accounts used for temporary depository for funds that are regularly transferred offshore are of high risk.

Account turnover or large transactions inconsistent with the size of the customer, are of higher risk.

3. Transaction

The transaction will be given a high risk score in the following conditions:

a. Deliberate structuring of banking transactions in order to avoid having them reported as threshold transactions.
b. Transaction behaviour that is out of character for the account, including unusual funds flows or an unexplained change in the pattern of transactions.
c. Origin of the transaction: Is the transaction an overseas or local one? This includes deposits and withdrawals.
d. The risk level of the other party of the transaction, if they are considered a high risk party, the transaction will be given a high risk score.

Figure 1. Data mining tree I: Individual clients decision tree

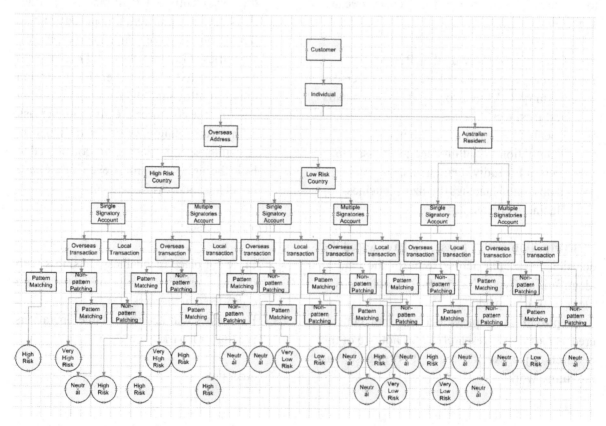

Test Results

The tree has been tested using a sample of the data and passing it through the relevant paths/ scenarios on the tree. We have found in the 92% of the cases match the category that the decision tree suggests. While this rate is acceptable at this level, further work is required to increase the success /confidence rate for the decision tree.

We need to enhance the decision tree to use it solely to identify the suspicious transactions. The tree also needs:

1. To be used in conjunction with other indicators that will enable a closer result
2. To include more classifiers and further scenario combinations.
3. To include various weightings to be given to various classifiers on the tree according to their importance and relevance.

FUTURE WORK

Money laundering life cycle goes through three stages, Placement, Layering and Integration. The decision tree developed as part of this research is mainly done in the Placement phase where the fund is being entered into the economy by being transferred into a bank account. However, Data Mining should be applied on transactions throughout their life cycle. Some transactions may not be detected in one phase, may be detected in the next phase.

Furthermore, in addition to having specific data mining activities for each phase separately, it would be very beneficial to use the data warehousing capabilities available in organisations. In case of large organisations, the creation of Data Marts with targeted parameters of data would be useful to conduct those data mining activities.

Figure 2 Data mining tree II: Business clients' decision tree

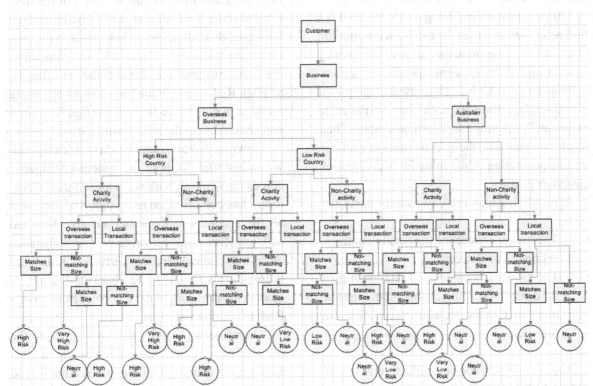

We may list our suggestions for further work as follows:

1. Further enhancement of the tree as indicated in the test findings.
2. Other classifiers to be explored that are relevant to the AML/CTF transactions.
3. Research to be conducted on the implementation side of the classification rules on the decision trees.
4. Research for ongoing review and enhancement of measures implemented to detect ML/TF transactions. An agile process is needed for the update of measures.

CONCLUSION

The aim of this research was to investigate the Money Laundering activities and try to identify the most critical classifiers that can be used in building a decision tree. The classifiers we have defined indicate a success rate of 92%.

Our results confirm Wang and Yang (2007)'s findings. They also used the Decision tree method to create the determination rules of the money laundering risk by customer profiles of a commercial bank in China. They used a sample of twenty-eight customers with four attributes to induce and validate the decision tree method. Their results also indicate the effectiveness of decision tree in generating AML rules from companies' customer profiles.

Data Mining may bring two major benefits:

- The higher chance for the fraudulent transactions to be detected.
- The more associations and relationships to be discovered. This enables the enhancement of current decision trees, logic and rules, etc...

Data mining can be very effective in the detection of ML/TF transactions. To be able to use it effectively, two main points need to be taken into consideration:

1. Trees and algorithms should be developed for each type of monetary transactions. For example, tree that applies to online transactions for e-commerce should be different to the one used in the Superannuation contributions done by employers or employees to their superannuation accounts.
2. Data Mining should be an ongoing process that is carried out at two dimensions, as follows:

Horizontal: Based on Customer, Account and Transaction

In this dimension, data is structured in a way that flags can be used to tag data at different levels starting from customer, going through the accounts and ending by single individual transactions.

The profiling of each level will feed further indicators into the subsequent levels of the tree. For example, if a customer is classified as a High Risk one, then all accounts belonging to the customer are flagged as High Risk ones. Similarly, since the customer and the accounts are flagged as High Risk ones, all the transactions occurring on those accounts are flagged as High Risk ones and should be on the monitoring list.

However this profiling should be working both ways, and that is where the system intelligence comes in. Working both ways mean that if a customer has been flagged as a High Risk one, and all the accounts and transactions are classified as High Risk ones, however no single instance of Money Laundering or Terrorism Financing is found, this should be fed back up the tree to change the profiling of the customer from a High Risk to a lower risk one.

Therefore, an activity that is essential to the effectiveness of tree success is the ongoing reassessment and re-profiling of customers and accounts is to be performed.

Vertical: Throughout the Phases of Money Laundering

Detection of fraudulent transactions can be done at any of the three phases of money laundering. Accounts and transactions should be monitored across their life cycles so that if a transaction was not identified as Money Laundry one in the Placement phase it may be identified in the layering or the integration phases.

ACKNOWLEDGMENT

Special thanks to the Commonwealth Bank, Wealth Management Department, Australia for the provision of data used in this research.

REFERENCES

Austrac E-learning. *(2009).* Introduction to Money Laundering. *RetrievedNovember27, 2009, from* http://www.austrac.gov.au/elearning/mod1/mod_1_money_laundering_11.html.

Campos, M.M., Stengard, P.J., & Milenova, B.L., (2005). *Data-centric automated data mining.* Proceedings of Fourth International Conf on Machine Learning and Applications, *15-17 Dec. 2005, (pp.8).*

Chen, H. (2006). *Intelligence and Security Informatics for International Security, Information Sharing and Data Mining.* Integrated Series in Information Systems, 10*(18).*

Chen & Lynch. (1992). Automatic constriction of networks of concepts characterizing document databases. *IEEE Transactions on Systems, Man, and Cybernetics, 22*(5), 885–902. doi:10.1109/21.179830

CRISP-DM. (2009). *Cross Industry Standard Process for Data Mining.* Retrieved November 27, 2009, from http://www.crisp-dm.org/

Goldberg, H. G., & Senator, T. A. (1998). Restructuring Databases for knowledge discovery by consolidation and link formation. In D. Jensen & H. Goldberg, (Eds.), *Proceedings of the 1998 AAAI Fall Symposium on Artuificial intelligence and link analysis,* (pp. 38-46). Menlo Park, CA: AAAI press.

Hauck, R. V., Atabakhsh, H., Ongvasith, P., Gupta, H., & Chen, H. (2002). Using COPLINK to analyse criminal justice data. *IEEE Computer, 35*(3), 30–37.

Kleissner, C. (1998). Data mining for the enterprise. *Thirty-First Hawaii International Conference on System Sciences,* January 6-9, Kohala Coast, HI, (Vol.7, pp.295-304).

Lin, S., & Brown, D. E. (2003). Criminal incident data association using the OLAP technology. In H.Chen, R, Miranda D., Zeng, C. Demchak, (Eds), *Proceedings of the First NSF/NIJ Symposium on Intelligence and Security Informatics (ISI'03),* Berlin, Springer, (pp. 13-26).

Luo, Q. (2008). Advancing Knowledge Discovery and Data Mining. In *First International Workshop on Knowledge Discovery and Data Mining.*

Schroeder, J., Xu, J., & Chen, H. (2003). CrimeLink Explorer: Using domain knowledge to facilitate automated crime association analysis. In H. Chen, R., Miranda, D., Zeng, C. Demchak, (Eds), *First NSF/NIJ Symposium on Intelligence and Security Informatics (ISI'03),* Berlin, Springer, (pp.168-180).

Sparrow, M. K. (1991). The application of network analysis to criminal intelligence: An assessment of the prospects. *Social Networks, 13,* 251–274. doi:10.1016/0378-8733(91)90008-H

Wang, S., & Yang, J. (2007). A money laundering risk evaluation method based on decision tree. *International Conforence on Machine Learning and Cybernetics,* 2007, 19-22 Aug. 2007, (Vol. 1, pp.283-286).

Wu, X. (2004). Data mining: artificial intelligence in data analysis. In *IEEE/WIC/ACM International Conference on Intelligent Agent Technology (IAT 2004)*, September 20-24, (pp. 7).

Zhang, Z. (2003). Applying data mining in investigating money laundering crimes.In P.M.D. Domingos, C. Falautsos, T. Senator, and L. Getoor (Eds), *The 9th ACM SIGKDD International Conference on Knowledge Discovery and Data Mining*, (pp. 747-752). New York: ACM.

ADDITIONAL READING

Berry, M. J., A., & Linoff, G., S. (2000). *Mastering data mining*. New York: Wiley.

Chung-Kwan, S. (2000). A hybrid approach of neural network and memory-based learning to data mining . *IEEE Transactions on Neural Networks*, *11*(3), 637–646. doi:10.1109/72.846735

de Callaos, B. (1994). Artificial organizational intelligence, *International Conference on Expert Systems for Development*, 3/28/1994 - 03/31/1994, Bangkok, Thailand, (pp.55-62).

Edelstein, H. A. (1999). *Introduction to data mining and knowledge discovery (3rd ed)*. Potomac, MD: Two Crows Corp.

Fan, Y., Zheng, Q., & Xiao-Ling, J. (2003). Data mining application issues in fraudulent tax declaration detection, *International Conference on Machine Learning and Cybernetics*, 2-5 Nov. 2003, Vol 4, (pp. 2202- 2206).

Fayyad, U. M., Piatetsky-Shapiro, G., Smyth, P., & Uthurusamy, R. (1996). *Advances in knowledge discovery & data mining*. Cambridge, MA: MIT Press.

Gao, S., Xu, D., et al. (2006). Intelligent anti-money laundering system, 2006. *SOLI '06. IEEE International Conference on Service Operations and Logistics, and Informatics*.

Han, J., & Kamber, M. (2000). *Data mining: Concepts and Techniques*. New York: Morgan-Kaufman.

Hastie, T., Tibshirani, R., & Friedman, J. H. (2001). *The elements of statistical learning: Data mining, inference, and prediction*. New York: Springer.

Holden, A. D. C. (1976). Trends in artificial intelligence . *Special Issue on Artificial Intelligence in the IEEE Transactions on Computers*, *C-25*(4), 313–316.

Kingdon, J. (2004). AI fights money laundering . *IEEE Intelligent Systems*, *19*(3), 87–89. doi:10.1109/MIS.2004.1

Luo, Q., (2008). Advancing knowledge discovery and data mining, F*irst International Workshop on Knowledge Discovery and Data Mining, IEEE Computer Society*, (pp. 3-5).

Pregibon, D. (1997). Data mining. *Statistical Computing and Graphics*, *7*, 8.

Simoudis, E. (1998). Industry applications of data mining: challenges and opportunities, *14th International Conference on Data Engineering*, 23-27 Feb 1998, (pp.105).

Weiss, S. M., & Indurkhya, N. (1997). *Predictive data mining: A practical guide*. New York: Morgan-Kaufman.

Westphal, C., & Blaxton, T. (1998). *Data mining solutions*. New York: Wiley.

Witten, I. H., & Frank, E. (2000). *Data mining*. New York: Morgan-Kaufmann.

Xindong, W. (2004), Data mining: artificial intelligence in data analysis, *WI 2004: Proceedings. IEEE/WIC/ACM International Conference on Web Intelligence*, 20-24 Sept. 2004, (pp. 7).

KEY TERMS AND DEFINITIONS

Data Mining: An analytic process designed to explore data in search of consistent patterns and/or systematic relationships between variables, and then to validate the findings by applying the detected patterns to new subsets of data.

Money Laundering: The process undertaken to conceal the true origin and ownership of the profits of criminal activities.

Terrorist Financing: The money raised to fund global terrorist activities.

CRISP-DM Methodology: The industry standard for data mining exercises.

Decision Tree: A decision tree is a decision support tool that uses a tree-like graph of decisions and their possible consequences. Decisions trees help identify a strategy most likely to reach a goal.

Decision Tree Learning: One of the most widely used methods for inductive inference.

Learning Classifier Systems: A machine learning technique which combines evolutionary computing, reinforcement learning, supervised/unsupervised learning, and heuristics.

Section 4
Early Warning Systems for Customer Services and Marketing

Chapter 13
Data Mining and Explorative Multivariate Data Analysis for Customer Satisfaction Study

Rosaria Lombardo
Second University of Naples, Italy

ABSTRACT

By the early 1990s, the term "data mining" had come to mean the process of finding information in large data sets. In the framework of the Total Quality Management, earlier studies have suggested that enterprises could harness the predictive power of Learning Management System (LMS) data to develop reporting tools that identify at-risk customers/consumers and allow for more timely interventions (Macfadyen & Dawson, 2009). The Learning Management System data and the subsequent Customer Interaction System data can help to provide "early warning system data" for risk detection in enterprises. This chapter confirms and extends this proposition by providing data from an international research project investigating on customer satisfaction in services to persons of public utility, like education, training services and health care services, by means of explorative multivariate data analysis tools as Ordered Multiple Correspondence Analysis, Boosting regression, Partial Least Squares regression and its generalizations.

INTRODUCTION

The necessity of systems of evaluation and assessment in many socio-economic fields together with the Learning Management System data (LMSD) have sparked a need in building early warning system (EWS) which produces signal for possible risks. Accordingly various EWSs have been established (Kim *et al.*, 2004): for detecting fraud, for credit-risk evaluation in the domain of financial analysis (Phua, *et al.*, 2009), to detection of risks potentially existing in medical organizations (risk aversion of nurse incidents, infection control and hospital management), to support decision making in customer-centric planning tasks (Lessman & Vob, 2009).

Enterprises are implementing systems of evaluation and assessment to demonstrate their com-

DOI: 10.4018/978-1-61692-865-0.ch013

mitment to efficiency, productivity, effectiveness and accountability (Volkwein, 1999). Managers are therefore under pressure to implement and demonstrate effective best practice. At the same time, their own performance as managers is under increasing government, public, and customers/ consumers scrutiny.

In this chapter we focus on EWS of LMSD for customer-centric planning tasks, to develop exploratory tools that identify at-risk customers and allow for more timely interventions.

Several data mining classifiers/predictors will be probed as training tools for detecting risks coming from Customer Interaction System data. The "Customer Interaction System" collects different information on customers/consumers by database and data-warehouse dealing with customers handled by the Consumer Affairs and Customer Relations contact centers within a company.

The maximization of lifetime values of the customer base in the context of a company's strategy is a key objective of customer relationship management (CRM). The role of CRM is in supporting customer-related strategic measures. Customer understanding is the core of CRM. It is the basis for maximizing customer lifetime value, which in turn encompasses customer segmentation and actions to maximize customer conversion, retention, loyalty and profitability. Hence, emphasis should be put on correct customer understanding and concerted actions derived from it, in order to reduce the risk to lose customers by loyalty increase.

The main aim of this project is to focus on customer satisfaction in services to persons of public utility, like training services and health care services.

The training services and the health care ones, as services of utility towards the public, are of relevant social interest. The main result of the supply process is not an output external to people, but it identifies itself with the effects of the service on consumers. For this reason the "product" is not simply an *output* (as result of a

short period), but an *outcome* (as result of a long period) which, in health care services, is given by the psychophysical state or condition of health of consumers/customers who perceived the service, while in training services, it can be identified with the success to find appropriate works (Goldstein & Spiegelhalter, 1996; Gori & Vittadini, 1999). The quality of health care services (Drummond *et al.*, 1997; Donabedian, 1985), supplied by a plurality of agents to consumer people, should be measured not only by quantitative-physic indicators (number of beds, number of operating rooms, number of high technologic instruments, number of training courses, number of teachers, etc.) and quantitative-monetary ones (input/output ratios, productivity indexes, etc.), but also by qualitative indicators which allow to measure the customer satisfactions, based essentially on the subjective evaluation of the quality service.

The availability of *customer satisfaction* measures is becoming as important as the corresponding objective measures, so it represents an early warning system data set, one of the essential component of the "optimal business management" following the approach of the Total Quality Management. The more reliable models for quality of services developed within a scientific framework agree on the necessity of a precise recognition of the fundamental perceptive dimensions on which the customer bases his or her judgment of the quality of particular public services. This evaluation of quality is typically express using ordinal categorical variables, which often require suitable transformation functions. Throughout this chapter with respect to different statistical methods, we consider different transformation functions of the ordinal categorical variables.

For the study of customer satisfaction, the theoretical models propose a system of five aspects of quality, these are: *tangibility, reliability, capacity of response, capacity of assurance and empathy*. These various aspects of the quality of the services in the so-called SERVPERF questionnaire (Parasuram, Zeithalm, & Berry, 1985) consist of items that form ordered categorical variables.

In particular the SERVPERF questionnaire was originally developed in a marketing context, and it measures the perceived quality of some important aspects of the quality of a particular service, using a response scale with ordered categories. In this chapter, this questionnaire has been employed to study CS in health care services.

Nevertheless in marketing literature the debate on defining quality aspects is open, not only the above mentioned five aspects of quality (*tangibility, reliability, capacity of response, capacity of assurance and empathy*) can be retained as characteristics of service quality but other different and important aspects can be highlighted (for example: *information/communication, organizations*, etc.). For this reasons in this chapter, to study the quality of training services we have pointed out a different questionnaire, not based on the five quality aspects of SERVPERF, but on some other perceived quality characteristics. All these questionnaires have in common the ordinal scale of responses (for example: bad service quality, sufficient service quality, high service quality, *Likert items*) which often require suitable transformations to be analyzed.

To support decision making in customer-centric planning tasks, explorative multivariate data analysis is an important part of corporate data mining.

In order to probe CRM data, one needs to explore the data from different perspectives and look at its different aspects. This should require application of different *tools* of DM.

At the beginning we investigate on the strength of variable associations by explorative Multiple Correspondence Analysis via polynomial transformations of ordered categorical variables (OMCA; Lombardo & Meulman, 2010; Lombardo & Beh, 2010). By Ordered Multiple Correspondence Analysis (OMCA), we will analyze a data set coming from a survey on the perception of various aspects of quality in an hospital of Naples (Italy)

using the SERVPERF questionnaire. The use of OMCA has a major advantage for this particular data set: we can easily monitor the overall (dis)satisfaction with the health care services the hospital provides, where ordered categorical variables or Likert items are involved. By OMCA we automatically obtain clusters of individuals ordered with respect to the ordered categories of responses (*no satisfaction, almost satisfaction, satisfaction, good satisfaction, optimal satisfaction*). By focusing on the discoveries of actionable patterns in customer data, the marketers or other domain experts make easier to determine which actions should be taken once the customer patterns are discovered.

In a second moment whenever the interest is on the study of dependence among variables, we could approach to studying customer satisfaction by means of linear and non-linear regressive models. Prediction with nonlinear optimal transformations of the variables is reviewed, and extended to the use of multiple additive components, much in the spirit of statistical learning techniques that are currently popular in data mining.

The present study will focus on the dependence relationships between quantitative and qualitative indicators through predictive and regressive techniques as Boosting regression, Partial Least Squares (PLS) and its generalizations. By Boosting regression (Buhlmann & Yu, 2003), we will analyze a data set with Likert items coming from a survey on students of master training courses of the university "L'Orientale" of Naples (Italy). The questionnaire has been based on the following quality aspects: process, teaching, materials and exercises, the rank transformation has been used to deal with the ordinal categorical variables (Hastie, Tibshirani & Friedman, 2001).

In the framework of Boosting regression in case of a low-ratio of observations to variables, the problem to evaluate the overall Customer Satisfaction (CS), in function of the above mentioned SERVPERF aspects of quality (tangibility, reliability, capacity of response, capacity of assurance and empathy) can be properly faced by non-linear

Discriminant Partial Least Squares (PLS, Wold, 1966; Tenenhaus, 1998) using B-spline transformations for the ordered categorical variables (Durand & Sabatier, 1997; Durand, 2001; Lombardo & Durand, 2005; Durand, 2008; Lombardo, Durand & De Veaux, 2009).

ORDERED MULTIPLE CORRESPONDENCE ANALYSIS TO STUDY CS VARIABLE INTERRELATIONSHIPS

A very common approach to analyze large survey data is to perform Multiple Correspondence Analysis (MCA, Benzecri, 1973; Greenacre, 1984, Lebart, Morineau & Warwick, 1984; Gifi, 1990). In multiple correspondence analysis, a variable is regarded as a set of category points. MCA, which is also known as Homogeneity analysis (Gifi, 1990), or dual scaling (Nishisato, 1980, 1996), is a powerful statistical tool used to assign scores to subjects and categories of discrete variables, displaying the association among more than two sets of categorical variables. MCA can be introduced in many different ways, which is probably the reason why it was reinvented many times over the years. Surely one of the hallmarks of correspondence analysis is the many ways in which one can derive the basic simultaneous equations which are related with the Pearson χ^2/n statistic (Gifi, 1990; van Rijckevorsel & de Leeuw, 1988; Lombardo & van Rijckevorsel, 1999). A possible interpretation of MCA is in terms of an optimal scaling technique, where the category quantifications are averages of object scores for objects within that category, and the object scores are proportional to the averages of the relevant category quantifications. Another possible interpretation is in terms of a principal component analysis of the quantified data matrix, where the original category labels in the multivariate categorical data matrix have been replaced by category quantifications obtained in the optimal scaling process. If we confine ourselves to ordered categorical variables, some variants of MCA are found by weighting the categories of variables (Nishisato & Arry, 1975) or by nonlinear transformation (Gifi, 1990, Heiser & Meulman, 1994, Meulman, van der Kooij & Heiser, 2004). Furthermore, over the past ten years, an alternative method of decomposition, called the bivariate moment decomposition, has been shown to be applicable for correspondence analysis as an important tool to take into account the information in ordered categorical variables (Best & Rayner, 1996; Beh, 1997; Lombardo, Beh, & D'Ambra, 2007). To do this, we focus on a confirmatory approach to MCA, called Ordered MCA (OMCA, Lombardo & Meulman, 2010; Lombardo & Beh, 2010) where explanatory tools are combined with inference ones. OMCA is based on the singular value decomposition (SVD) and on the bivariate moment decomposition (BMD). Specifically, correspondence analysis based on bivariate moment decomposition by orthogonal polynomials has been proposed for two-way and three-way contingency tables (Beh, 1997, 1998, 2001; Beh & Davy, 1998, 1999; Best & Rayner, 1996; D'Ambra, Beh, & Amenta, 2005; Lombardo, Beh, & D'Ambra, 2007; Beh, Simonetti, & D'Ambra, 2007). Ordered MCA maintains all the features of MCA, and allows for additional information about the structure and association of the ordered categories by separating the linear, quadratic and higher order components in the data. As graphical results, we obtain the same categorical variable display of MCA, but we add information on the relationships among the variable categories. Furthermore, we get more informative individual representations than MCA ones, as the individuals are automatically clustered in so many clusters as the number of ordered categories of the responses to a questionnaire.

At first, we briefly summarize Multiple Correspondence Analysis for evaluating survey data. Questionnaires often result in responses to a large number of questions with a limited number of answer categories. In a graphical representation, the association between the variables is represented by the closeness of the categories of different variables. The responses to these p questions, coded in complete disjunctive form, lead to different ways of classifying all the individuals in the sample. Let $\mathbf{X}=[\mathbf{X_1}|...|\mathbf{X_p}]$ be the indicator super-matrix of p ordered categorical variables observed on the same set of n individuals, with

$J = \sum_{k=1}^{p} j_k$ the total number of categories,

i.e. the number of columns in $\mathbf{X}$. Let $\mathbf{X_k}$ be the indicator matrix of the kth variable with margins $x_{.jk} = \{\sum_{t=1}^{n} x_{ij_k}\}$. Define $\mathbf{D}$ as the diagonal super-matrix of dimension $J \times J$, whose generic diagonal elements are given by the diagonal elements of the k different matrices $\mathbf{D_k} = x_{.j_k}$. To describing the relationships among the categories, we can perform: 1) a correspondence analysis on the $n \times J$ indicator super-matrix $\mathbf{X}$, i.e. the following singular value decomposition:

$$SVD\left(\frac{1}{p\sqrt{n}} \mathbf{X}\mathbf{D}^{-1/2}\right) = \Phi \Lambda \Upsilon'$$

where Λ represents the matrix of singular values in decreasing order, and where Φ and Υ denote the corresponding left and right singular vectors, respectively, subject to the ortho-normality constraints.; 2) a correspondence analysis of $J \times J$ Burt matrix, B. The Burt matrix B is a super-matrix that consists of diagonal blocks with the univariate margins on its main diagonal, and the collection of all tables with bivariate margins in the off-diagonal blocks. The Burt matrix can also be written as $B=\mathbf{X'X}$. The second approach to MCA involves the eigenvalue decomposition of $\frac{1}{p^2 n} D^{-1}B$.

Alternatively, multiple correspondence analysis is equivalent to homogeneity analysis (Gifi, 1990), which as conceived by Guttman (1941)

can be viewed as a nonlinear principal component analysis of categorical data.

Quick Review of OMCA

In customer satisfaction research and in general in service evaluations, we observe categorical variables whose categories are ordered, the amount of dissatisfied customers can represent an early warning system data useful to detect the risk to lose customers. To analyze variables with ordered categories through MCA, we propose a hybrid decomposition of the indicator super-matrix, which implies computing the orthogonal polynomials and singular vectors, by means of the bivariate moment decomposition (Beh, 1997) and the singular value decomposition, respectively. The computation of orthogonal polynomials for the ordered categorical variables is a key point of the analysis, we refer to a general recurrence formula to generate them that you can find in Emerson (1968), Beh (1997), Lombardo & Meulman (2010).

As highlighted by Emerson, the decomposition by orthogonal polynomials can be considered essentially equivalent to Gram-Schmidt orthogonal decomposition. Originally introduced in experimental design, the set of polynomials is orthogonal over a set of points with arbitrary spacing and weighting. The arbitrary spacing permits experiments where the categories are unequally spaced on the independent variable, and the arbitrary weighting system permits an unbalanced design, with unequal numbers of observations in the different categories.

The resulting polynomials are orthogonal with respect to the diagonal marginal matrix. After computing the orthogonal polynomials for each variable, we construct the super-matrix of orthogonal polynomials Ψ of dimension $(J \times J)$ whose block-diagonal elements are the orthogonal polynomial matrices $\psi_1 \cdots \psi_p$, while the off-diagonal elements are null. The use of orthogonal polynomials is not new, and recent applications can be found in ordered two-way and three-way correspondence analysis (Best & Rayner, 1996; Beh, 1997, 1998; Beh & Davy, 1998; Lombardo *et al.*, 2007; Beh *et al.*, 2007; Lombardo & Camminatiello, 2010).

Through the use of orthogonal polynomials that are associated with ordered categorical variables, the partition allows to analyze and decompose the total inertia (of the cloud of points) in terms of linear, quadratic and higher order polynomial components. Not only the total inertia, but also the contribution to the inertia by each singular vector can be partitioned in orthogonal polynomial components, showing the contribution of the dominant ones (linear, quadratic, cubic, etc). After computing the orthogonal polynomials with respect to the marginal distribution of the p ordered categorical variables and forming the diagonal super-matrix $\tilde{\psi}$, the hybrid decomposition (HD) for MCA on the basis of $\mathbf{X}$ can be applied (Lombardo & Meulman, 2010). At the heart of the analysis lies the matrix $\mathbf{Z} = \dfrac{1}{p\sqrt{n}} \Phi' \mathbf{X} \mathbf{D}^{-1/2} \tilde{\psi}$, by means of it the total inertia can be expressed as

$$trace\left(\mathbf{Z}'\mathbf{Z}\right) = trace\left(\mathbf{Z}\mathbf{Z}'\right) = \wedge^2 .$$

The (m, v_k)th value of $\mathbf{Z}$ defines the contribution of the v_kth-order bivariate moment between the categories of the kth ordered variable to the mth principal axis. When $v=1$, the element z_{m1_k} describes the importance of the location component for the kth variable on the mth axis of a classical MCA plot. Therefore, the overall location component of the categories of the kth variable can be determined by calculating $\sum_{m=1}^{m} z^2_{m1_k}$.

If this component is significant, then there is a significant variation in the location of those categories. The quadratic component of the categories can be calculated by $\sum_{m=1}^{M} z^2_{m2_k}$ which

reflects the spread of the categories of the k.th variable. The case for $p=2$ and both variables ordered, uses two sets of orthogonal polynomials (Beh, 1997; Lombardo & Beh, 2010).

Using the HD implies computing the singular vectors for the individuals and orthogonal polynomials for the ordered categorical variables. Therefore, the total inertia of the contingency table is not only partitioned into polynomial components, but can also be partitioned into m singular values and singular vectors. To test for statistically significant components in the decomposition of the total inertia using $\mathbf{Z}$, the mathematical equivalence between the inertia and the Pearson chi-squared statistic is considered. In fact, Bekker & de Leeuw (1988) show that the total sum of squares of the Burt matrix can be written as the sum of squares of all non-diagonal sub-matrices plus the sum of squares of all diagonal matrices. Note that the sum of squares of a diagonal matrix of the Burt matrix equals its trace and the sum of squares of a non-diagonal sub-matrix equals the Pearson chi-squared statistic divided by n. So the total sum of squares of the resulting matrix can be expressed in function of the element of the $\mathbf{Z}$ matrix and it can be shown that is asymptotically *chi-squared* distributed (for details see Lombardo & Meulman, 2010).

Under similar conditions, due to the relationship between the bivariate moment $z^2_{m(v_k)}$ and the eigenvalue λ_{B_m}, we assume the bivariate moment values are *chi-squared* distributed as well.

As the hybrid partition involves singular vectors and polynomial components, the inertia can be partitioned in terms of linear, quadratic and higher order components. In fact, one of the main advantages in OMCA is that not only the total inertia, but also the inertia associated with the m.th singular vector can be partitioned into the sum of squares of the *bivariate moments*. As shown before, these are defined by the elements of the matrix $\mathbf{Z}'\mathbf{Z}$. Differently from the matrix of singular values, the matrix $\mathbf{Z}'\mathbf{Z}$ is not diagonal.

The non-zero off-diagonal associations between the row and column categories allow us to identify important structures in the data not otherwise detected.

The inertia accounted for by the first axis is partitioned in terms of polynomials components, and establishing the relationship between λ_{B_m} and $z^2_{m(v_k)}$, we can test the significance of the components. In practice, when the linear component is dominant, then the representation using polynomials allows us to visualize the linear trend in the categories along the first polynomial axis. Unlike classical factorial analysis, the first and second polynomial axis are not necessarily the most important; for example, it may happen that the cubic or the forth polynomial is significant, while the linear and quadratic ones are not.

To display the association among variable categories and enhance the interpretation of the graphical display, a plotting system based on the orthogonal polynomials is employed. In these plots the dimensional style of interpretation is always valid. This applies to one axis at a time and consists in using the relative positions of one set of points on an axis giving the dimension a conceptual name. First, we will focus on the representation of the categories.

To compute category coordinates related to the **Z** matrix, we consider the super-matrix of orthogonal polynomials the computed coordinates for the categories in OMCA are identical to the coordinates obtained from a classical MCA. As consequence the interpretation of plots do not change: those categories that do not contribute to the association between the variables, will lie close to the origin of the correspondence plot, similarly, the distance of category points further from the origin indicates the relative importance of that variable to the association structure of the variables.

One of the possibilities of standard MCA is to represent categories and individuals simultaneously in the same map; but, if the number of objects is very large, the joint plot does not give a very clear display of the association between individuals and categories. The standard graphical display, which uses standardized coordinates for the individuals, leads to a scatter of points with very often no apparent pattern or structure (except for the so-called horse-shoe that points to a very dominant first dimension). Therefore, coordinates for individuals are often left out from a multiple correspondence analysis. Unlike classical MCA coordinates, the object coordinates obtained by using orthogonal polynomials are automatically arranged in distinct clusters, thereby giving a simple structure and classification of the objects. Assuming that all variables consist of the same number of ordered categories (as in data consisting of Likert items) such that $j_k=j$ for all $k=1,2,\ldots,p$, and that these categories are assigned equivalent scores to reflect the ordinal structure of the variable they belong to, the OMCA objects plot will consist of j clusters of objects. This particular feature makes very attractive OMCA to monitor (dis)satisfaction of each customer cluster in different time or spaces.

An Application: Customer Satisfaction in Health Care Services

The data concern a survey on the perception of various aspects of quality in an hospital in Naples, Italy, they can be seen as warning system data concerning the risk of poor quality services. The recent crisis in the public health system (welfare) calls for the necessity of deep human and technological restructuring, to improve customer satisfaction, and to recover efficacy and efficiency of health services. The health service, as utility towards the public, is of highly relevant social interest. The more reliable models for quality of service developed within a scientific framework agree on the necessity of a precise recognition of the fundamental perceptive dimensions on which the customer/patient bases his or her judgment of the quality of particular health services. For the study of patient satisfaction, the theoretical models propose a system of five aspects of quality that can be distinguished. These are *tangibility, reliability, capacity of response, capacity of assurance, and empathy*. In the present application of OMCA, we focus on data collected in a study at the Second University of Naples, in June 2008. Patient satisfaction was measured by the so-called SERVPERF instrument, we used the questionnaire

version presented by Babakus & Mangold (1992). The SERVPERF questionnaire was originally developed in a marketing context, and it measures the perceived quality of some important aspects of the quality of a particular service, using a response scale with ordered categories numbered from 1 to 5. In the health care context, "tangibility" refers to the structural aspects, "reliability" to trust and precision, "capacity of response" to

Table 1. Decomposition of the first two non-trivial eigenvalues and chi-square tests

Variable	Component	$z^2_{1(v_k)}$	χ^2	$z^2_{2(v_k)}$	χ^2	d.f.
Tangibility	Location	0.104	73.230***	0.030	2.093	8
	Dispersion	0.000	0.328	0.051	35.956***	8
	Skewness	0.001	0.362	0.008	2.398	8
	Kurtosis	0.002	1.567	0.000	5.936	8
Reliability	Location	0.140	98.781***	0.000	0.282	8
	Dispersion	0.000	0.219	0.099	69.999***	8
	Skewness	0.001	0.368	0.003	2.217	8
	Kurtosis	0.000	0.038	0.000	0.033	8
Capability of Response	Location	0.153	107.539***	0.002	1.154	8
	Dispersion	0.003	1.950	0.131	92.568***	8
	Skewness	0.001	0.523	0.008	5.806	8
	Kurtosis	0.000	0.027	0.002	1.748	8
Capability of Assurance	Location	0.151	106.328***	0.002	1.106	8
	Dispersion	0.005	3.313	0.119	84.106***	8
	Skewness	0.001	0.529	0.013	9.315	8
	Kurtosis	0.001	0.454	0.000	0.011	8
Empathy	Location	0.143	101.009***	0.003	2.094	8
	Dispersion	0.003	2.242	0.093	65.398***	8
	Skewness	0.001	0.615	0.016	11.082	8
	Kurtosis	0.002	1.665	0.000	0.020	8
	Total	0.711	501.088***	0.558	393.320***	160

emergency ready ward, "capacity of assurance" to competence and courtesy, and "empathy" to personal attention towards the patient. The data set consists of 705 patients, and 15 variables (Likert items), each having five ordered categories. Three items measure "tangibility" (Tang), three measure "reliability" (Rel), four items measure "response capacity" CRes), three "capacity of assurance" (CRas), and two "empathy" (Emp). As a composite measure for each of the five quality aspects, the respective medians for Tang, Rel, CRes, CRas, Emp were computed. To study patient satisfaction with respect to the five aspects, both MCA and OMCA have been applied to the median values across subsets. Categories of these composite variables will be indicated by the label number, for example, the composite responses "tangibility" on a five point scale are denoted by Tang1, Tang2, Tang3, Tang4 and Tang5. As previously discussed, to reflect the ordinal structure natural scores have been transformed in four orthogonal polynomials.

Using multiple correspondence analysis, the total inertia is 4.0, removing the redundancy in the p indicator matrices, since each row sums up to 1. The first two eigenvalues are $\lambda_B^2 = 0.711$

and $\lambda_B^2 = 0.558$, which are decomposed and tested in Table 1.

The graphical results obtained by OMCA are given in Figure 1a, b. The display consists of two panels. Figure 1a depicts the association across the 25 response categories of the five quality aspects. This representation is the same for MCA and OMCA. The plot shows that a low satisfaction level (response category 1) for one quality aspect is associated with a low level of satisfaction for the other quality aspects. Reversely, an aspect being judged as excellent (with response category 5) is associated with excellent ratings for the other aspects. Figure 1b shows the five classes of points for the 705 hospital patients who participated in the study. The horseshoe shape of the configuration of the coordinates suggests that there is a dominant one-dimensional structure in the data, which implies that the variables are very homogeneous (van Rijckevorsel, 1987). By applying OMCA, the total inertia representing the association between the variables, may be further partitioned into the sum of squares of the $z^2_{m(v_k)}$ values. Although the OMCA results for the category coordinates will not differ from those obtained by MCA, the OMCA results give further

Figure 1. a: Graphical displays of response categories in overall hospital; b: Graphical displays of patients in overall hospital

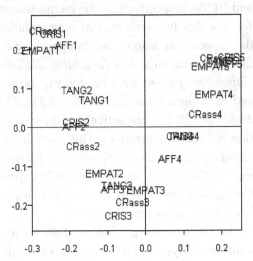
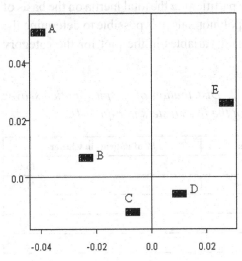

insight into the structure of the association between the variables.

But now consider Figure 1b), the OMCA representation for the patients. It is clear that there are five distinct clusters of patients, each associated with one of the five categories that form an ordered variable. It is evident that those in cluster **A** have an overall poor judgment of the quality of their hospital, while cluster **E** clearly shows those patients who gave an overall excellent rating to the hospital services. In fact, to better understand how dominant each of the response categories is, Table 2 shows the distribution of the patients over the five clusters representing an overall judgment from poor to excellent. This distribution shows that about the 72.3% of the patients evaluate the services in the hospital of middle-high quality, the 13.6% of the respondents qualified the services in the hospital of very-high quality. At the other end of the scale, only the 9.4% of the patients responded that the quality of the services was poor. Such an overall rating of the hospital services is not easily obtained when performing classical MCA. Thus the use of OMCA has a major advantage for this particular data set: we can easily monitor the overall (dis)satisfaction with the health care services the hospital provides. This advantage generalizes to other situations where ordered categorical variables or Likert items are involved.

By partitioning the total inertia on the basis of these polynomials, it is possible to determine the dominant variables in the plot for the category

Table 2. Distribution of hospital patients over each of the five clusters in Figure 1b

Cluster	% of Patients in Cluster
E	13,6%
D	41,7%
C	30,6%
B	4,7%
A	9,4%

points, and also the dominant sources in each variable. Table 1 provides a summary of the components that reflect the first four moments (location, dispersion, skewness and kurtosis) of each variable, and their contribution to the first and second principal axis of the MCA and OMCA plot. The statistically significant components are identified at three levels of significance: 0.01 (***), 0.05 (**) and 0.10 (*). The total degrees of freedom are equal to d.f.=160.

Table 1 shows that the variation between the categories of each variable is best explained in terms of the differences in their location and dispersion: the location component explains 97.1% of the inertia accounted for by the first dimension, while the dispersion component accounts for 88.4% of inertia accounted for by the second dimension.

These values of inertia accounted for can be further partitioned to identify those variables that dominate the solution for each dimension. If one considers the chi-squared inertia's for each dimension, in Table 1 the percentage of patients that lie in each of the 5 clusters in Figure 2b *Tangibility* accounts for 15% of the first principal inertia. Similarly, *Reliability, Capability of Response, Capability of Assurance* and *Empathy* contribute to 19.8%, 22.1%, 22.2% and 20.9% to the first principal axis, respectively. Similarly, for the second principal axis of Figure 1a), these variables contribute to 14.3%, 22.0%, 31.5%, 21.7% and 10.5%, respectively, to the inertia accounted for. For this two-dimensional representation of the association among the categories, we can therefore determine that *Tangibility, Reliability, Capability of Response, Capability of Assurance* and *Empathy* account for 15.9%, 18.3%, 25.6%, 24.6% and 20.1%, respectively, of the total variation between the variables. This result indicates that the patients consider that the most important aspect of quality is the hospital staffs capability to respond to the patients' needs, while tangibility is the least important factor.

To underline the usefulness of the technique, a further analysis of the same data is considered,

Figure 2. a: Graphical displays of response categories in gynecology division; b: Graphical displays of patients in gynecology division

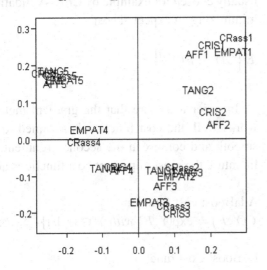
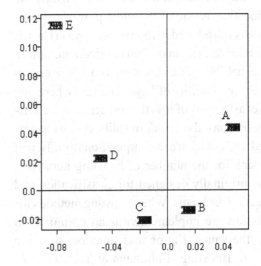

focusing on the patients within the gynecology division of the hospital. We investigate the perception of the same five quality aspects, but now only for this subset of patients, with $n= 216$. The graphical results are given in Figures 2a/2b. Figure 2a depicts the association between the 25 categories explaining the quality aspects, now judged only by a subgroup of the patients. As before, the display of the response categories is the same for MCA and OMCA.

In Figure 2b we consider the graphical display of the 216 patients of the gynecology division. As already underlined this display is useful only in OMCA, we can clearly distinguish five clusters of patients who were automatically classified with respect to their overall rating of the quality aspects from excellent (class **E**) to poor (class **A**).

The percentages of the subgroup of gynecology patients that lie in each of the five clusters are reported in Table 3. In the gynecology division we observe that the percentage of patients who found that the hospital offered very poor quality services is 9.7% (table 2), similar than that from the overall patients. Furthermore, about 15.3% of patients of gynecology thought that the hospital division offered excellent quality services, this

percentage is greater than that from the overall patients, and only 12.5% of the patients rated the hospital division services as bad-middle/bad. These unit percentages can represent early warning system data that help to identify at-risk customers/consumers and suggest for more timely interventions to improve service quality.

BOOSTING REGRESSION TECHNIQUES

In the framework of customer satisfaction studies, when the aim is to point out the dependence relationships between quantitative and qualitative indicators then predictive and regressive

Table 3. Distribution of gynecology patients over each of the five clusters in Figure 2b

Cluster	% of Patients in Cluster
E	15.3%
D	36.1%
C	36.1%
B	2.8%
A	9.7%

techniques as Boosting regressions can reveal their utility to examine causes of (dis)satisfaction.

Boosting is one of the most powerful learning ideas introduced in the last ten years (Hastie, Tibshirani & Friedman, 2001; Friedman, 2001). The possibility of this boosting procedure comes with the availability of large data sets where one can set aside part of it as the test set, or use cross-validation based on random splits, or use the corrected *AIC* criterion as a computationally efficient approach for the number of boosting iterations. It was originally designed for classification and regression problems. When boosting methods for regression are implemented as an optimization using the squared error loss function, they are called L_2 Boosting (Buhlmann & Yu, 2003). L_2 *Boosting* also characterizes PLS regression and its generalizations (Durand, 2008) as it will be discussed in the following section.

As a matter of fact simple variants of boosting with L_2 Loss have been proposed in literature (Buhlmann & Yu, 2003; Buhlmann & Hothorn, 2007). Like other boosting algorithms, L_2 Boost is an additive combination of simple functions of estimators and iteratively uses a pre-chosen fitting method called the learner. L_2 Boost is based on the explicit expression of refitting residuals. The improved performance through boosting of a fitting method, called the learner, has been impressive. It describes a procedure that combines the outputs of many "weak" model to produce a powerful model "committee". As proven (Buhlmann, 2006), L_2 Boosting for linear model yields consistent estimates in the very high-dimensional context. To explain boosting, as functional gradient descent techniques, consider the centered training sample $\{y_i, X_i\}_{i=1}^{n}$ where $y \in R$, and, $X = \left(x^1, \ldots, x^p\right) \in R$ the task is to estimate an additive parametric function

$$F\left(X, \alpha_m, \hat{\theta}_m\right)_{m=1}^{M} = \sum_{m=1}^{M} \alpha_m h(X, \hat{\theta}_m)$$

where M is the dimension of the additive model usually chosen for example by Cross-Validation, minimizing an expected cost

$$E\left\{C\left[Y - F(X)\right]\right\} \tag{1}$$

In order to ensure that the gradient method works well, the cost function is assumed to be smooth and convex in the second argument. In literature the most important cost functions are

AdaBoost cost function
$C(Y, F) = \exp(Y, F) \; with \; Y \in \{-1, 1\}$

L_2 Boost Cost function
$C(Y, F) = \{(Y, F)^2 \, / \, 2 \; with \; Y \in R$

Logit Boost cost function
$C\left(Y, F\right) = \log_2\left[1 + \exp\left(-2YF\right)\right] \; with \, Y \in \{-1, 1\}$

When the cost function is the squared loss, the minimizers for the expected cost (1) are

$$F\left(X\right) = E[Y \, / \, X = x]$$

Estimation of such function from data can be done by a constrained minimization of the empirical risk

$$n^{-1} \sum_{i=1}^{n} C[Y_i - F\left(X_i\right)] \tag{2}$$

applying functional gradient descent. The minimizer of (2) is imposed to satisfy a smoothness or regularization constraint in terms of an additive expansion of learners (i.e. fitted functions) $h(X, \hat{\theta})$ where $\hat{\theta}$ is an estimated parameter. For example least squares fitting yields

$$\hat{\theta}_{U,X} = min \sum_{i=1}^{n} [U_i - h(X_i, \theta_m)]^2$$

For some data $\{U_i, X_i\}_{i=1}^{n}$ where $U_1, \ldots, U_n$ denote some pseudo-response variables which are not necessarily the original $Y_1, \ldots, Y_n$

L_2 BOOSTING ALGORITHM.

- -Step1 (initialization) Set $m=1$, given the data apply the base procedure yielding the function estimate $F^{m=1}(.) = h(X, \hat{\theta}_{U,X})$

- Step2 compute residuals $U_i = Y_i - \widehat{F}^{m}(X_i)$ per $i=1, \ldots, n$ and fit the real-valued base procedure to the current residuals

- Update

  ∘ $F^{m+1}(.) = \widehat{F}^{m}(X_i) + h(X, \hat{\theta}_{U,X})$

- Step 3 (iteration) increase the iteration index m by one and repeat step 2 until a stopping iteration M is achieved.

The algorithm repeats M-1 times the least-squares fitting of residuals (pseudo-residuals) and seeks its improvements iteratively based on its performance on the training dataset (Friedman, 2001). With one boosting step it has already been proposed by Tukey (1977) under the name "twicing". The base learner $h(X, \hat{\theta})$ is usually a parametric function of X whose aim is to capture nonlinearities and interactions. L_2 boosting constructs additive regression models by sequentially fitting a simple parameterized function (base learner) to current pseudo-responses as the least-squares residuals.

We look at the L_2 boosting methodology from a practical point of view. The practical aspects of boosting procedures for fitting statistical models are illustrated by means of the dedicated open-source software package *mboost* in R. This package implements functions which can be used for model fitting, prediction and variable selection. It is flexible, allowing for the implementation of new boosting algorithms optimizing user-specified loss functions. The illustrations presented focus on a regression problem with a continuous re-sponse variable. The *mboost* package provides infrastructure for defining loss functions via boost family objects. For regression with continuous response, we use most often the squared error loss, this loss function is available in *mboost* as family *GaussReg*(). In particular, we employ the *glmboost* function from the package *mboost* to fit a linear regression model by means of L_2 Boosting with component-wise linear least squares. By default, the function *glmboost* fits a linear model (with optimal mstop = 100 and shrinkage parameter = 0.1) by minimizing squared error (argument family = *GaussReg*() is the default).

An Application: Evaluation of Student Satisfaction in Training Courses

To show the usefulness of L_2 Boosting regression we consider the data set resulting from a survey on student satisfaction concerning training master courses of the University of "L'Orientale" of Naples (October 2007). The questionnaire concerns the perceived quality of some important aspects of quality of training courses (*Likert items*), using a response scale with ordered categories numbered from 1 to 6 (for the questionnaire see Appendix A). The data set consists of 231 units, and 14 variables (*Likert items*), each having six ordered categories. At first the data were transformed in rank to overcome the problem of scale typical of this kind of data. The response variable is the overall satisfaction on the course organization transformed in continuous variable. The predictors are given by the 14 items which consist of four subsets: process, teaching, materials and exercises. Each subset measures one of the four quality aspects. Seven items measure the "process" (P), four items measure "teaching capability" (D) and three items measure quality aspects of "material" (M). In particular we indicate with **P2** the question: "Is the number of teaching hours enough?", **P3**: "Have been illustrated the contents of the course?"; **P4**: "Is the content of the course repeti-

Table 4. The Coefficients

Intercept	P2	P3	P4	P5	P6	P7	P8
-0.205	0.021	0.196	-0.019	0.000	0.000	0.237	0.021
	D1	D2	D3	D4	M1	M2	M3
	0.000	0.000	0.000	0.000	0.033	0.000	0.000

tive?; **P5**: "Have been respected the timetable of the course?"; **P6**: "Is the timetable adequate?"; **P7**: "has been the teaching method efficacious?"; **P8**: "Is the timetable suitable to learn the different subjects?"; **D1**: "Is the teacher in time?"; **D2**: "Is the teacher clear?"; **D3**: "Is the teacher capable to stimulate interest of students?; **D4**: "Is the teacher's capacity of response exhaustive?;

M1: "Do you feel the didactic material clear and complete?"; **M2**: "Are the slides clear and complete?"; **M3**: "Is the additional didactic material adequate?" (the questionnaire is reported in Appendix B).

Note that, by default, the mean of the response variable is used as an offset in the first step of the boosting algorithm. We center the covariates prior to model fitting. As mentioned above, the special form of the base learner, i.e., component-wise linear least squares, allows for a reformulation of the boosting fit in terms of a linear combination of the covariates. The estimated coefficients of covariates are given in table 4.

thus 6 covariates have been selected for the final model. By the *AIC* criterion (Buhlmann, 2006) we arrest at $m=100$ iteration, the most important predictors, which directly affect the satisfaction of students, result to be the process variables **P7**, and **P3** concerning the teaching method and the contents of courses, it follows the material information **M1**, and **P2**, **P3**. Inversely we notice the predictor **P4**, concerning the repetitive content of courses (less repetitive they are more the students are satisfied). All the other predictors do not play any important role in explaining the student satisfaction (see Figure 3).

LINEAR AND NON-LINEAR PLS

When there is a low-ratio of observations to variables and in case of multicollinearity in the

Figure 3. The predictor coefficients using the glmboost function

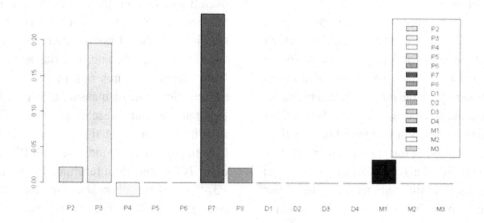

predictors, the problem to evaluate the Customer Satisfaction, in function of a large set of predictors (concerning tangible aspects, operator professionalism, organizations, information/communications, etc., of public services) can be properly faced by linear and/or non-linear Partial Least Squares (PLS, Wold, 1966; Tenenhaus, 1998; Durand, 2001; Lombardo Durand & De Veaux, 2009).

As recently pointed out (Durand, 2008; Lombardo Durand & De Veaux, 2009), the classic linear PLS regression belongs to the framework of L_2-boosting methods, when the base learner $h\left(X,\hat{\theta}\right)$ is expressed by the latent variable $t = h\left(X,\hat{\theta}\right) = \sum_{j=1}^{p}\theta^{j}X^{j}$, with $\hat{\theta} \in R^{p}$. In fact, PLS components that are linear compromises of pseudo-predictors built from centered design matrices, are based on the explicit refitting of residuals.

With a focus on observational data, originating from customer satisfaction research, we enhance, among different PLS regressions (Wold, Kettaneh, & Skagerberg, 1989; Wold, Martens & Wold, 1983; Tenenhaus, 1998; Bastien, Esposito Vinzi, & Tenenhaus, 2005; Esposito Vinzi, Guinot & Squillacciotti, 2007), non-linear PLS regression techniques (Durand, 2001; Durand & Lombardo, 2003, Lombardo, Durand & De Veaux, 2009). The aim is to evaluate the dependence between the satisfaction of customers and explicative variables which capture quality aspects of a service.

At the beginning one assumes that there exists an underlying linear relationship between response and predictor variables, but sometimes there is reason to doubt this assumption and a non-linear transformation of the variables might be useful to reveal the model underlying the data. So that non-linear relationships (PLS via Splines, i.e. PLSS; Durand, 2001) and interactions among predictors (Multivariate Additive PLSS, i.e. MAPLSS; Durand & Lombardo, 2003; Lombardo Durand & De Veaux, 2009) could drive at the choice of the model. To evaluate regression models of different complexities an heuristic strategy, consisting in increasing progressively the model parameters (degree and knot number) can be considered, as it often tends to work quite well giving a visually pleasing fit to a set of data.

In the framework of L_2-boosting methods, we can say that PLS components, as linear compromises of pseudo-predictors built from centered design matrices, maximize the covariance with the response variables. The function F, *depending on the dimension M,* is so defined

$$F(X,M) = \sum_{j=1}^{p}\beta^{j}(M)x^{j}$$

Whenever the base learner $h(X,\hat{\theta}_m)$ is a non-parametric function of $_{predictors}$, like in PLS via Splines, in short PLSS, then the base learner becomes a linear combination of the transformed predictors by B-spline functions $\left\{B_1^j(X^j),\ldots,B_{r_j}^j(X^j)\right\}$. We can write

$$t = h\left(X,\hat{\theta}\right) = \sum_{j=1}^{p}\sum_{k=1}^{r_j}\theta_k^j B_k^j(X^j)$$
$$= \sum_{j=1}^{p}s_j(x_j)$$

where $s_j(X_j)$ is the coordinate spline function measuring the influence of the predictor X_j on the component. The dimension of the base learner increases, it passes from p (of linear models) to $r = \sum_{i=1}^{p}r_i$

Furthermore when bivariate interactions are incorporated into the PLSS model, as in MAPLSS, the base learner becomes

$$t = h\left(X,\hat{\theta}\right) = \sum_{j=1}^{p}\sum_{k=1}^{r_j}\theta_k^j B_k^j(X^j) +$$
$$\sum_{(j,j')\in K_2}\left\{\sum_{k=1}^{r_j}\sum_{l=1}^{r_{j'}}\theta_{kl}^{jj'}B_k^j(X^j)B_k^{j'}(X^{j'})\right\}$$
$$= \sum_{j=1}^{p}s_j\left(X^j\right) + \sum_{(j,j')\in K_2}s_{j,j}(X^j,X^{j'})$$

Where $s_{j,j}(X^j, X^{j'})$ is the bivariate spline function of the interaction between X^j and $X^{j'}$. So the base learner (latent variable t) is a sum of univariate and bivariate spline functions. Furthermore when the learner is a linear combination of smoothing splines (Durand & Sabatier, 1997; Durand, 2001; 2008; Durand & Lombardo, 2003; Lombardo, Durand & De Veaux, 2009) the prediction from all of them can improve consistently by capturing non-linearity and interactions properly.

DISCRIMINANT PARTIAL LEAST SQUARES REGRESSION MODELS AND SOME EXTENSIONS TOWARDS MULTIVARIATE ADDITIVE MODELS

PLS has been promoted in the chemometrics literature as an alternative to ordinary least squares (OLS) in the poorly or ill-conditioned problems. When the response variable is categorical, coded in a disjunctive form, we refer to the technique as Discriminant PLS (Tenenhaus, 1998; Lombardo, Tessitore & Durand, 2007). Whenever we use B-spline transformations of predictors and include bivariate interactions between predictors, we perform **non-linear Discriminant PLS regression** (Lombardo & Durand, 2005).

Before presenting an application of non-linear discriminant PLS regression, a brief description of the techniques is due.

Let $Y = [Y^1 | \dots | Y^q]$ be the categorical $n \times q$ response matrix, coded in disjunctive form, where a column expresses an ordered category, and let $X = [X^1 | \dots | X^p]$ be the $n \times p$ matrix of the predictors observed on the same n statistical units. In the non-linear context of PLS via Spline (PLSS; Durand, 2001), the **X** design has been replaced by the centered supercoding matrix **B** obtained by transforming the predictors through a basis of B-spline functions. PLSS is defined as the usual linear PLS regression of **Y** onto the space spanned by the centered coding matrix **B** (new design matrix).

The PLSS regression can be viewed as a projection of response variables $Y = [Y^1 | \dots | Y^q]$ on latent structures (component scores from transformed predictor matrix by B-spline functions) that are of maximum covariance with **Y**. It constructs a sequence of centered and uncorrelated exploratory variables, i.e. the PLSS components $t^1, \dots, Y^M$, in three steps (refer to Durand, 2001, for a formal description).

Given the centered main effects coding matrix we get PLSS(**X**,**Y**)=PLS(**B**,**Y**) where the latent variables from **B** are of maximum covariance with **Y**. The PLSS regression, like PLS, is:

- efficient in spite of low ratio of observations on column dimension of **B**.
- efficient in the multi-collinear context for predictors (concurvity)

Furthermore, using B-spline basis functions, PLSS permits:

- to treat with continuous and categorical variables
- to be robust against extreme values of predictors (local polynomials).
- to evaluate non-linear relationships through main effects additive models.

The response Y^j is modeled as a sum of univariate spline functions transforming the set K_1 of the retained predictors.

The non-linear PLSS model for the generic response can be so expressed

$$\hat{Y}_A^i = F(X) = \sum_{j=1}^{p} s_j(X^j \hat{\beta}_i(A))$$
$$= \sum_{j=1}^{p} \sum_{k=1}^{r_j} \theta_k^j B_k^j(X^j)$$

Where $s_j(X^j \hat{\beta}_i^j(A))$ is the B-spline function expressing the main effect of x_i on the fitted response, also called the coordinate function of the predictor. The PLSS generalization towards multivariate predictors, called Multivariate Additive PLSS, i.e. MAPLSS (Lombardo, Durand & De Veaux, 2009) enhances the variable predictive power of PLSS including interaction terms. The MAPLSS model allows to include interesting interactions as predictors.

This kind of decomposition is particularly suitable to investigate in predictive models and identify the particular variables that enter into the model, whether they enter purely additively or are involved in interactions with other variables.

The use of interaction terms means looking for functions of two or more variables. The interaction degree depends on the number of variables involved in the analysis. We define the design matrix **B** from univariate and multivariate B-splines (tensor product of two or more functions). The MAPLSS model for the response j has been presented by using the ANOVA decomposition (Lombardo, Durand & De Veaux, 2009).

$$\hat{Y}_A^i = F(X) = \sum_{k \in K_1} s_j(X^k \hat{\beta}_i^k(A)) + \sum_{(j,j') \in K_2} s_{j,j'}(X^j, X^{j'}; \hat{\beta}_i^{j,j'}(A))$$

where K_1 and K_2 are index sets pointing out the main effects and the bivariate interactions, respectively. The higher interaction order in MAPLSS implies dimension expansion of design matrix. The risk of overfitting related to an increasing column dimension for the new design matrix **B** is well supported by MAPLSS like the standard PLS method.

Thanks to B-spline properties, the new base learner capture non-linearity and interactions, the price to be paid being the extension of the dimension M. This is generally well supported by PLS except when capturing interactions where the

explosion of the dimension needs an automatic selection of relevant terms stored in K_2 set. In MAPLSS, we do an automatic selection of interactions of degree two only, as it is true that models with interaction effects involving more than two variables become more difficult to interpret. This selection implies forward/backward phases which produce a sequence of models and estimate which one is the best, looking at a total criterion based on GCV index (Lombardo, Durand & De Veaux, 2009).

An Application: Evaluation of Patient Satisfaction in Health Care Service

To illustrate the usefulness of linear and non-linear discriminant PLS we consider the data set resulting from a survey on sanitary service of the Second University of Naples (October 2004). The questionnaire instruments considered to investigate on the patient satisfaction (PS) in an hospital of south Italy (Aversa, CE, Italy) is the SERVPERF (Parasuraman *et al.* 1985) adapted at the hospital services (for the questionnaire see Babakus & Mangold, 1992). Let be the response matrix coded in disjunctive form. It collects the degree of satisfaction on the perceived experience in the hospital, in an ordered scale: from 1 (very bad quality, dissatisfaction, **S1**) to 5 (excellent quality, optimum level of satisfaction, **S5**), in function of 15 ordered predictor variables (Likert items), whose natural scale is also coded by integers from 1 to 5. The predictors observed on 235 individuals are in relation with the five service quality dimensions of services, which are: 1) *Tangibility* with 3 items (**T1, T2, T3**); 2) *Reliability* with three items (**R4, R5, R6**); 3) *Response capacity* with 3 items (**C7, C8, C9**); 4) *Assurance capacity* with 4 items (**A10, A11, A12, A13**); 5) *Empathy* with 2 items (**E14, E15**). The aim is to predict the patient dissatisfaction (PS degree equal to 1) given the judgement of patients on the previous service quality dimensions (in total 15

Table 5. First experience: Linear PLS

GCV(α=3,1)=4.57" PRESS(leaving out proportion=0.1,A=1)=4.51	
dimension	Y var.
1	0.5490
2	0.0882

Table 6. Second experience: PLSS, degree=0, knots=4

GCV(5,2)=4.49 PRESS(0.1,2)=4.34	
dimension	Y var.
1	0.5538
2	0.3324

Table 7. Third experience: PLSS, degree=0 knots=4

GCV(8,2)=2.3042 PRESS(0.1,2)=2.1762	
Dimension	Y var.
1	0.6605
2	0.3384

Likert items). Performing usual linear PLS, we read in Table 5 the *PRESS* and *GCV* values, the dimension retained is 1. *PRESS*(0.1,1) denotes the *PRESS* with 10 percent of the observations out and A=1. Clearly the *GCV* criterion, is a surrogate of *PRESS*, their similar values can make reliable analysis results, difference in values of *GCV* can be due to the tuning parameter, α, that should be properly determined. The *reconstituted variance* according to this component is only 63.7%.

Passing to PLSS models (Table 6 and Table 7) we increase the goodness-of-fit and prediction of the models. In the present context of an opinion poll, the B-splines used to transform the predictors are local polynomials of degree 0 (piecewise

Figure 4. First experience, correlation circle of response

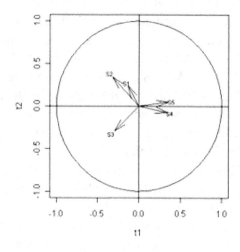

constant functions) with 4 knots at (1.5, 2.5, 3.5, 4.5).

Because no variable interaction was accepted in MAPLSS, we present the results of two different multi-response PLSS models. First, with all the 5 satisfaction response levels at hand, Table 2 shows the *PRESS* and *GCV* values, the dimension retained is 2. The *reconstituted variance* according to two components is increased to 88.6%.

Looking at the correlation circle (figure 4) of the response categories, we note that **S1** and **S2**, **S4** and **S5**, are highly correlated. So we perform a second PLSS experience, where the **Y** response has three ordered categories (**S1**=very satisfied; **S2**=medium satisfied; **S3**=not satisfied) and repeat the analysis. Reading the *PRESS* and *GCV* values (Table 3, Figure 5), the dimension retained is 2. The *reconstituted variance* according to two components is improved, it is now equal to 99.8%.

In Figure 6 we illustrate the importance of the predictors on the dissatisfaction degree (**S1**) measured by the range of the coordinate functions. The first important variable is related with the response capacity dimension, in particular with item **C9**, the second and third ones concern the tangibility aspects (**T3** and **T1**), etc.. The manage-

Figure 5. Second experience, correlation circle of response

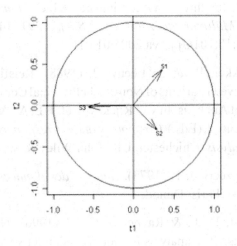

Figure 6. Influence of the predictors on the dissatisfaction S1

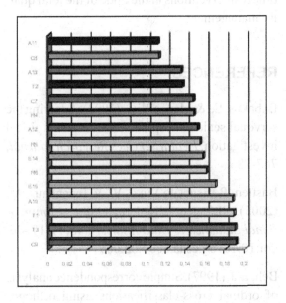

ment should take into account of the importance of variables in predicting the worst degree of satisfaction. In particular increasing attention should be paid at structure aspects (**T3, T1**), as well as at improving response and assurance capacities of professional operators (**C9, A10**).

CONCLUSION

The use of data mining has rapidly become widespread, with applications in domains ranging from credit risk, fraud detection, counter-terrorism, to marketing and decision making in customer-centric planning tasks. In all of these, data mining is increasingly playing a key role in decision making.

In this chapter the process of finding information in large data sets has been addressed to study information on customers/consumers by database dealing with customers handled by the Consumer Affairs and Customer Relations contact centers within a company. In particular we have paid attention on customer satisfaction in services to persons of public utility, as training services and health care services.

Explorative multivariate data analysis tools have been proposed to study and predict customer satisfaction developing an early warning system data that identify at risk customers/consumers who show high dissatisfaction for the quality service. Ordered MCA has allowed to get for additional information about the structure and association of the ordered categories (Likert items), that characterize CS questionnaires, and about the individuals who have been automatically clustered in so many clusters as the number of ordered categories.

Furthermore, boosting regression techniques (including PLS ones) have been particularly suitable to predict (dis)satisfaction of customers, in particular in presence of a large number of correlated variables, of predictors of mixed nature, permitting to get more accurate and parsimonious models. The applications on real data sets collecting the satisfaction levels of customers in public services in function of a lot variables characterizing the service quality have permitted to appreciate the usefulness of the techniques as predictive and decision models.

Customer (dis)satisfaction data can help to provide "early warning system data" in order to identify at-risk customers and allow for more timely interventions in the optic of the total quality management.

REFERENCES

Babakus, E., & Mangold, G. (1992). Adapting the servqual scale to hospital services: an empirical investigation. *Health Services Research Journal*, 767-786.

Bastien, P., Esposito Vinzi, V., & Tenenhaus, M. (2005). PLS generalised regression. *Computational Statistics & Data Analysis*, *48*(1), 17–46. doi:10.1016/j.csda.2004.02.005

Beh, E. J. (1997). Simple correspondence analysis of ordinal cross-classifications using orthogonal polynomials. *Biometrical Journal. Biometrische Zeitschrift*, *39*(5), 589–613. doi:10.1002/bimj.4710390507

Beh, E. J. (1998). A comparative study of scores for correspondence analysis with ordered categories. *Biometrical Journal. Biometrische Zeitschrift*, *40*, 413–429. doi:10.1002/(SICI)1521-4036(199808)40:4<413::AID-BIMJ413>3.0.CO;2-V

Beh, E. J. (2001). Partitioning Pearson's chi-squared statistic for singly ordered two-way contingency tables. *The Australian and New Zealand Journal of Statistics*, *43*, 327–333. doi:10.1111/1467-842X.00179

Beh, E. J., & Davy, P. J. (1998). Partitioning Pearson's chi-squared statistic for a completely ordered three-way contingency table. *The Australian and New Zealand Journal of Statistics*, *40*, 465–477. doi:10.1111/1467-842X.00050

Beh, E. J., & Davy, P. J. (1999). Partitioning Pearson's chi-squared statistic for a partially ordered three-way contingency table. *The Australian and New Zealand Journal of Statistics*, *41*, 233–246. doi:10.1111/1467-842X.00077

Beh, E. J., Simonetti, B., & D'Ambra, L. (2007). Partitioning a non-symmetric measure of association for three-way contingency tables. *Journal of Multivariate Analysis*, *98*(7), 1391–1411. doi:10.1016/j.jmva.2007.01.011

Bekker, P., & de Leeuw, J. (1988). Relations between Variants of Non-linear Principal Component Analysis. In van Rijckevorsel, J. L. A., & de Leeuw, J. (Eds.), *Component and Correspondence Analysis*. Chichester, UK: John Wiley & Sons.

Benzécri, J. P. (1973). *Analyse des données (2 vols)*. Paris: Dunod.

Best, D. J., & Rayner, J. C. W. (1996). Non-parametric analysis for doubly ordered two-way contingency tables. *Biometrics*, *52*, 1153–1156. doi:10.2307/2533077

Buhlmann, P. (2006). Boosting for high-dimensional linear models. *Annals of Statistics*, *34*(2), 559–583. doi:10.1214/009053606000000092

Buhlmann, P., & Hothorn, H. (2007). Boosting algorithms: regularization, prediction and model fitting. *Statistical Science*, *22*(4), 477–505. doi:10.1214/07-STS242

Buhlmann, P., & Yu, B. (2003). Boosting with the L2 loss: regression and classification. *Journal of the American Statistical Association*, *98*, 324–339. doi:10.1198/016214503000125

D'Ambra, L., Beh, E. J., & Amenta, P. (2005). CATANOVA for two-way contingency tables with ordinal variables using orthogonal polynomials. *Communication in Statistics*, *34*, 1755–1769. doi:10.1081/STA-200066325

Donabedian, A. (1985). *Explorations in quality assessment and monitoring. The findings of quality assessment and monitoring*. Ann Arbor, MI: Health Administration Press.

Drummond, M. F., Sculpher, M., Torrance, G. W., O'Brien, B. J., & Stoddart, G. L. (1997). *Methods of the economic evaluation of health care programs*. Oxford, UK: Oxford University Press.

Durand, J. F. (2001). Local Polynomial additive regression through PLS and Splines: PLSS. *Chemometrics and Intelligent Laboratory Systems, 58*, 235. doi:10.1016/S0169-7439(01)00162-9

Durand, J. F. (2008). La régression Partial Least-Squares boostée. *Revue MODULAD, 38*, 63–86.

Durand, J. F., & Lombardo, R. (2003). Interaction terms in Non-linear PLS via additive spline transformation. In Schader, P., Gaul, J., & Vichi, M. (Eds.), *Between Data Science and Applied Data Analysis* (pp. 22–30). Berlin: Springer.

Durand, J. F., & Sabatier, R. (1997). Additive pplines for partial least Squares regression. *Journal of the American Statistical Association, 92*, 440. doi:10.2307/2965425

Emerson, P. L. (1968). Numerical construction of orthogonal polynomials from general Recurrence Formula. *Biometrics, 24*, 696–701. doi:10.2307/2528328

Esposito Vinzi, V., Guinot, C., & Squillacciotti, S. (2007). Two-step PLS regression for L-structured data: an application in the cosmetic industry. *Statistical Methods & Applications, 16*(2), 263–278. doi:10.1007/s10260-006-0028-2

Fawcett, T., & Provost, F. (1997). Adaptive fraud detection. *Data Mining and Knowledge Discovery, 1*(3), 291–316. doi:10.1023/A:1009700419189

Friedman, J. H. (2001). Greedy function approximation: A gradient boosting machine. *Annals of Statistics, 29*, 1189–1232. doi:10.1214/aos/1013203451

Gifi, A. (1990). *Non-linear Multivariate Analysis*. Chichester, UK: Wiley.

Goldstein, H., & Spiegelhalter, D. J. (1996). League Tables and their limitation: statistical issues in comparisons of institutional performance. *Journal of the Royal Statistical Society. Series A, (Statistics in Society), 52*, 5.

Gori, E., & Vittadini, G. (1999). La valutazione dell'Efficienza e dell'efficacia per la valutazione dei servizi alla persona. In *Qualità e Valutazione nei servizi di pubblica utilità*. Milano: Etas Libri.

Greenacre, M. (1984). *Theory and applications of correspondence analysis*. London: Academic Press.

Guttman, L. (1941). The quantification of a class of attributes. In Horst, P. (Ed.), *The Prediction of Personal Adjustment* (pp. 321–347). New York: Social Science Research Council.

Hastie, T., Tibshirani, R., & Friedman, J. (2001). *The elements of statistical learning, data mining, inference and prediction*. New York: Springer series in Statistics.

Hastie, T. J., & Tibshirani, R. J. (1990). *Generalized additive models*. Boca Raton, FL: Chapman & Hall/CRC.

Heiser, W. J. (2004). Geometric representation of association between categories. *Psychometrika, 69*(4), 513–545. doi:10.1007/BF02289854

Heiser, W. J., & Meulman, J. J. (1994). Homogeneity analysis: exploring the distribution of variables and their nonlinear relationships. In Greenacre, M., & Blasius, J. (Eds.), *Correspondence Analysis in the Social Sciences: Recent Developments and Applications* (pp. 179–209). New York: Academic Press.

Kim, T. Y., Oh, K. J., Sohn, I., & Hwang, C. (2004). Usefulness of artificial neural networks for early warning system of economic crisis. *Expert Systems with Applications, 26*, 583–590. doi:10.1016/j.eswa.2003.12.009

Lebart, L., Morineau, A., & Warwick, K.M. (1984). *Multivariate descriptive dtatistical analysis*. Wiley series, 3.

Lessman, S., & Vob, S. (2009). A reference model for customer-centric data mining with support vector machines. *European Journal of Operational Research, 199*(2), 520–530. doi:10.1016/j.ejor.2008.12.017

Lombardo, R., & Beh, E. J. (2009). *Simple and multiple correspondence analysis for ordered-scale variables*. Applied Statistics Journal.

Lombardo, R., & Beh, E.J. (2009). Simple and multiple correspondence analysis for ordinal-scale variables using orthogonal polynomials. *Journal of Applied Statistics*.

Lombardo, R., Beh, E.J., & D'Ambra, L. (2007). Non-symmetric correspondence analysis for doubly ordered contingency table. *Computational Statistics & Data Analysis journal, 52* (1), 566-578.

Lombardo, R., & Camminatiello, I. (2009). CATANOVA for two-way cross classified categorical data. *Statistics: A journal of Theoretical and Applied Statistics, 1*(15).

Lombardo, R., & Durand, J. F. (2005). Discriminant Partial Least-Squares via Splines: An application to evaluate patient satisfaction. *Statistica & Applicazioni, 3*, 77–85.

Lombardo, R., Durand, J.F., & De Veaux, R. (2009). Model building in multivariate additive partial least squares splines via the GCV criterion. *Journal of Chemometrics*.

Lombardo, R., & Meulman, J. (2009). Multiple correspondence analysis via polynomial transformations of ordered categorical variables. *Journal of Classification*.

Lombardo, R., Tessitore, G., & Durand, J. F. (2006). Data mining and MAPLSS regression tools. A case study: the evaluation of trial duration. In *Metodi, Modelli e Tecnologie a Supporto delle Decisioni. Procida*, Napoli, 28-30 settembre 2006 Franco Angeli.

Lombardo, R., Tessitore, G., & Durand, J. F. (2007). Data mining and MAPLSS regression tools. A case study: the evaluation of trial duration. In D'Ambra, L., Rostirolla, P., & Squillante, M. (Eds.), *Metodi, Modelli e Tecnologie a Supporto delle Decisioni*. Milan, Italy: Franco Angeli.

Lombardo, R., & van Rijckervorsel, J. (1999) Interaction terms in homogeneity analysis: Higher order non-linear multiple correspondence analysis. In *Studies in Classification, Data Analysis and knowledge Organization*.

Macfadyen, L. P., & Dawson, S. (2009). Mining LMS data to develop an early warning system for educators: A proof of concept. *Computers & Education*. doi:.doi:10.1016/j.compedu.2009.09.008

Meulman, J., van der Kooij, A. J., & Heiser, W. H. (2004). Principal components analysis with non-linear optimal scaling transformations for ordinal and nominal data. In Kaplan, D. (Ed.), *Handbook of Quantitative Methods in the Social Sciences* (pp. 49–70). Newbury Park, CA: Sage Publications.

Nishisato, S. (1980). *Analysis of categorical data: Dual scaling and its applications*. Toronto, Canada: University of Toronto press.

Nishisato, S. (1996). Gleaning in the field of dual scaling. *Psychometrika, 61*(4), 559–599. doi:10.1007/BF02294038

Nishisato, S., & Arri, P. S. (1975). Non-linear programming approach to optimal scaling of partially ordered categories. *Psychometrika, 40*, 525–547. doi:10.1007/BF02291554

Parasuraman, A., Zeithaml, V. A., & Berry, L. L. (1985). A conceptual model of service quality and its implications for future research. *Journal of Marketing*, 49.

Phua, C., Gayler, R., Lee, V., & Smith-Miles, K. (2009). On the communal analysis suspicion scoring for identity crime in streaming credit applications. *European Journal of Operational Research, 195*, 595–612. doi:10.1016/j.ejor.2008.02.015

Tenenhaus, M. (1998). *La règression PLS, thèorie et pratique*. Paris: Editions Technip.

Tukey, J. W. (1977). *Exploratory data Analysis*. Reading, MA: Addison-Wesley.

van Rijckevorsel, J. L. A., & de Leeuw, J. (1988). *Component and correspondence analysis.* Chicester, UK: Wiley.

Volkwein, J. F. (1999). *The four faces of institutional research. What is institutional research all about? New directions for institutional research, 104.* San Francisco: Jossey-Bass.

Wold, H. (1966). Estimation of principal components and related models by iterative least squares. In Krishnaiah, P. R. (Ed.), *Multivariate Analysis.* New York: Academic Press.

Wold, S., Kettaneh-Wold, H., & Skagerberg, B. (1989). Non linear partial least squares modeling. *Chemometrics and Intelligent Laboratory Systems, 7,* 53–65. doi:10.1016/0169-7439(89)80111-X

Wold, S., Martens, H., & Wold, H. (1983). The multivariate calibration problem in chemistry solved by PLS method. In Ruhe A. and Kagstrom B. (Eds), *Lecture Notes in Mathematics, Proceedings of the Conference on Matrix Pencils,* (pp.286-293). Heidelberg, Germany: Springer-Verlag.

KEY TERMS AND DEFINITIONS

Learning Management System Data: Reporting tools that identify at-risk customers/consumers and allow for more timely interventions.

Customer Interaction System: Information system on customers/consumers by database and data-warehouse dealing with customers handled by the Consumer Affairs and Customer Relations contact centers within a company.

Early Warning System Data: Produces signal for possible risks: for detecting fraud, for credit-risk evaluation in the domain of financial analysis, for detection of risks potentially existing in medical organizations (risk aversion of nurse incidents, infection control and hospital management), to support decision making in customer-centric planning tasks.

Risk Detection in Enterprises: Detecting fraud, credit-risk evaluation in the domain of financial analysis, in medical organizations (risk aversion of nurse incidents, infection control and hospital management), in customer-centric planning tasks for risk detection to lose customers.

Customer Satisfaction: The perceived quality by customers/consumers of different quality aspects of services.

SERVPERF: It is a questionnaire originally developed in marketing context, it measures the perceived quality of some important aspects of quality of a particular service (*tangibility, reliability, capacity of response, capacity of assurance and empathy*), using a response scale with ordered categories.

Ordered Multiple Correspondence Analyses: Explorative and Confirmative Correspondence Analysis for ordered categorical variables (Likert items).

Boosting Regression: Powerful learning regression techniques to handle huge datasets.

Discriminant non-linear Partial Least Squares: Dependence analysis between a categorical response and a large set of predictors transformed via spline functions. It is suitable when there is a low-ratio of observations to variables and in case of multicollinearity and nonlinearities in the predictors.

APPENDIX

Table 8.

N	Service Quality aspects	Ordinal-scale (1=Min; 5= Max)		
P2	"Is the number of teaching hours enough?"	bad	1 2 3 4 56	excellent
P3	"Have been illustrated the contents of the course?"	bad	1 2 3 4 5 6	excellent
P4	"Is the content of the course repetitive?	bad	1 2 3 4 5 6	excellent
P5	"Has been respected the timetable of the course?"	bad	1 2 3 4 5 6	excellent
P6	"Is the timetable adequate?"	bad	1 2 3 4 5 6	excellent
P7	"Has been the teaching method efficacious?"	bad	1 2 3 4 5 6	excellent
P8	"Is the timetable sufficient to learn the different subjects?"	bad	1 2 3 4 5 6	excellent
D1	"Is the teacher in time?"	bad	1 2 3 4 56	excellent
D2	"Is the teacher clear?"	bad	1 2 3 4 56	excellent
D3	"Is the teacher capable to stimulate interest of students?	bad	1 2 3 4 56	excellent
D4	Is the teacher's capacity of response exhaustive?	bad	1 2 3 4 56	excellent
M1	"Do you feel the didactic material clear and complete?"	bad	1 2 3 4 56	excellent
M2	"Are the slides clear and complete?"	Bad	1 2 3 4 56	excellent
M3	"Is the additional didactic material adequate?	Bad	1 2 3 4 56	excellent

Chapter 14
Using POS Data for Price Promotions Evaluation:
An Empirical Example from a Slovenian Grocery Chain

Danijel Bratina
University of Primorska, Slovenia

Armand Faganel
University of Primorska, Slovenia

ABSTRACT

Price promotions have been largely dealt with in the literature. Yet there are just a few generalizations made so far about this powerful marketing communication tool. The obvious effect, that all authors who have studied price promotions emphasize, is quantity increase during price promotions. Inference studies about the decomposition of the sales promotion bump do not converge to a generalization or a law, but end in radically different results. Most of these studies use consumer panel data, rich of demographical characteristics and consumers' purchasing history. Companies that use such data, available from marketing research industry, usually complain that data is old and expensive. The authors start with literature review on price promotions in which they present existing models based on consumer panel data (Bell, et al., 1999; Mela, et al., 1998; Moriarty, 1985; Walters, 1991; Yeshin, 2006). Next they present existing POS analysis models and compare their findings to show the high level of heterogeneity among results. All existing models are based on powerful databases provided by professional research institutions (i.e. Nielsen or IRI) that usually cover the whole market for the analysed brand category geographically. The authors next apply existing models to find which best suits data available for Slovenian FMCG market. They show two models analysis – quantity (SCAN*PRO) and market share (MCI) and their power for explanatory and forecasting research using POS data. Having dealt with more than 30 brand categories within a wider research, they conclude that the models developed are usable for a fast decision making process within a company, but their exploratory power is still poor compared to panel data.

DOI: 10.4018/978-1-61692-865-0.ch014

INTRODUCTION

In the past 30 years marketing expenditures' monitoring is gaining a great deal of attention from academia and practitioners. Traditionally is the marketing budget among the first to be cut in crisis times, mostly because of lack of accountability and standardization of metrics. In terms of costs, price promotions rank high in marketing budgets (Mela et al.,1997) and since more than 90% (Abraham & Lodish, 1987) of FMCG (fast moving consuming goods) are sold on promotions, it is natural that a great part of marketing research is being spent on methods of price promotions accountability. Price promotions are also perceived to be the most powerful short-term marketing tool and, unfortunately, also the easiest to copy from the competition.

Brand managers, facing the shrinking of funding for their brands' marketing support, are striving to develop models that would help them determine the best price promotions strategies and supporting activities.

Even though price promotions are such a powerful tool, useful models have only started to appear in research papers since the year of 2000. van Heerde et al. (2001) and Bucklin & Gupta (1999) claim the reasons for such late researchers' interest for price promotions to be:

1. Lack of brand managers' time;
2. Undeveloped information technology for large scale analysis;
3. Unwillingness of brand managers' to search for accountability of their actions, that would shed light on marketing (brand) managers performance;
4. Data unavailability; and
5. Price concerns.

The three real problems (point 2., 4. and 5.), are successfully overcome, with the exponential development of computer processors' power and data storage capacities. Thus from year 2000 on

several models of price promotions effectiveness and efficiency have been developed. In terms of data used, price promotions models can be subdivided into three categories:

1. Models that use consumer (households) panels;
2. Models that use store panels and;
3. Models that use scanner level data on a store level.

Consumer panels' models (mostly basing on probability choice models) have been historically developed first. Such models can analyze a great deal of information (heterogeneity of consumers, heterogeneity of brands, and heterogeneity of stores). Their negative side is represented by their cost and data availability. The same is true for store panels.

It has been no more than a decade from the development of first scanner level data models, which use secondary data (POS scanner) to analyze price promotions. Models that use scanner level data have the advantage of being cheaper to use (once developed) and promptly available for decision making as data for model tuning is readily available within each retailer's information database. On the down side of these models is lack of consumer data, making them unusable for consumer heterogeneity analysis, and also store heterogeneity analysis as data from competitors' stores are unavailable for analysis.

In our paper we present two models (a share model and a sales model) that use scanner data to analyze price promotions effectiveness. We prove that some generalizations resulting from previous meta analysis (Assmus, et al., 1984; Bell et al., 1999; Bucklin & Gupta, 2000; Conchar, & Zinkhan, 2005; Tellis, 1988; van Heerde, 1999) can be done, while we also give support to some other research done with consumer panels.

This chapter is organized as follows. First we present the state of the art with main generalizations on price promotions and open questions. In the next paragraph we present the data used and model the two frameworks. At the end findings are gathered and commented with future research proposed.

PRICE PROMOTIONS: STATE OF THE ART

We divide the literature review into two areas:

1. Research that analyzes long and short term effects of price promotions and
2. Determinants of price promotion effectiveness.

The most widely acknowledged generalization in terms of price promotions effects is of course the short term promotion increase in sales common to all research studied. But already when we look at price promotion elasticities, we find a great deal of variety even though same types of products, consumers and market situations have been analyzed. Steenkamp et al. (2005) and Srinivasan et al. (2004) for example found the elasticity to be (-)4 (meaning that an 1% decrease in price results in a 4% increase in quantities). On the other hand high volume products (Narasimhan, et al., 1996; Raju, 1992), highly concentrated segments (Bell et al., 1999; Jedidi et al., 1999), poorly advertized segments (Jedidi et al., 1999; Raju, 1992) and segments with few new products (Nijs, et al., 2001) show fairly different elasticities.

The total effect of sales promotions increase of quantities can be split into (van Heerde,1999; Blattberg et al., (1995):

1. Increased consumption (Ailawadi & Neslin, 1998; Assuncao & Meyer, 1993),
2. Timing (incidence)– consumers start buying products before they do actually need to restock them (Bell, et al., 2002), and
3. Brand switching (Krishna, 1994).

Shares among the three categories vary between authors: Gupta (1988), van Heerde et al. (2002) and Steenkamp (2005) show that around 75% of the quantity increase during price promotions has to be accounted to brand switching within same category of products, around 15% is category increase and 10% goes to timing. It is of course very important to know the source of the promotion sales quantity increase, especially for the retailer, as brand switching doesn't really have an impact on retailer's sales (or even has a negative impact – as consumer get the products they need for lower prices), while increase consumption does. Shares between the three main categories of sales promotion effects are not fixed and vary between different papers. Table 1 shows the promotion effect split for different research.

The factors affecting such variations have been analyzed by Bell et al. (1999). Their findings are shown in Table 2. However an extensive research of the determinants still needs to be done.

Other, minor effects, of price promotions are:

4. Pre-promotion dip (customers buy less in expectations of sales promotion period) (Macé & Neslin, 2004; van Heerde, et a., 2004),
5. Post-promotion dip (customers buy less after price promotion due to stocking at home (Macé & Neslin, 2004; Neslin & Schneider, 1996; van Heerde et al., 2004),
6. Store switching (Bucklin & Lattin, 1992), and
7. Category switching (Walters, 1991).

While different authors study different effects, there is no sign of any generalizations for the above mentioned effects (i.e. some authors find great support for pre- and post- promotion dips, while other find none).

Authors use very different sources of data (consumer panels, scanner data, and store panels) to study the effects in very different product categories. Another problem, why authors can't

Table 1. Decomposition of the sales promotion increase. (Adapted from van Heerde (2005, 98))

Author	Brand category	Brand switching	Timing	Category increase
Gupta (1988)	Coffee	*84*	*14*	*2*
Chiang (1991)	Coffee	*81*	*13*	*6*
Chintagunta (1993)	Yogurth	*40*	*15*	*45*
Bucklin & Gupta (1999)	Yogurth	*58*	*20*	*22*
Bell et al. (1999)	Margarine	*94*	*6*	*0*
	Soft drinks	*86*	*6*	*9*
	Sugar	*84*	*13*	*3*
	Paper towels	*83*	*6*	*11*
	towels	*81*	*4*	*15*
	Softeners	*79*	*1*	*20*
	Yoghurt	*78*	*12*	*9*
	Ice cream	*77*	*19*	*4*
	Chips	*72*	*5*	*24*
	Bacon	*72*	*20*	*8*
	Washing powder	*70*	*1*	*30*
	Coffee	*53*	*3*	*45*
	Butter	*49*	*42*	*9*
Average		*74*	*11*	*15*

Table 2. Factors affecting price promotion elasticity. (Adapted from Bell et al. (1999, 519))

Secondary demand			Primary demand					
	Brand switching		Demand		Quantity		Total	
Factor	Coef.	p	Coef.	p	Coef.	p	Coef.	p
Category factors								
Share of budget	*-.599*	*<.01*	*.001*	*n*	*.148*	*<.01*	*-.409*	*<.01*
No. of brands	*-.031*	*n*	*.079*	*n*	*.583*	*<.01*	*.278*	*<.01*
No. of packagings	*.097*	*<.05*	*-.34*	*<.01*	*.386*	*<.01*	*.177*	*<.01*
Storability	*.586*	*<.01*	*.105*	*n*	*.486*	*<.01*	*.676*	*<.01*
Differentiation	*-.196*	*<.05*	*.305*	*<.05*	*.295*	*<.01*	*-.01*	*n*
Difficulty of purchase	*-.328*	*<.01*	*-.185*	*<.1*	*-.018*	*n*	*.247*	*<.01*
Frequency of purchase	*.003*	*n*	*.097*	*n*	*-.294*	*<.01*	*-.122*	*<0.5*
Brand factors								
Relative price	*-.099*	*<.05*	*-.027*	*n*	*.016*	*n*	*-.016*	*n*
Price variability	*-.129*	*<.05*	*-.185*	*<.05*	*-.146*	*<.01*	*-.157*	*<.01*
Frequency of promotions	*.025*	*n*	*.028*	*n*	*.025*	*n*	*.074*	*n*
Discount depth	*.076*	*n*	*-.007*	*n*	*-131*	*<.01*	*.035*	*n*
Brand knowledge	*-.059*	*n*	*.540*	*<.01*	*-.069*	*n*	*-.016*	*n*
Brand loyalty	*-.164*	*<.01*	*.096*	*n*	*.191*	*<.01*	*-.022*	*n*
Demographics								
Income	*-.070*	*n*	*-.025*	*n*	*-.018*	*n*	*-.066*	*n*
Age	*-.087*	*<.10*	*-.043*	*n*	*.044*	*n*	*-.066*	*n*
Level of education	*-.011*	*n*	*.135*	*<.05*	*-.047*	*n*	*.008*	*n*

confirm each other's findings could be that other marketing variables (uncontrolled marketing settings in their models) do have an impact on sales promotions effects. Up to date, there has been no research that accounted for all possible determinants of heterogeneity. This area still needs to get greater research attention.

Long term effects of price promotions studies deal with even more difficult challenges such as random events that happen during the period of study. Research on this field can be categorized into three groups:

1. Effects on sales and profits in the long run (Dekimpe & Hannsens, 1995, 2000; Martinez-Ruiz, et al., 2006; Nijs et al., 2001),
2. Effects on consumers' purchasing behavior (Blattberg, et al., 1981; Bucklin & Gupta, 1992; Currim & Schneider, 1991; Gupta, 1988; Neslin & Henderson, 1985), and
3. Changing consumer preferences (Bawa & Shoemaker, 1987; Dodson, et al., 1978; Guadagni & Little, 1983; Ortmeyer, et al., 1991).

Dekimpe & Hannsens (1995, 2000) and Nijs (2001) show that long term effects of most sales promotions is small. Only products in their early lifecycle could have a long term benefit from price promotions resulting in accelerated market penetration.

Lattin & Bucklin (1989) as well as Mayhew & Winer (1992) studied the impact on consumers' purchasing behavior. They show that increased exposure to price promotions shifts reference prices from regular to promoted and decreases price promotions efficiency, due to decreasing difference between regular and promoted price (due to the necessity of lowering regular prices because of changing consumers' perceptions).

Bawa & Shoemaker (1987) conducted a research on a large sample of customers before and after price promotion and found that user preferences for a brand is declining with increas-ing price promotions, while non-user preferences are increasing. Same results have been confirmed by Walters & Rinne (1986), Kumar & Leone (1988), Walters & MacKenzie (1988) and Grover & Srinivasan (1992).

The second area of research is determining the factors that affect the effectiveness of a price promotion (Bell et al., 1999). Research done so far is very heterogeneous in terms of factors used and proved to affect the effectiveness of a price promotion. The only determinant always used is discount amount (in %) and does always statistically positively affect sales or market share (depending on variable used as dependent). Already the deal effect curve (functional dependence of sales/market share on discount amount) can't be generalized. van Heerde et al. (2001) using semi-parametrical analysis prove it to be S-shaped, but that's all that is known about it. Their research shows that small discount have no effects and a promotion threshold needs to be reached in order to get a marginal increase in sales. Same is true if an already hugely discounted item is discounted even more (they claim the reason for this to be saturation effect). Authors realize that there is no general type of deal curve, but they do not dig deeper into analyzing the determinants of its shape. Such an analysis would be very difficult to conduct in a real world as setting different discounts (while keeping other parameters equal) would fuzzy the consumer resulting in an unnatural behavior. Laboratory experimentation, as an alternative, also shows no results.

Beside the ever used discount amount, these are the determinants used in explanatory research for price promotions:

1. Use of other marketing-communication tools (display, feature, advertising,…) (Blattberg & Wisniewski, 1989; Kumar & Leone, 1988; Woodside & Waddle, 1975),
2. Determinants of product category (size of category, durability of products, consumption speed, necessity of the product),

3. Brand determinants (relative price, price variability, price promotions frequency, loyalty, knowledge of the brand), and

4. Consumer's demography (income, age, level of education, …)

Different research shows that:

- Share of budget has a negative impact,
- Possibility of storage of the product at home has a positive impact,
- Necessity to buy the product has a positive impact,
- Price variability has a negative impact,
- Demographics has no impact,
- High market share brands are less elastic to price promotions,
- High market share brands have a greater impact on low market share brands
- Price promotion has an impact on brand awareness (positive) and perceived brand quality (negative).

Overall there is a general need of a more systematic approach to modeling price promotions, although our opinion is, that some findings will never be generalized, as there are too many factors affecting a consumer's purchasing process to be all included into a finite model.

The remaining of the paper will show two models used on scanner panel data, that do exploratory research to confirm some generalization on price promotions that have been done on consumer panel data.

Scanner Data Sales and Share Model

Price promotions have been largely dealt with in the literature. Yet there are just a few generalizations made so far about this powerful marketing communication tool. The obvious effect that all authors who have studied price promotions noticed is quantity increase, during price promotions.

Inference studies about the decomposition of the sales promotion bump do not converge to a generalization or law, but end in radically different results. Most of these studies use consumer panel data, rich of demographical characteristics and consumers' purchasing history. Companies, that use such data, available from marketing research industry, usually complain that data is old and expensive.

At the turn of the millennium, information technology advances and an intensified struggle to focus marketing resources resulted in dramatic advances in POS data analysis. POS (point of sale) data is usually readily available in decision makers' information systems, and it only needs to be stored properly thus offering the marketer an almost real-time assessment of their marketing activities allowing for fast adjustments.

Our study doesn't deal with the forecasting power of POS data analysis models, but shows, if and how POS data can compete with panel data when doing exploratory research. Slovenia is still far behind developed countries (Holland and USA being the 1st) when we deal with marketing data availability, being also the only EU country without a consumer panel available for research. Advanced price promotion databases with POS data usually combine nationwide sales of each UPC (EAN) code available on the market within a category including marketing variables values per period (i.e. advertising activity, display activity, features activity...), while in Slovenia this seems to be a problem at the company level. Our research builds a sales promotion effect model on relatively poor data from a single grocery chain. Such a model is usable for a decision maker within that company to adjust price promotion activities inside his company, ignoring competitive activity. We are well aware that cross store sales aren't a neglectible factor when analyzing price promotions, we offset with lower data gathering costs – virtually equaling zero as data is available inside the company's information system.

Data Used

The data we use is daily sales per EAN code aggregated per week for 4 different FMCG (fast moving consumer goods): beer, water, tooth paste and tuna. We present different models – SCAN*PRO (Wittink, et al., 1988), van Heerde's model (van Heerde et al., 2004) and a market share model (Steenkamp & Dekimpe, 2005), showing their power in explaining sales promotion effects. Factors used are price level of analyzed brand, price level of competitive brands, display and feature activity of analyzed brand, display and feature activity of competitive brands, brand power of analyzed brand (brand power being measured by a commercial model called PGM). Advertising activity levels aren't available for Slovenian retail market in time series but only by advertiser's funds spent per month (on different brands the advertiser carry), making the data unusable.

The collected data was raw files in .csv format from a major retailer's internal database. It needed extensive manipulation (using SQL server 2008, Excel and SPSS) to eliminate noise, clear incomplete data, filling in missing dates (such as holidays) with zeros. All data received was daily sales aggregated among four stores. We used simple SQL to aggregate it into weekly sales. Weekly sales contain much less noise, especially for products that have lower sales figures.

The Two Models

We've developed two models both basing on SCAN*PRO:

1. Sales model (using relative increase in sales as dependent variable), and
2. Market share model (using market share as dependent variable).

Pro and cons of both methods are extensively discussed in Besanko et al. (1998). The models (in their simplified versions) are defined as (Cooper & Nakanishi, 1996; Wittink et al., 1988):

$$Q_{it} = \left(\frac{P_t}{\tilde{P}}\right)^{\beta_i} e^{\delta PGM} \prod_{l=1}^{n} \gamma_l^{D_{lt}} \prod_{t=1}^{T} \delta_{it}^{X_t} \lambda_i e^{v_{it}}, \qquad (1)$$

and

$$A_i = \exp(\alpha_i + \epsilon_i)\prod_{k=1}^{K} f_k(X_{ki})^{\beta_k}, \qquad (2)$$

$$s_i = A_i \bigg/ \sum_{j=1}^{m} A_j,$$

where Q_{it} is quantity of brand i sold in period t, $\left(\frac{P_t}{\tilde{P}}\right)$ is the price ration of the brand t in period t relative to an average price, *PGM* represents the power of the brand (could be in terms of brand knowledge, perceived quality,…), $\prod_{t=1}^{T}\delta_{it}^{X_t}$ is the week dummy, and $\left(\prod_{l=1}^{n}[\![\gamma_l^{D_{lt}}]\!]\right)$ represents price promotion, feature, display and other marketing variables dummies for the period t for brand I, other factors are regression coefficients.

The SCAN*PRO model, developed by Wittink, et al. (1988), has more than 2000 commercial applications, some representative research using this model can be found here Foekens, et al. (1999), Christen, et al. (1997), Koppale, et al. (1999) and van Heerde et al. (2001)

In equation (2) A_i is attraction of brand i, X_{ki} is the k-th marketing communication variable for brand i, f_k is a positive monotone transformation of X_{ki}, in our case a power function, s_i is the brand share for brand i. The market share model is an MCI model, alternatively one could use a MNL model (using exponential function as the mono-

Table 3. Change of elasticity among loyal and non-loyal customers. (Adapted from Mela, et al. (1997, 257-259)

1% increase in	% of change with loyal customers			% of change with non-loyal customers		
1. Mid-term effects	*Price*	*Price promotions*	*Non-price promotions*	*Price*	*Price promotions*	*Non-price promotions*
Advertizing	*n*	*n*	*n*	*.15*	*n*	*.10*
Price promotions	*-.37*	*n*	*n*	*-1.20*	*.08*	*n*
Non-price promotions	*.35*	*n*	*n*	*-4.37*	*N*	*n*
2. Long-term effects						
Advertizing	*n*	*n*	*n*	*.30*	*n*	*.15*
Price promotions	*-.61*	*n*	*n*	*-2.50*	*.11*	*n*
Non-price promotions	*.57*	*n*	*n*	*-9.02*	*N*	*n*

tone function). Results would be nearly the same with regression coefficients varying only a little.

Determinants Used

Both models analyze how different marketing settings affect the dependent variable (market share or product sales). Different research use very different independent variables, but all use discount (or. price). For the remaining determinants we will modify the original SCAN*PRO model which uses also sales promotion tools (Table 3), by adding determinants of brand knowledge.

Having conducted a meta analysis of more than 50 models examining price promotions effectiveness and determinants, we came to a conclusion, that many models' determinants are set based on data availability, which poses to be a big problem. Our data has been collected from an internal database of a major Slovenian retail chain. We analyzed 4 stores' (out of more than 150, because other stores' data didn't meet the criteria of acceptable quality) daily sales of 30 product categories for a period of 1 year (2007). Data about non-price promotions activities was provided in a separate file (from strategic marketing department) and has been prepared manually, enhancing the possibility of human error. Data

included catalogue promotion, special displays, different types of in-store promotions and permanent promotions (such as every day low price…). Determinants of brand strength have been supplied as static data from PGM (product group manager) model – a cross-sectional research with time period 1 year based on Aaker's (1991) and Keller's (1998) brand equity models. The PGM model uses variables such as recognition, perceived quality, etc. to determine the strength of a brand. Given the fact, that it is the only brand equity measure available on Slovenian market that analyzes more than 8000 products, we had no choice but to use this model.

Advertizing data as an important determinant of price promotion effectiveness is unavailable on Slovenian market. There is a research (namely Mediana IBO) that shows EUR expenditure per month per advertiser based on TV time. Since such a research doesn't show which brand is being advertised and shows no frequency/day data, it is useless for marketing dynamics analysis.

One of the major downturns of POS analysis is in its inability to include consumer heterogeneity and demographics in the analysis. On the other hand, POS models, as mentioned in the introduction, offer nearly real-time processing of the data, giving the brand manager a powerful tool for

Table 4. Descriptive statistics for the categories used

Category	No. of time series available	Av. length of price promotion	No. of promoted brands (promotions)	Average discount in %
Beer	154	14	6 (26)	7.22 (4.89)
Water	135	14	4 (24)	10.01 (5.03)
Tooth pasta	70	14	5 (13)	11.50 (8.23)
Tuna	76	16	4 (24)	17.06 (7.92)

decision making, and it can be used as a proof of the power of marketing promotion activities. In fact, it was the unavailability of a consumer panel in Slovenia that has motivated us to analyze POS data for explanatory and forecasting purposes.

All the data from different sources was collected and sorted in MS SQL 2008 and exported to SPSS format where it was analyzed statistically. Table 4 shows descriptive statistics for the data analyzed. A total of 435 time series of 365 days aggregated to 52 weeks have been analyzed split into four categories – beer, water, tooth paste and tuna. A typical hypermarket chain has several contemporary ongoing sales promotions (whether price inducted or non-price), however we only analyzed catalogue sales which last 14 days (only in the tuna category, there were some brands being put in a 30-90 days every day low price promotions – thus the 16 days average length).

An average of 5 brands were promoted in each category (in reality there were more, but brands with a market share below 5% were eliminated from the analysis, because their time series were mostly filled with zeroes. An average brand was promoted 3-4 times in one year, topping 8 times with a tuna brand.

The models we propose are inference models. Initially we've conducted a preliminary univariate analysis presented in Table 5. Quantity sales in price promotion period (T) have been compared to sales in two periods (T-2), one period (T-1) before and one period (T+1) and two periods (T+2) after, where T-2 served as base sales. Brands with multiple promotion sales in the analyzed time span have been eliminated.

Table 6 shows t-test values for the above statistics showing statistically significant differences among period T and other periods, confirm-

Table 5. Univariate analysis of the price promotion

Category	T-2	T-1	T	T+1	T+2
Beer	1	1.01	**2.64**	1.55	1.17
	(0)	(0.22)	**(2.03)**	(0.72)	(0.68)
Water	1	1.09	**1.87**	1.24	1.08
	(0.17)	(0.17)	**(0.64)**	(0.45)	(0.41)
Tooth paste	1	1.19	**3.75**	1.16	1.20
	(0)	(0.56)	**(3.72)**	(0.73)	(0.79)
Tuna	1.00	1.12	**5.75**	1.80	1.19
	(0)	(0.49)	**(6.50)**	(2.08)	(2.03)

Table 6. T-test statistics for the univariate analysis

Category	T-2	T-1	T	T+1	T+2
Beer	1 *(p <.000)*	1.01 *(p <.000)*	**2.64**	1.55 *(p <.000)*	1.17 *(p <.000)*
Water	1 *(p<.000)*	1.09 *(p<.000)*	**1.87**	1.24 *(p<.000)*	1.08 *(p<.000)*
Tooth paste	1 *(p<.000)*	1.19 *(p<.000)*	**3.75**	1.16 *(p<.000)*	1.20 *(p<.000)*
Tuna	1 *(p<.000)*	1.12 *(p<.000)*	**5.75**	1.80 *(p<.01)*	1.19 *(p<.000)*

ing the generalization that for all brand categories during the sales promotion period there is a short term increase of sales. T-test statistics between other periods (seeking for post- and pre- promotions dips) show no consistence, thus from the univariate analysis it was impossible to determine the existence of any kind of pre- and post- promotion dips.

In multivariate inference statistics we used several variants of the quantity and share models. The first^t model used was intended to test non-price promotion tools effects. We used the model in equation 1:

$$Q = \left(\frac{P_t}{\tilde{P}}\right)^{\beta_i} \left(\prod_{l=1}^{n} [\![\gamma_l^{D_{lt}}]\!]\right) \left(\prod_{t=1}^{T} \delta_{it}^{X_t}\right) \lambda_i e^{v_{it}},$$

where β_i is the regressor coeficient for the price variance (discount), is the regressor coefficient for catalogue sales, $\ln \gamma_2$ is the regressor for instore promotion, $\ln \gamma_3$ is the regression for EDLP (every day low price) and $\ln \gamma_4$ is the

regressor for a discount given for the use of loyalty card.

Results are shown in Table 7. In order to solve the equation 1, a log -log transformation has been applied to get a simple OLS regression equation:

$$\ln Q_{it} - \ln \lambda_i = \beta \ln \left(\frac{P_t}{\tilde{P}}\right) + \sum_{l=1}^{n} D_{lt} \ln \gamma_l + \sum_{t=1}^{T} X_t \ln \delta_{it} + v_{it}$$

(3)

Elasticities are easily calculated:

$$\frac{dQ}{Q} \bigg/ \frac{dp}{P} = \frac{\beta \left(\frac{P_t}{\tilde{P}}\right)^{\beta-1} \left(\frac{1}{\tilde{P}}\right) dp}{\left(\frac{P_t}{\tilde{P}}\right)^{\beta}} \bigg/ \frac{dp}{P} = \beta$$

(4)

For γ_i, not being a continuous function, elasticities can't be calculated, but the values of the regressors shows conceptually a similar value.

Table 7. Regression coefficients for the SCAN*PRO model

Category	β_i	$\ln\gamma_1$	$\ln\gamma_2$	$\ln\gamma_3$	$\ln\gamma_4$
Beer	-2,90	0,146	--	--	
Water	-2,05	0,676	--	--	
Tooth paste	-3,28	0,497	0,165	--	0,113
Tuna	-1,34	0,988	--	0,056	1,301

Table 8. Correlation matrix for the PGM factors

	Awareness	Knowledge	Choice	Usage	Primary usage	Index of success	Power of the brand
Awareness	1	,991	,933	,923	,903	,967	,955
Knowledge		1	,971	,964	,950	,992	,984
Choice			1	,997	,997	,994	,997
Usage				1	,999	,990	,994
Primary usage					1	,983	,988
Index of success						1	,998
Power of the brand							1

Result show that a 1% increase in price would lower the quantities from 1, 34 (for tuna) to 2, 9 (for beer). Catalogue has a positive impact, while other marketing promotion tools have positive (as expected) but non-significant effects. Due to the lack of single brand promotion frequency, the heterogeneity of brands couldn't be taken into account. It is important to acknowledge, as we mentioned, that the elasticity β is not static and vary considerably with different discounts, its function taking an S-shape. Our β is an aggregated average value. For forecasting purposes we propose to include a varying parameter for β - use semiparametric analysis to determine its value for different discounts, although we advise to use good data with plenty of different discount settings – a very difficult task to achieve. Our categories had a discrete distribution of discounts that in no way would be usable for such analysis.

Brand Equity Factor

As a factor of brand heterogeneity we included into the equation brand equity factors from PGM. The new linearized equation is:

$$\ln Q_{it} - \ln \lambda_i = \delta PGM + \beta_i \ln\left(\frac{P_t}{\overline{P}}\right) + \sum_{l=1}^{n} D_{lt} \ln \gamma_l + v_{it}$$

$$(5)$$

where the new term δPGM represents a factor from PGM. We used several determinants of brand equity from the model, namely: awareness, knowledge, choice, usage, primary usage, index of success and power of the brand, the latest two being a linear combination of the former. Table 8 shows the correlation matrix between the factors, making our choice of the factor easy – use whichever.

Model results are shown in Table 9. The last two factors have not been analyzed as being a linear combination of the former ones.

Our next task was to try to find out the decomposition of the price promotion increase. We used a methor proposed by van Heerde et al. (2004) basing on a system of 4 equations:

$$OBS_{jt} = \alpha_j + \sum \beta_i X_i$$

$$CBS_t = \alpha'_j + \sum \beta'_i X'_i \text{ in}$$

$$TCS_{jt} = \alpha''_j + \sum \beta''_i X''_i$$

$$PPCS_{jt} = \alpha'''_j + \sum \beta'''_i X'''_i, \qquad (6)$$

where OBS_{jt} means sales of brand j in time t (*own brand sales*), CBS_t means cross brand sales in time t, TCS_{jt} is total category sales and $PPCS_{jt}$ shows

Table 9. Regression coefficient δ in equation 3

Product group	Awareness	Knowledge	Choice	Usage	Primary usage
Beer	**-,411**	**-,266**	-,066*	-,041*	-,482*
Water	**-,684**	**-,623**	**-,669**	**-,722**	**-1.037**
Tooth paste	**,155**	,316*	,749*	,--*	,--*
Tuna	**-,238**	**-,244**	,007*	,097*	,243*
Beer	**-,524**	**-,945**	-1,43*	-,845*	--*

the effect of price promotion pre- and post- promotion period (*pre- and post- category sales*). The equation connecting the system is:

$$OBS = CBS + TCS + PPCS, \qquad (7)$$

Where both *OBS* in *TCS* are defined as – (minus) sales. van Heerde et al. (2004) show that from equations 6 and 7 we get:

$$\beta_{ob,j} = \beta_{cb,j} + \beta_{ce,j} + \beta_{cp,j}, \qquad (8)$$

In other words the effect on the brand equals to the sum of brand switching and category increase. For the purpose of the analysis all but 5 biggest brands have been eliminated from the analysis. Percentage increase in sales has been used as dependent variable, to normalize the differences in quantities sold per brand. Results are shown in Table 10.

As in other analyses different effects vary considerably, although it is within the boundaries of other studies. van Heerde et al. (2004) pragmatically claim an even split of 1/3-1/3-1/3 be-

tween the three effects, a hazardous claim tough. For the retailer the most important regressor is the $\beta_{ce,j}$ that represents *TCS* (total category sales), while for brand managers, brand switching (when not cannibalization) is also an important determinant of stealing customers to their competition.

To test more directly a possible presence of a pre- or post- promotion dip, we couldn't rely on simple t-test statistics, but applied a time series analysis on daily data. We only did this for the beer category, as this category had far more daily sales than other categories analyzed, giving it a much better statistics than other categories.

Time series regression analysis (compared to normal regression analysis) requires a specific time-ordered equidistant data. Our interval was, as mentioned 1 day. We used ARMA modeling and found out (with PACF analysis) the model to be:

$$(1-L^7)(1-\varphi L)y_t = \mu + (1-L^7)(1+\theta L)\varepsilon_t \qquad (9)$$

where *L* represents the lag operator ($Ly_t = y_{t-1}$). Equation 9 clearly shows that sales in time t are correlated with sales from 7 days ago and the day

Table 10. Decomposition of the promotion sales increase

Category	$\beta_{ob,j}$	$\beta_{cb,j}$	$\beta_{ce,j}$	$\beta_{cp,j}$	$\beta_{cb,j}$	$\beta_{ce,j}$	$\beta_{cp,j}$
Beer	2,74	0,72	1,58	0,44	26,28%	57,66%	16,06%
Water	1,88	1,1	0,15	0,63	58,51%	7,98%	33,51%
Tooth paste	4,94	2,2	1,9	0,84	44,53%	38,46%	17,00%
Tuna	2,37	0,25	1,5	0,62	10,55%	63,29%	26,16%

before. A 7 days lag show a weekly pattern, while one day ago serves as normalization (if yesterday 1000 cans were sold, it is unrealistic to expect 10 or 100.000 to be sold today).

Applying the stochastic time series model to the deterministic variables we get the following regression model:

$$y_t = \mu + \varphi_1 y_{t-1} + \varphi_7 y_{t-7} + \varphi_8 y_{t-8} + \varepsilon_t + \theta_1 \varepsilon_{t-1} + \theta_7 \varepsilon_{t-7} + \theta_8 \varepsilon_{t-8} + \delta NEWYEAR + \omega SALESP_t + \omega_1 SALESP_{t-1} + \omega_2 SALESP_{t-2} + \lambda TEMPERATURE \qquad (10)$$

where y_t represents sales of brand y in time t, dummy NEWYEAR represents all holidays (closing dates) in the given year, TEMPERATURE is the outside temperature and SALESP is the sales price in time t. The model is not aggregated and analysis has been conducted for each time series available in the beer category. Should there be any pre- or post- promotion dip, $SALESP_{t-1}$ and $SALESP_{t-2}$ would be statistically significant.

All coefficients are statistically significant except SALESP and SALESP(-1). After eliminating these two variables also SALESP(-2) became statistically not-significant, which confirms that no long-term effects are to be expected from sales promotions. A two days only effect could be seen as too short for any meaningful significance and could catch the post-promotion dip effect (diminishing of sales immediately after the price promotion period due to stockpiling). We have tried to regress the sales by several lagged SALESP, none has significant statistics. By eliminating the terms SALESP(-1) and SALESP(-2) we get the equation:

$$y_t = 164 + 0.96 \cdot y_{t-1} + 0.98 \cdot y_{t-7} - 0.96 \cdot y_{t-8} + \varepsilon_t - 0.84 \cdot \varepsilon_{t-1} - 0.85 \cdot \varepsilon_{t-7} + 0.68 \cdot \varepsilon_{t-8} + 609 \cdot NEWYEAR + 132 \cdot SALESP + 4.93 \cdot TEMPERATURE \qquad (11)$$

R2 for the model in equation 11 was 0.67. It is of course beyond the scope of our research to draw any generalizations for post- and pre- promotion dips. Our research only confirms that daily sales

data (estimated as too noisy in other papers) can give useful conclusions.

Our second model is an MCI share model. It has some advantages over the quantity model. MS models are an aggregation of individual-level logit models used for consumer panels (Berry, et al., 1995). Such models are also not vulnerable to seasonal changes, as market share has a far lower variation if any through the seasons in comparison to quantity sold (i.e. beer product category sales increase considerably during hot months, but market shares for different brands do not). This fact, eliminates all weekly and season dummies from the research.

Our model used log(price), catalogue sales (as dummy) and brands (as dummies) in the regression analysis. Findings are shown in Table 11.

MCI model has (compared to quantity SCAN*PRO model) an average increase of .20 in R2 giving it more accuracy. Our findings are that most of the brand specific dummies were statistically significant and their correlation with the PGM (any variable) was positive and statistically significant. The regressor for these dummies can be understood as the utility of each brand. For the same brand sold in different packaging sizes, bigger packages have a higher value of the regressor which is consistent, as the consumer gets more of the item, usually for less price/unit.

The MCI model also gives the possibility to analyze the asymmetry of effects between brands (if brand A is on sales promotion, how this affects brand B sales and vice versa). Research shows there is asymmetry (meaning that if brand A has

Table 11. Regression coefficients of the MCI model

Category	Ln(price)	Sig.	Catalogue promotion	Sig.	R2
Beer	-1,948	.000	.380	.350	.830
Water	-1.165	.000	.271	.000	.851
Tooth paste	-1,344	.000	.026	.507	.824
Tuna	-1,958	.000	1.527	.000	.735

Table 12. Cross-brand regressors

Category beer		Brand 1	Brand 2	Brand 3	
	Brand 1	-9,73**	4,4**	8,34*	
	Brand 2	1,4*	-6,1**	7,5	
	Brand 3	1,1*	1,3	-17,1**	
Water		Brand 1	Brand 2	Brand 3	Brand 4	Brand 5
	Brand 1	-2,118	-	3,21	3,7	5,2
	Brand 2	-	-55,52	12,3	6	6,6
	Brand 3	7,028	5,12	-36,26	-	3,433
	Brand 4	0,006	1,23	-	-1,161	-
	Brand 5	1,017	0,34	-	1,995	-4,13
Milk		Brand 1	Brand 2	Brand3	
	Brand 1	-1,6**	10,5**	4**	
	Brand 2	1,05*	-0,55**	,9*	
	Brand 3	5,4**	2,36	-3,3**	

* $p<0.05$

a certain effect on brand B, when on sales promotion, the effect is different on A when B is on sales). Asymmetry is gainful for powerful brands (brands that have higher brand equity affect lower brand equity brands more). The regressors from equation 11 show the following asymmetry among brands (tested for beer, milk and water).

In Table 12 a positive coefficient shows the effect of brand in row x on brand in column y (for example in beer category – brand 1 has an elasticity of 1,4 on brand 2 sales promotion meaning that if price of brand 2 goes down by 1%, sales quantities of brand 1 go down by 1,4%). Of course the effects calculated is an average, again the cross-deal curve has an S-shape.

FUTURE RESEARCH

In our research we compared POS scanner data analysis with consumer panels. We show that most of the findings from consumer panel research can be analyzed also using POS data which is cheaper and more readily available than consumer panels (in-house vs. need to purchase a syndicated re-

search). We used two diffused models from econometrics the market share model and the purchase quantity model (SCAN*PRO). Both of them are multiplicative regression models that are easily linearised and processed with regression analysis.

Our analysis represents one of the first steps in terms of use of scanner time series in price promotion analysis. As in consumer panels, the whole field of price promotion analysis needs consolidations. The research done by various authors is too different in terms of data used, categories analyzed, methodology used and results found. Except for a few generalizations (price promotion quantity increase and its three sources), most of papers' results vary considerably. A more systematic approach accounting for all known determinants, using more than just a few brand categories is needed. Such a research approach of course poses a great problem in data collection and its quality.

Much effort has been spent on researching grocery or FMCG products, but there are few (van Heerde & Bijmolt, 2005), studies that research durable goods. It is unclear if products developed on grocery products could be applied also to non-grocery product categories. Our expectations are that deceleration effects (post promotion dips) are stronger than in grocery categories.

The current state of the art has been focusing on explanatory research, while forecasting models aren't really yet usable, thus a (brand) managers, hasn't yet been given a really usable tool for her decision making.

Determinants used in the current models are only a few (discount level, display, feature being among the most common). Other types of promotions haven't been extensively researched (such as rebates, bounded sales ...).

Our research included brand equity as an alternative to brand heterogeneity in the scanner data models. The model used (PGM) is a very primitive brand equity model (as the reader can see most of the variables used in the model are highly correlated). Our rationale is of course that PGM is at the moment the only available model providing data for so many different product categories. In this field a more extensive research is needed, to find out which determinants of brand equity, does affect the effectiveness of sales promotion the most.

At the end, no research has been conducted yet for web, online sales, which pose a special case in promotion analysis, due to its specific (click pass-through, e-mail effectiveness ...) purchasing process.

CONCLUSION

In this chapter we present two models for forecasting sales promotions effects based on given setting of initial determinants – the modified SCAN*PRO and the MNL model. Both models are useful for retailers before a price promotion actually starts to determine its total effect in terms of quantity or market share. In times, where price wars between big hypermarket chains are daily routine, managers start looking for basic profit-

ability of such promotions, as they can't afford to sell many items below certain profitability or even below cost. Since the competition is heavily selling using price promotions, managers of a hypermarket chain is also forced to use this marketing communication method.

Our models give a brand (or store) manager a relatively simple and powerful tool with which they can forecast price promotion effects on sales (and/or marketshare), giving them an early warning tool with which they can fine tune the discount, point of purchase activities and other promotion tools to maximize the effects while investing the lowest budget.

REFERENCES

Aaker, D. A. (1991). *Managing brand equity*. New York: The Free Press.

Abraham, M. M., & Lodish, L. M. (1987). An automated promotion evaluation system. *Marketing Science*, 6(2), 101–123. doi:10.1287/mksc.6.2.101

Ailawadi, K. L., & Neslin, S. A. (1998). The effect of promotion on consumption: Buying more and consuming it faster. *Journal of Marketing*, 65(1), 71–89. doi:10.1509/jmkg.65.1.71.18132

Assmus, G., Farley, J. U., & Leehmann, D. R. (1984). How advertising affects sales: A meta analysis of econometric results. *JMR, Journal of Marketing Research*, 21(February), 65–74. doi:10.2307/3151793

Assuncao, J. L., & Meyer, R. J. (1993). The rational effect of price promotions on sales and consumption. *Management Science*, 39(5), 517–535. doi:10.1287/mnsc.39.5.517

Bawa, K., & Shoemaker, R. W. (1987). The effects of a direct mail coupon on brand choice behavior. *JMR, Journal of Marketing Research*, 24(November), 370–376. doi:10.2307/3151384

Bell, R. D., Chiang, J., & Padmanabhan, V. (1999). The decomposition of promotional response: An empirical generalization. *Marketing Science, 18*(4), 504–526. doi:10.1287/mksc.18.4.504

Bell, R. D., Iyer, G., & Padmonbhan, V. (2002). Price competitoin under stockpiling and flexible consumption. *Marketing Research Journal, 37*(Aug.).

Berry, S., Levinsohn, J., & Pakes, A. (1995). Automobile prices in market equilibrium. *Econometrica, 63*(4), 841–890. doi:10.2307/2171802

Besanko, D., Gupta, S., & Jain, D. C. (1998). Logit demand estimation under competitive pricing behavior: An equilibrium framework. *Management Science, 44*(11, Part 1 of 2), 1533-1547.

Blattberg, R. C., Briesch, R., & Fox, E. J. (1995). How promotions work. *Marketing Science, 14*(3), G122–G133. doi:10.1287/mksc.14.3.G122

Blattberg, R. C., Eppen, G. D., & Lieberman, J. (1981). A theoretical and empirical evaluation of price deals for consumer nondurables. *Journal of Marketing, 45*, 116–129. doi:10.2307/1251725

Blattberg, R. C., & Wisniewski, J. (1989). Price-induced patterns of competition. *Marketing Science, 8*(4), 291–309. doi:10.1287/mksc.8.4.291

Bucklin, R. E., & Gupta, S. (1992). Brand choice, purchase incidence, and segmentation: An integrated approach. *Marketing Science, 18*(3), 247–273. doi:10.1287/mksc.18.3.247

Bucklin, R. E., & Gupta, S. (1999). Commercial use of UPC scanner data: Industry and academic perspectives. *Marketing Science, 18*(Fall), 247–273. doi:10.1287/mksc.18.3.247

Bucklin, R. E., & Gupta, S. (2000). Commercial adoption of advances in the analysis of scanner data. *Marketing Science, 15*.

Bucklin, R. E., & Lattin, J. M. (1992). A model of product category competition among grocery retailers. *Journal of Retailing, 68*(Fall), 271–293.

Christen, M., Gupta, S., Porter, J. C., Staelin, R., & Wittink, D. R. (1997). Using market level data to understand promotional effects in a nonlinear model. *Journal of Marketing Research, 34*(3 (August)), 322-334.

Conchar, M. P., Crask, M. R., & Zinkhan, G. M. (2005). Market valuation models of the effect of advertising and promotional spending: A review and meta-analysis. *Journal of the Academy of Marketing Science, 33*(4), 445–460. doi:10.1177/0092070305277693

Cooper, L. G., & Nakanishi, M. (1996). *Market-share analysis: Evaluating competitive marketing effectiveness*. Norwell, MA: Kluwer Academic Publishers.

Currim, I. S., & Schneider, L. G. (1991). A taxonomy of consumer purchase strategies in a promotion intensive environment. *Marketing Science, 10*(2), 91–110. doi:10.1287/mksc.10.2.91

Dekimpe, M. G., & Hannsens, D. M. (1995). The persistence of marketing effects on sales. *Marketing Science, 14*(1), 1–21. doi:10.1287/mksc.14.1.1

Dekimpe, M. G., & Hannsens, D. M. (2000). Time-Series Models in Marketing: Past, Present and Future. *International Journal of Research in Marketing, 17*.

Dodson, J. A., Tybout, A. M., & Sternhal, B. (1978). The effect of deals and deal retraction on brand switching. *JMR, Journal of Marketing Research, 15*(1), 78–81. doi:10.2307/3150402

Foekens, E. W., Leeflang, P. S. H., & Wittink, D. R. (1999). Varying parameter models to accommodate dynamic promotion effects. *Journal of Econometrics, 89*, 249–268. doi:10.1016/S0304-4076(98)00063-3

Grover, R., & Srinivasan, V. (1992). Evaluating the multiple effects of retail promotions on brand loyal and brand switching segments. *Journal of Marketing Resarch, 29*(Feb), 76–89. doi:10.2307/3172494

Guadagni, P. M., & Little, J. D. C. (1983). A logit model of brand choice calibrated on scanner data. *Marketing Science, 2*(3), 203–238. doi:10.1287/mksc.2.3.203

Gupta, S. (1988). Impact of sales promotions on when, what and how much to buy. *Journal of Marketing Reserach, 25,* 342–355. doi:10.2307/3172945

Jedidi, K., Mela, C., & Gupta, S. (1999). Managing advertising and promotion for long-run profitability. *Marketing Science, 19*(1), 1–22. doi:10.1287/mksc.18.1.1

Keller, K. L. (1998). *Strategic brand management - building, managing and measuring brand equity.* New Jersey: Prentice Hall.

Kopalle, P. K., Mela, C., & Marsh, L. (1999). The dynamic effect of discounting on sales: Empirical analysis and normative pricing implications. *Marketing Science, 18*(3), 317–332. doi:10.1287/mksc.18.3.317

Krishna, A. (1994). The impact of dealing patterns on purchase behavior. *Marketing Science, 13*(4), 351–373. doi:10.1287/mksc.13.4.351

Kumar, V., & Leone, R. P. (1988). Measuring the effect of retail store promotions on brand and store substitution. *Journal of Marketing Resarch, 25*(May), 178–185. doi:10.2307/3172649

Lattin, J. M., & Bucklin, R. E. (1989). Reference effects of pPrice and promotion on brand choice behavior. *JMR, Journal of Marketing Research, 26*(August), 299–310. doi:10.2307/3172902

Macé, S., & Neslin, S. A. (2004). The determinants of pre-andpost-promotion dips in sales of frequently purchased goods. *JMR, Journal of Marketing Research, 41*(August).

Martinez-Ruiz, M. P., Molla-Descals, A., Gomez-Borja, M. A., & Rojo Alvarez, J. L. (2006). Evaluating temporary retail price discounts using semiparametric regression. *Journal of Product and Brand Management, 15*(1), 75–80. doi:10.1108/10610420610650891

Mayhew, G. E., & Winer, R. S. (1992). An empirical analysis of internal and external reference prices using scanner data. *The Journal of Consumer Research, 19*(June), 62–70. doi:10.1086/209286

Mela, K., Gupta, S., & Lehmann, D. R. (1997). The long-term impact of promotion and advertising on consumer brand choice. *JMR, Journal of Marketing Research, 34,* 248–261. doi:10.2307/3151862

Mela, K., Jedidi, K., & Bowman, D. (1998). The long-term impact of promotions on consumer stockpiling behavior. *JMR, Journal of Marketing Research, 35*(May), 250–262. doi:10.2307/3151852

Moriarty, M. M. (1985). Retail promotional effects of intra- and interbrand sales performance. *Journal of Retailing, 61*(3), 27–47.

Narasimhan, C., Neslin, S. A., & Sen, S. K. (1996). Promotions elasticity's and category characteristics. *Journal of Marketing, 60*(2), 17–30. doi:10.2307/1251928

Neslin, S. A., Henderson, C., & Quelch, J. (1985). Consumer promotions and the acceleration of product purchases. *Marketing Science, 4*(2), 147–165. doi:10.1287/mksc.4.2.147

Neslin, S. A., & Schneider Stone, L. G. (1996). Consumer inventory sensitivity and the post-promotion dip. *Marketing Letters, 7*(1), 77–94. doi:10.1007/BF00557313

Nijs, V. R., Dekimpe, M. G., Steenkamp, J.-B. E. M., & Hannsens, D. M. (2001). The category-demand effects of price promotions. *Marketing Science, 20*(1), 1–22. doi:10.1287/mksc.20.1.1.10197

Ortmeyer, G., Lattin, J. M., & Montgomery, D. B. (1991). Individual differences in response to consumer promotions. *International Journal of Research in Marketing, 8*, 169–186. doi:10.1016/0167-8116(91)90010-5

Raju, J. S. (1992). The effect of price promotions on variability in product category sales. *Marketing Science, 3*, 207–220. doi:10.1287/mksc.11.3.207

Srinivasan, K., Pauwels, K., Hannsens, D. M., & Dekimpe, M. G. (2004). Do promotions benefit manufacturers, retailers, or both? *Management Science, 50*(5, May 2004), 617-629.

Steenkamp, J.-B. E. M., & Dekimpe, M. G. (2005). The increasing power of store brands: Building loyalty and market share. *Long Range Planning, 30*(6), 917–930. doi:10.1016/S0024-6301(97)00077-0

Steenkamp, J.-B. E. M., Nijs, V. R., Hannsens, D. M., & Dekimpe, M. G. (2005). Competitive reactions to advertising and promotion attacks. *Marketing Science, 24*(1, Winter 2005), 35-54.

Tellis, G. J. (1988). The price sensitivity of selective demand. A meta-analysis of econometric models of sales. *JMR, Journal of Marketing Research, 25*, 391–404. doi:10.2307/3172944

van Heerde, H. J. (1999). *Models for sales promotion effects based on store-level scanner data.* Ijsel, The Netherlands: Labyrint Publication.

van Heerde, H. J., & Bijmolt, T. H. A. (2005). Decomposing the promotional revenue bump for loaylty program members versus non-members. *Journal of Marketing Resarch, 42*(November), 443–457. doi:10.1509/jmkr.2005.42.4.443

van Heerde, H. J., Leefland, P. S. H., & Wittink, D. R. (2001). Semiparametric analysis to estimate the deal effect curve. *JMR, Journal of Marketing Research, 37*(May), 197–215. doi:10.1509/jmkr.38.2.197.18842

van Heerde, H. J., Leefland, P. S. H., & Wittink, D. R. (2004). Decomposing the sales promotion bump with store data. *Marketing Science, 23*(3), 317–334. doi:10.1287/mksc.1040.0061

van Heerde, H. J., Leeflang, P. S. H., & Wittink, D. R. (2002). *Flexible decomposition of price promotion effects using store-level scanner data.* Cambridge, MA: Marketing Science Institute.

Walters, R. G. (1991). Assessing the impact of retail price promotions on product substitution, complementary purchase, and interstore sales displacement. *Journal of Marketing, 55*(2), 17–28. doi:10.2307/1252234

Walters, R. G., & MacKenzie, S. B. (1988). A structural equations analysis of the impact of price promotions on store performance. *JMR, Journal of Marketing Research, 25*(1), 51–63. doi:10.2307/3172924

Walters, R. G., & Rinne, H. J. (1986). An empirical investigation into the impact of price promotions on retail store performance. *Journal of Retailing, 62*(3), 237–266.

Wittink, D. R., Addona, M. J., Hawkes, W. J., & Porter, J. C. (1988). *SCAN*PRO: The estimation, validation and use of promotional effects based on scanner data.* Cornell University.

Woodside, A. G., & Waddle, G. L. (1975). Sales effects of in-store advertising. *Journal of Advertising Research, 15*(3), 29–33.

Yeshin, T. (2006). *Sales Promotion.* New York: International Thomson Business Press.

KEY TERMS AND DEFINITIONS

Sales Promotion: A decrease in price usually short-term

Marketing Budgeting: Process of setting the amount of money spent for marketing activities on a yearly basis.

Scanner Level Data: Data of product sales that is generated by cashier UPC/EAN scanners and stored on a database server.

SCAN*PRO Model: A sales response model developed by AC Nielsen to study the effects of marketing promotion tools on sales.

MCI Model: Multiplicative competitive interaction model used for market share analysis.

Time Series Analysis: Regression analysis that uses past and future data for regression analysis.

Promotion Effectiveness: A measure for measuring the successfulness of promotion activity.

Compilation of References

Aaker, D. A. (1991). *Managing brand equity*. New York: The Free Press.

Abernathy, K. Q. (2001). *Speech to WCA*, June 25. Retrieved July 13, 2009, from http://www.fcc.gov/Speeches/Abernathy/2001/spkqa101.html

Abidogum, O. (2005). *Data mining, fraud detection and mobile telecommunications: Call patterns analysis with unsupervised neural networks*. PhD Thesis, University of the Western Cape, Capetown, South Africa.

Abouzeedan, A., & Busler, M. (2004). Typology analysis of performance models of small and medium size enterprises (SMEs). *Journal of International Entrepreneurship, 2*(1-2), 155–177. doi:10.1023/B:JIEN.0000026911.03396.2d

Abraham, M. M., & Lodish, L. M. (1987). An automated promotion evaluation system. *Marketing Science, 6*(2), 101–123. doi:10.1287/mksc.6.2.101

Abumustafa, N. I. (2006). Development of an early warning model for currency crises in emerging economies: An empirical study among Middle Eastern countries. *International Journal of Management, 23*(3), 403.

ACFE. (2008). *2008 report to the nation on occupational fraud and abuse*. Austin, TX: Association of Certified Fraud Examiners.

Acs, Z., & Audretsch, D. (1987). Innovation, market structure and firm size. *The Review of Economics and Statistics, 69*(4), 567–575. doi:10.2307/1935950

Acs, Z., Carlsson, B., & Thurik, A. R. (1996). *Small business in the modern economy*. Oxford, UK: Basil Blackwell Publishers.

Adam, N. R., & Wormann, J. C. (1989). Security-control methods for statistical databases: A comparative study. *ACM Computing Surveys, 21*(4), 515–556. doi:10.1145/76894.76895

ADBI Institute. (2010), *Enterprise risk management during the global financial crisis: Sharing global experience*. Presented at 2nd Annual Thought Leadership Conference, Bejing.

Agrawal, R., & Srikant, R. (2000). Privacy-preserving data mining. *2000 ACM SIGMOD International Conference Management of Data, 29*(2), (pp.439-450). New York: ACM Press.

Ailawadi, K. L., & Neslin, S. A. (1998). The effect of promotion on consumption: Buying more and consuming it faster. *Journal of Marketing, 65*(1), 71–89. doi:10.1509/jmkg.65.1.71.18132

Albrecht, W., Howe, K., & Romney, M. (1984). *Deterring fraud: The internal auditor's perspective*. Altamonte Springs, FL: Institute of Internal Auditors Research Foundation.

Alfaro, E., Garcia, N., Gamez, M., & Elizondo, D. (2008). Bankruptcy forecasting: An empirical comparison of AdaBoost and neural network. *Decision Support Systems, 45*(1), 110–122. doi:10.1016/j.dss.2007.12.002

Alker, H. R. (2009). *Conflict Early Warning Systems*. Received August 1, 2009 from http://www.usc.edu/dept/LAS/ir/cews/

Altman, E., & Hotchkiss, E. (2006). *Corporate financial distress and bankruptcy* (3rd ed.). New York: John Wiley & Sons.

Altman, E. I., Haldeman, G., & Narayanan, P. (1977). Zeta Analysis: A new model to identify bancrupcy risk of corporations. *Journal of Banking & Finance*, (June): 29–54. doi:10.1016/0378-4266(77)90017-6

Altman, E. (1968). Financial ratios, discriminant analysis and the prediction of corporate bankruptcy. *The Journal of Finance*, *23*(3), 589–609. doi:10.2307/2978933

Anghel, I. (2000). Predictia falimentului intreprinderilor romanesti – Scorul Anghel. *Tribuna Economica*, *40*, 33–35.

Apley, W. (2003). Principal componets and factor analysis. In Ye, N. (Ed.), *The handbook of data mining*. Upper Saddle River, NJ: Lawrence Erlbaum Associates Publisher.

Apoteker, T., & Barthelemy, S. (2005). Predicting financial crises in emerging markets using a composite non-parametric model. *Emerging Markets Review*, *6*(4), 363–375. doi:10.1016/j.ememar.2005.09.002

Arias, C. A., Martinez, A. C., & Gracia, J. (2003). *Capital structure and sensitivity in SME definition: A panel data investigation*. Retrieved December, 2009, from http://ssrn.com/abstract=549082.

Artis, M., Ayuso, M., & Guillen, M. (2002). Detection of automobile insurance fraud with discrete choice models and misclassified claims. *The Journal of Risk and Insurance*, *69*, 325–340. doi:10.1111/1539-6975.00022

Assmus, G., Farley, J. U., & Leehmann, D. R. (1984). How advertising affects sales: A meta analysis of econometric results. *JMR, Journal of Marketing Research*, *21*(February), 65–74. doi:10.2307/3151793

Assuncao, J. L., & Meyer, R. J. (1993). The rational effect of price promotions on sales and consumption. *Management Science*, *39*(5), 517–535. doi:10.1287/mnsc.39.5.517

Atallah, M., Elmagarmid, A., Ibrahim, M., Bertino, E., & Verykios, V. (1999). Disclosure limitation of sensitive rules. In *Proceedings of the 1999 Workshop on Knowledge and Data Engineering Exchange*, (pp. 45-52). Los Alamitos, CA: IEEE Computer Society.

Audretsch, D., van der Horst, R., Kwaak, T., & Thurik, R. (2009). *First section of the annual report on EU small and medium-sized enterprises*. Retrieved December, 2009, from http://ec.europa.eu/enterprise/policies/sme/files/craft/sme_perf_review/doc_08/spr08_anual_reporten.pdf

Austrac E-learning. *(2009)*. Introduction to Money Laundering. *Retrieved November 27, 2009, from* http://www.austrac.gov.au/elearning/mod1/mod_1_money_laundering_11.html

Ayres, R. U. (2000). On forecasting discontinuities. *Technological Forecasting and Social Change*, *65*, 81–97. doi:10.1016/S0040-1625(99)00101-8

Babakus, E., & Mangold, G. (1992). Adapting the servqual scale to hospital services: an empirical investigation. *Health Services Research Journal*, 767-786.

Baesens, B., Mues, C., Martens, D., & Vanthienen, J. (2009). 50 years of data mining in OR: Upcoming trends and chalanges. *Journal of the Orepational Research Society*, *60*, 16–23. doi:10.1057/jors.2008.171

Bailesteanu, G. (1998). *Diagnostic, risc si eficienta in afaceri*. Timisoara, Romania: Editura Mirton.

Balcaen, S., & Ooghe, H. (2006). 35 years of studies on business failure: An overview of the classic statistical methodologies and their related problems. *The British Accounting Review*, *38*(1), 63–93. doi:10.1016/j.bar.2005.09.001

Bank of Russia. (1999). *Russia bulletin on banking statistics, 11*, 19.

Bansal, R., & Papantoni-Kazakos, P. (1986). An algorithm for detecting a change in a stochastic process. *IEEE Transactions on Information Theory*, *32*(2), 227–235. doi:10.1109/TIT.1986.1057160

Bao, C. W., & Liao, W. (2005). Performance analysis of reliable MAC-layer multicast for IEEE 802.11 Wireless LANs. In *Communications, 2005, ICC 2005, IEEE International Conference*, (Vol. 2, pp.1378 – 1382).

Bardos, M. (1998). Detecting the risk of company failure at the Banque de la France. *Journal of Banking & Finance*, *22*, 1405–1419. doi:10.1016/S0378-4266(98)00062-4

Barniv, R., & Hathorn, J. (1997). The merger or insolvency alternative in the insurance industry. *The Journal of Risk and Insurance, 64*(1), 89–113. doi:10.2307/253913

Bartels, P. H., Montironi, R., Scarpelli, M., Bartels, H. G., & Alberts, D. S. (2009)... *Analytical and Quantitative Cytology and Histology, 31*(3), 125–136.

Basel Committee on Banking Supervision. (2005). *An explanatory note on the Basel II IRB risk weight functions.* Retrieved from http://www.bis.org/bcbs/irbriskweight. pdf.

Basel Committee on Banking Supervision. (2006). *Basel II: International convergence of capital measurement and capital standards: A revised framework.* Retrieved from http://www.bis.org/publ/bcbs128.htm.

Bastien, P., Esposito Vinzi, V., & Tenenhaus, M. (2005). PLS generalised regression. *Computational Statistics & Data Analysis, 48*(1), 17–46. doi:10.1016/j. csda.2004.02.005

Bawa, K., & Shoemaker, R. W. (1987). The effects of a direct mail coupon on brand choice behavior. *JMR, Journal of Marketing Research, 24*(November), 370–376. doi:10.2307/3151384

Beaver, W. (1966). Financial ratios as predictors of failure. *Journal of Accounting Research, 4*, 71–111. doi:10.2307/2490171

Beaver, W. H. (1966). Financial ratios as predictors of failure. *Journal of Accounting Research, 4*(3), 71–111. doi:10.2307/2490171

Beaver, W. H. (1966). Financial ratios as predictors failure. *Empirical Research in Accounting: Selected Studies. Supplement to Journal of Accounting Research, 4*, 71–111. doi:10.2307/2490171

Beck, T. (2007). *Financing Constraints of SMEs in developing countries: Evidence, determinants and solutions.* Working Paper. World Bank.

Beck, T., Kunt, A., & Peria, M. S. (2008). *Bank financing for SMEs around the world, Policy Research Working Paper,* 4785. Retrieved October, 2009, from https://www. researchgate.net/publication/23970207_Bank_Financing_for_SMEs_around_the_World_Drivers_Obstacles_Business_Models_and_Lending_Practices

Beh, E. J. (1997). Simple correspondence analysis of ordinal cross-classifications using orthogonal polynomials. *Biometrical Journal. Biometrische Zeitschrift, 39*(5), 589–613. doi:10.1002/bimj.4710390507

Beh, E. J. (1998). A comparative study of scores for correspondence analysis with ordered categories. *Biometrical Journal. Biometrische Zeitschrift, 40*, 413–429. doi:10.1002/(SICI)1521-4036(199808)40:4<413::AID-BIMJ413>3.0.CO;2-V

Beh, E. J. (2001). Partitioning Pearson's chi-squared statistic for singly ordered two-way contingency tables. *The Australian and New Zealand Journal of Statistics, 43*, 327–333. doi:10.1111/1467-842X.00179

Beh, E. J., & Davy, P. J. (1998). Partitioning Pearson's chi-squared statistic for a completely ordered three-way contingency table. *The Australian and New Zealand Journal of Statistics, 40*, 465–477. doi:10.1111/1467-842X.00050

Beh, E. J., & Davy, P. J. (1999). Partitioning Pearson's chi-squared statistic for a partially ordered three-way contingency table. *The Australian and New Zealand Journal of Statistics, 41*, 233–246. doi:10.1111/1467-842X.00077

Beh, E. J., Simonetti, B., & D'Ambra, L. (2007). Partitioning a non-symmetric measure of association for three-way contingency tables. *Journal of Multivariate Analysis, 98*(7), 1391–1411. doi:10.1016/j.jmva.2007.01.011

Bekker, P., & de Leeuw, J. (1988). Relations between Variants of Non-linear Principal Component Analysis. In van Rijckevorsel, J. L. A., & de Leeuw, J. (Eds.), *Component and Correspondence Analysis.* Chichester, UK: John Wiley & Sons.

Bell, R. D., Chiang, J., & Padmanabhan, V. (1999). The decomposition of promotional response: An empirical generalization. *Marketing Science, 18*(4), 504–526. doi:10.1287/mksc.18.4.504

Bell, R. D., Iyer, G., & Padmonbhan, V. (2002). Price competitoin under stockpiling and flexible consumption. *Marketing Research Journal, 37*(Aug.).

Benzécri, J. P. (1973). *Analyse des données (2 vols)*. Paris: Dunod.

Berenguela, R., & Pescetto, C. (2003). *Improving the measurement of poverty in the Americas health adjusted poverty lines: background materials – a literature review*. Pan American Health Organization. Working Paper (Draft).

Berg, A., Borensztein, E., & Pattillo, C. (2004). *Assessing early warning systems: How have they worked in practice? IMF Working Paper*, March 2004. Retrieved October, 2009, from http://www.ksri.org/bbs/files/research02/wp0452.pdf.

Berger, A., Udell, G. (2005). A more complete conceptual framework for financing of small and medium enterprises. *World Bank Policy Research Working*, Paper 3795.

Berliet, J. (2008). *Lessons from the financial crisis for directors and CEOs of insurance companies, risk management: The current financial crisis, lessons learned and future implications*. Institute of ActuARies

Bermúdez, L., Pérez, J., Ayuso, M., Gómez, E., & Vázquez, F. (2007). A Bayesian dichotomous model with asymmetric link for fraud in insurance. *Insurance, Mathematics & Economics, 42*, 779–886. doi:10.1016/j.insmatheco.2007.08.002

Berry, S., Levinsohn, J., & Pakes, A. (1995). Automobile prices in market equilibrium. *Econometrica, 63*(4), 841–890. doi:10.2307/2171802

Berson, A., Smith, S., & Thearling, K. (2000). *Building Data Mining Applications for CRM*. New York: McGraw-Hill.

Besanko, D., Gupta, S., & Jain, D. C. (1998). Logit demand estimation under competitive pricing behavior: An equilibrium framework. *Management Science, 44*(11, Part 1 of 2), 1533-1547.

Best, D. J., & Rayner, J. C. W. (1996). Nonparametric analysis for doubly ordered two-way contingency tables. *Biometrics, 52*, 1153–1156. doi:10.2307/2533077

Beynon, V. H., & Seibet, P. D. (2003). Detecting abandoned packages in a multi-camera video surveillance system. In *2003 IEEE International Conference on Advanced Video and Signal Based Surveillance (AVSS'03)*, Miami, FL. FIPS-197, National Inst. Of Standards and Technology, Federal Information Processing Standard 197. (2001, November). *Advanced Encryption Standard*. Retrieved from http://csrc.nist.gov/publications/fips/fips197/fips-197.pdf

Bhaird, C., & Lucey, B. (2006). *Capital structure and the financing of SMEs: Empirical evidence from an Irish survey*. Working Paper, Retrieved October, 2009, from http://www.cebr.dk/upload/ciaranmacanbhaird.pdf

Bhairdi, C., & Lucey, B. (2005). Determinants of the capital structure of SMEs: A seemingly unrelated regression approach. *Small Business Economics*. doi:.doi:10.1007/s11187-008-9162-6

Biggs, T. (2002). *Is small beautiful and worthy of subsidy? Literature Review*. IFC.

Bilderbeek, J. (1979). De continuïteitsfactor als beoordelingsinstrument van ondernemingen. *Accountancy en Bedrijfskunde Kwartaalschrift, 4*(3), 58–61.

Birch, D. L. (1987). *Job creation in America: How our smallest companies put the most people to work*. New York: Free Press.

Bitzenis, A., & Nito, E. (2005). Obstacles to entrepreneurship in a transition business environment: The case of Albania. *Journal of Small Business and Enterprise Development, 12*(4), 564–578. doi:10.1108/14626000510628234

Blackburn, K., & Sola, M. (1993). Speculative currency attacks and the balance of payments crises. *Journal of Economic Surveys, 7*, 119–144. doi:10.1111/j.1467-6419.1993.tb00162.x

Blattberg, R. C., Briesch, R., & Fox, E. J. (1995). How promotions work. *Marketing Science, 14*(3), G122–G133. doi:10.1287/mksc.14.3.G122

Blattberg, R. C., Eppen, G. D., & Lieberman, J. (1981). A theoretical and empirical evaluation of price deals for consumer nondurables. *Journal of Marketing, 45*, 116–129. doi:10.2307/1251725

Blattberg, R. C., & Wisniewski, J. (1989). Price-induced patterns of competition. *Marketing Science, 8*(4), 291–309. doi:10.1287/mksc.8.4.291

Bologna, G., & Lindquist, R. (1995). *Fraud auditing and forensic accounting.* New York: John Wiley & Sons.

Bolshakova, N., Azuaje, F., & Cunningham, P. (2005). An integrated tool for microarray data clustering and cluster validity assessment. *Bioinformatics (Oxford, England), 21*(4), 451–455. doi:10.1093/bioinformatics/bti190

Bolton, R., & Hand, D. (2001). *Unsupervised profiling methods for fraud detection.* Credit Scoring & Credit Control VII.

Bonchi, F., Giannotti, F., Mainetto, G., & Pedreschi, D. (1999). A classification based methodology for planning audit strategies in fraud detection. *Fifth ACM SIGKDD International Conference on Knowledge Discovery and Data Mining.* San Diego, CA: ACM Press.

Booth, P., Chadburn, R., Haberman, S., James, D., Khorasanee, Z., Plumb, R. H., & Rickayzen, B. (1999). *Modern actuarial theory and practice.* Boca Raton, FL: Chapman and Hall/CRC.

Box, G. E. P., Jenkins, G. M., & Reinsel, G. C. (2008). *Time series analysis, forecasting and control.* New York: Wiley.

Brause, R., Langsdorf, T., & Hepp, M. (1999). Retrieved July 6, 2009, from Goethe Universität - Frankfurt am Main: http://www.uni-frankfurt.de

Breiman, L. (1996). Bagging predictors. *Machine Learning, 24*, 123–140. doi:10.1007/BF00058655

Breiman, L. (1999). Prediction games and arcing algorithms. *Neural Computation, 11*(7), 1493–1517. doi:10.1162/089976699300016106

Breiman, L., Friedman, J., Olshen, R., & Stone, C. (1984). *Classification and regression trees.* Wadsworth.

Brockett, P. L., Golden, L. L., Jang, J., & Yang, C. (2006). A comparison of neural network, statistical methods and variable. *The Journal of Risk and Insurance, 73*(3), 397–419. doi:10.1111/j.1539-6975.2006.00181.x

Brockett, P., Derrig, R., Golden, L., & Levine, A., & M., A. (1998). Using Kohonen's self-organizing feature map to uncover automobile bodily injury claims fraud. *The Journal of Risk and Insurance, 69*, 245–274. doi:10.2307/253535

Brockett, P., Derrig, R., Golden, L., Levine, A., & Alpert, M. (2002). Fraud classification using principal component analysis of RIDITs. *The Journal of Risk and Insurance, 69*, 341–371. doi:10.1111/1539-6975.00027

Brown, M. E. (2008). *Famine early warning systems and remote sensing data.* Berlin: Springer.

Bucklin, R. E., & Gupta, S. (1992). Brand choice, purchase incidence, and segmentation: An integrated approach. *Marketing Science, 18*(3), 247–273. doi:10.1287/mksc.18.3.247

Bucklin, R. E., & Gupta, S. (1999). Commercial use of UPC scanner data: Industry and academic perspectives. *Marketing Science, 18*(Fall), 247–273. doi:10.1287/mksc.18.3.247

Bucklin, R. E., & Gupta, S. (2000). Commercial adoption of advances in the analysis of scanner data. *Marketing Science, 15*.

Bucklin, R. E., & Lattin, J. M. (1992). A model of product category competition among grocery retailers. *Journal of Retailing, 68*(Fall), 271–293.

Buhlmann, P. (2006). Boosting for high-dimensional linear models. *Annals of Statistics, 34*(2), 559–583. doi:10.1214/009053606000000092

Buhlmann, P., & Hothorn, H. (2007). Boosting algorithms: regularization, prediction and model fitting. *Statistical Science, 22*(4), 477–505. doi:10.1214/07-STS242

Buhlmann, P., & Yu, B. (2003). Boosting with the L2 loss: regression and classification. *Journal of the American Statistical Association, 98*, 324–339. doi:10.1198/016214503000125

Bukvic, V., & Bartlett, W. (2003). Financial barriers to SME growth in Slovenia. *Economic and Business Review, 5*(3), 161–181.

Bull, M., Kundt, G., & Gierl, L. (1997). Discovering of health risks and case-based forecasting of epidemics in a health survellance systems. In Komorowski, J., & Zytkow, J. (Eds.), *Principles of Data Mining and Knowledge Discovery, 1263* (pp. 68–77). Berlin: Springer-Verlag.

Burge, P., & Shawe-Taylor, J. (2001). An unsupervised neural network approach to profiling the behavior of mobile phone users to use in fraud detection. *Journal of Parallel and Distributed Computing, 61*, 915–925. doi:10.1006/jpdc.2000.1720

Burleson, R. (2009). *Information to insight in a counterterrorism context.* Retrieved August 1, 2009, from http://www.ipam.ucla.edu/publications/gss2005/gss2005_5484.pdf

Buse, L., Pirvu, C., Siminica, M., & Circiumaru, D. (2006). A model for assessing the performances of the company using financial and non-financial measures. *Brno International Conference on Applied Business Research 2006* (pp. 130-138). Brno, Czech Republic: Mendel University and Forestry.

Bussiere, M., & Fratzscher, M. (1996). Towards a new early warning system of financial crises. *Journal of International Money and Finance, 25*, 953–973. doi:10.1016/j.jimonfin.2006.07.007

Bygrave, L. A. (2002). *Data protection law - approaching its rationale, logic and limits (Information law series Vol: 10).* The Hague, The Netherlands: Kluwer Law International.

Bygrave, L. A. (2004). Privacy protection in a global context – A comparative overview. *Scandinavian Studies in Law, 47*, 319–348.

Cabena, P., Hadjinian, P., Stadler, R., Verhees, J., & Zanasi, A. (1997). *Discovering Data Mining: From Concept To Implementation.* Upper Saddle River, NJ: Prentice Hall PTR.

Cahill, M., Lambert, D., Pinheiro, J., & Sun, D. (2000). *Detecting fraud in the real world.*

Cajueiro, D. O., Tabak, B. M., & Werneck, F. K. (2009). Can we predict crashes? The case of the Brazilian stock market. *Physica A, 388*, 1603–1609. doi:10.1016/j.physa.2008.12.010

Campos, M.M., Stengard, P.J., & Milenova, B.L., (2005). *Data-centric automated data mining.* Proceedings of Fourth International Conf on Machine Learning and Applications, *15-17 Dec. 2005, (pp.8).*

Canovas, G. H., & Solano, P. M. (2006). Banking relationships: Effect on debt terms for Spanish firms. *Journal of Small Business Management, 44*(3), 315–334. doi:10.1111/j.1540-627X.2006.00174.x

Canuto, A. M. P., Abreu, M. C. C., De Melo Oliverira, L., Xavier Jr, J. C., & Santos, A. D. M. (2007). Investigating the influence of the choice of the ensemble members in accuracy and diversity of selection-based and fusion-based methods for ensembles. *Pattern Recognition Letters, 28*(4), 472–486. doi:10.1016/j.patrec.2006.09.001

Caragata, P. J. (1999). *Business early warning systems:Corporate Governance for the New Millennium.* Wellington, New Zealand: Butterworths.

Carbó-Valverde, S., Fernández, R. F., & Udell, G. F. (2008). *Bank lending, financing constraints and SME investment.* Federal Reserve Bank of Chicago, Working papers.

Casta, J. F., & Zerbib, J. P. (1979). Prévoir les défaillances des entreprises. *Revue Française de Comptabilité, 97*, 506–527.

Cervone, G., Kafatos, M., Napoletani, D., & Singh, R. P. (2006). An early warning systems for coastal earthquakes. *Advances in Space Research, 37*, 636–642. doi:10.1016/j.asr.2005.03.071

Chan, N. H., Wong, H. Y., & Wong, H. Y. (2007). Data mining of resilience indicators. *IIE Transactions*, *39*(6), 617–627. doi:10.1080/07408170600899565

Chang, G., Healey, M. J., McHugh, J. A. M., & Wang, J. T. L. (2001). *Mining the world wide web: An information search approach*. Boston: Kluwer Academic Publisher.

Chang, S., Chang, H., Lin, C., & Kao, S. (2003). The effect of organizational attributes on the adoption of data mining techniques in the financial service industry: An empirical study in Taiwan. *International Journal of Management*, *20*(4), 497–503.

Chen, Y., Guo, J. J., Healy, D. P., Lin, W. D., & Patel, N. C. (2008). Risk of hepatotoxity associated with the use of telithromycin: A signal detection using data mining algorithms. *The Annals of Pharmacotherapy*, *42*(12), 1791–1796. doi:10.1345/aph.1L315

Chen & Lynch. (1992). Automatic constriction of networks of concepts characterizing document databases. *IEEE Transactions on Systems, Man, and Cybernetics*, *22*(5), 885–902. doi:10.1109/21.179830

Chen, H. (2006). *Intelligence and Security Informatics for International Security, Information Sharing and Data Mining*. Integrated Series in Information Systems, 10*(18)*.

Cheng, T. X., Qi, X., & Jiang, W. T. (2008). The DM based DSS for risk pre-warning in tender evaluation of civil projects. In Xia, G. P. & Deng, X. Q. (Eds.), *Proceedings of the 38th International Conference on Compuers and Industrial Engineering*, (Vol. 1-3, pp. 487-492). Beijing: Publishing House Electronics Industry.

Chernoff, H., & Zacks, S. (1964). Estimating the current mean of a normal distribution which is subject to changes in time. *Annals of Mathematical Statistics*, *35*, 999–1018. doi:10.1214/aoms/1177700517

Chien, C.-F., & Chen, L. (2008). Data mining to impove personnel selection and enhance human capital: A case study in hig-technology industry. *Expert Systems with Applications*, *34*, 280–290. doi:10.1016/j.eswa.2006.09.003

Christen, M., Gupta, S., Porter, J. C., Staelin, R., & Wittink, D. R. (1997). Using market level data to understand promotional effects in a nonlinear model. *Journal of Marketing Research*, *34*(3 (August)), 322-334.

Chuang, C. L., & Lin, R. H. (2009). Constructing a reassigning credit scoring model. *Expert Systems with Applications*, *36*(3), 1685–1694. doi:10.1016/j.eswa.2007.11.067

Clifton, C. Kantarcioglu. M. & Vaidya, J. (2002). Privacy for data mining. In *National Science Foundation Workshop on Next Generation Data Mining*, Baltimore, MD.

Coady, D., Grosh, M., & Hoddinott, J. (2003). *The targeting of transfers in developing countries: review of experience and lessons*. World Bank.

Cocx, T., Kosters, W. A., & Laros, J. F. J. (2008). An early warning system for the prediction of criminal careers. In Gelbukh, A., & Morales, E. F. (Eds.), *Mexican international conference on artifical intelligence 2008: Lecture notes in artifical intelligence* (pp. 77–89). Berlin: Springer-Verlag.

Collard, J. M. (2002). Is your company at risk? *Strategic Finance*, *84*(1), 37–39.

Commission Recommendation of 6 May 2003 Concerning the Definition of Micro, Small and Medium-sized Enterprises (2003/361/EC), L 124/36 2003. *Official Journal of the European Union*. Retrieved December, 2009, from http://eur-lex.europa.eu/LexUriServ/LexUriServ.do?uri=OJ:L:2003:124:0036:0041:en:PDF

Conan, J., & Holder, M. (1979). *Variables explicatives de performances et contrôle de gestion dans les PMI*. Thèse d'Etat en Sciences de Gestion Université, Universite Paris Dauphine.

Conchar, M. P., Crask, M. R., & Zinkhan, G. M. (2005). Market valuation models of the effect of advertising and promotional spending: A review and meta-analysis. *Journal of the Academy of Marketing Science*, *33*(4), 445–460. doi:10.1177/0092070305277693

Cooper, L. G., & Nakanishi, M. (1996). *Market-share analysis: Evaluating competitive marketing effectiveness*. Norwell, MA: Kluwer Academic Publishers.

Cortes, C., Pregibon, D., & Volinsky, C. (2002). Communities of interest. *Intelligent Data Analysis, 6*, 211–219.

Council of Europe. (1981). *Convention for the protection of individuals with rRegard to automatic processing of personal data.* Strassburg, January 28. ETS no. 108. Retrieved July 13, 2009, from http://conventions.coe.int/treaty/EN/Treaties/Html/108.htm

Cox, D. R., & Snell, E. J. (1989). *Analysis of binary data.* London: Chapman & Hall.

Cox, K., Eick, S., Wills, G., & Brachman, R. (1997). Visual data mining: Recognizing telephone calling fraud. *Data Mining and Knowledge Discovery, 1,* 225–231. doi:10.1023/A:1009740009307

CRISP-DM. (2009). *Cross Industry Standard Process for Data Mining.* Retrieved November 27, 2009, from http://www.crisp-dm.org/

Crompton, M. (2002). *Under the gaze, privacy identity and new technologies.* International Association of Lawyers, 75th Anniversary Congress, Sydney. Retrieved July 13, 2009, from http://www.privacy.gov.au/news/speeches/sp104notes.doc

Currim, I. S., & Schneider, L. G. (1991). A taxonomy of consumer purchase strategies in a promotion intensive environment. *Marketing Science, 10*(2), 91–110. doi:10.1287/mksc.10.2.91

Daily, C. M., & Dalton, D. R. (1994). Bankruptcy and corporate governance: The impact of board composition and structure. *Academy of Management Journal, 37*(6), 1603–1617. doi:10.2307/256801

D'Ambra, L., Beh, E. J., & Amenta, P. (2005). CATANOVA for two-way contingency tables with ordinal variables using orthogonal polynomials. *Communication in Statistics, 34,* 1755–1769. doi:10.1081/STA-200066325

Danset, R. (1998). *Comparison between the financial structures of SME versus large enterprises.* Final Report for the DG II European Community.

Daskalakis, N., & Psillaki, M. (2008). Do countries or firm factors explain capital structure? Evidence from SMEs in France and Greece. *Applied Financial Economics, 18*(2), 87–97. doi:10.1080/09603100601018864

Daskalakis, N., & Psillaki, M. (2005). *The determinants of capital structure of the SMEs: Evidence from the Greek and the French firms.* Paper presented at the XXIInd Symposium on Banking and Monetary Economics, Strasbourg.

Dasu, T., & Johnson, T. (2003). *Exploratory data mining and data cleaning.* New York: Wiley-Interscience. doi:10.1002/0471448354

Davey, N., Field, S., Frank, R., Barson, P., & McAskie, G. (1996). The detection of fraud in mobile phone networkds. *Neural Network World, 6,* 477–484.

Davia, H., Coggins, P., Wideman, J., & Kastantin, J. (2000). *Accountant's Guide to Fraud Detection and Control.* New York: John Wiley & Sons.

Davis, E. P., & Karim, D. (2008). Could early warning systems have helped to predict the sub-prime crisis? *National Institute Economic Review, 206*(1), 35–47. doi:10.1177/0027950108099841

Deakin, E. B. (1972). A discriminat analysis of predictors of business failure. *Journal of Accounting Research, 10*(1), 167–179. doi:10.2307/2490225

Deakin, E. (1977). *Business Failure Prediction: an empirical analysis, Financial Crisis Institutions and Marlets in a Fragile Environment.* Chichester, UK: John Wiley&Sons.

Deconinck, E., Hancock, T., Commans, D., Massart, D. L., & Heyden, Y. V. (2005). Classification of drugs in absorption classes using the classification and regression trees (CART) methodology. *Journal of Pharmaceutical and Biomedical Analysis, 39*(1-2), 91–103. doi:10.1016/j.jpba.2005.03.008

Dekimpe, M. G., & Hannssens, D. M. (1995). The persistence of marketing effects on sales. *Marketing Science, 14*(1), 1–21. doi:10.1287/mksc.14.1.1

Dekimpe, M. G., & Hannsens, D. M. (2000). Time-Series Models in Marketing: Past, Present and Future. *International Journal of Research in Marketing, 17*.

Delmater, R., & Hancock, M. (2001). *Data mining explained: A manager's guide to customer-centric business intelligence*. Digital Press.

Derby, B. L. (2003). Data mining for improper payments. *The Journal of Government Financial Management, 52*(1), 10–13.

Derrig, R., & Ostaszewski, K. (1995). Fuzzy techniques of pattern recognition. *The Journal of Risk and Insurance, 62*, 447–482. doi:10.2307/253819

Deshmuck, A., & Talluru, L. (1998). A rule-based fuzzy reasoning system for assessing the risk of management fraud. *International Journal of Intelligent Systems in Accounting Finance & Management, 7*, 223–241. doi:10.1002/(SICI)1099-1174(199812)7:4<223::AID-ISAF158>3.0.CO;2-I

Diamond, H. (1976). *Pattern recognition and detection of corporate failure*. PhD Dissertation, New York University.

Dian-Min, Y., Xiao-Dan, W., Yue, L., & Chao-Hsien, C. (2007). Data mining-based financial fraud detection: Current status and key issues. In Qi, E. (Ed.), *Proceedings of the 14th International Conference on Industrial Engineering and Engineering Management, Vols A and B – Building core competencies through IE&EM* (pp. 891-896). Beijing: Chine Machine Press.

Djeraba, C., & Fernandez, G. (2003). Mining image data. In Ye, N. (Ed.), *The handbook of data mining* (pp. 637–656). Mahwah, NJ: Lawrence Erlbaum Associates Publisher.

Dodig-Crnkovic, G. (2006). *Privacy and protection of personal integrity in the working place*. Department of Computer Science and Electronics, Mälardalen University, Västerås, Sweden, February 2006. Retrieved July 13, 2009, from http://danskprivacynet.files.wordpress.com/2008/08/privacy_personalintegrity_workplace.pdf

Dodson, J. A., Tybout, A. M., & Sternhal, B. (1978). The effect of deals and deal retraction on brand switching. *JMR, Journal of Marketing Research, 15*(1), 78–81. doi:10.2307/3150402

Donabedian, A. (1985). *Explorations in quality assessment and monitoring. The findings of quality assessment and monitoring*. Ann Arbor, MI: Health Administration Press.

Dorronsoro, J., Ginel, F., Sanchez, C., & Santa Cruz, C. (1997). Neural fraud detection in credit card operations. *IEEE Transactions on Neural Networks, 8*, 827–834. doi:10.1109/72.595879

DPT - CPO. (2001). Rehabilitation of income distribution and fight against poverty, Special Interest Group Report, Ankara, Turkey.

Drewes, B. (2005). Some industrial applications of text mining. In Sirmakessis, S. (Ed.), *Knowledge mining: Proceesings of the NEMIS 2004 final conference* (pp. 233–238). Berlin: Springer.

Drummond, M. F., Sculpher, M., Torrance, G. W., O'Brien, B. J., & Stoddart, G. L. (1997). *Methods of the economic evaluation of health care programs*. Oxford, UK: Oxford University Press.

Dudding, B. P., & Jennett, W. J. (1942). *Quality control charts, British Standard 600R*. London: British Standards Institution.

Dunham, M. H. (2003). *Data mining introductory and advanced topics*. Upper Saddle River, NJ: Prentice Hall/Pearson Education.

Durand, J. F. (2001). Local Polynomial additive regression through PLS and Splines: PLSS. *Chemometrics and Intelligent Laboratory Systems, 58*, 235. doi:10.1016/S0169-7439(01)00162-9

Durand, J. F. (2008). La régression Partial Least-Squares boostée. *Revue MODULAD, 38*, 63–86.

Durand, J. F., & Sabatier, R. (1997). Additive pplines for partial least Squares regression. *Journal of the American Statistical Association, 92*, 440. doi:10.2307/2965425

Durand, J. F., & Lombardo, R. (2003). Interaction terms in Non-linear PLS via additive spline transformation. In Schader, P., Gaul, J., & Vichi, M. (Eds.), *Between Data Science and Applied Data Analysis* (pp. 22–30). Berlin: Springer.

E&Y. (2006). *9th Global fraud survey, fraud risk in emerging markets*. Technical Report, Ernst&Young.

E&Y. (2007). *A survey into fraud risk mitigations in 13 European Countries*. Technical Report, Ernst&Young.

EC – European Commission. (1995). *Directive 95/46/EC of the European Parliament and of the Council of 24 October 1995 on the protection of individuals with regard to the processing of personal data and on the free movement of such data,* No L 281/31. Retrieved July 13, 2009, from http://ec.europa.eu/justice_home/fsj/privacy/docs/95-46-ce/dir1995-46_part1_en.pdf

EC – European Commission. (1997). *Directive 97/66/EC of the European Parliament and of the Council the Council, December 1997 concerning the processing of personal data and the protection of privacy in the tele-communications sector.* Retrieved July 13, 2009, from http://www.legaltext.ee/text/en/T50023.htm

EC – European Commission. (2000a). Data protection: Commission adopts the "safe harbor" decision – Adequate protection for personal data transfer to US. *Single Market News, 23* (October 2000). Retrieved July 13, 2009, from http://ec.europa.eu/internal_market/smn/smn23/s23mn27.htm

EC – European Commission. (2000b). *The Charter of Fundamental Rights of the European Union.* Retrieved July 13, 2009, from http://www.eucharter.org/

EC – European Commission. (2001). *Regulation (EC) No 45/2001 of the European Parliament and of the Council of 18 December 2000 on the protection of individuals with regard to the processing of personal data by the institutions and bodies of the Community and on the free movement of such data.* Retrieved July 13, 2009, from http://europa.eu/legislation_summaries/information_society/l24222_en.htm

EC – European Commission. (2002). *Directive 2002/58/EC of the European Parliament and of the council of July 2002, concerning the processing of personal data and the protection of privacy in the electronic communications sector (Directive on privacy and electronic communications).* Retrieved July 13, 2009, from http://mineco.fgov.be/internet_observatory/pdf/legislation/directive_2002_58_en.pdf

EC – European Commission. (2008). *Opinion 2/2008 on the review of the Directive 2002/58/EC on privacy and electronic communications (ePrivacy Directive).* Retrieved July 13, 2009, from http://ec.europa.eu/justice_home/fsj/privacy/docs/wpdocs/2008/wp150_en.pdf

Edge, M. E., & Dampaio, P. R. (2009). A survey of signature based methods for financial fraud detection. *Computers & Security, 28,* 381–394. doi:10.1016/j.cose.2009.02.001

Edison, H. J. (2003). Do indicators of financial crises work? An evaluation of an early earning system. *International Journal of Finance & Economics, 8*(1), 11–53. doi:10.1002/ijfe.197

Edmister, R. (1972). An empirical test of financial ratio for Small business failure prediction. *Journal of Financial and Quantitative Analysis, 2,* 1477–1493. doi:10.2307/2329929

Edwards, S. (1998). Interest rate volatility, contagion and convergence: An empirical investigation of the cases of Argentina, Chile and Mexico. *Journal of Applied Econometrics, 1,* 55–86.

Eichengreen, B., Rose, A., & Wyplosz, C. (1995). Exchange market mayhem: The antecedents and aftermath of speculative attacks. *Economic Policy, 21,* 249–312. doi:10.2307/1344591

Eichengreen, B., Rose, A., & Wyplosz, C. (1996). Contagious currency crisis. *Scandinavian Economic Review, 98,* 463–484. doi:10.2307/3440879

Eklund, T., Back, B., Vanharanta, H., & Visa, A. (2003). Using the self- organizing map as a visualization tool in financial benchmarking. *Information Visualization, 2*(3), 171–181. doi:10.1057/palgrave.ivs.9500048

El-Shazly, A. (2006). Early warning of currency crises: An econometric analysis for Egypt. *The Middle East Business and Economic Review*, *18*(1), 34–48.

Emerson, P. L. (1968). Numerical construction of orthogonal polynomials from general Recurrence Formula. *Biometrics*, *24*, 696–701. doi:10.2307/2528328

Esposito Vinzi, V., Guinot, C., & Squillacciotti, S. (2007). Two-step PLS regression for L-structured data: an application in the cosmetic industry. *Statistical Methods & Applications*, *16*(2), 263–278. doi:10.1007/s10260-006-0028-2

Estévez, P., Held, C., & Perez, C. (2006). Subscription fraud prevention in telecommunications using fuzzy rules and neural networks. *Expert Systems with Applications*, *31*, 337–344. doi:10.1016/j.eswa.2005.09.028

Estivill-Castro, V., & Brankovic, L. (1999). Data swapping: Balancing privacy against precision in mining for logic rules. In Mohania, M., & Min Tjoa, A. (Eds.), *DaWaK '99 Proceedings – Data Warehousing and Knowledge Discovery* (pp. 389–398). Berlin: Springer.

EU. Europen Commission. (2003). *2003 Observatory of European SMEs: SMEs in Europe*. Technical Paper No.7.

European Association of Craft. Small and Medium-Sized Enterprises (UEAPME). (2009). *European SME Finance Survey*. Retrieved October, 2009, from http://www.ueapme.com/IMG/pdf/090728_SME-finance_survey.pdf

Ezawa, K., & Norton, S. (1996). Constructing Bayesian networks to predict uncollectible telecommunications accounts. *IEEE Expert: Intelligent Systems and Their Applications*, *11*, 45–51.

Falkingham, J., & Namazie, C. (2002). *Measuring health and poverty: A Review of approaches to identifying the poor*. London: DFID Publishing.

Fan, W. (2004). Systematic data selection to mine concept-drifting data streams. In *Tenth ACM SIGKDD International Conference on Knowledge and Discovery and Data Mining*, Seattle, (pp. 128-137).

Fanning, K., & Cogger, K. (1998). Neural network detection of management fraud using published financial data. *International Journal of Intelligent Systems in Accounting Finance & Management*, *7*, 21–41. doi:10.1002/(SICI)1099-1174(199803)7:1<21::AID-ISAF138>3.0.CO;2-K

Fawcett, T., & Provost, F. (1997). Adaptive fraud detection. *Data Mining and Knowledge Discovery*, *1*(3), 291–316. doi:10.1023/A:1009700419189

Fawcett, T. (2003). *ROC graphs: notes and practical considerations for data mining researchers*. Technical Report HPL-2003–4. Palo Alto, CA: HP Laboratories.

Fawcett, T., & Provost, F. (1999). Activity monitoring: Noticing interesting changes in behavior. *Fifth ACM SIG-KDD: International Conference on Knowledge Discovery and Data Mining*, (pp. 53-62). New York: ACM Press.

Fayyad, G., Piatetsky-Shapiro, P., & Symth, P. (1996). From data mining to knowledge discovery in databases. *AI Magazine*, *17*(3), 37–54.

FDPIC - Federal Data Protection and Information Commissioner. (2005). Montreux declaration: The protection of personal data and privacy in a globalised world: a universal right respecting diversities. In *27th International Conference of Data Protection and Privacy Commissioners*, Montreux (14 - 16 September 2005). Retrieved July 13, 2009, from http://www.privacy.org.nz/assets/Files/22718821.pdf

Feldman, R., & Sanger, J. (2007). *The text mining handbook*. Cambridge, MA: Cambridge University Press.

Feldman, R. (2003). Mining text data. In Ye, N. (Ed.), *The handbook of data mining* (pp. 481–518). Mahwah, NJ: Lawrence Erlbaum Associates Publisher.

Field, F. (1983). *The minimum wage*. London: Policy Studies Institute.

Flavian, C., & Guinaliu, M. (2006). Consumer trust, perceived security and privacy policy. *Industrial Management & Data Systems*, *106*(5), 601–620. doi:10.1108/02635570610666403

Flood, R., & Garber, P. (1984). Collapsing exchange rate regimes: Some linear examples. *Journal of International Economics, 17,* 1–13. doi:10.1016/0022-1996(84)90002-3

Foekens, E. W., Leeflang, P. S. H., & Wittink, D. R. (1999). Varying parameter models to accommodate dynamic promotion effects. *Journal of Econometrics, 89,* 249–268. doi:10.1016/S0304-4076(98)00063-3

Fong, A. C. M., & Hui, S. C. (2001). Web-based intelligent surveillance system for detection of criminal activities. *Journal of Computing & Control Engineering, 12*(6), 263–270. doi:10.1049/cce:20010603

Frankel, J. A., & Rose, A. K. (1996). Currency crashes in emerging markets: An empirical treatment. *Journal of International Economics, 41*(3-4), 351–366. doi:10.1016/S0022-1996(96)01441-9

Frawley, W., Piatetsky-Shapiro, G., & Matheus, C. (1992). Knowledge discovery in databases: An overview. *AI Magazine,* (Fall): 213–228.

Friedman, J. H. (2001). Greedy function approximation: A gradient boosting machine. *Annals of Statistics, 29,* 1189–1232. doi:10.1214/aos/1013203451

Frisen, M. (2008). *Financial surveillance.* New York: Wiley.

Fu, L. M. (1994). *Neural networks in computer intelligence.* New York: McGraw-Hill.

Fule, P., & Roddick, J. F. (2004). Detecting privacy and ethical sensitivity in data mining results. In V. Estivil-Castro (Ed.), *Twenty-Seventh Australasian Computer Science Conference (ACSC2004).* Dunedin, Australia: Australian Computer Society, Inc.

Gao, W., & Zhang, G. (2007). An IDS early-warning model based on data mining technology. In *ISCRAM CHINA 2007: Proceedings of the Second International Workshop on Information Systems for Crisis Response and Management* (pp. 99-104). Harbin, China: Harbin Engineering University.

Gasparini, P., Manfredi, G., & Zschau, J. (2007). *Earthquake early warning systems.* Berlin: Springer. doi:10.1007/978-3-540-72241-0

Gaytan, A., & Johnson, A. J. (2002). *A review of the literature on early warning systems for banking crises.* Central Bank of Chile Working Papers no: 183.

Gerlach, S., & Smets, F. (1995). Contagious speculative attacks. *European Journal of Political Economy, 11,* 5–63. doi:10.1016/0176-2680(94)00055-O

Gifi, A. (1990). *Non-linear Multivariate Analysis.* Chichester, UK: Wiley.

Gilad, B. (2003). *Early warning: using competitive intelligence to anticipate market shifts, control risk, and create powerful strategies.* New York: AMACOM.

Giudici, P. (2003). *Applied data mining: statistical methods for business and industry.* New York: John Wiley.

Giurca Vasilescu, L. (2008). A SWOT Analysis of the SMEs Development in Romania. *Journal of Applied Economic Sciences, 4*(6), 396–404.

Giurca Vasilescu, L., Pirvu, C., & Tapordei, D. (2008). Challenges for the Romanian SMES regarding the cmpetitiveness. *microCAD. International Scientific Conference* (pp. 91-98). Miskolc, Hungary: University of Miskolc.

Glantz, M. H. (2009). *Heads up!: early warning systems for climate-, water- and weather-related hazards.* Tokyo: United Nations University Press.

Goldberg, H. G., & Senator, T. A. (1998). Restructuring Databases for knowledge discovery by consolidation and link formation. In D. Jensen & H. Goldberg, (Eds.), *Proceedings of the 1998 AAAI Fall Symposium on Artuificial intelligence and link analysis,* (pp. 38-46). Menlo Park, CA: AAAI press.

Goldstein, M., Reinhart, C., & Kaminsky, G. (2000). *Assessing financial vulnerability: an early warning system for emerging markets.* Washington, DC: Institute for International Economics.

Goldstein, H., & Spiegelhalter, D. J. (1996). League Tables and their limitation: statistical issues in comparisons of institutional performance. *Journal of the Royal Statistical Society. Series A, (Statistics in Society), 52*, 5.

Gori, E., & Vittadini, G. (1999). La valutazione dell'Efficienza e dell'efficacia per la valutazione dei servizi alla persona. In *Qualità e Valutazione nei servizi di pubblica utilità*. Milano: Etas Libri.

Grabert, M., Prechtel, M., Hrycej, T., & Gunther, W. (2004). An early warning systems for vehicle related quality data. In Perner, P. (Ed.), *Advances in Data Mining – Applications in Image mining, Medicine and Biotechnology, Management and Environment Control, and Telecommunications, 3275* (pp. 88–95). Berlin: Springer-Verlag.

Grammatikos, T., & Gloubos, G. (1984). Predicting bankruptcy of industrial firms in Greece. *Spoudai, The University of Piraeus Journal of Economics, Business. Statistics and Operations Research, 3-4*, 421–443.

Green, B., & Choi, J. (1997). Assessing the risk of management fraud through neural network technology. *Auditing, 16*, 14–28.

Greenacre, M. (1984). *Theory and applications of correspondence analysis*. London: Academic Press.

Greenleaf, G. W. (2009). Five years of the APEC privacy framework: Failure or promise? *Computer Law & Security Report, 25*(1), 28–43. doi:10.1016/j.clsr.2008.12.002

Greenleaf, G. W. (1996). Privacy and Australia's New Federal Government. *Australasian Privacy Law & Policy Reporter, 3*(1), 1-3 and 4-7.

Grover, R., & Srinivasan, V. (1992). Evaluating the multiple effects of retail promotions on brand loyal and brand switching segments. *Journal of Marketing Resarch, 29*(Feb), 76–89. doi:10.2307/3172494

Guadagni, P. M., & Little, J. D. C. (1983). A logit model of brand choice calibrated on scanner data. *Marketing Science, 2*(3), 203–238. doi:10.1287/mksc.2.3.203

Guba, E. G., & Lincoln, Y. S. (2005). Paradigmatic controversies, Contradictions, and emerging confluences. In Booth, C., & Harrington, J. (Eds.), *Developing Business Knowledge* (pp. 295–319). London: SAGE.

Gunther, J., W. & Moore, R. R. (2003). Early warning models in real time. *Journal of Banking, 27*(10), 1979–2001. doi:10.1016/S0378-4266(02)00314-X

Gupta, S. (1988). Impact of sales promotions on when, what and how much to buy. *Journal of Marketing Research, 25*, 342–355. doi:10.2307/3172945

Gurr, J. L., & Davies, T. R. (1998). *Preventive measures: building risk assessment and crisis early warning systems*. Lanham, MD: Rowman and Littlefield Publishers, Inc.

Guttman, L. (1941). The quantification of a class of attributes. In Horst, P. (Ed.), *The Prediction of Personal Adjustment* (pp. 321–347). New York: Social Science Research Council.

Gutwirth, S., Poullet, Y., De Hert, P., de Terwangne, C., & Nouwt, S. (2009). *Reinventing data protection?* Berlin: Springer. doi:10.1007/978-1-4020-9498-9

Han, J., & Kamber, M. (2006). *Data mining: Concepts and techniques* (2nd ed.). New York: Elsevier Publisher.

Han, J., & Kamber, M. (2001). *Data mining: Concepts and Techniques*. San Diego.

Hand, D. J., Mannila, H., & Smyth, P. (2001). *Principles of data mining*. Cambridge, MA: MIT Press.

Hanley, J. A., & McNeil, B. J. (1982). The meaning and use of the area under a Receiver Operating Characteristic (ROC) curve. *Radiology, 143*, 29–36.

Harrell, F. E., & Lee, K. L. (1985). A comparison of the discrimination of discriminant analysis and logistic regression. In Se, P. K. (Ed.), *Biostatistics: Statistics in Biomedical, Public Health, and Environmental Sciences*. Amsterdam: North-Holland.

Hastie, T. J., & Tibshirani, R. J. (1990). *Generalized additive models*. Boca Raton, FL: Chapman & Hall/CRC.

Hastie, T., Tibshirani, R., & Friedman, J. H. (2001). *The elements of statistical learning*. New York: Springer New York Inc.

Hastie, T., Tibshirani, R., & Friedman, J. (2001). *The elements of statistical learning, data mining, inference and prediction*. New York: Springer series in Statistics.

Hauck, R. V., Atabakhsh, H., Ongvasith, P., Gupta, H., & Chen, H. (2002). Using COPLINK to analyse criminal justice data. *IEEE Computer, 35*(3), 30–37.

Hayashi, Y., & Setiono, R. (2002). Combining neurla network predictions for midical diagnosis. *Computers in Biology and Medicine, 32*(4), 237–246. doi:10.1016/S0010-4825(02)00006-9

He, H., Wang, J., Graco, W., & Hawkins, S. (1997). Application of neural networks to detection of medical fraud. *Expert Systems with Applications, 13*, 329–336. doi:10.1016/S0957-4174(97)00045-6

He, Y., Huang, Z., & Liu, J. S. (2007). An application of self-organizing data mining method in early-warning of industrial economy. In Xu, J., Jiang, Y. & Yan, H. (Eds.), *Proceedings of 2007 International Conference on Management Science and Engineering Management* (pp. 163-167). Liverpool, UK: World Acad Union-World Acad Press.

Heisenberg, D. (2005). *Negotiating privacy: The European Union, The United States, and personal data protection (Politics/Global Challenges in the Information Age)*. Boulder, CO: Lynne Rienner Publishers.

Heiser, W. J. (2004). Geometric representation of association between categories. *Psychometrika, 69*(4), 513–545. doi:10.1007/BF02289854

Heiser, W. J., & Meulman, J. J. (1994). Homogeneity analysis: exploring the distribution of variables and their nonlinear relationships. In Greenacre, M., & Blasius, J. (Eds.), *Correspondence Analysis in the Social Sciences: Recent Developments and Applications* (pp. 179–209). New York: Academic Press.

Hilas, C., & Mastorocostas, P. (2008). An application of supervised and unsupervised learning approaches to telecommunications fraud detection. *Knowledge-Based Systems, 21*, 721–726. doi:10.1016/j.knosys.2008.03.026

Hilas, C. S. (2009). Designing an Expert System for Fraud Detection in Private Telecommunications Networks. *Expert Systems with Applications, 36*, 11559–11569. doi:10.1016/j.eswa.2009.03.031

Hlaciuc, E., Socoliuc, M., & Mates, D. (2008). Bankruptcy risk analysis through financial management. *Buletin stiintific, Publicatie stiintifica de informare a academiei fortelor terestre, 2* (26).

Ho, J. M., Chang, R. I., Juang, J. Y., & Wang, C. H. (2000). Design and implementation of a web-based surveillance system using internet multicast communications. In *SoftCOM 2000*. Washington, DC: IEEE.

Hoare, R. (2004). *Using CHAID for classification problems*. Paper presented at New Zealand Statistical Association 2004 Conference, Wellington.

Hodorogel, R. G. (2009). The economic crisis and its effects on SMEs. *Theoretical and Applied Economics, 5*(34), 79–89.

Hoffmann, F., Baesens, B., Mues, C., Gestel, T. V., & Vanthienen, J. (2007). Inferring descriptive and approximate fuzzy rules for credit scoring using evolutionary algorithms. *European Journal of Operational Research, 177*, 540–555. doi:10.1016/j.ejor.2005.09.044

Hoogs, B., Kiehl, T., Lacomb, C., & Senturk, D. (2007). A genetic algorithm approach to detecting temporal patterns indicative of financial statement fraud. *Intelligent Systems in Accounting. Financial Management, 15*, 41–56.

Hoppszallern, S. (2003). Healthcare benchmarking. *Hospitals & Health Networks, 77*, 37–44.

Hormozi, A. M. & Giles, S. (2004). Data mining: A compatetive wepon for banking and retail industries. *International Systems Management*, 62-71.

Hosmer, D. W., & Lemeshow, S. (1989). *Applied logistic regression*. New York: Wiley Publications.

Hsieh, N. C. (2005). Hybrid mining approach in the design of credit scoring models. *Expert Systems with Applications, 28*, 655–665. doi:10.1016/j.eswa.2004.12.022

Hu, M. Y., & Tsoukalas, C. (2003). Explaining consumer choice through neural networks: the stacked generalization apporach. *European Journal of Operational Research, 146*(3), 650–660. doi:10.1016/S0377-2217(02)00368-5

Hua, Z., Wang, Y., Xu, X., Zhang, B., & Liang, L. (2007). Predicting corporate financial distress based on integration of support vector machine and logistic regression. *Expert Systems with Applications, 33*(2), 434–440. doi:10.1016/j.eswa.2006.05.006

Huang, C. L., Chen, M. C., & Wang, C. J. (2007). Credit scoring with a data mining approach based on support vector machines. *Expert Systems with Applications, 33*(4), 847–856. doi:10.1016/j.eswa.2006.07.007

Huang, S. M., Tsai, C. F., Yen, D. C., & Cheng, Y. L. (2008). A hybrid financial analysis model for business failure prediction. *Expert Systems with Applications, 35*(3), 1034–1040. doi:10.1016/j.eswa.2007.08.040

Hughes, G., Dawson, S., & Brookes, T. (2008). Considering new privacy lLaws in Australia. *IEEE Security and Privacy, 6*(3), 57–59. doi:10.1109/MSP.2008.60

Hung, S. Y., Yen, D. C., & Wang, H. Y. (2006). Applying data mining to telecom churn management. *Expert Systems with Applications, 31*(3), 515–524. doi:10.1016/j.eswa.2005.09.080

Inegbenebor, A. U. (2006). Financing small and medium industries in Nigeria-case study of the small and medium industries equity investment scheme: Emprical research finding. *Journal of Financial Management and Analysis, 19*(1), 71–80.

International Centre for Geohazards (ICG). (2009). *Project 12: monitoring, remote sensing and early warning systems.* Retrieved August 1, 2009 from http://www.geohazards.no/projects/project12_monitor.htm

International Council Of Nurses. (2004). *Nurses: Working with the poor; Against Poverty. Information and action tool kit.* Geneva, Switzerland: International Council of Nurses.

Ionascu, C. M., & Radu, C. (2008). Comparative analysis at the level of countries from European Union regarding the development potential of companies population. *Annals of University of Craiova. Economic Sciences Series, 36*(1), 203–210.

Iseri, M., Caglar, H., & Caglar, N. (2008). A model proposal for the chaotic structure of Istanbul stock exchange. *Chaos, Solitons, and Fractals, 36*, 1392–1398. doi:10.1016/j.chaos.2006.09.041

Ishikawa, K. (1982). *Guide to quality control.* Tokyo: Asian Productivity Organization.

Ito, N., Onoda, T., & Yamasaki, H. (2009). Interactive abnormal condition sign discovery for hydroelectric power plants. In Chawla, S., Washio, T., Minato, S. I., Tsumoto, S., Onoda, T., Yamada, S., & Inokuchi, A. (Eds.), *New Frontiers in Applied Data Mining, 5433* (pp. 181–192). Berlin: Springer-Verlag. doi:10.1007/978-3-642-00399-8_16

Ivonciu, P. (1998). Analiza riscului de faliment prin metoda scorurilor. *Revista finante banci, asigurari, 4*, 17-19.

Jacobs, L. J., & Kuper, G. H. (2004). *Indicators of financial crises do work! An early-warning system for six Asian countries.* CCSO Working Paper 13. Department of Economics, University of Groningen, the Netherlands.

Jacobs, L. J., & Kuper, G. H. (2004). *Indicators of financial crises do work! An early-warning system for six Asian countries.* CCSO Working Paper 13. Department of Economics, University of Groningen, the Netherlands.

Jager, R., & Kalber, S. (2005). GNSS/GPS/LPS based online control and alarm system (GOCO) – Mathematical models and technical realization of a system for natural and geotechnical deformation monitoring and hazard prevention. In Cygas, D. & Froehner, K. D. (Eds.), *6th International Conference Environmental Engineering, Vols 1 and 2* (pp. 882-890).

Jang, J.-S. R. (1992). Self-learning fuzzy controllers based on temporal back propagation. *IEEE Transactions on Neural Networks, 3*(5), 714–723. doi:10.1109/72.159060

Jang, J.-S. R. (1993). ANFIS: adaptive-network-based fuzzy inference system. *IEEE Transactions on Systems, Man, and Cybernetics, 23*(3), 665–685. doi:10.1109/21.256541

Jang, J.-S. R. (1996). Input selection for ANFIS learning. In *Proceedings of the IEEE International Conference on Fuzzy Systems,* (pp.1493-1499).

Jans, M., Lybaert, N., & Vanhoof, K. (2009). *International Journal of Digital Accounting Research,* 1-29.

Jedidi, K., Mela, C., & Gupta, S. (1999). Managing advertising and promotion for long-run profitability. *Marketing Science, 19*(1), 1–22. doi:10.1287/mksc.18.1.1

Johnson, D. R., & Post, D. G. (1996). Law and borders - The rise of law in cyberspace. *Stanford Law Review, 48*(5), 13–67. doi:10.2307/1229390

Jones, F. (1987). Current techniques in bankruptcy prediction. *Journal of Accounting Literature, 6,* 131–164.

Jones, O., & Tilley, F. (2003). *Competitive advantage in SME's: Organising for innovation and change.* New York: John Wiley & Sons.

Jorion, P. (2004). *Value at risk* (3rd ed.). New York: McGraw-Hill.

Juang, C. F., & Chang, C. M. (2007). Human body posture classification by a neural fuzzy network and home care system application. *IEEE Transactions on Systems, Man, and Cybernetics, 37*(November), 984–994.

Juszczak, P., Adams, N., Hand, D., Whitrow, C., & Weston, D. (2008). Off-the-peg and bespoke classifiers for fraud detection. *Computational Statistics & Data Analysis, 52,* 4521–4532. doi:10.1016/j.csda.2008.03.014

Kamath, C. (2003). Mining science and engineering data. In Ye, N. (Ed.), *The handbook of data mining* (pp. 550–572). Mahwah, NJ: Lawrence Erlbaum Associates Publisher.

Kamin, S. B., Schindler, J., & Samuel, S. (2007). The contribution of domestic and external factors to emerging market currency crises: An Early Warning System. *International Journal of Finance & Economics, 12*(3), 317–322. doi:10.1002/ijfe.314

Kaminsky, G., Lizondo, S., & Reinhart, C. (1998). Leading indicators of currency crisis. *International Monetary Fund Staff Papers, 45*(1).

Kane, G. D., & Velury, U. (2004). The role of institutional ownership in the market for auditing services: an empirical investigation. *Journal of Business Research, 57*(9), 976–983. doi:10.1016/S0148-2963(02)00499-X

Kapetanovic, I. M., Rosenfeld, S., & Izmirlian, G. (2004). Overview of connonly used Bioinformatics methods and their applications. *Annals of the New York Academy of Sciences, 1020,* 10–21. doi:10.1196/annals.1310.003

Karim, D. (2006). *Comparing early warning systems for banking crises.* Unpublished doctoral dissertation, Brunel University, UK.

Kass, G. V. (1980). An exploratory technique for investigating large quantities of categorical data. *Applied Statistics, 29*(2), 119–127. doi:10.2307/2986296

Katz, M. (2006). *Multivariable Analysis: A Practical Guide for Clinicians.* New York: Churchill-Livingstone. doi:10.1017/CBO9780511616761

Kay, O. W., Warde, A., & Martens, L. (2000). Social differentiation and the market for eating out in the UK. *International Journal of Hospitality Management, 19*(2), 173–190. doi:10.1016/S0278-4319(00)00015-3

Keen, M., & Smith, S. (2007). VAT fraud and evasion: What do we know, and what can be done? IMF Working Paper, WP/07/31.

Keller, K. L. (1998). *Strategic brand management - building, managing and measuring brand equity.* New Jersey: Prentice Hall.

Kennedy, G., Doyle, S., & Lui, B. (2008). Data protection in the Asia-Pacific region. *Computer Law & Security Report, 25*(1), 59–68. doi:10.1016/j.clsr.2008.11.006

Kim, T. Y., Oh, K. J., Shon, I., & Hwang, C. (2004). Usefulness of artificial neural networks for early warning system of economic crisis. *Expert Systems with Applications, 26,* 583–590. doi:10.1016/j.eswa.2003.12.009

Kim, T. Y., Oh, K. J., Sohn, I., & Hwang, C. (2004). Usefulness of artificial neural networks for early warning system of economic crisis. *Expert Systems with Applications, 26*, 583–590. doi:10.1016/j.eswa.2003.12.009

Kim, E., Kim, W., & Lee, Y. (2002). Combination of multiple classifiers for the customer's purchase behavior prediction. *Decision Support Systems, 34*(2), 167–175. doi:10.1016/S0167-9236(02)00079-9

Kim, H., & Kwon, W. (2006). A multi-line insurance fraud recognition system: A government-led apporach in Korea. *Risk Management & Insurance Review, 9*, 131–147. doi:10.1111/j.1540-6296.2006.00090.x

Kim, T. Y., Oh, K. J., Sohn, I., & Hwang, C. (2004). Usefulness of artificial neural networks for early warning system of economic crisis. *Expert Systems with Applications, 26*, 583–590. doi:10.1016/j.eswa.2003.12.009

Kimura, F., & Shridhar, M. (1991). Handwritten numeral recognitioni based on multiple algorithms. *Pattern Recognition, 24*(10), 969–983. doi:10.1016/0031-3203(91)90094-L

Kirkos, E., Spathis, C., & Manolopoulos, Y. (2007). Data mining techniques for the detection of fraudulent financial statements. *Expert Systems with Applications, 32*, 995–1003. doi:10.1016/j.eswa.2006.02.016

Klapper, L., Allende, V. S., & Zaidi, R. (2006). *A firm level analysis of small and medium size enterprise financing in Poland*. World Bank Policy Research Working Paper No: 3983.

Kleissner, C. (1998). Data mining for the enterprise. *Thirty-First Hawaii International Conference on System Sciences*, January 6-9, Kohala Coast, HI, (Vol.7, pp.295-304).

Kloptchenko, A., Eklund, T., Karlsson, J., Back, B., Vanhatanta, H., & Visa, A. (2004). Combining data and text mining techniques for analysing financial reports. *Intelligent Systems in Accounting Finance and Management, 12*(1), 29–41. doi:10.1002/isaf.239

Kloptchenko, A., Eklund, T., Karlsson, J., Back, B., Vanhatanta, H., & Visa, A. (2004). Combining data and text mining techniques for analysing financial reports. *Intelligent Systems in Accounting Finance and Management, 12*(1), 29–41. doi:10.1002/isaf.239

Koh, H. (1992). The sensitivity of optimal cutoff points the misclassification costs of type I and type II errors in the going concern prediction. *Journal of Business Finance & Accounting, 19*(2), 187–197. doi:10.1111/j.1468-5957.1992.tb00618.x

Koh, H., & Killough, L. (1980). The use of multiple discriminant analysis in the assessment of the going concern status of an audit client. *Journal of Business Finance & Accounting, 17*(2), 179–192. doi:10.1111/j.1468-5957.1990.tb00556.x

Koksal, G., Batmaz, I., & Testik, M. C. (2008). *Data mining processes and a review of their applications for product and process quality improvement in manufacturing industry. Technical report No: 08-03, Supported by TÜBİTAK, Industrial Engineering Department*. Ankara: METU.

Kopalle, P. K., Mela, C., & Marsh, L. (1999). The dynamic effect of discounting on sales: Empirical analysis and normative pricing implications. *Marketing Science, 18*(3), 317–332. doi:10.1287/mksc.18.3.317

Kovalerchuk, B., & Vityaev, E. (2002). *Data mining in finance*. Hingham, MA: Kluwer Academic Publiher.

Koyuncugil, A. S., & Ozgulbas, N. (2007). Detecting financial early worning signs in Istanbul stock exchange by data mining. [IJBR]. *International Journal of Business Research, 5*(3).

Koyuncugil, A, S., & Ozgulbas, N. (2006a). Is there a specific measure for financial performance of SMEs. *The Business Review, Cambridge, 5*(2), 314–319.

Koyuncugil, A. S., & Ozgulbas, N. (2008). A data mining model for detecting financial and operational risk indicators of SMEs. *World Academy of Science. Engineering and Technology, 46*, 88–91.

Koyuncugil, A. S., & Ozgulbas, N. (2006a). *Financial profiling of SMEs: An application by Data Mining. The European Applied Business Research (EABR)*. Conference, Clute Institute for Academic Research.

Koyuncugil, A. S., & Ozgulbas, N. (2006b). Is there a specific measure for financial performance of SMEs? *The Business Review, Cambridge, 5*(2), 314–319.

Koyuncugil, A. S., & Ozgulbas, N. (2006c). *Determination of factors affected financial distress of SMEs listed in ISE by Data Mining. In 3rd Congress of SMEs and Productivity*. Istanbul: KOSGEB and Istanbul Kultur University.

Koyuncugil, A. S., & Ozgulbas, N. (2007b). Detecting financial early warning signs in Istanbul Stock Exchange by data mining. *International Journal of Business Research*, VII(3)

Koyuncugil, A. S., & Ozgulbas, N. (2008a). Strengths and weaknesses of SMEs listed in ISE: A CHAID Decision Tree application. *Journal of Dokuz Eylul University. Faculty of Economics and Administrative Sciences, 23*(1), 1–22.

Koyuncugil, A. S., & Ozgulbas, N. (2007). Detecting financial early warning signs in Istanbul Stock Exchange by data mining. *International Journal of Business Research, 7*(3).

Koyuncugil, A. S., & Ozgulbas, N. (2006a). *Financial profiling of SMEs: An application by Data Mining. The European Applied Business Research (EABR)*. Conference, Clute Institute for Academic Research.

Koyuncugil, A. S., & Ozgulbas, N. (2006b). Is there a specific measure for financial performance of SMEs? *The Business Review, Cambridge, 5*(2), 314–319.

Koyuncugil, A. S., & Ozgulbas, N. (2006c). *Determination of factors affected financial distress of SMEs listed in ISE by Data Mining. In 3rd Congress of SMEs and Productivity*. Istanbul: KOSGEB and Istanbul Kultur University.

Koyuncugil, A. S., & Ozgulbas, N. (2009). Early warning system for SMEs as a financial risk detector. In Rahman, H. (Ed.), *Data mining applications for empowering knowledge societies* (pp. 221–240). Hershey, PA: Information Science Reference.

Koyuncugil, A, S., & Ozgulbas, N. (2006b). Financial profiling of SMEs: An application by data mining. *European Applied Business Research (EABR) Conference*.

Koyuncugil, A. S. (2006). *Fuzzy Data Mining and its application to capital markets*. Unpublished doctoral dissertation, Ankara University, Ankara.

Koyuncugil, A. S. (2006). *Fuzzy Data Mining and its application to capital markets*. Unpublished doctoral dissertation, Ankara University, Ankara.

Koyuncugil, A. S. (2006). *Fuzzy data mining and its application to capital markets*. Unpublished doctoral dissertation, University of Ankara, Turkey.

Koyuncugil, A. S. (2009). *The financial crisis and its impact on international business from statistics and data mining approached early warning systems perspective*. Paper presented at the Financial Crisis and its Impact on International Business Panel Discussion in World Summit on Economic-Financial Crisis and International Business (WSEFCIB2009), Washington, DC.

Koyuncugil, A. S., & Ozgulbas, N. (2006c). Determination of factors affected financial distress of SMEs listed in ISE by data mining. In *3rd Congress of SMEs and Productivity*, KOSGEB and Istanbul Kultur University (pp.159-170).

Koyuncugil, A. S., & Ozgulbas, N. (2007). Detecting financial early warning signs in Istanbul Stock Exchange by data mining. *International Journal of Business Research, 7*(3)

Koyuncugil, A. S., & Ozgulbas, N. (2008). Early warning system for SMEs as a financial risk detector. H. Rahman (Ed), *Data mining applications for empowering knowledge societies* (pp. 221-240). Hershey, PA: Idea Group Inc.

Koyuncugil, A. S., & Ozgulbas, N. (2007a). *Developing financial early warning system via data mining*. Paper presented in 4th Congress of SMEs and Productivity, Istanbul.

Koyuncugil, A. S., & Ozgulbas, N. (2008b). Early warning system for SMEs as a financial risk detector. H. Rahman (Ed), *Data mining applications for empowering knowledge societies* (pp. 221-240). Hershey, PA: Idea Group Inc. Global.

Koyuncugil, A. S., & Ozgulbas, N. (2009). An intelligent financial early warning system model based on data mining for SMEs. In *IEEE Proceedings of the 2009 International Conference on Future Computer and Computation,* (pp. 662-666.)

Koyuncugil, A. S., & Ozgulbas, N. (2009). Early warning system approach to SMEs Based on data Mining as a financial risk detector. In H. Rahman (Ed), *Data mining applications for empowering Knowledge societies* (pp.221-240). Hershey, PA: Idea Group Inc., USA

Koyuncugil, A. S., & Ozgulbas, N. (2009a). *Measuring and hedging operational risk by data mining.* Paper presented in the World Summit on Economic-Financial Crisis and International Business, Washington, DC.

Koyuncugil, A. S., & Ozgulbas, N. (2009b). An intelligent financial early warning System model based on data mining for SMEs. *International Conference on Future Computer and Communication, Kuala Lumpur, Malaysia.*

Krenker, A., Volk, M., Sedlar, U., Bester, J., & Kos, A. (2009). Bidirectional Artificial Neural Networks for Mobile Phone Fraud Detection. *ETRI Journal, 31,* 92–94. doi:10.4218/etrij.09.0208.0245

Krishna, A. (1994). The impact of dealing patterns on purchase behavior. *Marketing Science, 13*(4), 351–373. doi:10.1287/mksc.13.4.351

Krugman, P. (1979). A model of balance-of-payments crises. *Journal of Money, Credit and Banking, 11,* 311–325. doi:10.2307/1991793

Krzysztof, J. C., Pedrycz, W., Swiniarski, R. W., & Kurgan, L. A. (2007). *Data mining: A knowledge discovery approach.* Springer.

Kuenzer, C., Zhang, J., Voigt, J. L., Mehl, H., & Wagner, W. (2007). Detecting unknown coal fires: synercy of coal fire risk area delination and improved thermal anomaly extraction. *International Journal of Remote Sensing, 28*(20), 4561–4585. doi:10.1080/01431160701250432

Kumar, N., Krovi, R., & Rajagopalan, B. (1997). Financial decision support with hybrid genetic and neural based modeling tools. *European Journal of Operational Research, 103,* 339–349. doi:10.1016/S0377-2217(97)00124-0

Kumar, P. R., & Ravi, V. (2007). Bankruptcy prediction in banks and firms via statistical and intelligent techniques – a review. *European Journal of Operational Research, 180*(1), 1–28. doi:10.1016/j.ejor.2006.08.043

Kumar, N., Krovi, R., & Rajagopalan, B. (1997). Financial decision support with hybrid genetic and neural based modeling tools. *European Journal of Operational Research, 103,* 339–349. doi:10.1016/S0377-2217(97)00124-0

Kumar, V., & Leone, R. P. (1988). Measuring the effect of retail store promotions on brand and store substitution. *Journal of Marketing Resarch, 25*(May), 178–185. doi:10.2307/3172649

Kumar, T. S., Kumar, C. P., Kumar, B. A., Mulukutla, S., & Vittal, T. S. (2009). *Geospatial technology solution for Indian national tsunami early warning system.* August 1, 2009 from http://www.gisdevelopment.net/application/natural_hazards/floods/mwf09_srinivasa.htm

Kusiak, A. (2006). Data mining: Manufacturing and service applications. *International Journal of Production Research, 44*(18/19), 4175–4191. doi:10.1080/00207540600632216

Kusiak, A., & Smith, M. (2007). Data mining in design of products and production systems. *Annual Reviews in Control, 31,* 147–156. doi:10.1016/j.arcontrol.2007.03.003

Kyong, J. O., Tae, Y. K., Chiho, K., & Suk, J. L. (2006). Using neural networks to tune the fluctuation of daily financial condition indicator for financial crisis forecasting. In *Advances in Artificial Intelligence.* DOI: 10.1007/11941439_65 Volume 4304/2006

Ladner, R. Show, & Abdelguerfi, K. (2002). *Mining spatio-temporal information systems.* Boston: Kluwer Academic Publisher.

Lai, T. L. (1995). Sequential change point detection in quality control and dynamical systems. *Journal of the Royal Statistical Society. Series B. Methodological, 57,* 613–658.

Lai, T. L. (1998). Information bounds and quick detection of parameter changes in stochastic systems. *IEEE Transactions on Information Theory, 44,* 2917–2929. doi:10.1109/18.737522

Lai, T. L., Liu, H., & Xing, H. (2005). Autoregressive models with piecewise constant volatility and regression parameters. *Statistica Sinica, 15*, 279–301.

Lai, T. L., & Shan, J. Z. (1999). Efficient recursive algorithms for detection of abrupt changes in signals and systems. *IEEE Transactions on Automatic Control, 44*, 952–966. doi:10.1109/9.763211

Lai, T. L., & Wong, S. P. (2009). Statistical models for the Basel II internal ratings-based approach to measuring credit risk of retail products. *Statistics and Its Interface, 1*, 229–241.

Lai, T. L., & Xing, H. (2009a). *A simple Bayesian approach to multiple change-points. To appear in.* Statistica Sinica.

Lai, T. L., & Xing, H. (2009b). *Sequential change-point detection when the pre- and post-change parameters are unknown. To appear in.* Sequential Analysis.

Lai, T. L., & Xing, H. (2010). *Risk management and surveillance: Financial models and statistical methods.* Boca Raton, FL: Chapman & Hall/CRC.

Lai, T.L. & Xing, H. (2009c). A Bayesian approach to sequential surveillance in exponential families. To appear in *Communications in Statistics, Theory and Methods* (Special issue in honor of S. Zacks).

Laitinen, K., & Chong, H. G. (1998). Early warning system for crisis in SMEs: Preliminary evidence from Finland and the UK. *Journal of Small Business and Enterprise Development, 6*(1), 89–102. doi:10.1108/EUM0000000006665

Laitinen, E. K., & Laitinen, T. (2000). Bankruptcy prediction: application of the Taylor's expansion in logistic regression. *International Review of Financial Analysis, 9*(4), 327–349. doi:10.1016/S1057-5219(00)00039-9

Larose, D. T. (2005). *Discovering knowledge in data.* Mahwah, NJ: Wiley and Sons.

Larose, D. T. (2006). *Data mining methods and models.* Mahwah, NJ: Wiley and Sons.

Larose, D. T. (2005). *Data mining methods and models.* New York: John Wiley & Sons. doi:10.1002/0471756482

Larsen, K., & Bjerkeland, K. M. (2005). Are unexpected loan losses for small enterprises than for large enterprises? *Norges Bank Economic Bulletin, 76*(3), 126–133.

Lattin, J. M., & Bucklin, R. E. (1989). Reference effects of pPrice and promotion on brand choice behavior. *JMR, Journal of Marketing Research, 26*(August), 299–310. doi:10.2307/3172902

Laxman, S., & Sastry, P. S. (2006). A survey of temporal data mining. *Sadhana, 3*, 173–198. doi:10.1007/BF02719780

Lebart, L., Morineau, A., & Warwick, K.M. (1984). *Multivariate descriptive dtatistical analysis.* Wiley series, 3.

Lee, K. C., Han, I., & Kwon, Y. (1996). Hybrid neural network models for bankruntcy predictions. *Decision Support Systems, 18*, 63–73. doi:10.1016/0167-9236(96)00018-8

Lee, S. J., & Siau, K. (2001). A review of data mining techniques. *Industrial Management & Data Systems, 101*(1), 41–46. doi:10.1108/02635570110365989

Lee, K., Booth, D., & Alam, P. (2005). A comparison of supervised and unsupervised neural networks in predicting bankruptcy of Korean firms. *Expert Systems with Applications, 29*(1), 1–16. doi:10.1016/j.eswa.2005.01.004

Lee, T. S., Chiu, C. C., Chou, Y. C., & Lu, C. J. (2006). Mining the customer credit using classification and regression tree and multivariate adaptive regression splines. *Computational Statistics & Data Analysis, 50*(4), 1113–1130. doi:10.1016/j.csda.2004.11.006

Lee, K. C., Han, I., & Kwon, Y. (1996). Hybrid neural network models for bankruntcy predictions. *Decision Support Systems, 18*, 63–73. doi:10.1016/0167-9236(96)00018-8

Lefebvre, E., & Lefebvre, L. A. (2000). *SMEs, exports, and job creation: A firm level analysis. CIRANO and Polytechnique de Montreal.* Retrieved from http://www.strategis.ic.gc.ca/SS1/ra/op26_e.pdf.

Legovini, A. (1999). *Targeting methods for social programs. Poverty & Inequality Technical Note 1.* Washington, DC: Inter-American Development Bank.

Lensberg, T., Eilifsen, A., & McKee, T. E. (2006). Bankruptcy theory development and classification via genetic programming. *European Journal of Operational Research, 169*(2), 677–697. doi:10.1016/j.ejor.2004.06.013

Lessman, S., & Vob, S. (2009). A reference model for customer-centric data mining with support vector machines. *European Journal of Operational Research, 199*(2), 520–530. doi:10.1016/j.ejor.2008.12.017

Levy, M. (2008). Stock market crashes as social phase transitions. *Journal of Economic Dynamics & Control, 32*, 137–155. doi:10.1016/j.jedc.2007.01.023

Li, C. T., & Tan, Y. H. (2006). Adaptive control of system with hysteresis using neural networks. *Journal of Systems Engineering and Electronics, 17*(1), 163–167. doi:10.1016/S1004-4132(06)60028-5

Li, C. S. (2006). Survey of early warning systems for environmental and public health applications. In Wong, S., & Li, C. S. (Eds.), *Life science data mining.* Singapore: World Scientific Publishing. doi:10.1142/9789812772664_0001

Liang, L. F., & Yu, S. Y. (2001). Real-Time duplex digital video surveillance system and its implementation with FPGA. In *Proceedings off International Conference on ASIC,* (pp. 471-473).

Lin, C. S., Khan, H. A., Chang, R. Y., & Wang, Y. C. (2008). A new approach to modeling early warning systems for currency crises: Can a machine-learning fuzzy expert system predict the currency crises effectively? *Journal of International Money and Finance, 27*, 1098–1121. doi:10.1016/j.jimonfin.2008.05.006

Lin, S. W., Ying, K. C., Chen, S. C., & Lee, Z. J. (2008). Particle swarm optimization for parameter determination and feature selection of support vector machines. *Expert Systems with Applications, 35*(11), 1817–1824. doi:10.1016/j.eswa.2007.08.088

Lin, J., & Hwang, M., & becker, J. (2003). A fuzzy neural network for assessing the risk of fraudulent financial reporting. *Managerial Auditing Journal, 18*, 657–665. doi:10.1108/02686900310495151

Lin, C., Khan, H. A., Wang, Y., & Chang, R. (2006). A new approach to modeling early warning systems for currency crises: Can a machine-learning fuzzy expert system predict the currency crises effectively? *CIRJE-F, 411.*

Lin, S., & Brown, D. E. (2003). Criminal incident data association using the OLAP technology. In H. Chen, R, Miranda D., Zeng, C. Demchak, (Eds), *Proceedings of the First NSF/NIJ Symposium on Intelligence and Security Informatics (ISI'03),* Berlin, Springer, (pp. 13-26).

Linn, A. (2005). Amazon has a big memory. *Philadelphia Inquirer,* E12.

Lipton, M., & Ravallion, M. (1995). Poverty and policy. In Behrman, J., & Srinivasan, T. N. (Eds.), *Handbook of development economics.* Amsterdam: Elsevier.

Liu, S., & Lindholm, C. K. (2006). Assessing early warning signals of currency crises: A fuzzy clustering approach. *Intelligent Systems in Accounting. Financial Management, 14*(4), 179–184.

Lo, W. S., Hong, T. P., Jeng, R., & Liu, J. P. (2009). Intelligent agents in supply chain management as an early warning mechanism. In *2006 IEEE International Conference on Systems, Man, and Cybernetics, Vols 1-6, Proceedings* (pp. 2161-2166). New York: IEEE Pub.

Lombardo, R., & Beh, E. J. (2009). *Simple and multiple correspondence analysis for ordered-scale variables.* Applied Statistics Journal.

Lombardo, R., & Durand, J. F. (2005). Discriminant Partial Least-Squares via Splines: An application to evaluate patient satisfaction. *Statistica & Applicazioni, 3*, 77–85.

Lombardo, R., Tessitore, G., & Durand, J. F. (2007). Data mining and MAPLSS regression tools. A case study: the evaluation of trial duration. In D'Ambra, L., Rostirolla, P., & Squillante, M. (Eds.), *Metodi, Modelli e Tecnologie a Supporto delle Decisioni.* Milan, Italy: Franco Angeli.

Lombardo, R., & Beh, E.J. (2009). Simple and multiple correspondence analysis for ordinal-scale variables using orthogonal polynomials. *Journal of Applied Statistics.*

Lombardo, R., & Camminatiello, I. (2009). CATANOVA for two-way cross classified categorical data. *Statistics: A journal of Theoretical and Applied Statistics, 1*(15).

Lombardo, R., & Meulman, J. (2009). Multiple correspondence analysis via polynomial transformations of ordered categorical variables. *Journal of Classification.*

Lombardo, R., & van Rijckervorsel, J. (1999) Interaction terms in homogeneity analysis: Higher order non-linear multiple correspondence analysis. In *Studies in Classification, Data Analysis and knowledge Organization.*

Lombardo, R., Beh, E.J., & D'Ambra, L. (2007). Nonsymmetric correspondence analysis for doubly ordered contingency table. *Computational Statistics & Data Analysis journal, 52* (1), 566-578.

Lombardo, R., Durand, J.F., & De Veaux, R. (2009). Model building in multivariate additive partial least squares splines via the GCV criterion. *Journal of Chemometrics.*

Lombardo, R., Tessitore, G., & Durand, J. F. (2006). Data mining and MAPLSS regression tools. A case study: the evaluation of trial duration. In *Metodi, Modelli e Tecnologie a Supporto delle Decisioni. Procida*, Napoli, 28-30 settembre 2006 Franco Angeli.

Lopez, A. S. (2007). *Improving access to credit of SME's in Puerto Rico: Exploring variables to Forceast small business loan events*. Retrieved October, 2009, from http://selene.uab.es/dep-economia-empresa/Jornadas/Papers/4-12-2007/Alizabeth_Sanchez.pdf

Lorden, G. (1971). Procedures for reacting to a change in distribution. *Annals of Mathematical Statistics, 42*, 1897–1908. doi:10.1214/aoms/1177693055

Lundheim, R., & Sindre, G. (1993). Privacy and computing: A cultural perspective. In Sizer, R. et al. (Eds.), *Security and Control of Information Technology in Society, IFIP WG 9.6 Working Conference*, St. Petersburg, Russia. New York: Elsevier Science Publishers.

Luo, S. T., Cheng, B. W., & Hsieh, C. H. (2008). Prediction model building with clustering-launched classification and support vector machines in credit scoring. *Expert Systems with Applications, 36*(4), 7562–7566. doi:10.1016/j.eswa.2008.09.028

Luo, Q. (2008). Advancing Knowledge Discovery and Data Mining. In *First International Workshop on Knowledge Discovery and Data Mining.*

Lynch, A., & Gomaa, M. (2003). Understanding the potential impact of information technology on the susceptibility of organizations to fraudulent employee behaviour. *International Journal of Accounting Information Systems, 4*, 295–308. doi:10.1016/j.accinf.2003.04.001

Macé, S., & Neslin, S. A. (2004). The determinants of pre- and post-promotion dips in sales of frequently purchased goods. *JMR, Journal of Marketing Research, 41*(August).

Macfadyen, L. P., & Dawson, S. (2009). Mining LMS data to develop an early warning system for educators: A proof of concept. *Computers & Education.* doi:.doi:10.1016/j.compedu.2009.09.008

Maes, S., Tuyls, K., Vanschoenwinkel, B., & Manderick, B. (2002). Credit card fraud detection using Bayesian and neural networks. In *First International NAISO Congress on Neuro Fuzzy Technologies*, Havana, Cuba.

Magidson, J. (1993). The use of the new ordinal algorithm in CHAID to target profitable segments. *The Journal of Database Marketing, 1*, 29–48.

Magidson, J., & Vermunt, J. K. (2004). An extension of the CHAID tree-based segmentation algorithm to multiple dependent variables, ed. Classification – the ubiquitous challenges, studies in classification, data analysis and knowledge organization. In *Proccedings of the 28ᵗʰ Annual Conference of the Gesellchaft für Classification e.V.* (pp.176-183). University of Dortmund.

Magnusson, C., Arppe, A., Eklund, T., & Back, B. (2005). The language of quarterly reports as an indicator of change in the company's financial status. *Information & Management, 42*, 561–570. doi:10.1016/S0378-7206(04)00072-2

Maher, M., & Andersson, T. (2000). *Corporate governance: Effects on firm performance and economic growth, convergence and diversity of corporate governance regimes and capital markets*. London: Oxford University Press.

Major, J., & Riedinger, D. (2002). EFD: A hybrid knowledge/statistical-based system for the detection of fraud. *The Journal of Risk and Insurance, 69*, 309–324. doi:10.1111/1539-6975.00025

Manecuta, C., & Nicolae, M. (1996). Construirea si utilizarea functiei scor pentru diagnosticarea eficientei agentilor economici. *Revista Finante. Credit si Contabilitate, 5*, 47–54.

Marcenaro, L. F., et al. (2001). Distributed architectures and logical-task decomposition in multimedia systems. In *Procedings of IEEE,* (pp.1419-1440).

Marko, Z., & Larose, D. T. (2007). *Data mining the web.* Mahwah, NJ: Wiley and Sons. doi:10.1002/0470108096

Martens, D., Baesens, B., Gestel, T. V., & Vanthienen, J. (2007). Comprehensible credit scoring models using rule extraction from support vector machines. *European Journal of Operational Research, 183*(3), 1466–1476. doi:10.1016/j.ejor.2006.04.051

Martinez, W. L., & Martinez, A. R. (2002). *Computational statistics handbook with MATLAB.* Boca Raton, FL: Chapman and Hall.

Martinez-Ruiz, M. P., Molla-Descals, A., Gomez-Borja, M. A., & Rojo Alvarez, J. L. (2006). Evaluating temporary retail price discounts using semiparametric regression. *Journal of Product and Brand Management, 15*(1), 75–80. doi:10.1108/10610420610650891

Mauro, P. (2002). *The persistence of corruption and slow economic growth,* IMF Working Paper, WP/02/213.

Mayhew, G. E., & Winer, R. S. (1992). An empirical analysis of internal and external reference prices using scanner data. *The Journal of Consumer Research, 19*(June), 62–70. doi:10.1086/209286

McMichael, A. J. (2000). The urban environment and health in a world of increasing globalization: issues for developing countries. *Bulletin of the World Health Organization, 78*(9), 1117–1126.

McNelis, P. D. (2005). *Neural networks in finance: Gaining predictive edge in the market.* New York: Elsevier Academic Press.

Meier, P. (2006). *Towards an early warning system for preventing environmental conflicts. Natural Resources Related Conflict Management in Southeast Asia.* Khon-Khaen, Thailand: Institute for Dispute Resolution.

Mela, K., Gupta, S., & Lehmann, D. R. (1997). The long-term impact of promotion and advertising on consumer brand choice. *JMR, Journal of Marketing Research, 34*, 248–261. doi:10.2307/3151862

Mela, K., Jedidi, K., & Bowman, D. (1998). The long-term impact of promotions on consumer stockpiling behavior. *JMR, Journal of Marketing Research, 35*(May), 250–262. doi:10.2307/3151852

Mena, J. (2003). *Investigative data mining for security and criminal detection.* New York: Elsevier Science.

Meng, Y., & Dunham, M. H. (2006). Online mining of risk level of traffic anomalies with user's feedbacks. In *2006 IEEE International Conference on Granular Computing,* (pp. 176-181). New York: IEEE Pub.

Meredith, G. (2007). *Debt dynamics and global imbalances: some conventional views reconsidered,* IMF Working Paper, WP/07/4.

Meulman, J., van der Kooij, A. J., & Heiser, W. H. (2004). Principal components analysis with nonlinear optimal scaling transformations for ordinal and nominal data. In Kaplan, D. (Ed.), *Handbook of Quantitative Methods in the Social Sciences* (pp. 49–70). Newbury Park, CA: Sage Publications.

Meyer, P. A., & Pifer, H. W. (1970). Prediction of bank failures. *The Journal of Finance, 25*(4), 853–886. doi:10.2307/2325421

Meyer, P. A., & Pifer, H. W. (1970). Prediction of bank failure. *The Journal of Finance, 25*(4), 853–868. doi:10.2307/2325421

Ministry for SMEs, Trade and Business Environment (MSMETBE).(2008). *Annual report.*

Mirkin, B. (2005). *Clustering for data mining: a data recovery approach*. New York: Chapman and Hall.

Mohnen, A., & Nasev, J. (2005). *Growth of small and medium-sized firms in Germany*. Retrieved October, 2009, from http://ssrn.com/abstract=852785

Monk, E., & Wagner, B. (2006). *Concepts in Enterprise Resource Planning* (2nd ed.). Boston: Thomson Course Technology.

Moriarty, M. M. (1985). Retail promotional effects of intra- and interbrand sales performance. *Journal of Retailing, 61*(3), 27–47.

Morrisson, C. (2001). *Health, education and poverty reduction. Policy Brief No. 19*. OECD Development Centre.

Moss, L. T., & Atre, S. (2003). *Business intelligence roadmap: the complete project lifecycle for decision-support applications* (p. 576). Reading, MA: Addison-Wesley Publishing.

Murad, U., & Pinkas, G. (1999). Unsupervised profiling for identifying superimposed fraud. *Lecture Notes in Computer Science, 1704*, 251–262.

Nanni, L., & Lumini, A. (2009). An experimental comparison of ensemble of classifiers for bankruptcy prediction and credit scoring. *Expert Systems with Applications, 36*(2), 3028–3033. doi:10.1016/j.eswa.2008.01.018

Narasimhan, C., Neslin, S. A., & Sen, S. K. (1996). Promotions elasticity's and category characteristics. *Journal of Marketing, 60*(2), 17–30. doi:10.2307/1251928

National Credit Union Administration. (2007). *National Credit Union Administration Year-end Statistics, 2007; Statistics on Banking, 2007*. Retrieved from http://www.census.gov/compendia/statab/tables/09s1136.xls

National Health Care Anti-Fraud Association (NHCAA). (2009). *Anti-Fraud Resource Center - Fighting Health Care Fraud: An Integral Part of Health Care Reform*. Retrieved July 1, 2009, from National Care Anti-Fraud Association: http://www.nhcaa.org

National Insurance Crime Bureau (NICB). (2009). *Theft & Fraud Awareness - Fact Sheets - Insurance Fraud*. Retrieved July 1, 2009, from National Insurance Crime Bureau: http://www.nicb.org

Nazem, S., & Shin, B. (1999). Data mining: New arsenal for strategic decision making. *Journal of Database Management, 10*(1), 39–42.

Nazem, S., & Shin, B. (1999). Data mining: New arsenal for strategic decision making. *Journal of Database Management, 10*(1), 39–42.

Neslin, S. A., Henderson, C., & Quelch, J. (1985). Consumer promotions and the acceleration of product purchases. *Marketing Science, 4*(2), 147–165. doi:10.1287/mksc.4.2.147

Neslin, S. A., & Schneider Stone, L. G. (1996). Consumer inventory sensitivity and the postpromotion dip. *Marketing Letters, 7*(1), 77–94. doi:10.1007/BF00557313

Newberry, D. (2006). *The role of small and medium sized enterprises in the futures of emerging economies*. World Resource Institute.

Newman, A. L., & Bach, D. (2004). Self-regulatory trajectories in the shadow of public power: Resolving digital dilemmas in Europe and the U.S. *Governance: An International Journal of Policy, Administration, and Institutions, 17*(3), 387–413.

Nguyen, D. K., & Ramachandran, N. (2006). Capital structure in small and medium sized enterprises: The case of Vietnam. *ASEAN Economic Bulletin, 23*(2), 192–208. doi:10.1355/AE23-2D

Nijs, V. R., Dekimpe, M. G., Steenkamp, J.-B. E. M., & Hannsens, D. M. (2001). The category-demand effects of price promotions. *Marketing Science, 20*(1), 1–22. doi:10.1287/mksc.20.1.1.10197

Nishisato, S. (1996). Gleaning in the field of dual scaling. *Psychometrika, 61*(4), 559–599. doi:10.1007/BF02294038

Nishisato, S., & Arri, P. S. (1975). Non-linear programming approach to optimal scaling of partially ordered categories. *Psychometrika, 40*, 525–547. doi:10.1007/BF02291554

Nishisato, S. (1980). *Analysis of categorical data: Dual scaling and its applications.* Toronto, Canada: University of Toronto press.

Nomenclature statistique des activités économiques dans la Communauté européenne (NACE). (n.d.). Retrived October, 2009, from http://epp.eurostat.ec.europa.eu/statistics_explained/index.php/SMEs

Nooteboom, B. (1994). Innovation and diffusion in small firms: Theory and evidence. *Small Business Economics, 6*(5), 327–347. doi:10.1007/BF01065137

Nunan, F., Grant, U., Bahigwa, G., Muramira, T., Bajracharya, P., Pritchard, D., & Vargas M. J. (2002). *Poverty and the environment: Measuring the links.* Environment Policy Department Issue Paper No. 2

O'Brien, S. P. (2003). *Near-term forecasts of crisis and instability using text-based events.* Bethesda, MD: Center for Army Analysis, Report Number: A363824.

OECD – Organisation for Economic Co-operation and Development. (2007). *Recommendation on Cross-Border Co-operation in the Enforcement of Laws Protecting Privacy.* Paris: OECD – Committee for Information, Computer and Communications Policy.

OECD. (2003). The measure of non-observed economic activity. In *The Guide.* Paris: OECD.

OECD. (2008). The measure of non-observed economic activity. In *The Guide.* Paris: OECD.

OECD. (2001). *Poverty reduction. The DAC guidelines.* Retrieved December, 2009, from http://www.oecd.org/poverty.

OECD. (2005). *SME and Entrepreneurship Outlook.* Centre for Entrepreneurship, SMEs and Local Development OECD.

OECD. (2009 c). *The impact of the global crisis on SME and entrepreneurship financing and policy* Responses. Retrieved December 2009, from http://www.oecd.org/dataoecd/40/34/43183090.pdf

OECD. (2009a). *Policy responses to the economic crisis: Investing in innovation for long-term growth.* Retrieved December 2009, from http://www.oecd.org/dataoecd/59/45/42983414.pdf.

OECD. (2009b). *The observatory of European SMEs, 2007 observatory survey.* Retrieved from http://ec.europa.eu/enterprise/policies/sme/facts-figures-analysis/sme-observatory/index_en.htm#h2-2007-observatory-survey

Ogiujiba, K. K., Ohuche, F. K., & Adenuga, A. O. (2004). *Credit availability to small and medium scale enterprises in Nigeria: Importance of new capital base for banks.* Retrieved October, 2009, from http://129.3.20.41/eps/mac/papers/0411/0411002.pdf

Oh, K. J., Kim, T. Y., & Kim, C. (2006). An early warning system for detection of financial crisis using financial market volatility. *Expert Systems: International Journal of Knowledge Engineering and Neural Networks, 23*, 83–98. doi:10.1111/j.1468-0394.2006.00326.x

Ohlson, J. A. (1980). Financial ratios and the probabilistic prediction of bankruptcy. *Journal of Accounting Research, 18*(1), 109–131. doi:10.2307/2490395

Ohlson, J. A. (1980). Financial ratios and the probabilistic prediction of bankruptcy. *Journal of Accounting Research, 18*(1), 109–131. doi:10.2307/2490395

Ong, C.,S., Huang, J.J., & Tzeng, G., H. (2005). Building credit scoring models using genetic programming. *Expert Systems with Applications, 29*, 41–47. doi:10.1016/j.eswa.2005.01.003

Ooghe, H., & Van Wymeersch, C. (2006). *Traité d'analyse financière.* Intersentia/Anthemis.

OpenIVS. (2009). Retrieved 2009, http://OpenIVS.dyndns.org

Organisation for Economic Co-operation and Development (OECD). (2009). *Conflict and fragility preventing violence, war and state collapse: the future of conflict early warning and response*. Paris: OECD Publishing.

Organization for Economic Cooperation and Development (OECD). (2003). *Emerging systemic risks in the 21st century: an agenda for action*. Paris: OECD Publishing.

Ortiz, I. D. (2001). *Social protection in Asia and the Pacific*. Asian Development Bank.

Ortmeyer, G., Lattin, J. M., & Montgomery, D. B. (1991). Individual differences in response to consumer promotions. *International Journal of Research in Marketing, 8*, 169–186. doi:10.1016/0167-8116(91)90010-5

Ozdamar, K. (2004). *Paket programlar ile istatistiksel veri analizi 1*. Eskisehir, Turkey: Kaan Kitabevi.

Ozgulbas, N., Koyuncugil, A. S., & Yilmaz, F. (2006). Identifying the effect of firm size on financial performance of SMEs. *The Business Review, Cambridge, 5*(2), 162–167.

Ozgulbas, N., & Koyuncugil, A. S. (2009). Financial profiling of public hospitals: An application by Data Mining. *The International Journal of Health Planning and Management, 24*(1), 69–83. doi:10.1002/hpm.883

Ozgulbas, N., & Koyuncugil, A. S. (2006). Profiling and determining the strengths and weaknesses of SMEs listed in ISE by the Data Mining Decision Trees Algorithm CHAID. In *10th National Finance Symposium, Izmir.*

Ozgulbas, N., & Koyuncugil, A. S. (2006). Profiling and determining the strengths and weaknesses of SMEs listed in ISE by the Data Mining Decision Trees Algorithm CHAID. In *10th National Finance Symposium, Izmir.*

Ozgulbas, N., & Koyuncugil, A. S., (2006). Profiling and determining the strengths and weaknesses of SMEs listed in ISE by the data mining decision trees algorithm CHAID. *10th National Finance Symposium*, Izmir, Turkey.

Ozgulbas., et al. (2006).Identifying the effect of firm size on financial performance of SMEs. *Economics & International Business Research Conference*, Miami, FL.

Ozkan, F. G., & Sutherland, A. (1995). Policy measures to avoid a currency crisis. *The Economic Journal, 105*, 510–519. doi:10.2307/2235508

Paass, G., Reinhardt, W., Rüping, S., & Wrobel, S. (2007). Data Mining for Security and Crime Detection. *NATO Advanced Research Workshop on Security Informatics & Terrorism - Patrolling the Web.* Beer-Sheva, Israel.

Page, E. S. (1954). Continuous inspection schemes. *Biometrika, 41*, 100–114.

Panigrahi, S., Kunda, A., Sural, S., & Majundar, A. (2009). Credit Card Fraud Detection: A Fusion Approach Using Dempster-Shafer Theory and Bayesian Learning. *Information Fusion, 10*, 354–363. doi:10.1016/j.inffus.2008.04.001

Pantalone, C., & Platt, M. (1987). Predicting failures of savings and loan associations. *AREUEA Journal, 15*, 46–64.

Paranque, B. (1995). *Equity and rate of return: Are small manufacturing firms handicapped by their own success?* Paper presented at the meeting International Council for Small Business 40th World Conference, Sydney.

Parasuraman, A., Zeithaml, V. A., & Berry, L. L. (1985). A conceptual model of service quality and its implications for future research. *Journal of Marketing, 49*.

Park, C. S., & Han, I. (2002). A case-based reasoning with the feature weights derived by analytic hierarchy process for bankruptcy prediction. *Expert Systems with Applications, 23*(3), 255–264. doi:10.1016/S0957-4174(02)00045-3

Pastena, V., & Ruland, W. (1986). The merger/ Bankruptcy alternative. *Accounting Review, 61*(2), 288–302.

Pastena, V., & Ruland, W. (1986). The merger/bankruptcy alternative. *Accounting Review*, (April): 288–301.

Pathak, J., Vidyarthi, N., & Summers, S. (2003). A fuzzy-based algorithm for auditors to detect element of fraud in settled insurance claims. *Odette School of Business Administration Working Paper No. 03-9.*

Patil, G. P. (2005). Geoinformatic hotspot systems (GHS) for detection, prioritization, and early warning. In *Proceedings of the 2005 national conference on digital government research* (pp. 116-117). Digital Government Society of North America.

Peltonen, T. A. (2006) Are emerging market currency crises predictable? A test. *European Central Bank, Working Paper Series*, No. 571.

Pendharkar, P. C. (2008). A threshold varying bisection method for cost sensitive learning in neural networks. *Expert Systems with Applications, 34*(2), 1456–1464. doi:10.1016/j.eswa.2007.01.011

Peneder, M. (2001). *Entrepreneurial competition and industrial organization.* Cheltenham, UK: Edward Elgar.

Peng, Y., Kou, G., & Shi, Y. (2009). Knowledge-rich data mining in financial risk detection. Allen, G. Seidel, E., Dongarra, J., Nabrzyski, J., VanAlbada, G. D. & Sloot, P. M. A. (Eds.), *Computational Science, ICCS 2009, Part II, LNCS 5545* (pp. 534–542). Berlin: Springer-Verlag.

Petrushin, V. A., & Khan, L. (Eds.). (2006). *Multimedia data mining and knowledge discovery.* London: Baker & Taylor Books. RFC-3489. (n.d.). *STUN - Simple Traversal of User Datagram Protocol (UDP) Through Network Address Translators (NATs).*

Pettersson, M. (2004). SPC with applications to churn management. *Quality and Reliability Engineering International, 20,* 397–406. doi:10.1002/qre.654

Phua, C., Gayler, R., Lee, V., & Smith-Miles, K. (2009). On the communal analysis suspicion scoring for identity crime in streaming credit applications. *European Journal of Operational Research, 195,* 595–612. doi:10.1016/j.ejor.2008.02.015

Phua, C., Alahakoon, D., & Lee, V. (2004). Minority report in fraud detection: Classification of skewed data. *SIGKDD Explorations, 6,* 50–59. doi:10.1145/1007730.1007738

Phua, C., Gayler, R., Lee, V., & Smith-Miles, K. (2009). On the communal analysis suspicion scoring for identity crime in streaming credit applications. *European Journal of Operational Research, 195,* 595–612. doi:10.1016/j.ejor.2008.02.015

Piatetsky-Shapiro, G., & Frawley, W. (Eds.). (1991). *Knowledge discovery in databases.* Cambridge, MA: AAAI/MIT Press.

Pietravalle, S., Van der Bosch, F., Shaw, M. W., & Parker, S. R. (2002). Towards an earl warning system for winter wheat disease severity. In *BCPC Conference – Pests & Diseases 2002,* (Vol. 1-2, pp. 897-902).

Pirvu, C., Giurca Vasilescu, L., & Mehedintu, A. (2008). *Banking financing for Romanian SMEs – challenges and opportunities. Munich Personal RePEc Archive.* MPRA.

Pollak, M. (1985). Optimal detection of a change in distribution. *Annals of Statistics, 18,* 1464–1469.

Ponniah, P. (2001). *Data warehousing fundamentals: Comprehensive guide for IT professionals.* New York: John Wiley & Sons, Inc., (Electronic).

Privacy International. (2007). *Overview of privacy.* Retrieved July 9, 2009, from http://www.privacyinternational.org/article.shtml?cmd[347]=x-347-559062

PwC. (2007). *Economic Crime: People, culture and controls. The 4th biennial global economic crime survey.* New York: PriceWaterhouse&Coopers.

Pyle, D. (1999). *Data preparation for data mining.* San Francisco, CA: Morgan Kaufmann Publishers.

Quah, J., & Sriganesh, M. (2008). Real-time credit card fraud detection using computational intelligence. *Expert Systems with Applications, 35,* 1721–1732. doi:10.1016/j.eswa.2007.08.093

Raab, C. D. (2005). The future of privacy protection. In Mansell, R., & Collins, B. S. (Eds.), *Trust and crime in information societies* (pp. 282–318). Cheltenham, UK: Edward Elgar Publishing Ltd.

Raju, J. S. (1992). The effect of price promotions on variability in product category sales. *Marketing Science, 3,* 207–220. doi:10.1287/mksc.11.3.207

Rao, C. R. (2001). Statistics: reflections on the past and visions for the future. *Communications in Statistics Theory and Methods, 30*(11), 2235–2257. doi:10.1081/STA-100107683

Ravi Kumar, P., & Ravi, V. (2007). Bankruptcy prediction in banks and firms via statistical and intelligent techniques – A review. *European Journal of Operational Research, 180*, 1–28. doi:10.1016/j.ejor.2006.08.043

Requejo, M. (2002). *SME vs. large enterprise leverage: Determinants and structural relations*. Retrieved October, 2009, from http://ssrn.com/abstract=302400 or DOI: 10.2139/ssrn.302400

Richardson, F. M., Kane, G. D., & Lobingier, P. (1998). The impact of recession on the prediction of corporate failure. *Journal of Business Finance & Accounting, 25*(1-2), 167–186. doi:10.1111/1468-5957.00182

Ross, S., Westerfield, R., & Jaffe, J. (2008). *Corporate finance* (8th ed.). New York: McGraw Hill Ryerson Limited.

Rosset, S., Murad, U., Neumann, E., Idan, Y., & Pinkas, G. (1999). Discovery of fraud rules for telecommunications: Challenges and solutions. In *Fifth ACM SIGKDD: International Conference on Knowledge Discovery and Data Mining*, (pp. 409-413). New York: ACM Press.

Ruhashyankiko, J., & Etienne, B. Y. (2006). *Corruption and technology-induced private sector developpment*. IMF Working Paper, WP/06/198.

Rygielski, C., Wang, J. C., & Yen, D. C. (2002). Data mining techniques for customer relationship management. *Technology in Society, 24*(4), 483–502. doi:10.1016/S0160-791X(02)00038-6

Salas, V., & Saurina, J. (2002). Credit risk in two institutional regimes: Spanish commercial and savings banks. *Journal of Financial Services Research, 22*(3), 203–224. doi:10.1023/A:1019781109676

Salcedo-Sanz, S., Fernandez-Villacanas, J. L., Segovia-Vargas, M. J., & Bousono-Calzon, C. (2005). Genetic programming for the prediction of insolvency in non-life insurance companies. *Computers & Operations Research, 32*(4), 749–765. doi:10.1016/j.cor.2003.08.015

Sanchez, A., & Marin, G. S. (2005). Strategic orientation, management characteristics, and performance: A study of Spanish SMEs. *Journal of Small Business Management, 43*(3), 287–309.

Sánchez, D., Vila, M., Cerda, L., & Serrano, J. (2009). Assocation rules applied to credit card fraud detection. *Expert Systems with Applications, 36*, 3630–3640. doi:10.1016/j.eswa.2008.02.001

Sanders, T., & Wegener, C. (2006). *Meso finance filling the financial service gap for small business in developing countries*. Retrieved from http://www.bidnetwork.org/download.php?id=40005

Sarno, D. (2005). Liquidity constraint on the production of firms in Southern Italy. *Small Business Economics, 25*(2), 133–146. doi:10.1007/s11187-003-6452-x

Sarr., A., & Lybek, T. (2002). *Measuring liquidity in financial markets*. IMF Working Paper, WP/02/232.

Schonbucher, P. J. (2000). *Factor models for portfolio credit risk*. Manuscript, Department of Statistics, Bonn University.

Schroeder, J., Xu, J., & Chen, H. (2003). CrimeLink Explorer: Using domain knowledge to facilitate automated crime association analysis. In H. Chen, R., Miranda, D., Zeng, C. Demchak, (Eds), *First NSF/NIJ Symposium on Intelligence and Security Informatics (ISI'03)*, Berlin, Springer, (pp.168-180).

Sedita, S., & Subramanian, R. (2006). Trends and issues in global information security – a comparison of US and EU cybercrime laws. In *Proceedings of the Conference on Trends in Global Business- Doing Business in the European Union: Yesterday, Today and Tomorrow* (pp. 214-228). Hamden, NJ: Quinnipiac University.

Sharkey, A. J. K. (1996). On combining artificial neural nets. *Connection Science, 8*(3), 299–314. doi:10.1080/095400996116785

Shea, C. (2008). A need for a swift change: The struggle between the European Union's desire for privacy in international financial transactions and the United States' need for security from terrorists as evidenced by the Swift scandal. *Journal of High Technology Law, 8*, 143.

Shekhar, S., & Vatsavai, R. R. (2003). Mining geospatial data. In Ye, N. (Ed.), *The handbook of data mining* (pp. 520–548). Mahwah, NJ: Lawrence Erlbaum Associates Publishers.

Shewhart, W. A. (1925). The application of statistics as an aid in maintaining quality of manufactured product. *Journal of the American Statistical Association, 20*, 546–548. doi:10.2307/2277170

Shewhart, W. A. (1931). *Economic control of quality of manufactured product.* New York: D. Van Nostrand Company.

Shin, K. S., Lee, T. S., & Kim, H. J. (2005). An application of support vector machines in bankruptcy prediction model. *Expert Systems with Applications, 28*(1), 127–135. doi:10.1016/j.eswa.2004.08.009

Shin, K. S., & Lee, Y. J. (2002). A genetic algorithm application in bankruptcy prediction modeling. *Expert Systems with Applications, 23*(3), 321–328. doi:10.1016/S0957-4174(02)00051-9

Shirakawa, M. (2009). Coping with financial crisis - Japan's experiences and current global financial crisis. *BIS Review, 23*.

Shirata, C. Y. (1999). *Financial ratios as predictors of bankruptcy in Japan: an empirical research.* Tsubuka College of Technology.

Shiryaev, A. N. (1963). On optimum methods in quickest detection problems. *Theory of Probability and Its Applications, 8*, 22–46. doi:10.1137/1108002

Shiryaev, A. N. (1978). *Optimal stopping rules.* Berlin: Springer.

Shyu, M. L., Chen, S. C., Sarinnapakorn, K., & Chang, L. (Eds.). Foundations and novel approaches in data mining. *Studies in Computational Intellegence, 9*.

Simchera, V. (2003a). *M* (pp. 91–116). Federalizm Magazine.

Simchera, V. M. (2003a). *Introduction to financial and actuarial calculations.* Moscow: Financy i Statistika Publishing House.

Siminica, M. (2005). Model de analiză a riscului de faliment la nivelul firmelor industriale româneşti. *Revista de Politica Ştiinţei şi Scientometrie*, CNCSIS, 1-6.

Simoff, S., Böhlen, M. H., & Mazeika, A. (Eds.). (2008). *Visual data mining: Theory, techniques and tools for visual analytics.* Berlin: Springer.

Singleton, T., Singleton, A., Bologna, J., & Lindquist, R. (2006). *Fraud Auditing and Forensic Accounting.* New York: John Wiley & Sons.

Sintchenko, V., Gallego, B., Chung, G., & Coiera, E. (2009). Towards bioinformatics assisted infectious disease control. BMC *Bioinformatics, 10*(2). Retrieved August 1, 2009, from http://www.biomedcentral.com/1471-2105/10/S2/S10

Sivanandam, S. N., Sumathi, S., & Deepa, S. N. (2007). *Introduction to fuzzy logic using matlab.* Berlin: Springer. doi:10.1007/978-3-540-35781-0

Soava, G., Mehedintu, A., Buligiu, I., & Buse, R. (2008). *Sisteme informatice economice. Teorie şi aplicaţii.* Craiova, Romania: Editura Universitaria.

Sogorb-Mira, F. (2005). How SME uniqueness affects capital structure: Evidence from A 1994–1998 Spanish data panel. *Small Business Economics, 25*(5), 447–457. doi:10.1007/s11187-004-6486-8

Sogorb-Mira, F. (2001). *On capital structure in the small and medium enterprises: The Spanish case.* working paper series, Instituto de Estudios Europeos – Universidad San Pablo CEU, Madrid. Retrieved October, 2009, from http://ssrn.com/abstract=277090 or DOI: 10.2139/ssrn.277090.

Sohn, S. Y., & Lee, S. H. (2003). Data fusion, ensemble and clustering to improve the classification accuracy for the severity of road traffic accidents in Korea. *Safety Science, 41*(1), 1–14. doi:10.1016/S0925-7535(01)00032-7

Solove, D. J. (2008). *Understanding Privacy.* Cambridge, MA: Harvard University Press.

Solove, D. J., & Hoofnagle, C. J. (2005). *A model regime of privacy protection* (Version 2.0). GWU Law School Public Law Research Paper No. 132. GWU Legal Studies Research Paper No. 132. Retrieved July 9, 2009, from at SSRN: http://ssrn.com/abstract=699701

Song, M., & Parry, M. (1997). A cross-national comparative study of new product development processes: Japan and the USA. *Journal of Marketing, 61*(2), 1–18. doi:10.2307/1251827

Sookman, B. B. (2000). *Sookman: Computer, Internet and Electronic Commerce Law*. Toronto, Canada: Carswell Legal Publications.

Sormani, A. (2005). Debt causes problems for SMEs. *European Venture Capital & Capital Equity Journal, 1*, 1.

Sparrow, M. K. (1991). The application of network analysis to criminal intelligence: An assessment of the prospects. *Social Networks, 13*, 251–274. doi:10.1016/0378-8733(91)90008-H

Springate, G. (1978). *Predicted the possibility of failure in a Canadian firm. Unpublished MBA research project*. Simon Fraser University.

SPSS. (2001). *AnswerTree 3.0 User's Guide*. Chicago: SPSS Inc.

Srinivasan, K., Pauwels, K., Hannsens, D. M., & Dekimpe, M. G. (2004). Do promotions benefit manufacturers, retailers, or both? *Management Science, 50*(5, May 2004), 617-629.

Stanley, J. D., & DeZoort, F. T. (2007). Audit firm tenure and financial restatements: An analysis of industry specialization and fee effects. *Journal of Accounting and Public Policy, 26*(2), 131–159. doi:10.1016/j.jaccpubpol.2007.02.003

Steenkamp, J.-B. E. M., & Dekimpe, M. G. (2005). The increasing power of store brands: Building loyalty and market share. *Long Range Planning, 30*(6), 917–930. doi:10.1016/S0024-6301(97)00077-0

Steenkamp, J.-B. E. M., Nijs, V. R., Hannsens, D. M., & Dekimpe, M. G. (2005). Competitive reactions to advertising and promotion attacks. *Marketing Science, 24*(1, Winter 2005), 35-54.

Stolfo, S., Fan, W., Lee, W., Prodromidis, A., & Chan, P. (2000). Cost-based modeling for fraud and intrusion detection: Results from the JAM project. In *DARPA Information Survivability Conference & Exposition 2,* (pp. 1130-1144). New York: IEEE Computer Press.

Sun, J., & Li, H. (2008). Data mining method for listed companies' financial distress prediction. *Knowledge-Based Systems, 21*, 1–5. doi:10.1016/j.knosys.2006.11.003

Szathmary-Miclea, C. (2003). *Evaluarea si gestionarea riscului in intreprinderile mici si mijlocii* (de Vest, U., Ed.). Timisoara, Romania.

Taffler, R. J., & Tisshaw, H. (1977). Going, going, gone-four factors which factors which predict. *Accountancy*, (March), 50-54.

Tagoe, N., Nyarko, E., & Amarh, E. A. (2005). Financial challenges facing urban SMEs under financial sector liberalization in Ghana. *Journal of Small Business Management, 43*(3), 331–343.

Taleb, N. N. (2007). *The black swan: The impact of the highly improbable*. New York: Random House.

Tam, K. Y., & Kiang, M. Y. (1992). Managerial applications of neural networks: The case of bank failure predictions. *Decision Sciences, 38*, 926–948.

Tam, K. Y., & Kiang, M. Y. (1992). Managerial applications of neural networks: The case of bank failure predictions. *Decision Sciences, 38*, 926–948.

Tan, P. N., Steinbach, M., & Kumar, V. (2006). *Introduction to data mining*. New York: Pearson Education.

Tan, Z., & Quektuan, C. (2007). Biological brain-inspired genetic complementary learning for stock market and bank failure prediction. *Computational Intelligence, 23*(2), 236–242. doi:10.1111/j.1467-8640.2007.00303.x

Tan, P.-N., Steinbach, M., & Kumar, V. (2006). *Introduction to Data Mining*. New York: Pearson Education, Inc.

Taniar, D. (Ed.). (2007). *Research and trends in data mining technologies and applications*. Hershey, PA: IGI Global.

Tellis, G. J. (1988). The price sensitivity of selective demand. A meta-analysis of econometric models of sales. *JMR, Journal of Marketing Research, 25*, 391–404. doi:10.2307/3172944

Tenenhaus, M. (1998). *La règression PLS, thèorie et pratique*. Paris: Editions Technip.

Teruel, P. J. G., & Solano, P. M. (2007). Effects of working capital management on SME profitability. *International Journal of Managerial Finance, 3*(2), 164–177. doi:10.1108/17439130710738718

The Hankyoreh. (2009). *The financial crisis and South Korea one year after*. Retrieved October, 2009, from http://english.hani.co.kr/arti/english_edition/e_business/376783.html

The Istanbul Stock Exchange. (2009). Retrieved 2009, from http://www.ise.org

The MathWorks. (2008a). *MATLAB: Getting Started Guide*.

Thearling, K. (2004). *Data mining and analytic technologies*. Retrieved October, 2009, from hhtp://www.thearling.com/.

Theodoridis, S., & Koutroumbas, K. (2006). *Pattern recognition*. Amsterdam: Academic Press.

Thuraisingham, B. (2003). *Web data mining with applications in business intelligence and counter-terrorrism*. Boca Raton, FL: CRC Press. doi:10.1201/9780203499511

Thurik, A. R. (1996). Introduction: economic performance and small business. *Small Business Economics, 8*(5), 327–328. doi:10.1007/BF00389551

Tibshirani, R. (1997). The Lasso method for variable selection in the Cox model. *Statistics in Medicine, 16*, 385–395. doi:10.1002/(SICI)1097-0258(19970228)16:4<385::AID-SIM380>3.0.CO;2-3

Toktas, P., & Demirhan, M. B. (2004). *Risk analizinde veri madenciliği uygulamaları*. Paper presented at the meeting of the YA/EM'200-Yöneylem Araştırması/ Endüstri Mühendisliği-XXIV Ulusal Kongresi, Gaziantep-Adana.

Tou, J. T., & Gonzalez, R. C. (1974). *Pattern Recognition Principles*. Reading, MA: Addison-Wesley.

Tran, E., & Atkinson, M.-A. (2002). Security of personal data across national borders. *Information Management & Computer Security, 10*(5), 237–241. doi:10.1108/09685220210446588

Trappey, C. V., & Wu, H. (2008). An evaluation of the time-varying extended logistic, simple logistic, and Gompertz models for forecasting short product lifecycles. *Advanced Engineering Informatics, 22*, 421–430. doi:10.1016/j.aei.2008.05.007

Trumbach, C. C., Payne, D., & Kongthon, A. (2006). Technology mining for small firms: Knowledge prospecting for competitive advantage. *Technological Forecasting and Social Change, 73*, 937–949. doi:10.1016/j.techfore.2006.05.018

Tsai, C. F. (2003). Stacked generalization: a novel solution to bridge the semantic gap for content-based image retrieval. *Online Information Review, 27*(6), 442–445. doi:10.1108/14684520310510091

Tsai, C. F. (2009). Feature selection in bankruptcy prediction. *Knowledge-Based Systems, 22*(2), 120–127. doi:10.1016/j.knosys.2008.08.002

Tsai, C. F., & Wu, J. W. (2008). Using neural network ensembles for bankruptcy prediction and credit scoring. *Expert Systems with Applications, 34*(4), 2639–2649. doi:10.1016/j.eswa.2007.05.019

Tsai, C. F. (2008). A review of bankruptcy prediction models: the machine learning perspective. In Peters, H., & Vogel, M. (Eds.), *Machine Learning Research Progress*. New York: Nova Science Publishers.

Tsakonas, A., Dounias, G., Doumpos, M., & Zopounidis, C. (2006). Bankruptcy prediction with neural logic networks by means of grammar-guided genetic programming. *Expert Systems with Applications, 30*(3), 449–461. doi:10.1016/j.eswa.2005.10.009

Tsumoto, S., & Washio, T. (2007). Risk mining – Overview. In Washio, T., Satoh, K., Takeda, H., & Inokuchi, A. (Eds.), *New frontiers in artificial intelligence* (pp. 303–304). Berlin: Springer-Verlag. doi:10.1007/978-3-540-69902-6_26

Tsumoto, S., Tusumoto, Y., Matsuoka, K., & Yokoyama, S. (2007). Risk mining in medicine: Application of data mining to medical risk management. In Zhong, N., Liu, J. M., Yao, Y. Y., Wu, J. L., Lu, S. F., & Li, K. C. (Eds.), *Web Intelligent Meets Brain Informatics, 4845* (pp. 471–493). Berlin: Springer-Verlag. doi:10.1007/978-3-540-77028-2_28

Tsumoto, S. Maksuoka, K. & Yokoyama, S. (2008) Application of data mining to medical risk management – art. No. 697308. In Dasarathy, B. V. (Ed.), *Data Mining, Intrusion Detection, Information Assurance, and Data Networks Security, 6973* (pp. 97308-97308). Bellingham, WA: Spei-Int. Soc. Optical Engineering.

Tsung, F., Zhou, Z., & Jiang, W. (2007). Applying manufacturing batch techniques to fraud detection with incomplete customer information. *IIE Transactions, 39,* 671–680. doi:10.1080/07408170600897510

Tsuruta. D., & Xu, P. (2005). *Capital structure and survival of financial distressed SMEs in Japan.* Retrieved April, 2009, From (2005). http://www.rieti.go.jp/users/uesugi-iichiro/cf-workshop/pdf/tsuruta-xu.pdf

Tukey, J. W. (1977). *Exploratory data Analysis.* Reading, MA: Addison-Wesley.

Turkish Statistic Institute (TSI). (2002). *General industrial enterprise census, April 2006.* Retrieved April, 2009, from hhtp://www.die.gov.tr/TURKISH/SONIST/GSIS/gsisII141003.pdf

U.S. Federal Deposit Insurance Corporation. (2007). *Statistics on Banking,* Tables 696, 1136. U.S. Federal Deposit Insurance Corporation. Retrieved from http://www.fdic.gov/index.html.

U.S.Census Bureau. (2009). Statistical Abstract of the United States: 2008, Table 651, *Statistical abstract of the United States: 2008.* www.census.gov.

UN. (2010). *United nations millennium declaration.* Retrieved January 2010, from http://www.un.org/millennium

UNDP. (1997a). *Poverty measurement: Behind and beyond the poverty line.* Technical Support Document. Poverty Reduction. Module 3.

UNDP. (1997b). *Poverty indicators.* Technical Support Document. Poverty. Module 1.

United Nations. (1990). *Guidelines concerning Computerized personal data files.* Geneva: UN, Office of the high commissioner for human rights. Retrieved July 13, 2009, from http://www.unhchr.ch/html/menu3/b/71.htm

US – United States. (1791). *The United States Constitution.* Washington, DC: US Department of Justice. Retrieved July 13, 2009, from http://www.usconstitution.net/const.html

US – United States. (1966). *The Freedom of Information Act.* Washington, DC: US Department of Justice. Retrieved July 13, 2009, from http://www.usdoj.gov/oip/foia_guide07.htm

US – United States. (1974). *The Privacy Act.* Washington, DC: US Department of Justice. Retrieved July 13, 2009, from http://www.usdoj.gov/opcl/1974privacyact-overview.htm

US – United States. (1986). *The Computer Security Act of 1987.* Washington, DC: US Department of Justice. Retrieved July 13, 2009, from http://epic.org/crypto/csa/csa.html

US – United States. (1986). *The Electronic Communications Privacy Act of 1986.* Washington, DC: US Department of Justice. Retrieved July 13, 2009, from http://www.usiia.org/legis/ecpa.html

US – United States. (2001). *Uniting and Strengthening America by Providing Appropriate Tools Required to Intercept and Obstruct Terrorism Act of 2001* (USA PATRIOT Act). Washington, DC: US Department of Justice. Retrieved July 13, 2009, from http://www.gpo.gov/fdsys/pkg/PLAW-107publ56/content-detail.html

US – United States. (2002). *Homeland Security Act of 2002*. Washington, DC: US Department of Homeland Security. Retrieved July 13, 2009, from http://www.dhs.gov/xlibrary/assets/hr_5005_enr.pdf

Vaitilingam, R. (2007). *Guide to using the financial pages*. London: FT Pitman Publishing.

Van Gestel, V., Baesens, B., Suykens, J. A. K., Van den Poel, D., Baestaens, D. E., & Willekens, M. (2006). Bayesian kernel based classification for financial distress detection. *European Journal of Operational Research*, *172*(3), 979–1003. doi:10.1016/j.ejor.2004.11.009

van Heerde, H. J. (1999). *Models for sales promotion effects based on store-level scanner data*. Ijsel, The Netherlands: Labyrint Publication.

van Heerde, H. J., & Bijmolt, T. H. A. (2005). Decomposing the promotional revenue bump for loaylty program members versus non-members. *Journal of Marketing Resarch*, *42*(November), 443–457. doi:10.1509/jmkr.2005.42.4.443

van Heerde, H. J., Leefland, P. S. H., & Wittink, D. R. (2001). Semiparametric analysis to estimate the deal effect curve. *JMR, Journal of Marketing Research*, *37*(May), 197–215. doi:10.1509/jmkr.38.2.197.18842

van Heerde, H. J., Leefland, P. S. H., & Wittink, D. R. (2004). Decomposing the sales promotion bump with store data. *Marketing Science*, *23*(3), 317–334. doi:10.1287/mksc.1040.0061

van Heerde, H. J., Leeflang, P. S. H., & Wittink, D. R. (2002). *Flexible decomposition of price promotion effects using store-level scanner data*. Cambridge, MA: Marketing Science Institute.

van Rijckevorsel, J. L. A., & de Leeuw, J. (1988). *Component and correspondence analysis*. Chicester, UK: Wiley.

Velasco, A. (1987). Financial crises and balance of payments crises: A simple model of the southern cone experience. *Journal of Development Economics*, *27*, 263–283. doi:10.1016/0304-3878(87)90018-6

Venetianer, Z., & Yin, L. (2007). Stationary target detection using the object video surveillance system. In *2007 IEEE Conference on Advanced Video and Signal Based Surveillance,* (pp. 242-247).

Verykios, V. S., Elmagarmid, A. K., Bertino, E., Saygın, Y., & Dasseni, E. (2004). Association rule hiding. *IEEE Transactions on Knowledge and Data Engineering*, *16*(4), 434–447. doi:10.1109/TKDE.2004.1269668

Viaene, S., Ayuso, M., Guillén, M., Gheel, D., & Dedene, G. (2007). Strategies for detecting fraudulent claims in the automobile insurance industry. *European Journal of Operational Research*, *176*, 565–583. doi:10.1016/j.ejor.2005.08.005

Viaene, S., Dedene, G., & Derrig, R. (2005). Auto claim fraud detection using Bayesian learning neural networks. *Expert Systems with Applications*, *29*, 653–666. doi:10.1016/j.eswa.2005.04.030

Viaene, S., Derrig, R., Baesens, B., & Dedene, G. (2002). A comparison of state-of-the-art classification techniques for expert automobile insurance claim fraud detection. *The Journal of Risk and Insurance*, *69*, 373–421. doi:10.1111/1539-6975.00023

Volkwein, J. F. (1999). *The four faces of institutional research. What is institutional research all about? New directions for institutional research, 104*. San Francisco: Jossey-Bass.

Wahyu, I., & Swadaya, B. (2009). *Impact the financial crisis for SMEs in Indonesia*. Paper presented at the Regional Conference on the Impact of Financial Crisis on Vulnerable Sectors: Civil Society Voices and ASEAN, Jakarta.

Wallace, J., & Cermack, T. (2004). Text mining warranty and call center data: Early warning for product quality awareness. *SUGI 29 Proceedings, Analytics, 003-29*. Cary, NC: SAS Institute Inc. Retrieved August 1, 2009, from http://www2.sas.com/proceedings/sugi29/003-29.pdf

Walters, R. G. (1991). Assessing the impact of retail price promotions on product substitution, complementary purchase, and interstore sales displacement. *Journal of Marketing, 55*(2), 17–28. doi:10.2307/1252234

Walters, R. G., & MacKenzie, S. B. (1988). A structural equations analysis of the impact of price promotions on store performance. *JMR, Journal of Marketing Research, 25*(1), 51–63. doi:10.2307/3172924

Walters, R. G., & Rinne, H. J. (1986). An empirical investigation into the impact of price promotions on retail store performance. *Journal of Retailing, 62*(3), 237–266.

Wang, W., & Yang, J. (2005). *Mining sequential patterns from large data sets*. New York: Springer.

Wang, C. H., Chang, R. I., & Ho, J. M. (2003). An effective communication model for collaborative commerce of Web-based surveillance services. In *IEEE International Conference on E-Commerce* (CEC 2003), 24-27 June, (pp. 40 -44).

Wang, C. H., Li, M. W., & Liao, W. (2007). A distributed key-changing mechanism for secure voice over IP (VOIP) service. In *IEEE 2007 International Conference on Multimedia & Expo (ICME 2007),* July 2-5, Beijing, China.

Wang, K., Yu, P. S., & Chakraborty, S. (2004). Bottom-up generalization: A data mining solution to privacy protection. In *Fourth IEEE International Conference on Data Mining (ICDM'04)* (pp. 249-256). Brighton, UK: IEEE.

Wang, S., & Yang, J. (2007). A money laundering risk evaluation method based on decision tree. *International Conforence on Machine Learning and Cybernetics,* 2007, 19-22 Aug. 2007, (Vol. 1, pp.283-286).

Wang, T., & Liu, L. (2008). Butterfly: Protecting output privacy in stream mining. *2008 IEEE 24th International Conference on Data Engineering* (pp.1170-1179). Cancun, Mexico: ICDE.

Ward, T. J., & Foster, B. P. (1997, July). A Note on Selecting a Response Measure for Financial Distress. *Journal of Business Finance & Accounting, 24*(6), 869–879. doi:10.1111/1468-5957.00138

Warner, J. (1977). Bankruptcy costs: some evidence. *The Journal of Finance, 32,* 337–347. doi:10.2307/2326766

Wasserman, S., & Faust, K. (1998). *Social Network Analysis: Methods and Applications*. Cambridge, UK: Cambridge University Press.

Waters, N. (2008). *The APEC Asia-Pacific privacy initative – a new route to effective data protection or as Trojan horse for self-regulation?* Paper 59. University of New South Wales, Faculty of Law Research Series. Retrieved July 13, 2009, from http://law.bepress.com/cgi/viewcontent.cgi?article=1134&context=unswwps

Webb, P. (2003). A comparative analysis of data protection laws in Australia and Germany. *Journal of Information, Law and Technology, 2.* Retrieved July 13, 2009, from http://www2.warwick.ac.uk/fac/soc/law/elj/jilt/2003_2/webb/

Wei, W. W. S. (2006). *Time series analysis: univariate and multivariate methods*. Boston: Addison-Wesley.

Wei, C. P., & Chiu, I. T. (2002). Turning telecommunications call details to churn perdiction: A data mining approach. *Expert Systems with Applications, 23*(2), 103–112. doi:10.1016/S0957-4174(02)00030-1

Weiler, K. (1954). A new type of control chart, limits for means, ranges and sequential runs. *Journal of the American Statistical Association, 40,* 298–514. doi:10.2307/2280936

Wells, J. (2005). *Principles of Fraud Examination*. Chichester, UK: John Wiley & Sons.

West, D. (2000). Neural network credit scoring models. *Computers & Operations Research, 27*(11/12), 1131–1152. doi:10.1016/S0305-0548(99)00149-5

West, D., Dellana, S., & Qian, J. (2005). Neural network ensemble strategies for financial decision applications. *Computers & Operations Research, 32*(10), 2543–2559. doi:10.1016/j.cor.2004.03.017

Westin, A. F. (1967). *Privacy and freedom*. New York: Athenenum.

Westin, A. F. (2003). Social and political dimensions of privacy. *The Journal of Social Issues, 59*(2), 431–453. doi:10.1111/1540-4560.00072

Wilmott, P. (2006). *Paul Wilmott on quantitative finance*. London: John Wiley & Sons.

Withrow, C., Hand, D., Juszczak, P., Weston, D., & Adams, N. (2009). Transaction Aggregation as a Stragey for Credit Card Fraud Detection. *Data Mining and Knowledge Discovery, 18*, 30–55. doi:10.1007/s10618-008-0116-z

Witten, I. H. (2005). *Data mining: practical machine learning tools and techniques*. Boston: Morgan Kaufman.

Witten, I. H., & Frank, E. (2005). *Data mining: Practical machine learning tools and techniques* (2nd ed.). San Francisco, CA: Morgan Kaufmann Publishers.

Wittink, D. R., Addona, M. J., Hawkes, W. J., & Porter, J. C. (1988). *SCAN*PRO: The estimation, validation and use of promotional effects based on scanner data*. Cornell University.

Witzner, D. J., Abelson, H., Berners-Lee, T., Hanson, C., Hendler, J., Kagal, L., et al. (2006). *Transparent accountable data mining: New strategies for privacy protection*. MIT CSAIL Technical Report-2006-007. Retrieved July 13, 2009, from http://dig.csail.mit.edu/2006/01/tami-privacy-strategies-aaai.pdf

Wold, S., Kettaneh-Wold, H., & Skagerberg, B. (1989). Non linear partial least squares modeling. *Chemometrics and Intelligent Laboratory Systems, 7*, 53–65. doi:10.1016/0169-7439(89)80111-X

Wold, H. (1966). Estimation of principal components and related models by iterative least squares. In Krishnaiah, P. R. (Ed.), *Multivariate Analysis*. New York: Academic Press.

Wold, S., Martens, H., & Wold, H. (1983). The multivariate calibration problem in chemistry solved by PLS method. In Ruhe A. and Kagstrom B. (Eds), *Lecture Notes in Mathematics, Proceedings of the Conference on Matrix Pencils*, (pp.286-293). Heidelberg, Germany: Springer-Verlag.

Wolpert, D. H. (1992). Stacked generalization. *Neural Networks, 5*(2), 241–259. doi:10.1016/S0893-6080(05)80023-1

Woodside, A. G., & Waddle, G. L. (1975). Sales effects of in-store advertising. *Journal of Advertising Research, 15*(3), 29–33.

World Bank. (2003). *Turkey, poverty and coping after crises*. Human Development Unit Europe and Central Asia Region Report No: 24185- TR Vol.1-2.

World Bank. (WB). (2009a). *The financial crisis: Implications for developing countries*. Retrieved December, 2009, from http://econ.worldbank.org/WBSITE/EXTERNAL/EXTDEC/0,contentMDK:21974412~isCURL:Y~pagePK:64165401~piPK:64165026~theSitePK:469372,00.html

World Bank. (WB). (2009b). *Survey: Eastern European businesses report long-term impact of financial crisis*. Retrieved December, 2009, from http://www.enterprise-surveys.org/FinancialCrisis/

Worldbank. (2010a). *Official list of MDG indicators*. Retrieved January 2010, from http://siteresources.worldbank.org/DATASTATISTICS/Resources/MDGsOfficialList2008.pdf.

Worldbank. (2010b). *Overview: Understanding, measuring and overcoming poverty*. Retrieved January 2010, from http://web.worldbank.org/WBSITE/EXTERNAL/TOPICS/EXTPOVERTY/0,contentMDK:20153855~menuPK:373757~pagePK:148956~piPK:216618~theSitePK:336992,00.html)

Worldbank. (2010c). *What can poverty maps be used for?* Retrieved January 2010, from http://web.worldbank.org/WBSITE/EXTERNAL/TOPICS/EXTPOVERTY/EXTPA/0,contentMDK:20239110~menuPK:462100~pagePK:148956~piPK:216618~theSitePK:430367,00.html

Wu, C. H., Tzeng, G. H., Goo, Y. J., & Fang, W. C. (2007). A real-valued genetic algorithm to optimize the parameters of support vector machine for predicting bankruptcy. *Expert Systems with Applications, 32*(2), 397–408. doi:10.1016/j.eswa.2005.12.008

Wu, T., & Li, X. (2003). Data storage and management. In Ye, N. (Ed.), *The handbook of data mining* (pp. 393–408). Mahwah, NJ: Lawrence Erlbaum Assoc. Publishers.

Wu, X. (2004). Data mining: artificial intelligence in data analysis. In *IEEE/WIC/ACM International Conference on Intelligent Agent Technology (IAT 2004)*, September 20-24, (pp. 7).

Xie, J., Nandi, A., & Gupta, S. A. K. (2006). Improving the reliability of IEEE 802.11 broadcast scheme for multicasting in mobile ad hoc networks. *Proceedings of Communications IEE*, *153*(2), 207–212. doi:10.1049/ip-com:20045271

Xing, D., & Girolami, M. (2007). Employing Latent Dirichlet Allocation for Fraud Detection in Telecommunications. *Pattern Recognition Letters*, *28*, 1727–1734. doi:10.1016/j.patrec.2007.04.015

Yang, B., Ling, X. L., Hai, J., & Jing, X. (2001). An early warning system for loan risk assessment using artificial neural Networks. *Knowledge-Based Systems*, *14*(5-6), 303–306. doi:10.1016/S0950-7051(01)00110-1

Yang, W.-S., & Hwang, S.-H. (2006). A process-mining framework for the detection of healthcare fraud and abuse. *Information and Security*, *18*, 48–63.

Yang, J. M., Liang, P. H., & Chen, A. H. (2007). Applying text mining for extracting non-structural information in corporate financial report- A study of financial early-warning system. *Proceedings of Bussiness and Information*, 4. Retreived August 1, 2009, from http://ibacnet.org/bai2007/proceedings/Papers/2007bai7427.doc

Yao, Y. (1984). Estimation of a noisy discrete-time step functions: Bayes and empirical Bayes approach. *Annals of Statistics*, *12*, 1434–1447. doi:10.1214/aos/1176346802

Yeshin, T. (2006). *Sales Promotion*. New York: International Thomson Business Press.

Zaslavsky, V., & Strizhak, A. (2006). Credit card fraud detection using self-organizing maps. *Expert Systems with Applications*, *31*, 56–68.

Zastrow, C., & Bowker, L. (1984). *Social problems*. Chicago: Nelson-Hall.

Zavatta, R. (2008). *Financing technology entrepreneurs & SMEs in developing countries*. Retrieved June 2008, from http://www.infodev.org/en/Publication.542.html

Zavgren, C. (1985). Assessing the vulnerability to failure of American industrial firms: A logistics analysis. *Journal of Accounting Research*, *22*, 59–82.

Zavgren, C. (1983). The prediction of corporate failure: The state of the art. *Journal of Accounting Literature*, *2*, 1–33.

Zhai, L., Khoo, L., & Fok, S. (2002). Feature extraction using rough set theory and genetic algorithms—an application for the simplification of product quality evaluation. *Computers & Industrial Engineering*, *43*(4), 661–676. doi:10.1016/S0360-8352(02)00131-6

Zhan, G., Patuwo, B. E., & Hu, M. Y. (1998). Forecasting with artificial neural network: The state of the art. *International Journal of Forecasting*, *14*(1), 35–62. doi:10.1016/S0169-2070(97)00044-7

Zhang, Z. (2003). Applying data mining in investigating money laundering crimes. In P.M.D. Domingos, C. Falautsos, T. Senator, and L. Getoor (Eds), *The 9th ACM SIGKDD International Conference on Knowledge Discovery and Data Mining*, (pp. 747-752). New York: ACM.

Zhou, D., & Zhang, J. (2002). Face recognition by combining several algorithms. *Pattern Recognition*, *3*(3), 497–500.

Zmijewski, M. E. (1984). Methodological issues related to the estimation of financial distress prediction models. *Journal of Accounting Research*, (Supplement), 59–82. doi:10.2307/2490859

Zwick, D., & Dholakia, N. (2001). Contrasting European and American approaches to privacy in electronic markets: Property right versus civil right. *Electronic Markets*, *11*(2), 116–120. doi:10.1080/101967801300197034

About the Contributors

Ali Serhan Koyuncugil is working as a statistician for Capital Markets Board of Turkey. He had his B.Sc., M.Sc. and Ph.D. degrees in statistics from Ankara University Department of Statistics. His current research interests are design and development of fraud detection, risk management, early warning, surveillance, information, decision-support and classification systems, design and development of datawarehouses and statistical databases, development of indicators, models and algorithms, conducting analysis on capital markets, finance, health, SMEs, large scale statistical researches (e.g. census), population and development, socio-economic and demographic affairs based on data mining, statistics, quantitative decision making, operational research, optimization, mathematical programming, fuzzy set, technical demography theory and applications. He is elected member (fellow) of the International Statistical Institute (ISI) and member of the IASC and IASS sections of ISI, Turkish Statistical Association, Turkish Informatics Society and was former vice head of Turkish Statisticians Association. He has been taking part in a lot of international and national projects (UN, IBRD, EU, etc.). He has been taking part in a lot of international and national journals, conferences as an editorial board member, organizer, reviewer and advisor. His latest researches are about early warning systems based on data mining.

Nermin Ozgulbas is associate professor of finance at Baskent University in Turkey. She taught financial management, financial analysis and cost accounting in Baskent University, distance education program of Anadolu University and Turkish Ministry of Health. Her research and publication activities include finance, cost accounting, risk management, early warning systems, and data mining in especially SMEs, capital markets, health care organizations, and social security. She has been participating in a lot of international and national projects and conferences as an organizer, reviewer and advisor. Her latest researches are about early warning systems based on data mining.

* * *

Murat Acar is currently a Master of Science student in Computer Engineering Graduate Program at Bahcesehir University in Istanbul. He is a computer engineer and has been working in ISE Settlement and Custody Bank Inc. for 11 years. He is a Project Leader at IT Division. He has worked in many software projects as a software engineer and managed many software projects. His research interests are database management systems, data mining, machine learning and software project management. In his research, Acar has been focused on Early Warning Systems for Stock Market Crashes Based on Machine Learning Forecasting.

Inci Batmaz is a faculty member at the Department of Statistics, Middle East Technical University (METU), Turkey, since 2002. She graduated from the Department of Statistics at METU in 1985. She received her MS (1986) and PhD (1993) degrees in Computer Science at Ege University, Turkey. She pursued her PhD thesis at Carnegie Mellon University (CMU), USA, as a Fulbright Scholar. She worked as a research and teaching assistant at both CMU (1988-1991) and Ege University (1985-1994). She was a faculty member at the Department of Statistics, Ege University during 1994-2002. Her research interests include statistical (intelligent) software development, statistical computing, computational statistics, statistical modeling and data mining.

Danijel Bratina is a senior lecturer for the courses in Marketing, Marketing services and Marketing research at the Faculty of management in Koper. His main field of research is marketing research models of discrete choice and marketing efficiency modeling. He is currently preparing a doctoral thesis about sales promotion efficiency determinants. His bibliography includes papers from marketing budgeting, effectiveness and efficiency. His work was presented on several international conferences. Beside his research and pedagogical experience, he also has extensive background in industry, where he operated in the business of knowledge and production outsourcing to low labor cost countries.

Ray-I Chang received his Ph.D. degree in Electrical Engineering and Computer Science from National Chiao Tung University in 1996. Dr. Chang was the editorial board member of International Journal of Applied Metaheuristic Computing, Management and Information Science, and Journal of the Chinese Institute of Industrial Engineers. His current research interests include real-time and distributed multimedia systems. Dr. Chang is a member of IEEE.

Armand Faganel has been gathering working experience in both FMCG and industrial business as sales manager, marketing manager, and director of manufacturing company for 13 years. He graduated and took his MSc degree in Marketing, now he is in the process of defending his PhD at the University of Primorska (UP), Faculty of Management Koper, Slovenia. As Senior lecturer at the UP he is teaching several marketing related classes since 2004; he is also acting as the Head of Marketing Institute at the UP. His bibliography consists of scientific papers, independent scientific chapters and contributions to scientific conferences. Main areas of research include services quality perception, market orientation in the higher education, and qualitative market research.

Ibrahim George is currently working for the Commonwealth Bank of Australia. He completed his Masters by coursework at the Department of Computing, Macquarie University in 2008 and focused on money laundering and terrorist financing as a research project topic.

Jan-Ming Ho received his Ph.D. degree in electrical engineering and computer science from North-western University in 1989. Dr. Ho joined the Institute of Information Science, Academia Sinica as associate research fellow in 1989, and was promoted to research fellow in 1994. In 2004-2006, he was jointly appointed by National Science Council, Taiwan, where he served as Director General of Division of Planning and Evaluation. Dr. Ho is Associate Editor of IEEE Transaction on Multimedia. He was Program Chair of Symposium on Real-time Media Systems, Taipei, 1994 - 1998, General Co-Chair of International Symposium on Multi-Technology Information Processing, 1997 and will be General Co-Chair of IEEE RTAS 2001. He was also steering committee member of VLSI Design/CAD Symposium, and program committee member of several previous conferences including ICDCS 1999, and IEEE Workshop on Dependable and Real-Time E-Commerce Systems (DARE'98), etc.

Yu-Feng Hsu got his Master degree at the Department of Accounting and Information Technology, National Chung Cheng Univeristy. He currently is a Ph.D student at the Department of Information Management from National Sun Yat-Sen University. He has published a paper in Expert Systems with Applications. His research interests include data mining applications and real estate price prediction.

Costel Ionascu Assoc Prof, University of Craiova, Faculty of Economics and Business Administration, Department of Analysis, Statistics and Mathematics, is involved in research and teaching activity, as follow: author or coauthor of many articles on Statistics, Business Statistics, International Statistics, Informatics and e-learning; member of various professional associations: AGER, INFOREC, RAQAHE; editor in chief of Young Economists Journal Research interest: statistics, business statistics, informatics, international statistics, SMEs.

Mieke Jans earned her PhD in Applied Economic Sciences in 2009 by a dissertation 'Internal Fraud Risk Reduction by Data Mining and Process Mining'. After first researching earnings management in an accountancy field, she turned to the accounting information systems area by researching internal fraud risk reduction by means of data mining and process mining techniques. At this thesis, she explored several data mining techniques and their applicability in the context of internal fraud detection and prevention. Later on, she turned to the field of process mining as an extension of het methodology. Currently Mieke is active in the field of Accounting Information Systems where IS techniques are investigated on their use for business applications.

Adem Karahoca is head of Software Engineering Department of Engineering Faculty at Bahcesehir University in Istanbul. His research interests are web based learning systems and intelligent web based education tools, software standards, human computer interaction, data mining and web mining, mobile information systems and hospital information systems. He has 23 ICT related books in Turkish language. He has edited a data mining book in English. Also, he has written 10 articles that indexed in SCI and engineering index, and more than 100 proceeding papers. He has already supervised 40 Master of Science students.

Dilek Karahoca is social anthropologist and interested in human computer interaction, web based education systems, and blended learning methodologies. She has articles about hospital information systems, tourism information systems, education information systems in SCI, and engineering index. She has a book, Management Information Systems as a co-author with Adem Karahoca in Turkish. She has already supervised 10 Master of Science students' projects. She is teaching HCI and Software Project Management courses in Software Engineering Department.

Manolya Kavakli is an Associate Professor at the Department of Computing, Macquarie University. She gained her BSc (1987), MSc (1990) and PhD (1995) degrees from Istanbul Technical University. In 1996, Dr. Kavakli was awarded a NATO Science Fellowship in UK. In 1998, she received a Postdoctoral Fellowship from the University of Sydney, Australia. After working as an Associate Professor at Istanbul Technical University until 1999, she moved to Australia and became the course coordinator of the first

Computer Science (Games Technology) degree at the School of Information Technology, Charles Sturt University. Dr Kavakli established a Virtual Reality (VR) Lab at Macquarie University in 2003 and brought researchers together as a multidisciplinary and international research team with the establishment of VISOR (Visualisation, Interaction and Simulation of Reality) Research Group.

Gulser Koksal is currently a faculty member at the Industrial Engineering Department, Middle East Technical University (METU). She received her BS (METU, 1985), MS (METU, 1987) and PhD (North Carolina State University (NCSU), 1993) all in Industrial Engineering. Her work experience includes teaching and research positions at METU, NCSU and SPAC Six Sigma Consulting Company. Her research interests include integration of quality and production management, robust design, six sigma, statistical process control and data mining. She has worked as a consultant and researcher on several projects on textiles, health care, education, construction, manufacturing, R&D management, retailing, telecommunications, energy planning, and software development.

Tze Leung Lai is Professor of Statistics, and by courtesy, of Health Research and Policy and of the Institute of Computational and Mathematical Engineering at Stanford University. He is the co-director of the Biostatistics Core of the Cancer Center and of the Center for Innovative Study Design at Stanford University Medical School, and is also the director of the Financial Mathematics Program at the university. He received his Ph.D. degree from Columbia University in 1971, where he remained on the faculty until moving to Stanford University in 1987. He received the Committee of Presidents of Statistical Societies Award in 1983 and is an academician of Academia Sinica. He is an elected Fellow of the American Statistical Association and of the Institute of Mathematical Statistics, and is an elected member of the International Statistical Institute. He has published over 240 papers in sequential analysis, time series, econometrics, quantitative finance and risk management, signal processing and engineering control, probability theory and stochastic processes, biostatistics and clinical trials. A complete list of his publications can be found at http://lait.web.stanford.edu. He has supervised over 50 Ph.D. theses and has written eight books.

Rosaria Lombardo In 1995 Rosaria Lombardo, coming from an Economics faculty, gained the PhD in Computational Statistics and Data Analysis. In 1995 she became Researcher in Statistics and in 2001 Associate professor in Statistics. She was elected in the board of directors of International Association of Statistical Computing of the European regional section (IASC-ERS) for the period 2006-2010. Prof. Rosaria Lombardo has carried out an intense didactic activity in: Statistics, Applied Statistics, Data Mining. Her main research fields are: Data Mining and Explorative Multivariate Data Analysis. Linear and non linear Multiple Correspondence Analysis, Non-linear Principal Component Analysis. Three-way Data Analysis: Tucker3, Parafac, Candecomp, Statis, SumPca, Indscal, etc.. Analysis of dependence: linear and non-linear regression models, Partial Least Squares via Splines, Multiple Additive Regression Tree. Applications for the evaluation of Efficiency, Efficacy and Customer Satisfaction, in the framework of public services of social interest.

Yu-Hsin Lu received her Bachelor (Feng Chia University) and Master (National Chunghua University of Education) degrees in 1999 and 2005 respectively, all majoring in Accounting. She is now a PhD student at the Department of Accounting and Information Technology of the National Chung Cheng

University, Taiwan. During her PhD study, she has published 3 international journal and 2 international conference papers. Her research interests are financial accounting and data mining applications.

Nadine Lybaert became Doctor in the Applied Economics in 1995 at the Catholic University of Brussels. Her PhD dealt with the problems of SMEs. After working several years at the University of Maastricht, she moved to Hasselt University in 2000. There she is Associate Professor of Accounting. As such, she is project leader of the Accounting research group. Her research interests lie in the broad area of financial accounting. She is also guest professor at the University of Antwerp.

Anca Mehedintu, Assoc. professor, University of Craiova, Faculty of Economy and Business Administration, Department of Economic Information Systems, is involved in research and teaching activity, as follows: author of many books and articles on information systems, databases, applied economic informatics and globalization; member of various professional associations: CECCAR, ANEVAR, AGER; member of editorial and scientific board at national journals, such as: Annals of the University of Craiova, Young Economists Journal.Research interests: information systems, databases, information and communication technology, globalization, project management for information systems.

Cerasela Pirvu Professor, University of Craiova, Faculty of Economy and Business Administration, Department of Accounting, is involved in research and teaching activity, as follows: author of many books and articles on managerial accounting, financial accounting and banking accounting; member of various professional associations: EAA, CEDIMES, IAAER, CECCAR, AGER; Research interests: management accounting, financial accounting, banking accounting

Bo Shen is a graduate research assistant in the Department of Statistics at Stanford University. His current research interests are empirical Bayes modeling, statistical methods in risk management, algorithm trading and quantitative finance in general. He is currently writing his Ph.D. thesis on evaluating probability forecasts and early warning systems. He received his undergraduate education in mathematical science at Oxford University, where he graduated with a B.A. degree with First Class Honors. He has worked as an intern with a hedge fund to develop statistical methods for high frequency trading.

Vassiliy M. Simchera. Born on 26th of February 1940 in Transcarpathia (former Hungary, Ukraine at present). In the age of 24 he has received PhD degree (thesis – Conversion coefficients of overlapping statistical sets), in the age of 35 - Doctor's degree (thesis - Techniques on multivariate international comparisons). From 1976 he is professor. In the period of 1965-1983 he has headed different statistical sections and departments in the State structures of the U.S.S.R. From 1983 up to 2000 he is head of chair of statistics in All-Russian distant financial and statistical institute. From February 2000 he is a director of Russian State Scientific and Research Statistical Institute of Rosstat (Russian Federation). He is honored scientist of Russian Federation (2001) and Full member of the International Statistical Institute (ISI) from 2001. He had published over 50 books and 350 articles. From 1961, he is living in Moscow, and has scientific, educational and social practices.

Marian Siminica Professor PhD, University of Craiova, Faculty of Economy and Business Administration, Department of Analysis, Statistics and Mathematics, is involved in research and teaching activity, as follows: author of many books and articles on financial analysis, financial management and statistics; member of various professional associations: ANEVAR, CECCAR, CCFR, AGER; member of editorial and scientific board at international and national journals, such as: E-Journalnet issue Economy and Business, European Research Studies Journal, Vol. XI, Issue 4, 2008, Annals of the University of Craiova, Young Economists Journal,. Research interests: financial analysis, financial management, risk analysis, SMEs.

Chih-Fong Tsai obtained a PhD at School of Computing and Technology from the University of Sunderland, UK in 2005 for the thesis entitled "Automatically Annotating Images with Keywords". He is now an assistant professor at the Department of Information Management, National Central University, Taiwan. He has published more than 20 refereed journal papers including ACM Transactions on Information Systems, Pattern Recognition, Information Processing & Management, Applied Soft Computing, Neurocomputing, Knowledge-Based Systems, Expert Systems with Applications, Expert Systems, Online Information Review, International Journal on Artificial Intelligence Tools, Journal of Systems and Software, etc. In 2008, he received the 'Highly Commended Award' (Emerald Literati Network 2008 Awards for Excellence) for a paper published in Online Information Review ("A Review of Image Retrieval Methods for Digital Cultural Heritage Resources"). His current research focuses on multimedia information retrieval and data mining applications.

Koen Vanhoof attained a master in Physics in 1982 and a master in Computer Science in 1985 at the Katholieke Universiteit Leuven. His major research interests lie in the areas of data mining, statistics, knowledge engineering and modelling, computational intelligence methods, decision support systems and soft computing applications to information management, marketing and finance. He has authored and/or co-authored over 30 peer-reviewed journal articles and about 6 book chapters and 60 conference papers on his research topics. He is co-editor of the International Journal of Information Theory and Applications. He has been appointed as a guest professor at Jagilionski University (Cracow, Poland), the University of Antwerp (Antwerp, Belgium), the University of Maastricht (Maastricht, the Netherlands), the University of Economics (Sofia, Bulgaria), the Technical University (St. Petersburg, Russian Federation) and the Academy of Economics (Wroclaw, Poland). He is project leader of the Data Mining research group at Hasselt University in Belgium.

Laura Giurca Vasilescu, Assoc. professor PhD, University of Craiova, Faculty of Economy and Business Administration, Department of Finance, is involved in research and teaching activity, as follows: member of various professional associations: CEDIMES, IAAER, ERDS, AGER; member of editorial and scientific board at international and national journals, such as: MIBES Transactions International Journal, Journal of Humanities and Social Sciences, E-Journalnet issue Economy and Business, African Journal of Business Management, Journal of Administrative Sciences, Annals of the University of Craiova, Young Economists Journal, Management&Marketing. Research interests: corporate finances, financial management, banking, international finance, SMEs, real estate, investment, regional development.

Chia-Hui Wang received the B.S degree in Computer Science from Tamkang University in 1986 and received the M.S. degree in Computer Science from New Jersey Institute of Technology, U.S.A., in 1991. Then, he received the Ph.D. degree in Computer Science and Information Engineering from National Taiwan University in 2002. His industry experience included four years as a software developer in the high-tech industry. Now, he is an Assistant Professor of the Department of Computer Science and Information Engineering, Ming Chuan University. His research interests include multimedia communications, multimedia security and embedded systems. He is a member of IEEE and ACM.

Index